P9-DCT-968

YELTSIN

YELTSIN
A Life

Timothy J. Colton

A Member of the Perseus Books Group
New York

Published by Basic Books,
A Member of the Perseus Books Group

Books published by Basic Books are available at special discounts
for bulk purchases in the United States by corporations, institutions,
and other organizations. For more information, please contact the
Special Markets Department at the Perseus Books Group,
2300 Chestnut Street, Suite 200, Philadelphia, PA 19103, or call
(800) 255-1514, or e-mail special.markets@perseusbooks.com.

Designed by Trish Wilkinson
Set in 10.5 point Electra

Library of Congress Cataloging-in-Publication Data

Colton, Timothy J., 1947–
Yeltsin : a life / Timothy J. Colton.
p. cm.
Includes bibliographical references and index.
ISBN 978-0-465-01271-8 (alk. paper)
1. Yeltsin, Boris Nikolayevich, 1931–2007. 2. Presidents—Russia
(Federation)—Biography. I. Title.
DK290.3.Y45C65 2008
947.086092—dc22
[B]

2007051367

10 9 8 7 6 5 4 3 2 1

For Samuel P. Huntington

Contents

Introduction
Hero As Paradox

At twelve noon, Friday, December 31, 1999, Moscow time, on the cusp of the new year, the new century, and the new millennium, a surprise announcement from the president's office was televised across Russia from the Baltic Sea, where the sun had crept above the horizon, to the Bering Strait, where it had just dipped below. Boris Yeltsin, attired in a charcoal-gray suit and silver tie, with a tinseled holiday tree in the background, had videotaped it that morning. He was retiring seven months before the expiration of his mandate, he said hoarsely, and was handing over power to the prime minister and now acting president, Vladimir Putin, pending confirmation by the electorate. As the terse clip rolled, the presidential suite, paraphernalia, and "nuclear briefcase" were already in Putin's hands and Yeltsin was clinking glasses at a leave-taking luncheon.[1]

Most viewers could not help recall a telecast from the Kremlin eight winters earlier, at seven P.M. on Western Christmas, December 25, 1991.[2] In that funereal tableau, Mikhail Gorbachev, the resolute liquidator of the Cold War and the Iron Curtain and the irresolute reformer of communism, declared his resignation from the presidency of the Soviet Union and, with utmost reluctance, his acquiescence in unraveling the once mighty union itself. He abdicated to the same human being who would star in the 1999 presentation.

The uncanny thing is that vanquisher and vanquished, Yeltsin and Gorbachev, had so much in common. They came into the world twenty-nine days apart in 1931, Yeltsin on the first day of February and Gorbachev on the second of March. They were born to lowly parents in out-of-the-way villages on the Russian perimeter—at the fringe of the craggy Urals, almost in Siberia, for Yeltsin, and on the Caucasus isthmus, between the Caspian and the Black seas, for Gorbachev—at a time when those communities were hungry and under siege by the communist regime. Regardless, as grown men they served the regime and carved out vocations in its core as apparatchiks, members of the administrative machine of the Communist Party of the Soviet Union (CPSU).[3] In the 1980s they strained every sinew to reform that machine: Gorbachev, in the top job as general secretary, recruited Yeltsin to a senior post for that very purpose. How odd, then, for them to wind up on either side of the barricades in 1991. And so they would remain until Yeltsin's death sixteen years after.

In 1999 Yeltsin began his valedictory on a sunny note. He commended the constitutionally correct transfer of power and the advances in political, economic, and cultural freedoms while he was head of state, all running against the grain of Russia's autocratic heritage. The solid showing of pro-government candidates in the recent parliamentary election had left him confident he could bow out in peace. "I have attained the goal of my life: Russia will never return to the past, Russia from now on will proceed only forward."[4]

In midstream, though, Yeltsin switched gears and delivered a curiosity for any politician—a mea culpa:

> I would like to say a few words more personal than I am accustomed to saying. I want to apologize to you. I beg your forgiveness for not making many of your and my dreams come true. What seemed simple to do proved to be excruciatingly difficult. I beg your forgiveness for not vindicating some of the hopes of those who believed that in one leap, with one stroke, we could jump from the gray, stagnant, totalitarian past into a cloudless, prosperous, and civilized future. I myself believed this. I thought we could overcome everything in one go.
>
> One leap was not enough to do it. I was in certain respects naïve. Some problems revealed themselves to be exceptionally complicated. We slogged ahead through trial and error. Many people were shaken by these trying times.
>
> But I want you to know what I have never spoken about before and what it is important for me to say today. The pain of each of you called forth pain in me and in my heart. I went through sleepless nights and torturous self-doubts about what to do so that people might live easier and better. For me no task outweighed this.
>
> I am departing. I did all I could do.[5]

For anyone wishing to retrace the Yeltsin saga, his soul-baring farewell raises as many questions as it answers. It stays away from how he, a child of totalitarianism, got to dismantle it, and whether the project was quixotic or feasible. It does not offer a scoresheet of his or the other players' experience in government. If the exercise to date had been that torturous, it does not tell why Russians should have been hopeful about going forward.

In the library on the transition from Soviet-type communism, the Yeltsin bookshelf is slender. Almost all the works on it by Westerners were written before he stepped down, some long before; none was done with access to him; and together they miss out on "the submerged nine-tenths of the personality iceberg."[6] In Russia, no writer has so much as attempted an authoritative life of Yeltsin. As was bemoaned on his penultimate birthday in 2006, the existing publications are "politicized and maudlin" and "often slip into opinion pieces *[publitsistika]* not of the highest order."[7]

Why this apathy? In Yeltsin's native land, biography has never been a mainstream art form or the halfway house between academic and popular history that it is in the West.[8] It was frowned upon under communism as irreconcilable with the struggle between monolithic social classes outlined by Marx and Engels in the *Communist Manifesto.* Poking into any Soviet citizen's life and provenance—exposing details like socioeconomic, religious, and ethnic lineage, accusations against a relative, hidden enthusiasms or grudges—was treacherous for the subject. In post-Soviet Russia, biography and the search for roots are more in vogue. But books on political figures, at least so far, tend toward gimcrack sensationalism and the regurgitation of press clippings. As for Yeltsin, official attitudes cooled after Putin took over, and popular interest waned. A Russian would have thought twice about undertaking a serious tome on Yeltsin and would have been hard-pressed to get inside information about him.[9]

In the West, it has been suggested that Yeltsin scared authors off because he was sui generis and so hulking a presence.[10] This argument does not pass muster. Historians have not ignored such unique, outsized figures as Washington, Lincoln, Churchill, and Hitler.[11]

The inverse possibility is not readily brushed aside. Maybe all individual actors would be insignificant in a scene scoured by large-scale social and political forces, as this one was. Yeltsin pointed out in *Presidential Marathon,* the last in his trilogy of memoirs, that as paramount leader he did not fly solo. "Much of what occurred depended on my actions, right or wrong," he averred. "But in the end history is not written by individuals. There are general and sometimes cryptic patterns in the lives of nations."[12]

The surreal events that ripped asunder a superpower are comparable to angry eruptions in the natural world. Mere interrogation of Soviet officialdom's political monopoly in the late 1980s was for a snugly encased society "as if a meteorite had hit the planet, after which the climate changed and floods and earthquakes broke out," wrote a Moscow essayist.[13] The passing of the Soviet partocracy in 1991, a nanosecond in political time, has been equated with the extinction of the dinosaurs. A communist bloc guided in varying degrees by the USSR was omnipresent in the affairs of the twentieth century. As a Berkeley professor wrote in 1992, "We have thought in terms of East and West," and now "there is no East as such."[14]

Although vast collective forces were involved in its creation and development, communism was also an artifact of leadership, of concerted action to mobilize people for a joint purpose. So, at the outset, was the effort to save communism from its own follies—Gorbachev's *perestroika*, or "restructuring" of the system. Gorbachev reminds us that "perestroika started from above. It could not have been otherwise in totalitarian conditions."[15] The Soviet old guard warded it off as best they could. Newcomers to the corridors of power gave it impetus and vied over its direction. They set the terms under which non-leaders, in concentric circles, entered into it. Not always alert to the effects, they let change snowball from reform to revolution. Thereupon, Yeltsin, and the subset of leaders who had hitched their chariot to his, came to constitutive choices about the future after communism and after the USSR.

The downplaying of Yeltsin, therefore, can be ascribed neither to his having too much stature and influence nor to his having too little. The clincher is something else again: that his odyssey from *Homo sovieticus* to *Homo antisovieticus* and *Homo postsovieticus* confronts us with one paradox after another. The Oxford English Dictionary gives a pair of primary definitions for "paradox": "a phenomenon that exhibits some contradiction or conflict with preconceived notions of what is reasonable or possible" and "a person of perplexingly inconsistent life or behavior." Yeltsin squares with both.

Yeltsinism scorned canonic wisdom in and about his motherland and flouted policies he had previously embraced. It has rightfully been said that no other contemporary leader "has played this many political roles" in a single lifetime.[16] The scion of an agrarian household dispossessed by the Stalinists, Yeltsin led a hardscrabble Soviet childhood. Somehow, he became a

CPSU stalwart and rose to a seat on its Politburo. He then turned out, phantasmagorically, to renounce his party card and be the communists' nemesis. On October 21, 1987, he made what I call his "secret speech," a phrase coined originally for Nikita Khrushchev's denunciation of Joseph Stalin at the Twentieth Congress of the CPSU on February 25, 1956. His critique of Gorbachev's policies led to dismissal from the party inner circle only two years after he had been admitted into it and to Yeltsin becoming leader of the opposition to Gorbachev, seeking to change the system radically from without. Innocuous as it might appear by comparison, the 1987 speech was as momentous a chapter in the history of communism as Khrushchev's in 1956. On August 19, 1991, Yeltsin, this former party prefect in Sverdlovsk province, a beehive of the USSR's military-industrial complex, stared down a hard-line coup d'état from the armor of a battle tank manufactured in that same province, and in a factory he knew inside out. "Life presents us with surprising paradoxes," marvels one Muscovite raconteur. "Isn't it amazing that destiny prepared the part of executioner of the Soviet system for . . . a Yeltsin who . . . was the archetypal *Soviet* man?"[17] This dragon slayer sallied forth from the belly of the beast.

Paradoxes proliferated in the new Russia. Gorbachev in charge had distended cherished institutions and identities; Yeltsin shattered them and devised substitutes. While the changes he instituted were revolutionary in their scope and consequences, he recoiled from pronouncing them that. "The quintessential anti-revolutionary revolutionary,"[18] he was as bent on moderating the revolution as on making it, and inducted into his administration a battalion of the functionaries from the party elite, the *nomenklatura,* he had been busy attacking as hoary reactionaries. Having catapulted to power as a populist critic of official privilege and arrogance did not deter Yeltsin from building a grossly unequal capitalist economy or ordering his conscript army to wage war in the breakaway republic of Chechnya. And his seasoning in the Communist Party apparatus predisposed him to construct a Russian "superpresidency" that fit uneasily with the democratic way.

All that said, Yeltsin refused to set up a disciplined post-communist party allegiant to him and in the parting act of his presidency he voluntarily relinquished power. In decisions like the privatization of industry, territorial devolution, and support for autonomous communications media, he frequently employed power to disperse power. In 1999, withal, the person to whom he ceded his position was a product of an organization that was an embodiment of Soviet values as staunch as the defunct CPSU: the KGB, the secret police that in Yeltsin's youth had oppressed his kinfolk. As if that were not mystifying enough, Yeltsin, baptized Orthodox at birth and having been responsible in the 1970s for demolishing the house in which the Romanovs, Russia's last royal family, were executed, gave them a Christian burial as president in 1998, and, in retirement, rediscovered religion and was interred amid full church rites in 2007.

Looking back at this dialectic with all the benefit of 20/20 hindsight, it is far from obvious what to take from it. And it is far from easy to escape the impression that one is chasing a slippery and constantly moving quarry.

Likewise, Yeltsin the man teemed with inner complexities. Bill Clinton, who saw him at close quarters in eighteen negotiating sessions, likened him to "an Irish poet" or an artist who "sees politics as a novel he's writing or a symphony he's composing."[19] Clinton, a person of some complexity himself, and also given to reinvention and to questioning general frameworks, is an approving observer. In researching this volume, I have heard an earful of other similes, and not all are as appreciative of Yeltsin. A sampling would be those drawn to:

- *Roles and occupations:* aerialist, architect, boss, builder, chef, chess master, chieftain, Cossack, criminal, crusader, deceiver, demagogue, democrat, diva, drummer, foreman, godfather, grandpa, hedonist, hermit, jester, knight, lord of the manor, magus, man on a white horse, martyr, mutineer, neo-Bolshevik, patriarch, pied piper, prizefighter, reformer, revolutionary, roughneck, shock worker, sorcerer's apprentice, sultan, surgeon, thespian, tsar, Viking;
- *Historical personages:* Alexander the Great, Muhammad Ali, Julius Caesar, Fidel Castro, Cincinnatus, Christopher Columbus, Deng Xiaoping, Galileo, Charles de Gaulle, Boris Godunov, Harry Houdini, Ivan the Terrible, Andrew Jackson, Jesus, Lyndon Johnson, Judas, Nikita Khrushchev, Lenin, Abraham Lincoln, Huey Long, Mao Zedong, Napoleon, Richard Nixon, Peter the Great, Augusto Pinochet, Vidkun Quisling, Franklin Roosevelt, Pëtr Stolypin, Margaret Thatcher;
- *Characters from literature and folklore:* King David, Faust, Gulliver, Hamlet, Haroun al-Rashid, Hercules, Robin Hood, Icarus, Ivanushka, Lazarus, King Lear, Il'ya Muromets, Oedipus, Don Quixote, Samson, Tom Sawyer, Leonard Zelig, Zeus;
- *Physical objects and forces:* battering ram, cyborg, electric shock, false-bottom suitcase, hurricane, mannequin, puppet, sledgehammer;

- *Animal species:* bear, boa constrictor, bull, bulldog, chameleon, crocodile, eagle, elephant, phoenix, tiger, tortoise, wolf.

Many of these will be discussed in the chapters that follow. It can be said here that no one image captures the whole man. As those who worked closely with him can confirm, the qualities that made Yeltsin tick always eluded others: "Much about him is arcane and under figurative lock and key."[20] The ideological doyen of perestroika, Aleksandr Yakovlev, noted that Yeltsin had "not a little of the extravagant" to him and regularly incorporated polar opposites. "He was too credulous *and* too suspicious, too daring *and* too careful, too open *and* too inclined to crawl back into his shell."[21] The same politico who at incandescent moments, especially of risk and crisis, could move mountains, could on other days be maddeningly indecisive or self-indulgent. In demotic memory, unfair as it is, the snapshot of Yeltsin on the tank in Moscow in August 1991, the valiant defender of democracy, collides with the Yeltsin of August 1994, when he tipsily conducted a German band alfresco at Berlin's city hall. He could be "both a very big man and a very bad boy," in the breezy epigram of Strobe Talbott, a fly on the wall at all of President Clinton's summits with Yeltsin.[22]

The biography of this singular person provides an interpretive prism for the decline and fall of Soviet communism, the grandest of the past century's failed social experiments, and for the harrowing genesis of post-communism.[23] Yeltsin leaves nobody indifferent. He needs to be understood if we are to understand the age we inhabit and how we got here.

When Yeltsin made his debut in high Soviet politics in 1985, many onlookers, in the West in particular, misconstrued him as a bumpkin, or at best as a cat's paw in a game controlled by others more gifted than he. When he parted ways with Gorbachev in 1987, they were overhasty to write his political obituary.[24] There were those who saw him as a flash in the pan in his recusant phase and who thought he was fading out as Gorbachev and the USSR were sidelined in 1991.[25] When these prognoses were refuted, the tenor changed to flattery, and Yeltsin as president was valorized as a veritable archangel of reform. At first at home and then abroad, this vision segued into one of haplessness and aloofness. His growing unpopularity, a deadly altercation with parliament in 1993, and health issues in 1995 prompted predictions of an imminent cessation of Yeltsin's reign. Most cognoscenti foresaw an ignominious defeat in the 1996 presidential election, were he to hazard it—but he ran for re-election, won a dazzling victory, and was saluted as a political maestro. After 1996 the pendulum swung yet again. With political and economic crises peaking in 1998–99 and the hourglass running out on his second term, he was pilloried as a national embarrassment and his Russia as "a disastrous failure . . . threatening other countries with multiple contagions."[26]

On the personal and moral level, there were those who maintained early on that Yeltsin did not hold a candle to his great rival, Gorbachev. President George H. W. Bush, underwhelmed when he first met Yeltsin in 1989, was incensed by Yeltsin's demand in February 1991 that Gorbachev leave office. "This guy Yeltsin," he muttered to staffers, "is really a wild man, isn't he?"[27] Bush came around on Yeltsin, but in the middle and late 1990s two other character leitmotifs gained currency. One brought to the forefront Yeltsin's frailties and foibles and depicted him as someone "at the mercy of the pettiest passions,"[28] notably his fondness for strong drink. The other latched onto what Russian wordsmiths titled "the Family" (with a capital "F"): supposedly a camarilla of advisers, officials, and big-business oligarchs associated with his daughter Tatyana Dyachenko and the plutocrat Boris Berezovskii, and, it was said, the force behind the throne in the twilight years of the Yeltsin presidency.

While these pictures are all overblown, some fudge the truth worse than others. For example, although he overindulged in alcohol, the habit must be seen in perspective and most of the time was not central to his public activities. And although the nexus between wealth and power in the Yeltsin period has to be of concern, he was no marionette of the oligarchs, whom he invented sociologically, and the idea of the late Yeltsin fronting for a palace-cum-business consortium has little relation to reality.

In the 1980s and 1990s, acting in spurts and out of intuition more than a panoramic master plan, Yeltsin made fateful decisions that put his society on a much more promising road than it had been on since 1917. He did so under arduous circumstances and avoided the apocalyptic scenarios—anarchy, nuclear blackmail, famine and industrial collapse, ethnic strife—that had haunted forecasts about the demise of one-party rule. For what he wrought, and for pulling it off in the main by ballots rather than bullets, he belongs with the instigators of the global trend away from authoritarianism and statism and toward democratic politics and market-based economics. As a democratizer, he is in the company of Nelson Mandela, Lech Wałesa, Mikhail Gorbachev, and Václav Havel. It is his due even when allowance is made for his blind spots and mistakes. As against those who would shrug him off as an oddball or an antihero, or who cannot get beyond his welter of contradictions to come to a summary judgment, my net assessment of Yeltsin is as a hero in history—enigmatic and flawed, to be sure, yet worthy of our respect and sympathy.[29]

I initially intended to restrict myself to a portrait of Yeltsin's leadership of Russia as its elected president and to treat everything before that as preface. The further I got, however, the more I asked myself what those tumultuous years had to do with precedent, what molded the man and his instincts, and how the new Yeltsin, if that is what he was, ever emerged from the chrysalis of the old. It is anything but self-evident how the virtuoso product and agent of a dictatorship could end up as its hangman.

A 1995 skit in *Kukly* (Puppets), the political satire on Russian television, lampooned Yeltsin's shifting loyalties. "Boriska," the Yeltsin doll, plays Faust, situated in a medieval scholar's laboratory thick with books and test tubes. Tongue in cheek, he intones:

> *Once I was a communist*
> *Faithful to the marrow of my bones:*
> *From all three deities [Marx, Engels, and Lenin] I drank*
> *And ate of the constituent parts.*
> *I kept watch at the [party] congresses,*
> *But really I was a democrat in spirit,*
> *I was brother to the wind and sun*
> *And godmother to the people of Sverdlovsk.*
> *Lo and behold, when the clock struck and the moment came—*
> *I was president of Russia!*[30]

In real life, the tale was not nearly so simple—not with Yeltsin's abilities, not with his relationship to the ancien régime, not with his scorpions-in-a-bottle fight with Gorbachev or his conquest of power, and assuredly not with his use of power to make a new beginning.

My overarching aim in this "history made personal"[31] is to submit Boris Yeltsin and his career to a textured scrutiny that does justice to their many-sided humanity. Years of fieldwork that afforded eye-opening interviews with Yeltsin, with family members, and with about 150 other principals, declassified files from the Soviet archives, and new memoirs shed fresh light on the extended drama of his life. It is necessary to explain why the lunge toward a better tomorrow did not cross the chasm with finality, as by his admission it did not. Indivisible from that, we must see why it was mounted, why by Boris Yeltsin, and why it took him and the former Soviet Union as far as it did.

Chapter One

Self-Reliance

The Urals, among the most ancient mountain ranges in the world, are the physiographic frontier between Europe and Asia. They rise 1,500 miles from the grasslands above the inland Caspian Sea, in present-day Kazakhstan, to the icebound coastal plain of the Arctic Ocean. Their creases push gelid northern air, and with it northern flora and fauna, southward. They are highest in the upper segment; in the lower segment, the Urals comprise parallel folds of hills and stony crests. The middle segment, which by convention runs from 55° 30' to 61° north, consists largely of low plateaus trenched by ravines. Here are located most of the mountain belt's deposits of ferrous and nonferrous metals, salt, gemstones, and bauxite. It was this subterranean bounty that, beginning in the 1550s, drew Russians in from the west and north. Metallurgy dominated the Urals economy by the eighteenth century—three-quarters of the Russian Empire's iron and almost 100 percent of its copper were smelted there at century's end—but regressed in the nineteenth under competition from the mills of the Donbass and Dnieper Valley, in southern Ukraine, where coal rather than wood was used for heat. Agrarian migrants also flocked to the mid-Urals' lowlands, most of which bear a load of rich humus that responds well to the plow.

The sleepy community of Butka nestles just inside the southern and the eastern, Asiatic, margin of the middle Urals in undulating countryside mantled in birch, larch, red pine, and poplar. It lies at 56° 43' north, the same line of latitude as the Alaska panhandle and Dundee, Scotland, and at 63° 46' east, the approximate longitude of Herat, Afghanistan. It is 1,100 miles (two time zones) to the east of Moscow, 170 miles east of the continental divide, and 150 miles east of the largest Urals city, Yekaterinburg, known from 1924 to 1991 as Sverdlovsk. Butka is not as well-endowed agriculturally as many corners of the Urals, and there are few minerals nearby. The name means "porridge" in the languages of the Tatars and Bashkirs, the Turkic groups whose tribes, before their subjugation to the Russian crown, held sway in the swath of territory straddling the southern and central Urals. The reference is to the swampiness of the site, on the Belyakovka River.[1] The shallow and silty Belyakovka, less than fifty miles in length, curls southwest to northeast through Butka, where it was fifty feet wide in 1900; it is twenty or thirty feet wide there today. Through the Pyshma, it drains lazily into the Tobol, Irtysh, and Ob Rivers in west Siberia (the Irtysh and Ob form the world's fourth longest river system) and on to tidewater at the Arctic 700 miles away.

Legend has it that the Russians who initially settled at Butka were deserters from the host of Yermak Timofeyevich, the Cossack buccaneer who carried Ivan the Terrible's writ over the Urals in the 1580s. Be that as it may, we know from the state chronicle that on November 1, 1676, the governor of Tobol'sk, the Russian fort at the junction of the Tobol and the Irtysh, granted a petition by the peasants Ivashka Sylvenets and Tereshka Ivanov for leave to found a *sloboda*, a government-chartered village, at Butka. They were to survey the spot, construct a palisade against raiders, and "invite free and unattached people" to move there.[2] Built to secure Russia's borderlands, villages of this type offered peasants arable land, tax exemptions, and a measure of self-government. Butka had expanded bit by bit to a hundred souls when the German naturalist and explorer Johann Georg Gmelin came upon it in 1746, and to 825 in the imperial census of 1897. The nearest towns of any size were Shadrinsk, the district seat, fifty miles to the south on the Iset River, and Talitsa, on the Pyshma, twenty miles north of Butka and astride the highway and railroad to Siberia. Transport to and from the village was either by water or, if by land, along a horse trail to Talitsa, which it took ten or eleven hours to cover most seasons of the year and twice as long during the vernal and autumnal muddy seasons.[3]

Unpretentious Butka in 1900 shared much with the habitat of most of the tsar's subjects. It was now a regular village *(selo)*, a category for a relatively large settlement with a parish church and some government offices. There was no trace of the palisade. One-story wood cabins, thatched and with hand-carved window frames, and heated by tiled clay stoves, hugged several main streets and the rutted byways that meandered off from them. Everyone kept a dairy cow and tilled the fields rimming the village and the potato and vegetable patches out their back doors. The average growing season in Butka being 150 days and the soil being saline, seldom did the surfeit for the market amount to much. The young and strong cut timber or worked in the sawmill opened in 1914, which had 100 employees. Handicraftsmen made barrels, pottery, coal-tar soap, boots, and fur hats and put together sledges, carts, and spinning wheels. Amenities were sparse. The Orthodox Church of the Presentation of the Blessed Virgin, built in stone around 1800, had a wood attic and a belfry adjacent. Water was taken from wells and roadside pumps, and women did their laundry by hand in the river. There was a small library as of 1908 but no school and no doctor. A few clerks were the only representation from government.

In other respects, Butka was uncharacteristic of Russian rural society. People in it and its rustic surroundings, going back to the order of 1676 and the welcome mat to the free and unattached, had been spared the serfdom that stultified most of European Russia from the sixteenth century until abolition in 1861. Like most agriculturalists in the Urals and Siberia, they were classified as "state peasants," who were at liberty to change abode and marry as they wished, were judged in the civil courts, and owed a fixed rent to the government, not manorial service to a landlord's estate. In mentality, they were more like pioneers than like the serfs, whose status differed little from the black slaves in the United States.[4] Two pre-1914 ethnographic portraits of the Russians in these parts were fully applicable. "Our peasant," wrote one, "is sturdy beyond belief," toiling in the fields sunup to sundown, rain or shine, and "will not complain until things have become completely unbearable."[5] Said the other, "The population is bright and clear of mind and possesses accuracy of speech and an unflappable, playful sense of humor. While not devoid of the widely known [peasant] slyness, it is keen and imitative. It masters its favorite tasks and is good at accommodating itself to any kind of labor."[6] The asperity of the climate, rugged topography, isolation from central Russia, and low population density bred the virtue encapsulated in a noun resonant in Urals lore: *samostoyatel'nost'*, or self-reliance (self-rule in the group context), literally the ability to stand on one's own feet. At river fords and crossroads that were the merest specks of light in a vacuity, nothing except gumption and hardiness under adversity stood between the colonists and extinction.

Religion backed up legal categories and geography. Many Slavic settlers in the Urals were disciples of the Old Belief, the purist sect that seceded from Russian Orthodoxy in the 1650s in a schism over liturgical practices. There was an eschatological streak to the Old Believers; a spirit of outback resistance to the absolutist state and its bailiffs, foresters, and military recruiters; and a line of self-willed martyrs, "men who could keep silent no longer" in the face of ungodliness and injustice.[7] Their reserve, frugality, and diligence in all things economic were "to a certain extent . . . reminiscent of the Protestant ethic" in the West.[8] In all of the *guberniya* (province) of Perm, the largest in the Urals in the late tsarist period, the Shadrinsk district was one of the three with the heaviest concentration of dissidents.[9] There were pious and not-so-pious Old Believers up and down the Belyakovka Valley. They prayed with their brethren in peasant houses, there being no chapels or ordained clergy for them, and often participated in Orthodox parishes.[10]

The Yeltsin surname derives from *yel'*, Russian for "fir tree," and is a fairly common one in the region.[11] The ancestors of Boris Yeltsin were age-long inhabitants of the Urals and adjoining parts of Russia's north, probably since the fifteenth century. They are thought to have migrated from Novgorod, the principality opening out to the Baltic and distinguished by its local assembly, private property, and trade with Scandinavia and the Hanseatic League; Novgorod was devoured by Muscovy in 1478. Courtesy of the archivist Dmitrii Panov, there is a genealogy on the father's side spreading back eight generations to one Sergei Yeltsin, a state peasant registered at the start of the eighteenth century in the village of Basmanovo, or Basmanovskoye. Basmanovo was half again as big as Butka (its 1897 population was 1,307) and is located eight miles south, upriver on the Belyakovka. The connotations of the name were better than those of Butka. *Basman*, imported from the Tatar, refers to a loaf of bread baked for the royal court and stamped with its badge.[12] Sergei's son Anika made his home in Butka, his grandson Pëtr in Basmanovo, and his great-grandson Ivan in Beregovaya, two miles downriver from Butka. Commencing with Boris Yeltsin's great-great-grandfather, Savva, whose year of birth was 1807, and his great-grandfather, Yekim, born the fifth of Savva's eight children in 1841, the family hearth was in Basmanovo.[13] Another branch of the Yeltsins hailed from the hamlet of Konovalovaya, on a tributary of the Belyakovka fifteen miles to Butka's east. Except for the odd soldier (an Ivan Yeltsin fought against Napoleon at Borodino in 1812, in the Yekaterinburg Regiment), the menfolk did not stray from the Basmanovo-Butka-Beregovaya-Konovalovaya quadrangle.[14] The Basmanovo subgroup originally spelled the name "Yeltsyn," and in Konovalovaya it was "Yel'tsyn." The name was standardized to "Yel'tsin" after 1900. (I use the anglicized "Yeltsin.")

Yekim Yeltsin had three sons, and Ignatii Yekimovich Yeltsin, evidently the oldest of them, born in Basmanovo in 1875, was to be Boris Yeltsin's paternal grandfather. His paternal grandmother, the future Anna Dmitriyevna Yeltsina, was born there in 1877.[15] Ignatii's religious pedigree, it can be established secondhand, was Old Believer.[16] The family's dissidence had dimmed with time, as he was baptized Orthodox and worshiped in the Holy Trinity Orthodox congregation in Basmanovo (some say he was a deacon). But the telltale asceticism and industriousness of the sect endured. Wiry and bearded, Ignatii Yeltsin was a self-made man, a backwoods capitalist who, by Urals and Russian standards, prospered before the 1917 revolution. Shortly after marrying Anna in 1900 or 1901, he built a sizable framed house, trimmed in white, on the left bank of the Belyakovka; it stands to this day, a TV antenna jutting up between it and the toolshed. On twelve hectares (thirty acres) leased from the local land commune, he planted rye, wheat, and fodder. He had about five farmhands and owned a combine harvester, a thresher, five horses, four milk cows, and sheep and goats. In an outbuilding to his house, Ignatii worked as the Basmanovo blacksmith, shoeing horses, forging farm implements, and repairing mechanical equipment. He was also the proprietor of a water-powered flour mill on the Belyakovka and a larger windmill on the brow of the hill above the Yeltsin homestead. He was firm in the belief that, as one of his daughter-in-laws—Boris Yeltsin's mother—was to put it after his death, good land and good economic results in this world fell to those who earned them: "People who worked lived well. And then there were lazybones and drinkers; they lived poorly."[17]

A half-decade of accumulation was sacrificed to the Bolshevik Revolution of 1917 and Russia's civil war, when platoons of Red and White troops marauded through Basmanovo and Butka and helped themselves to horses and loot. Admiral Aleksandr Kolchak's anti-Bolshevik cavalry were driven from the middle Urals in late 1919. The requisitioning of grain by Moscow under War Communism eased off in 1920, although food was in short supply in 1921–22. Resilient Ignatii picked up where he had left off. By terms of the liberalized New Economic Policy enacted by Vladimir Lenin in 1921, which let private entrepreneurs operate in farming, light industry, and commerce, he cultivated twelve acres and rehabilitated the windmill. Doubled over time from four to eight sails, the mill was the only one that peasants for miles around could use to process grain. To minimize envy and taxation, Ignatii Yeltsin relied on family members for manpower and in 1924 divvied up title to many of his assets among his three oldest sons.[18]

Nikolai Ignat'evich Yeltsin, the father of Boris Yeltsin, was born in Basmanovo in June 1906. He was the middle of the five offspring Ignatii and Anna produced between 1902 and 1912. From eldest to youngest, the others were Mariya, Ivan, Dmitrii, and Andrian. Nikolai was schooled in reading, writing, and arithmetic for four years—Basmanovo, unlike Butka, had a one-room school—and went into the Yeltsin businesses about 1920. Of the four sons, he and Andrian did carpentry and odd jobs, Ivan worked as a blacksmith with his father, and Dmitrii tended to the windmill on the hill. With an ear for music and a dulcet voice, Nikolai sang in the church choir with his father and brothers and played the harmonica and accordion in the evenings. He appears to have tried to assist with the Communist Party–sponsored government in Basmanovo; according to an autobiographical essay written in the 1950s, he worked from 1924 to 1928 "in an elective post attached to the village soviet [council]." In that same text, he said he "worked as a carpenter in a district workshop" in 1928 and 1929.[19] But both these positions, so far as one can tell, were accessorial to his base activity, which was to labor with his father and brothers in the private sector.

In early 1928, bowing to Ignatii's wish that he terminate a dalliance with a married woman,[20] Nikolai wed the nineteen-year-old daughter of a family of lesser means, which had been farming in Basmanovo since the 1670s. The bride's name was Klavdiya Vasil'evna Starygina. Unschooled, she and her younger sister had been relegated to spinning, sewing, and field chores while waiting for husbands. "My mama would say," she once told a journalist, "'For what does a maiden need to be literate? To write letters to boys? She needs to think about getting married.'"[21] Klavdiya, who was not much over five feet tall and had braided hair down to her waist, had known Nikolai since age fifteen. When he came courting, they decided to tie the knot immediately, during the Christmas season, and did without a church wedding. She was gladdened to enter the Yeltsin family, with its "golden hands" and property, but her people were not penniless. Vasilii Yegorovich Starygin, her father (born in 1877), was an accomplished carpenter and cabinetmaker who built houses in Basmanovo with the aid of relatives and wage workers; Afanasiya Kirillovna Starygina, her mother (born in 1881), was a needleworker of local acclaim.[22]

Nikolai could afford a matrimonial home in Basmanovo, which Klavdiya festooned with tablecloths and other hand-crafted textiles. It was across the lane from Ignatii's and from the humbler cabin built by Nikolai's brother Ivan. (Dmitrii's place was on another street, and Mariya and husband Yakov lived with her in-laws, the Gomzikovs.) Boris Nikolayevich Yeltsin saw the light of day on February 1, 1931—in Butka. Nikolai and Klavdiya's firstborn was brown-haired and had his mother's sparkling blue eyes. In the Russian folk calendar, it was the time of the "Epiphany frosts" *(kreshchenskiye morozy)*, the nippiest of the winter. Why a child conceived in Basmanovo was born in Butka—and why in an overcrowded little house, on marshy land on the far side of the Belyakovka from the village green—I shall explain shortly.[23] As his mother told him, and as he retold in his first autobiographical volume, *Confession on an Assigned Theme*, the baby all but drowned at christening when the priest, bibulous on homebrew, let him drop to the bottom of the font. Hearing the gurgles, Klavdiya retrieved him from the water, and the cleric proposed he be named Boris, from the same root etymologically as "struggle" and "fighter" (and also the name of one of Russia's first two saints and one of its earliest tsars).[24] The family domicile in Butka, about fifteen feet by twenty, was filled to the rafters by a ménage of a dozen Yeltsins in three generations, most of whom slept on straw mattresses and overgarments. It still rests crookedly beneath a rusting iron roof at 22 Toilers Street. No plaque or sign immortalizes Yeltsin or his birth. When I ferreted out the house in September 2005, some denizens of the street did not know that the family had ever lived there.[25]

At this juncture, the clan's luck had taken a calamitous turn. In 1928 Stalin and his allies applied pressure on the Soviet peasantry to increase deliveries to government granaries. In 1929–30 they unleashed a social revolution in town and country, swinging from the market-oriented New Economic Policy to breakneck, state-led industrialization. In village Russia, the communists set neighbor against neighbor, divested well-to-do peasants, the *kulak*s, of their property, and corraled independent growers into *kolkhoz*es and *sovkhoz*es, bureaucratized collective and state farms.

Collectivization did not go unopposed. The young Leonid Brezhnev, who was to lead the Soviet Union from 1964 to 1982, worked in the 1920s as a land surveyor and organizer of collective farms in Bisert district, to the west of Sverdlovsk; he became a probationary member of the party there in 1929. In his memoirs, he wrote that irate farmers "railed at us with ropes, pitchforks, malicious notes, and stones heaved through the window"—prompting government agents to "lead the onslaught against the hated kulaks" with ever more fervor.[26] It was an unequal contest and one in which, toward the end of 1929, the ruling party pressed its advantage with fury. If 1 percent of peasant households in the unified Urals region were collectivized in May 1928, that ratio went up to 7 percent in October 1929, 19 percent by late November 1929, and 67 percent by March 1930; many of the new collectives fell apart in 1930 and had to be reorganized in 1931 and 1932.[27]

In Yeltsin's birthplace, as at many a Urals address, symbols of the past came thudding down: The Church of the Presentation, shorn of its icons and its seven-point Orthodox cross, and the bronze bells in its belfry melted down, was converted into the district House of Culture and, in the 1950s, into a movie theater.[28] In 1932 and 1933, the leanest years, when crops failed and many peasants slaughtered their livestock, residents say there was cannibalism in Butka.[29] The population stagnated, coming to 1,007 in the Soviet census of 1939, only 182 more than in 1897. Lenin had envisioned communism in an amaranthine slogan as "Soviet government plus the electrification of the whole country." Butka was to be wired into the national electric grid only in 1946, after World War II. The first macadam road to Talitsa came in 1936 (asphalting waited until 1976), the first Butka school in 1937, and a spur line from the railroad, laid by corvée labor, in 1949.

In *Confession on an Assigned Theme*, composed hurriedly in 1989 and published in still-Soviet Russia in 1990, Boris Yeltsin sketched the Butka scene in one solitary page and without proper names, identifying individuals only by their position in the line of descent (father, mother, grandfather). He writes of "dekulakization" (as nasty a word as any in the Soviet lexicon) of "one and all";[30] of bread and seed grain running out; of armed brigands roving the village; of his grandfather, seeing the family's last cow and horse starve, installing home stoves for cash in 1935.

Some paragraphs down, we read how the teenaged Yeltsin decided in 1949 to get his grandfather's blessing for his plans to study construction engineering in Sverdlovsk. Grandpa had the boy build a home steambath single-handedly as a show of his commitment. As for Nikolai, the word was that in 1935, "to save the family," he fled Butka with them to drudge in construction in the city of Berezniki, which is in the vicinity of Perm, on the western, European incline of the Urals. Later in the memoir, Boris referred in a single disarming sentence to an arrest in the 1930s. "I well remember when my father was taken away in the night, and I was six years old," which would date it in 1937.[31] The Sverdlovsk journalist Andrei Goryun, who had conversations with Yeltsin's mother, quoted her in 1991 as saying her father-in-law, Ignatii, going on eighty, was "sent away to certain death" on the northern taiga in 1931 and made it for only several months. Goryun also quoted a statement by Boris Yeltsin at a news conference in Sverdlovsk in 1989 that his father sat "several months in prison" in 1937.[32]

Hamstrung by incomplete data and by Yeltsin's taciturnity, analysts long recited these bits and pieces as gospel truth. Unwittingly, they misstated and understated the family's tribulations.[33] Some shards, it transpires, were correct and some were not. Even in the accounts as of 1990, there were gaps and discrepancies. Ignatii Yeltsin could not have been eighty in 1931; if so, he would have been fifty when he sired his first child, most unlikely in a peasant family. Boris Yeltsin speaks in *Confession* of his grandfather surviving wraithlike in Butka until 1934–35, while his mother has him deported in 1931. Yeltsin describes meeting with his grandfather in 1949, almost two decades after he reputedly died in the north, and gives his age then as "over seventy," another inconsistency. Yeltsin also states that both grandfathers got into their nineties, which would belie what his mother said about Ignatii Yekimovich. And nothing was ever said about what befell Anna Dmitriyevna Yeltsina—her very name was missing from the narrative.

The missing links in the chain of events can now be filled in, thanks to informational nuggets from family members and, for Nikolai Yeltsin, his unpublished autobiographical note and the forensic research of Aleksei Litvin, a historian from Kazan State University. The fate of the Yeltsin paterfamilias and his spouse was as harsh as Klavdiya Yeltsina presented it to Goryun, though different in some of the particulars. The die was cast when the Basmanovo village council in 1928 or 1929 slapped a punitive tax on Ignatii Yeltsin and disenfranchised him under a clause in the Soviet Russian constitution of 1918. The elections in which he had lost the right to vote were by now bogus affairs without competition; the real penalty was being fixed a member of a social category hostile to the regime and ineligible for all state benefits and services.[34] In 1930 the authorities officially branded Ignatii a kulak. He was triply vulnerable, as a profit-making cultivator, a mill owner, and a blacksmith—all of them in the regime's black book.

Dekulakization scarred one and all indirectly but a substring of the rural population directly and viciously. A decision of the party Politburo, in Moscow, in January 1930 delineated three categories of kulak. The first were the "counterrevolutionary kulak activists," persons who had been in the White armies or were against the regime; they were to be arrested and sent to concentration camps. Category two was "rich" kulaks, who had property but had not committed political offenses; their punishment was to be sent to boreal exile in "special settlements." Ignatii was slotted into the third, smallest, and least nefarious category. Third-class kulaks were to be expropriated and resettled, serflike, on inferior land in their home districts, and could keep some of their farm tools and possessions on the say-so of the local government. The boundaries between the three categories of kulak were indistinct, as was the line between kulaks and the "middle peasants" below. The typical dekulakized family in the Urals owned a house, one cow, and three domestic fowl, worked five to eight acres of land, and was "far from prosperous."[35] These assets were considerably less than Ignatii and Anna Yeltsin had had in the 1920s and much less than they had before 1917, so they were at risk for being put into the second category. But the third category was bad enough. In August or September of 1930, at harvest time, the village leaders impounded Ignatii's farmstead and ran him, Anna, and his sons and daughters-in-law (one of them the pregnant Klavdiya Yeltsina) out of the community and sent them to Butka, which had been made the district seat for the area in the early 1920s. As he was put on a horse-drawn cart for the ride to Butka, the heartsick Ignatii wept and wrung his hands. He asked his daughter, Mariya, the only one of his progeny to stay behind, to pray for him: "Why am I being forced to go? For what I built with my own hands!"[36] His windmill and smithy would quickly fall into ruin, their remnants hauled off for scrap by neighbors.

This was the act of spoliation, expulsion, and spite that drove the Yeltsins to rent the rough-hewn, poorly situated cottage in Butka from an elderly widow. It was a lacerating demotion from their four houses and assorted farm buildings in Basmanovo. They were among the 4,200 Urals families, or roughly 21,000 people, subjected to local deportation in 1930; 100,000 people were put in camps or sent to the north. The upper Urals by January 1932 held almost a half million deported peasants, about one in three of the USSR total.[37] In Butka, Ivan, Nikolai, Dmitrii, and Andrian Yeltsin were admitted to the new Red May kolkhoz; Ignatii was not. For a year or two, like many Soviet peasants in his position, he went on the lam, hiding out with relatives and scavenging for handyman's jobs to earn his keep.[38] With the stress and despair this begat, Klavdiya Vasil'evna could well have *remembered* him as eighty years old.

Four years later—and this Boris Yeltsin never acknowledged openly—the noose was tightened. Sometime in 1934, Ignatii and Anna Yeltsin were rounded up in Butka and banished again. It is unclear why, since the mass deportation of peasants ended in 1931. The Soviet norm was for third-category kulaks to work in supervised crews doing heavy labor the government valued, especially in woodcutting and construction. There was no such work at Butka, which perhaps drew official attention to the Yeltsins. Ignatii's refusal to report to the police may have provoked them to act, and there could possibly have been a connection with the problems his son Nikolai was having that spring in the city (see below). One guesses that Ignatii, beggared in 1930, was reclassified in 1934 as a second-category kulak. Even that device would have created an anomaly. The regulations in effect in the Urals exempted from deportation kulak families that did not include an able-bodied male younger than fifty, and in 1934 Ignatii Yeltsin was fifty-nine.[39]

Whatever the pretext, what came next was a long journey in convoy to the verge of nowhere: the uninviting and unfarmable environs of Nadezhdinsk, an ironworking center in the far north of Sverdlovsk province (1939 population 65,000), on the Kakva River 400 miles below the Arctic Circle. The Yeltsins and the ten or twelve other households removed with them could each bring only several sacks of belongings; tools and most of their cash and clothing, peasants' sheepskin coats *(tulupy)* included, were taken away.[40] In the special settlements, exiles worked under police oversight and had 15 percent of their wages garnisheed to maintain the guard force. The outstations used people up: "The [housing] . . . was unfit for habitation. The lack of food and medical care consigned people to malnourishment and wasting away. Unsanitary conditions spread infections and epidemics of typhus, scarlet fever, and scurvy. All of this led to high mortality rates among the settlers."[41] In the worst years, 1932 and 1933, peasants in some remote northern places had to eat fallen draft animals, moss, and birch leaves.[42]

Nadezhdinsk, which in a cruel jest means City of Hope in Russian (it was assigned the name Serov in 1939), held out not an iota of hope to the Yeltsins.[43] The outcasts subsisted in a dugout *(zemlyanka)*, a concavity scooped out in the earth, with a wood coal fire for heat and a twig blind against the elements. The only organized industries in the virgin land around Nadezhdinsk were forestry and mining, which Ignatii was too old and arthritic to do. By grace of the police, he was given a few trips back to Butka to fix farm machinery for the kolkhoz. That was his only comfort. Destitute and distraught, he lost his sight and went into mental collapse. Ignatii Yekimovich died a broken man in 1936, at the age of sixty-one, far short of ninety. His widow was let out of the area in 1936 and moved to Berezniki to live with her eldest son, Ivan, and died there before her time in 1941.[44]

The story did not end with the deaths of Ignatii and Anna. The gruesome truth is that *all four* of Yeltsin's grandparents were victims in their own way of the terror. Vasilii Starygin had hired workmen in his homebuilding business, which was enough for him, too, to be dekulakized and deposited in Butka in 1930. In 1934, the same year the Yeltsins were transported north, the OGPU (the appellation of the Soviet political police in the first half of the 1930s) marooned Vasilii and Afanasiya Starygin in the selfsame subarctic precinct. At Nadezhdinsk/Serov they eked out a threadbare existence for eleven years. They apparently had some contact with the elder Yeltsins in the two years Ignatii and Anna spent in the area. A little younger and in better health, the Starygins were more adaptable than their relations by marriage. Vasilii built himself and his wife an above-ground cabin. He kept his sanity and kept afloat economically by making furniture and cabinets and selling them locally.[45] Boris Yeltsin and his mother, he was to say in an interview, paid calls on the grandparents in the summertime and helped out with the gardening.[46]

The riddle of how the grandfather could die in the 1930s and miraculously reappear in the 1940s is thus solved: The first grandfather in Yeltsin's transcription is his father's father, Ignatii Yeltsin; the second is his mother's father, Vasilii Starygin. Starygin was the master carpenter, not the blacksmith and mill owner, which would explain why his opinion would have been so treasured by Boris Yeltsin as he pondered going into construction and why Starygin would have wanted his grandson to prove himself with the steambath project. Dekulakized peasants and many administrative deportees in the Soviet Union were allowed out of their places of servitude after the war, especially if a close relative had fought in it; the rest were to be freed after Stalin breathed his last in 1953.[47] Possibly since several family members had been in the army, the Starygins, both of them still spry, were discharged in 1945. Nikolai and Klavdiya Yeltsin fetched her parents in Serov and brought them to Berezniki to share quarters with them and their children. They were to live to the ripe old age of ninety-one (for Vasilii Yegorovich, who would die in 1968) and eighty-nine (for Afanasiya Kirillovna, who died in 1970). From the same peasant stock and locale as Ignatii and Anna Yeltsin, they outlasted them by three decades.[48]

Another bolt of lightning hit Boris Yeltsin's parents. Nikolai, while admitted to the Butka kolkhoz, was looking even before his son's birth for something better. This search led him to Nadezhdinsk, of all places, the little town near which his parents were to land in 1934. There he joined the great wave of peasants in quest of work in the new factories burgeoning in the Soviet Union's first five-year plan. His 1950s autobiography tells us he "worked from 1930 to 1932 as a foreman" in Nadezhdinsk, presumably in the construction of a factory there.[49] His presence in Nadezhdinsk could not have been continuous. He was in Basmanovo to father Boris Nikolayevich in May or June of 1930, he was in Butka for the baptism in February or March of 1931, and he was attached to the Butka kolkhoz after Boris's birth.[50] Spotty evidence suggests that Nikolai, Klavdiya, and their newborn spent the winter of 1931–32 in Nadezhdinsk and returned to the village after that.[51] In December 1932 the kolkhoz chairman let Nikolai and his kid brother, Andrian, go somewhere else. The train they boarded was not to Nadezhdinsk or to Berezniki, as Yeltsin's first book of memoirs says, but to Kazan, the polyglot capital of the republic of Tatariya, on the Volga River equidistant from Sverdlovsk and Moscow.

Ivan the Terrible conquered the Volga Tatar khanate at Kazan in 1552, annexed its territories, and opened it to Russian settlers and to Orthodoxy (the Tatars are Sunni Muslims). Lenin lived there for a few months in 1887 and was expelled from the local university for revolutionary activity. The population was a quarter million in 1932. The Yeltsin men signed on as woodworkers in Aviastroi, the syndicate constructing Works No. 124, an aviation plant, at the hamlet of Karavayevo, five miles north of the Kazan kremlin. The works was going to produce gleaming military aircraft designed by the illustrious aeronautical engineer Andrei Tupolev.[52] Those who put it up were limited to pick and shovel, flatbed trucks, and hand tools. Nikolai was promoted to leader of a crew that built housing, an equipment depot, and a workshop in the assembly hangar. He also, it would seem, studied in the evenings in a technical school *(tekhnikum)* for construction personnel.[53] Klavdiya and her toddler lived with him in Barracks No. 8 in the settlement of Sukhaya River. A Russian "barracks" *(barak)* is a ramshackle wood shack, either unpartitioned or ranging bedrooms off of a long corridor; the Sukhaya River building had the latter plan. Nikolai and his wife and son had an unadorned family room to themselves; Andrian's bachelor room was one door down. "Like nomads," Klavdiya and Boris again flitted to Butka in the spring and back to Kazan when the snow flew. They kept up their shuttling between village and city, which was commonplace in nineteenth- and early twentieth-century Russia, for several years.[54]

On April 27, 1934—not in 1937—the young family's world was turned topsy-turvy. OGPU officers, let in by the barracks commandant, collared Nikolai and Andrian Yeltsin and took them off in a "black crow" paddy wagon to the Kazan political prison. The arrest report said all their rooms contained were sticks of furniture and a smattering of letters and identification papers.[55] Six Aviastroi workers from Urals and Volga farm families had been under observation since January 1934. In conspiratorial mode, the OGPU gave them the code name *Odnosel'chane*, Countrymen, implying that they were from the same village or district. But they were not. Besides the two Yeltsins, there were Prokofii Gavrilov and his son Ivan, ethnic Russians from another part of the Urals, plus Vasilii Vakhrushev, whose nationality was Udmurt, a Finno-Ugric minority, and who was from Udmurtiya, and Ivan Sokolov, a Russian from Tatariya. The file bulged with materials from their home villages and the Kazan workforce. Three weeks of bullyragging led to accusations of "anti-Soviet agitation and propaganda," a crime under the infamous Article 58, Section 10 of the Russian penal code. On May 23 an OGPU tribunal, ruling on Case No. 5644, found them guilty as charged and sentenced five of the six (the Yeltsins, the Gavrilovs, and Vakhrushev) to three years in a forced-labor camp, minus one month for time served; Sokolov, fingered as the inciter, got five years. If they had come into the police's clutches in 1930 or 1931 or after 1935, they would have been much more liable to be tortured or put to death.[56]

The investigation and summary trial were a travesty, a paranoid era in microcosm. It is plain from Aleksei Litvin's sleuthing, though, that the defendants had "an ill-concealed dissatisfaction with conditions at the construction site."[57] This provided the OGPU with ammunition for prosecution as a deterrent to their coworkers. The six, the formal indictment alleged, had underhandedly preyed on "the actual difficulties" with food and supplies at the factory. They grumbled about scarcity of their rationed provisions, soup made from rancid meat, a ban on solemnizing Orthodox Easter, and deductions from their pay packets for state bonds and to make donations to communists imprisoned in Austria. OGPU interrogators trolled for more political articulations, dragooning a laborer from Basmanovo, Sergei Kudrinskii, into testifying under oath to the Yeltsins' kulak origins and to the twenty-two-year-old Andrian having said the people would be better off if a war broke out and the Soviet government was toppled. For Nikolai Yeltsin, no such words were hit upon, although his and Klavdiya's bedroom in the tumbledown Barracks No. 8 was where the most inculpating conversations were said to have taken place. The canard that most occupied the inquisitors was offered by Maksim Otletayev, a Tatar carpenter, who gave information that Nikolai had prevented the workers from reading Soviet newspapers out loud at the Aviastroi site. The dossier shows the presiding officer staging an in-person meeting between Nikolai and Otletayev and peppering Yeltsin with queries on this and other venial offenses:

INTERROGATOR: Did you tell Otletayev not to read the newspaper and that he would not find anything in it anyway, and then tear it away from him?
YELTSIN: To say that there was nothing in the newspaper—I did not say that. As far as ripping the newspaper out of Otletayev's hands is concerned, I did that unintentionally.
INTERROGATOR: Did you say we do not need to help workers who are rotting in prisons in capitalist countries?
YELTSIN: I don't exactly remember. But I guess I said that because I am a simpleton.
INTERROGATOR: And with respect to the dining arrangements, [did you complain] when the dinner was bad?
YELTSIN: We discussed this in our crew when the food was lousy.[58]

These equivocations and a steadfast denial of any lawbreaking, recorded in his signature on the indictment, were the best Nikolai Yeltsin could do in the OGPU snake pit. That he felt disaffection with the Soviet regime in 1934 is beyond question. It was anchored in the ravages of collectivization and forced-draft urbanization and in the lot of the Yeltsin and Starygin families. But it was his grousing about Aviastroi that got him into the police's bad books. He faulted the newspaper readings mostly as a drag on productivity, as tallies with his crusty personality.[59] He and his brother, unlike many Soviets in Stalin's time, begged off collusion with the police. When the OGPU approached them, the reed they grabbed was the same artifice of peasant simple-mindedness that Nikolai had pleaded in his interrogation. The OGPU papers sent to the camp specified they were "not subject to recruitment" as stool pigeons and were to be watched with special vigilance.[60]

Boris Yeltsin cried himself to sleep the night his father was taken into custody. He was too young to follow it but "could see my mother was sobbing and how petrified she was."[61] The two were imperiled when the Aviastroi barracks prepared to kick them out after Nikolai's sentencing. A Good Samaritan—Vasilii Petrov, a sixty-year-old medical orderly and World War I veteran who was Nikolai's cell mate as they awaited trial—took pity on them and asked his wife, Yelizaveta, and young daughter, Nina, to help out. Help they did. They came upon mother and child crouched in the hallway, locked out of their room, and gave them sanctuary in the Petrov cottage on Sixth Union Street. Klavdiya Vasil'evna would scrape by, working as a seamstress at a Kazan garment factory, where she learned to read and write in an evening class, and as a baker's helper at Bread Factory No. 2. The boy, Nina said in the 1990s, was "skinny, calm, and obedient." "When his mama would say to him, 'I'm going to work, sit here quietly,' he did not fuss. . . . The only toy he had was a doll. He wasn't to touch it, only to look at it. But kids will be kids. Borya played with little pyramids he made out of pieces of wood. In the winter he and I loved to go on toboggan rides."[62] In 1936–37 Boris attended a kindergarten in Kazan, perhaps one attached to the bakery.[63]

Nikolai Ignat'evich did his time at the Dmitrov camp on the Moscow-Volga Canal, the Suez-size dig to open up the capital to Volga water and shipping, which was the most pharaonic project in Stalin's Gulag. The work, as a bearer and carpenter, was backbreaking and hellishly unsafe. Death rates among the canal's almost 200,000 inmates were high. One in six was claimed by exposure, accidents, and disease in 1933 alone, so Nikolai's chances of making it through three years were maybe fifty-fifty.[64] He did make it, however, and was released seven months early. Aleksei Litvin is convinced there was an explicit deal for him to do post-Gulag work duty in Berezniki, and his discharge form from the Dmitrov camp did say he was bound for Berezniki.[65] This, though, would not explain why Nikolai did not go there directly.

In October 1936 Nikolai Ignat'evich was restored to his wife and son at the Petrovs' in Kazan. His registration papers said he was unemployed, that is, not formally signed up at a state workplace, in 1936–37. He must have found some work in the informal sector to put bread on the table. He may also have re-enrolled at the construction tekhnikum where he had taken classes before his arrest.[66] Further reason to tarry in Kazan was Klavdiya's pregnancy with their second child. Mikhail Yeltsin was born in July 1937. The six-year-old Boris was godfather at his christening. Right after, on July 31, the four pulled up stakes for Berezniki and the Urals, trundling their every possession in a wood laminate trunk. Vasilii Petrov was released from captivity and died in late 1937; his wife lived until 1966 and Nina until 2002. Klavdiya Yeltsina and the Petrovs corresponded and then lost track of one another during the war. As a mark of gratitude, Boris Yeltsin's wife, Naina, bought Nina and her family a two-room apartment in Kazan in 1999, using Yeltsin's book royalties; in 2006, on a visit to the city, she laid flowers on Nina's grave.[67]

The Yeltsins' destination in 1937 was on the upper Kama River, some 400 miles northeast of Kazan (which is near where the Kama, flowing south, empties into the Volga) and 100 miles north of the major city of Perm. Berezniki lay over the proverbial Russian salt mines. First at the mouth of the small Zyryanka River on the left bank and later in the right-bank town of Usol'e, the Stroganovs, a monied merchant family from Novgorod, had begun in the sixteenth century to extricate unpurified sodium chloride out of the ground and refine it through desiccation and boiling. The saltworks went into decline in the eighteenth century, undersold by product from the Volga basin. In the nineteenth century, admixtures of calcium and magnesium chlorides were discovered in the local brine; these could be separated out through ammonia treatment and used as ingredients for fertilizers, industrial chemicals, and pharmaceuticals. The Belgian company Solvay and a Russian shipbuilder, Ivan Lyubimov, constructed a soda plant in the village of Churtan in 1883. Communist planners were taken with the area's potential after 1917, and opened Russia's first radium mill there in the 1920s. In the first five-year plan, they made it the epicenter of the Soviet chemical industry—a "republic of chemistry," in a shibboleth of the day. The municipality of Berezniki was formed in March 1932 as an amalgamation of Churtan, the other four villages over the salt beds on the left bank of the Kama, and Usol'e, which was to be severed from it in 1940.

As a sign of the times, the city had its own penal colony, an arm of the camp complex at the conflux of the Kama and the Vishera, the first Gulag outpost in the Urals. The encampment on Adamova Hill, assigned in May 1929 to build the Berezniki Potash Combine on log piles driven into a bog, had as many as ten thousand workers in the early 1930s. Convicts were needed because free laborers did not want to go to Berezniki, which was short of housing and food and had had an outbreak of typhus in 1930. As the OGPU (renamed the NKVD in 1934) reassigned the prisoners to new building sites, other workers, many of them former inmates or indigent deportees under police restrictions, took their place. "The mass of the builders of the city were exiles and resettled people—dekulakized peasants from central Russia, Tatariya, and Ukraine, politically unreliable elements, counterrevolutionaries, intellectuals, and so forth. Later [during World War II] they would be joined by [deported] Volga Germans, Crimean Tatars, et cetera."[68] Berezniki was a venue for the dregs of society, as those who ruled Soviet society defined it.

Nikolai Yeltsin's older brother, Ivan, was already in Berezniki, having been sent to involuntary labor there in 1935 for "subverting" grain procurement in Butka (he could not meet his quota despite selling all he had to make up the difference); he checked in with the NKVD but was not in lockup. Before 1936 was out, Nikolai and Ivan's bereaved mother, Anna, had come to be with Ivan after burying her husband at Nadezhdinsk. Dmitrii and Andrian Yeltsin were soon to join them from Butka and Dmitrov. Nikolai got work in 1937 at Sevuraltyazhstroi, the North Urals Heavy Industry Construction Trust, and was assigned to the potash combine project. As an ex-convict, he would be banned until the mid-1950s from residing in Perm, Sverdlovsk, and the USSR's principal cities and from membership in the Communist Party. Within those limits, he and his family lived a humdrum Soviet life unmolested. Only on July 15, 1989, was he to be exonerated of the 1934 charges, twelve years after his death, by a Gorbachev-era commission.[69]

Boris Yeltsin's reaction to this palimpsest of misery is more important to his development than the raw facts are. Until the *glasnost'* of the 1980s, censorship and political conformism bottled up many neuralgic truths about the Soviet past. The removal of restraints on the exterior did not do away with restraints on the interior. Klavdiya Yeltsina, replying to Andrei Goryun at the highwater mark of revelations about Soviet history, clammed up about the detention of her husband and their sojourn in Kazan. More astounding, she did not mention her parents' loss or their stolen decade at Nadezhdinsk/Serov. The years may have dulled an old woman's memory; it is hard to believe that she did not remember the plight of, and her separation from, her mother and father. Boris Yeltsin cannot be blamed a half-century later for mistaking his age upon the jailing of his father for six rather than three. But a person could not as easily forget that the parent's sentence, and time out of the nest, was measured in years and not in months. Yeltsin did not say anything about Kazan in *Confession on an Assigned Theme;* in autobiographical forms dating from the 1960s and 1970s, stored in the Communist Party archive, he had listed it as a place of residence.[70] Later, in the second volume of his memoirs, *Notes of a President,* and in visits to the city in the 1990s and in retirement, he was to recount having lived there.[71] He had only fuzzy memories of Ignatii Yekimovich, although he did know Anna Dmitriyevna, who died in Berezniki when he was ten. Whatever he retained about his paternal grandparents, he knew that his maternal grandparents had been uprooted from Basmanovo and Butka and languished in the penumbra of the Gulag until moving to Berezniki and into his parents' house in 1945. Yeltsin skirted the subject in *Confession* even though the book was rushed into print in time for his campaign for a seat in the Russian parliament in 1990 and word of his family would have been electorally useful. He still shied away from making known his grandparents' fate in *Notes of a President*, which went to press in post-Soviet 1994. (Volume three, *Presidential Marathon*, was all about the 1990s.) For him, as for his mother, recall was selective and not only blurred.

Why the amnesia? A misplaced shame about trouble with the powers-that-be, implanted in the Yeltsins by Soviet education and propaganda, was surely part of it.[72] A sense of proportion, a mental barometer of sorrow, was also involved. For Klavdiya Yeltsina, having let Goryun in on her father-in-law's wretched death, it would have been indecent to speak in the same breath about her parents, who got through their purgatory alive. Another dampener, symptomatic of the times, was a conspiracy of silence inside the nuclear family. A nephew of Nikolai and Klavdiya's from Butka who boarded with them in Berezniki for two years in the late 1950s never heard them refer to Nikolai's arrest, and in an interview with me in 2005, in Butka, swore that it was a fiction.[73] About the incarceration, Yeltsin wrote in *Notes:* "My father never spoke with me about it. He erased this piece of his life from his memory as if it had never been. The family was forbidden to talk about the subject." When I asked him about it, he repeated these words almost verbatim.[74] The autobiographical note Nikolai wrote in Berezniki did not mention the OGPU and the Gulag.[75] Klavdiya Yeltsina was more loquacious and more agitated. Goryun concludes on the basis of his contact with her that she "felt herself innocently wronged" and "could not have failed to tell her children . . . about the tragic occurrences of the 1930s."[76] To my question in 2002 about whether his mother was more unforgiving of the family's pain than her husband, Yeltsin nodded yes but did not go into detail. And he indicated his familiarity with the Yeltsins and Starygins having been pauperized and stigmatized: "I did not approve of dekulakization, I did not support it. I was hurt for my grandfather [Starygin], whom I loved, and for my father and mother."[77] But being hurt and verbalizing the source of the hurt were two different responses.

We can take Yeltsin at his word that until he held Nikolai Yeltsin's OGPU interrogation file in his hand in the 1990s he was uninformed about many details of the victimization of his family. He also says in *Notes* that, if he had come by this information earlier, he would have understood the "banal horror" of Stalinism and his life might have "taken a different turn."[78] This is more problematic, in that Yeltsin was not unaware of the police state and knew generally how it had impinged on his kin. A different political turn in the Soviet 1930s or 1940s would have been impossible. The Urals, like Russia and the USSR as a whole, were bombarded with word of the misdeeds of saboteurs and spies. The Urals party leadership under Ivan Kabakov was purged by Stalin in 1937 as a "right-wing and Trotskyite center," and officials, intellectuals, and factory directors were arrested by the thousands. Agitprop encouraged citizens to pass on to the police anonymous tips about loose talk. "People had to answer for it if they made remiss statements about Soviet reality or maintained relations with friends or relatives who had been condemned as 'enemies of the people.'"[79] In 1937 and the first nine months of 1938, when the Perm area was still part of Sverdlovsk region, most political prisoners under sentence of death were convoyed to the provincial capital for execution. At a killing field just west of Sverdlovsk, some seven thousand men and women from places like Perm and Berezniki were shot in those twenty-one months, an average of eleven a day. A memorial cross was put up there in the 1990s.[80]

For those who came of age in the shadow of such barbarism, Yeltsin among them, putting a lid on the recapitulation of terror was a psychological defense mechanism and insurance against repercussions from babbling about it. The trouble was that over the years and the decades the repression fed on itself. The later the sufferings of the elders were owned up to, the more the silence had to be explained, which in turn raised the cost of making a clean breast of it and finally moving on.

CHAPTER TWO

Scripts

Nikolai and Klavdiya Yeltsin, their vagabondage over, settled down in Berezniki, as did Nikolai's three brothers. Boris lived with his parents there until he headed for Sverdlovsk and a higher education in 1949.

Berezniki was the second city of Perm *oblast'*, the principal Soviet term for province after 1929. At 59° 24' north, it is set in taiga of spruce, silver fir, and the spindly birches that lend it its name (*bereznik* or *bereznyak* is birch wood), and has only 100 to 110 frost-free days a year. In population, it was 65,000 in 1939, not counting internees, and maybe 80,000 in 1950. The Perm area, having been part of a region centered in Sverdlovsk since 1923, was made an oblast in 1938, the last section of the Urals freed from the control of Sverdlovsk. From 1940 to 1957, it and its capital would bear the name Molotov, after Stalin henchman Vyacheslav Molotov.

The enveloping forest has a pellucid, rustling beauty, and every June and July it has "white nights" as enchanting as those of St. Petersburg or Stockholm. But as factory towns go it would be hard to think of one much bleaker than Berezniki when the Yeltsins made their way there. Decades before, an 1890 travelogue, describing an approach by vessel up the Kama from Perm, drew a panorama of man-made desolation: "The closer you get to Usol'e, the grimmer and more mournful the riverbanks. You no longer see forest; the fields are without greenery. . . . On both banks . . . you find salt barns, linked by dark, cold tunnels. Great black saltworks stand out against the pewter sky and create an impression of gloom."[1] By the 1930s the new city's factories were turning out soda, mineral fertilizers, dyes, and pesticides. Its residential center was built about five miles inland, to keep travel time to the workplaces there to a minimum. During World War II (the Great Patriotic War of 1941 to 1945, as the Russians knew it), a magnesium and titanium mill was added to the chemical works. Berezniki was awash in refugees and wounded servicemen, several schools served as rehab hospitals, and evacuated factory machinery was stored in mine shafts and chutes. In addition to gunpowder and conventional explosives, Berezniki was one of five cities in the Soviet Union to produce toxic compounds for chemical weapons. Workers made mustard gas, lewisite, hydrogen cyanide, and adamsite and decanted thousands of tons of them into canisters for the army and air force. The ecological byproducts were horrendous. Contaminants spewed unfiltered into the water, atmosphere, and soil; puddles of brine and effluent pockmarked the townscape; tailings coughed up by the mines, ashes, and chemicals all sprawled in windblown dunes up to 250 feet high; houses and factories could sink into karsts and mining cavities. All these years later, Berezniki is one of the most polluted cities in Russia. Industrial smoke and fumes still foul the air. A containment pond for liquid wastes, built next to the Kama after the war, glows an iridescent green and does not ice over in wintertime. Berezniki's children have abnormal rates of morbidity and are eight times likelier to have blood ailments than those in other urban centers.[2]

Never far away in the Yeltsins' allotted hometown were the barbed wire, watchtowers, and guard dogs of the Gulag. A stockade for 11,000 German and Axis prisoners of war was set up in 1943. A new strict-labor camp for Soviet convicts came in 1946 to expand a chemical plant, and to build another in 1950, when its workforce capped off at 4,500. Across the Kama artery in Usol'e lay a camp specializing in lumbering (with 24,900 inmates in 1940 and 3,600 in 1953). Twenty miles upriver at Solikamsk, the location of the Stroganovs' first salt pit, was a small camp for building a pulp and paper mill (4,300 inmates in 1938) and a big one for lumbering (32,700 in 1938); at Kizel, forty miles south, captives logged and built hydro dams in two waves (with peaks at 7,700 in 1946 and 21,300 in 1953).[3] Taken together, this unfree labor dwarfed the legally free workforce of Berezniki.[4]

Soviet cities were cauldrons for social change and for the conversion of peasants into proletarians. But the size of the inflow from the villages, the tenacity of agrarian identities, and the systematic underinvestment in urban infrastructure meant that the cities themselves were substantially peasantized in the 1930s and 1940s.[5] When the Yeltsins first walked its streets, Berezniki had almost no pavement, no sewage system, and no public transit. It had some asphalt and sewage mains by 1950, though still no buses or streetcars. And yet, Berezniki had been laid out by planners from Leningrad as a "socialist city," and there was some attention to culture and leisure: the Avangard cinema, a live theater, a museum, several stadiums, a park and arboretum on Stalin Prospect (Lenin Prospect today). Postwar apartment houses had "elements of the classical orders, immense window apertures reminiscent of Roman triumphal arches," and "obelisk-like turrets in memory of those who had fallen" in the crusade against fascism.[6]

Nikolai Yeltsin made the best of the situation. He bootstrapped himself during and after the war from woodworker at the bench to foreman, work superintendent, dispatcher, planner, and head of several technical bureaus at Sevuraltyazhstroi. In wartime Klavdiya Yeltsina did twelve-hour shifts as a dressmaker. After 1945 she was that rarity in the urban USSR, a housewife who worked wholly in the home. She reared their two sons and a daughter, Valentina, born in July 1944, took in sewing to pad out Nikolai's income, and cared for her parents, who did not work once they were out of exile.

Debarking in 1937, the family found lodgings for several months in Usol'e, from where Nikolai commuted to work by ferry (there was no bridge over the Kama until the 1950s). After about a year shoehorned with three other households into a scruffy timber cottage in Berezniki, they were given one of the twenty rooms in a new two-story wood barracks, in the adjacent Zhdanovo Fields section of town. It had outdoor plumbing (privies and a well) and was so leaky and drafty that the children huddled on winter nights with a nanny goat. The animal, Polya, was also a source of fresh milk. In *Confession on an Assigned Theme*, Yeltsin fastened on the auditory porousness of the thin walls. Were any tenant to mark a name day, birthday, or wedding, someone would put on the windup gramophone "and the whole barracks would be singing. . . . Quarrels, conversations, scandals, secrets, mirth—the entire barracks could hear, everyone knew everything. It could be that is why I still remember the barracks with such revulsion."[7] Across the street was the city's only public bathhouse, where a weekly soaping and soaking could be had for pennies. Next to it was the bustling farmers' bazaar, one of the thousands in Soviet towns where peasants since 1935 had been allowed to sell, at unregulated prices, food they grew in plots behind their homes. On another side were sheds for the barracks dwellers' goats, chickens, and geese, while cattle grazed in the unbuilt portion of

Zhdanovo Fields. The log house and the barracks have long since been torn down.[8]

In 1944, in anticipation of Valentina's birth, Nikolai used his construction skills and tools and, it may be hazarded, his connections with materials suppliers to erect a private house, as was permissible under Soviet legislation. It was in brick and stood on a parcel of land known as the Seventh Block, facing First Pond, the water reservoir for the old Stroganov mine. The home's four rooms and a kitchen were enough to accommodate the Starygins comfortably when they arrived from Serov in 1945. Boris Yeltsin did not note this change of circumstances in his autobiography, saying only that they lived in the Berezniki barracks for ten years (the actual figure was about six) and passing over how they were housed after that. More than likely, he feared some readers would impute the family's acquisition of such an asset to greed or privilege. A private house (but not the land beneath it, which was owned by the state) was a valuable nest egg, and protection against the inflation that ate into cash savings.[9]

A decade and a half after dekulakization, the Yeltsin house, which is still in use, was palpable betterment, and it spoke well of the esteem Nikolai was earning in the urban world. Ironically, it also re-created the rural ambience the family had lost and felt the need of. Grandfather and grandmother Starygin having moved in, the three generations cohabited, much as they would have in the Russian village, where they would have shared a house or lived within walking distance. Out in the yard were a woodpile, a vegetable garden, some poultry—and the small steambath Boris built for Vasilii Starygin in 1949. But the village continued to tug at the family's heartstrings. In 1955 Nikolai was asked to act as chairman of a Urals collective farm—in the village of Urol, Molotov oblast—during an all-USSR campaign to recruit urban specialists for positions in the agrarian economy. He accepted, but the experiment failed, and he took back his technical job in the Sevuraltyazhstroi construction trust in two months.[10] In 1959 he was sent to represent the trust at the USSR Exhibition of Economic Achievements, the trade fair and amusement park in Moscow lorded over by Vera Mukhina's steel statue of a brawny male worker and a peasant woman holding aloft a hammer and a sickle. When he received the invitation to the capital, which he had never laid eyes on, he could not believe his good fortune: "He read it out, grabbed his head, and bounded off to the office [to check it], although by the standards of those years he cut a figure that corresponded [to the honor]."[11] But the bright lights were not really for him. In 1962 Nikolai was to take a pension and, after a thirty-year absence, to repatriate to Butka with his wife, turning the wheel full circle. Klavdiya's aging parents made the move with them. The sale of the Berezniki home allowed them to purchase a cozy cabin at 1 Korotkii Lane with cash.[12]

The family's mores were rooted in communism and in the austerity of the Urals countryside and of their Old Believer and Russian Orthodox forerunners there. While Klavdiya was "devoutly religious" from first to the last, the Yeltsins, in the land of official atheism, were not observant. Churchgoing was impossible in Berezniki, as the only Orthodox temple, the Church of the Beheading of John the Baptist, was closed by the government in 1937 and did not open again for worship until 1992. Valentina Yeltsina, unlike her brothers, was not christened as a babe in 1944. A layman could have administered the sacrament, or the Yeltsins could have gone to a village church outside of Berezniki, but they took neither option. The living room of the home had no icons on display, although the Starygins did keep icons in their bedroom and Klavdiya Vasil'evna prayed before a miniature icon she hid from prying eyes.[13] Boris grew up with no religious beliefs and developed a regard for Christianity only in the 1980s and 1990s.[14]

Nikolai and Klavdiya, she said in 1991, two years before her death, agreed that it was a big job "raising a good person who does not run around the streets like a waif or come into bad company."[15] None of the siblings smoked, played cards or dice, used smutty language, or touched liquor. Any trespass on this code would have been condemned in the classroom as well as in the home. Teachers at the schoolhouse where Boris studied after the war would order the pupils to shun for an entire month any pupil with the odor of tobacco on his or her breath; for the smell of alcohol, the penalty was a one-week suspension from classes and a stern note to the parents. At the age of sixteen, Yeltsin intercepted another adolescent in the act of buying a glassful of vodka at a roadside stand; he prudishly poured the liquid on the sidewalk, paid the vendor for it, and walked off. Unlike cigarettes, gambling, and swearing, drinking was one thing in which he would indulge in later life. His old classmate Sergei Molchanov, who lived in Berezniki until his death in 2006, was sure that the first alcohol that Yeltsin ever touched was the glass of champagne he was given to sip at his secondary-school graduation party in 1949.[16]

The growing boy had his mother's square physiognomy. To her, whom he had all to himself during Nikolai's interlude in the Gulag and then frequent stays at construction jobs, were his warmest attachments. "My mother," he said in a judgment echoed by everyone who knew her, "was a very kind woman, tender and caressing." "I . . . loved her considerably more than my father," he added.[17] In disposition, Boris Yeltsin always stressed how much he took after the man of the house: "My father's character was gruff [*krutoi*], like my grandfather's, and I suppose this was passed on to me." The context indicates the grandfather referred to here is Ignatii Yeltsin (Nikolai's father), but Vasilii Starygin (Klavdiya's father), whom Boris Yeltsin knew far longer and better, did not give up much to Ignatii in the gruffness department. In the late 1940s, he was "an imposing codger with a long beard and an original mind," Yeltsin wrote, and as "unregenerate and obstinate" as they come.[18] In a press interview on turning seventy-five in 2006, Boris Yeltsin attributed "my emotionalism and explosive character" to Starygin: "This was inborn. It was handed on to me from my grandfather [Starygin]. My grandmother was afraid to cross him."[19]

Between father and son, Nikolai and Boris, bullheadedness on both sides and a rivalry for Klavdiya's affection, aggravated by Nikolai's absences, by his binge drinking, and by the wide spacing of the children, made for a fraught relationship. In his first memoir volume, Yeltsin tells of Nikolai strapping him with a leather belt and of the arguments this kicked up between his parents. He would endure it mutely—and his father for his part would also say nothing—until his mother, "my constant protector," came to the rescue and shooed Nikolai away.[20] In one theory about the beatings, Yeltsin's submission is said to point to masochism in his makeup.[21] It is a cockamamie theory: Russian peasant boys took corporal punishment without a murmur; girls could cry, but not boys. Yeltsin took no joy in it and finally pushed back. At fourteen or fifteen, he demanded that Nikolai refrain from pummeling him and leave him in charge of his own character formation. "We are not in the time of the tsars," Klavdiya remembered him saying to his father, "when it was all right to thrash people with birch rods." It was then that Nikolai stopped the beatings.[22] There is no way to know how often these whippings were administered or at what age they began. Boris Yeltsin's account says his father brought him into the bedroom, closed the door, and laid him on the bed as he pulled out the strap. This would have had to be in the family house, built in 1944, since in the barracks they had only one room. One might infer from this that the punishment did not begin until the boy was around the age of puberty and did not last more than a year or two.

While the nurturing Klavdiya Vasil'evna took his side against her husband, she should not be turned into a cardboard saint. A boyhood friend,

Vladimir Zhdanov, told a reporter in 2001 that Auntie Klava, as the local children called her, had teeth beneath the smile and did not coddle her son: "She was very strong-willed and strict. . . . [He] could not disobey her on anything. If she said, 'Do your lessons,' he sat right down and did them."[23] The mature Boris was to take a similar stance toward non–family members subordinate to him.

Nor did everything with Nikolai Ignat'evich have a sharp edge. There was an imaginative side to him, which Boris admired. Here is how he puts it in *Confession:*

> My father was always trying to invent something. One of his dreams was to come up with an automated machine that would lay bricks. He would sketch it out, do drawings, think it over, make calculations, and then produce another set of drawings. It was a kind of phantom for him. Alas, no one has ever invented such a gizmo, although even now whole research institutes rack their brains over it. He would describe to me what his machine would be like and how it would work: how it would mix the mortar, put down the bricks, clean off the excess, and move along. He had worked it all out in his head and had drawn the general plan for it, but never realized the idea in metal.[24]

Nikolai bequeathed to his son this restlessness, his work ethic, a knowledge of carpentry, and the art of the folk percussion instrument, the wood spoons *(lozhki)*, played by slapping one spoon against another and against the bended knee. He also handed the boy a love of the *banya*, the wet steambath that alternates sweating with cooling in fresh water or a pool and cleanses the skin, relaxes the mind, and, as Russians see it, strengthens the organism and prepares the bather for life's trials. The bath is often taken in single-sex groups and in the culture can be conducive to male bonding, as it was at various times for Boris Yeltsin.

Yeltsin's exegesis of the years in Berezniki is the most novelistic section of his memoirs, yet it skimps on details and is not always reliable. Two years, 1937 to 1939, were inactive, a respite from education, at home with his mother and baby brother, after the kindergarten in Kazan.[25] Six years, 1939 to 1945, were passed at Railway School No. 95, an elementary school operated by the transport ministry (Yeltsin does not name the school), and four, 1945 through 1949, at the municipal Secondary School No. 1, or the Pushkin

School (this one he does name), which offered ten years of instruction. The company Boris kept was almost exclusively male. Many of his friends in the first school were the sons of army officers stationed at a military college moved to safety in Berezniki from Leningrad.[26] The Pushkin School, under Soviet policy, was converted to an all-boys school in 1946, his second year there.[27] Above him, though, at school as at home—and more widely in a society where tens of millions of able-bodied men were in military service or had given their lives in it—those in authority were often female. Of 26 to 27 million Soviet deaths in the war, about 20 million were male. In 1946 women in their twenties outnumbered men by about 50 percent. Two million soldiers from the Urals served in the war and more than 600,000 died.[28]

Yeltsin as memoirist vouched for the importance to him of the formative phase of his life—of "childhood, out of which come all the models that the person assimilates firmly and forever."[29] It is at this labile time that we find him evincing what I think of as his personal scripts, characteristic bunches of attitudes and behaviors that recur in his adult life.[30] He acted out five of them, turning on survival, duty, success, testing of his powers, and rebellion.

Grinding poverty, acquaintance with oppression, and a punitory father all dictated that Boris Yeltsin take care of brute survival and the basics of life. From the outbreak of war with Germany in 1941 until 1947, Berezniki schools had no central heating, only stoves fed with firewood, and the inkwells froze in the winter months. Like the other pupils, Yeltsin frequently wrote his lessons on scissored-up paper wrappings. The family "made ends meet as best they could," his friend Zhdanov remembers.[31] The phasing out of food rationing in the mid-1930s went with a slight improvement in supply in Berezniki, although to levels below the experience of most Westerners.[32] Rationing was reimposed during the war. His mother would say much later:

> Hunger returned to us in the first winter of the war [1941–42]. Borya would come home from school, sit in the corner of the room, and begin to moan inconsolably, "I'm h-u-n-g-r-y, I c-a-n-'-t take it." At moments like this, my heart would bleed because I had nothing to feed him with, not even a stale crust. All foodstuffs were being distributed through ration cards, and they were calculated at a minimal level. The daily norm for bread, practically the only thing they gave out, was 800 grams [about two pounds] for [manual] workers and 400 grams for their dependents. On the black market, they asked one-quarter of a month's pay for a baguette.

> From time to time, I had to send the children to the restaurant in our neighborhood so they would be fed out of kindness. The children and I had to swallow no small amount of pride because of this.[33]

One can see how every drop of Polya's warm milk was precious to the Yeltsins. Boris and his mother mowed hay in the summers, sold their half of the harvest to whoever wanted it, and bought bread with the proceeds. The year he was twelve, he herded sheep on a local farm. He carried pails of water, cooked, and darned his own socks and underwear. "My childhood went by rather cheerlessly," he says in summary. "There weren't delights or delicacies, nothing like that. We just wanted to survive, survive, and survive."[34]

The second, closely related script the boy lived by revolved around duties. In the family setting, he was a devoted son, especially in relation to his mother. A half-century after the fact, Klavdiya Yeltsina was to tell a journalist about the thirteen-year-old Boris—not Nikolai—coming to see her in the maternity ward after she gave birth to Valentina, bringing her tasty meals and embroidering a rug with a goldfish theme for her homecoming. When they planted their family garden with potatoes, "My older son would go to hill it and hoe it, without ever having to be reminded."[35] Yeltsin also provided protection to his mother in the home. As he and his mother withheld from the published accounts, Nikolai, who beat Boris, also struck Klavdiya Yeltsina. When his mother was the victim, it was Boris's turn to stand guard over her. He precociously took moral responsibility for a parent, following a pattern detectable in the younger years of many leading individuals.[36]

In wider context, Soviet society swaddled its members, young and old, and taught them to put collective over individual needs. Not to do so was to woo disaster. Boris Yeltsin cites his father as his role model in dutifulness. Fragmentary remarks and body language implied that Nikolai Yeltsin had no use for those who had inflicted such pain on him and his. As Boris pictured it in an interview, choosing his words with care:

> He never was close to the communists and he never was a communist. This mirrored his conviction that communism was not the line Russia should take. . . . In general, it was not customary in our family to have conversations . . . about the Soviet regime, about the communists. But we did talk in a restrained way, in a very restrained way. In this connection, my father was more guided by principle [than my mother] and had a greater influence on me. He had his opinion, his point of view, and he

> defended it. And he taught me about being principled, for sure. He taught me a lot.[37]

For the father, then, being "principled" meant, on the one hand, never praising those who had done you wrong. On the other hand, it meant bearing one's cross stoically, a moral he had set aside in Kazan. And it meant abiding by the established rules and giving society and the Soviet behemoth their due. Nikolai Yeltsin did not wear a soldier's uniform in the war; he most likely was needed more in Berezniki. His brother, Boris's uncle Andrian, did serve and was killed at the front; brother Dmitrii was invalided home to Berezniki with an amputated leg and died of complications in the 1950s. Hard feelings from some of these events lingered for decades. Andrian's son (Boris Andrianovich Yeltsin), who has spent all his life in Berezniki, said to a journalist shortly before Boris Nikolayevich's death that Nikolai "used tricks to get out of going to the front, at the same time as my father died in battle." Because they were ashamed, he claimed, Nikolai and his family turned their back on Andrian's widow and son afterward.[38] Despite the strikes against him politically, Nikolai, the inventor manqué, did not back down in work-related disagreements. In the early 1940s, he paid from his own wages for specialists to take the train from Moscow to check a factory design he said was unsound; the outsiders bore him out. "He held his ground. . . . He risked his neck, even though, in the case of success, he had nothing to gain."[39] At the construction site, he was a taskmaster, intolerant of the unproductive and the unpunctual, though never profane or screaming.[40]

Boris Yeltsin knew about the iniquities of communism, which might in principle have turned him away from the Soviet dictatorship in toto. Asked in retirement about whether this was so, he said point-blank that it was not:

> In those early years, when I was in school, I was not yet conscious of [the system]. I hardly could have been. It may be that awareness was forming subconsciously *[podspudno]*, but I did not formulate it for myself, or I did not formulate it with any clarity. I was not that conscious of the perniciousness of Soviet power or of the communist regime. . . . Propaganda and ideology were everywhere. They took a person down one and the same track. There was no chance for him to deviate to the left or the right.[41]

Far from bucking the system, the adolescent Yeltsin was an amenable cog in it. He enlisted in the red-scarved Young Pioneers, the official Soviet organization for building character in young children, in 1939 or 1940, and in the Komsomol, the Communist Youth League, after his fourteenth birthday in 1945. He participated energetically in Pioneer and Komsomol assemblies and hobby circles, without taking a leadership position in either organization.[42] When war broke out, he and his buddies "wanted to go to the front but, of course, we were not allowed." So they played soldier games, making faux pistols, rifles, and cannon to act out their patriotic fantasies.[43]

About male child Yeltsin and the received wisdom, the most that can be said is that he was youthfully inquisitive and entertained half-formed representations of abuse. He purchased at a bookstore and borrowed from the Berezniki town library volumes out of the collected papers of Lenin—of whom there was (and is) a life-sized statue in the courtyard of the Pushkin School—so as to understand for himself the revolution of 1917. He had found the answers in the textbooks unsatisfying and was thrown by citations in Lenin of revolutionaries who were nonpersons under Stalin. He did not read the sterilized, Stalin-edited *Short Course* of party history: "I understood I would not find the answers there. I wanted to get an answer from Lenin." He gave his notebooks to brother Mikhail when he left for college.[44] Boris's concern with Lenin fit with the general style of a Stalinist political education, which "was based on devotion not so much to ideas as to *specific leaders* who were identified with them."[45]

It was at this point that a political demigod not in the Marxist-Leninist pantheon enthralled him. That was Peter I, or Peter the Great, the tsar who reigned from 1682 to 1725, built St. Petersburg (Leningrad in the Soviet period), and brought Russia into the community of European powers. Yeltsin read Aleksei Tolstoy's historical novel *Peter I*, which was studied in all Soviet schools, and saw the film based on it, directed by Vladimir Petrov and starring Nikolai Simonov, which came out in two parts in 1937–38. Peter, Yeltsin said in 2002, for him wore a halo and was "one of my teachers by example" in school.[46]

Along with bare-bones survivalism and compliance with duty, Yeltsin was responding to a third script—for personal success through the development and assertion of self. In his memoirs, he writes of his prowess in the classroom: "I stood out among the other youngsters for my activism and vigor. From first grade to tenth . . . I was always elected class monitor [*starosta*]. I always did well at my studies and got 5s," the highest mark on the five-point Russian scale.[47] Vladimir Zhdanov, his fellow pupil in the railway school, concurs:

> He had authority. We often turned to him for advice, and every year we elected him class monitor. He always studied hard and willingly. Every subject came easy to him. He would often be called to the blackboard, particularly when someone was not able to answer. His best subject was mathematics. Borya had a mathematical cast of mind. He was always the first to finish his quizzes and would then pass his exercise book around the class. He never minded if we copied the answers. . . . [He] was a good comrade to all.

That Yeltsin's sharing of his problem sets was not only an unselfish but a corrupt act, and one against the norms of any Soviet school, seems not to have occurred to Zhdanov. Cheaters in the class would have had a leg up on the others and would have owed Yeltsin a favor. Did Yeltsin call in his debts? Zhdanov does not say. Instead, he goes on to recollect that Yeltsin was an effective if not an artful communicator: "He spoke in a vivid Urals accent. Dragging out his syllables, he expressed himself in the way of simple people. In his gesticulations and manner of contact, it was the same."[48]

The awakening to his own talents, coalescing with awareness that others benefited from the stratified Soviet order more than he and his parents, spurred a desire in Yeltsin to gain standing in the system. Klavdiya Yeltsina gave Andrei Goryun the telling vignette of her son learning in the war years, before he was old enough to shave, that the store where they exchanged their ration coupons for food had a closed subdivision for "the upper echelons" in the town. Borya found his way in and gawked at the white bread, cheese, and American canned spam on the shelves. "This was when I heard him say, 'Mama, no matter what, I'm going to be a boss.' Yes, yes, 'boss' *[nachal'nik]*, I remember it well."[49] In another version, Boris tells Klavdiya he wants to become an engineer when he grows up.[50]

The rub was that Railway School No. 95 was an unsatisfactory springboard for any youth's career. Built of logs near the Berezniki train station, it was founded in 1906 to bestow literacy on the sons and daughters of railroad workers; after 1917 its clientele widened to the children of all blue-collar workers, but the mission stayed the same. It became a seven-year school only in 1932. Most graduates went either into a trade school or into manual labor for the railroad or the saltworks. It says a lot about the Yeltsins' tenuous status that in 1939, two years out of kindergarten, Boris was assigned to School No. 95, on Vainer Street, a twenty-minute walk from their barracks, and not to School No. 1, which was on Shkol'naya Street five minutes away.

School No. 1, where Yeltsin moved in 1945, was better known by the second name, Pushkin School, appended to it in 1937 in observance of the centenary of the death of the national poet, Alexander Pushkin (1799–1837). Built by the potash combine in 1931–32 as a "model" *(obraztsovaya)* school for Churtan village, it was donated to the city when Berezniki was established. This was the school for the city's best and brightest youngsters, and admittance was by examination. Its physical plant, in brick and with indoor plumbing and a gymnasium, outclassed the railway school's. The teachers exacted more at Pushkin, it had a student orchestra and after-school activities, and it had an evening branch and a boarding unit for village children. Doing well was promoted by staff and at meetings between students and parents, where World War II veterans "spoke about the usefulness of being educated."[51] Punning on the name, the Pushkin School boys were spoken of as *pushkari*—"gunners" or, as we might say, hotshots. Girls from Berezniki's two ten-year institutions for females, the Gorky and Ostrovsky Schools, "counted it pure happiness to stroll with the gunners along the local Broadway," the well-lit stretch of Stalin Prospect near the Berëzka café.[52] Pushkin graduates could qualify for a post-secondary education and entry into white-collar employment. First they needed the diploma, and that was no sure thing. In 1948–49, Yeltsin's final year, there were 660 boys in first through fourth grades, 214 in fifth through seventh grades, seventy-two in eighth and ninth, and a mere nineteen left in tenth grade. Five of the twenty-six pupils in his ninth-year class were not promoted to tenth grade, and two of the remaining twenty-one did not enroll in September 1948.[53]

In this bracing environment, Boris Yeltsin thrived. Antonina Khonina, the young literature instructor who was his homeroom teacher in eighth through tenth grades, was a demanding educator who "treated all of us like adults" and would hear of no alibis for uncompleted assignments. She took a shine to Yeltsin, and he was one of her stars.[54] In ninth grade, he split seven 5s with seven 4s. In tenth, he improved to eight 5s and six 4s: 5s in the three math subjects (algebra, geometry, and trigonometry) and in biology, "The Constitution of the USSR," geography, astronomy, and German language; 4s in Russian language, literature, Soviet history, world history, physics, and chemistry.[55]

In the railway school, Yeltsin had been gangly and often sick, with nagging throat and ear problems for which his mother wound his neck in a coarse bandage. As an upperclassman at the Pushkin School, he was broad-shouldered, hale, and the tallest in class by a head. He was long-waisted, to boot, possessing a torso that accentuated his height when seated. To some of the younger Pushkin boys, he was a ruffian. One who started first grade in 1948 remembers Yeltsin uncivilly barring him from the second-floor lavatory, which was unofficially reserved for the big boys.[56] Boris had grown interested in sports and especially in volleyball, a game in which Soviet athletes excelled. He was captain of the school squad, which played against students and adults. He and a cluster of friends bought their own volleyball and net and practiced serves and rallies in the schoolyard after hours. On the court, he was forward-leaning *(napadayushchii)*, always scouting for opportunities to attack.[57] The team were city champions in 1948 and were all presented with wristwatches as prizes. "For postwar boys this was the same as if pupils today were given automobiles."[58] Yeltsin in future, perhaps inspired by this generosity, was to make it a practice of giving wristwatches away.

Yeltsin's influence with the others had only increased since the early grades. Khonina has left an affectionate cameo stressing this point:

> Boris Yeltsin [was] a tall, dignified, and studious youth. His gaze was direct, attentive, and intelligent. He was a good athlete. He never violated any of the rules of school life. Boris did not tolerate lies and made his arguments animatedly and persuasively. He read a lot and loved poetry. When he answered [in class], he would furl an eyebrow and look out at you. He spoke with conviction, making his point without empty words. You could sense a brusque character, a torrid temperament. He was sincere and big-hearted toward his comrades.[59]

Khonina was not the only member of the faculty to hold him in warm regard. In April 1948 Yeltsin was one of but two pupils, out of a total of more than nine hundred, to be selected by headmaster Mikhail Zalesov to sit on the teachers' committee organizing the assembly for the May Day holiday. Classmates Robert Zaidel and Viktor Nikolin, the other boy named to the May Day committee, qualified for the school's gold medal in 1949, with straight 5s in tenth grade. Yeltsin was a tier down, in a cohort that was mobile into social strata closed to the older generation. The adult occupations of thirteen members of the Pushkin class of 1949 are known. Among them were seven engineers—one of them Yeltsin—a physicist (Zaidel), a professor of engineering (Nikolin), an architect, an agronomist, an army officer, and a dentist.[60]

Yeltsin was rambunctious as well as proficient and a striver. In his brief reminiscences with me about Berezniki, fifty-odd years afterward, he said it was into his relations with the educational system that such discomfort as he had with Soviet reality spilled over:

> I did have a certain alienation from the school system. I waged war, if you like. Throughout my time as a pupil, I warred with my teachers—with their dictates, with their pedantry, with the absence of any freedom of choice. I might like [Anton] Chekhov, but they would force me to read [Leo] Tolstoy. I read Tolstoy also, yet still I liked Chekhov more. . . . You may say that, to the extent I opposed the system of instruction, I did it as a sign of protest against something.

The concise stories and plays of Chekhov (1860–1904), with their epiphanies and their argumentative and misunderstood characters, struck much more of a chord with Yeltsin than the voluminous, fatalistic novels of Leo Tolstoy. Chekhov was to be his favorite author: "In one short story he could describe an entire life. He had no need of the tomes that Leo Tolstoy wrote."[61] In 1993, as president of Russia, he spoke with literary critic Marietta Chudakova and her husband, Aleksandr Chudakov, who is a Chekhov scholar. Yeltsin led off with his thoughts on a Chekhov short story that neither of the Chudakovs was familiar with. When they got home, they found it in Chekhov's collected works.[62]

In *Confession on an Assigned Theme*—a title suggestive of a student or employee who departs from the appointed ways and owns up to it—Yeltsin waxed more eloquent about being the ringleader *(zavodila)* behind group hijinks than about being the class monitor or an exemplary pupil. The text chronicles no fewer than eight pranks and acts of derring-do:

1. At age eleven, in third or fourth grade, he crawled under a fence and purloined two live RGD-33 hand grenades from an arms depot in a derelict church (the John the Baptist temple, it turns out), "to learn what was inside them."
2. As a fifth grader, he goaded his class to jump out a second-floor window and hide in an outbuilding in the schoolyard.
3. Around that time, motivated by the anti-German emotions rampant during the war, he hammered phonograph needles bottom-up through the seat of a German-language teacher's desk chair, exposing her to the sharp points.
4. In the springtime, he participated in races over slithery logs on the runoff-swollen Zyryanka River.

5. He led mêlées with fists and clubs and up to a hundred combatants.
6. In 1945 or 1946 (the timing is unclear), he raked his elementary-school homeroom teacher over the coals, before a packed auditorium at graduation from School No. 95, for tormenting the class.
7. In 1948, after ninth grade in the Pushkin School, he went AWOL for weeks in the forest with chums.
8. In 1949 he contested the school's ruling that he repeat tenth grade after missing time recuperating from his backpack hike.[63]

And there unquestionably were others, as Yeltsin said to me in an interview. Sergei Molchanov has recounted how the two of them lit a sooty wood fire in a home steambath in their neighborhood; Sergei left for dinner, and Boris blacked out from inhaling the fumes.[64]

Three of the bravado incidents described by Yeltsin resulted in injury or illness: the thumb and index finger (and tip of the middle finger) of his left hand blown off by a grenade fuse (he hit it with a hammer while his partners in crime looked on from a safe distance), and surgery to stop the spread of gangrene; a broken, crooked nose from a fight; and three months in the hospital to cure typhoid fever from drinking impure water on the hike. In retrospect, many were death-defying feats. After all, the hand grenade could just as well have sprayed its hunks of steel into his skull as into his left hand. In a medical system with no antibiotics, one in five typhus patients dies, and unchecked gangrene can also be fatal. The scramble across the logs could have drowned the frisky boys. In the nose-breaking fight, he was whacked by a cart axle and thought he was done for—"But I came to, pulled myself together, and was carried home."[65] Molchanov saw smoke engulfing the steambath, ran back, and pulled Yeltsin unconscious into the open air—saving his friend's life, he says. In Yeltsin's account, four actions incurred disciplinary penalties at school: grades of 2 out of 5 on the day for going out the window; a reprimand for the phonograph needles; suspension of his elementary-school diploma for the graduation philippic; and the refusal to register him for tenth grade following his recovery from the typhoid infection.

These events follow a two-pronged logic. The river race and the trio ending in bodily harm (and the steambath fire as a marginal case) bespeak what we can term a testing script. Here Yeltsin willingly underwent the risks for no reason other than the thrill of it and to demonstrate his mettle—urges for which pubescent hormones were surely responsible in part. In the tests detailed in *Confession,* the adversary is nature or his compeers and he narrowly deflects crippling wounds or death. In the literally most stomach-churning test, Boris and schoolmates set out up the western foothills of the Urals, in scorching heat, to find the headwaters of the Yaiva River, a feeder of the Kama; they carried neither an accurate map nor provisions enough to last the trip. The sulphurous spring at the river's source found, the lads traded their gear for a dinghy, roughed it and straggled aimlessly for a week, and floated in delirium downriver toward Berezniki. Yeltsin docked the boat beneath a railroad trestle before passing out. That and other footloose moments were more unsettling to his mother than to his father, maybe because Nikolai Yeltsin was so frequently away and she dreaded being left alone. As a friend of Klavdiya's later years noted, since Nikolai was often gone, and since Boris was his mother's defender upon Nikolai's return, "A heavy burden was laid on Boris. He helped his mother out at this time but was always trying to get away, run off, vanish, cavort, even in his youngest years. . . . She would say [to me], 'Why did he do such things, to get some kind of revenge?' She was always asking this question."[66]

The remaining stunts were juvenile protests against authority figures, with hormones as impetus and maybe politics as subtext. In this rebellion script, the lines are tidily drawn and have the schoolboy clashing with callous pedagogues and educational bureaucrats. The most glaring case of hooliganism, as drawn by Yeltsin, is the speech at his graduation from elementary school. He asked for the floor, spoke courteous words about several of his teachers, and then surprised the audience by lighting into his homeroom teacher as "not fit to be a teacher and a rearer of children." "I went at her hammer and tongs," giving examples of her insensitivity such as the requirement that boys and girls gather food scraps for her pet pig. "Fury, uproar—the whole event was sullied. The next day the teachers' council sent for my father and told him my diploma was being canceled."[67] In Yeltsin's retelling, the enemy mostly crumpled under the force of his salvos. The 2 grades were annulled; his diploma was reinstated and the obnoxious homeroom teacher retired; and he took his tenth-grade finals at the Pushkin School after completing four semesters of course work in two on home study (his pals were not given this privilege). Only the teacher of German, perforated though not seriously injured, did not cave. The crises roped in his father, not his mother, as enforcer of decorum; it was during the graduation ruckus, when Boris would have been fifteen (if his memoir account is correct), that Nikolai last tried to beat his son with a strap. And they gave Yeltsin his first contact with political actors. To resolve the dispute over his diploma, he did an end run around his new headmaster, Vasilii Zanin, to the municipal school directorate and then to the arbiter of all things in Berezniki, the Communist Party apparatus: "That was when I first came to know what the *gorkom* [city committee] of the party was."[68]

The tales of puckishness and delinquency from *Confession* are required reading for anyone seeking to comprehend Yeltsin's life, but he was not above embellishing them. The Zyryanka, dammed to form First Pond, is about the width of a city street downstream (where it is five minutes down the hill from John the Baptist church). Even in the annual snow melt, it is not the raging torrent Yeltsin depicts—which is not to rule out jousting on the logs. Vladimir Zhdanov has no remembrance of the fifth graders going out the window; the railway school, he points out, was all on one floor, and it would have been easier to play hooky than to follow a showoff outside. Some of Yeltsin's defiance of his teachers may have been more impish than impudent. When Zhdanov was asked by the reporter if teachers had tongue-lashed Yeltsin for passing his problem sets around, he replied, "They are only finding out about it now."[69] For some events, memoirist Yeltsin mistakes the fine points yet not the main meaning. The jump out the window seems indeed to have occurred, but at the Pushkin School, which has two stories and where Yeltsin's homeroom (which I saw in 2005) was on the second floor.[70] While the mean trick on his elementary school German teacher is uncorroborated, again there appears to have been such an incident with a chair at the Pushkin School. A boxer's nose and a maimed hand, about which he was always self-conscious, were fleshly mementos of his adventures. Conversations in 2005 with clergy and parishioners at the reopened Church of the Beheading of John the Baptist substantiated that it was used as a furniture factory and munitions warehouse during the war, and that a daredevil could have slipped in and made off with small projectiles. None doubted that Yeltsin had done so. For the wilderness trek and the infection in 1948, we have verification by a fellow pupil.[71]

The episode that remains mysterious is the one to which Yeltsin gives the most import: the stand against his oafish teacher at School No. 95 and the struggle for exculpation that followed. Yeltsin's own account does not quite add up. He writes that after the fracas he "decided not to return" to the school and to enroll at Pushkin, the place that was to open doors for him. But School No. 95 offered seven years of classes only, and so he would have had no choice but to move on to a secondary school had he finished the seventh grade there; the one secondary school in Berezniki that accepted boys was School No. 1, the Pushkin School. Muddying the waters is a prosaic detail: Pushkin School records, and the commemorative plaque outside, show Boris Yeltsin to have transferred there in 1945—in the second half of or at the end of sixth grade or in the first half of seventh grade—and not, as he says, after seventh grade, which would have been in mid-1946.[72] The acting up with his teacher, if it happened, could not have been at his graduation, since he never passed out of School No. 95.[73] But *something* got Yeltsin in hot water there. His mother told relatives later that he left his first school because of a disagreement with a female teacher. It was unheard-of for a pupil to quit a Soviet elementary school without completing the sequence of instruction in it. Teachers at the Pushkin School believed that the decision was mutual, that friction over behavior such as the theft of the grenades had coiled to a level where young Boris was happy to go and the exasperated staff of School No. 95 was relieved to see the last of him.[74]

A bloodline in the free and religious peasantry, a proud and individualistic family, the confiscation of hard-earned property, the arbitrary arrest and loss of loved ones, a closet anti-communist of a father—any one ingredient would have shortened the odds that Yeltsin would eventually strike out on another road. He was not unique in any one of these respects, and not in the millstone of hardship he carried. Other Soviet leaders had poverty and politically driven private tragedies in their blood. For Yeltsin, it is not the particulars but the gestalt that commands our attention.

Already his life's plotline diverged from that of his future ally and antagonist, Mikhail Gorbachev. Although the Gorbachevs of Privol'noye, Stavropol province, had their share of tears, the family had been dirt poor and supported the collectivization drive that was at its climax when Gorbachev and Yeltsin were born in 1931. Gorbachev's maternal grandfather, Pantelei Gopkalo, was a communist, the organizer of a peasant cooperative in the 1920s, and the first chairman of the local kolkhoz; his father, Sergei, to whom he was close, joined the party at the front during World War II.[75] While still in Privol'noye, in 1948, young Gorbachev was awarded the Order of the Red Banner of Labor, one of the USSR's highest laurels, for his norm-busting work at bringing in the harvest (Sergei, a tractor driver, won the Order of Lenin), and won a medal in school for a hagiographic essay about Stalin.[76] Yeltsin, the son and grandson of kulaks, would be torn from the village by collectivization, grew up in a city, had a twinge of doubt about Stalin, had strained relations with his father, and would wait until 1971 to win his first

Order of the Red Banner. In 1950, still a teenager and about to leave Privol'noye for university in Moscow, Gorbachev applied for the Communist Party and was made a probationary member; he was promoted to full membership in 1952, with Stalin still in the Kremlin.[77] Yeltsin was to take out probationary membership ten years after Gorbachev and full membership nine years after him.

To deal with the demands of his provincial youth, Boris Yeltsin developed a repertoire of life scripts. They were not mere coming-of-age stereotypes but were to be of ongoing relevance in later life. The scripts implied various relationships with the social environment. Survival was for the lonely individual, and the few others he trusted, to achieve, leaving nothing to chance and saying not a word more about it than needed to be said. Duty was about conforming to conditions and meeting the standards of family, equals, and superiors. Success was earned in contestation with others, not primarily through the pursuit of security at all costs or through cooperation. Testing was also a comparative exercise, though more about the capability of acting than the doing. And rebellion, in the confines of the Soviet system, required a break with convention and with lines of subordination. Artistry in one role did not negate the next. The boy with the mathematical cast of mind also had a Tom Sawyer–like taste for adventure. Yeltsin could give teacher Khonina the sense that he "never violated" the rules, and get faculty approval as class monitor year after year, while showing her a "fiery temperament" and coming on to the other young people as someone who could contravene the rules to his and sometimes their benefit. As his friend Sergei Molchanov put it, "He stood out, without a doubt. He . . . was someone who made things a little dangerous."[78] As both propagator of and occasional scoffer at the constituted ways, he was more than a face in the crowd. One comparative study of modern rulers finds that as youths 61 percent of them tended to conform to authority and 16 percent were nonconformists. Yeltsin in a sense was these two things together.[79]

The common denominator in all five scripts is the ethos of flinty self-sufficiency and willpower that suffuses the vibrant subculture of the Urals. As Yeltsin commented, he was a person "who incessantly needs to prove his strength and ability to overcome, to breathe deep . . . to load himself up to total exhaustion." Until his health nosedived in the 1990s, he was what Russians call a *morzh*, a walrus—a devotee of swimming in icy water. Healthy and unhealthy, he started his day's regimen with a cold shower. He yoked this passion to his rural beginnings and the reflexes nourished there: "My childhood was tied to the village, to physical burdens and labor. If you don't develop your strength there, you fall by the wayside."[80] To stay alive, meet filial and societal obligations, impose one's ego on others, demonstrate one's abilities, and hit back at unfeeling authority, one had to be strong and appear to be strong. Physical power and the ability to overcome would in most societies be typecast as masculine traits. But it should not be forgotten that family realities and the demographics of gender imbalance in the Soviet Union put women disproportionately in positions of authority over the young Yeltsin. Of the abilities he was to manifest in politics, the greatest—the intuition for grasping a situation holistically, as he was learning to do in Berezniki—is one we normally categorize as feminine.

In 1949 Yeltsin prepared to leave town for manhood and a higher education in Sverdlovsk. He had stargazed about shipbuilding—his beau ideal, Peter the Great, worked for some time as a shipwright in Holland in the 1690s—but changed the plan in order to follow his father's footsteps into the construction industry, only at a higher level of expertise, influence, and remuneration. His mother's father gave Boris his curmudgeonly lesson in the self-reliance of the *uralets*, the man of the Urals—the job of putting up a backyard steambath for the family, which uncoupled them from the city's collective bathhouse and went farther to reproduce village living conditions. Vasilii Starygin was well cut out to teach the lesson, as his ability to live hand to mouth in northern exile had spared him and his wife the sad end of Yeltsin's paternal grandparents. Boris Yeltsin related without criticism how he did Starygin's bidding. "You must build it yourself from beginning to end," the graybeard said to him, "and I will not come near you." Beyond getting approval from the Berezniki timber trust for his grandson to fell some conifers, Vasilii did not lift a finger. Boris cut the logs, hauled them two miles to their yard, dried them, sawed boards, dug footings, fitted the frame, roofed the structure and caulked it with moss, and added a porch. He was at it the whole summer long. "At the finish, my grandfather said gravely that I had passed the test and had his full permission to enter the construction division" in the polytechnic across the mountains. Yeltsin's mother did not object. "Oh how I cried," she told a woman friend forty years later, "but he had to learn."[81]

Chapter Three

Only Forward

In September 1949 Boris Yeltsin matriculated at the Urals Polytechnic Institute (UPI) in Sverdlovsk, a sixteen-hour train ride through Molotov (the once and future Perm) and over the ridge of the mountains toward Siberia. He went there because there was no technical college in Molotov province and Moscow and Leningrad, the centers of higher learning in the USSR, were more than he could aspire to.[1] Unlike his parents and his maternal grandparents, who went from Berezniki back to Butka, Boris accepted city life. He was to be a Sverdlovsker for thirty-six years, thrice the time he spent in Berezniki, and to go on from there to twenty-two years in Moscow.

Sverdlovsk was founded as Yekaterinburg and is called that once again. The city lies in the eastern foothills of the mid-Urals, on the banks of the Iset River, which the Russians dammed up to form reservoirs and ponds. It was set up in 1723 by the soldier and historian Vasilii Tatishchev, commissioned by Yeltsin's hero Peter the Great to prospect for ores and to open mines and metalworks, and named Yekaterinburg in honor of Catherine I, Peter's second wife. Before the 1917 revolution, it was a considerable place for mining (iron, gold, and gemstones), industry (foundries and machinery), transportation (the Trans-Siberian Railroad), education (the Urals Mining College), and administration but was overshadowed by the Urals guberniya seats of Perm, Orenburg, and Ufa. It was also where the last tsar of Russia, Nicholas II, his wife, Alexandra, and their five children were executed in

1918. The new regime made Yekaterinburg capital of the Urals section in 1923, replacing Perm, which it considered a more bourgeois, backward-looking place.[2] In 1924 Yekaterinburg was renamed Sverdlovsk, after Yakov Sverdlov, the Bolshevik based there before the revolution who authorized the killing of the Romanovs. A more compact Sverdlovsk oblast was demarcated in January 1934 and took its final contours with the severance of the Perm area in 1938. With the exception of a hump in the southwest, it was to the east of the spine of the Urals.

Local communists lobbied for state investment in the metallurgical sector and in 1930 put forward a Great Urals plan that would have had the Urals, and Sverdlovsk within it, displace the south of Ukraine as the powerhouse of Soviet heavy industry.[3] The plan as such was never adopted, but its showpiece, the processing of Urals metals by means of coking coal transported from west Siberia and Kazakhstan, did come about. Joseph Stalin's five-year plans stimulated growth. "It didn't matter where you went," Leonid Brezhnev, who was in those days a bureaucrat in Sverdlovsk province, was to recall, "all around you rose factory chimneys and plumes of smoke pouring out of them."[4] Up-to-date blast furnaces transformed the eighteenth-century Upper Iset Works in Sverdlovsk and the Demidov Works in Nizhnii Tagil, the province's second city, into throbbing combines putting out pig iron and steel. New plants smelted copper, nickel, aluminum, and titanium. Uralmash, the Urals Heavy Machinery Works, opened in Sverdlovsk in 1933, was the largest of its kind in the USSR, a "factory of factories" making equipment for mining, oil extraction, manufacturing, and construction. The Urals Wagon Works in Nizhnii Tagil, opened in 1936, led the Soviet Union in the assembly of rolling stock. By the late 1930s, plants like Uralmash were changing over to the production of matériel for the armed forces. An influx of factories evacuated eastward from front-line cities in 1941–42 raised Sverdlovsk's profile and gave its economy a more militarized cast.[5] Urals Wagon, merged with an enterprise from Kharkov, Ukraine, was the top maker of tanks on Soviet territory, and Uralmash converted to tanks, howitzers, and self-propelled artillery. Urals Wagon, Uralmash, and the Tankograd Works in Chelyabinsk, south of Sverdlovsk oblast, made all of the Red Army's heavy tanks in 1942–45 and 60 percent of the medium tanks. Conversion back to civilian uses after 1945 was halting. In the Cold War, branches of the military-industrial complex based on high technology, such as atomic energy and rocketry, took root, shielded from foreign eyes.

The population of the oblast capital, powered by the boom in smokestack industry and armaments, roared from 150,000 in 1929 to 426,000 in

1939 and 600,000 by midcentury. The deracinated peasants who were the majority of Sverdlovskers lived in factory housing toward the city limits, as higgledy-piggledy as Berezniki's. Downtown was a different sliver of Soviet reality. An Australian-born American historian who visited as it was opening up to Westerners in 1990 said that, never mind the industrial wasteland in the outlying areas, the center of Sverdlovsk was citified and a lot like Victorian Melbourne—"solid, civic, self-respecting."[6] When Yeltsin detrained in 1949, he saw landmarks from the eighteenth and nineteenth centuries, avant-garde Constructivist creations from the 1920s, pompous government buildings, and the accessories of urbanity—an opera and ballet house, a philharmonic hall, a movie studio, Urals State University, a unit of the USSR Academy of Sciences. A clutter of cultural and research establishments from central Russia sat out the war in Sverdlovsk. Many artists, performers, and scientists settled there, and partly for that reason the Jewish community was one of the largest in Russia.[7] For a country lad a few years out of the barracks on the Zhdanovo Fields, it was a far richer environment than any he had known.

Created in 1920 and with 5,000 undergraduates in 1949, UPI was the best school of its type in the Urals and one of the better ones in the Soviet Union. It educated specialists for civilian and for classified, defense-related tasks.[8] The construction division was located in the institute's Stalin-Gothic headquarters on Lenin Prospect, on a hilly campus, Vtuzgorodok (Technical College Town), in the east end of Sverdlovsk. The division prepared construction engineers, architects, and town planners. The students into the 1930s were manual workers selected by party cells and trade unions without regard for educational attainment; some were unversed in arithmetic. During the war, many UPI men and women were rushed to the front or to munitions factories without graduating, and a clinic and quarters for army wounded took up part of the main dormitory. Come the postwar years, entrants were chosen by examination, were required to have passed high school mathematics and science, and completed their diplomas without interruption. Professors were encouraged to take up scientific research and supervise postgraduate dissertations. Several hundred students from the new Soviet bloc in Europe and East Asia were in each UPI cohort.[9]

The qualifying examinations Yeltsin took in August 1949 were considered relatively easy, as a chemistry portion was not required for the construction division—many students had not taken it in secondary school, although Yeltsin had. He had to pass a twenty-five-meter swimming test and a timed

100-meter run, neither of which gave him difficulty. Originally in the class of 1953, he was to finish the industrial- and civil-engineering stream in June of 1955, one of forty-nine (thirty-three men, sixteen women) to get out that year. The course of study was lengthened by one year in 1951, as the education ministry, wanting to improve engineering cadres, upped the time spent in all Soviet technical institutes from four years to five. Yeltsin lost more ground in the spring of 1952 when tonsillitis and rheumatic fever caused him to drop out of his third year; he was readmitted that fall and completed the year's courses in 1952–53. The construction curriculum emphasized mathematics, physics, materials and soil science, and draftsmanship. The seven or eight hours of lectures per day were mandatory, as was a diploma project.

The polytechnic's boarding students got by on measly stipends of 280 rubles a month—the price of a pair of men's shoes—but there was no tuition and the residence halls, in a first for Yeltsin, had tap water and flush toilets. The canteen food was edible; if you had the rubles to spare, you could dine in a smart café where young women waited on the tables in starched white aprons and peaked caps. The discontinuation of wartime rationing and the efflorescence of "the spirit of victory" over Germany, a reminder of which was the POWs slaving away on the Sverdlovsk streets, kindled optimism in the student body. "There was confidence in the future, confidence that things would work out okay," a schoolfellow of Yeltsin's recounted. "We were not that demanding toward life, that is, it took little to satisfy us."[10] Fifteen percent of the students' time was earmarked for military drills (Yeltsin's specialty was tank operator) and 20 percent for instruction in the recondite science of Marxism-Leninism. Yeltsin met the foreign-language requirement by continuing to study German. It had little effect: He was to write in his Communist Party file that he read German and translated it with a dictionary, but in conversation he could not tell it and English apart.[11]

Although national politics did not seep much into the student life at UPI, this was not always so. In 1949–50 Stalin's xenophobic propaganda campaign against "rootless cosmopolitan"—read, Jewish—influence made a stir, and several students of Jewish descent were expelled from UPI or forced out of dormitories.[12] In 1953 the police arrested a twenty-year-old UPI student and Komsomol member, V. L. Okulov, for making disrespectful comments about Stalin. He was found guilty of anti-Soviet agitation and propaganda in April 1953 and imprisoned for a year.[13] March 9, 1953, the day of Stalin's funeral, was a day of mourning at UPI. Classes were canceled and students and faculty, many of them weeping, gathered in front of the main building to hear eulogies.[14] UPI students had one outlet for sometimes fairly risqué expression, *BOKS* (*Boyevoi organ komsomol'skoi satiry*, Battle Organ of Komsomol Satire), a wall newspaper by Komsomol members that printed uncensored spoofs and limericks.

The costume Yeltsin donned almost every day of his first several years at the institute bespoke his origins: waterproofed canvas boots, hirsute wool trousers, and a velveteen jacket. He got an irregular allowance from his parents and potatoes and vegetables from their garden plot. Only once a month could he treat himself to the café. For pocket money, he unloaded railcars and did other menial jobs; during most summer breaks, he took paid internships. The puritanism breathed in at Berezniki had begun to mellow. Yeltsin entered into wagers about not cussing for a year at a time, and always collected, but he now drank beer and vodka in moderation. A fun-loving companion, he was disposed to gestures and the gifts his budget allowed. He was a practical joker and the life of the party at the "Komsomol weddings" into which many Soviet students, barely out of their teens, entered in the year or two before graduation. To impress a group of acquaintances, he dove clothed into a swimming pool. On a students' steamer cruise on the Kama, he led three of his male friends in a knockabout *Swan Lake* ballet, all of them splendiferous in white women's slips, tutus made of towels, and gauze headgear.[15]

The UPI students bunked eight to a room in the first year and five to a room in the upper classes. Coeducation brought close contact with the opposite sex. Yeltsin had a crush on Margarita Yerina, a student from Berezniki and a figure skater. Yeltsin, the story goes, requested that an acquaintance of both from home, Mikhail Ustinov, help Yerina with a work assignment. "Misha carried out his friend's request so enthusiastically that he took up with Rita himself and beat Boris to the punch." One thing led to another and the two married early in the 1952–53 school year. "Boris was invited to the wedding. Congratulating them, he half-jokingly said to Ustinov, 'So this is the kind of friend you are! I got you to watch over Rita and look what you did!'"[16]

In November 1952 Yeltsin and five roommates and neighbors (three females and two males) pooled resources to form a self-help collective that they facetiously called the Troublemaker (Shkodnik) Kolkhoz. Yeltsin, who had suggested it, chaired the group, and each member assumed some responsibility. In the "charter" they signed, the friends agreed to sub for one another in lectures, buy and cook food jointly, go to the movies or to a sports event weekly, visit the bathhouse once a week (where the boys were to drink beer and the girls champagne), and celebrate holidays and birthdays together. With several substitutions, the sextet stayed together until graduation. All were from towns and villages quite remote from Sverdlovsk, and so from parents' gardens, and much of Shkodnik's activity focused on food. To save money, the members skipped breakfast, used coupons to buy a cheap lunch, and gathered for a supper cooked on a hotplate in the kitchen cubicle on the residence floor, the ingredients bought by contributions from their stipends.[17]

In charge of "sanitation" in the group was Naina Iosifovna Girina, a female student born on March 14, 1932, who had enrolled in the hydraulics department of the construction division in 1950. Naina, baptized Anastasiya and nicknamed Naya, was from the city of Orenburg in the south Urals hills, the eldest of six children of a Cossack family in which some Russian Orthodox religious practices had survived. Her mother kept small icons and every Easter prepared ritual foods (painted eggs and *kulich* and *paskha* cakes) and lit candles; from her grandmother she learned two prayers which she memorized and would recite thereafter at times of distress. Naina had wanted to enter medicine, an impecunious and feminized profession in the Soviet Union, but chose engineering, higher-status work in which males were prevalent. She came to UPI not much better clad than Yeltsin: All she owned was two dresses and a flannel track suit hand-sewn by her mother.[18] In 1951–52, the year Yeltsin had to take medical leave, he and Girina had been in a group that took waltz, tango, and foxtrot lessons together. They began a courtship in 1953. Girina "was distinguished by her amicability, affability, and cleanliness. It was impossible to break her composure, and she was able to put out all conflicts in the female collective. . . . She was always neatly dressed and coiffed and was willing to sacrifice an hour of lectures in the institute for a more attractive undertaking."[19]

Yeltsin took away idyllic memories of the camaraderie and "giddy romanticism" shared at the polytechnic. "Never since can I remember feeling such fabulous energy, and against the background of a half-starving, Spartan, almost garrison-like existence."[20] Besides finding his future wife, he made friends there for the duration. The schoolmates were to do a summer journey with their families in 1960 and every five years after that.

A slug of the energy Yeltsin felt was injected into his studies, in which he got almost all 4s and 5s, the honors grades. He was known for a fire-and-ice pattern of work, cramming for exams and handing in assignments in the nick of time. "He studied in quite a strange way—by snatches, convulsively, whatever you want to call it. For the days when the most intense exercises or examinations were scheduled, he would manage to master a mound of information. Then he would take a long break, which did not appeal in the slightest to his teachers."[21] It foreshadowed his style as president of Russia four decades later.

The frolicking and jousting with classroom instructors that were so frequent in Berezniki tailed off. Yeltsin's tiff with a lecturer in political economy, a dour communist by the name of Savel'ëva (the students nicknamed her *Sova,* the Owl), was trivial by comparison. He was turned off more by her unbending pedagogy than by the conservatism of her lectures. His grade of 3 in the course barred him from graduating with distinction, and he waived the chance to retake the exam and try for a higher grade.[22] Yeltsin cut classes in favor of athletic and other interests, but his friend, group monitor Yurii Poluzadov, who filled out attendance sheets with the dean's office, covered for him. Poluzadov and Yeltsin both had their stipends docked one September for late filing of their reports on summer activities.[23] Yeltsin allows in *Confession on an Assigned Theme* that some of his teachers were hard on him out of disapproval of the time he put into athletics. The example he gives is not Savel'ëva but Stanislav Rogitskii, the head of the department of construction mechanics. In a course on elasticity, Rogitskii once gave him a snap quiz, saying that a great athlete like him would need no preparation, and did not let him use the formulas recorded in his notebook. Yeltsin was not up to the exercise, and the two "fought for a long time." One day, though, Yeltsin found the solution to a mathematical problem set by the professor, which, he said, had baffled students for ten years. Rogitskii worked up "a true affection" for Yeltsin—repaid in Yeltsin's memoirs—but still gave him a grade of 4, not the 5 Yeltsin expected. As with Savel'ëva, Yeltsin refused an offer to retake the final exam.[24]

Yeltsin shunned all political topics and involvements at Urals Polytechnic and did not talk about the regime's maltreatment of his family. His attitude makes for a ringing contrast with his rival-to-be, Mikhail Gorbachev. Gorbachev, a Komsomol organizer in his village school, served as a Komsomol secretary in the Moscow State University law division and took out full membership in the governing party in 1952, in his second year of study. Yeltsin gave wide berth to the UPI committee of the Komsomol, in which participation was necessary for anyone intending to work in the guilds of the Communist Party apparatus and the Soviet security services. Committee documents cite his name but two or three times, in connection with his favorite extracurricular activity: sports, and specifically volleyball.[25]

Games sublimated Yeltsin's need to prove himself, at an age when boyish capers were no longer appropriate. At the Pushkin School in Berezniki, he had conditioned muscles and nerves to compensate for the gash in his left hand and to get firmer control of the all-white leather sphere. His love for volleyball was quasi political: "I liked the way the ball obeyed me, the way I could pounce on it and return the most awesome of volleys."[26] That he was tall and strong helped. He also liked volleyball's cooperative dimension. In the other games he tried out (cross-country skiing, decathlon, gymnastics, boxing, and wrestling), the competitors were individuals; only this was a team endeavor, with six per side and a need for synchronization on the compact playing surface. Versatility and waiting one's turn were required, since volleyball players rotate through the positions. Yeltsin's favorite move was the downward "spike" of the ball over the net after it had been set on a high flight. Impatient with waiting, he had the squad work out maneuvers that let him spike from the back court as well as the normal location, the two hitter's places in the front row.[27] He made the divisional and institute-wide teams his freshman year, captaining both and coaching several other teams for extra income. He gleefully noted in his memoirs that he logged six hours at the gymnasium daily and, between that and homework, pared his sleeping time to four hours a night—a figure confirmed by contemporaries.

But the schedule took its toll. In 1952 overexertion made Yeltsin ill. It cost him a year in the program and "nearly put me in the grave" at the age of twenty-one. An untreated streptococcal infection of the throat grew into inflammation of his tonsils, joints, and coronary valves. It would have responded to penicillin; there is no mention of an antibiotic or any drug in Yeltsin's writeup. By his account, he went to the hospital only when his temperature surged to 104 degrees and his pulse to 150 beats per minute. The physician prescribed four months in sick bay to allow his heart to recover. Still feverish, says Yeltsin, he skipped out several days later—lowering himself out the window on a cable of knotted bed sheets—and went to his parents' house in Berezniki. Fellow students have recollected that Yeltsin had earlier sneaked out of his sickroom to play in a big game, then returned to the hospital before making his final escape. After shinnying down the sheets to leave for home, he was given a sendoff by the team. "Our team consoled him and promised to write him letters. And we kept our word. Each day one of the eight of us took a turn and wrote him."[28]

When not reading his mail, Yeltsin soon started taking volleyball serves in the Berezniki gym:

> My friends would put me down on a bench and I would lie there. I felt trapped: I might never break out of this situation, my heart would be permanently damaged, I would be washed up as a player. Nonetheless, I decided to fight and to go only forward. At first I took the court for a minute at a time, and after that two and then five, and within a month I was able to make it through a whole game. When I got back to Sverdlovsk, I went to the doctor. "Well, even though you gave us the slip," she said, "it would appear that you have spent the entire time in bed, and now your heart is fine." I have to admit I had taken a colossal risk, because my heart could have been ruined. But there was no point feeling self-pity. No, I was better off loading myself up and letting like cure like.[29]

While not every detail may be dead-on here, Yeltsin's illness and furlough were real and were entered into his student file.[30] The scene with the doctor testifies to openness to risk and neglect of his health, patterns that were to recur.

Sports brought out another talent in Yeltsin, according to his lifelong friend Yakov Ol'kov:

> Captaincy of the [UPI] team was his first manifestation of leadership qualities. It was a small team, but a team. . . . He was a good organizer. He knew how to stir people up. As we would use the term today, he had charisma. . . . He was quite an impulsive organizer. He was able to draw people in and get results. . . . He knew how to make decisions on the run that would push the cause forward. And if a loss was threatened, then he would come up with something that would catch everybody on fire.[31]

As a side venture, Yeltsin organized his study group's participation in the UPI relay race held every May. To get the students out of bed for calisthenics on spring mornings, he had a professor of geology, Nikolai Mazurov, go to the dormitory hall with his trumpet and blow reveille. Boris Furmanov, a freshman in the construction division in the spring of 1955 and later a Russian government minister, remembered Yeltsin jabbering before his class about past victories in the relay and about "the need to stick up for the division's honor." "Not just anyone, when you first hear and see him, manages to make a mark on 'the multitude' (there were one hundred of us), compel you to believe him, and then influence you in accord with his will."[32]

As with the mischief-maker in Berezniki, the athlete and cheerleader at UPI attested to qualities Yeltsin would later apply to political causes. For now, the applications were exclusively apolitical, and those who knew him assumed his interests would keep it that way. As Ol'kov put it, "To say that he was going to be a political boss or someone like that would have seemed quite unreal to me. We simply could not have foreseen it."[33]

Yeltsin's biggest self-reported adventure came to pass on summer vacation in 1953. It was a two-and-a-half-month hobo's tour of the Volga and central Russia (taking him to Kazan for the first time since 1937), Belorussia, Ukraine, and Georgia. A UPI friend who had agreed to tag along bailed out after one day on the road. Yeltsin, in his telling, stowed away on trains, scrounged for meals, and played strip poker with ex-convicts. Several times policemen took him off the train and asked him where he was going. "I would say something along the lines of, I am on my way to Simferopol [in Crimea] to see my grandmother. They would ask me what street she lived on. I knew there was a Lenin Street in every Soviet city, so I would give that answer every time. And they would let me go."[34] Yeltsin's poker mates, imprisoned for common criminal offenses, had been released from jails and camps in the amnesty after Stalin's death. They were banned from Moscow, so he went on his own to see Red Square and the mausoleum holding Lenin's body (and Stalin's, which was to be removed in 1961 and buried in the ground behind the mausoleum) and the walls and towers of the Kremlin, which, because it was closed to nonofficials until 1955, he could not enter. Yeltsin writes that in Zaporozh'e, a steel town on the Dnieper River in Ukraine, he earned his keep by teaching a one-week course in mathematics to an army colonel who wanted to enter a local polytechnic—with twenty hours of drill a day. He got word at the next stop that his tutee had won a place in the institute.[35]

In the fall of 1954, Yeltsin had a mini-adventure on a trip with the UPI volleyballers. To procure some food for his famished teammates, he set down at the station in Lozovaya, near the big Ukrainian city of Kharkov. He did not make it back to the train on time, and his coach gave him up for lost and sent a telegram to that effect back to UPI. Their next stop was Tbilisi, Georgia. Two days after the team got there, Yeltsin rapped on the door of the coach's hotel room, bushy-tailed but bearing two shopping bags laden with provisions. Fearing that his cargo would be pilfered, he had come from Lozovaya to Tbilisi, about 700 miles, on the roof of one of the passenger cars.[36]

Upon reading Yeltsin's prose about the main conflictual episodes at UPI, one cannot but see the progression in his ego and attitude toward authority. When he gives short shrift to his studies and fences with Rogitskii, he engages in the mildest of rebellions, checked by his respect for the learned professor. A point of pride in the narration of his illness is when he pulls the wool over the physician's eyes—he did not lie to her but did not act to correct her misconception, either—and so outfoxes authority rather than defy it. In the summer of 1953 he rides the rails with the ex-cons, only to turn the student's role on its head and become a source of knowledge in the crash course with the Ukrainian officer twice his age: "The colonel had his doubts: Would we be able to do it? I told him there was no other way to get ready in one week. [He showed himself to be] a person of perseverance, with a character that kept the pace of *the lessons I gave him.*"[37] To be able to give lessons and hold up in a competitive world, Yeltsin worked at learning self-restraint and mental toughness. "Boris Nikolayevich worked a lot, consciously, on his character. At first it seemed to contain a good deal of personal sensitivity, but he did much to counter this, saying he had to squeeze the flabbiness out of himself. If he felt sorry for someone, he would express it in reverse—he would say words of support yet, intentionally, in a harsh fashion."[38]

Yeltsin's diploma assignment had to be carried out in one month rather than the allotted five, since he had blown a semester on traveling with the volleyball team. "I still can't figure out how I did it," he burbles in *Confession.* "It was unreal how much of a mental and physical effort I had to make." His project was an undistinguished design for an overhead bucket line to transfer waste materials out of a coal mine. In the memoir, he was to misrepresent it as a plan for a television tower, so avant-garde that assistance from faculty and students was out of the question and only Urals self-reliance would save the day. "Until then there were almost no [towers] around, and so I had to sort everything out myself. . . . No one . . . could help me with this new and unknown theme. I had to do the drawings myself, do the calculations myself, do everything from beginning to end myself."[39] Whether this was a fib or an inadvertency,[40] Yeltsin was attracted to futuristic undertakings and to the emerging medium of television, which was to play a big part in his political life. One of his pet projects as leader of the province's party organization in the 1980s was to build a TV transmission tower at the midpoint of the Sverdlovsk skyline, not far from the city's large circus building. Only the conical concrete column of the structure, and not the planned restaurant and metal spire, was up when work stopped around 1990. It is 725 feet high. The plan was for the tower to soar up to 1,300 feet, which would have made it the sixth or seventh tallest in the world.[41]

Graduates of Soviet universities and institutes were assigned to their first jobs by the educational bureaucracy and were free to seek other employment after two or three years. The year Yeltsin graduated was the last in which many young civil engineers, including UPI students, were ordered to projects in the Gulag, which was liquidated by 1956. He was fortunate not to have drawn such an assignment. Before getting into the work world, he spent ten weeks after graduation in June 1955 playing with UPI's varsity volleyball team at tournaments in Tbilisi, Leningrad, and Riga, Latvia. He presented himself at the Lower Iset Construction Directorate in Sverdlovsk in September. The appointment augured well. Reacting against decades in which construction was a backwater of makeshift methods and unqualified, often convict, labor, the post-Stalin leadership was determined to give it a trained proletarian workforce, effective supervision, and the capital investment to press ahead with building factories and cities. The industry was to flourish under Khrushchev and Brezhnev.

His UPI pedigree gave Yeltsin the right to go straightaway to project foreman. Instead, he chose to work for a year as a trainee in the building trades with the men and women he would later oversee. Several analysts have reasoned that it was a financial decision, since junior-grade engineers in the Soviet Union were paid less than construction workers.[42] They are mistaken: Yeltsin's wage as an apprentice worker was lower than what he would have gotten starting as a foreman. The decisive motivation was self-sufficiency. Some of the book knowledge from UPI would have been a dim guide to "the real life of the workplace." Worse would be dependence on other people's judgment. "I was certain that it would be very rocky for me if any crew leader [*brigadir*] could consciously or unconsciously wrap me around his finger because his practical knowledge of the job outstripped mine."[43] Yeltsin waded through twelve hard-hat specialties—carpenter, plasterer, stonemason, painter, crane operator, and the like—and secured a rudimentary competence in each. He helped build factory workshops, apartments, and schools. The job sites were filthy and hazardous, and he did not shy away from danger in Sverdlovsk any more than he had as a youth in Berezniki. In

Confession on an Assigned Theme, he tells of a fall from scaffolding, a locomotive just missing him as he sat in a stalled truck, and having to secure a runaway crane.

The Iset building trust took Yeltsin on as a foreman *(master)* in June 1956. From there, he climbed sure-footed up the organizational ladder, rung by rung: work superintendent *(prorab)* in June 1957, senior work superintendent *(starshii prorab)* in June 1958, head engineer *(glavnyi inzhener)* of SU-13 (Construction Directorate No. 13) in January 1960, and chief *(nachal'nik)* of the directorate in February 1962. The first project he completed, in time for the November 7 holiday in 1957, was a five-story apartment house on Griboyedov Street, which ran by Uralkhimmash, the Urals Chemical Machinery Works, on the southeastern extremity of Sverdlovsk. In 1957–58 he finished construction at a textile-mill project that had been incomplete for several years and had been ransacked by the workers. But he went back to residential construction. Housing was a political priority for Moscow, dictated by the need to gain favor with the populace.

Shelter for the masses had gotten the short end of the stick under Stalin, whose preference was for office blocks and luxury apartments destined for elite groups. The war and the postwar military buildup had exacerbated the shortfall. Griboyedov Street was part of the first wave of the new consumerism in Soviet housing. The new self-contained flats in houses like this one, informally dubbed *khrushchëby* (a play on Khrushchev's surname and *trushchoba,* an old Russian word for "slum"), were built to standardized designs. Minimalist as they were, they were a real step up from barracks and communal apartments and gave families spaces in which to store and improve possessions, and a kitchen where they could talk, laugh, and grieve in privacy. Five stories was the maximum that could be completed in one building season, and, under the regulations, could be commissioned with neither an elevator nor garbage chute. By the early 1960s a second wave of innovation was toward *korobki,* or "boxes," much taller structures out of prefabricated reinforced-concrete slabs, generally on bulldozer-cleared outer areas of the cities. There was one production cycle for the lookalike product, from mixing the cement to fitting the doorknobs and the kitchen sink.[44]

In June 1963 Yeltsin was reassigned to the Sverdlovsk House-Building Combine, the high-profile enterprise for housing construction in the city, as head engineer. In December 1965 he was elevated to director of the combine. "He knew," Naina Yeltsina remembers, "that it was time to move on when the [post] he was in had started to bore him. So when he was chief of the construction directorate, for example, he found it was getting repetitive, he had done everything he could, and he wanted more challenging work."[45] The need was satisfied temporarily, as Yeltsin now held Sverdlovsk's most salient administrative post associated with popular welfare. "Being 'first' was probably always in my nature," he was to observe in *Notes of a President*, "although I perhaps did not realize it in the early years."[46] Ten years after leaving the polytechnic, now that he was in his mid-thirties, he and everyone around him realized it.

Meantime, Yeltsin made shifts in his personal life. He stopped playing league volleyball in 1956, limiting himself to coaching a local women's team. That year, he and his college sweetheart, Naina Girina, who had returned to Orenburg after graduation, were reunited in Sverdlovsk and married in a civil ceremony on September 28, 1956, celebrating the nuptials with 150 friends in a local reception hall. Boris had to borrow his grandfather Starygin's copper wedding band to give Naina. He did not buy her a gold band until their fortieth anniversary in 1996.

The couple soon joined the Soviet baby boom, parents to Yelena (Lena, born in August 1957) and Tatyana (Tanya, born in January 1960). The son Boris earnestly hoped for never materialized. After the birth of Yelena, all the peasant prescriptions for conceiving a boy were followed, such as putting an axe and workman's cap under the pillow: "My friends, experts on customs, told us that for sure we would now have a son. The verified methods were of no use." The new arrival "was a prim, smiling child, who maybe took after her mother's character, where our elder daughter takes after me."[47] When they were still young girls, their maternal grandmother, Mariya Girina, had a priest secretly baptize them at a home chapel in Orenburg, there being no officially recognized Orthodox church in the vicinity. Their father was not informed about the procedure. Their mother not only approved but brought each child to Orenburg for the purpose. Naina Iosifovna, in her words, "lived all her life with God in my soul," although active practice was impossible. Like Klavdiya Yeltsina, she owned several small icons, and stood one of them on her night table, a talisman of pre-Soviet ways and beliefs.[48]

The Yeltsins' first connubial home was a space in a dormitory owned by Uralkhimmash. They graduated from there to a single room in a two-room apartment owned by the plant and in 1958, after Yelena was born, to a two-room apartment of their own—twenty-eight square meters (300 square feet), with the bathtub in the kitchen, and not far from Vtorchermet, a scrap-iron plant. There they shared a tiny icebox with their next-door neighbors. On Sundays they cooked Boris's favorite dishes, *pel'meni* (Siberian dumplings stuffed with ground meat), *blinchiki* (fritters), and walnut cake, with them and sang folk music. The Yeltsins were among the first in their building to acquire an electric washing machine. A UPI comrade of theirs lived up the stairwell, and the two families used the machine alternate weeks, toting it back and forth. In 1959 Yeltsin's job as head engineer of SU-13 got him a company car and driver. In 1960, having been issued another two-room apartment in the settlement of Yuzhnyi, closer to his work, they bought their first family refrigerator.[49]

As was the woman's lot in the USSR, Naina balanced a job—hers was in Vodokanalproyekt, a bureau that drafted blueprints for water and drainage utilities, where she was promoted to head engineer—with running a household and raising children without much husbandly assistance. Nor, unlike umpteen Soviet mothers, could she fall back on a live-in *babushka*, a grandmother who would hold the fort as she worked: Grandma Girina was in Orenburg and grandma Yeltsina back home in Berezniki and then, beginning in 1962, in Butka. Boris was relieved to delegate money and the care of belongings to his wife: "Never in his life did Boris Nikolayevich concern himself with the family budget, and he had no idea what I was spending the money on. When I ironed his suit, I always put some cash in the pocket, because every respectable man should have cash in his pocket. . . . He never tried to control me and he purchased nothing on his own but books."[50]

Boris was largely an absentee father, although when his daughters were teenagers he did review their grades on the weekend and, if they were less than a 5, he would zing the underachiever's school diary across the living room of the apartment. Of their childhood he writes, "I must honestly admit I do not remember the details—when they took their baby steps, when they started to talk, or the rare moments when I tried to help raise them—since I worked almost without a break and we would meet only on Sunday afternoons."[51] Naina was as candid about the imbalance between the spouses in a press interview in retirement: "If a woman marries and has children, she has to make sacrifices. . . . You can rarely expect the husband to sacrifice anything on behalf of the family. For the man, the big thing is work. I always tried to make things go smoothly in the family." She acknowledged in the 1990s that she, too, made less time for the children than she should have and was caught between opposing demands. Friends accused her of negligence, while "at work they chuckled, 'Here you are guiding them across the street on the telephone.'"[52] When Yeltsin's work demanded it, the family's comfort suffered. Having briefly lived in their first three-room apartment in the south of the city after Tatyana's birth, they moved to a *smaller* flat, of two rooms only, around 1965, so he could be handier to the construction sites where he was needed. They transferred several years after that to a sunlit three-room apartment on Voyevodin Street, in the city center. In the first eleven or twelve years of their marriage, Boris and Naina had called seven different places home.[53]

Romantic gifts and festivities were primarily how Yeltsin expressed affection and salved a guilty conscience. Naina, he wrote, "loves my surprises." As examples he cited the nosegay and several verses of poetry he sent to the maternity home where she had Yelena in 1957—in Berezniki, where his mother could help with the diapers—and his daughters "squealing from joy" when he picked them up at eleven one night to go a friend's birthday party.[54] They all would have loved to see him in the home more. When Yelena and Tatyana were young, the couple took summer holidays at one of the Soviet Union's Caucasus resorts, dropping the girls off with Yeltsin's parents and grandparents in Butka. The village was bigger and a little more prosperous than they had left it in the 1930s, although it lost the status of district seat in 1962 and was put under the town of Talitsa. A carpet manufactory, a creamery, and starch mill had opened in the 1950s, and the kolkhoz specialized in breeding hogs. Returning to pick the children up, Boris and Naina would remain in Butka for up to a week to bring in the hay and pick berries and mushrooms.[55]

The other departure in Yeltsin's life had bigger implications. In March 1960 he applied for and was granted probationary membership in the CPSU; he was made a full member, with Card No. 03823301, on March 17, 1961. The Khrushchev thaw had made it permissible for the relatives of former political prisoners and deportees to enter the ranks of the party, subject themselves to its discipline, and be certified as model citizens. Yeltsin was to state in his autobiography in 1990 that he "sincerely believed in the ideals of justice the party espoused and enlisted in the party with equal sincerity." This sentence stressed attentiveness to duty and ideals and the ideal he as a politician made his signature issue in the 1980s—justice for all and the elimination of privileges. He also tried to impart in the memoir that not all communists, even then, were as sincere as he. At the meeting that formalized his membership in 1961, the head bookkeeper of SU-13, with whom he had professional differences, asked a pharisaical question about the exact volume and page in Marx's *Das Kapital* where a certain doctrinal problem was discussed. Yeltsin made up a flippant reference, which was accepted. The insinuation was that party doctrine was already being perverted for contemptible ends.[56]

Interviewed in 2002, though, Yeltsin stated that his decision about the party was half-hearted, ideals were of secondary moment, and it came down to a career calculus:

> More than once, they urged me [to join]. I was doing well at work, and naturally they hung around me all the time. But I always held back. I did not want to bind myself to the party. I did not want it. I had, you see, a gut feeling about it. But then I was in a dead end. I was required to join the party to become chief of the construction directorate. They made me a simple proposition: If you are willing to do it [join the CPSU], we will promote you. I could still not be a party member when I was head engineer. . . . To be chief, no, for this you needed to be a communist.[57]

These revised words are more consonant than his memoirs with the fact that, while a young Yeltsin had soaked up mainstream Soviet values, he had not bought into the party qua organization. Unlike his wife, whose father (an official in railroad security) and many relatives in Orenburg were communists, none of the Yeltsins or Starygins was a member of the party. Yeltsin was thirty years of age when he received his party card, significantly older than the mean for that rite of passage. Roughly 10 percent of the adult population, but about 50 percent of all men with a higher education, were CPSU members in the late decades of the Soviet regime. Those bound for work in administration usually enrolled in their mid-twenties, and Gorbachev was twenty-one when admitted as a student.[58] The description of Yeltsin's standoffishness from the party and of his commonsensical decision to join it also comports with the chronology. He filed the application two months after his designation as head engineer of SU-13; he was promoted to SU-13 chief eleven months after his party admission. Unlike Gorbachev, who was a delegate to the Twenty-Second CPSU Congress in Moscow in 1961 (Yeltsin did not go to any congress until 1981), Yeltsin makes no memoir reference to the political headlines of the 1950s and 1960s: the death of Stalin in 1953, the attack on the Stalin cult at the Twentieth CPSU Congress in 1956, Khrushchev's overthrow by Brezhnev in 1964. Having left

Urals Polytechnic in 1955, he had missed the outbreak of student unrest in post-secondary institutions in Sverdlovsk and other Soviet cities in 1956, after the Twentieth Congress.[59] It is of interest that his brother, Mikhail, a construction worker and UPI dropout, never belonged to the party and said that people only took out cards for selfish reasons. Mikhail, wrote Andrei Goryun in 1991 after getting to know him, "does not conceal his critical attitude toward the communists and asserts that most members whom he knows use their membership in the CPSU for mercenary purposes. He acknowledges he has never discussed these problems with Boris. The brothers have generally avoided conversations on touchy political themes, assuming, it would seem, that their views are too divergent."[60] If they had talked politics in depth, they might in fact have agreed on some matters. Naina Yeltsina entered the party only in 1972, at age forty, for the same reasons that Boris entered in 1961. She served as secretary of the party bureau in her firm, which she described to me as tedious work.

What made the party pursue Yeltsin were his production accomplishments. In remembrances of the building industry, he credited them to a grueling schedule and ramrod organizational techniques. He was, he says, "exacting" *(trebovatel'nyi)*: "I required people to keep strict discipline and to stick to their word. Since I never used profanity and . . . did my best not to raise my loud and piercing voice in front of people, my arguments in the fight for discipline were my own dedication to the job, my unflagging high standards and checking on the work done, plus people's trust in the fairness of what I was doing. Whoever worked better would live better."[61] There is a truth to this chesty self-description. Eyewitnesses are in agreement that Yeltsin worked marathon days (and six of them a week), ran a tight ship, and stayed away from the swear words that sprinkled workplace communication in the industry. He was unfailingly punctual and levied fines for truancy and malingering. He accepted criticism, so long as it was made to his face. And he valued effort: He gave morning pep talks that singled out productive employees, dispensed yearly incentive pay, and, after his promotion in 1965, issued workers overalls lettered with "DSK," the Cyrillic initials for House-Building Combine.[62] At the combine, which because of its importance was staffed by older engineers and foremen, "At first no one perceived Yeltsin as a serious person—he was 'a young whippersnapper.' But, by demonstrating his competency, he very soon compelled people to take notice of him. Many listened to him more and more."[63] This regard was as common below as at the top: "Yes, he was feared, but we respected him for his fairness and attention toward people. He knew every crew leader by name. He demanded discipline from all and forced each to put his shoulder to the wheel, while sparing no effort himself."[64]

Yeltsin's rise was meritocratic, made without the windfall of a well-connected parent, spouse, or friend. The measure of merit was performance within the Soviet administrative system. For all managers in the USSR, the motto was "Fulfill the Plan!"—which meant "Fulfill the Plan or Else!" Fulfillment was computed in inelastic physical indicators—for housing, it was square meters completed—while quality, durability, and monetary cost were subsidiary. Leaders who met their targets were recompensed and promoted; those who did not were penalized or demoted. In the construction sector, the visibility of the product, unpredictable weather, and a lackadaisical labor force made for a notoriously campaign-driven work ethos. Two pieces of Soviet slang express the culture of the industry: *shturmovshchina* or "storming" to complete a project on time; and *avral*, a hard-to-translate term for "all hands on deck" or "hurry up and finish." Thirty to forty percent of the entire annual housing plan in Sverdlovsk was completed in December.

Given what is known of his behavior as a student and athlete, Yeltsin was well suited by character to the frenetic aspect of the Soviet construction business. One afternoon in 1959, about to commission a worsted-wool mill, he discovered that SU-13 had not built a fifty-yard tunnel between two buildings and had mislaid the drawings. By six the next morning, he and his charges redid the drawings, excavated the passageway, and poured the concrete. In 1962–63 Yeltsin formed a model brigade (work crew) consisting of about one tenth of SU-13's personnel. He opened up a cache of scarce construction supplies to the workers and enabled the brigade to shine and to set a USSR record by doubling its rate of completion. It was another feather in Yeltsin's cap: As much a tutelary as a production feat, it got him and the brigade accolades in the Sverdlovsk press.[65]

The pattern continued in the house-building combine from 1963 to 1968. Yeltsin himself writes of the mad dash to finish the plan and of how he was in his element in it: "The hardest part of building housing came at the end of the year and at the end of a quarter, when we had to work practically twenty-four hours. Often, especially on the night shifts, I visited the work crews, mostly the female ones."[66] Without self-consciousness, he discloses that as head engineer he sponsored a successful "experiment" to slap up a five-story apartment house in five days flat. The building yard was equipped with three cranes, a network of transport rails, and large stocks of pre-positioned materials; it was the "industrial equivalent of street theater."[67] In March 1966, in his first year as director, a five-story building being completed by the DSK on Moscow Street keeled over. A slipshod subcontractor had not correctly gauged the time needed to allow the foundation to set in the winter months. There was a criminal probe; no charges were laid and Yeltsin was not held culpable. But plans to give him an Order of Lenin for his work were scrubbed, and in April the Sverdlovsk party committee hit him with a formal reprimand. The combine hauled off the detritus and did the building a second time. It was known from then on as the *desyatietazhka*—Ten-Story House.[68]

Yeltsin's evolving relationships within the layer of CPSU appointees, or nomenklatura, of the post-Stalin Soviet system brought him advantage and vulnerability both. In no time, he learned how to deploy and manipulate incentives. Yakov Ryabov, the first secretary of the party gorkom (city committee) since 1963, was impressed at how he jawboned Sverdlovsk factory directors into lending hundreds of workers to the combine every year to help it meet its housing plan. The Soviet rules required that the resource quotas for any apartments not finished by December 31 be deleted from the coming year's plan. Yeltsin cagily made the directors see they would be better off assigning the labor and getting housing in exchange. They received their apartments; Yeltsin and his employees met their plans and pocketed year-end bonuses.[69]

At the same time, Yeltsin raised hackles. He scrapped tirelessly with Nikolai Sitnikov, his boss in SU-13, who had ordered him to give up volleyball coaching. They stayed at the feud when Sitnikov went on to higher things and Yeltsin succeeded him in the directorate. Ryabov and his second secretary, Fëdor Morshchakov, the official behind the creation of the DSK, were sympathetic to Yeltsin, seeing him as a diamond in the rough. They did not write him off when he received his party reprimand in 1966. Ryabov saw to it that Yeltsin was put on the list to be granted a Badge of Honor, his first state award.

Yeltsin needed a mentor. He was on good terms with the head of the construction department of the party gorkom, Boris Kiselëv, a former UPI classmate. Kiselëv saw promise in Yeltsin and introduced him to the party apparatus.[70] But the crucial patron was Ryabov. Born in 1928 in the province of Penza, Ryabov labored at the bench in the Urals Turbine Works, assembling diesel engines for tanks, and took his UPI diploma in mechanical engineering by correspondence. Bantam-sized, he was as much of a go-getter as Yeltsin but had a loutish edge. The teenaged Tatyana Yeltsina saw him as one of the more unpleasant of her father's associates and was slightly afraid of him.[71] Ryabov was drawn into work in the CPSU apparatus in 1960 by Andrei Kirilenko, an outsider from the Ukrainian party machine who had been first secretary of the Sverdlovsk *obkom*—oblast committee of the party—since 1955. Kirilenko drew praise from Nikita Khrushchev for sharply increasing shipments of meat to the central authorities. He did so by ordering the slaughter of calves, lambs, and piglets, which then depressed production in the region for a decade. Yeltsin would later describe Kirilenko's part in the meat scam as shameful. "Kirilenko is still known for this. People have forgotten any good things he did [in Sverdlovsk], but this kind of thing is not forgotten."[72]

Khrushchev and his then deputy, Leonid Brezhnev, brought Kirilenko back to Moscow in 1962 for a position in the Central Committee Secretariat. His replacement in Sverdlovsk, on Kirilenko's recommendation, was Konstantin Nikolayev, a local who graduated from the UPI construction division in the 1930s and was secretary of the institute's party committee during the war. Nikolayev, a 300-pound diabetic, depended heavily on Ryabov because of his disabilities and promoted him in 1966 to second secretary of the obkom. In January 1971 Nikolayev retired and Ryabov took over as first secretary; Nikolayev died several months later. Kirilenko, as a member of the Politburo, seems not to have figured in the decision, although he kept a hand in Sverdlovsk politics until 1982. Ryabov was happy Moscow accepted the need for an industrial expert and Urals man to have the job and not to repeat the experience of sending in a *varyag* (Viking) like Kirilenko.[73]

You would never know Yeltsin's dependence on Ryabov from the Yeltsin memoirs, which hardly mention him. Yeltsin was not one to concede indebtedness to another, and this feeling was strengthened in Ryabov's case by their rupture of relations in 1987, when Ryabov took part in the attack on Yeltsin as Mikhail Gorbachev pushed him out of his high position.

Ryabov made up his mind in April 1968 to recruit Yeltsin into the regional party apparatus. He wanted to turn a page in the obkom's department for construction, which had been run for years by the ineffective Aleksei Guseletov. When Ryabov raised Yeltsin as a potential head, some functionaries, aware of the belatedness of his admittance into the CPSU and of his past noninvolvement in Komsomol and party activity, were dumbfounded. The least Yeltsin could do, they thought, was earn his party spurs at the factory or district level, as Ryabov had.[74] They may not have known that he had paid his dues the past five years on nominally elected "soviets" (legislative councils) and local party committees or that a 1966 review of his work appreciated him as "politically literate" *(politicheski gramotnyi)*, taking part in public service, and "having authority" in the collective.[75] In his memoir account, Yeltsin specifically links his 1968 appointment to his political activities: "I was not especially surprised to receive this offer, since I had been engaged constantly in public service."[76] Partocrats consulted by Ryabov objected that Yeltsin was headstrong and abrasive. Ryabov would not leave it at that. "I asked, 'And how do you assess him from a work perspective?' They gave it some thought and answered, 'Here there are no problems. He . . . will carry out what the leadership assigns him to do.'" No powderpuff himself, Ryabov swore he would get the most out of Yeltsin and, "if he were 'to kick off the traces,' would put him in his place."[77] He was not the last to think he could domesticate Yeltsin and harness him for his purposes.

Ryabov ran the appointment by Nikolayev and made the overture to Yeltsin. "To be objective about it, he was not dying to have this job," writes Ryabov, "but after our chat he gave his agreement."[78] Yeltsin says parsimoniously that he consented for no better reason than he "felt like taking a new step."[79] But he did not do it on a lark. He knew full well that it was a wise career move—onward to fresh experiences and upward in the pyramid of power. "I became not merely a boss but a man of power. I threw myself into a party career as I had once thrown myself into hitting the volleyball."[80]

Sverdlovsk oblast's party committee and regional government were in a low-slung building on Lenin Prospect, across the Town Pond from where Vasilii Tatishchev established his ironworks in the eighteenth century. An Orthodox cathedral was demolished to make way for it in the 1930s. The six-man construction department was one of several offices the obkom, as in other provincial capitals, had for palliating the numberless frictions and contradictions built into the Soviet planned economy. It acted as a watchdog on personnel, oversaw the logistics for mundane and showcase projects, and encouraged "socialist competition" among work units to outdo one another in attaining output targets. Yeltsin considered this meddling in line management unexceptionable. By hook or by crook, "with the aid of pumped-up resolutions, reproofs, and whatnot," the party organs would take care of nuts-and-bolts problems. "This was the gist of the existing system, and it raised no questions."[81]

The first half of the 1970s were the last time the economy of the Soviet Union, buoyed by high world oil prices, met its growth norms. The fledgling party worker met his in spades. Yeltsin prided himself, as in SU-13 and the DSK, on an orderly work environment. Making a sales pitch to a young engineer, Oleg Lobov, to sign on as his deputy in 1972, he called the department "a structure in which discipline has been maintained," not disguising that he viewed it as wilting elsewhere.[82] Yeltsin would work nonstop as a troubleshooter, as he did in 1973 during completion of a cold-rolling mill (a mill for reprocessing plate and sheet metal to make it thinner and harder) at the Upper Iset Works. For this exploit, which involved 15,000 workers and intercessions with head offices in Moscow, he won an Order of the Red Banner of Labor, his second. Yeltsin "worked conscientiously and responsibly," Ryabov was to relate—no mean encomium in a book written a decade after the two fell out.[83]

Yeltsin also had a nose for publicity. In 1970 he had builders retread his earlier experiment of putting up an apartment house in five days, and went one better by organizing a national conference on "the scientific organization of labor" around the project.[84] He butted into projects to be commissioned and was at Nikolayev's or Ryabov's side when the ribbon was cut. Yeltsin even listened to advice from Ryabov on softening his manner. "He changed tactics in his bearing and started to foster sociable ties with his colleagues in the obkom [staff] and to put out feelers to the members of the bureau, the obkom secretaries, the oblast executive panel, and other well-placed cadres."[85] Yeltsin was not on a particularly fast track. He occupied the same departmental position in the obkom apparatus for seven years, which was as long as it took him to progress from foreman to chief of SU-13.

Here a providential event interceded. In the spring of 1975 Eduard Shevardnadze, the party boss in the Caucasus republic of Georgia, asked for and received the Politburo's permission to hire away Gennadii Kolbin, the second secretary in Sverdlovsk and heir presumptive to Ryabov, as his second-ranking secretary in Tbilisi. Ryabov's preferred candidate for second secretary, Vyacheslav Bayev, the head of the obkom's machine-building department, was happy where he was and not tempted by the offer. Ryabov then approached Yevgenii Korovin, the secretary for industry, a diffident and sickly official from Kamensk-Ural'skii, who recommended Yeltsin—a mere department head—for the position. "He told me he could not handle it, it would be hard on him, but Boris Nikolayevich was high-powered and assertive, and I would be good in a secondary role." Ryabov thought Yeltsin lacked the experience, and accepted a compromise recommended by Kolbin: that Korovin be made second secretary and Yeltsin be made one of the five obkom secretaries. Yeltsin may have expected more, but accepted. His new portfolio took in the forest and pulp-and-paper industries as well as construction, and he was given a seat on the bureau, the obkom board comprising ten to twelve party and state officials.[86]

Speculation was rampant that Ryabov himself was going to graduate to other duties. Yeltsin smelled an opportunity for the taking. Ryabov shuddered when he described the situation twenty-five years later:

> So the step was taken and Boris Nikolayevich became the obkom's secretary for construction. This gave him more independence and scope in dealing with the issues he was responsible for, and as a member of the obkom bureau he could be bolder in addressing them. There was gossip galore that I was going to be moved up or transferred, and people even drew up various scenarios. Boris came to understand the subtleties and knew how to conduct himself, in view of the fact that . . . Korovin was not a competitor for him and was not spoiling for power. Boris understood he had to position himself closer to me, as he had already been doing in recent years, which is what earned him the promotion to secretary. He kept his head down. As before, we went together to important construction sites. He could still not do without me, because for [the projects] to be completed he needed additional construction manpower and the use of workers from the factories. Many of the oblast's problems had to be taken care of in Moscow, and for that you couldn't manage without the first secretary of the obkom. As I figured out only later, Boris, in trying so hard to carry out all my wishes, was behaving like a sycophant and careerist. But I was impressed and did not suspect that for him this was a tactic to achieve a breakthrough in his career. On the contrary, I considered that this fine fellow Boris had at long last come to understand the oblast's needs and was doing everything he could to satisfy them. We and our families continued to be on amiable terms.[87]

There is something disingenuous to Ryabov's imputation of malevolence. In a hierarchical political order, the *only* way to gain traction was to carry out one's superior's wishes, as officials at all levels in the USSR strove to do and as Ryabov himself was no stranger to. Had Yeltsin held fast to the illiberal path Ryabov favored, Ryabov would not have characterized his behavior with such odium.

In real time, Ryabov, enjoining Yeltsin to be more collegial,[88] groomed him to be his successor. Ryabov got his big promotion out of Sverdlovsk in

October 1976, when he was selected for the post of secretary supervising the Soviet defense industry in the Central Committee Secretariat in Moscow. To fill the vacancy, Ryabov saw Korovin and Yeltsin as the main alternatives and did not doubt which one he preferred. "Korovin," he said, "was very diligent and finicky, and he had a lot of knowledge, but he did not have an iron grip, and the leader of such an organization has to have an iron grip and has to be strong of will. I consulted with my comrades and with the other secretaries, and with people from other provinces, and decided to recommend Yeltsin."[89] There was some opposition at home. The obkom secretary for ideological questions, Leonid Ponomarëv, had had it with Yeltsin's two-fisted approach and convoked the obkom bureau off-the-record. Ryabov was in Moscow for the plenum of the Central Committee (which confirmed him in the Secretariat position on October 25) and Yeltsin, by chance, was there for a month-long training course at the party's Academy of Social Sciences. Ponomarëv moved that the bureau speak out against Yeltsin and endorse Leonid Bobykin, the first secretary of the city party committee. It reached no consensus and would have had a hard time of it had it voiced an opinion different from the outgoing first secretary's, especially once it was clear that Yeltsin had support in the Kremlin.[90]

Ryabov won General Secretary Brezhnev over to the candidacy, subject to vetting by party elders and forty minutes of chin-wagging between Brezhnev and Yeltsin. The central secretary for personnel questions, Ivan Kapitonov, had wanted Korovin as first secretary, and Brezhnev at first protested that "we in the Central Committee do not know [Yeltsin]." Brezhnev gave his seal of approval in their interview on October 31. "Even though I had always felt deep down that such a conversation might take place," Yeltsin says, "I had tried not to dwell on it." Brezhnev warned him that he would carry "additional responsibility" before the party because he had leapfrogged over Korovin.[91]

On November 2, 1976, a plenum of the Sverdlovsk obkom was convened to discuss "the organizational question." "Everything went as planned," Yeltsin remembered. Yevgenii Razumov, the apparatchik sent by Moscow to represent the Central Committee, moved on its behalf that Yeltsin be chosen first secretary. "As always, the vote was unanimous." Yeltsin had written out a short speech, "feeling that it was necessary to do this," and read it out to the obkom, which listened and adjourned.[92]

Chapter Four

A Boss with a Difference

At forty-five, Yeltsin was one of the youngest provincial first secretaries in the Russian core of the Soviet Union. The seventh of twelve apparatchiks to fill this post in the unofficial capital of the Urals between World War II and 1991, he would reign supreme in Sverdlovsk for eight and a half years, as many as he was to be president of post-communist Russia. Yeltsin's kingdom was pear-shaped, with its capital city at the middle of the base and his native Butka tucked in its southeast corner. In area it was an amplitudinous 75,000 square miles. That was more than eight of the USSR's fifteen union republics and about the size of the six New England states in the United States or, in Europe, of Austria, Switzerland, and Ireland combined. Its population of 4,483,000 put the oblast fourth among Soviet Russian provinces in 1979. Eighty-five percent of its people were urban—1,225,000 in Sverdlovsk, 400,000 in Nizhnii Tagil, and 189,000 in Kamensk-Ural'skii—and only 15 percent lived on the land.

The local bosses of the ruling party originally functioned as its "law-and-order prefects," tasked with projecting the center's power and maintaining political stability.[1] This function continued to make demands on Boris Yeltsin's time in the 1970s and 1980s. The territorial subunits of the CPSU paralleled the institutions of local government. Sverdlovsk oblast contained thirty districts (*raions*), each of which had a party committee; there were districts within the three largest cities; and a mass membership of 221,000 communists (as of 1976) formed a base. The obkom and its leader decided on about 20,000 personnel appointments and supervised all entities that policed, educated, and informed the population and mobilized it for the purposes of the regime. For emergencies, Yeltsin's duty officer had prolix instructions on liaison with the KGB, the Committee on State Security (the OGPU and the NKVD under Stalin). Yurii Kornilov, the head of the Sverdlovsk KGB and a former raion party secretary, escorted him on his railcar and helicopter incursions into the backcountry.[2] "I often came by the agency," Yeltsin writes in *Confession on an Assigned Theme*. "I asked to be informed about the KGB's work, studied how it functioned, and acquainted myself with its departments."[3] Yeltsin also sat on the civil-military collegium of the Urals Military District and attended field exercises. Ministry of Defense brass conferred the rank of colonel on him in October 1978, presenting him with a dress uniform and an astrakhan hat.

Not that law-and-order obligations were ever forsworn; the party chiefs with the passage of time defined themselves more as "developmental prefects" for coordinating economic growth and ensuring that some of the benefits trickled down. Administrative intervention for harmony of operation was bound to happen in an economy where market mechanisms had been squashed by the state. In economic indices, Sverdlovsk oblast ranked third among Soviet provinces. The Urals staples of mining and metallurgy continued to expand, slowly. Beloyarsk, the Soviet Union's first nuclear power station, powered by a sodium-cooled breeder reactor, started up in 1964 at the town of Zarechnyi, north of Sverdlovsk (it was disabled by fires in 1977 and 1978). In the 1981–85 five-year plan, Yeltsin and the oblast were active in the crash campaign to transport natural gas from the middle and lower Ob in west Siberia to customers in Europe; five pipelines and twenty compressor stations were constructed in the taiga.

In Sverdlovsk civilian pursuits paled before the production of armaments. The oblast had 350,000 military-industrial employees, more than any other Soviet province.[4] Defense plants could not be mentioned by exact name or whereabouts in the media, and the province was off-limits to Westerners throughout the Cold War. The Urals Wagon Works in Nizhnii Tagil was the highest-volume maker of tanks anywhere in the world; its product is still wheeling around the former Soviet Union, Eastern Europe, India, the Arab world, and North Korea. Two of the ten cloistered "atomic cities" in the USSR lay north of the oblast capital: Sverdlovsk-44, known today as Novoural'sk, home to the Urals Electrochemical Combine, which was the largest factory for enriching uranium in the world; and Sverdlovsk-45, later Lesnoi, whose

Electrochemical Instrumentation Combine was the country's premier facility for serial assembly of nuclear warheads. Yeltsin as first secretary was accountable for the well-being of the atomic towns, whose very existence was a state secret. A number of flagships of military industry were situated in Sverdlovsk city. The Kalinin Machinery Works, for example, was an artillery plant retooled to rockets in the 1950s; it cranked out surface-to-air missiles (such as the one that downed Francis Gary Powers's U-2 spy plane over Sverdlovsk in 1960), medium-range ballistic missiles, and torpedoes. The Urals Turbine Works manufactured tank engines, the Urals Transportation Machinery Works armored vehicles, the Vektor Works missile guidance systems and radars, and Uralmash, the biggest employer in Sverdlovsk, artillery pieces. Military Compound No. 19, built in the Chkalov raion of Sverdlovsk in 1947 with blueprints from Japan's Unit No. 731 in Manchuria, was the busiest of the USSR's three centers for producing biological weaponry. An accidental emission of aerosolized anthrax spores from its dryer took nearly a hundred lives in April 1979. Moscow attributed it to tainted meat.[5]

If the early part of the Brezhnev period, when Yeltsin broke into party work, were halcyon days for the nomenklatura, the later years were not. The economy was in the doldrums, and there were signs of creeping social and political crisis. Urals minerals were increasingly expensive to mine, the labor to work its antiquated factories was running low, and agricultural production was stagnant. In no region of the USSR had negligence of consumers for the benefit of heavy and military industry been as bad. Per-capita supply of housing, food, and retail goods was below average. Of the thirty-seven worst-polluted cities in Soviet Russia in the 1980s, eleven were in the Urals and six were in Sverdlovsk oblast (Kamensk-Ural'skii, Kirovgrad, Krasnoural'sk, Nizhnii Tagil, Revda, and Sverdlovsk).[6]

Yeltsin had good reason to depict the first secretary in his autobiography as "god, tsar, and master" of the province, head and shoulders above the lesser mortals around him. "[His] word was law, and barely anyone would dare not to heed a request or assignment from him. . . . On practically any question, the first secretary's opinion was final." Yeltsin wielded his influence in Sverdlovsk, he insisted, only to benefit society. "I made use of this power, but to benefit others and never for myself. I forced the wheels of the economic machine to spin faster. People submitted to me, people obeyed me, and owing to that, it seemed to me, work units performed better."[7]

Two hundred obkom staffers were at Yeltsin's beck and call, dishing out guidance, punishment, and favors. He had a finger in every pie of political relevance, although he would stay away from organizational trivia unless procedures broke down or higher-ups wanted a report. He had the self-assurance to be open to his associates' input. Taking a procedure from the construction industry, on Monday mornings he chaired a planning session *(planërka)* of members of the bureau of the obkom, where they were invited to raise their concerns casually. The formal convocation of the bureau on Tuesday (every second week, on average) was more crisply run. At several meetings a year, it was time for "personal responsibility"; bureau members did a self-evaluation in front of their colleagues, followed by a Yeltsin report card. As it tended to be in the Soviet Union, the party boss's word was most conclusive when it was spoken, not written. If the two ever deviated, the verbal held. In countries with rule of law, formal understandings on paper take precedence. In the communist system, the primacy of informal oral commands and handshake agreements reflected the weakness of law, insidious secrecy and mistrust, and the need for authority figures able to cut through the thicket of often conflicting administrative requirements.

Yeltsin made short work of the ineffectual Yevgenii Korovin, sending him to the trade unions; Leonid Ponomarëv soon found himself an academic dean in Moscow; it took several more years to get rid of Leonid Bobykin.[8] For the circle of obkom secretaries, Viktor Manyukhin, an apparatchik who worked with Yeltsin for fifteen years, notes in a vinegary memoir about him, "The principles of selection were cut-and-dried: good training, knowledge of the work, and, the main criterion, devotion *[predannost']* to the first [secretary]."[9] The two party officials on the best terms with Yeltsin, Oleg Lobov and Yurii Petrov, both construction specialists, were each to make it to obkom second secretary, and Petrov would succeed him as number one in 1985 after several years in Moscow. But Yeltsin did not reward fawning praise, and for most appointments he was results-oriented. To head the oblast government, he picked the distinguished director of the Kalinin Works, Anatolii Mekhrentsev, in 1977. Yeltsin had an affinity for technocrats like him and for eager younger candidates whom he could promote—if they played second fiddle. With Mekhrentsev, although Yeltsin respected him, he fretted when Mekhrentsev was introduced that his awards and production medals would be listed. At an early meeting, Yeltsin cut off the introducer: "Don't announce any awards; there should be no heroes among us."[10] There were interpersonal rivalries, and an intercity competition between Sverdlovsk and Nizhnii Tagil, but in the main the political elite of the oblast was tight-knit. Most obkom officials were alumni of either UPI or Urals State University; they communicated on a first-name-and-patronymic basis; they partied on one another's birthdays and attended the last rites of family members. If there was a disagreement, the first secretary resolved it. When Manyukhin, as first secretary of the city of Sverdlovsk, criticized Petrov, a Nizhnii Tagil native, for bias toward the second city, Yeltsin sided with Manyukhin and had Petrov right the balance.[11]

Force of personality amplified administrative levers. A strapping six foot two, 220 pounds by the 1970s, his hair parted on the right into a formidable cowlick, First Secretary Yeltsin oozed *vlast'*, that untranslatable Russian epithet for power and rule. He enunciated laconically and emphatically in a husky baritone. He elongated his syllables—as his classmates in Berezniki had noticed—flattened his vowels, and thrummed his r's in the Urals manner. Interest was added by either picking up the pace or pausing for dramatic effect. When riled at windy speeches or untoward news, he would raise an eyebrow—as teacher Antonina Khonina saw in the 1940s—poke a pencil through the forefinger and little finger of his right hand, and rat-a-tat-tat it; should they persist, he whammed his hand on the desk or lectern and snapped the pencil into thirds.

A ward in Sverdlovsk's Hospital No. 2 was put on standby before plenums of the obkom, as insurance against an acerbic report from the rostrum—one that "really made the malachite ashtrays quiver"—putting any members in need of therapy.[12] A spit-and-polish dress code prevailed. The chief wore a two-piece suit, with necktie and tie clip, and had his shoes burnished to a glint. Heaven help the clerk or factory manager who did not wear a tie, even on the muggiest summer day, or who stood before Yeltsin with hands in his pockets: He would be sent home without ado.

It was not wise to cross the boss on substance. *Ural'skii rabochii*, the Sverdlovsk daily newspaper, ran a story about a Yeltsin visit to a local factory that rubbed the first secretary the wrong way. "We gave it [the newspaper] to you," Yeltsin threw at editor-in-chief Grigorii Kaëta, "and we can take it away." Yeltsin's smoldering glare cut into Kaëta "like a knife."[13] Engineer Eduard Rossel was chief of the Nizhnii Tagil construction combine in 1978 and was asked by Yeltsin to take on the job of mayor of that city. Rossel said he preferred to stay put. Yeltsin was tight-lipped for a full sixty seconds—an eon to Rossel, who was only six years younger but very much the junior player—splintered his pencil, and blurted out ill-naturedly, "Very well, Eduard Ergartovich, I won't forget your refusal."[14] Both Kaëta and Rossel found, though, that if they patiently accepted the talking to and did their work well, it was possible to get out of the doghouse. Kaëta remained as editor until after Yeltsin's departure for Moscow. Rossel got several promotions from him and after communism was to be elected governor of Sverdlovsk oblast.

Ex officio, Yeltsin was his bailiwick's spokesman in USSR-wide politics. As its unwritten rules prescribed, he was elected without opposition to the Supreme Soviet, the Soviet Union's rubber-stamp parliament, in 1978. (Andrei Kirilenko continued to occupy another seat from Sverdlovsk oblast.) In February 1981 Yeltsin made his first speech to a quinquennial party convention in Moscow, the Twenty-Fifth CPSU Congress. He was on pins and needles, as the KGB was looking into the suicide of Vladimir Titov, a key operative on his staff, several days before. Titov, the head of the obkom's "general department," which answered for confidential records and correspondence, shot himself with a pistol he kept in his office safe, and some secret materials were missing. Yeltsin had to return to Sverdlovsk midway through the congress to meet with officers.[15] On the congress's last day, Yeltsin was selected to the CPSU Central Committee, whose plenums he had been attending and speaking at since 1976 as a guest (and which Mikhail Gorbachev had joined in 1971). He met on a regular basis with members of the "Sverdlovsk diaspora," officials from the province who had been transferred to Moscow. In bureaucratic encounters, he had the reputation of someone who was as good as his word and was a bulldog guardian of his home turf. Viktor Chernomyrdin, who was to be Russian prime minister in the 1990s, met up with him on gas pipeline projects in the early 1980s and was struck by his addiction to speaking first, assertively, at meetings with central officials.[16]

Yeltsin and Yakov Ryabov, his predecessor and booster, were at first in frequent contact. "He often phoned me," Ryabov said, "and sought my advice on all serious questions." When Yeltsin was in Moscow, he visited Ryabov at his Central Committee office and dacha. "We had a friendship that was not only official but informal, family."[17] In February 1979 Ryabov tripped up politically over unguarded comments on Brezhnev's medical condition. He made them in Yeltsin's presence at a semipublic meeting in Nizhnii Tagil and, says Ryabov, someone passed them on to Brezhnev—he believed it was Yurii Kornilov, the general in charge of the Sverdlovsk oblast KGB. His words were then used by the defense minister of the USSR, Dmitrii Ustinov, to turn Brezhnev against Ryabov. Ustinov had earlier held Ryabov's slot in the Central Committee Secretariat, where he had several disputes with him about tank production; he had wanted the position for one of his clients in

1976 and saw Ryabov as a threat. Within a week, Brezhnev informed Ryabov he was being bumped to a position in Gosplan, the state planning committee. Ryabov was officially removed from the Secretariat at the Central Committee plenum of April 17, 1979.[18] He served as first deputy chairman of Gosplan until 1983 and subsequently as minister of foreign trade, deputy premier, and Soviet ambassador to Paris—significant posts all, but mediocre compared to the appointment he held from 1976 to 1979.

Yeltsin, his ties to Ryabov common knowledge, feared for his own seat. "Boris Nikolayevich took Ryabov's failure badly" and had "long conversations in the evenings" at his dacha with Sverdlovsk colleagues. Yeltsin appreciated that the fall of Ryabov "would for some time close off the road . . . out of Sverdlovsk," and was on his guard.[19] Two months after the firing of Ryabov came the Sverdlovsk anthrax outbreak, in which Marshal Ustinov was also a player. Yeltsin "was so enraged by the lack of cooperation he received [from the military] that he stormed over to Compound [No.] 19 and demanded entry." He was excluded on the personal order of Ustinov. As a Politburo member who had known Stalin, Ustinov "far outranked a provincial party boss."[20] Yeltsin was to contend in a press interview in 1992 that the matter did not stop there. He went to see Yurii Andropov, the chairman of the KGB, in his office on Lubyanka Square in Moscow. According to Yeltsin, Andropov "phoned Ustinov and ordered him to take this facility down." Andropov could not literally have given an order to Ustinov, his political equal, but could have pressed him to make the decision—or the scene could have been flimflam put on for Yeltsin's benefit. In any event, it was Yeltsin's understanding that Andropov had interceded and the program was discontinued. He found out in the 1980s that it was only moved elsewhere.[21] The germ-processing plant was evacuated to the Central Asian republic of Kazakhstan and Compound No. 19 was continued as a proving range and storage dump. Yeltsin as leader of post-Soviet Russia was to inform U.S. President George H. W. Bush in February 1992 of the full story.

Not without guile, the vulnerable Yeltsin protected himself by turning to Andrei Kirilenko, the crony of Brezhnev's who had been Sverdlovsk first secretary before Konstantin Nikolayev and Ryabov. Ryabov had looked up Kirilenko when Brezhnev gave him the bad news; Kirilenko was shocked and seemed to fear that he, too, would feel the effects.[22] But Kirilenko's high offices and long links to Brezhnev—they first worked together in Ukraine in the 1940s—kept him in the game until Brezhnev's death in 1982. Kirilenko advocated as a priority continued investment in heavy industry and was not popular in the Sverdlovsk elite. Neither those problems nor the encroaching senility of Uncle Andrei, the obkom staffers' moniker for him, deterred Yeltsin from paying recurring visits and tracking him down every year for a telephone call on his birthday, September 8.[23]

General Secretary Brezhnev, who had worked as an agricultural functionary in the Sverdlovsk region from 1929 to 1931, at the time of collectivization and dekulakization, took no particular interest in Sverdlovsk or the Urals. The one time he scheduled a visit to the city when Yeltsin was first secretary was the night of March 29–30, 1978, en route to Siberia. The local leadership, waiting with bouquets in hand at the main railroad station, looked like dolts when his train whizzed through the junction with the blinds drawn, no excuses offered. Behind closed doors, Yeltsin was contemptuous of Brezhnev's vanity and sloth, and he professes to have foiled a suggestion from Moscow to create a Brezhnev museum in Sverdlovsk premises where he once had an office.[24] For public consumption, he played along with the Brezhnev personality cult, although he was less rhapsodic than some of the provincial potentates and toadied less over time.[25] But as Brezhnev's seventy-fifth birthday, in December 1981, neared, Yeltsin ordered that words about Brezhnev as a leader "of genius" *(genial'nyi)* be folded into the obkom salutation. He later agreed to suggestions from the scribes to tone down the language, aware that blarney could be overdone. Sverdlovsk's gift for the birthday was a kitschy likeness of Brezhnev in full regalia, done in semiprecious Urals stones. Craftsmen had to be flown to Moscow to update it when the Politburo padded out his chestful of medals before the mosaic could be presented.[26]

It has been intimated that Yeltsin's attitude to the perks of office at the start of his career was one of indifference.[27] Perhaps this was so, but that attitude was soon inoperative. He was permitted what corresponding members of the nomenklatura had in other parts of the USSR. Soon after he went to the obkom apparatus in 1968, the Yeltsins were allotted a four-room apartment, their largest yet, in a shiny new building on downtown Mamin-Sibiryak Street. Yelena and Tatyana studied at the close-by School No. 9, the best in Sverdlovsk, where the program was heavy in mathematics and science. For summers and weekends, they had use of a two-family dacha, their first, in Istok, east of Sverdlovsk.

As oblast party secretary, Yeltsin in 1975 was given four rooms in the House of Old Bolsheviks at 2 Eighth of March Street, built for revolutionaries from the Urals and Siberia, many of whom during Stalin's purges were led off from their apartments to the Gulag or death. Better-appointed digs in the building were assigned in 1977. In 1979 the family moved into a high-ceilinged, five-room apartment (living room, dining room, study, and two bedrooms) in a sepulchral new VIP edifice at 1 Working Youth Embankment—palatial for the Soviet Union. The house gave out onto the Town Pond and 1905 Square, the promenade where the Sverdlovsk leadership reviewed the May 1, May 9, and November 7 parades.[28] The household had no domestic help: Naina Yeltsina cooked, took out the trash to a bin in the courtyard, and ironed Boris's shirts and pants. The shabbily built House of Soviets, the twenty-four-story party and government tower on Ninth of January Street, begun by Ryabov and opened in 1982, was a stroll away. Here was Yeltsin's first office with air conditioning, which was exotica in the Urals.[29] Without leaving the building he could place orders for foods unavailable in local stores or have himself fitted for clothing chargeable to his personal allowance. A stone's throw from Yeltsin's front door, the secluded Hospital No. 2, infested with KGB bugs, ministered to several thousand elite clients.[30]

A twenty-minute ride north of Ninth of January Street would take Yeltsin to the obkom bureau's dacha hideout at Baltym, to which he was admitted in 1975. Dacha No. 1, just inside the gatehouse, was booked for him in 1976. In earshot of a growling highway, its charms again were not lush: three sleeping rooms, a parlor, a kitchen and eating area with a fireplace, and a billiards hall. Other families were put up two to a dacha, sharing latrines and kitchens. Outside lay a swimming pool, a volleyball court, and a canteen. In the temperate months, Yeltsin had the cottagers and their wives don gym togs for Wednesday evening and Sunday volleyball matches. Volleyball facilities figured large in obkom resolutions about mass athletics and fitness.[31] In winter, there were cross-country ski runs and volleyball in a Sverdlovsk gym. Indoors at Dacha No. 1, there was billiards, with the first secretary showing off behind-the-back and left-handed shots. Yeltsin was a crabby loser in these contests. After his side was outpointed in several hard-fought volleyball matches, he sulked and made ready to depart. Oleg Lobov, captain of the opposing team, defused the situation by inviting Yeltsin to join him as a twosome against a full six. They won the rematch—with some help from their opponents—and Yeltsin went to the showers with his dignity unharmed.[32]

Over time, Yeltsin indulged in a more baronial taste—for hunting. As deputy chairman of the oblast government, his former guardian angel in the party apparatus, Fëdor Morshchakov, an avid marksman, organized the shooting of ducks in the spring and fall and wild elk in the winter. Yeltsin had a collection of guns, preferring a Czechoslovak-made Ceská Zbrojovka carbine—bought for him as a gift by obkom staff in Prague in 1977—and gave chase in a UAZ all-terrain vehicle fitted out with racks and heaters.[33] He went over the guest list name by name, saw to the bird limit of five per person, and began the pleasantries at mealtime. It is not small-minded to agree with Viktor Manyukhin that the bonhomie likely had an ulterior political motive as well: "The tactic of keeping all under vigil . . . helped Boris Nikolayevich know everything about his colleagues [and] . . . see for himself that there were no groupings against him."[34]

Liquor flowed at these events, especially when a session in the steambath was part of it for the males in the company. It was imbibed in the dressing room before and after and in the cooling-off intervals during the bath. The effects of alcohol are felt quickly in such heat. Yeltsin's temperance had given way to drinking at or above the average level within the party elite. Thursday and Friday evenings were often taken up with banquets for "delegations" from Moscow or other provinces. It not infrequently fell to Yeltsin to act as *tamada,* toastmaster. He had high tolerance and a formidable capacity. The cosmonaut Vitalii Sevast'yanov, a native of Sverdlovsk oblast, once told of Yeltsin, on a stressful trip to Moscow in this period, knocking back three water tumblers of vodka, which might have held a cup of fluid each, to start off a repast at Sevast'yanov's apartment.[35] But Manyukhin, no yes-man for Yeltsin, portrays his conduct as unimpeachable:

> Did Yeltsin drink when he worked in the Urals? Yes, he drank, like all normal people, and perhaps a mite more. With his expansive nature and character, on festive occasions Boris Nikolayevich loved to sit down to a good table with friends and comrades. Sometimes this would happen when he was out hunting, as is the practice with hunters. Yet, even after a "blowout," Boris Nikolayevich, healthy and youthful as he was, was fresh and cheerful the next morning and made it to work on time.[36]

There were exceptions. Ryabov noted in his diary in February 1976, when Yeltsin was still obkom secretary for construction, that he had been flat on his back in bed for a couple of days after "a tempestuous celebration of his [forty-fifth] birthday."[37] A deputy chairman of KGB central, Gelii Ageyev, was apoplectic when Yeltsin diverted him to interminable receptions and dinners after he landed at Sverdlovsk's Kol'tsovo airport during the

1979 anthrax crisis. Local notables hypothesized this was his way to prevent Ageyev from obstructing and from holding Yeltsin accountable for the outbreak. The general considered a written report to Brezhnev on Yeltsin's conduct but backed off the idea.[38] To larger questions, the drinking was tangential. Yeltsin had no pity for office drunks, as Manyukhin points out, and fired several factory directors for inebriation.

There was some political dissent in Sverdlovsk in the Brezhnev years, by individuals and, rarely, by very small organizations. A memo sent to the Central Committee Secretariat by Yurii Andropov on June 12, 1970, detailed the arrests in Sverdlovsk of seven members of a Party of Free Russia, later renamed the Revolutionary Workers Party. In 1969 they had run off 700 anti-Soviet pamphlets, stuck some to walls, and pelted 200 of them, from a viaduct over Cosmonauts Prospect, onto the official parade during the November 7 festivities. Student A. V. Avakov was jailed in 1975 for distributing 300 leaflets at Urals State University and reading out a speech made by Leon Trotsky in the 1920s. Around the same time, a League for the Liberation of the Urals put out flyers calling for a popular referendum on "autonomy of the Urals." No culprits were found. In February 1979, during the election campaign for the USSR Supreme Soviet, an unnamed Sverdlovsk group called on citizens to vote against the official nominees: "Comrades, let us cross out the names of the sellout candidates. They will forget about us right after the election. It doesn't bother them that the party has put itself above the people and above the law, that prices are rising and the stores are empty." This, too, went into the cold-case file.[39]

Yeltsin would have been within eyeshot of the 1969 protest and would have heard about some of these incidents through party channels. After November 1976, as first secretary, he was more fully informed and had to invest in the cultural domination and ideological hygiene that engross all authoritarian regimes. As came with the job description, his reports to CPSU meetings were now flecked with paeans to political conformity and harangues against Western imperialism. In September 1977 he carried out a Politburo directive to raze the building on Karl Liebknecht Street in whose cellar Tsar Nicholas II, his family, and four of their retainers were killed after the Bolshevik Revolution by a firing squad. Ipat'ev House was the two-story mansion of Nikolai Ipat'ev, a Urals merchant; the Romanovs lived in it as captives from April 1918, when they were brought there by horse and carriage from Tobol'sk, until the execution the night of July 17–18.[40] It was in connection with this place that Yeltsin came to the attention of Andropov, the leading Kremlin hawk on demolition. An Andropov letter to the Politburo is dated July 26, 1975; the bureau's resolution assigning the Sverdlovsk obkom to tear the house down, and present it as part of "the planned reconstruction of the city," is dated August 4. Since 1918 the building had been variously an anti-religious museum, dormitory, and storehouse. Andropov noted that it had attracted unwanted curiosity from Soviets and foreigners. Other sources say there was fear it would become an anti-communist shrine or a cause célèbre abroad, and that there might be trouble in 1976, the eightieth anniversary of Nicholas's coronation.[41] Why the act waited two years, and waited until Yeltsin replaced Ryabov, is uncertain, but scholars of the city and region told me in 2004 that local conservationists prevailed upon Ryabov to temporize. Brezhnev, says Viktor Manyukhin, sent a note to Yeltsin in 1977 telling him to go ahead, as a United Nations committee was planning to discuss conservation of the home. Yeltsin was away on vacation when the destruction occurred.[42] The foundation was filled with gravel and asphalted over.

The fifteen months Andropov was Soviet leader in 1982–84 were to bring out greater verbal rigor in Yeltsin. He huffed and puffed about imported films and pop music and about "duplicitous Januses" who debauched Urals youth with foreign culture and ideas. Yeltsin had subordinates detain in conversation party members who in the past wrote recommendations for Jewish acquaintances who later tried to emigrate to Israel. The hard-shell culture department of the obkom prevented one theater from staging a Russian play and banned six non-Soviet movies from local cinemas, while the department of propaganda and agitation stiffened controls over photocopiers.[43] In May 1983 a hue and cry in the Central Committee apparatus led Yeltsin to haul on the carpet the editor of *Ural* magazine, Valentin Luk'yanin, whose infraction had been to publish "Old Man's Mountain," a novella by Sverdlovsk writer Nikolai Nikonov about social decay in the Russian countryside. The work was already bowdlerized, having been worked over by the Sverdlovsk branch of Glavlit, the Soviet censorship agency, but even in that form it was too close to the bone for the apparat. Yeltsin forced Luk'yanin to own up to wrongdoing before the obkom bureau but left him in the editorship. At the July 1983 plenum of the oblast party committee, Yeltsin also denounced Valerian Morozov, an engineer from Nizhnii Tagil committed to a psychiatric hospital in 1982 for writing political letters to officials (in one to the Soviet procurator general he called the CPSU "a careerist mafia that has usurped power") and for trying to send a manifesto abroad. Morozov, Yeltsin pointed out sternly, composed "a plump revisionist manuscript" and went to the city of Gorky to try to meet with "the not unknown anti-Soviet element *[antisovetchik]* Sakharov."[44] Andrei Sakharov, the father of the USSR's hydrogen bomb, human rights advocate, and 1975 winner of the Nobel Peace Prize, had been exiled to Gorky in 1980 for protesting the invasion of Afghanistan. Luk'yanin later painted Yeltsin's doublespeak at conclaves such as these as typical of the man: "He always knew in advance what decision needed to be taken and moved toward it like a tractor or tank. . . . He spoke very authoritatively and unconditionally. . . . This was the essence of the party's policy. He was a glorious executor of it."[45]

A quarter-century after graduating from Urals Polytechnic, Yeltsin had achieved levels of status and prosperity in excess of what he could have envisaged. And he had experienced the personal passages, sweet and sour, that midlife brings. Vasilii Starygin passed away in Butka in 1968. Yeltsin's last surviving grandparent, Afanasiya Starygina, lost her bearings and tried several times to make her way back to her birthplace, Basmanovo. She died after wandering off in 1970; the body was never found.[46] In 1973 Nikolai Yeltsin suffered a stroke. He and Klavdiya moved from the Butka house to Sverdlovsk to live with their divorced and childless son, Mikhail, in his apartment on Zhukov Street. Nikolai died in May 1977. Between Boris and Mikhail, a construction foreman, there were hard feelings about parental care and other family business, and Boris averted the appearance of favoritism. He is said to have commented to a colleague, "I earned everything in life on my own, so let him do the same."[47] Their sister completed her studies at UPI in the late 1960s, moved home to Berezniki, and, as Valentina Golovacheva, worked as an engineer and raised two children. She was to divorce her husband and migrate to Moscow in 1995 to work in a low-level Kremlin position, when Boris was president of Russia,[48] but Mikhail took early retirement and did not leave Sverdlovsk. Naina Yeltsina's widowed mother, Mariya Girina, was also in Sverdlovsk, having moved from Orenburg. After the deaths of her father, Iosif, and two of her five siblings in road accidents, Naina developed a claustrophobic fear of cars and airplanes.[49]

Yeltsin, as workaholics will do, suffered from health issues of his own. Only expert medical intervention, some sources say, was to help him overcome symptoms of rheumatic valvular heart disease and acute angina in the mid-1960s.[50] Before Moscow he had fainting spells from hypertension and from labored breathing in airless rooms. He was deaf on the right side, the result of a middle-ear infection that grew out of an untreated head cold. The arches in his feet had fallen and he had lower back pain from volleyball and other insults. And he had been operated on for an intestinal ailment. In 1977 Yeltsin visited Hospital No. 2 for a bad infection of the second toe in his right foot. The swollen foot would not fit into his shoe—but Ivan Kapitonov of the Central Committee Secretariat was arriving at Kol'tsovo for an inspection tour. Yeltsin took a scalpel from the surgeon, made two slits in the leather, and limped off to his limousine.[51] With his selection to the Central Committee in 1981, Yeltsin's health was in the charge of the "Kremlin hospitals" of the Fourth Chief Directorate of the Ministry of Health. He told friends that a Gypsy fortune-teller predicted he would die at age fifty-three. In 1984, the year he was fifty-three, he lost weight and muscle tone; a medical exam in Moscow came up dry, and he put it out of his mind.[52] He would go to outlandish lengths, and not always successful ones, to cloak infirmities. One time, an otolaryngologist performed a small surgical procedure on him and he was groggy from the anesthetic. Rather than appear unsteady, Yeltsin had the orderlies roll him through the waiting room on a gurney, shrouded head to toe in a white sheet. The ruse backfired, and for days, it was rumored in Sverdlovsk that he had died.[53]

The vicissitudes of the younger generation ensured that Boris and Naina Yeltsin would rarely be alone in their spacious apartment. Their daughter Yelena enrolled in civil engineering at UPI after high school. Early in the course, and against her parents' wishes, she married a school friend, Aleksei Fefelov. They parted and divorced shortly after the birth of daughter Yekaterina in 1979, and she and Yekaterina moved back in with Boris and Naina. Her father, nervous that Yelena's problems might sully his reputation, sought the advice of Pavel Simonov, the subdepartment head for the Urals in the Central Committee Secretariat. Simonov calmed him down: For his CPSU superiors in Moscow, such things were personal, but, just in case, Simonov would brief them. "If Boris Nikolayevich had known at the time about the murky relationships within many other leadership families, he would not have worried. [He] never mentioned the topic again."[54] Several years later, Yelena married an Aeroflot pilot, Valerii Okulov; their daughter Mariya was born in 1983.

Then there was Tatyana Yeltsina, who was to be a political player after communism. As a girl, she was "a dreamer" who wanted to become a sea captain, and learned Morse code in preparation, but girls were not taken into the Nakhimov schools (for naval cadets). She then, like her father in the 1940s, longed to be a shipbuilder, and she figure skated and inherited his love for volleyball. Teachers and schoolmates have testified that she was weighed down by high expectations and illness. Graduating from School No. 9 in 1977, she announced to her parents that she planned to study in far-off Moscow. She did not want to repeat the experience of her sister, whose 5s at UPI, she said, were unjustly devalued as having been awarded *po blatu*—as part of the Soviet web of reciprocal favors: "I wanted to go away, to where no one knew my father." He overruled Naina, and Tatyana went off to study computer science and cybernetics at Moscow State University. There she married fellow student Vilen Khairullin, an ethnic Tatar, in 1980 and had a son, Boris, in 1981. This union, too, failed, and she spent the year after the birth with her parents in Sverdlovsk before returning to Moscow to finish her diploma.[55] Boris Nikolayevich at last had a male offspring. He was exhilarated that his grandson bore the legal name Boris Yeltsin.[56]

Professionally, Yeltsin was every inch the boss he had told his mother he would become. He savored the chief apparatchik's role. His time as Sverdlovsk first secretary, he was to say in 1989, brought him "the best years of my life" up to then.[57] Receipt of the Order of Lenin upon his fiftieth birthday in 1981, with a crimson flag, crimson star, and hammer-and-sickle surrounding a disc portrait of Lenin in platinum, rounded out his set of official awards. It came with an ode to "services rendered to the Communist Party and the Soviet state" and was presented in the Moscow Kremlin. Yeltsin's personal records in the Sverdlovsk archive of the CPSU show him receiving one award while in the construction industry—his Badge of Honor in 1966—and nine as a party official. These included medals honoring the Lenin centenary in 1970, the thirtieth anniversary of victory over Germany in 1975, the centenary of Felix Dzerzhinsky (the founder of the Soviet secret police) in 1977, and the sixtieth anniversary of the Soviet Army in 1978; Orders of the Red Banner of Labor in 1971 and 1974; the Order of Lenin in 1981; a gold medal for his contribution to the Soviet economy in 1981; and a certificate of thanks from the obkom upon his departure in April 1985. Yeltsin held onto these medals after 1991, still proud of having earned them. They were stored in his home study and put on display at his wake in 2007.[58]

The boss Yeltsin of the second half of the 1970s and the first half of the 1980s must be evaluated in the context of the political and social order of the day. Roving far from the approved path was not in the choice set for the proconsul of the Soviet empire in a strategic province. The Ipat'ev House decision underlines the point. Yeltsin "could not imagine" balking at the Kremlin's order. Had he, he "would have been fired" and whoever replaced him would have knocked down the building.[59]

A picture that incorporated nothing but orthodoxy, however, would overlook traits that differentiated Yeltsin from the typical CPSU secretary of his generation. There were signs of him holding back from the tedium of rites and routines. In television footage, he never wears his gold stars and medallions or busses dignitaries Brezhnev-style, although he does give out back-slapping bear hugs. He seems more attentive than most to his wardrobe. His hair is suspiciously long for a member in good standing of the nomenklatura, and every few minutes he brushes a hank of it from his forehead. Ennui plays on his face as he drones on at conferences and sits through commemorations.

Substantively, Yeltsin nibbled at the edges of what was admissible in late Soviet conditions and presaged what he was to do in the reform era. He was a compliant activist—accepting of the system and ready to put body and soul into making it work, and yet able to make judicious intrasystemic innovations and accommodations.[60]

As the Soviet economy went downhill after 1975, Yeltsin repulsed calls to strangle what little Stalin had left of free markets in the USSR. When irate Sverdlovskers agitated in 1982 for caps on the prices of meat and fruit in the farmers' bazaars, he branded them economic nonsense and lauded competition and self-sufficiency. "Prices in the marketplaces," he said, "depend on supply and demand. In order to lower them, we mostly have to move more farm products to the bazaars and to develop the personal gardens of the province's residents. Then . . . prices will fall."[61] In the state sector, Yeltsin adopted a device called the "complex brigade," which decentralized some economic operations to small labor collectives and let them qualify for wage premiums. The formula, found here and there in the provinces since the 1960s, was "the closest approximation to entrepreneurial initiative the official Soviet economy ever tolerated."[62]

Where he had wiggle room, Yeltsin made extensive use of the tool kit of the communist state to improve physical and social infrastructure and consumer welfare. He addressed these issues because of a desire to do the right thing, because he liked playing sugar daddy, and because, in a flip of his dictum in the construction industry ("Whoever worked better would live better"), he felt that employees who lived better would put out more in their work for the state. A partial list of Yeltsin's projects would take in: a start on a subway for the city of Sverdlovsk; eradication of its squalid barracks housing; near-completion of a south-north road artery through Nizhnii Tagil to Serov (this project began under Nikolayev in the 1960s, and Ryabov had been unable to complete it); "youth housing complexes" which gave younger families first crack at apartments and down payments, on condition of putting in two years of labor on the construction; pressure on heavy and defense industry to manufacture scarce household goods;[63] new theaters and a circus in Sverdlovsk and refurbishment of the 1912 opera house; a line for the province in the agricultural program for the Non–Black Soil Zone of European Russia (an acrobatic feat, since Sverdlovsk oblast is not in European Russia); and a City Day festival in Sverdlovsk, instituted in 1978, and neighborhood fairs to distribute food and consumer wares before winter. Yeltsin borrowed good ideas from others. The youth housing complexes had been pioneered in Moscow oblast; he tweaked the model by reserving spots for blue-collar workers, invalids, and army officers. The first City Day had been organized in Nizhnii Tagil in 1976 by Yurii Petrov. Compared to the world-shaking decisions Yeltsin was to be privy to after 1985, this may seem like small potatoes; to those affected, it was not.

Ventures like these would make headway only if clearances and means not written into the binding economic plan could be procured. For getting to the Soviet pork barrel, Yeltsin's intensity and connections were irreplaceable. "For our industrial province I hauled in from the center freight cars full of meat, butter, and other foods," he says. "I telephoned, demanded, strong-armed." He did the same for housing.[64] His critics do not deny his deftness. Manyukhin pays homage to him for "beating out resources from the center" for local initiatives and extra goods and medicines. When push came to shove, "Boris Nikolayevich went all the way up to the general secretary."[65]

Yeltsin's worldview did evolve in the late Soviet period. To a degree, the evolution was intellectually based. He and Naina subscribed to five or six of the monthly "thick journals." He had begun signing up for series of literary books while still a student at UPI, and the family continued this practice. The home library they kept on handmade shelves in his apartment study was to number some 6,000 volumes when they shipped it to Moscow in 1985. He often initiated discussions at the office about those social questions that could be debated in the Soviet media.[66] Yeltsin even familiarized himself with a few dissident works. He told me that in the late 1970s he read *The Gulag Archipelago*, Alexander Solzhenitsyn's unmasking of Stalinist cruelties (published in the West in 1973 but not in Russia until 1989), in a *samizdat* (underground) typescript that he got through his wife, who obtained it at work. When I asked him whether the KGB was aware of his reading, he replied, "Of course not. How would they know? They weren't looking in my direction."[67] Yeltsin began to open up at reunions of old UPI classmates and with others about the misfortunes of his family in the Stalin period. The travel to foreign shores for which his position qualified him also helped widen his horizons. Andrei Goryun reports that as long ago as the late 1960s, having arrived back from his first Western trip, to France, Yeltsin told associates in the Sverdlovsk House-Building Combine about how the capitalist economy was humming along there, and that he was "very strictly warned" to watch his tongue.[68] Naina Yeltsina's opinions contained seeds of doubt similar to his. "We are all children of the system," she said to an American television correspondent after her husband's retirement. "But I was not a good one, to be honest. I was outraged by many things."[69]

For the most part, Yeltsin's concerns were more bread-and-butter than philosophical or historical. He was moved not by some metaphysical thirst for reform, democracy, or the market but by a visceral sense that the autocratic methodology of the Soviet order was losing effectiveness and rot was setting in little by little. "I began to feel," he noted in *Confession on an Assigned Theme,* "that quite good and proper decisions . . . were turning out more often not to be implemented. . . . It was obvious that the system was beginning to malfunction."[70] This would have been more obvious when the book came out in 1990, but the harbingers were there in 1980—before Ronald Reagan entered the White House and escalated the arms race and before Mikhail Gorbachev started perestroika. Yeltsin caviled to friends that there was no limit to the time he sank into his work: The people around him shared a mystical belief in the power of ranking officials to fix problems by command. He begged off a get-together with UPI friends on the azure Lake Baikal in east Siberia because agricultural bureaucrats feared that without him there would be delays with the harvest. "They tell me," he said acidly to a friend, "that after I speak [to farm workers] the cows give more milk and the milk is creamier."[71] Yeltsin, needless to say, saw the problem as evolutionary rather than revolutionary. As Oleg Lobov said, "He was thinking about how to utilize the capacities of the system that was. He expressed great dissatisfaction not with the system in general but on concrete issues."[72] The bacillus was there, gnawing away at Yeltsin *before* he left for Moscow in 1985. Asked in 1988 about his acceptance of an Order of Lenin in 1981, he said he valued that kind of recognition at the time, but, "The Brezhnev system was always a mental irritant, and I felt a sense of inner reproach."[73] The next year, while a deputy in the Soviet parliament, he was challenged to explain how his opinions had changed in a reformist direction. They had, he stated, "gradually transformed" over the past six to eight years—a gestation starting in the early 1980s in Sverdlovsk.[74]

In this connection, Yeltsin was in step with parts of his constituency. A critical spirit was afoot in the middle Urals. Sverdlovsk had larger communities of academics, researchers, students, and artists than any city in Soviet Russia except Moscow and Leningrad. Despite Yeltsin's imperiousness toward Luk'yanin and the censoriousness of the obkom culture department, the authorities purposely overlooked unregistered amateur *(samodeyatel'nyye)* organizations dedicated to reading poetry and discussing movies. The Sverdlovsk Komsomol committee not only tolerated mass songfests and bohemian clubs for jazz, rock, and film but allocated rooms and equipment to them. Experimental discussion circles were found in several Sverdlovsk universities and institutes. One, in the philosophy department of UPI, was organized by Gennadii Burbulis, who later would be a high-level official in Yeltsin's Russia. The youth housing complexes were wired for cable television, which was not subject to official censorship. In short, "In Sverdlovsk and Sverdlovsk oblast, changes in the atmosphere of public life began to take place before the advent of perestroika."[75] Yeltsin was mindful and did not fight them. He exhorted CPSU and Komsomol organizations to make their activities more relevant to impressionable young people by offering programs that matched their tastes and the values sainted in Soviet propaganda: "When there is a gap between word and deed . . . this has an especially baleful influence on our youth."[76]

A concrete problem that increasingly distressed was the top-heaviness of Soviet government. In late communist times, decisions responsive to local interests awaited years of special pleading with Moscow. Sverdlovsk planners first petitioned the center to approve a subway in 1963; a preliminary edict was issued in 1970; to get shovels in the ground in 1980, it took entreaties via Andrei Kirilenko and a Yeltsin pilgrimage to Brezhnev's office, where Brezhnev asked him to handwrite a Politburo resolution; the first stations did not come into service until 1994.[77] To get things done took pluckiness and ingenuity. The Serov highway was built on the fly over twenty years without any central largesse. Yeltsin badgered factory directors and district personnel for the materials, equipment, and labor. The first secretary, who was god and tsar on some scores, had to be a nagger and a supplicant on others. Through the obkom, he had at his disposal thousands of personnel; thousands more were out of his reach, among them all the holders of top positions in the military-industrial complex. The state industrialists in the factories could not be obliged to contribute, only persuaded. And when they did chip in, Moscow might suddenly reverse direction and take away local gains. In 1980 Yeltsin and Yurii Petrov inveigled twenty Sverdlovsk factories, mostly in the defense sector, to jointly manufacture for use in the oblast heavy-duty harrows, which are toothed steel tools for tilling, aerating, and weeding fields. They were beside themselves when mandarins in Gosplan appropriated the harrows and carted them off to farms in Ukraine, with the statement that Sverdlovsk land was fit only for pasturage. Yeltsin's telephone calls to Gosplan, the minister of agriculture, and Mikhail Gorbachev, by then the Central Committee's secretary for agrarian affairs, were in vain.[78]

These machinations brought Yeltsin up against a question pregnant for the future: the place of "Russia" in the Soviet federation. A reason Sverdlovsk fared so badly in the byplay with Moscow was that the regions of the Russian Soviet Federative Socialist Republic, RSFSR, lacked the mediating structures available to the non-Russian republics. The RSFSR had a toothless government and no CPSU machinery at all. In the party, provinces like Sverdlovsk reported to USSR-level officials; in places like Ukraine and Kazakhstan, there was a republic-level party committee, bureau, and first secretary. An inconsequential Bureau of the Central Committee for RSFSR Affairs had existed in 1936–37, under Stalin, and was resuscitated by Khrushchev in 1958, only to have Brezhnev terminate it in 1965. The Russians "were always the Soviet Union's awkward nationality, too large either to ignore or to give the same institutional status as the Soviet Union's other major nationalities."[79]

What Yeltsin digested on the job in the Urals—again, well before his move to Moscow—was that Russia was an "accessory" or "appendage" of the imperial Soviet center, an unsung "donor" to the rest. "In Sverdlovsk I thought about this and began to talk about it . . . not loudly but, you would say, under my breath."[80] Naina Yeltsina and the engineering institute where she worked preferred contracts with clients in Kazakhstan, where she had lived as a girl, to work with RSFSR organizations: The Kazakhs, unlike the Russians, could make decisions expeditiously.[81] At the beginning of the 1980s, Yeltsin and Petrov jotted down a tripartite scheme for change: decentralizing the USSR's federal system; making Russia institutionally whole by strengthening its government and giving it a CPSU central committee or some such structure; and carving the RSFSR into seven or eight regional republics, one of them a Urals republic, strong enough to make a go of it. They kept the sketch to themselves. Petrov summarized it two decades afterward in that Urals nostrum *samostoyatel'nost'*, self-reliance. Smacking of autonomist ideas that have long swirled in the Urals, the scheme points toward the position Yeltsin was to take on Soviet federalism in 1990–91.[82]

The other area of probing that was a bellwether of the politics of perestroika dealt with relations between the leader and the mass of the population. Soviet partocrats rarely rubbed shoulders with ordinary people. When they did, it was at perfunctory affairs before docile viewers, pegged to state holidays or single-candidate elections, and more ritualized after about 1960 than before.[83] As first secretary, Yeltsin did all in his power to spice up these rituals.

At the groundbreaking for the Sverdlovsk subway in August 1980, he invited Young Pioneers to attend, play the bugle and drum, and distribute flowers to the mud-splattered construction workers—and to the members of the obkom bureau, who lined up long-faced behind the first secretary.[84] To mark the 1984 campaign for the USSR Supreme Soviet, Yeltsin organized a rail tour of remote districts of the oblast, in the dead of winter. The locomotive pulled two cars: a political coach full of obkom officials and an artistic coach containing twenty-two singers and musicians shanghaied for the journey from Sverdlovsk theaters:

> Every day of the agitation outing, from February 20 to 25, 1984, through the soiled and almost uninhabitable towns of the north, followed the same program. In the morning, the travelers from the political coach went off to the next kolkhoz or sovkhoz, where Yeltsin would summon the peasants to keep their cattle stalls as spotless as their own homes. In the afternoon, he would give a report on political and economic themes to the local communists. But in the evenings, like balsam on the soul after wearisome speeches, reproval, and criticism from the first secretary, the long-awaited concert would begin. . . . [The performers] were surprised at Yeltsin's abilities. As it happened, he not only knew by heart ditties from the operettas of Offenbach but reeled off the names of the workers at the enterprises that those on the agitation train had visited.[85]

In various appearances, Yeltsin departed by inches from the ceremonial. One way for which he had a fancy was spur-of-the moment gift giving. The gift of choice was a watch—remember the high value he and his Berezniki teammates placed on the watches they received as city volleyball champions—often unfastened from his own or an aide's wrist. The first occasion of which I am aware occurred in 1977. Yeltsin had implored the director of the Nizhnii Tagil construction organization, Eduard Rossel, to help him win a "socialist competition" with the Severstal iron-and-steel plant in Cherepovets, Vologda province. Severstal had signed up to complete a large mill for making steel plate by December 25, six days before the end of the year. Yeltsin and Rossel assigned 25,000 workers in three shifts to the Nizhnii Tagil Metallurgical Works in order to commission their mill by a week before and qualify it as the largest industrial construction project to be finished in the year of the sixtieth jubilee of the Bolshevik Revolution. On December 18 the job was done, and Yeltsin spoke before a rally of the entire workforce. At the microphone, he took the gold watch off his left wrist and put it on Rossel's. He told the crowd the day could have never have been won without them and Rossel, and explained that the watch had been given to him as a birthday present earlier that year by none other than General Secretary Brezhnev. The workers clapped madly.[86]

Yeltsin took to handing out watches and other keepsakes to rank-and-file employees. Naina Yeltsina gave him a wristwatch for many of his birthdays, only to find that the latest timepiece had disappeared a week or two later.[87] The presents, and wry oratorical throwaways, were the public equal of the surprises he loved to spring on his wife at home. As an example of the latter, he concluded his report to a party conference at Uralkhimmash by opening up the floor. Employees hollered that housing was impossibly short. Not skipping a beat, Yeltsin redirected the plea to the USSR government minister responsible for the plant, seated beside him, with the dig that "surely you cannot refuse" it. The minister said meekly he would boost housing quotas for the factory, and did.[88] Yeltsin's replies to questions dripped with sarcasm about "those in Moscow who, so he said, understood little yet consumed much."[89]

By 1980 Yeltsin also had a knack for appearing unannounced in factories, shops, and public transit. "Maybe it was partly for show, but he could on any day of the week sit down on a streetcar or bus, go around the route, and listen to what the passengers were saying, see for himself how well transportation was organized, how the city looked. . . . When he was at a workplace, he would think nothing of taking a cage down a mine shaft, or going over to a smelting furnace, talking with people, visiting the workers' cafeteria." In one eatery, he grabbed a spoon and asked a worker if he could taste his lunch; when he found it to be slop, he ordered an aide to ride herd on the place's food service.[90] Some visits took the form of raids on sites where Yeltsin thought there had been malfeasance. To these live forms was added television—"the blue screen," as Russians call it—the electronic medium now piped into virtually every Soviet home.

A pair of events took the unmediated and mediated modes of contact to a higher plane: a question-and-answer session with college students in the Sverdlovsk Youth Palace on May 19, 1981, and a television broadcast to the region on December 18, 1982. There were several similar encounters before April 1985. The in-person and mass-media variants served several purposes at once. They relayed party policy, allowed the people to let off steam, hyped Yeltsin's image, and gave him leverage vis-à-vis third parties.

Nothing was left to chance in the Youth Palace. A call for written questions for the first secretary went out six weeks beforehand. Nine hundred and thirty of them, deposited in receptacles at Sverdlovsk's universities and institutes, were compiled and given to city and oblast administrators, who drafted answers. Obkom staff and then the first secretary pored over the draft responses. The 1,700 attendees received printed invitations, embossed with an effigy of Lenin, and were assigned seats in the banked hall. The meeting was five hours long. Yeltsin read out canned responses that were riffs upon the official line. But there were fresh ingredients that made the meeting an anomalous event for the Soviet Union of the day. With verve—in a verveless time—Yeltsin provided information about when this or that local improvement was going to be finished and promised to expedite overdue projects. He varied many of the prearranged responses ad lib and had the students pass 144 supplementary questions to the front of the hall. He let slip remarks about his disputatious nature. Asked why the Soviet Union was technologically inferior to the United States, he brashly gave as one of the reasons that "capitalist competition greatly stimulates labor efficiency, that is, only the strongest survive." Most of all, he encouraged the students to speak their minds and communicated that he was on their side. They touched on everything from the paucity of tablecloths and schoolbooks to price gouging in the Shuvakish flea market and the losses of the Uralmash soccer club. They gave Yeltsin a standing ovation when he finished.[91]

The blue screen had transfixed Yeltsin since his early months as first secretary. In September 1978 he used it to urge city dwellers to help bring in the fall harvest, which was wasting away in the fields because of bucketing rains. Some 85,000 Sverdlovskers are said to have responded to his plea to enlist in "the battle for grain."[92] If this was Soviet mobilizational propaganda with a human touch, the television programs of the early 1980s, which were the brainchild of Igor Brodskii, the director of the Sverdlovsk television studio, had a different slant. They were organized around letters, which gave scope for startlingly frank appraisals. Some older apparatchiks who feared television had to be placated. They need not have worried, for the broadcasts could be minutely planned and prerecorded. The bevy of officials assigned to the December 1982 event spelled out in exquisite detail the camera angles, the topics to be discussed (in thirteen categories), and the towns and villages to be named (forty-five of them). But there was something new about the broadcast. Unlike anonymous agitprop, this was an acutely personalized dialogue. Brodskii's "scenario plan":

The video will be taped from the working office of B. N. Yeltsin.

Once the title of the broadcast has been flashed, the camera pans over envelopes spread out on the desk. We see that B. N. Yeltsin has been going through his mail. At this point, a crawler along the bottom of the screen reminds viewers about who is participating in the broadcast [First Secretary Yeltsin] and commenting on their letters.

The magnification changes from medium to high. In the picture is B. N. Yeltsin. He speaks directly to us:

"Good evening, comrades. The letters now on my desk are only part of the large amount of mail I will be commenting on. . . ."[93]

In July 1984, when the obkom did a second big telecast, staff did alternate draft scenarios—every one of them devised to place Yeltsin in the limelight. In one, he would be shot watching film of interviews with 1982 letter writers. "Watching these interviews together with the television audience, B. N. Yeltsin could use them by way of illustration in the course of his conversation." In another, he would stand on a factory floor and field questions from workers; the catch there was that the participants in the meeting might "upstage" Yeltsin. Then there was the scenario they adopted:

A monologue. The broadcast comes from the office of the first secretary of the obkom of the CPSU, comrade B. N. Yeltsin.

The kinks have been worked out of this form. It allows us to show comrade B. N. Yeltsin as a party and state figure in his usual working surroundings.

The reactions received by [Sverdlovsk] TV after the December [1982] broadcast show that people watched with great interest and listened intently to the direct appeal to them on the part of B. N. *Yeltsin. The meeting was a 100 percent success.*[94]

On television, the first secretary was more argumentative than at the in-person meetings. The programs were notable for the passel of gripes vented, now taking in insufficiencies of a catalogue of everyday articles (matches, dry cell batteries, bed linen, tea kettles, caramels), bribe taking, inflation, miserly pensions, pollution, and sore points of every description. Replying to questions about the unauthorized use of limousines and about bureaucrats who constructed houses with misappropriated materials, Yeltsin cautiously brought up the issue of the privileges of officialdom. The follow-up was a set of unobtrusive countermeasures to curb the use of official cars for driving children to school and wives to shop; family members of the leaders of the oblast party committee and government were now taken to their dachas in a minivan.[95] In Moscow several years later, the response was to be more up-front.

Yeltsin admitted that he might be inciting unrealistic hopes. He had received, he said in December 1982, a squall of letters from Sverdlovskers begging him to advance them in the waiting line for government-built apartments. This was impossible, since the function had to be done by the book. He would check the correspondence and right any wrongs done. Other than that, he counseled honesty about the problem and forbearance until the housing supply could be increased: "I am not a magician. Neither are the central organs of government magicians. . . . It is hard to take when your request is refused, but I believe that the bitter truth is better than the sweet lie."[96] That aphorism was to take Yeltsin a long way.

Still captive to the communist paradigm, Yeltsin was declaring that the performance of the regime left something to be desired and he was simultaneously putting *himself* forward as the agent of change. This was the jumping-off point for role aggrandizement in the future.

Not everyone was taken by an approach that threw other local leaders into shadow. Gennadii Bogomyakov, the CPSU first secretary in Tyumen, the adjacent, oil-rich oblast in west Siberia, carped to party officials that Yeltsin was pandering and acting like a clown, not a proper Soviet solon.[97] Ryabov was to write in hindsight that Yeltsin had begun "to play a phony game," although he had to concede that his antics hoodwinked "simple people." "'Look what sort of leader we have,' they said."[98] No alarm bells jangled where it counted—in the inner sanctum of the party in Moscow. Pavel Simonov in the Central Committee apparatus had admonished Yeltsin soon after his appointment to keep his photograph off the front page of *Ural'skii rabochii*.[99] No one seemed unhappy with his playing to the crowd or at seeing his face splashed on the television screen hour after hour. Either official awareness was lagging or, more likely, there was an opinion at the center that the party would be better off if all local leaders were as popular as its man in Sverdlovsk.

Boris Yeltsin's flight to prominence in a communist framework was by dint of his intelligence, drive, ability to communicate and call attention to himself, and "iron grip." And it owed much to an instinct for timely decisions. The portrait in *Confession* of his log hopping on the Zyryanka River as a teenager may serve as an allegory for how he made his way in an uncharitable environment. "If you figured everything just right" and had "incredible dexterity," he says, "you had a chance to cross over to the far bank." Leap soon or late, or misconstrue another boy's motion, and you would plop into the water, gasping for air, and have to clamber onto a new log to resume your quest, "not sure if you would save yourself."[100] In the work world, Yeltsin chose well when to spring and when to stand pat. If not—if, say, he had been unadventurous about trying out party work or had committed political hara-kiri by disobeying the Politburo on Ipat'ev House—he would occupy history's footnotes and not its central narrative. Minus Yeltsin as a driving force, the narrative itself would be considerably different.

There were times when the self-interested actions of others, like Ryabov in pushing him for first secretary, propelled Yeltsin forward. Still other times, it was dumb luck and contingency. He might have come to a different end if Eduard Shevardnadze had not lured away Gennadii Kolbin in 1975, if Vyacheslav Bayev had taken the second secretaryship, if Moscow had listened to Leonid Ponomarëv in 1976, or if Dmitrii Ustinov or someone else had settled scores for his toying with General Ageyev, his witticisms with the workers, or his affiliation with the fallen Ryabov. If his patrons had known ex ante what they were to know ex post, it would have ended poorly for him. Ryabov, for one, believes the Yeltsin of the 1990s to be a turncoat, and says it all started in Sverdlovsk. These are the pangs of a Victor Frankenstein beholding his monster. Ryabov is not the only old-school communist who feels them today.

The sachem of Sverdlovsk no longer needed to be a survivalist; his testing was routinized; his rebellious urges were in abeyance. The primary script in his mature life was success—being first—constrained by duty to the vertical structures hegemonic in Soviet society. Although the regime was dictatorial, agents could implement its will only if they could recruit and promote on merit and if they were given some leeway and some space to advocate for themselves and their organizations. Yeltsin was an effective regional prefect, a hard-boiled boss with a difference, because he used to his advantage the liberties granted. Doing so made him less convinced than when he started of the soundness and perfectability of the system. Serious policy questions could only be settled in a "supercentralized" fashion, he was to recall. But the center's attention span was short and its strategic sense vitiated by aged leaders and the opaqueness of decision making. Get away from its priorities, and the problems were yours to handle: "All you could place your trust in was yourself and the oblast. . . . The center did little to help. . . . We decided the other questions by ourselves, self-reliantly *[samostoyatel'no]*."[101] What was more, the reflexive "self" was becoming an elastic category for comrade B. N. Yeltsin. Populism and a nonethnic Russianism were working their way into his thinking. And he was beginning to realize there were means—politically rewarding means—to deal in the populace on the conversation about government and change. That realization would bring about an activism that was not compliant.

Chapter Five

Megalopolis

Boris Yeltsin was not going to count in the main game of Soviet politics unless he relocated from the fringes of the system to the metropole. Did he want to? He denies it in his memoirs: "I never had the dream or so much as the wish to work in Moscow." He had received a series of proposals to resettle there, "some of them" as minister in the central government, and turned them all down. A son of Sverdlovsk and the Urals, he wanted to stay with his friends and colleagues and loathed how Muscovites created prettified façades, Potemkin villages, and looked down their noses at country cousins.[1] His Sverdlovsk patron, Yakov Ryabov, spins it differently. Sverdlovskers frequently moved to Moscow and to other regions, and thought it "a normal part of the selection and assignment of cadres." Yeltsin studied with interest several offers in the provinces and the capital before he was lifted to obkom secretary in 1975, and used them to importune Ryabov to advance his career locally.[2] He also, Ryabov claims, felt envious of some of the promotions given to others—for example, Nikolai Ryzhkov, the director of Uralmash, who moved to a high ministerial position in 1975.[3] Information is lacking on the jobs Yeltsin may have turned down after 1975. If he did so, it was not out of a refusal to leave Sverdlovsk.

As a reputable regional administrator, Yeltsin was a surefire candidate for inclusion in any effort to revivify the Soviet leadership. Generational kinetics bolstered the case for him. In November 1976 only three of seventy-two first secretaries in RSFSR regions were younger than he, and he was ten years younger than the average fifty-five-year-old provincial leader. By January 1985 he was at the median in seniority—thirty-six officials had been chosen earlier than he and thirty-five later—but *still* five years more youthful than the average first secretary, whose age was now up to fifty-nine.[4] In that way, he offered an attractive combination of combat-hardened experience and energy.

Yeltsin's rise out of Sverdlovsk came in three steps in 1985. All were questioned by Muscovites with political clout. Personalities and niggling jealousies, not grand visions of reform, were behind it. There were to be consequences, however.

The change to change in the USSR started in the abbreviated Kremlin reign of Yurii Andropov, the onetime KGB chairman who succeeded Leonid Brezhnev in November 1982 and died of kidney failure in February 1984. Andropov sounded the alarm about the regime's problems and tried to inculcate "order and discipline" in the bureaucracy and the workforce. His disciplinarian line was in those days very much to the liking of Yeltsin, who was to voice "the highest and the best opinion" of him.[5] One may conjecture also that Yeltsin's grizzled supporter in the Politburo, Andrei Kirilenko, expounded his qualities to Andropov before Kirilenko's retirement in late 1982.

In December 1983 Andropov, bedridden in the hospital, had a conversation about Yeltsin with Yegor Ligachëv, the new organizational secretary of the Central Committee. Andropov had selected Ligachëv, a straitlaced Siberian partocrat who had been on the outs with Brezhnev, on the advice of his lieutenant, Mikhail Gorbachev. By Ligachëv's testimony, Andropov instructed him to go to Sverdlovsk and "have a look at" the local strongman. Ligachëv visited on January 17–21, 1984, inspecting farms and factories and attending the oblast party conference. He was smitten: "I will not conceal it: The liveliness of Yeltsin's relations with people, his vigor, and his decisiveness appealed to me. It was obvious that many had heartfelt respect for him."[6] Andropov's assistant for economic policy, Arkadii Vol'skii, remembered Ligachëv proposing to Andropov that they hand Yeltsin the construction department of the CPSU Secretariat, the Soviet-wide equivalent of what he oversaw in Sverdlovsk from 1968 to 1975. Andropov was for it, with the sidelong compliment that Yeltsin was "a good builder"—even though he had been a multifunctional party prefect since 1976. Andropov probably saw Yeltsin as fit for no more than the departmental slot, but Ligachëv saw it as probationary and leading to bigger things.[7]

Yeltsin's appointment to the Central Committee apparatus was on hold during the interregnum of the Brezhnev epigone Konstantin Chernenko. Kremlin workhorses like Dmitrii Ustinov, the defense minister who forced out Yakov Ryabov in 1979, may have had it in for Yeltsin. If so, Marshal Ustinov's death in December 1984 was well-timed. Chernenko died of emphysema three months later, and Yeltsin participated in the Central Committee plenum of March 11, 1985, which made Gorbachev general secretary of the party.

Gorbachev was initially not a Yeltsin fan. He knew little of him, and "What I did know made me leery." They made their acquaintance in the two years after Yeltsin became Sverdlovsk first secretary in late 1976. Gorbachev had been first secretary in the breadbox province of Stavropol since 1970, and they swapped Stavropol foodstuffs for metals and lumber from the Urals. As Central Committee secretary for the Soviet farm sector from 1978 to 1985, Gorbachev crossed swords with Yeltsin two or three times over Yeltsin's surliness with emissaries of Moscow. At a plenum of the obkom to discuss a Central Committee memorandum that took a swipe at the Sverdlovsk livestock industry, Yeltsin exchanged words with Gorbachev's representative, Ivan Kapustyan. "I noted for myself," writes Gorbachev in his memoirs, *Life and Reforms*, "that the Sverdlovsk secretary reacted inadequately toward remarks directed at him." Besides, Gorbachev had seen Yeltsin wobbly on his feet in the Soviet parliament; from hearsay, he ascribed it to a drinking spree.[8] To hear Gorbachev tell it, Ligachëv did not need to be asked by Andropov to go for the look-see in Sverdlovsk. He volunteered to do it and phoned Gorbachev late at night to tell him, "Mikhail Sergeyevich, this is our kind of person, we have to pick him!"[9]

When Gorbachev and Ligachëv did summon Yeltsin to Moscow in the first week of April 1985, their prize enlistee gummed up the works by playing hard to get. As Yeltsin says in *Confession on an Assigned Theme*, he spurned the offer relayed by Vladimir Dolgikh, a junior member of the Kremlin leadership. He relented only when Ligachëv stepped in the morning after and invoked party discipline.[10] Yeltsin's liking for Sverdlovsk and dislike of Moscow, where he had never lived and had almost no friends, argued against the move. He was assuaged some by his younger daughter, Tatyana, and his grandson, Boris, being in Moscow and by the willingness of elder daughter Yelena to move with them. As Tatyana said in a 2001 interview, her mother was to be homesick but not her father: "For him, the principal thing is work. Where he works is where he makes his home."[11] The issue was what Yeltsin would work at in Moscow. He had ruled the roost in Sverdlovsk for most of a decade, and two of his three predecessors in the obkom, Kirilenko in 1962 and Ryabov in 1976, had been appointed a Central Committee secretary out of Sverdlovsk. (Nikolai Ryzhkov was made a secretary in November 1982, seven years after leaving Sverdlovsk, taking Kirilenko's slot.) To Yeltsin, that, or at the lower limit, a position as deputy prime minister of the Soviet Union, was his due, and one of the CPSU's economic departments, further down the pecking order, was not.

It was unhelpful, as historians have not appreciated, that Yeltsin *already* had doubts about Gorbachev. Stylistically, the two were oil and water. Gorbachev, from the sun-drenched plains bordering the Caucasus Mountains, had become a communist in his early twenties, received a law degree at Moscow State University (the oldest and most prestigious university in Russia), made his career in the Komsomol and in general party leadership, and was married to a Marxist philosopher. Yeltsin, from the frigid and rock-ribbed Urals, entered the CPSU late, studied at a provincial polytechnic, was a production specialist, and married another engineer. Gorbachev was sedentary and balding; Yeltsin was a half-foot taller, athletic, and had a full head of hair. Gorbachev was garrulous and even-tempered; Yeltsin was spare with words and irascible. Gorbachev's favorite authors were the Romantic writer and poet Mikhail Lermontov (1814–41) and Vladimir Mayakovsky (1893–1930), the Futurist bard of the Bolshevik Revolution who died a suicide; Yeltsin preferred Chekhov, Pushkin, and Sergei Yesenin (1895–1925), a poet who wrote of love and village life, married five times (including once to Isadora Duncan), and who also died by his own hand. In music, Gorbachev's taste ran to symphonies and Italian opera; for Yeltsin, it was folk songs and pop tunes.[12]

After Gorbachev moved to Moscow as Central Committee secretary, Yeltsin found him controlling and patronizing, although he kept lines of communication open. Gorbachev hailed workmates in the Russian language's familiar second person singular, *ty*; Yeltsin winced at this liberty and always used the more correct plural, *vy*.[13] As we saw in the last chapter, Gorbachev for Yeltsin connoted overcentralization on questions such as locally manufactured farm machinery. At a deeper level, Yeltsin had qualms about Gorbachev's grasp of the issues and his ability to lead the country. "Notes of disesteem for Gorbachev" wafted through his patter at meetings of the Sverdlovsk party bureau.[14] Stoking Yeltsin's unhappiness was his belief that Gorbachev, his exact contemporary, had overachieved. Stavropol was known for its wheat farms and its mineral-waters spas, at the ritziest of which, in Kislovodsk and Pyatigorsk, Gorbachev had been innkeeper to the holidaying

Brezhnev, Andropov, and Chernenko. Stavropol had half of Sverdlovsk's population and, as Yeltsin wrote in his memoirs, was "significantly inferior" to it economically.[15] But Gorbachev had come to Moscow as a secretary in 1978 and by 1985 was general secretary—and Gorbachev had not deigned to phone in April 1985 to recruit Yeltsin.

Nor was there any love lost with Ligachëv. Eleven years older than Yeltsin and a party member since 1944, he had a dossier replete in propaganda and personnel work; his service in the party apparatus dated from 1949, nineteen years before Yeltsin's and four years before the end of the Stalin era. So many of Ligachëv's choices as CPSU director of personnel, Yeltsin groaned to Ryabov, were from backwaters, "provinces not comparable to ours."[16] With 900,000 people, Tomsk, where Ligachëv was first secretary for seventeen years, was the fifty-eighth most populous Russian region; Sverdlovsk was fourth and even Stavropol was fourteenth.[17] The January 1984 reconnaissance trip to Sverdlovsk that so gratified Ligachëv only got Yeltsin's dander up. The one thing he had heard, Yeltsin informed the obkom secretaries before Ligachëv flew in, was that Ligachëv fancied buckwheat porridge for breakfast; they were to feed him well, show him around the oblast, and not darken Yeltsin's door until the oblast's scheduled party conference later in the week.[18] True to his word, Yeltsin met Ligachëv at the airport and told him he would be too busy to squire him on his rounds, but looked forward to some conversations and to seeing Ligachëv at the conference. Several days later, informed that Ligachëv had shared tips on sowing and harvesting at a local kolkhoz, Yeltsin chortled that everyone should take the Trans-Siberian to Tomsk to "see how great things are there."[19] He at one point compelled the first secretary of the Sverdlovsk gorkom, Sergei Kadochnikov, to take "this idiot" off his hands, as Ligachëv had demanded to know why the city's storefronts were not painted as nicely as in Tomsk.[20] The day of the oblast party conference, Ligachëv, a saturnine Yeltsin at his side, queried Sverdlovskers in front of the opera house about what they made of their first secretary.[21] Not disheartened by Yeltsin's petulance—possibly even heartened by it, since here was a man who put business before public relations—Ligachëv led him to believe he would soon be reassigned to Moscow at an appropriate grade.[22]

Yeltsin was crestfallen when it sank in that he was to be a department head, a subaltern. He arrived untypically late at the Sverdlovsk House of Soviets for the Monday planning session of the obkom bureau on April 8. He had been detained by a red-eye flight from Moscow, where he got the details and the most fugitive of audiences with Gorbachev.[23] He had an aide fetch a pencil and cracked it in three, as was his habit when peeved. He squinted at the group. "Yeltsin said, 'Do you know who is sitting there [in Moscow]? They are doddering half-wits *[staryye nedoumki]*. . . . We have to chase them away.' We all froze and blanched. . . . We could see what it was about: the first secretary of such an oblast was being given the position of head of a department. . . . He said it right out."[24] Everyone in those chairs understood that his contempt encompassed not only the geriatric Brezhnevites but Gorbachev, Ligachëv, and the arriviste group. All it would have taken to derail his career was one telephone call to Moscow from the local KGB chairman, Yurii Kornilov—the person Yakov Ryabov thought tattled on him in 1979—or any other person on the bureau. That none was made is testament to Yeltsin's hold on the grandees of Sverdlovsk.

This tempest in a teapot rings true in context. In the estimation of Yeltsin, the supreme leaders had been exposed as poor judges of talent and tepid agents of change. He left for Moscow with a two-ton chip on his shoulder.

On Friday, April 12, 1985, Yeltsin reported for work at the Central Committee enclosure on Old Square, down the block from the Spasskii Gate of the Kremlin. The party center's construction department had ten sections and about a hundred staff, a comedown from twice that many in the Sverdlovsk obkom. Yeltsin's attention as head went to a housecleaning of personnel and to flagging projects to lay pipelines and build housing for workers in the west Siberian oil patch. Gorbachev was content. The pickings in the CPSU apparatus were slim: "We were looking everywhere to 'spy out' people who were active, unhesitating, and responsive to new things. Not too many of them were nearby, in the upper stratum. Yeltsin impressed me."[25]

Boris and Naina were issued a nomenklatura apartment at 54 Second Tverskaya-Yamskaya Street, in a congested quarter of the downtown near the Belorussia Station. Its windows looked out at Transformation of the Savior, a long-closed Old Believers monastery. There the Yeltsins opened their doors to Tatyana, grandson Boris, and Tatyana's second husband, Leonid Dyachenko. Since graduating from the university, Tatyana had been working at Salyut, a closed military institute where her job was to track space vehicles in orbit. Yelena and her family lived with the rest for a year or two and then went to party-supplied housing a short distance away.[26]

Before three months had lapsed, Gorbachev was happy enough with Yeltsin's labors to put him up for the title Yeltsin had coveted in April: secretary of the Central Committee for construction and capital investment.

Questions came up at the Politburo on June 29 from Nikolai Tikhonov, Brezhnev's comrade from pre–World War II Ukraine whom he had made prime minister of the Soviet Union in 1980. The octogenarian Tikhonov, born one year before Yeltsin's father, demanded to know his qualifications for a secretaryship. Gorbachev rattled off the Yeltsin résumé and emphasized his energy, experience, and inside-out knowledge of the construction industry. "Somehow," sniffed Tikhonov, "I don't have a feel for him." Ligachëv rushed to Yeltsin's aid, explaining that he had gotten off to a fast start in Moscow and had been doing the rounds of the ministries, where "people have reached out to him." Vladimir Dolgikh, the Central Committee secretary for the whole heavy-industrial sector and Yeltsin's supervisor since April, said Yeltsin had shown he could work satisfactorily with central bureaucrats and regional party officials: "Having gotten to know him better, I have not noticed any weak spots." Mikhail Solomentsev, the head of the party's disciplinary arm, the Control Commission of the Central Committee, added a flaccid endorsement: "Comrade Yeltsin . . . is going to grow. He has all the right attributes: a good education and tempering as a civil engineer. This is a person with a future." Another elderly member, Foreign Minister Andrei Gromyko, expressed support. Tikhonov pulled in his horns and the Politburo consented to the designation, which was approved by Central Committee plenum on July 1, 1985.[27]

Yeltsin took the secretaryship as his due. Still running the construction department, he was relieved that he no longer communicated with the administrative and political summit through a go-between, which had been for him "a severe trial." All spring he had fidgeted at meetings of department heads where he was meant to write down every pearl Dolgikh dropped. Other than a tour of the oil boomtowns of Tyumen province with Gorbachev in September 1985 and the odd meeting, his only communication with number one was by the Kremlin's high-frequency telephone line.[28]

It was the third promotion that lofted Yeltsin into the political stratosphere. On Tuesday, December 24, 1985, the Moscow gorkom (city committee) of the CPSU, the relative of the Sverdlovsk obkom, installed him as its first secretary. Gorbachev, who moved the resolution on behalf of the Politburo, had been weighing the move since July, when he had Yeltsin promoted to Central Committee secretary: "I was 'trying him out for size' for Moscow."[29]

In *Confession*, Yeltsin writes that the first he heard about the Moscow opening was at the Politburo meeting that discussed it and that he was reluctant to take it, offered the names of alternative candidates, and agreed only out of regard for party discipline. Gorbachev, Yeltsin recounts, said he wanted him to take the job. "For me, this was a bolt from the blue. I stood up and spoke out about the inappropriateness of such a decision." He was a builder, an unassuming construction engineer, and would contribute more as a Central Committee secretary. "And also I did not know cadres so well in Moscow, so it would be difficult for me to work in the position." But, Yeltsin says chastely, Gorbachev pressed the case. "The conversation in the Politburo was not simple . . . for me. Again [as in April], they said to me that party discipline applied and they knew better where I would be of most use to the party. In general, once again puzzling over it, understanding full well that the Moscow party organization could not be left in such a state, and throwing out suggestions as I went about whom it would be better to send there, I agreed."[30]

Most of this is to be taken with a grain of salt. We know that Yeltsin and a Sverdlovsk confrère compared notes on the Moscow job a few days before the Politburo meeting. On that occasion, Yeltsin was champing at the bit and agreed with the suggestion that "for the second time only the Urals can save Moscow"—the first being in World War II, when munitions factories were evacuated there and it became an arsenal for the country.[31] The transcript in the archives for the Politburo session of December 23 shows unequivocally that Yeltsin took the change in stride and said nothing about other likely appointees. Gorbachev was quoted, in the tradition of the spoken word taking precedence over the written, as having talked the position over with him. The only other members who spoke on the motion, all briefly and all in favor, were Gromyko, now head of the executive board of the Soviet parliament; Solomentsev of the control commission; Vitalii Vorotnikov, the prime minister of the RSFSR and its representative on the Politburo; and Viktor Grishin, the incumbent Moscow leader.

Gorbachev opened with word that he had received a letter of resignation from Grishin and wanted him to be given an honorific post as adviser to Gromyko:

GROMYKO: It should say in the text of the resolution that comrade Grishin will be assigned to the group of advisers.

SOLOMENTSEV: That's right.

VOROTNIKOV: Yes, it has to be written up like that.

GORBACHEV: If the comrades have no objections, I am available to take part in the plenum of the Moscow gorkom of the CPSU. Now, let us talk about who should be the candidate for the post of gorkom first secretary. The question is about the party organization of our capital. This makes it appropriate to recommend for this post someone from the Central Committee who has work experience in a major party organization and knows about the economy, science, and culture. There is a suggestion that we recommend comrade B. N. Yeltsin.

VOROTNIKOV: Good idea.

SOLOMENTSEV: Sure.

GORBACHEV: I have had a conversation with comrade Yeltsin. He understands the place and significance of the Moscow party organization, how thorny and complex work as first secretary of the Moscow city committee would be. The capital, after all, is the capital. It is our administrative, economic, scientific, and cultural center.

GROMYKO: In population size alone, Moscow is like a real country.

VOROTNIKOV: Yes, a country like Czechoslovakia.

GORBACHEV: Do the comrades have any other suggestion?

MEMBERS OF THE POLITBURO: No.

GORBACHEV: In that case, comrade Yeltsin, we will be recommending you as first secretary of the Moscow party committee.

The retirement of Grishin from the Politburo and Yeltsin's shedding of his duties in the Secretariat were to be straightened out at the next plenum of the Central Committee. Grishin was given a minute to offer unctuous thanks to Gorbachev, and then all eyes turned to Yeltsin:

YELTSIN: Five and a half months ago, I was elected a secretary of the Central Committee. I exerted every effort to master my new duties. Now I am being given an extraordinary assignment. I shall do all I can in order to participate actively in every innovation taking place in the party and the country, in dealing with the problems Mikhail Sergeyevich has been speaking about. I will try to justify your confidence.

GORBACHEV: We certainly hope so, or else we would not be making such a decision. Do we all approve of this motion?

MEMBERS OF THE POLITBURO: We approve.

The motion was adopted.[32]

At 8.7 million people, Yeltsin's new domain was the megalopolis of the USSR. Moscow was, as Gorbachev said, the hub of government, business, education, science, and culture—in the Soviet constellation of things, it was

Washington, New York, Boston, and Los Angeles rolled into one. Unlike other Soviet cities, it answered to the central authorities and not to the province around it. Its party boss was the senior local politico in the power structure and sat on the highest councils of the CPSU. Among the major figures who had held its first secretaryship in the past were Vyacheslav Molotov, Lazar Kaganovich, and Nikita Khrushchev. The office building of the Moscow party committee was 6 Old Square, cheek by jowl with the Central Committee reception at 4 Old Square; the two had been built around 1910 as matching luxury apartment houses for the Moscow bourgeoisie. Yeltsin was to make it onto the second tier of the Politburo as a candidate (nonvoting) member on February 18, 1986, which was when he officially left the Central Committee Secretariat so as to concentrate on Moscow. Moving up from a Volga sedan to a ZIL-115 limousine, he was now one of the fifteen or twenty most powerful people in the second most powerful country in the world.[33] Under Brezhnev-era understandings on continuity in office, he would have occupied it carefree for two decades.

Control of Moscow was as sensitive an issue as any in Soviet politics in 1985–86. Viktor Grishin, a phlegmatic, half-educated mainstay of the Brezhnev Politburo now in his seventies, had been its first secretary since 1967 and had promoted the capital under his hand as the "model communist city." His authority had been sapped by a string of scandals, exposed by Ligachëv and others, alleging falsification and thievery in Moscow's trade and housing networks. Grishin sealed his fate in 1984–85 with an inapt play to present himself as the deathbed pick of Chernenko for general secretary.[34]

The selection of Yeltsin to dislodge the antediluvian Grishin was, once again, contested. The disapproval came this time not from a relic of the past like Tikhonov but from the likes of Nikolai Ryzhkov, the youngish technocrat who, with Gorbachev behind him, had supplanted Tikhonov as Soviet prime minister in September 1985. Ryzhkov, born in 1929 in Ukraine, was well acquainted with Boris Yeltsin. A UPI alumnus who made his career in Sverdlovsk, he had been director of Uralmash, the Urals Heavy Machinery Works, and sat on the oblast party committee from 1971 to 1975, when Yeltsin was head of the obkom construction department. Although Yeltsin had personal respect for him and the two talked civilly until 1990, Ryzhkov thought Yeltsin was egocentric and quarrelsome and that, as head of department, he had improperly "commanded" Uralmash to carry out tasks the party apparatus wanted done.[35] Not being on the Politburo until some weeks after Yeltsin was brought to Moscow, Ryzhkov was out of the loop on that decision. Now that he was chairman of the government and a full member of the Politburo, he could not be circumnavigated. In a colloquy at Old Square before the December 23 meeting, Gorbachev and Ligachëv asked him if he approved of Yeltsin being made the Moscow party chief. Ryzhkov did not mince words. Yeltsin, he warned, while well and good for a party department or one of the construction ministries, could not be entrusted with a more sensitive, political mission. Yeltsin was by nature cut out for brawls. "He will chop wood," said Ryzhkov, using a rural maxim as warning, "and it will be your elbows that will smart." Not wanting a fight, he agreed to keep mum in the Politburo unless a fellow member asked his opinion, which none was to do. Some years later, Gorbachev would admit to him that he rued the day he snubbed Ryzhkov's advice about Yeltsin.[36]

Ryzhkov's doubts were about Yeltsin's character and style, not about policy or obeisance to the regime. No one, not even Yeltsin, saw him as a prospective apostate and leader of the opposition. In December 1985, like Ryabov in his day, Gorbachev considered Yeltsin a force he could tame. Yeltsin knew the terms of the bargain: "I understood perfectly that I was being used to knock down the Grishin team."[37]

But Ryzhkov was not the only queasy one. Yevgenii Razumov, the deputy head of the Secretariat's personnel department, had known Yeltsin since 1976, when he was the Politburo's representative at the plenum of the Sverdlovsk obkom that confirmed Yeltsin as first secretary. He is said to have spoken out against all three of Yeltsin's 1985 promotions.[38] Anatolii Luk'yanov, the then head of the Central Committee's general department, says that when Moscow for Yeltsin was under review, he received many letters from Sverdlovsk lambasting Yeltsin and saying "you will weep" if he were to be given a lofty position.[39]

One issue that did not harm Yeltsin's chances was his physical condition. Ligachëv in early 1985 had Yevgenii Chazov, the chief of the Kremlin medical service, do a briefing on it, saying he had heard that it was poor (Dolgikh said the same to Chazov). Chazov gave him a clean bill of health.[40] Alcohol would have been one of the subjects covered. Luk'yanov has noted that "in Russia nobody is ever hired or fired exclusively on the basis of his attitude toward alcohol,"[41] but there were limits to this leniency. Ligachëv, Yeltsin's protector in 1985, was a teetotaler and, with Solomentsev, conceived the "dry law" of May 1985, the short-lived attempt to curb drunkenness and alcoholism among the citizenry. Ligachëv said to friends in the 1990s that Yeltsin did not touch a drop on his trip to Sverdlovsk in 1984 and no excess was ever in evidence.[42] Had Yeltsin been a problem drinker, there would have been no invitation to Moscow or its party committee.

The Moscow position was an opportune outlet for Yeltsin's urban and regional expertise, hankering for recognition, and love of a good fight. As citadel of the Soviet regime, the city stood for all that was amiss with communism and for its potential for redemption through reform. For a month after December 24, Yeltsin galloped through its factories, architectural monuments, and housing projects. His slow-ripening disaffection was giving way to political wanderlust and an itch to speak "the bitter truth" instead of "the sweet lie," as he had put it on Sverdlovsk television in 1982. He committed wholeheartedly to the reform project and was determined to make his mark on it, repressing any reservations he had about Gorbachev as an individual. As Aleksandr Korzhakov, a former attendant to Brezhnev and Andropov assigned to Yeltsin by the Ninth Directorate of the KGB as one of his three bodyguards, recollected, Yeltsin was "the sincerest member of the party" in cleaving to the general course of perestroika. He "tried harder than the other party bosses to change life for the better."[43]

On January 24, 1986, Yeltsin surveyed Moscow's woes in a stentorian two-hour report to its party conference, held in the glittering convention hall of the Soviet trade unions—the place where Soviet leaders from Lenin to Chernenko had lain in state and Stalin's show trials were held in the 1930s. Yeltsin wove his points into a parable of broader import. Under Grishin and Brezhnev, the city had been "infected by window dressing, an overemphasis on successes, and a hushing up of shortcomings [through] cooking the books . . . [and] fakery." So inveterate was the illness, he said, that even calls for improvement "have been to a great extent perceived formulaically . . . lamely, at times cravenly." "There may be some who think these judgments sound indelicate," Yeltsin added, but "they had to come out."[44] Grishin, still a member of the Politburo, sat with a poker face on the podium, within spitting distance of Yeltsin. He did not ask to speak in self-defense: "This is how we were raised, not to contradict the opinion of the [leadership], which was where the assertions of the keynote speaker [Yeltsin] were coming from."[45] He never grasped that the Yeltsin and Gorbachev messages might be appreciably different. Grishin was to lose his advisory post in 1987 and died in 1992.

The words from the Moscow soapbox were the talk of the town. Yeltsin's speech was a "strong fresh wind" for the party, Gorbachev told him. The general secretary, Yeltsin adds, said this "without an approving smile and with a blank look on his face."[46] "From that moment," says Anatolii Chernyayev, the perspicacious foreign-policy aide to Gorbachev from 1985 to 1991, "dates [Yeltsin's] glory." He wrote in his diary that "in spirit, in vocabulary, and in approaches" the speech was putting forth "new norms of life and activity" for the regime. Chernyayev noticed lines at newsstands for that day's *Moskovskaya pravda*, the Moscow newspaper that carried the text.[47]

Yeltsin on February 26, 1986, regaled the delegates to the Twenty-Seventh Congress of the whole CPSU. Orthodox in some ways, heterodox in others, his missionary speechifying broadened the discourse about Soviet reform by flogging "the infallibility of officialdom," its "special blessings" (material privileges), and the smothering of innovation by an "inert stratum of time servers with party cards." Yeltsin was the first spokesman at this level to propose some revision to political structures ("periodic accountability" of leaders from the general secretary on down) and to say that the regime's very continuance depended on disinfecting changes taking hold. In his best line, he also gave the national audience a taste of the theatricality so well known in Sverdlovsk. Why had he not been as forthright at the last party congress in 1981? "I can answer and answer sincerely. I did not then have enough courage and political experience."[48] By inference, he now had both.

The priority in Moscow was a cadres shakeup. "Conservatism has gone way too far among us," Yeltsin fumed before several thousand agitprop workers, officials who propagated the party line in the media and the education system, at the House of Political Enlightenment on April 11, 1986. "The city authorities have been playing make-believe [*zanimalis' pokazukhoi*]: 'We know what we are doing, everything is A-plus here, we are the tops in the world, there is no need to wash Moscow's dirty laundry in public.' Those who keep on thinking this way should vacate their places and clear out."[49] Many did. His first week as viceroy, Yeltsin gave Vladimir Promyslov, who had been mayor since Khrushchev's day and was politically independent of Grishin, until noon the day after to leave. When Promyslov stalled for time, Yeltsin telephoned him and "suggested that he depart the easy way and not the hard way"; twenty minutes later, Promyslov had quit. To succeed him, Yeltsin tapped Valerii Saikin, the director of the ZIL Works, the biggest auto plant in the USSR; he had to talk Gorbachev out of appointing Saikin Soviet minister of the automobile industry.[50] In twenty-two months, Yeltsin retired all of the Grishin-appointed secretaries of the gorkom, two-thirds of the raion first secretaries, and, with Saikin, about 90 percent of the leaders in the Promyslov municipal machine. The replacements, better trained technically and up to twenty-five years younger, were often plucked from nonstandard channels, particularly, as in Sverdlovsk, from the ranks of factory management. Yeltsin, an interloper in the capital, had to rely on locals for personnel advice, but he did not always take it: "Like a wild animal, he had a feel for any imprecision, for any falseness in tonality, and was always on his guard. . . . If he asked you whom to appoint to some post and you gave a name right away, before you knew it that person would be appointed. If you said you needed to think about it, he would set to thinking himself whether to make the appointment or not."[51]

He was in almost as big a rush to tackle policy problems. Often it came down to what Yeltsin had tried out in Sverdlovsk, such as youth housing complexes, the City Day festival (the first in September 1987), and street fairs. On other issues, his preferred remedy was an action bundle linked to numbered targets and deadlines, to emphasize the urgency: twenty-six "multipurpose programs" for socioeconomic issues; letters to forty-two central agencies laying down the law on industrial automation and manufacture of consumer goods; thirty-nine superfluous research institutes and laboratories he wanted closed down forthwith; retrenchment in the residency permits issued to rural and small-town migrants (*limitchiki*, persons admitted on governmental "limits") who were overloading the Moscow housing supply. Yeltsin pestered the Politburo and the Soviet cabinet for tons of meat, fish, and produce; on city hall, he foisted heavier burdens and tauter plans.[52] There was some clucking at the highest level at his demands but nothing to indicate a deep split.[53] When Saikin shared with the gorkom bureau a plan to expand the subway and, under a Politburo directive, provide every Moscow family with an apartment by the year 2000, Yeltsin whipped out his pen, drew a line through Saikin's numbers, and superimposed more demanding ones: apartments for all by 1995 and a third more metro track than projected. Saikin could not believe his eyes.[54] Objectives such as these would have been hard to attain under the best of circumstances. Most of them were to remain on paper as the Soviet and then Russian economy went into free fall, and not to be feasible until after Yeltsin's retirement in 1999.

Yeltsinesque populism, a nascent motif in Sverdlovsk, found its way onto the front burner in Moscow. While he continued with impromptu gifts of wristwatches—bodyguard Korzhakov had to keep a spare in his overcoat pocket—the focus shifted to rides on public transit and visitations to trouble spots. The rides were well-rehearsed trips of two or three stops on a subway car, bus, or tramcar. On a fixed destination such as a retail store, workers' or students' dining hall, or apartment house basement, Yeltsin would swoop down in his limousine; he bantered with the crowd; if corruption or skullduggery was uncovered, the wrongdoers were chewed out and in the direst cases fired. Managers of food stores on main boulevards learned to keep an attractive assortment of produce in their glass cases. Tipped off to that, Yeltsin had his guards look for places to be audited off the beaten track, which required the KGB to allot extra conveyances to steer the first secretary through the traffic.[55] As the columnist Vitalii Tret'yakov was to write as an early champion of Yeltsin in 1989, these field trips were in the manner of Haroun al-Rashid, the caliph from *Arabian Nights* who roamed Baghdad in the dress of a commoner, spreading assurance that he knew what to do about the people's problems.[56]

In the Moscow media, Mikhail Poltoranin, the new *Moskovskaya pravda* editor-in-chief who was moved at Yeltsin's behest from *Pravda*, printed titillating, dirt-digging exposés of the illicit benefits of the nomenklatura—of the spouses of party secretaries being chauffeured to stores, of nepotism in august universities and institutes, and of fat-cat buffets, order desks, dachas, and clinics. In his question-and-answer meeting with the agitprop staff in April 1986, Yeltsin related how he had removed a raion second secretary, I. V. Danilov, for illegally converting his apartment into "a palace" with a fireplace that blew smoke into his neighbors' flats. Officers of the city party committee had out of their own free will waived their limos and chauffeurs. "See," Yeltsin deadpanned, "the [six] gorkom secretaries are smiling. Today they came here together in one car."[57] That July Yeltsin initiated the ouster of Nikolai Lebedev, the rector of the Moscow State Institute for International Relations, the undergraduate training school for the Soviet diplomatic service. Lebedev's offense had been to show preference in admissions to the children of nomenklatura officials.

In the age of glasnost, the homespun and pungent locutions of Yeltsin made him the darling of journalists. An interview with him guaranteed splashy copy and a cruise along the frontier of permissible speech. During his first year in the Moscow hot seat, Yeltsin the gadfly and moralist concentrated on the capital city; in year two, he generalized from its experience and went farther afield. Vladimir Mezentsev, a correspondent for Ostankino, the primary Soviet television studio, collared him at a youth league meeting at ZIL in April 1987. Yeltsin expostulated for the camera that the time had come for young workers to be "unfettered" and granted "creative freedom" to dance or listen to music as they liked. He castigated the Komsomol for being "covered in bureaucratic moss and cobwebs" and for hackneyed methods, like organizing forty-six overtime shifts before the branch's forty-sixth conference. Mezentsev was agog: "He was saying words no one was then saying about the canonized Komsomol and by extension about the party. He was saying what they didn't let me say at Ostankino. He was speaking for all of us who wept at the hypocrisies of the communist way of life."[58] As sympathetic Muscovites saw it, he was taking the discussion of the nomenklatura and its incompetence out of their kitchens and onto the streets of the *novostroiki*, the tracts of cookie-cutter, high-rise housing where most of them lived and raised their children. Yeltsin further pushed the envelope by meeting with foreign newspapermen. In May 1987 he gave his first interview on non-Soviet television. He was filmed in action and then in a long conversation in his office with Diane Sawyer of *CBS News*, for the news special "The Soviet Union—Seven Days in May." He was won over to scheduling it by seeing a photograph of the winsome Sawyer.[59]

Yeltsin's policies in 1985–87 were not always iconoclastic. He cautioned that cultural activity had to observe some limits of propriety. Despite the abuse of his family in the Stalin years, he was against "throwing stones into the garden of the past," though he was for unfreezing debate and calmly reassessing errors and crimes.[60] He continued for some time to tout remedies within the old paradigm over ones that might disturb it. In July 1986, with him in the chair, the party caucus in the Moscow Soviet, the city's municipal council, gave the newly chosen chief of its trade directorate, Nikolai Zav'yalov, fourteen days to make a "turnaround" in the supply of vegetables; when he did not achieve the impossible, he was sent packing.[61] At a symposium on mass transit in 1987—to which, as a good showman, he rode a trolley bus—Yeltsin charted a plan to mark off the city into sectors and lay down hard passenger quotas in them all. The dean of economics at Moscow State University, Gavriil Popov, retorted that this evaded the core problem: In a planned economy, there was no housing market that would let Muscovites lessen their daily commutes by moving closer to work; the only way to fix the problem was to create a market. Yeltsin harrumphed and had Popov—who several years later would be an important supporter of his—struck from the guest list for future meetings.[62] Asked at his consultation with the propagandists whether restraints on migration into Moscow would spawn a labor shortage, Yeltsin shot back, "We need not to bring in new people but to force Muscovites to work" through a police dragnet to roust out "spongers." He defended the decree shuttering some research institutes as a wakeup call to laggards: "Closing down the first ten or fifteen . . . will have quite an effect in activating the others."[63]

Two years after losing the Moscow post, Yeltsin was to explain his ham-handed techniques as determined by education, situational needs, and necessity:

> In Moscow, there was no alternative. This is a bewildering city, I had a difficult legacy to deal with. And you have to take into account that all of us who today are over fifty grew up in the time of administrative-command methods. You can't get away from this. Thus far we have no other methods. We educate ourselves and try to find something different, but it all goes very slowly. When I worked in the gorkom, 90 percent of the problems that arose had to be dealt with immediately and decisively. The situation demanded it.[64]

Some years later, Vitalii Tret'yakov, by then a critic of Yeltsin's, was to deprecate the latter's experience as Moscow boss as the flailing of a gung-ho but dim-witted Soviet *udarnik*—the "shock worker" or Stakhanovite of Stalinist mythology.[65] There was something of the norm-busting shock worker to the Yeltsin of 1985–87, but to pigeonhole him as that is to lose sight of the tactility that was opening him up to new viewpoints and to flushing out new allies of change. Even in Sverdlovsk, he had leavened command methods with understanding of the Soviet economy's residual private sector. As inhospitable as ever to blatantly illegal activities, such as the sale of scarce goods under the counter at inflated prices, Yeltsin in Moscow referred with increased respect to what nonstate producers and distributors could bring to the table. At the 1986 meeting with propaganda workers, he sympathized with the charge that prices in the farmers' bazaars were sky-high, yet went on to make different points:

> I have been to many Moscow bazaars. I have never seen such prices. . . . A pathetic sprig of parsley costs fifty kopeks or maybe a ruble. A kilogram of meat goes for eight rubles. [Note: The average monthly salary in the USSR in 1985 was 190 rubles.] But we mustn't put a ceiling on prices, since this method has been tried before and gave no results. The vendors will just move on to other cities and provinces. The way to apply pressure on the

> marketplace is through trade. What we need to do is build a cooperative store at every bazaar. It doesn't matter if sausage is sold in those stores for eight rubles. I have a list of people who can pay a high price. At the very least, they will be purchasing sausage that actually smells like meat.[66]

If the only case Yeltsin made for free commerce in the Urals had been that it would keep food prices down, he now hinted that it might meet demand from comparatively well-off consumers, boost supply, and improve quality.

The same explorative mood came through on political topics. Most Soviet officials held their noses and tolerated the liberalizing measures the party espoused under the rubric of *demokratizatsiya*, democratization, at the Central Committee plenum of January 27–28, 1987; to Yeltsin, they were yeast for reform. In September 1987 he was at his seat in the Moscow Soviet when a young deputy named Arkadii Murashov, a physicist by profession, stood up to announce that he was planning to do something never before done in Soviet legislatures for the past sixty years: He was breaking unanimity to vote against a resolution sponsored by the executive. Yeltsin balled the chamber over by defending Murashov's freedom to differ and calling for the draft motion to be referred back to committee.[67] Another example would be his warming to environmental and urban-conservation issues. Hearing voices from below, Yeltsin halted construction of an eyesore World War II memorial on Poklonnaya Hill, evicted about thirty unhealthful factories from Moscow, and had a batch of pre-Soviet street names restored and pre-Revolution mansions saved from the wrecking ball. Ecopolitics brought him into contact with the *neformaly* (informals), the extra-governmental organizations that sprouted as curbs on grassroots activity slackened. The Moscow informals advocated a variety of causes, everything from free speech to arms control and animal rights, but not every group was progressive or liberal. On May 6, 1987, Yeltsin and Mayor Saikin met with a delegation from Pamyat, an ultranationalist, anti-Semitic organization illegally created in the 1970s. Five hundred Pamyat activists had been waving placards on Manezh Square, in Moscow's first wildcat demonstration since the 1920s. In August, representatives of fifty Soviet informals, most of them liberal in orientation, gathered in a Moscow hall under the protection of the gorkom.[68]

The city of Moscow was a far tougher nut than Sverdlovsk for Yeltsin to crack as leader. Its economy was less militarized, its intellectual and expert classes were more influential, and it was home to the bloated central bureaucracy. At a time of ferment, it was being tugged to and fro. That is, it was both a hotbed of reformism and a stronghold for the old ways. Yeltsin's problem was the latter and what, in an unpublished speech to the Central Committee, he decried as the snobbery of "pampered people who think they are bigwigs."[69] With rare empathy, Gorbachev said afterward, in the mid-1990s, that he understood "it was not easy to work in Moscow and Yeltsin very likely *felt more acutely than others* the resistance of the party and economic nomenklatura to perestroika. . . . Yeltsin happened upon obstacles that in Sverdlovsk he did not suspect existed."[70]

To light his path through the Moscow labyrinth, the new maestro had neither the local knowledge nor the cohesive team he had in the Urals. The Sverdlovsk factotums in tow to Yeltsin were few; many of the Muscovites with whom he worked saw him as a hick. As in Sverdlovsk, he strategized Monday mornings with a kitchen cabinet, which by the end of 1986 included Valerii Saikin, Mikhail Poltoranin, his second secretary (the Sverdlovsker Yurii Belyakov) and secretary for ideological questions (Yurii Karabasov), and the head of the Moscow KGB (Nikolai Chelnokov). The official bureau of the gorkom congregated on Wednesdays. To keep it on its toes, Yeltsin again resorted to criticism and self-criticism, with the difference that he now shared his associates' inadequacies with the press. The shared recreation that pumped up élan in Sverdlovsk would have been out of place in Moscow. Spinal and foot problems kept Yeltsin from playing volleyball after May 1986, when he scrimmaged at a Georgian vacation spot.[71] His dacha was far from the cottages of gorkom staffers. There was no hunting range at which he could dish out quotas for fowl and game.

Yeltsin's sense of responsibility to the regime and to the project of reforming communism spurred him on. And he craved personal success as ardently as he ever had, seeing no inconsistency between it and the reform cause. The Moscow assignment also elicited the testing script, as we have called it. As never before in his political work, Yeltsin after December 1985 felt the compulsion to show strength and proficiency. He recalls in *Notes of a President* how he "began to breathe in an utterly different way," energized by the demands his new post made on him.[72] In *Confession on an Assigned Theme,* he lays it on thick in describing the close of his workday. Arriving home, rarely before midnight, he would sit five or ten minutes in the limousine: "I was so worn out that I did not have the strength to raise my arm."[73] His sleep budget, he declared to underlings, was four hours a night; he was up at the crack of dawn to exercise, read, and prepare for work. (Aleksandr Korzhakov confirms the schedule.)[74] Yeltsin, Korzhakov states, put great effort into memorizing names, facts, and figures: "Yeltsin came from the wilds and felt the need when he got the chance to underscore that there are people there who are as good as Muscovites."[75] Symptomatic of the testing mode was the puffing up of the objects of his wrath into extra-large beings. Thus the district secretary drummed out for his apartment renovations was cast as comporting himself like "a prince"; others were preening "princelings" or "his majesty the worker of the apparatus."[76]

Yeltsin drew a connection between his efforts on behalf of reform and the determination of opponents to scotch them and even to do him in. In the Q&A at the House of Political Enlightenment in 1986, he selected for off-the-cuff reply questions that highlighted the point,[77] and hammered it home by quoting from an incendiary memorandum from another file:

> [I have been asked] what privileges of officials of the Moscow city committee of the party we have abolished. . . . The question is well put. But why only abolish? We have added certain things—we have increased the amount of work and the number of bureau sessions, for instance. Gorkom officials no longer work from 9:00 A.M. to 6:00 P.M. but until 10:00 or 11:00 P.M. and sometimes until midnight. So far as abolition is concerned, for a start we have closed the [gorkom's] commissary for manufactured goods. I think this is very useful. Gorkom workers will have a better feeling for our problems. . . .
>
> I get letters like this, for example: "Khrushchev long ago tried to dress us in [inmates'] padded jackets. Nothing came of it, and nothing will come of you. We have been stealing and we will go on stealing." Comrades, we can break up this cycle only through common efforts. . . .
>
> I am being reminded that in three years I will have to give an account and answer for the promises I have made. I am ready for this and intend to devote these years entirely to the struggle.
>
> And here I see a note of this sort: "Your plans are Napoleonesque. You are in over your head. . . . Go back to Sverdlovsk while you can." (Cries of "Shame" from the audience.) Stay calm, comrades, I think the question did not come from this audience and that a note I received earlier has gotten mixed in. Looks like it was written by someone sick. . . .
>
> Some people are concerned about how long I will have the strength to work on so killing a schedule. I can reassure the comrades my health is

> fine, I have nothing to snivel about. If it gives out, I will grab several extra hours of rest. Meanwhile, we need to work full bore, otherwise we will not turn things around.
>
> And then another note: "We hope that a year from now you will, in the Bolshevik way, tell us what you have not managed to get done." Sure, agreed, one year from now I will tell you.[78]

What Yeltsin was presenting was the complex that Erik Erikson labels personal and occupational "overobedience." Erikson's thumbnail description of the overobedient Martin Luther is evocative of Yeltsin at this crossroads—"a certain zest in the production of problems, a rebellious mocking in dramatic helplessness, and a curious honesty (and honest curiosity) in the insistence on getting to the point, the fatal point, the true point."[79] Overobedience, as the Luther of Wittenberg shows, can be the antechamber to mutiny if the excitable concentration on means coincides with the setting in of incertitude about ends. And that is how it was with Yeltsin in Moscow.

Chapter Six

The Mutineer

He was never at ease on the Soviet Olympus. The starchy protocol grated on Yeltsin. Unlike in Sverdlovsk, his coworkers' homes were not close by, and they rarely socialized or played games together. "It was almost impossible," to quote from the autobiographical *Confession on an Assigned Theme,* "to meet with or contact anyone," such was the security bubble. "If you went out in public to the movies, the theater, or a museum, a whole advance guard would be sent. First they would check out and encircle the place, and only then could you make your appearance."[1]

If his memoirs are any guide, Yeltsin was unsure what to make of the accoutrements provided him. His housing was middling and noisy, he said, and he implied that it was discrimination when he was not given quarters in the leafy neighborhood of Kuntsevo, in Moscow's west end. Yet the "yellow brick building" on Second Tverskaya-Yamskaya Street in which the Yeltsins were accommodated—to Muscovites, the bricks and their hue bespoke a nomenklatura dwelling—was no hovel, and the family had as many square feet as on Working Youth Embankment in Sverdlovsk. As Yeltsin did not then understand, most apparatchiks assigned to Kuntsevo were lower in station than he and did not qualify for dachas. Yeltsin was supplied with one gratis in April 1985, a cottage shared with Anatolii Luk'yanov, the party department head who had just vetted him for the transfer to Moscow. If he at first thought his living conditions were too modest, they soon seemed

Lucullan. Once in the Secretariat in July, he took Moskva-reka-5, the "state dacha" at the village of Usovo that had been occupied for several years by Gorbachev. He was "dismayed" at its ostentation. Set behind a stone wall, it was several times larger than Dacha No. 1 at Baltym, floored in marble, luxuriously furnished, and surrounded by a garden and playing courts. Yeltsin also professes to have been troubled by the dacha staff—three cooks, three waitresses, a chambermaid, and a groundskeeper, all of them on the roster of the KGB's Ninth Directorate—who were his as soon as he was raised to the status of candidate member of the Politburo.[2]

Introduction to the innermost circle of power nudged Boris Yeltsin to think more globally about the regime's raison d'être and its stance toward society. Naina Yeltsina was to use an intriguing culinary metaphor to explain how improbable mutiny would have been if her husband had not decamped from the Urals and gained the metropolitan perspective. "Chances are, if he had not come to Moscow he would not have carried out that act [his speech to the October 1987 plenum of the Central Committee]. That is because you learn more about the layer cake of life in Moscow than on the periphery. Out there, life is simpler. There is no layer cake there, by job and by level of life. There, although he had his high post, I don't think we lived all that much better than other people."[3] Like many ex-provincials adjusting to the capital, he began the process a tad starry-eyed about those who had admitted him to the club. Some recruits over the years had set about conforming to it and finding a way to benefit. For Yeltsin, though, as Vitalii Tret'yakov puts it, naïveté curdled into aggressiveness. "At first it was a positive, constructive aggressiveness, the wish to do what it seemed to him Gorbachev expected, and to do it better and faster than the others. . . . But when it came to light that the general secretary did not view Yeltsin's zeal and *udarnichestvo* [shock-workerness] with gratitude . . . [Yeltsin] took a turn toward an aggressiveness that was destructive of the power of the leader of perestroika."[4]

Most of all, then, it was the fraying of his bond with Mikhail Gorbachev that disaffected Yeltsin. In his early months as Moscow chief, they spoke regularly. This tapered off over the course of 1986. A nitpicking point was the place of the Soviet first lady, Raisa Gorbacheva. Yeltsin felt she put on airs, and he was convinced that her husband told her more than was appropriate about political issues (often on long walks upon Gorbachev's return from the Kremlin) and that she had more say on them from behind the curtains than was appropriate. In the summer of 1987, she hatched a project to convert the gigantic GUM department store on Red Square into an art museum. Yeltsin and Mayor Saikin were aghast and intervened with central planners to kill the idea.[5] In one of his interviews with me, Yeltsin said he did not refer to Raisa in his letter or his October disquisition to the Central Committee (see below), but he had talked about her with Gorbachev face to face.[6] Others confirmed this and said Gorbachev was furious that the question was raised in any form.[7] When the U.S. ambassador asked Yeltsin in 1989 if he would bring Naina Yeltsina with him on his forthcoming visit to the United States, he said, "No. Absolutely not! I'll not have her acting like Raisa Maximovna."[8] Yeltsin's grousing about Mrs. Gorbachev was not only about her personally; it also indicates a certain sexism, one that was and is shared by many Russians.

More apropos were the two leaders' styles and policy positions. To Yeltsin, after their political honeymoon in 1985–86, Gorbachev was vacillating, long-winded, and conceited: "You could not talk of any democracy in the Politburo. After the general secretary's preamble, everybody was supposed to get up and read out from a little card, 'Hooray, I agree with everything.'"[9] Yeltsin had little experience in a collegial decision-making organ he did not head. In Sverdlovsk he was a member of the obkom bureau for only eighteen months before becoming first secretary, and in the Moscow city committee he was in the chair from the start. For his part, Gorbachev thought Yeltsin was playing the prima donna, and in mid-1986 he instructed the editor-in-chief of *Pravda*, Viktor Afanas'ev, to mute coverage of him in the paper.[10] Gorbachev also thought Yeltsin was overstrung and that he was running scared when his intense tactics in Moscow did not bring results. It was generally believed when Yeltsin was made capital-city boss, and it was his expectation, too, that he would be a full member of the CPSU Politburo, with voting rights, as Viktor Grishin had been from 1971 to 1986.[11] He was hurt when Gorbachev refused to make it happen. Gorbachev was to concede in his memoirs that Yeltsin had reason to feel affronted, as there were still "mastodons and dinosaurs" from the Brezhnev era on the bureau.[12] And there were those who passed Yeltsin by. Of the three individuals promoted to full member of the Politburo in June 1987, one had been a candidate member for the same amount of time as Yeltsin, the second had spent less time than he as a candidate, and the third overleaped the candidate stage altogether. Ligachëv, whom Yeltsin more and more saw as a mastodon, has maintained that Yeltsin at some point in 1987 expressed anger directly to the voting members of the Politburo that the Grishin precedent had not been applied. Yeltsin retired from the room, and Ligachëv said he was categorically against such a promotion and would resign if Gorbachev made it. Gorbachev did not make it.[13]

On the nitty-gritty of within-system reform and its prospects, the perceptions of Yeltsin and Gorbachev came to vary. In retrospect, Yeltsin made it sound like a neat breach, where he questioned Gorbachev's scheme for turning the country and the regime around and Gorbachev stayed with the tried and true: "Despite what seemed to be changes for the better, despite the upsurge of emotion that was roiling the whole country, I sensed that we were running up against a brick wall. The thing was, this time we could not get away with pretty new phrases about perestroika and renewal. We needed concrete actions, new steps forward, but Gorbachev did not want to take such steps."[14] At the time, the break was messier and more tentative than this passage implies, and more discomfiting to those on the ground. Yeltsin was to tell the Politburo in October 1987 that he first grew disconcerted in the summer of 1986. However, there were few public or semipublic clues of it until 1987, and it took most of 1987 for his mood to work itself out.

The bad blood between Yeltsin and Gorbachev showed in the weekly meetings of the Politburo in the autumn of 1986. It was unmistakable there, though not yet on the outside, when the Politburo sat on January 19, 1987, to deliberate Gorbachev's report to the Central Committee plenum on political change, just around the corner.[15] Yeltsin heard out Gorbachev on the draft report and then recited a litany of twenty suggestions for improvement. Several were bellicosely worded. The manuscript, he said, oversold the accomplishments of reform, and bureaucratic foot-dragging made it unwise "to succumb to optimism." Comparisons of perestroika with the 1917 revolution, such as Gorbachev was given to, were "worthless," since the Soviet social structure was not being transfigured. "It would be better to say simply that perestroika has something of a revolutionary character." Even as moderate reform, Yeltsin continued, perestroika, or "restructuring," had been more buzzword than reality. "Certain people are disinclined toward revolutionary changes. It is best to appraise the current period as one of new forms of work *leading toward perestroika*." Yeltsin detoured to belittle a paragraph in the Gorbachev document claiming that the fundamentals of the regime guaranteed success: "The guarantees enumerated—the socialist system, the Soviet people, the party—have been around for lo these seventy years! So none of them is a guarantee against a return to the past." The only insurance policy would be "democratization of all spheres of life," and that had been barely put in motion, especially in spheres, such as local government, that dealt directly with people. Yeltsin ended with demands for identification by name of the authors of wrongful decisions in the present and past Soviet governments, for term limits for leaders, and for a discussion of ethnic relations in the USSR. Gorbachev said that Yeltsin's time was up and stormed out of the room.[16]

When he resumed the chair a half hour later, Gorbachev made a scathing attack on the Moscow dynamo. "Boris Nikolayevich," he observed, "deviates from our common assessment" by throwing out "loud and vacuous" reproofs. Personalized judgments had their place, but Yeltsin often lost sight of more general points and in Moscow was overseeing endless staff turnover and reorganization. "We cannot break the knees of the party and society. We need to speak respectfully about the party members who have been carrying and will carry the load and who are experiencing losses. They may have weaknesses but they have strengths, too."[17] The two swapped comments about Yeltsin's overheated style, in which Yeltsin accepted Gorbachev's rebuke only to hear Gorbachev restate it:

GORBACHEV: Let us not overdramatize, but this kind of conversation has been good for Boris Nikolayevich's practical work. He cannot be immune to the criticism that he calls on all of us to make. . . .

YELTSIN: I am a novice on the Politburo. For me this has been a lesson. I don't think it came too late.

GORBACHEV: You and I have already had words on this subject. By all means, take the lesson to heart. This conversation has been necessary. But you are an emotional person. I don't think your observations will change our attitude toward you. We have a high opinion of your work. Just remember that we have to work together. You are not to set yourself [apart from us] or to show off in front of your comrades.

"I was beside myself," Yeltsin recounts, at Gorbachev's "almost hysterical" reaction to his well-intentioned statement.[18] In a birthday call to Vitalii Vorotnikov, the head of the Russian government, on January 20, Gorbachev confided that the Politburo skirmish had left him with a "sour aftertaste." Yeltsin was getting too big for his britches, pinning the blame for every snafu on predecessors and superiors, and "playing around with the masses."[19] Yeltsin paid his respects to Vorotnikov and asked if he had been too abrupt at the meeting. You have every right to take part, Vorotnikov answered, but you should do it more calmly and self-effacingly. "You are forever the accuser, the exposer. You speak acerbically, categorically. You can't get away with that."[20]

And so it went until October 1987. At some gatherings of the leadership, the archives reveal, Yeltsin and Gorbachev butted heads; at others, Yeltsin kept silent or limited himself to needling. He was, he says, the odd man out or a queer fish *(chudak)* in the collective.[21] In the Politburo on March 24, he sniped at the foreign-language "special schools" for the offspring of Moscow VIPs, which drew an answering fusillade from Gorbachev and Ligachëv. On April 23 Gorbachev denounced press articles on limousines, clinics, and other nomenklatura privileges, such as had been printed in the pages of *Moskovskaya pravda;* Yeltsin replied that reasonable explanations of the privileges, if justified by higher need, had to be given to the media and the people. In Politburo discussions in April and May, Yeltsin gave an equivocal signal in favor of deep economic reform. He supported retention of central planning but composition of the plan "from below," with slack targets whereby efficient firms, once they had met their output quotas, would hold back surplus production for reuse or sale at unregulated prices. It was a branching out from the "complex brigade" model he had favored in Sverdlovsk. On September 28 Yeltsin proclaimed at a Politburo session that the party had been caught with its head in the sand by the emergence of the *neformaly*, the extra-governmental, informal organizations, and that the Komsomol was ossified and was proving incapable of offering Soviet youth alternatives to them. "It does nothing itself and only interferes with others." Mobilization of old-style party propagandists into the youth league, as had been advised, "will bring no results." And the sputtering economy was turning the population away from perestroika: "We said that in two years there would be an improvement. But there have not been any discernible changes. So questions arise. 'There was one period when it got better [people say], but once again . . . '"[22]

At the marathon Politburo meeting of October 15, by which time their relations were on the rocks, Gorbachev refuted commentary Yeltsin made on the 120-page draft of his address marking the seventieth anniversary of the Bolshevik Revolution on November 7. In *Life and Reforms,* Gorbachev characterizes Yeltsin's comments as "saturated by a spirit of great caution and conservatism," in contrast to his own latitudinarian views.[23] So black-and-white an interpretation is hard to sustain from the archival record.

Both Gorbachev and Yeltsin were unsure about how far to go in revising the Soviet past. In the October 15 discussion, Gorbachev differed from the communist catechism on many issues.[24] Yet he defended Stalin's crushing of Trotskyism and other intraparty opposition groups, his wartime leadership of the fatherland, and "the liquidation of the kulaks as a class" during collectivization, reminiscing here about the organizing efforts of his grandfather in their birthplace of Privol'noye. Yeltsin—from a family of dispossessed kulaks—avoided collectivization and Stalin's attacks on the opposition and wartime leadership, but spoke on a host of other historical issues. One unifying point for him was the need to recognize the past contribution of rank-and-file citizens and communists. In 1917 the party found out "how to win over the majority of the population and of the soviets [elected councils]" to its side; Germany would not have been defeated in 1945 without the unselfishness of anonymous workers and foot soldiers. Yeltsin asked for elucidation of the role of Lenin and—shades of his adolescent inquiries in Berezniki—for inclusion in the jubilee report of some evaluations of Lenin's revolutionary contemporaries. Toward the end, he telegraphed irritation at the effort being spent on the past, since what mattered most to society was a decent life in the present. His plea was for a stock taking, a summary in Gorbachev's speech about the Soviet experiment and the path ahead.

The declassified transcript shows Gorbachev taking to heart the question about the velocity of reform, though not quite as Yeltsin did. On other items, he tut-tutted Yeltsin for artlessness with reference to Lenin and, in Aesopian language, for his self-centeredness:

YELTSIN: I think that besides Lenin we need to name [in the report] his closest comrades-in-arms.

GORBACHEV: Whom do you have in mind?

YELTSIN: I have in mind [Yakov] Sverdlov, [Felix] Dzerzhinsky, [Mikhail] Kalinin, [Mikhail] Frunze.

GORBACHEV: Look, don't be so simplistic. Here in my briefcase I have a list of members of the Politburo under Lenin. Wouldn't those be his closest comrades-in-arms? Yes, that is right. And you wish to give names from today's point of view, whom you like and whom you do not. That would be incorrect. . . . [Gorbachev speaks of some personalities from the 1920s and 1930s and reviews their policy positions.] The question being settled here was where the country was headed. . . . But personal needs were folded into these struggles. . . . When it comes to subjective aspects at the level of high politics, and when it touches on big-time politicians, then frequently these personal ambitions, pretensions, the inability to work in the collective, and so on and so forth are capable of warping the person's political position. All of this, you have to understand, is not a simple thing, it is a delicate interaction. . . .

YELTSIN: A very important theme is . . . the time frame in which perestroika, now that it has begun, is to occur. People are looking for a very stringent formulation. But we are still writing out that perestroika is going to take fifteen to twenty years, that is, it is a long-range policy. We have to solve our most crying problems in two, three, five years, that's all there is to it. We must say this.

GORBACHEV: I am the one who thought it best to say perestroika would take fifteen to twenty years, but the report has a line about it taking a generation . . . and a generation is longer than fifteen or twenty years. Thank you. It is good that you paid attention to this. The question about time frame is worth thinking about, because it is very important. You are right, people are watching this. . . .

YELTSIN: The last thing I would say is, we have a ton of experience on all these matters. So what have these seventy years brought us? What suggests itself is a section that sums things up.

GORBACHEV: We took the correct road, that is what I would conclude.

Gorbachev's greater attachment to the road taken, and to theories of socialism, rings out. Yeltsin's emphasis was on how effectively or ineffectively systems *worked*. If they did not, he implied, society would have to find ones that did.

An antagonism with Yegor Ligachëv, the second-in-command to Gorbachev, also ballooned. The two already differed on minor patronage and organizational issues. In late 1986, for example, Yeltsin walked out of a Politburo session when Ligachëv presented his choice for president of the Urals branch of the Academy of Sciences, located in Sverdlovsk. Yeltsin had not been asked his opinion, and the appointee, physicist Gennadii Mesyats, was from Tomsk, where Ligachëv had been party leader, and was given the job over the Sverdlovsker whom Yeltsin had in mind.[25] So far as the Moscow first secretaryship went, Ligachëv was resolved not to let Yeltsin evade Kremlin scrutiny and control, as he was persuaded Viktor Grishin had done under Brezhnev. Once Ligachëv and his operatives had determined to keep a close eye, physical propinquity on Old Square allowed them to do so.[26] As the organizational vicar of the CPSU, Ligachëv disliked what he saw as Yeltsin's smears of the party apparatus on issues such as privilege, corruption, and dogmatism. Yeltsin in turn felt Ligachëv was braking progress and using his staff to undercut him.

For Yeltsin, it especially rankled that he had far less autonomy in the Moscow position than in Sverdlovsk and less, for that matter, than when he served as a Central Committee department head in 1985. At the Central Committee plenum in June 1987, he blasted Ligachëv: "We know, Yegor Kuz'mich, that the Secretariat is working hard. But still [we see] a profusion of petty questions, no letup in the volume of paper, undue tutelage, administration by command, over-regulation of the party organs, and continual visits by commissions chiefly to dig up negative examples." "Practically nothing" had changed here since 1985 and nothing would until the party center gave local leaders room to exercise that distinctive Urals quality, self-reliance.[27] Things were such, he told Prime Minister Nikolai Ryzhkov in a chat, that Ligachëv had phoned him to complain that the lawn in front of Luzhniki, the city's main soccer stadium, was poorly mowed.[28] To *Moskovskaya pravda*'s Mikhail Poltoranin, Yeltsin said that Ligachëv had him "account for every pencil and scrap of paper" and "put him in the shoes of a little boy."[29]

The tiebreaker for Yeltsin was a microissue in political reform. Gorbachev being away on summer vacation in the south, Ligachëv chaired the Politburo session of September 10, 1987. In the Politburo in early August, following rallies by the Pamyat nationalists and by representatives of the Crimean Tatars, a Turkic minority exiled to Central Asia by Stalin, Yeltsin had promised Gorbachev to consider how to regulate street demonstrations. In a memorandum, he proposed to take a permissive approach to citizens who wished to march and congregate but to limit meetings to Izmailovo Park in the east end, which would become a Moscow Hyde Park. Some guidelines had since been promulgated in the city press.[30] On September 10 Ligachëv and other standpat members criticized Yeltsin for not checking back with the Kremlin, and said the document was unnecessary and would invalidate police controls. Yeltsin replied that he had made an effort to clear the decision and that such matters were best left to Moscow and other city councils to legislate. Ligachëv waved him off pedantically. The old, centrally run system, which banned meetings other than official rallies, prevented "harm to society, the state, and other citizens." "There is no need to pass other 'rules,'" he stated, "and the document adopted in Moscow is to be repealed."[31] A Politburo commission merely tweaked the USSR-wide regulations. They would be redone in a much more liberal direction only in 1988–89.

The rigors of the Moscow party position, and the tugging and hauling with Gorbachev and Ligachëv, wore Yeltsin down. Toward the end of 1986, he checked into a Kremlin clinic with a hypertensive attack and symptoms of anxiety. The doctors concluded that he was overworked and that a principal health issue was that in reaction to the nervous tension he "had begun to abuse sedatives and sleeping pills and to be enamored of alcohol." The patient reacted cantankerously: He had no intention of curbing his workload and "no need of moral lectures."[32] It is to be noted that individuals who worked closely with Yeltsin in those years, and whom I interviewed, seem to have seen few or no effects of psychological dislocation, overmedication, or overconsumption of alcohol. For instance, Valerii Saikin, the mayor of Moscow from 1986 to 1990 and not well disposed toward Yeltsin, said the first secretary never ran out of energy. He might plead a headache at their planning meetings on Monday mornings and refer jocularly to staying up late to work on his weekly report. Beyond that, Saikin saw nothing out of the ordinary.[33]

It was on September 10, the day of the Politburo brouhaha over street marches, that Yeltsin decided to fire off a letter to Gorbachev. He came home late to the Usovo dacha and sat with Naina in his study. He told her he intended to write the general secretary and to get out of the CPSU leadership: "I am not going to work with this band *[s etoi bandoi]* any longer. They are ruining the country" (the country at this time still being the Soviet Union). She was not surprised at his anger, as she had felt it for months, but was taken aback by the solution he proposed. Where would he work? she asked. Yeltsin said it was possible that Gorbachev would let him continue to run the Moscow party committee, without a Politburo seat, although his formal request was to give up both positions. If not, he would go back to the construction industry, perhaps as chief of a building trust. The party would never let him do that, she replied. Then he would work as a foreman, as he had in the 1950s, or perhaps they would move to the far north and start a new life there. Maybe it would be simpler to go on pension, Naina thought, and let their grown-up children feed them. Then came a pause: "He sat and sat and finally said, 'No.' I [Naina Yeltsina] thought the continuation of his thought would be, 'I am not going to write it.' But he said, 'No, I *am going to write* my statement. And we will just see about work later.' He did not say a thing after that."[34] He drafted the letter that night and sent it to Gorbachev on Saturday, September 12, after what one must assume was further introspection.

Half of the missive was a swipe at Ligachëv, whom Yeltsin painted as a boor and a hat-throwing partisan of Tomsk. Party committees like Yeltsin's in Moscow, restrained by Ligachëv and his minions, "are losing their self-reliance *[samostoyatel'nost']*," even as the leadership was beginning to ease up on factory and farm directors.[35] Yeltsin also underlined "the disparity between revolutionary words and [unrevolutionary] deeds," as had been a theme of his all year, and notified Gorbachev that people felt the inconsistency but were reticent to talk about it.

The novelty of the September document was not the compendium of allegations but the quandary it laid before the Soviet leader. Yeltsin's undiplomatic request to quit his official posts was certain to cause consternation. The letter only magnified it by telling the general secretary that unnamed officials were shamming agreement with his reforms and blocking them on the sly. Gorbachev, Yeltsin said, had grown inured to the pseudo reformers' game and was an accomplice in it: "This suits them and, if you will pardon me, Mikhail Sergeyevich, it seems to me [these people] are coming to suit you." The author was not good at stroking his boss's ego: "I am an infelicitous person and I know it. I realize it is hard for you to know what to do about me." If he were to stay in place and nothing else changed, he would be a nuisance, and the problems "will grow and will hobble you in your work." Most striking for the member of a collective leadership, Yeltsin raised the possibility of taking unilateral action. It was best if Gorbachev dealt with Ligachëv's obstinacy, one way or the other: "To 'decode' all of this would be deleterious if it went public. Only you personally can make a change in the interests of the party." Between the lines, Yeltsin was asking Gorbachev to throw overboard his second secretary and not Yeltsin, and to speed up reform. The closing sentence of the memorandum was a saber-rattling ultimatum about a widening of the arena of internecine conflict: "I *do not think I will find it necessary* to turn directly to the plenum of the Central Committee."

Gorbachev was troubled enough by the letter to dial Yeltsin from his seaside villa in Pitsunda, Georgia. He agreed to discuss it with Yeltsin in Moscow but wanted the meeting to wait almost two months, until after the November 7 holiday break. Gorbachev's hauteur was strange. One would have thought he would hasten to fix the problem. It was not every day that a candidate member of the Politburo resigned his position. Gorbachev has maintained that Yeltsin accepted his timing. Yeltsin says they agreed to confer "later," and he assumed that meant in one or two weeks.[36] Yeltsin stewed when Gorbachev did not contact him. He feared that the planned October plenum of the Central Committee, the third of the year, was where Gorbachev was going to take up the question, and that he would be confronted there by a motion from Gorbachev and the voting members of the Politburo to purge him.[37] He got intelligence from Poltoranin of *Moskovskaya pravda* and others that Ligachëv was stockpiling data and poised for a preemptive strike against him. On injunction from Ligachëv, Yurii Sklyarov, the head of the Central Committee propaganda department, instructed Poltoranin to write a memorandum "showing that Yeltsin was a populist, that he got in the way of normal work, and so on." Poltoranin turned him down and took the news to Yeltsin.[38]

As Yeltsin gave his letter to the courier on September 12, he was to recall, he foresaw two options: "If they ousted me, . . . I would take up independent political activity. . . . If they did not oust me, I would appeal to the plenum of the Central Committee."[39] His upbeat attitude is hard to fathom. Basmanovo or Butka homesteaders and maybe Sverdlovsk civil engineers could forage on their own—the word Yeltsin used for "independent" *(samostoyatel'nyi)* is the adjectival form of "self-reliance." What, however, would *political* independence be in a country where one centralized party still controlled government and its means of violence, the media, and the economy? As for the Central Committee as a court of appeal, Yeltsin did not know if he would be afforded the floor. If he were able to speak, he might find some committee backing, but to suborn members would have been "sacrilegious," as he was to say to the plenum, and would not have gone undetected.[40] He mulled over a third course and mentioned it to Naina: to write a special letter to the members of the Politburo. He rejected it; a letter could influence no one except possibly for Aleksandr Yakovlev, the Central Committee secretary who was the most change-acceptant of Gorbachev's wards.[41]

The Central Committee met two or three times a year in Sverdlov Hall, in the eighteenth-century Building No. 1 of the Kremlin. The hall was a magnificent rotunda, ninety feet high and ringed in light Corinthian pillars and pilasters and a narrow gallery above. The plenum of Wednesday, October 21, was billed as a sedate affair. It was to consist of hearing out the Politburo-approved text of Gorbachev's report commemorating the revolution, which was scheduled for delivery on November 2, and party etiquette prescribed early adjournment without discussion, followed by a pleasant luncheon together. Yeltsin was seated in the front row; only the full members of the Politburo were on the presidium, or presiding panel, which looked down on the Central Committee members, alternates, and guests across a skirted desk. He was unsure until the last about whether to try to speak. At about eleven A.M., as Gorbachev finished up, Yeltsin scribbled a few "theses" on one of the red cards used to register votes at Soviet committees and assemblies. He raised his good, right hand shakily in the air. Stage fright hit and he took it down. Gorbachev pointed him out to Ligachëv, who was chairing. Ligachëv asked the members if they wanted to open discussion of the report; when several said they did not, he motioned to Yeltsin that he would not get to speak. Yeltsin took to his feet and was again repelled by Ligachëv. Gorbachev interjected a second time: "Comrade Yeltsin has some kind of announcement." Only then did Ligachëv surrender the microphone.

Why ever did Gorbachev override Ligachëv? He had to know Yeltsin was up to no good. The circumstances prompt the surmise that the general secretary thought he would kill two birds with one stone by letting the Moscow boss have the floor. One benefit would be to apply pressure on the party to get with the program of reform, on the rationale that incremental change was to be preferred to the shocks favored by Yeltsin. The other potential advantage was the chance for Gorbachev and his followers in the Central Committee to reply to and chasten the hotheadedness of Yeltsin, which could have led to further sanctions.[42] Like Yeltsin's decision to speak out, Gorbachev's decision to allow him to speak carried its own heavy risks.

No drumroll announced Yeltsin's cri de coeur. In Vitalii Vorotnikov's words, he "strode up onto the dais. Clearly agitated, he took a pause and began to speak. He talked at first confusedly and then with more assurance, but without his usual force. Somehow, he was semi-apologetic and semi-accusatory, trying continuously to contain his passions."[43] Gorbachev remembers in his memoirs a similarly "strange composite" of feelings on Yeltsin's face. The combination, he says in one of his off-the-shelf digs at Yeltsin, was what you got from "an unbalanced nature."[44]

Yeltsin's nine hundred words—his secret speech—lasted all of six or seven minutes.[45] In form, they will not put anyone in mind of Pericles' Funeral Oration or the Gettysburg Address or even of the original secret speech by Nikita Khrushchev in 1956, with its gripping, four-hour narrative of arrest, torture, and gore under Stalin. Yeltsin gave mostly a rambling rerun of the letter of September 12 and of oral statements at meetings, open and closed.[46] Items about Ligachëv and hidebound Soviet bureaucracy tripped out pell-mell. The only concrete anecdote Yeltsin gave of messed-up reform was the workaday one of his inability to cut back on the number of research institutes in Moscow, as he had promised to do in 1986.[47]

What was lacking in fluency and lawyer's points Yeltsin made up for in audacity and heat. He wanted "to say everything that is in my soul, what is in my heart, and what is in me as a communist." He unloaded three bombshells. The first was a sharpened position on how the mass of the population was tuning out the reform process. "People's faith has begun to ebb." Unless results were hewed to match promises, "we may well find that the authority of the party as a whole will diminish in the people's eyes." Yeltsin made the point clumsily, pushing both a stronger effort to make good on promises and a move away from the two- or three-year period he had spoken of in the Politburo on October 15. The second point was a call for "democratic forms" in Soviet politics, especially in the Communist Party, and disapproval of the growing sycophancy toward Gorbachev, which he said had the ring of a Stalin- or Brezhnev-like personality cult. Political deformations of this sort, Yeltsin asserted, accounted for the failures of the seventy years reviewed in Gorbachev's report:

> I must say that the lessons that come out of these seventy years are painful lessons. Yes, there have been victories, as Mikhail Sergeyevich has said, but there also have been . . . harsh lessons, serious defeats. These defeats took shape gradually. They happened because there was no collegiality [in the party], because cliques were formed, because the party's power was delivered into a single pair of hands, because this one man was protected from all criticism.
>
> Myself, I am disturbed that there is still not a good situation within the Politburo and that recently there has been a noticeable growth in what I can only call adulation of the general secretary on the part of certain members of the Politburo, certain members of long standing. This is impermissible now, at a time when we are introducing properly democratic and honorable relations toward one another, true comradely relations. . . . This is impermissible. I am all for criticizing people to their faces, eye-to-eye, but not for being carried away by adulation, which can again become the norm, a cult of personality.[48]

These broadsides landed, Yeltsin's peroration made his third point—repetition of the request to get him off the Politburo that he had initially made in writing on September 12. It was offered with an addendum that was not in the letter to Gorbachev but was part of his September 10 conversation with Naina: the afterthought that his position as Moscow first secretary should be considered by the city committee of the party and not solely by the Central Committee, which would have made it possible for him to remain Moscow party boss after departing the Politburo. Catcalls rang out when he made the last statement. As he took his seat again, "My heart was pounding and seemed ready to burst out of my chest."[49]

Looked at in the sweep of Yeltsin's life, the soliloquy was an instant of truth. He reflected on it in an interview fifteen years later as lonely and intimidating: "It was an expression of protest. . . . I had a venturesome attitude but no support. . . . I was all alone against this armada, this bulky and cumbersome communist thing, their KGB system."[50] There is some self-dramatization here, and not for the only time, but there is no denying that Yeltsin was tempting fate. Irrespective of the cries from the hall after he spoke that he was consumed by vainglory, the eruption was not the result of naked power-seeking, for, absent something to defuse the situation, retribution was foreordained as soon as he had gone through with it. As Anatolii Chernyayev dryly put it to Gorbachev in early November, Yeltsin "was not aiming for the top spot: He was smart enough not to count on it."[51]

Even pushing on Gorbachev to change policy was dicey, given past Soviet practice. Nor was Yeltsin adhering to a well-defined program or set of ideas. His perception that Gorbachev was acting timidly, and that he as a result should recalibrate his position, was grounded more in an almost feline instinct for the moment than in ideology. Gorbachev's feet were still firmly planted in Marxism-Leninism. Now and over the next four years, inasmuch as he resonated to instincts at all, they were, in a manner of speaking, canine—trained, trainable, tied to the known and to the previously rewarded.[52]

Once the hunch took with Yeltsin, he acted as he had at times in the past, going beyond survival, duty, success, and testing to revisit the dormant rebellion script. In *Confession*, he explicitly drew the parallel to a simple act of defiance back in his adolescence—at his commencement from elementary school. In the school hall, he had piped up, "almost as at the October plenum of the Central Committee,"[53] and announced to horrified parents and staff that his homeroom teacher was not fit for her job. But Sverdlov Hall in the Moscow Kremlin was, to say the least, a more consequential stage for rebellion than Railway School No. 95 in inconspicuous Berezniki. And, although Yeltsin concentrated in 1987 on his immediate superior, Ligachëv, as he said it had been on his teacher in 1945 or 1946, this time he also went after the headmaster. The Khrushchev secret speech was about the Stalinist past and attempted to absolve the current leadership of responsibility for that past. The Yeltsin secret speech was about the Gorbachevian present and attempted to make the person and the group in charge responsible for the malpractice of reform.

When Yeltsin was back in his seat, Gorbachev took control from Ligachëv. He was, noticed Valerii Boldin, his chief of staff, "livid with rage" at the monkey wrench Yeltsin had thrown and at the claim about kowtowing to Gorbachev as general secretary.[54] Still, Gorbachev did have options. He could have voiced receptivity and asked Yeltsin to explicate his points. He could have picked some of them apart. Yeltsin had cast aspersions on Gorbachev for exalting palaver over action; the same could have been shown to apply to some degree to Yeltsin's speech. Or Gorbachev could have finagled the matter by undertaking to review it with Yeltsin or to refer it to the Politburo. That he did not do so is proof that by the time Yeltsin's speech was over Gorbachev had shifted to giving his uppity associate a dose of his own medicine.

In high dudgeon, Gorbachev rejected Yeltsin's position that the Moscow party organization should be left to decide on his standing there: "We seem to be talking here about the separation of the Moscow party organization [from the party as a whole] . . . about a desire to fight with the Central Committee." Under the "democratic centralism" bolted in place by Lenin and Stalin, local and regional leaders served for the good of the whole and bowed to the will of higher-ups. It was anathema for the Moscow committee, and not the Politburo and the Central Committee apparatus, to choose the city's party boss.[55] Gorbachev then solicited opinions, signaling that he had made willingness to berate Yeltsin a badge of loyalty to him.[56]

Nine Politburo members—Ligachëv, Prime Minister Ryzhkov, Vitalii Vorotnikov, Eduard Shevardnadze of Georgia (Gorbachev's foreign minister), and Viktor Chebrikov (the chairman of the KGB), inter alia—spoke against Yeltsin. All were willing and even happy to oblige, although later Ryzhkov and some others would hold it against Gorbachev that he had not let them in on Yeltsin's September letter.[57] A parade of fifteen officials and two blue-collar workers then had at Yeltsin. It was four hours' worth of imprecations, with time off for a recess in which Yeltsin stood alone. Some committee members approached Gorbachev at the break to demand that Yeltsin be expelled from the Central Committee; Gorbachev refused.[58] Several members long affiliated with Yeltsin, such as Yurii Petrov, his successor in the Sverdlovsk obkom, and Arkadii Vol'skii, who had tried to bring him to Moscow in the Andropov years, did not respond to Gorbachev's invitation to attack him verbally. Several others, notably Mayor Saikin, Politburo member Aleksandr Yakovlev, the Sverdlovsker Gennadii Kolbin (now party first secretary in Kazakhstan), and academician Georgii Arbatov, showed some fellow feeling for him even as they got in their digs. Saikin truly stuck his neck out. He was opposed to Yeltsin's speech and underlined that he had no forewarning of it (he was right off a plane from Beijing), but said there had been some achievements in Moscow since 1985 that Yeltsin had "worked around the clock" to bring about.[59] The rest ranged from the admonitory to the abusive. These rejoinders were as new as Yeltsin's almost unrehearsed piece. Since Stalin's time, would-be speakers at Central Committee plenums had requested a place on the docket weeks ahead, written out their remarks, and filed them with the Secretariat before meeting day.

Ligachëv led off by demanding to know why Yeltsin had been unengaged at many Politburo meetings; the answer must be that all along Yeltsin had knavishly been collecting materials for use in his speech to the plenum.[60] If Ligachëv's venom was predictable, some blows smarted more—they were acts of "betrayal," Yeltsin later said.[61] They came from several provincial party bosses, from Yakov Ryabov, and from Politburo members Ryzhkov and Yakovlev. Boris Konoplëv, the first secretary in Perm oblast, where Yeltsin grew up, wrote Yeltsin's presentation off to "either cluelessness about life or an effort to shove us aside and distort reality." Ryabov, sponsor to Yeltsin in Sverdlovsk in the 1960s and 1970s and now ambassador to France, said he should never have drafted him into the party apparatus and promoted him, and ought to have been awake to his "delusions of grandeur."[62] Ryzhkov parroted Ligachëv's charges and added ones of his own about "political nihilism" and a desire to split the Politburo. Yakovlev found that Yeltsin had displayed panic, "petit-bourgeois attitudes," and an infatuation with "pseudo-revolutionary phrases." Mikhail Solomentsev, a backer in 1985, faulted him for a tendency to accumulate hostilities the way a snowball does bits of gravel. Vorotnikov, also an early supporter, saw it differently: "At Politburo sessions, Boris Nikolayevich, you mostly keep to yourself. There is some kind of mask on your face the whole time. It was not that way when you were in Sverdlovsk. . . . You seem to feel malcontent with everyone and everything." Chebrikov of the KGB reproved the sinner for never having "loved the people of Moscow" and for blabbing to foreign journalists.[63]

Shooting through the proceedings was paternalistic and pedagogical imagery. When Yeltsin toward the end tried a hangdog rebuttal, Gorbachev interrupted midsentence: "Boris Nikolayevich, are you so politically illiterate *[bezgramotnyi]* that we should be organizing a reading and writing class for you right here?" No, Yeltsin gulped. Gorbachev then pontificated on Yeltsin's "hypertrophied self-love" and puerile need to have the country "revolve around your persona," as the city had since 1985. Several accusers said Yeltsin would do well to think of the plenum and similar conclaves as a rectifying "school" for his "political immaturity *[nezrelost']*." Shevardnadze, after Yakovlev the most liberal member of the Politburo, inveighed against his "irresponsibility" and "primitivism." Stepan Shalayev, the chairman of the Soviet trade unions, said Yeltsin should have been heedful of Ligachëv, whose apparatus was "a great school for each communist who takes part in its work," a point also taken up by Ryzhkov. Yeltsin dawdled in enlisting in the party in the 1960s, stated Sergei Manyakin, and never was tempered as a communist and citizen; Ligachëv had erred in coddling Yeltsin and not "thumping the table with his fist" at Yeltsin's roguery.[64]

Yeltsin got with the spirit in his closing by describing the plenary as "a severe school . . . that will do me for my whole life." He tried gamely to recycle several of his propositions in conciliatory form, saying, for instance, that his barb about hosannas to Gorbachev applied to only "two or three comrades." And he allowed that he generally agreed with the assessment of him: "In speaking out today and letting down the Central Committee and the Moscow city organization, I made a mistake." Gorbachev then asked if Yeltsin was capable of continuing with his work—a giveaway that he was open to a rapprochement, provided Yeltsin ate his words. Yeltsin would not and said again he wanted to be discharged. In his wrap-up, Gorbachev retracted the lifeline and moved that Yeltsin be censured for his "politically erroneous" outburst and that the Politburo and the Moscow committee meet to examine his status.[65] Yeltsin, like everyone else, voted for the resolution.

There was still time to salvage something from the debacle. The Moscow party bureau met several days later, excoriated Yeltsin for putting them on the spot by speaking out without consultation, but passed a resolution that he should be permitted to stay as gorkom first secretary. They delegated the estimable Saikin to press this position with Gorbachev, yet the general secretary considered the case closed and would not meet with him. Yeltsin attended the Politburo meeting of October 31 and again asked pardon for his conduct ten days before. He informed members he would agree to the Moscow bureau's proposal that he remain in his local position—an initiative that went unmentioned in his memoirs:

> I am suffering keenly from the criticism of my presentation to the [Central Committee] plenum. The reason for my statement was my worry that perestroika had gained momentum and now we are losing that momentum. I am prepared to continue to work. We need to hold course on perestroika. I confess that I took too much upon myself, that I am guilty [in this regard]. I had still not seen or really felt what I was guilty of. Since the middle of 1986, I have felt a powerful psychological overload. I should have gone openly with this to my comrades on the gorkom and Politburo. But my self-love interposed, and that was my main mistake. I am now

ready to speak with Yegor Kuz'mich [Ligachëv], Aleksandr Nikolayevich [Yakovlev], and Georgii Petrovich [Razumovskii, a deputy of Ligachëv's]. My gorkom comrades have not turned away from me. They are asking me to stay, although they also condemn my speech.

Gorbachev listened impassively.[66]

On November 3 Yeltsin sent the general secretary a letter repeating his request. Gorbachev consulted with several Politburo members and called him at work to turn it down summarily. He was fed up with indulging Yeltsin and now had a new plaint: Yeltsin had not disavowed bastard versions of his October 21 speech that were popping up in Moscow and in the world press. "He [Yeltsin] ostensibly perceives himself a 'popular hero,'" the general secretary exclaimed to staff.[67] The underlying worry was that Yeltsin's conceit was shared by the crowd.

It is mind-boggling how close the two gladiators came to a compromise. On October 21, even after Yeltsin refused to withdraw his resignation request, Gorbachev said to the plenum that the position of Moscow party chief might not be "beyond his powers" in the long term, if Yeltsin were "able to draw the correct conclusions" and work well.[68] Yeltsin did eat humble pie on October 31 and November 3. As late as November 10, Anatolii Chernyayev was recommending to Gorbachev in a letter that he conserve Yeltsin as an ally, in a manifestation of magnanimity and reformism, and not drive him into the ranks of the outcast.[69] Yeltsin could have been left in the Moscow position with a slap on the wrist—not a kick in the groin. And he could have been wheedled into signing a nonaggression pact that would take him out of the Politburo, something he had wanted since September, with eligibility for a return. Had this been done, as Yeltsin theorized in an interview in 2002, "History might have veered in a different direction."[70]

On November 7, the anniversary of the revolution, Yeltsin was on the Lenin Mausoleum reviewing stand with the other Soviet leaders, waving at the tanks and rockets in the military parade. Fidel Castro of Cuba, who admired his spunk (and later was to despise his policies), came up and gave him a rib-crunching hug. At the Kremlin reception for the diplomatic corps, Yeltsin, U.S. Ambassador Jack Matlock wrote, stood apart from his Politburo colleagues, "bore a rather sheepish smile, and periodically shifted his stance from one foot to the other, rather like a schoolboy who had been scolded by the teacher."[71]

During the holiday—reading by now off of a primordial script for survival—Yeltsin got the family together to ponder his plight. Would he get work in industry, be rusticated to Sverdlovsk, or worse? His distress took a morbid turn on November 9. He was found dripping in blood in the dressing room off of his Old Square office and whisked by ambulance to the TsKB (Central Clinical Hospital, the main Kremlin hospital) on Michurin Prospect. He had slashed the left side of his rib cage and stomach with office scissors. The weapon chosen and the injury, too superficial to require stitches, indicate it was a howl of anger, frustration, and perhaps self-hate rather than an act of suicide. Of his hospitalization, Yeltsin has said no more than that he had "a breakdown" *(sryv)*, headaches, chest pains, and heart palpitations: "My organism could not stand the nervous strain."[72] Naina Yeltsina cared sufficiently about her husband's mental state to have his head bodyguard, Yurii Kozhukhov, remove hunting knives, guns, and glass objects from their home and dacha before his return, and to tell a friend later she had taken precautions against an overdose with prescription drugs.[73]

The nadir for Yeltsin was the city party plenum called by Gorbachev and Ligachëv for the evening of Wednesday, November 11. Gorbachev phoned him in his TsKB room that morning to tell him KGB officers would come for him. He cut short Yeltsin's protestations that he was too ill even to walk unassisted to the toilet; the doctors would help, Gorbachev retorted. Only at this stage did the general secretary canvass Yevgenii Chazov, by this time the Soviet minister of health, who warned him that participation in any public meeting would be a danger to Yeltsin's health; Gorbachev replied that the matter was settled and Yeltsin had given his agreement.[74] Naina was in her husband's room when the guards arrived at Michurin Prospect, and she wanted him to refuse to cooperate. He disagreed because he still hoped against hope that some would side with him, and even that he might win a vote of confidence, and because he was afraid that not to go would be taken as cowardice and would leave pro-Yeltsin members of the Moscow bureau in the lurch. Yeltsin feared a replay of the post–World War II Leningrad affair, when the leadership of the USSR's second city was decapitated on Stalin's orders. Until he mentioned this to Naina, she had urged him to stay in the hospital, "And then there was nothing I could do."[75] In light of later events, it is of note that one of Stalin's accusations against the Leningraders in 1949–50 was that they were scheming to set the Russian republic against the central government.[76]

Yeltsin arrived at Old Square bandaged, his face and lips of a violet color, and dazed by the medication. Aleksandr Korzhakov and Chazov both write in their books that he had received a potent shot of baralgin, an analgesic and antispasm agent. He felt so poorly, Yeltsin was to say in 2000, "that it seemed like I would die right there, in the meeting hall."[77] KGB officers had roped off the first three rows of the gorkom's auditorium. Pre-selected speakers filed in and filled up the seats—"flushed, quaking, like borzois [Russian wolfhounds] before the hunt."[78] In his introduction to the meeting, Gorbachev said his erstwhile protégé had taken "an exclusive position" on political issues and "put his personal ambitions above the interests of the party." Yeltsin's October speech "did not contain a single constructive suggestion" and showed he had forfeited the party's trust.[79]

Twenty-three borzois then subjected Yeltsin to yet another round-robin hazing. No one from the bureau or the parent city committee, not Mayor Saikin or any of the party secretaries, emitted a benevolent peep, which cut Yeltsin to the quick. A select few were temperate. Alla Nizovtseva, a secretary of the gorkom, said she had met many times with the first secretary and never heard him say anything unfaithful. But he had swerved off the rails, and they had not seen it coming: "We really deluded ourselves, we . . . overestimated his savvy and knowledge."[80] One brave soul, cosmonaut Aleksei Yeliseyev, now the rector of the Bauman Technical University, flayed committee members for coming out against Yeltsin only when it was politically convenient and for denying responsibility for his errors. Most of the other speakers would not take any of the blame.

Some of the vitriol came from officials whom Yeltsin had demoted or dressed down since December 1985. "You have ground everything into dust and ashes," Vladimir Protopopov, a professor of economics, formerly a raion first secretary, declared, "but when it was time for something creative all you did, Boris Nikolayevich, was stumble around." Yurii Prokof'ev, a party apparatchik banished to city hall, reminded Yeltsin of his comments to the Twenty-Seventh CPSU Congress in 1986, when he said he had lacked the courage and political experience to speak out before then. "So far as courage goes, you have it, but you have never had political maturity and you do not have it now. The only way to explain that is by reference to your character." A. N. Nikolayev of Bauman raion stated that Yeltsin had committed "a party crime" and "blasphemy" and "qualified for the same bossman syndrome against which he spoke so angrily at the [1986] party congress." As an example of the syndrome, A. I. Zemskov from Voroshilov district cited Yeltsin's inattentiveness to the courtesies Viktor Grishin had been master of: "It is repugnant when not a single raikom [district party committee] secretary . . . has been able to phone the city secretary direct. Over the course of two years, we have had to report to an assistant why the first secretary of a raikom wants to have a word with the first secretary of the gorkom." Consecutive orators bandied about invidious comparisons: to Napoleon again ("elements of Bonapartism"); to a prancing general on horseback ("on your steed in front of the man on the street"); to Julius Caesar ("'I came, I saw, I conquered' is not the motto for us"); even, with a snicker, to Christ (anti-communists "are trying to make out of Boris Nikolayevich a Jesus Christ who has been tortured for his frightfully revolutionary love of social renewal and democracy"). Some of these speakers were later to ask Yeltsin's pardon,[81] but that evening the schadenfreude hung over the hall.

Yeltsin went up to the microphone, Gorbachev holding him by the elbow. As he spoke, communists in the first three rows stamped their feet and hissed "*Doloi!*"—"Down with him!" Gorbachev motioned them down and said, "That's enough, stop it."[82] Yeltsin recanted more abjectly than he had at the Central Committee plenum or the Politburo—before the party, before his Moscow comrades, and "before Mikhail Sergeyevich Gorbachev, whose authority is so high in our organization, in our country, and in the entire world." "The ambition talked about today" had been his siren song. "I tried to struggle with it, without success." Were he to transgress in the future, he said, he ought to be expelled from the party.

When the meeting was over and Gorbachev and the audience were gone, Yeltsin, overwrought, put his head down on the presidium table.[83] Back at the hospital, Naina exploded that the guards were no better than Nazis—the worst abuse that could be hurtled by a Soviet citizen of her generation—and asked them to tell Gorbachev, whose orders they had carried out, that he was a criminal.[84]

The resolution of the city committee gave Yeltsin's position to Lev Zaikov, the blimpish Central Committee secretary for the military-industrial complex, the same job Yakov Ryabov had held in the 1970s. Zaikov, a former mayor of Leningrad, had been appointed a CPSU secretary in July 1985, the same day as Yeltsin, and to the Politburo in February 1986. The morning of November 13, *Pravda* led with an abridged transcript of the November 11 meeting. On February 18, 1988, two years to the day after the Central Committee elevated him to candidate member of the Politburo, it voted him out. Zaikov crowed to editor Mikhail Poltoranin that "the Yeltsin epoch is over."[85]

Chapter Seven

The Yeltsin Phenomenon

Yeltsin was moved in early December 1987 from the principal Kremlin hospital in the city to the forest calm of the Soviet government's sanitarium in Barvikha, west of Moscow. He was there through February 1988. His mother visited from Sverdlovsk. Student friends from Urals Polytechnic sent flowers, get-well cards, and one caller a week. Yeltsin depicts the stay in *Confession on an Assigned Theme* as a fugue of obsessional self-analysis and indifference to normal temporal rhythms:

> It is hard to describe the state I was in. . . . I was analyzing every step I had ever taken, every word I had spoken, my principles, my views of the past, present, and future . . . day and night, day and night. . . . I summoned up the images of hundreds of people, friends, comrades, neighbors, and workmates. I reviewed my relationships with my wife, children, and grandchildren. I reviewed my beliefs. All that was left where my heart had been was a burnt-out cinder. Everything around me and within me was incinerated. Yes, it was a time of fierce struggle with myself. I knew that if I lost that fight, everything I had worked for in my life would be lost. . . . It was like the torments of hell. . . . I later heard gossip that I had contemplated suicide. . . . Although the position in which I found myself might drive someone to that simple way out, it was not in my character to give up.[1]

Confession was thrown together as a book in the fall of 1989, when Yeltsin was aiming for a political effect, and contains a certain amount of self-mythologization. There is some of that in this passage. From what I have heard from family members, however, Yeltsin's torments were not feigned. His dissociation from reality was a kind of "moratorium," as some psychoanalysts term it: a time away for cleansing and reorientation that in many cultures is reserved for the young.[2] It was necessary to Yeltsin's recovery, personal and political.

As Boris Yeltsin exorcized his private demons, his Central Committee gambit was having far-reaching reverberations in the public square. That a ranking politico had summarily fallen from grace was standard stuff for those who knew their Soviet history. But the synergy with reforming communism gave a new twist to this Icarus crash. In the game of transitional politics, the short-term loser had seized what a game theorist would categorize as a "first-mover" advantage. Just as the Soviet Union steamed off into the uncharted waters of democratization, Yeltsin had established a strategic edge that would outbalance the penalties levied on him.[3]

A Russian who read between the lines in *Pravda* on November 13, 1987, could have extracted six claims about the political situation:

Obstructed reforms. Change in Soviet communism was being thwarted by know-nothings in the nomenklatura. Real as opposed to rhetorical change was going at a snail's pace.

An impatient nation. Ordinary people's hopes had been raised and their patience was wearing thin. They were a constituency for a different course.

Gorbachev in the middle. The originator of perestroika was a gradualist who knew about the impediments to reform but was unwilling to dislodge them.

A radical alternative. A maverick, Yeltsin, had championed a speedier course. This marked him for payback by vested interests.

Not just talk. The bellwether of change was not a chatterer but a doer. He had street smarts. He knew from the inside how the wheels turned, in the provinces and in the Kremlin. Forgoing an influential post demonstrated his willingness to give something up for the common good.

Something to hide. The authorities had persecuted Yeltsin for puncturing the verities of the regime. Now they were muzzling him and were not putting out a complete account.

For Mikhail Gorbachev, the short-term victor, some of these claims were more easily countered than others. When students in the capital city passed around pro-Yeltsin petitions and marched in the streets, the uniformed and secret police kept watch on them. Several hundred demonstrators gathered on November 14 in downtown Sverdlovsk; on November 15 Yurii Petrov, Yeltsin's friend and the first secretary of the obkom, received a delegation and accepted a protest letter addressed to the Politburo. Afraid of rallies "in the guise of preparations for the New Year's holiday," the obkom would in December cordon off 1905 Square.[4]

The censors decreed a media blackout on these events, and Kremlin agitprop was able to circulate an airbrushed account of the affair. But word of the petitions and demonstrations, and rumors of what Yeltsin had said to the Central Committee, spread like wildfire through the Moscow political underground and the foreign media. One of the more cockeyed simulations of the speech was prepared by Mikhail Poltoranin of *Moskovskaya pravda.* He was about to be dismissed as editor, but before he was, the Secretariat directed him to speak to 700 personnel from the Soviet local press gathered in a Central Committee academy in Moscow. The newspapermen wanted to know what Yeltsin had actually said to the October plenum, which Poltoranin was not of the rank to have attended. In his apartment that night, he pecked out on his typewriter an apocryphal speech—the one he would have wanted Yeltsin to make. Knowing how unloved Raisa Gorbacheva was, he put into Yeltsin's mouth words about how she had telephoned him with peremptory instructions on party business. Poltoranin ran off several hundred copies and distributed them the next day without anyone stopping him.[5]

Gorbachev would have done well to release the transcript of the plenum. His more enlightened advisers held that declassification would confute the untruths being told about it and that news about Yeltsin's disjointed performance would be unflattering to him. To stonewall, they said, would put the nimbus of "a martyr for justice" around his head.[6] The original secret speech by Khrushchev, circulated in redacted form to party members in 1956, was not published in full in the USSR until 1989. Gorbachev moved more quickly than that, but not quickly enough. It took until March of 1989 for the plenum transcript to appear on the page.

Draconian measures against Yeltsin were not feasible at a time when Gorbachev was liberalizing the Soviet system. Criminal proceedings were out of the question. Yeltsin had parliamentary immunity as a member of the USSR Supreme Soviet. This never stopped Stalin's OGPU or NKVD, but for a deputy to be arrested in 1987, the Soviet would have had to vote to lift the exemption and spark a national and international furor.[7] And glasnost would have been no panacea. The unvarnished truth would only verify that in-house foes of reform existed, that Gorbachev was hugging the political center, and that Yeltsin had a more forward posture and was waylaid for it. And full disclosure of the context would have shown that Yeltsin's diagnosis of perestroika was onto something—that the Soviet economy and society were deteriorating. Petroleum production of the USSR had gone into decline in 1985, petrodollars from exports were sharply down (mostly due to a dropoff in world oil prices), and the finances of the government were under strain more than since the 1940s.[8] In the teeth of this, the firing of Yeltsin and even his penance, which most would have assumed was offered under duress, made him a magnet for popular discontent. "In the Russian tradition," as one former Soviet publicist was to write of him, "the aggrieved mutineer earns the sympathy and benevolence of the common people."[9]

The great Cossack mutineers of the seventeenth and eighteen centuries, Stenka Razin and Yemel'yan Pugachëv, paid for their impudence with their heads.[10] This twentieth-century mutineer kept his. The executioner's axe and the Gulag being unavailable, what was Gorbachev going to do with him?

If history were the touchstone, Gorbachev had little to worry about. As far back as the 1920s, the also-rans in personality and factional quarrels within the party had never recouped their losses. The renunciation of violence after Stalin left general secretaries with ample means for sidelining an opponent. Gorbachev made it plain to Yeltsin that he was ostracized from upper-level political activity. How the ban was expressed depends on whose memoir one reads. Yeltsin says it was permanent and general: "I will no longer let you take part in politics *[politika]*." Gorbachev writes in his *Life and Reforms* of saying to Yeltsin that he "could not return to the sphere of big-time politics *[sfera bol'shoi politiki]* any time soon," which connotes a door ajar.[11] Gorbachev might have wielded a much heavier truncheon than this. He could have pensioned Yeltsin off, a possibility that surfaced in irritable conversations between them in November 1987. Gorbachev did not want this solution. He wisecracked to Yeltsin that he was against retirement since, they being the same age, it might be thought appropriate for him as well.[12] Yeltsin was still a member of the CPSU Central Committee. Under the rulebook, only a congress of the party could expel him against his will, but Gorbachev was capable of forcing him to resign. In fact he did that to ninety-eight long-in-the-tooth members of the committee in April 1989, but not to Yeltsin. Another device forsworn was to make Yeltsin ambassador to a distant capital—as Nikita Khrushchev did in 1957 when he made Vyacheslav Molotov, who had been prime minister under Stalin, Soviet envoy to Outer Mongolia.[13] Yeltsin believed Gorbachev preferred to keep him in Moscow and in his sights: "He thought I was less of a risk nearby. It is always best to keep a free-thinker close at hand, so you can keep him under observation. And what would an ambassador be up to? Who knew?"[14]

So why the lenience? In his memoirs, Gorbachev credits it to his chivalry ("It is not in me to make short work of people") and collectivism ("the strong belief that with us everything had to be done on the basis of comradeship").[15] But it was not all about the kindliness of the general secretary. Yeltsin points to a more political theory, that Gorbachev wanted him to survive as a balance against conservatives and fence-sitters: "It seems to me that if Gorbachev had not had a Yeltsin he would have had to invent one."[16] Gorbachev's desire to use Yeltsin as a counterweight dovetailed with his reading of the past record, which was that no one in Yeltsin's unenviable predicament could pose a threat. To these, there needs to be added an attitudinal factor: cocksureness. Georgii Shakhnazarov, Gorbachev's main political aide, several times implored him to expatriate Yeltsin, to an ambassadorship, and absent him from the upcoming USSR elections. Gorbachev would not countenance it. "He regarded Yeltsin as semiliterate, as understanding nothing, as a drunkard." He sorely misjudged Yeltsin and, says the cerebral Shakhnazarov, refused to see that Yeltsin's personality, the festering grudge Yeltsin bore, and the pent-up appetite for change might commix into "an explosive force."[17]

Had the Soviet rules of the game still applied, Yeltsin's political career would have been well and truly over. But the game was in kaleidoscopic motion, and soon was to provide undreamt-of opportunities outside the iron cage of the bureaucracy. His intuition in 1987 about which way the wind was blowing, the action of speaking out before the Central Committee, and Gorbachev's overkill reaction to it constituted an inflection point in the breakup of the communist system. The juncture set up a robust alignment of political forces on the macro issue of how fast the system should change: Yeltsin in the van as the apotheosis of change, party conservatives in the rear, Gorbachev in the spongy middle. Successive crises and feedback loops were to fortify it even as the political spectrum was displaced in a more revolutionary direction. Originally limited to the elite, the fatal alignment would reproduce itself in the population when electoral freedom made it relevant to them, which in turn widened the fissures at the elite plateau. As one of the directors of Yeltsin's eventual campaign for president of Russia was to remark in 1991, "This campaign began in 1987."[18]

On November 19, 1987, a bulletin from the TASS news agency said Yeltsin had been appointed first deputy chairman of Gosstroi, the State Construction Committee of the Soviet Union. His blackest fears had gone unrealized. He was not to be banished to Ulan Bator or Addis Ababa, or to a muddy Soviet construction site, or to a cottage in Moscow oblast. The new position was a sinecure, on a rank with minister in the USSR government, and was at the summit of an industry Yeltsin had known since his twenties.

Licking his wounds, Yeltsin started work at Gosstroi on February 8, 1988. Once ejected from the Politburo, he kept the VIP flat on Second Tverskaya-Yamskaya but lost his bodyguards and was downgraded to a mid-sized Chaika limousine and a cramped dacha. Gosstroi was in a modern building on Pushkin Street, later to house the Federation Council, the upper house of the Russian parliament. Not what he was used to in space or conveniences, the office there was all he had.

The pressure on Yeltsin did not abate. The chief of Gosstroi, Yurii Batalin, a pipeline specialist and a Sverdlovsker with a UPI diploma, was under orders to report any wayward activity. The KGB eavesdropped on Yeltsin's phone calls; plainclothes officers lurked in the foyer to see who was visiting.[19] As he settled in, Yeltsin took lynx-eyed note of the surveillance: He would turn on the radio or pour water in the washbasin to muffle sensitive conversations. His first ever desk job bored him no end. He gave one visitor the impression that he was permanently stifling a scream.[20] He was to write a memorandum to Prime Minister Ryzhkov proposing that Gosstroi be done away with as a fifth wheel and its significant functions transferred to other agencies.[21] "My work with real, live people has been replaced by the office," was his plaint later that year. "I shuffle papers."[22]

Yeltsin was at sea psychologically for months. He took it hard when the February plenum of the Central Committee confirmed his demotion from the Politburo. His Gosstroi assistant, Lev Sukhanov, was stunned at his condition the next day: "When he got to work that morning, his face was vacant. It looked to me like the finale of a burial service staged by his Politburo colleagues. He suffered from all of this, but somehow found strength within himself and worked the entire day."[23] Yeltsin's memoirs painted his Gosstroi entr'acte as "a nightmarish year-and-a-half" and "perhaps the most difficult days of my life." All was "dead silence and emptiness" in the office. It was "torture" to watch his cream-colored Kremlin telephone in the hope of an expiatory call from Gorbachev. He felt like tearing it out of the wall, lest the appliance "spout new miseries" for him.[24] Dejected at work, and with time on his hands, Yeltsin took up the game of tennis in 1988 and bought with cash savings his first automobile, a tiny, silver-colored Moskvich. Aleksandr Korzhakov, a KGB bodyguard to Yeltsin when he was Moscow party boss, helped teach him how to drive the vehicle. Yeltsin was a poor pupil who often mistook brake for gas pedal. "It was after this that my hair began to go gray," Korzhakov says.[25]

Politically, until the elections for the Soviet parliament in the spring of 1989, Yeltsin was in a netherworld. He was banned from the Moscow media, and the only interviews he granted were to reporters from abroad and from the Baltic republics of the USSR. The chairman of the Party Control Commission, Mikhail Solomentsev, hauled him on the carpet in the spring of 1988 for contact with the foreign press. "He rudely cut me off," says Solomentsev, "and asserted that he had no need to ask anyone's permission, that he was a free man and had the right to give his opinion wherever he liked and to whomever he liked."[26] The interviews did subside for a spell. In May Yeltsin spoke with two Russian publications; the party Secretariat blocked publication. He then resumed interviews with the foreign media, going on the BBC in May and on the three American television networks in June.

The Nineteenth CPSU Conference in June–July 1988 was convened to showcase Gorbachevian political reform. Yeltsin, who could have sat in by right as a Central Committee member, held out for nomination by a territorial subunit of the party. Stymied in Moscow and in Sverdlovsk (where Gorbachev and Ligachëv had just made Leonid Bobykin, a competitor of Yeltsin's, the first secretary), he snagged a ticket from Kareliya, a minority republic of the RSFSR located on the Finnish border. As in October, he had to exert himself at the conference to speak. Two notes to Gorbachev, in the chair, did not do the trick. On the fifth and last morning of the conference, July 1, Yeltsin announced to the Karelian delegation, seated to the back of the mezzanine, that he was taking the floor by storm, "like the Winter Palace" falling to the Bolsheviks and the workers in 1917. He trooped to the foot of the dais and stood there, staring at the presidium and brandishing his red card. Looking daggers, Gorbachev had a staffer tell him he would be recognized if he sat down and waited his turn. Yeltsin did so and was given the floor.[27]

The gatecrashing paid off. To the 5,000 conferees, Yeltsin gave a feisty fifteen-minute speech that he had massaged for weeks. Excerpts were broadcast on Soviet television, and it was published in the press. It contained no jabs at Gorbachev and few words about Yegor Ligachëv, with whom he said he had tactical differences only. But his wad of accusations got larger, as he added the need for transparency in the party's finances and for a downsizing of the apparatus. Yeltsin was more recalcitrant than in 1987 on the issues of mass benefit from reform and the privileges of the well-fed Soviet elite. Perestroika had been configured "under the hypnosis of words" and had "not resolved any of the tangible, real problems of people"; to go on this way was to "risk losing grip on the steering wheel and on political stability." On elitist patterns, where he had previously limited himself to those counter to party norms, he now hacked away at the norms per se. Communists' monthly dues, he observed, paid for food packets for "the starving nomenklatura" and for "luxurious residences, dachas, and sanatoriums of such an amplitude that you are ashamed when the representatives of foreign parties visit." All political initiatives, said Yeltsin, ought to be discussed without preconceptions and put to national referendums. The CPSU general secretary, the Politburo, and party officers down the line should be elected by the rank-and-file, restricted to two terms in office, and retired at sixty-five.[28]

About October 1987, Yeltsin was obdurate. He demanded restitution, contrasting that to the posthumous amends being made to people purged by Stalin decades before:

> Comrade delegates, rehabilitation after fifty years has become the norm, and this has a healthy effect on our society. But I am requesting my political rehabilitation while I am alive. I consider this a question of principle. . . . You all know that my speech to the October plenum of the Central Committee was found to be "politically erroneous." But the questions I brought up at the plenum have since that time been raised repeatedly in the press and by communists. Here virtually all of these questions have sounded in the reports and speeches given from the tribune. I consider the only error in my presentation to have been that I spoke out at an inopportune time, right before the seventieth anniversary of October 1917. . . . We all have to master the rules of political discussion, to tolerate opponents, as Lenin did, and not rush to hang labels on them or to brand them heretics.

In one swoop, Yeltsin had publicly affiliated himself with diversification of the political system and justice for the ghosts of the Soviet past—and had tarred Gorbachev and those who laid him low in 1987 with intolerance and rigidity. As Vitalii Tret'yakov was to put it, "These two words, 'political rehabilitation,' intuitively found by Yeltsin, were a godsend—a wondrous public-relations move, we would say today, one that a thousand first-class political technologists and image makers would never have come up with."[29]

After Yeltsin left the stage, every second speaker roasted him. Most had been put up to it by Lev Zaikov and the Moscow party staff, who assumed that Yeltsin would find a way to get to the microphone. Ligachëv, whom some of Gorbachev's men tried to dissuade from speaking, was the most vituperative, maximizing their differences and saying he and Yeltsin diverged not only in tactics but in strategy. "Boris, you *[ty]* are wrong," he said in a concluding sentence that would be flung back in his face over the next two years. A Sverdlovsk delegate, Vladimir Volkov, the party secretary of the Kalinin missile plant, extolled Yeltsin and won applause for it. Gorbachev had wanted to concentrate on his leaderly agenda, but expended almost half of his conference encore on Yeltsin. "Here he has some kind of a complex," Anatolii Chernyayev entered in his diary.[30]

For the Yeltsin story, the striking thing about the conference was the entrenchment of the political cleavage opened up by his secret speech in October 1987. The party did not rehabilitate its freelancer. Beyond the crenellated Kremlin walls, Lev Sukhanov said, he had achieved "the popular acclaim any politician can only dream about."[31]

Yeltsin did not see it this way at first. He once again felt sorry for himself over the invective by Ligachëv and the conservatives: "A feeling of apathy washed over me. I did not want struggle, not explanations, not anything. All I wanted was to forget it all and be left in peace." The heartsickness lasted only a few weeks. He was cheered up by the thousands of letters and telegrams that arrived from all over the Soviet Union. The subject matter of most of them was not any particular political line but, says Yeltsin, compassion for him as having been mistreated. Through these communications from afar, people "stretched out their hands to me, and I was able to lean on them and get back on my feet."[32] Yeltsin's dislike of elite privilege did not keep him from leaving for vacation at a government rest house in Jurmala, Latvia. When he returned, citizens began showing up in droves to see him. Batalin had a reception area installed near the Gosstroi checkpoint where those not admitted to his office could write out questions for him.[33]

The new Yeltsin was sought after by other agents of change. In August 1988, for example, he agreed to join the supervisory board of the Memorial

Society, the new nongovernmental organization for promoting construction of a monument in Moscow to the millions imprisoned and murdered under Stalin. He was chosen for this honor on write-in ballots by readers of the newspaper *Literaturnaya gazeta* and the magazine *Ogonëk*. These publications were favorites of the Russian intelligentsia, with whom Yeltsin had few connections.[34] Yeltsin was also seeing how reporters and editors could be allies. Jonathan Sanders, a Moscow producer for CBS News, arranged several Yeltsin interviews and decided to buy him a red-striped Brooks Brothers necktie while on home leave in New York. He spotted Yeltsin walking down the Gosstroi steps, explained that he had to be punctilious about giving a politician a present, but handed him the tie anyway. Yeltsin put it on admiringly and wrapped his own tie around Sanders's neck, turning the scene into an exchange of tokens of respect.[35] An invitation by students to answer questions at the Higher Komsomol School on November 12, 1988, gave him further scope. Shortly after the session, Sukhanov found a counterfeit transcript of Yeltsin's remarks for sale on Arbat Street. "I showed him this 'commercial copy' and he asked, 'Why have we not made our own transcript?' A very good question. So he put his daughters Tanya and Lena to work and they typed up a tape of the session that Sasha Korzhakov had made." Twelve carbon copies were distributed through informal networks. Cooperative journalists used every trick in the book to get the text published. In the Perm youth paper, they got the editor to agree by giving it the title "Politician or Roughneck?"[36]

Yeltsin was increasingly willing to moor his critique in unblinking views of the Soviet past. Russians, he said to the Komsomol students, were submissive because they learned to be that way from "parasitic" party and state structures that monopolized power, hid behind a veil of secrecy, and taught individuals to make "a ritual of the bearing of sacrifices" at every turn. It all went back to a history in which one cannot help see the experience of the Urals and of the Yeltsin family: "First the people were forced to put on the altar an inhuman agricultural policy [collectivization], then they were required to give up such timeless values as spirituality and culture, and finally they were divested of the ability to define their goals self-reliantly *[samostoyatel'no]* and to go about attaining them self-reliantly."[37]

When the talk turned to remedies, Yeltsin was not a flaming militant. Besides his now faddish populism, the pillars of his approach were outspokenness, the need for reform to show results, and support for political competition and inclusiveness. His forté was not the clairvoyant pronouncement but the folksy verbalization of what many others were already thinking and had been subdued from saying in public. Yeltsin, as a Moscow academic was to say after one of his more plain-spoken statements, was giving voice to "what the people have freely talked about for ages" in their kitchens or at their dachas.[38] To put it in the more formal language of anthropology, he was a leader in the "discursive deconstruction" of the late Soviet system, taking apart meanings that were increasingly disconnected from reality.[39] On the economic and social front, he was for a cooling of the polemics and for brass-tacks improvements in living standards. Although he mentioned a few action steps, such as a hike in the output of consumer goods and building supplies to be funded by cuts to the construction and space budgets, he laid out no general conception of reform. At the Komsomol academy, he held his thoughts on it for his edification alone: "I have stuffed them far down in the archives, in a safe, so that no one sees them."[40] It was a subterfuge his enraptured listeners let him get away with. In a New Year's interview with newspaperman Pavel Voshchanov, who would be his press secretary in 1991–92, Yeltsin said he wanted to annul the "double privileges" built into the Soviet system, so that a ruble earned by a government minister would buy the same goods and services as a ruble earned by the janitor in the ministry's headquarters.[41] But this was more a design for redressing past abuses than for building a productive and equitable economy.

In the political realm, Yeltsin was for the liberalization of electoral laws enacted after the Nineteenth Conference and fought measures, such as Gorbachev's provision to have party secretaries chair local councils, that might adulterate the reform. What about the Communist Party and its "leading role"? At the conference in July, Yeltsin favored "socialist pluralism," Gorbachev's shorthand for heterogeneity within the ruling party, and came out against a system containing two socialist parties. By late 1988, he was telling his wife over the dinner table that *multi*party democracy, without limitations, was inescapable. Naina was quizzical: "I told him, 'Borya, what are you talking about? It is too early. Why say such a thing?' And he said, 'Well, you see, all this will come about, it will all come to this.'"[42] But at the Komsomol school Yeltsin dodged questions about the supremacy of the CPSU and made seven well-behaved references to Lenin. He was asked, since "your popularity with the people is not less" than Gorbachev's, "could you be head of the party and state?" Once there was full-fledged competition, Yeltsin answered demurely, "I may participate a little, as they say."[43] He was still denying advocacy of multipartism in mid-March 1989, right before the Soviet parliamentary elections, while calling for a discussion of its advisability.

Coyness about an overt challenge to Gorbachev fooled no one. Yeltsin had by this time traversed the threshold dividing dissidence, or criticism of those in power, from opposition, or activity aimed at gaining power.[44] And the general secretary could hear his footfall. "Indubitably," recalled Georgii Shakhnazarov, "Gorbachev saw in Yeltsin his principal rival for the future. Possessing a low opinion of [Yeltsin's] intellect and his other qualities, he feared not the person-to-person competition but the very fact of the appearance of a leader of the opposition."[45] Shakhnazarov did not share Gorbachev's complacency about Yeltsin and repeated the advice to send him to a cushy, faraway embassy and so keep him out of the 1989 national elections. Gorbachev turned a deaf ear.

One of the reasons Yeltsin accepted speaking engagements, and stood on the stage for hours, was to prove that he was out of his sickbed. Of the encounter at the Komsomol school, Sukhanov writes: "In speaking without a gap, he was able to exhibit that he was in good shape physically. He was rumored to be seriously ill, and he did not want to look impotent and pitiable."[46] The students asked how he had handled the slings and arrows of the past year. He answered in high testing mode and educed Russia's revolutionary past:

> In theory, after shocks like this I should be six feet under. But, the way it turned out, I slowly got over this moral blow, thanks to my athletic past, my good physical health, et cetera. Is this all too much for me? No, categorically no. So what is it with me? I am not the type to take the easier or more pleasing course, to go by the satiny paved road rather than the rough footpath. I believe, and this is no empty phrase, that public activity or any other work counts for immeasurably more than personal considerations. . . . Look at people like the revolutionaries who died or the Decembrists [organizers of a revolt against Tsar Nicholas I in 1825] who were exiled to Siberia. What about us? Have we lost the moral capacity for self-sacrifice? [When I was Moscow first secretary] I worked from eight A.M. to midnight. . . . At a time of reconstruction, for three years or so everyone should work to the limit and make sacrifices. Then we will pull together and perestroika will have been given a push.[47]

Under terms of the political reforms agreed to in 1987–88, Soviet parliamentary bodies were to be reshaped. A new USSR Congress of People's Deputies, with 2,250 members, was to be instituted. Two-thirds of its members were to be elected in territorial districts. One-third were to be chosen by the cartel of officially recognized and controlled associations. The CPSU filled its quota of 100 seats in a retrograde procedure: The Politburo nominated Gorbachev and ninety-nine others in a plenum of the party Central Committee on January 10, 1989, and a second plenum on March 16 approved all 100. As was barely noticed at the time, Boris Yeltsin in the January plenum cast the very *first* dissenting vote in the Central Committee, on any issue, since the 1920s by abstaining on support for the nomination of Yegor Ligachëv. In the vote on the nominations in March, he was one of seventy-eight committee members to vote against Ligachëv, and may have voted against other nominees of the in-group.[48]

As the party's bogeyman, Yeltsin had no chance at a protected spot. He could get into the congress only by standing in one of the 1,500 geographic districts. Gorbachev chewed over entering a district race but did not, out of fear that Yeltsin would run against him and beat him.[49] Gorbachev's self-doubt did not make the electoral Rubicon one that Yeltsin could cross lightly. Government ministers, unlike party workers, were barred from the congress. To take up a seat if elected, Yeltsin would have to leave the Gosstroi position. The congress would name a new, compact standing parliament from among its members—the old name, Supreme Soviet, stayed—and only those on the Soviet would draw salaries as legislators. If Yeltsin got into the 2,250-member congress and was not one of the 542 chosen for the Supreme Soviet, he would be without a livelihood. It did not stop him. Sentient that the decision had "ripened long ago," in mid-December 1988 he threw his hat in the ring.[50]

Scouting out nomination possibilities took Yeltsin two months. Papers were filed on his behalf in fifty localities, and on February 11 he was nominated as a native son in Berezniki, traveling there by a circuitous air route through Leningrad to throw CPSU monitors off. He related his embarrassment of riches to Anatolii Luk'yanov, the Central Committee secretary with whom he had shared a dacha in 1985. Yeltsin was duty-bound, Luk'yanov said, to leave the decision to the Politburo—to which Yeltsin snorted that this was "a conversation right out of the 1930s" that he would sooner forget.[51] His competitive juices raised, he took his chances by gunning for a seat in Moscow and not in the Urals. During the prescribed winnowing-down period, as the party organs tried to keep him off the ballot or shunt him to the boondocks, he pounded home his core message. "In Boris Yeltsin there is certainly more than an ounce of Huey Long," David Remnick of *The Washington Post* noted; he half-expected Yeltsin to break out in song on the Louisianan's motto, "Every Man a King." Remnick also saw a parallel with another American icon. "When [Yeltsin] stands in front of a television camera, he will sometimes stop in midsentence, comb his thick mane of white hair, smile ironically into the lens, and then continue. Muhammad Ali used to pull the same cocky move after an easy fight."[52] On February 22, 1989, following a twelve-hour nomination meeting, the local electoral commission registered Yeltsin in National-Territorial District No. 1, Moscow's at-large district—the most populous and the most visible in the country. He took his name off the Berezniki ballot.

A ragged troupe headed by Aleksandr Muzykantskii, a Gosstroi engineer and friend of Lev Sukhanov, ran the campaign. Several were to stick with Yeltsin afterward. Valerii Bortsov, a junior apparatchik in the south Russian city of Rostov, took the train to Moscow in January to offer his services. He got a meeting with Yeltsin, who decided to make him an unpaid assistant. At a rally in February, Yeltsin teasingly asked Valentina Lantseva, a *Pravda* correspondent from Kazakhstan who was carrying a basket of flowers she had bought for her husband's birthday, if they were for him. They struck up a conversation and exchanged telephone numbers. Three days later, she agreed to be his press spokesperson, also without pay.[53]

Yeltsin's campaign brochure, "Perestroika Will Bring Changes," came out on March 21, only five days before the vote. Yeltsin posters were pasted in apartment stairwells, on lampposts, and at public-transit stops. A committee of activists in nineteen factories and institutes spread the word at the workplace level.[54] Digging for the public-speaking skills honed in Sverdlovsk and the Moscow gorkom, Yeltsin darted across the city, giving several talks daily and answering reams of questions, town meeting–style. The crowds in parks, hockey arenas, and stadiums reached into the tens of thousands by the last week. Many fans wore sandwich-boards, had "Fight, Boris!" (*Boris', Boris!*) buttons on their lapels, or carried hand-lettered signs blaring "Hands Off of Yeltsin," "Boris Is Right," "We Are with You, Comrade Yeltsin," "Not the People for Socialism but Socialism for the People." Yeltsin lapped up the attention. His war cry was the "struggle for justice" and against moribund practices and privilege. Bill Keller of the *New York Times* caught the flavor of an open-air rally in front of 7,000 shivering urbanites:

> Mr. Yeltsin has a rapport with an audience that is rarely seen in Soviet politics and is a bit frightening even to some of his supporters. Today the crowd greeted him with an outpouring of protective emotion, warning him not to risk trouble by answering "provocative" questions passed up to

> him from the crowd, and at one point ordering him to put on his fur cap so he would not catch cold in the rising breeze. He did.
>
> He has turned the party's attacks on him to his advantage, using them to underline his underdog status and his bond with the common man. That is now part of Mr. Yeltsin's standard speech, along with populist demands that the bigshots give up their privileges, that the people be allowed to decide issues by referendum, and that the Communist Party be brought under the control of an elected government.[55]

All appearances concluded with Yeltsin clapping his hands, then clasping them in front of his forehead and wagging them in the direction of the audience.

Yeltsin's one opponent was the old-line director of the ZIL auto plant, Yevgenii Brakov; more than twenty potential candidates, including Politburo member Vitalii Vorotnikov, withdrew. Brakov made an ideal personal foil, but Yeltsin sanctimoniously refused to stoop to unsportsmanlike "American" methods. Planted questions—asking him to explain, for instance, the Ipat'ev House demolition in Sverdlovsk or how his daughter Yelena had been issued a nomenklatura apartment in 1987—caused him heartburn but were lost in the shuffle.[56] And the party's dirty tricks—defacing Yeltsin signs, cooking up pro-Brakov letters to *Moskovskaya pravda*, sending claques to Brakov rallies—backfired and played into his David-versus-Goliath image. In early March, the long-delayed publication in a CPSU journal of the record of the October 1987 plenum was manna from heaven. Vitalii Tret'yakov, who would eventually repent of his support, gushed that the transcript showed Yeltsin to be prescient ("he alone said yesterday what everyone is discussing now"), an information democrat ("the destroyer of secrets always ingratiates people"), and civic-minded (he "is not fighting for power for his own sake").[57] Ten days before the election, the Central Committee took the misguided decision to impanel a commission, chaired by Politburo member Vadim Medvedev, to see if Yeltsin had deviated from the Communist Party line. The three largest rallies of the race—and the largest public gatherings in Moscow since the 1917 revolution—were called to protest the commission, which was to be quietly dropped in May. Yeltsin gauged it and the ersatz letters to the editor (Lantseva showed many were counterfeit) to have fattened his vote total by 15 to 20 percentage points.

Other candidates hopped on the bandwagon. The thirty-five-year-old Sergei Stankevich, a historian specializing in the U.S. Congress who was in a neck-and-neck race in the Cherëmushkii area of Moscow, sent Yeltsin a telegram of endorsement and then photocopied it and used it as an advertisement for himself. Twenty-six other liberal candidates, mostly professors, scientists, and literati, did the same. Some distributed pictures of themselves shaking hands with Yeltsin. Stankevich, who had organized a pro-Yeltsin demonstration at a Moscow subway stop in November 1987, could not because he had never met him.[58] Across the city, "The main orienting points were opposition to all the bosses and support for everyone who was for Yeltsin. All candidates with a lower rank than their main opponents did everything they could to emphasize their ordinariness, almost as if it were a nobleman's title, and all who had the slightest basis for doing so played up their nearness to Yeltsin."[59]

Yeltsin glided home in District No. 1 with 89 percent of the popular vote on March 26—5,117,745 out of 5,736,470 votes cast, with little variation across districts. Since Moscow had 1.1 million CPSU members and Brakov's take was less than 400,000, Yeltsin netted the ballots of most of Moscow's *communists*, to say nothing of noncommunists. Even in neighborhoods peopled by high-ranking party workers and bureaucrats, Brakov did not rise above 30 percent.[60] Intimates of Gorbachev told the American ambassador, Jack Matlock, they had been sure Yeltsin would win but were "astonished by how much."[61] Yeltsin's personal absolution and his drubbing of the nomenklatura candidate stole headlines from the change in institutions and political process represented by the holding of a semifree election. Candidates who had put their names on the Stankevich telegram polled 20 percentage points more on average than candidates who did not. First Secretary Lev Zaikov, like Gorbachev, took election as part of the Central Committee hundred rather than try his chances in a Moscow district. Second Secretary Yurii Prokof'ev ran in a district and was trounced, with 13 percent of the votes; Valerii Saikin, the mayor, got 42 percent in his district and pulled out of the runoff that was required when no one had secured a majority in the first lap.

In a lucid election postmortem, Tret'yakov reported how Yeltsin's win made explicit every one of the implicit lessons of October–November 1987. People were connecting the dots:

> Many people identify with Yeltsin. He is a victim of the higher-ups. Who of us has not been in the same position? And he is being slighted for refusing to seek their approval. Who has not dreamt of doing this? The main thing is that he speaks with everyone, with those below and those above,

> in the same way and as an equal, breaking the hierarchical barriers that everyone, especially below, is sick of.

Even his detractors, Tret'yakov continued, "never tire of reiterating his positive features," and Yeltsin came across as "contradictory but likeable in a human way even in his gaffes and inconsistencies." Most important were the mass perceptions of the gravitas that accrued to Yeltsin from his background in the governing elite:

> A hallmark of the Yeltsin phenomenon is his relations with the apparatus. This phenomenon could have sprung up only inside the apparatus because until now the apparatus has been the real and stable part of power, and people need stability. But the stability and strength of officialdom annoy people and restrict their freedom. Therefore, their sympathies go to the one who shakes up this apparatus. However, so far any serious revamping of the apparatus *will be feasible only if it comes from someone who himself constitutes part of it and is thence a credible force.* The circle closes and the Yeltsin phenomenon moves in this circle. I am sure that, had Yeltsin run for the post of director of some research institute or factory, his success could not have been guaranteed. On March 26, 1989, Yeltsin was voted in by a lopsided majority not as "boss for the people" but as "boss for the bosses." The oneness in voting for Yeltsin is the people's retort to the apparatus for its high-handed omnipotence.

Tret'yakov prognosticated that the groundswell would persist as long as the regime showed itself incapable of making improvements. "Even Yeltsin's failures will be blamed not on him but on the [Soviet] administrative-command system and on his critics."[62]

Three days after gaining his seat, Yeltsin set out for a month-long vacation in Kislovodsk, in the North Caucasus. The decision removed him from the runoff stage, where some pro-reform nominees needed help. It struck some as eccentric. Aleksandr Muzykantskii also detected that Yeltsin wanted other players to make do without him for a time, and so to feel the need to approach him with offers of cooperation on his, the winner's, terms.[63] Back from Kislovodsk, Yeltsin orated at rallies in the Moscow suburb of Zelenograd and in front of the Luzhniki stadium.

From the first day of operations of the USSR Congress of People's Deputies, May 25, 1989, it was to be a little more than two years until the life-and-death crisis of the Soviet regime. Most of this caesura Yeltsin spent either in unproductive legislative activity or in campaigning for office. Time and initiative were on his side because he had the ace in the hole—people power—that other contestants did not have.

The congress's organizing parley, televised live, showed the difficulty of translating charisma into institutional influence. High on the docket was selection of a chairman of the Supreme Soviet. It would be the cardinal office in the Soviet state, and Gorbachev meant to have it. In a conversation with Yeltsin in mid-May about their plans, Gorbachev offered him a ministerial post; Yeltsin refused and said, "Everything will be decided by the congress." At a Politburo meeting days after that, Gorbachev instructed aides to offer Yeltsin the position of first deputy premier of the RSFSR and to craft an "intermediate response" to questions about Yeltsin's dependability.[64] The offer seems not to have been made. Yeltsin abstained on the motion at the May Central Committee plenum to nominate Gorbachev for the chairmanship—the only member to do so—and then declared he would vote for it in the congress because he was bound by party discipline. The Soviet Union, he said, was in a "revolutionary situation" which the party did not seem capable of facing.[65] At the congress, he behaved coquettishly. He said in his maiden speech on May 26 that he was jobless as of the day before and might possibly agree to "some kind of nomination." That night a Yeltsin representative consented to the urging of deputies from Sverdlovsk that his name be offered from the floor. Aleksandr Obolenskii, a little-known engineer from Leningrad, said he would do it—only to flipflop and nominate himself. Yeltsin distanced himself from the attempt, and 96 percent of the deputies voted on May 27 to elect Gorbachev.[66]

After this comedy of errors came a more pressing problem: Yeltsin having given up his Gosstroi post, unfriendly deputies blocked him from so much as a seat in the Supreme Soviet. Of the twelve deputies nominated for the RSFSR's eleven seats in the Council of Nationalities (the section of the Supreme Soviet for which Yeltsin was eligible), he finished dead last in the congressional voting, his 5 million popular votes notwithstanding. The day was saved by Gavriil Popov, the Moscow economic thinker whom Yeltsin had cold-shouldered in 1987. He sold Gorbachev on a resolution. Aleksei Kazannik, a jurist from Omsk, Siberia, freed up a seat for him, and the congress on May 29 approved. Gorbachev wanted a vote on whether Yeltsin would fill the vacancy. Kazannik would not budge on the package deal and received more than 100,000 congratulatory telegrams.[67] In his first speech to the congress on May 31, Yeltsin called for a yearly country-wide referendum on confidence in the chairman of parliament and for conversion of the Kremlin medical directorate into a service for mothers and children.

When the Supreme Soviet met in June, Yeltsin, with Gorbachev again in acquiescence, was made chairman of its committee on construction and architecture.[68] It was a dead end, Gorbachev seemed to think, and it tied Yeltsin to housekeeping matters more than to politics. Yeltsin did not disagree and invested little in the position. Its real utility was visibility and the midtown workspace and telephones put at the disposal of Lev Sukhanov, now his paid parliamentary assistant, and volunteers. Yeltsin said in October 1989 he was thinking of giving up the committee because it had no staff and pulled him into citizen petitions and bureaucratic red tape.[69] As lawmaker, he was listless. He introduced no bills and did not affect policy. He built his everyman image by signing himself out of the Kremlin health clinic and into City Polyclinic No. 5. Naina Yeltsina did her part by shopping in neighborhood grocery stores not reserved for the elite. Vladimir Mezentsev, a press aide to Yeltsin in 1989–90 and a critic ever since, had the sense that she did all her shopping in such places. "I was a bachelor at the time, and Naina Iosifovna constantly gave me advice on the shops where sausages would be available."[70] During his campaign for Russian president in 1991, Yeltsin was able to advertise that she "spends three to four hours a day chasing around shops, like all the other unfortunate Moscow women."[71]

What should not be missed in all this is that Yeltsin's year in the last Soviet parliament extended his horizons in more ways than one. The catalyst was the Interregional Deputies Group (MDG), the pioneering democratic caucus, with about 250 members, formed against Gorbachev's wishes on July 29–30, 1989. The conscience of the group was Andrei Sakharov, the erudite atomic physicist, advocate of human rights, and Nobel laureate who had been freed from house arrest in 1986; its arranger was Gavriil Popov.

During the spring campaign, Sakharov acceded to Yeltsin's request to stay out of District No. 1, but considered him to be "of a completely different [lesser] caliber than Gorbachev," and bumptious at that.[72] His attitude eased after the election, as he came to know Yeltsin and to see how much he had changed. "I don't understand how Yeltsin arrives at his decisions," Sakharov said to an American friend in the autumn, "but he usually arrives at the right answer."[73]

As formation of the Interregional group was being discussed, some of the founders wanted Yeltsin excluded as an ex-partocrat and a rabble rouser. Yeltsin wanted not just to join but to be sole *leader*. That was fine with Popov.

At the organizing meeting, in the Moscow Cinema House, he and a petroleum engineer from Orenburg named Vladislav Shapovalenko put forward Yeltsin as chairman. Sergei Stankevich said he could support Yeltsin if his position were open to review after one year. Yurii Boldyrev, an engineer elected in a district in Leningrad, led a countercharge: "If you want to create a centralized party, go right ahead and create one. I will not participate. We will not fall in behind a leader." Viktor Pal'm, an Estonian natural scientist, said choosing Yeltsin or anyone else as boss would be "a fatal mistake." Effective leaders "are not appointed or elected" but "come into being" in the course of solving collective problems. Pal'm proposed the designation of equal co-chairmen. Popov agreed, and five were elected: Yeltsin (first, with 144 votes), historian Yurii Afanas'ev (143 votes), Popov (132 votes), Pal'm (73 votes), and Sakharov (69 votes). Popov and Shapovalenko then tried to have one among the quintet made the "main" chairman, or to have the position rotate.[74] It was a fool's errand. Yeltsin, Afanas'ev stated, was "the second figure after Gorbachev on the country's political stage," but the Interregional group could not be a one-man band. The result was not pleasing to Yeltsin. "A USSR-wide opposition party or movement could at that time only have been a leader-centered one, and the only leader capable of heading it was Yeltsin. But the role the Interregionals were willing to assign, which was not even first among equals but equal to four other leaders, could not have been attractive to him. The MDG showed it was not prepared to be building material for a political organization that would smooth Yeltsin's road to power."[75]

For all his eagerness to lead them, Yeltsin's initial reaction to the Interregional luminaries as people had been one of culture shock. At the summer meetings, he "looked on them as something alien" and did not want to be photographed in their company.[76] The secretary of the group, the same Arkadii Murashov who cast the objecting vote in the Moscow council in 1987, says Yeltsin kept a sphinx-like silence in caucus and almost never spoke in the steering committee.[77] Nevertheless, as the only co-chairman to sit in the Supreme Soviet, Yeltsin represented the group's views in that body. More vitally, he metabolized heretical ideas—by osmosis and in exchanges brokered by Popov, Mikhail Poltoranin, and Murashov, all of whom stressed that interlocutors were never to take a professorial attitude toward him. Yurii Afanas'ev, the economist Nikolai Shmelëv, the aeronautics specialist Yurii Ryzhov, and the theater director Mark Zakharov were among those who found a common language with Yeltsin. Excited to be in out of the cold, Yeltsin awakened to the need to have a modicum of system and coherence in his thoughts.[78] He was playing with the kind of ideas it had once been his duty as a Communist Party boss to suffocate. What Popov and the Interregionals were now saying about the regime, and Yeltsin with them, was scarcely less damning of Soviet ways than what Yeltsin had execrated the political prisoner Valerian Morozov for saying in Sverdlovsk in 1983. One of Morozov's misdemeanors had been to go to Gorky in search of the castaway Sakharov, who now, a few years later, was in harness with deputy Yeltsin.

For Popov, the man from Sverdlovsk, warts and all, was the answer to a prayer. He personified the longing for change and had the reassuring quality of hailing from the ranks of the establishment. "We reconnoitered for a very long time, we picked them over. But here in fact was life throwing Yeltsin into our hands. *They themselves* kicked him out, they themselves made him a renegade."[79] Popov was sure Yeltsin would find a way around the queasiness of the intellectuals in the MDG. Any possibility of the saintly Sakharov becoming Russia's Václav Havel was extinguished when he died of a heart attack on December 14, 1989, at the age of sixty-eight. Yeltsin garnered respect by walking behind the bier in a sleet storm, speaking briefly at Luzhniki, and then going to the graveyard and to the funeral repast. The entente with Russia's Westernizers was contemporaneous with the fall of the Berlin Wall and of satellite regimes in Eastern Europe in the autumn of 1989. For the first time, Yeltsin's statements were emphasizing democracy and some species of market economy as facets of "de-monopolization."

The learning process was accelerated by a whirlwind tour of the United States from September 9 to 17, 1989, sponsored by the Esalen Foundation of California. In New York, Yeltsin did a walkabout in Manhattan, went to the top of the Empire State Building, helicoptered twice around the Statue of Liberty (he was "doubly free," he told Sukhanov), gave lectures at Columbia University and the Council on Foreign Relations and to Wall Street investors (wowing some and offending others),[80] and was interviewed on *Good Morning, America.* He spoke at Johns Hopkins in Baltimore, the World Affairs Council of Dallas, and the University of Miami, met corporate executives at several stops, wore a white ten-gallon hat in Texas, and stopped in on an Indiana hog farm, the Johnson Space Center, Ronald Reagan's hospital room at the Mayo Clinic, and a Florida beach house. Yeltsin had been to Western Europe as a representative of the CPSU; this was his first encounter with the United States and his first with any capitalist country as a private citizen.

Itching to establish international credentials, Yeltsin wangled an invitation to the White House office of President George H. W. Bush's national security adviser, Brent Scowcroft, with the promise of a "drop by" from the president. He had to enter by the West Basement entrance and was waspish with Scowcroft and Scowcroft's assistant, Condoleezza Rice. Yeltsin lightened up when Bush came by for fifteen minutes of small talk. Vice President Dan Quayle followed and liked him. "He may not have had Gorbachev's polish, but I could immediately see how confident he was." Quayle was taken that Yeltsin was well enough briefed to poke fun at the bad press the two of them had been receiving. "My feeling was mixed with a whit of annoyance: Was my press so bad that it made its way to everyone's attention?"[81] The Russian "emerged from the West Wing to tell the press corps that he had presented Bush and Quayle with a 'ten-point plan' to 'rescue perestroika.' Inside, Scowcroft complained that Yeltsin was 'devious' and a 'two-bit headline-grabber.'" James A. Baker formed a similar appraisal at the State Department.[82] For Yeltsin, it had been gainful exposure: Much to Gorbachev's chagrin, he had his foot in the door of official Washington.

Yeltsin was bowled over by the variance between what he saw, communist stereotypes of American life, and the dreariness of Soviet reality. He and his party felt almost like characters in a science fiction novel. "Don't forget," Sukhanov wrote about the tour, "that we were travelers from the 'anti-world' and in our heads the U.S.A. was the country where universal chaos reigned."[83] They did find some scenes that conformed to their expectations—the filth and overcrowding of the New York subway, for one—but many more that did not.[84] Yeltsin was most moved by the cornucopia at a Randalls discount supermarket in a suburb of Houston, which he asked to inspect when he saw it next to the expressway between the space center and Love Field. He went over its shelves—video taken by a member of the group shows him examining onions and potatoes under a sign "You Just Can't Buy It Better"—and to its bar-coded checkout stand, and was in disbelief when the manager said it inventoried "only" 30,000 products. Yeltsin's eyes were watery as he reboarded the bus. In the air between Houston and Miami, he remarked to Sukhanov that the grocery market for ordinary Americans, far better stocked than VIP dispensaries in Moscow, pointed up the fatuity of the "fairy tales" fed to his generation by Marxist-Leninist propaganda. "They had to deceive the population. . . . And now it is plain why Soviet citizens were not permitted to go abroad. They [the bosses] were afraid that their eyes would be opened."[85]

Sukhanov suspected that the exchange aboard the Miami-bound jet was when "the last prop of Yeltsin's Bolshevik consciousness decomposed," and with it the vestiges of his belief in the Soviet model.[86] Asked by a close associate in the 1990s what most turned him against the old system, Yeltsin said it was "America and its supermarkets."[87] Yeltsin records the scales falling off his eyes several weeks after the U.S. trip. Aides, seeing him disconsolate after the press skewered his U.S. tour, tried to lift his spirits by organizing a visit to a public steambath in a Moscow district. There were forty nude men in the sultry room, lathering one another on the back with water-soaked birch branches, to improve the circulation. "Hang in there, Boris Nikolayevich," they cried, "we are with you!" It was then and there, Yeltsin was to claim in *Notes of a President*, that "I changed my worldview" and came to the understanding "that I had been a communist by Soviet tradition, by inertia, and by upbringing, but not by conviction."[88]

If ever there was a eureka moment when Yeltsin separated himself from the Soviet state of mind, either the flight from Texas to Florida or the scene in the steambath might have been it. It is more cogent to visualize the shift, cognitive and affective, as cumulative and as taking months rather than hours. Rethinking communism and kissing it good-bye was one of those exercises in "innovative uncommon sense" that, as James MacGregor Burns writes, "transcends routine problem solving to address the deep human needs and crises from which it emerges."[89] It happened as the economy of the USSR, beginning in the winter of 1988–89, went from stagnation to recession. Lower production and excessive currency emission disordered consumer markets and made for empty shelves in the stores, longer lines, more squirreling away of consumer staples, barter, and by 1990 spot rationing.[90] Millions of citizens puzzled it all out in their own way. Gorbachev did, too, but always with a lag and clinging to the dying embers of the faith.[91]

Less attached to communism's ideology and more moved by its failures—more like the members of his children's generation than like his and Gorbachev's—Yeltsin passed through the stages of realignment during a liminal period lasting from the summer of 1989 to the summer of 1990. In a few years, he had gone from frowning at Soviet difficulties, to doubts about the system, and onward to assent in a new framework for society and politics.[92] He had not "become somebody else," he said when asked in January 1990 to compare his political position in 1990 with 1985–87. "But there has undoubtedly been a change [in me], a change leftward. . . . I am today disposed toward more radical change than at that time."[93] Reassessment of methods of rule escalated to reassessment of overarching goals and of the paradigm that framed them. In February 1990 Yeltsin would notify British writer Barbara Amiel that he now saw Lenin's division of world socialism into communist and social-democratic wings in 1919 as a tragedy, and that "in my heart I am really more of a social democrat" than a communist.[94] In January he was chosen to join the coordinating committee of the Democratic Platform in the CPSU, a ginger group that favored transmuting the Communist Party into a social-democratic movement—with a family resemblance to Labour in Britain or the German SPD—and institutionalization of jostling factions within it. It was a way station on Yeltsin's road out of the party. He was transiting from the Gorbachev-in-a-hurry he had been in 1986–87, to the Gorbachev-with-a-difference he was in 1988–89, to the forget-about-Gorbachev of 1990–91.

There were off-key notes as Yeltsin's political reputation grew. About one of them—purported to be a fatal car accident with him behind the wheel—we know only a claim made many years later by a far from neutral observer. Aleksandr Korzhakov, Yeltsin's former KGB bodyguard, had continued to see the family after November 1987 and after his discharge from the KGB's Ninth Directorate in February 1989.[95] He writes in the second edition of his memoirs, published in 2004, eight years after he became Yeltsin's mortal enemy, that at some point between May 1989 and the spring of 1990 Yeltsin drove his Moskvich into a two-seat motorcycle idling at sunrise on a country road near Korzhakov's dacha at the village of Molokovo, close by Moscow. Korzhakov had given him driving lessons and found him a slow learner. In the Molokovo accident, the motorbike passenger, Korzhakov claims, was injured and died a half year later without the authorities knowing about the accident and perhaps without Yeltsin himself knowing the man had died. Yeltsin, Korzhakov, and a companion, says Korzhakov, had been drinking at Korzhakov's dacha the previous evening.[96] Although a biographer is obliged to note the report, it is an unconvincing one, since Yeltsin was being tailed and wiretapped by KGB officers, and Gorbachev would have pounced on the mere suspicion of such an incident to crucify him politically. Korzhakov did not mention the event in the first edition of his memoirs, published in 1997, or in my interview with him in 2002, and it has been left out of other accounts written in the spirit of his book.[97] The presumption of innocence must remain with Yeltsin.

The U.S. junket caused Yeltsin more immediate pain. In Miami Beach, Dwayne Andreas of the food-industry conglomerate Archer Daniels Midland, one of the large companies to which Yeltsin was introduced, loaned him the waterfront property at the Sea View Hotel normally occupied by his two daughters. Yeltsin did not know this detail and threw a fit when he found women's lingerie in the bedroom drawers. Scared that American intelligence was trying to set him up with a call girl and blackmail him, he placed irate calls to his hosts. Robert S. Strauss, the Washington lawyer and political broker, had to spend an hour calming him by telephone.[98]

The greater blight was that Yeltsin attracted unpropitious publicity at several of his ports of call. The tour was originally scheduled for two weeks, but CPSU officials refused to give him an exit visa for more than eight days, since he needed to attend a Central Committee plenum on agricultural policy. James Garrison of Esalen compressed the program into the eight days, saying Yeltsin "would have to sleep less."[99] At Johns Hopkins University on September 12, jet lag, sleeping pills, and perhaps the aftereffects of evening-before libations left him the worse for wear. Sukhanov had to admit it was "not his most successful meeting."[100] *The Washington Post*'s Paul Hendrickson chronicled "Yeltsin's Smashing Day" and identified bourbon as the main source of the grief, which was an overstatement if not a falsehood. Hendrickson was a prize-winning feature writer; the *Post* did not think the Yeltsin story important enough to fly its Moscow bureau chief, David Remnick, in for it. Hendrickson would later be contrite about the piece, but the damage was done. On September 18, the day after Yeltsin landed back in Moscow, *Pravda* reprinted a five-day-old story by Vittorio Zucconi, the Washington correspondent of the Italian newspaper *la Repubblica,* portraying the voyage as one long orgy of shopping and drinking. It was a mishmash of a few facts and much fiction and innuendo. Videotape of the Johns Hopkins appearance shown on Soviet television appears to have been doctored to garble Yeltsin's words. His son-in-law Valerii Okulov delivered a letter from Yeltsin to *Pravda* denouncing the article as libelous. An outcry in Italy and Russia forced the paper to publish a retraction.[101] At the Central Committee plenum shortly afterward, Yeltsin accosted *Pravda* editor Viktor Afanas'ev for publishing the article. It was too bad, he said about their conversation, "that the time of duels has passed."[102]

Another barrage of flak was fairer to link to Yeltsin's behavior. About ten P.M. on September 28, 1989, he showed up drenched and bruised at the guardhouse of the Uspenskoye dacha compound for VIPs, on the Moskva River west of Moscow. He informed police that he had been forced to swim for his life after a carful of thugs waylaid him and dumped him off a bridge with a sack over his head. Yeltsin had been driven from a political rally in Ramenki, the Moscow neighborhood he represented in the city council, bearing two bouquets he took from the meeting, to the dacha of Sergei Bashilov, another construction bureaucrat from Sverdlovsk, with whom he was social. (He had known Bashilov, Yurii Batalin's predecessor as chairman of Gosstroi, since the 1960s.) Aleksandr Korzhakov, called in by the family, went to the guardhouse, gave Yeltsin a shot of vodka, and took him home. Yeltsin's purpose in going to Uspenskoye is unclear, as the Bashilovs were not home and their steaambath room was locked. Press speculation centered on a tryst, although there is no proof of that and womanizing is a charge his enemies have almost never aimed at him. Speaking the day after to the Soviet interior minister, Vadim Bakatin, he retracted his statement about a plot to drown him. Today Bakatin, in retirement, says Yeltsin was doused in a pond near the dacha (by whom or for what he will not say) and what ensued was a KGB caper to embarrass him.[103]

If that was the plan, it misfired. Bakatin and Gorbachev reported to the Supreme Soviet that the reasons for the incident were not known and that there had been no attempt to murder Yeltsin, and Yeltsin issued a statement fulminating at infringement on his "private life." Yeltsin called off several public appearances, and some of his amateur helpers, fearing he was losing his touch, had "nervous eruptions verging on frenzy."[104] But nerves calmed, and the uproar blew over. Korzhakov offered to be his full-time security man and chaperone, to prevent further misadventures. Yeltsin soon perked up and was back on track.[105] Greener pastures beckoned.

Chapter Eight

Birth of a Nation

Gorbachev's decision to begin political reform with his central government had a prodigious effect on the course of change. Because the society beneath was ever more restive—"moving to the left," as Yeltsin put it, using "left" to mean hunger for change rather than in the socialist-capitalist dimension—and because curbs on contestation were breaking down, the next wave of change, in the fifteen constituent republics of the Soviet Union and their provincial and local governments, was predestined to be more radical. Boris Yeltsin was checkmated at the USSR level. The Interregional Deputies Group was a minority in the Soviet congress, and he was not its unchallenged leader. With good reason, he felt he was in better sync than his adversaries, and even than his allies, with the times and with a popular constituency. Power and principle conjoined on a strategy of outflanking the general secretary and away from the moderation that had characterized Yeltsin's views when he first took up the reform banner. It was "a classic polarizing game" intended to box Gorbachev in "and to create the conditions for a decisive break with the old order."[1]

Several members of the 1989 campaign team wanted Yeltsin to catch the coming political wave in Moscow. There he would have taken control of city hall and revenge on the local party machine. Yeltsin decided to train his sights on Russia. It was against Soviet law to sit in more than two elected legislatures. Yeltsin thus had to choose between Moscow and the RSFSR, unless he wanted first to resign his seat in the USSR Supreme Soviet. It was not a hard choice. "This maximal program" of going for Russia, wrote Lev Sukhanov, "was more to Yeltsin's taste. He does not like to take the same track twice: monotony nauseates him."[2] The Russian Soviet Federative Socialist Republic was a much grander prize than Moscow. It accounted for half of the Soviet Union's population, two-thirds of its economy, and three-quarters of its landmass. The RSFSR Congress of People's Deputies was to be elected on March 4, 1990, under rules eased up from the USSR election: The filters for candidates were simplified, and there were no seats earmarked for the CPSU or other organizations.

Yeltsin sought nomination in his home province and was registered in District No. 74, comprising Sverdlovsk city and the industrial town of Pervoural'sk. His return to Sverdlovsk in the last days of January was front-page news, despite moves by the CPSU obkom, now headed by his old enemy Leonid Bobykin, to hush it up. "He met with electors in halls filled to bursting. Whenever possible, an audio feed onto the street was organized."[3] At one rally, three social scientists from the Urals Polytechnic Institute—Aleksandr Il'in, Gennadii Kharin, and Lyudmila Pikhoya—walked up to Yeltsin and told him his statement had been haphazard and he was too dependent on Q&A repartee. They offered to write a sample speech with greater thematic richness. Yeltsin liked the result and asked them to draft his candidate's program in February.[4]

For half of the campaign, Yeltsin was on the stump for candidates outside of Sverdlovsk oblast. The lion's share of them subscribed to Democratic Russia, a protoparty formed in January 1990 on the basis of the Interregional caucus, which listed nominees in several hundred urbanized districts. Yeltsin offered his signature on leaflets and posters, "creating a giant coattails effect from Boris Yeltsin on down to the city district level."[5] Russia was the only Soviet republic where the CPSU was without a committee, bureau, and first secretary. Reluctantly, Gorbachev in October 1989 reconstituted the Khrushchev-era Russian Bureau within the Central Committee apparatus. He accepted a Russian Communist Party only in the new year. It did not have its founding congress until June of 1990, three months after the election. So it was that the Communist Party was hit-or-miss in the RSFSR campaign and candidates who were members of it (as 70 percent were) were left to sink or swim. Vitalii Vorotnikov, the Politburo member who answered for the RSFSR, met with yawns when he tried to get Gorbachev to send heavy hitters into the fray. He offered his resignation to Gorbachev in January, and then agreed to stay through the election.[6]

The Yeltsin campaign offered a mélange of the familiar and the new. In pushing populism and calling for a blanket prohibition on nomenklatura privilege, he was aided by publication in February of the best-selling *Confession on an Assigned Theme*, with its purple prose about the lifestyles of the CPSU elite. It was widely quoted in the provincial press.[7] The new ingredients had to do mostly with the governance of Russia and its place in a reformed federal system. Here Yeltsin preached making the RSFSR over into a "presidential republic" with an elective president, a full-time parliament, a constitutional court, a state bank, an academy of sciences, a territorial militia, and multiple political parties. A democratic constitution adopted by referendum would enshrine these provisions as well as "the principle of the paramountcy of law" and freedoms of expression, assembly, association, and worship. The Soviet state, de jure federal but de facto unitary, ought to be decentralized, Yeltsin's program said, "because monopoly and the overcentralization of political and economic power have led our country to its present state." The heavy hand of Moscow stultified natural communities of interest as surely as dictatorship stultified political freedom and command planning stultified economic enterprise. "We have to give the maximum possible self-reliance [or self-rule—*samostoyatel'nost'*] to the republics," beginning with the RSFSR. "We have to see to it that we have strong republics, which should *decide themselves* what functions to give up to [the center] and which to keep for them."[8] The same held within Russia, where regions had to have more autonomy. Devolution, based on liberal, nonethnic Russian nationalism, augmented democratization and market reform as a third and equal strand in Yeltsin's de-monopolization project. How the wish would be made reality, or what would happen if the strands came into conflict or were internally inconsistent, was not specified.[9]

March 4 brought another electoral landslide. Yeltsin toted up 84 percent of the votes in his Sverdlovsk district against eleven no-name candidates. He told a journalist friend he would now "go only to Golgotha"—to a reckoning in some form with the old regime. The look on his face was both elated and fearful.[10]

Gorbachev hurried to prop up his position by carpentering a new institutional framework for governing the Soviet Union. In early February he had the party Central Committee approve a motion to repeal Article 6 of the 1977 Brezhnev constitution, which stipulated that the CPSU was the only legal party—"the leading and guiding force of Soviet society and the nucleus of its political system." It was an overdue concession to the opposition and to democratic principles. On March 13, 1990, the USSR congress approved the measure. At the same sitting, on March 14, it introduced a Soviet presidency, to which it elected Gorbachev on March 19. The change was an acknowledgment that the Communist Party, whose general secretary he remained, was no longer plausible as the sole basis for political authority. At the Politburo session of March 7, Anatolii Luk'yanov, who was to succeed Gorbachev as USSR parliamentary chairman, asked him why they were acting in such unseemly haste. "So as to put them [the republics and the Russian democrats] in their place," Gorbachev rejoined. Luk'yanov predicted, accurately, that the republics would counterpunch with presidencies of their own. He then brought up a deadlier point—about legitimacy. Why should Gorbachev be made president by the legislature and not by the whole people? "Why should the people not be the electors? This betokens mistrust of the people. All this will be exaggerated by [the opposition]." Gorbachev was unswayed, a blunder of biblical proportions.[11] Until June–July 1990, when Yeltsin streaked past him in the opinion polls, he would have won a general election.[12]

A couple of weeks after the election, Yeltsin, as Gorbachev noted with satisfaction at a Politburo meeting, requested and received a spa ticket from the Soviet parliament; he had notified Luk'yanov that he was worn to the bone and had to get away. The effort to make Yeltsin speaker of the RSFSR congress, which was to open in May, would have to begin without him.[13] Once he was back from vacation, however, Yeltsin worked methodically on getting the position and agreed to put off formation of the Russian presidency until 1991. On the question of chairing the legislature, about 40 percent of the deputies were pro-Yeltsin (in the USSR congress, only 10 to 15 percent by this time adhered to the Interregional group) and 40 percent were anti-Yeltsin; the rest were known as the "swamp." Hopeful of success, the Democratic Russia bloc nominated Yeltsin for the chair.

In camera, Nikolai Ryzhkov from Sverdlovsk, who was still Gorbachev's prime minister, had a foreboding at the Politburo meeting of March 22, 1990, of a domino effect if Yeltsin and his allies were to succeed in their quest: "If they take Russia, they need not try hard to destroy the [Soviet] Union and cast off the central leadership: party and legislative and governmental. In my view, once they have taken Russia, everything else, the entire federal superstructure, *will very quickly go to pieces*."[14] The inhabitants of what had been an impregnable castle were pressing the panic button, this at a time when many analysts still asserted that Russia could never be a threat to Soviet stability. Bootlessly, Ryzhkov pushed the Politburo to nominate and promote a reliable candidate for Russian parliamentary chairman. At the April 20 meeting of the Politburo, Gorbachev expressed incredulity at

Yeltsin's growing standing in Russian society. "What Yeltsin is doing is incomprehensible. . . . Every Monday his face doubles in size [due to his self-importance]. He speaks inarticulately, he often comes up with the devil knows what, he is like a worn-out record. But the people repeat over and over, 'He is our man!'"[15] Gorbachev could not understand why and could not bring himself to imitate Yeltsin.

On April 27 Yeltsin flew to London for a foreign diversion, the British book party for the English translation (as *Against the Grain*) of *Confession on an Assigned Theme*. Margaret Thatcher received him for forty-five minutes at 10 Downing Street. He tried to draw her out on a channel between the United Kingdom and "the new, free Russia" that would bypass the Soviet government. First, she replied suavely, Russia would need to be new and free in more than words. The Iron Lady had notified Gorbachev "to make it clear that I was receiving Mr Yeltsin in the way I would a Leader of the Opposition." She found her guest "far more my idea of the typical Russian than was Mr Gorbachev—tall, burly, square Slavic face and shock of white hair." He was sure-footed and mannerly, "with a smile full of good humour and a touch of self-mockery." What most struck her was that Yeltsin "had . . . thought through some of the fundamental problems much more clearly than had Mr Gorbachev" and, "unlike President Gorbachev, had broken out of the communist mindset and language." Thatcher shared her rave reviews with President Bush, who answered that "the Americans did not share them."[16]

Yeltsin left the next day to give a talk at a symposium in Córdoba, Spain. The six-passenger airplane chartered to take him from there to Barcelona ran into engine and electrical trouble and had to make a rough landing at the Córdoba airport. Yeltsin suffered a slipped disk and numbness in his legs and feet. He had three hours of spinal surgery in Barcelona on April 30. Within two days, he was on his feet; on May 5 he was in Moscow, met at the airport by a crowd chanting "Yeltsin for President!" Never one to baby an injury, he made it on May 7 to a pre-congress meeting of reform-minded deputies in Priozersk, a lakeside resort near Leningrad. He and Lev Sukhanov sat in a pavilion and downed a liter of Armenian brandy, his preferred drink at that time—before repairing to the main party for toasts.[17] If Yeltsin had been operated on in a Soviet hospital, he would have been bed-bound for weeks and might well have lost the contest for Russian parliamentary chief on that account.

Only on May 16 did Gorbachev nominate Aleksandr Vlasov, a lackluster apparatchik recently promoted to Vorotnikov's place as head of the RSFSR government, as congress chairman. Gorbachev spoke on Vlasov's behalf on May 23 and dropped the ball, packing his bags for a visit to Canada and the United States. He and the Central Committee men sent to twist the deputies' arms could not conceive of losing—"as Nicholas II might have thought on the eve of the revolution," to quote Georgii Shakhnazarov.[18] But, straw polls showing his support to be soft, Vlasov backed out and left Yeltsin to face Ivan Polozkov, a regional secretary from Krasnodar in the North Caucasus similar in mentality to Ligachëv—but to Gorbachev more appetizing than Yeltsin.

A lot was riding on Yeltsin's May 25 opening speech to the deputies. He and his team put the finishing touches on it past midnight. Discovering at daybreak that the ribbon from the office typewriter on which they had worked was missing, they were anxious that one of his opponents might read it and steal a march on Yeltsin, "and then there would be nothing for him to do on the podium."[19] It was a false alarm. Deputies made their way from the Rossiya Hotel to the Kremlin gates through lines of picketers bearing Yeltsin signs. In his self-introduction, Yeltsin conceded that attitudes toward him among the representatives ran the full gamut, and pledged "dialogue with various political forces" and give-and-take with Gorbachev. In the first round of voting, tabulated the morning of May 26, he polled 497 votes to Polozkov's 473. On May 27 he tiptoed up to 503 votes, Polozkov drooping to 458. On Tuesday, May 29, with Vlasov back in the game, Yeltsin sat breathless through a third round. He squeaked through with 535 votes, outpolling Vlasov by sixty-eight and landing exactly four more than the compulsory 50-percent-plus-one.[20] Gorbachev heard the ill tidings midway across the Atlantic to Ottawa. He said in retirement that he might have been better off egging the deputies on to vote for Yeltsin, which would have motivated contrarians to vote against him: "They wanted to show their independence."[21] Independence from established authority was indeed the zeitgeist in 1990, and Yeltsin was channeling it.

In the afterglow of his cliff-hanger victory, Yeltsin moved into the Russian White House, the spanking new granite-and-marble skyscraper for the RSFSR's legislature and executive on the Moskva River embankment, down a hill from the U.S. embassy. His cavernous office was on the fifth floor, with a private elevator, and had been occupied until then by Vitalii Vorotnikov. As parliamentary speaker, he got to form a small secretariat and to put on the payroll Aleksandr Korzhakov and irregulars from the provinces such as Valerii Bortsov, Valentina Lantseva, and the UPI speech writers, some of whom had lived out of suitcases and put themselves up in hotels, suburban hostels, and even railway stations.[22] He asked Viktor Ilyushin, an apparatchik from Sverdlovsk oblast who had also worked with him in the Moscow party committee, to head the group. Under the revised RSFSR constitution, Yeltsin was to nominate candidates for head of government. On June 15, 1990, Ivan Silayev, formerly one of Ryzhkov's deputy premiers and before that the head of the Soviet aviation industry, was confirmed as the first of his prime ministers. He and Yeltsin nominated ministers for the cabinet and secured parliamentary confirmation for them. Mikhail Bocharov, Yeltsin's deputy in the USSR legislative committee and the point man for his election as chairman of the Russian parliament, had been led to believe the job would be his. Bocharov had been an active member of the Interregional group and finished sixth in the contest to elect its five co-chairmen. He was the principal liaison between Democratic Russia and the first session of the Russian congress, applying himself to this work while Yeltsin was out of Moscow on vacation. He says Yeltsin at first invited him to be prime minister, but was miffed when he drew up a list of cabinet members. Bocharov adds that at one point Yeltsin suggested that he himself become prime minister and Bocharov chair the parliament. Bocharov turned into a caustic critic, the first of many office seekers to become embittered.[23]

The triumph, and the conservative drift within the party, also affected Yeltsin's withdrawal from the communist fraternity. The Russian Communist Party elected Polozkov—the paleo-communist out of central casting—its first secretary on June 19. Yeltsin's man Oleg Lobov, a political centrist, finished second in the balloting. Lobov, who had moved from Sverdlovsk to Moscow in 1987, had been sent to Armenia in 1989 as CPSU second secretary and was not an official delegate to the Russian party congress. Had he been better prepared and won, Yeltsin might have tried to work out an accommodation.[24] Yeltsin had indicated that if chosen as leader of the Russian congress he would ensure evenhandedness by quitting the party or putting his membership in abeyance. At the Twenty-Eighth CPSU Congress in early July, he called for the party's conversion into a Party of Democratic Socialism or Union of Democratic Forces that would take its place in a multiparty democracy. Yeltsin wagged a finger at those unable to part with the "apparatus party" of yesteryear: "Let those who would think of any other variant look at the fate of the communist parties of the countries of Eastern

Europe. They cut themselves off from the people, misunderstood their role, and found themselves left behind."[25]

Gorbachev would not take the bait. Expecting deadlock, Yeltsin had bargained with Gavriil Popov and the Moscow liberals over a collective going-away letter—in the woods outside Popov's dacha, to block KGB snooping.[26] But as usual he did things his way. He "wore out his speech writers" in drafting and redrafting his remarks and went over "all the details of the definitive moment—how he would mount the rostrum, how he would leave the hall after his statement, which doorway he would use."[27] On July 12 he asked Gorbachev to let him speak and then said to the hall that he was leaving the party. The umbilical cord was snipped after twenty-nine years. "Taking into account our transition to a multiparty society," he said, "I cannot carry out only the decisions of the CPSU."[28] He then stalked up the center aisle of the Kremlin Palace of Congresses, guffaws and whistles resounding in his ears. Soviet television broadcast the congress with a delay. When his statement began to play, Yeltsin came out of his White Office study into the corridor to watch the only large-screen set in the building. "His face was strained. He noticed no thing or person. . . . All that was important to him was to see himself from the side. As soon as the picture changed, he walked noiselessly to his desk—looking at no one, greeting no one, saying good-bye to no one. No doubt about it, this was one of the turning points of his life."[29] Yeltsin seems to have left his party card at the meeting hall. Family members did not see it again, and, unlike his Soviet-period medals, which he kept, it was not found with his personal effects in 2007.[30]

That evening Gorbachev's guru, Anatolii Chernyayev, wrote a note to Gorbachev about Yeltsin's "musical moment." "You pulled teeth so as to keep the position of general secretary of the party. Yeltsin spit in its [the party's] face and went to do what it was up to you to do."[31] Later in the congress, those leaders most at odds with Yeltsin—Yegor Ligachëv, Nikolai Ryzhkov, Vitalii Vorotnikov, and Lev Zaikov, who in 1988 had proclaimed the Yeltsin epoch to be over—were taken off the Politburo. The party as such would linger another thirteen months.

The Gorbachev group's take on Yeltsin's Russianism was that it was a smoke screen for his power-seeking. "All at once," party secretary Vadim Medvedev said acridly to the Politburo in May, "he has become a Russian patriot, although he never gave a thought to Russia until now. This . . . is a dishonorable political game." "Why is Yeltsin picking up this question?" Gorbachev

The house Yeltsin's paternal grandfather, Ignatii, built in the village of Basmanovo around 1900. The home of his uncle Ivan is in the rear. His father, Nikolai's, house was across the lane but no longer stands.

The small cottage in Butka in which Yeltsin was born in 1931.

The workers' barracks in Berezniki where Yeltsin and his immediate family occupied a single room from 1938 to 1944. (YELTSIN FAMILY ARCHIVE.)

Vasilii and Afanasiya Starygin, Yeltsin's maternal grandparents, in a 1950s photo. (YELTSIN FAMILY ARCHIVE.)

Boris with parents Klavdiya and Nikolai and brother Mikhail in Berezniki, 1939. (YELTSIN FAMILY ARCHIVE.)

Railway School No. 95, where Yeltsin was a pupil from 1939 to 1945. (YELTSIN FAMILY ARCHIVE.)

The Pushkin School, which Yeltsin attended from 1945 to 1949. (YELTSIN FAMILY ARCHIVE.)

Yeltsin as a ninth grader, 1948.
(YELTSIN FAMILY ARCHIVE.)

Creatively eating buckwheat porridge with a friend at the Urals Polytechnic Institute in the early 1950s. (YELTSIN FAMILY ARCHIVE.)

Airborne (on the left) on the volleyball court at UPI, 1953.
(SERGEI SKROBOV.)

Yeltsin (fourth row, third from left) in his student group at UPI, 1953.
(SERGEI SKROBOV.)

Boris and Naina Yeltsin, early 1960s. (YELTSIN FAMILY ARCHIVE.)

The Yeltsin daughters in 1965; Yelena (left) was about seven, Tatyana five. (YELTSIN FAMILY ARCHIVE.)

Reviewing a document as one of the secretaries of the Sverdlovsk obkom (regional committee of the Communist Party), 1975 or 1976. Yakov Ryabov, Yeltsin's mentor, is second from left. Vladimir Dolgikh, a Central Committee secretary, is third from left. (YELTSIN FAMILY ARCHIVE.)

Taking charge at a construction site as obkom first secretary, around 1980. Yurii Petrov, who later headed Yeltsin's presidential office, is third from left. Oleg Lobov, who also served in high positions in the 1990s, is second from right, foreground. (YELTSIN FAMILY ARCHIVE.)

Tending to the harvest, around 1980. Anatolii Mekhrentsev, chairman of the provincial government, is third from left. (YELTSIN FAMILY ARCHIVE.)

Discussing city planning issues in Sverdlovsk, around 1980. (YELTSIN FAMILY ARCHIVE.)

At an exercise of the Urals Military District, around 1980. (YELTSIN FAMILY ARCHIVE.)

With Politburo colleagues at a session of the USSR Supreme Soviet, November 1986. First row, left to right: Yegor Ligachëv, Nikolai Ryzhkov, Andrei Gromyko, Mikhail Gorbachev. Second row: Vitalii Vorotnikov, Lev Zaikov, Mikhail Solomentsev. Third row: Vladimir Dolgikh, Yeltsin, Eduard Shevardnadze. (RIA-Novosti/S. Guneyeva.)

As Moscow Communist Party leader, with constituents from the district he represented in the city council, June 1987. (RIA-Novosti/ A. Petrushchenko.)

Orating at Luzhniki stadium, May 21, 1989. Gavriil Popov is first from left; Andrei Sakharov is second from right. (RIA-Novosti/ I. Mikhaleva.)

Speaking to the Interregional Deputies Group, December 1989, with co-chairmen (left to right) Andrei Sakharov, Yurii Afanas'ev, Gavriil Popov, Viktor Pal'm. (RIA-NOVOSTI/ V. CHISTYAKOVA.)

Leaving the hall after announcing his resignation from the Communist Party to the party congress, July 12, 1990. (RIA-NOVOSTI/V. BABANOVA.)

Before a large gathering in Novokuznetsk, May 1, 1991. (RIA-NOVOSTI/D. KOROBEINIKOVA.)

Yeltsin's first prime minister, Ivan Silayev, 1991. (AP IMAGES/CARL DUYCK.)

Atop Tank No. 110 during the attempted coup, August 19, 1991. Aleksandr Korzhakov is next to Yeltsin on the machine. (AP Images/ Boris Yurchenko.)

Deflating Gorbachev's authority before the Russian Supreme Soviet, August 23, 1991. (AP Images/ Boris Yurchenko.)

Signing the Belovezh'e Forest accord, December 8, 1991. Gennadii Burbulis (far right) co-signs for Russia. Leonid Kravchuk of Ukraine (second from left) and Stanislav Shushkevich of Belarus (third from left) are also signatories. (RIA-Novosti.)

inquired at the same session. "He is picking it up in order to play games. [He wants] to use it to make his way to power in Russia, and through Russia to blow up the CPSU and the country."[32]

Although expediency was a factor, it did not make Yeltsin a political mad bomber and it was not nearly the whole story. Yeltsin was no neophyte to Russia-firstism. In Sverdlovsk he had discoursed on Russia as ugly stepchild of the Soviet Union and dreamed up paper schemes for giving it status and devolving some powers to its regions. While Russian rights had not been his priority before the 1990 election, in his first speech to the USSR congress in May 1989 he had advocated "territorial sovereignty" and "economic and financial self-reliance" for all Soviet republics, specifically endorsing a proposal from the Baltic republic of Latvia.[33] By now, although the potshots from Medvedev and Gorbachev tried to obfuscate it, Russianist sentiment was quite widespread in the RSFSR elite. Partly it was contagion from nationalist movements in the Baltic and elsewhere and partly it pushed back against the Soviet congress's decision on April 26, 1990, to put on a legal par with the fifteen "union" republics of the USSR the thirty-odd "autonomous" republics, the ethnic homelands implanted within the union republics, most of which were within Russia. "No other action could have so dramatized Yeltsin's claim that the center ignored and repressed Russia and that Russia needed a strong leader and the right to abrogate USSR laws on Russian territory."[34] The clarion statement on the part of the RSFSR was its congress's declaration on June 12, 1990, of Russia's "sovereignty" *(suverenitet)*, meaning national self-determination, territorial integrity, and, once a new Soviet constitution or federative agreement was in place, the primacy of its laws over federal legislation.[35] Indicative of the breadth of feeling, the motion was first made by Vorotnikov and the communists and went through in a one-sided roll call (907 yeas, thirteen nays, nine abstentions). Yeltsin remembered the vote and the ear-splitting ovation as the acme of all his years in Moscow. "For me and for everyone . . . in the hall, this was a moment of rejoicing."[36] The genie was out of the bottle. Six union republics, starting with Estonia in November 1988, had adopted such a manifesto, and the remainder were to do so later in 1990 (Kirgiziya or Kyrgyzstan in Central Asia was the last, in December).

The opening of the RSFSR's books was salt on the wounds of Russian rancor over the economic terms of Soviet federalism. Prime Minister Silayev persuaded himself that the center had for seven decades been robbing Russia blind. He was scandalized to find that the RSFSR subsidized the federal budget to the tune of 46 billion rubles (about $30 billion at the official exchange rate). With Yeltsin's backing, he tried to pare the figure in the 1991 budget to 10 billion rubles and to pass that sum to sister republics through an RSFSR-controlled account and collect some of what was owing in kind as consumer goods.[37] As talk grew of market pricing, Russia's mammoth reserves of hydrocarbons and minerals looked increasingly like a pot of gold to be protected from the center and from poorer Soviet republics. And Yeltsin voiced sympathy with the labor movement that had taken shape in Russian and Ukrainian heavy industry in 1989 and gone on strike in favor of workers' control over productive assets.

Crisscrossing the regions of Russia for three weeks in August 1990—flying on scheduled Aeroflot flights—Yeltsin was in tip-top populist form. In Sterlitamak, Bashkiriya, in the southern Urals, an invitation-only audience gathered in the House of Culture of the Caustic Soda Works:

> Watching Yeltsin's chemistry with a crowd, it is easy to see why local officials are eager to grab his coattails. . . . Yeltsin had just begun his remarks when an aide interrupted to tell him that the outdoor loudspeakers were not working and that the thousands of people gathered in the square outside were getting restless.
>
> A few minutes later, Yeltsin left the elite stewing in the stuffy auditorium and squeezed through a window onto a low rooftop. The reception was thunderous. He doffed his suit coat and mugged for the delighted crowd until technicians could run a microphone out to him.
>
> "Well, I think this event could have been better organized," he teased, with a glance back at his embarrassed hosts.[38]

At several stops, Yeltsin was mobbed by well-wishers and had to step onto a streetcar or truck bed to get out of the press of people. In the hamlet of Raifa outside Kazan, Tatariya, where he had lived for five years before the war, he went for a half-hour swim in the local lake and then donated his striped swimsuit to his hosts, who made it the centerpiece of "one of the main legends of the village," brought out for discussion once a year.[39]

In the minority homelands, Yeltsin catered to the anti-Moscow mood. If he were a Tatar, he told writers in Kazan, he would be going after "the self-sufficiency of the Tatar republic." At Kazan State University on August 5, where he was met with pickets who bore signs reading *Azatlyk* (Freedom, in the Tatar language), he put forth his famous summons to the Tatars to "take as much sovereignty as you can swallow." In Ufa, the capital of Bashkiriya, he rephrased the call: "We say to the Bashkir people: 'You take the share of power which you yourselves can swallow!'"[40] The catchy phrase was minted by his new adviser on nationality questions, the ethnographer and sociologist Galina Starovoitova. It corresponded with Yeltsin's take on the issue, and he unsheathed it to great effect. On the same expedition, he deplored the cost to Russians of the USSR as a superpower. "Charity begins at home," he declared, "and Russia will not help other states" or keep up the Soviet Union's defense, space, and foreign-aid budgets.[41]

Russia-USSR tensions were taken to the boiling point in 1990–91 not by this or that issue but by the intertwining of all the main issues dividing them. For the insurgent Yeltsin, devolution of power was a precondition of pursuing political and economic reform. He meant to become Russia's first elected head of state and up the pace of economic change, toward a terminus he now would not put in the Marxist compartments: "I think you find in the real world neither the capitalism about which the classics spoke nor the socialism about which they spoke. . . . I am not for socialism for the sake of socialism. I am for the people living better."[42] The prelude to market reform would be an anti-crisis package to counter shortages and hoarding. And Russia would need to be paid a fair price by Soviet and foreign purchasers for its fuels and raw materials. Only self-direction would permit his government to take this route.

Gorbachev was more emphatic than Yeltsin in commingling devolution, politics, and economics. The play for sovereignty, he charged in May 1990, was a design for killing state socialism (communism) as an ideology and social model. "It contains an attempt to excommunicate Russia from socialism. . . . The program's author . . . wants to invite us with one stroke of the pen to say farewell to the socialist choice we made in 1917."[43] In defending the central power, Gorbachev saw himself as carrying on sacrosanct Soviet beliefs as much as constitutional stability.

Did this all make for an ineluctable collision between the two? High-level actors feared it did and tried to talk Gorbachev into co-opting Yeltsin by offering him a plum political position. Aleksandr Yakovlev and Georgii Shakhnazarov—who had earlier begged Gorbachev to send Yeltsin abroad—lobbied him after the Russian election to make Yeltsin vice president of the USSR. Gorbachev demurred, saying Yeltsin's ambitiousness was too insatiable for him ever to accept.[44] In December 1990 he handed the post to Gennadii Yanayev, a former Komsomol official whom he said he could trust; Yanayev would be one of the leaders of the plot to depose him in August

1991. While Yeltsin would have turned down the vice presidency—it would lower him to "personal assistant to Gorbachev," he said in an interview—he would have considered the meatier job of prime minister if it had been offered in 1989. Once he was RSFSR leader, it was out of the question.[45]

Common ground was more likely to be found on policy than on the allocation of positions. Yeltsin's ideas about economic and socioeconomic change continued to be sketchy. For some months in 1990, he backed a wacky plan, put forward by economic counselors Igor Nit and Pavel Medvedev, for motivating workers through the emission of a counter-currency they termed "red money." Implementation in the agrarian sector divided the Silayev cabinet, and a more presentable alternative came up. The Five Hundred Days Program for economic reform furnished the last best chance for collaboration with the center. Drawn up between February and August of 1990 by a group of economists headed by Stanislav Shatalin and Yevgenii Yasin of Gorbachev's camp and Grigorii Yavlinskii of Yeltsin's, it called on Russia and the Soviet Union to move decisively to market harmonization of economic activity. In the space of a year and a half, it would have nullified most price controls, made a start on privatization of property (for which it used the euphemism "destatization"), scrapped the USSR's industrial ministries, and relegated regulatory and overhead functions to an "interrepublic economic committee," after agreement on a "treaty of economic union." The project, Yeltsin assured crowds in the Volga basin and the Urals in August, would stabilize the economy in two years and lead to growth and improved consumer welfare in the third year. The Russian Supreme Soviet passed on it on September 11, at which point Gorbachev got cold feet. On October 16 he abandoned Five Hundred Days, saying it would emasculate the federal government. Yeltsin declared Russia would have to make reform on its own, which Kremlin conservatives took as evidence that it was impossible ever to cooperate with him.[46] Yavlinskii left his position as deputy premier of the RSFSR in frustration with Gorbachev but also with Yeltsin. Yeltsin was to vow in a private aside to Yelena Bonner, Andrei Sakharov's widow, that "I will not play the dupe *[durachkom ne budu]* the next time."[47]

Gorbachev's backpedaling bore on more than economics. He bit off extra powers for his executive presidency, promoted hard-liners to positions such as prime minister (where he replaced Ryzhkov with the Soviet finance minister, Valentin Pavlov), and made spasmodic use of troops against nationalist unrest in the Baltic and Caucasus areas. In the consultations on a new "union treaty" for the Soviet federation, the necessity for which he announced on June 11, 1990, the day before the Russian sovereignty declaration, Gorbachev ceded nothing to the republics.

In November 1990 Yeltsin visited Kiev, the capital of Ukraine, the second-ranking Soviet republic, where he addressed its parliament and dealt with Ukrainian officials as equals. He signed a ten-year cooperation treaty with his counterpart, Leonid Kravchuk, on November 19. It recognized existing borders, which gave weight to Ukraine's claim to Crimea, the idyllic peninsula in the Black Sea, populated chiefly by Russian speakers and home to the Black Sea Fleet, arbitrarily shifted from the RSFSR to the Ukrainian republic by Nikita Khrushchev in 1954. Yeltsin, said a leading nationalist, Vyacheslav Chornovil, had "injected a very constructive note" by holding out the prospect of greater Ukrainian autonomy from Moscow without severing ties with Russia.[48] A month later, Yeltsin's Russia and Kravchuk's Ukraine, with Belarus (Belorussia) and Kazakhstan (the fifth- and fourth-ranking republics, Uzbekistan being the third), formed a "council of four" to work on a bottom-up treaty as a counter to Gorbachev's. In January 1991 the Soviet military put on a show of force in Lithuania and Latvia, slaying twenty people in firefights at a television tower in Vilnius and an office building in Riga. In fear of a crackdown that would be lethal to democratization, Yeltsin called down hellfire on it and issued an appeal to Russian soldiers in the Baltic garrisons not to take "a wrong step." Anatolii Chernyayev, in a draft letter he kept to himself, reproached Gorbachev: "You started the process of returning the country to civilization, but it has come up against your line on the 'unified and indivisible [USSR].' You have said many times to me and other comrades of yours that the Russians will never forgive anyone for 'breaking up the empire.' But here is Yeltsin insolently doing it in Russia's name, and very few Russians are protesting."[49] On February 19 Yeltsin issued his first call for Gorbachev to resign. Gorbachev assured his assistants that "Yeltsin's song has been sung" and time was working against him.[50]

A related topic was Russia's right to act in world affairs. U.S. Secretary of State James Baker was in Moscow on March 14–16, 1991, and refused to meet with Yeltsin privately; Yeltsin then refused to come to the embassy dinner party. Ambassador Matlock thought his handling of Baker "petty and self-defeating."[51] In mid-April he got a chilly reception at the European Parliament in Strasbourg, leaving after several days of snubs, and was unable to get President François Mitterrand to meet with him at the Élysée Palace.[52] After France, he tried again in the United States. Through Ambassador Jack Matlock, he stated his wish to visit Washington a second time and be guaranteed that he would be properly received by the president. He went shortly before his swearing in as Russian president, but at the bipartisan invitation of Senators Robert Dole and George Mitchell, not of George Bush. Hosting Yeltsin in the Rose Garden on June 20, Bush stressed relations with the Soviet government and mentioned Gorbachev's name more often than Yeltsin's. Strasbourg and Washington were both reminders "that the West only had eyes for Gorbachev."[53]

Or at least most of those in authority in the West did. Margaret Thatcher had been an admirer since their meeting, and John Major, her replacement, took a like view. They were joined by Richard Nixon, the thirty-seventh president of the United States. Nixon went to Moscow right after Baker and paid a call on Yeltsin. Yeltsin had been misinformed by staff members about the family history of his guest and held forth about Nixon's grandfather having lived for a time in Yekaterinburg. Nixon's grandfathers had never traveled outside the United States; he listened without comment, and they moved on to the current political situation.[54] Nixon, who had traded observations about the future of communism and capitalism with Nikita Khrushchev in the celebrated Kitchen Debate of July 1959, liked what he saw and heard in 1991. The Russia trip had held but one surprise, he told an assistant back in New Jersey. "What was that?" she asked:

> He pointed a finger in the air. "One word. Yeltsin."
>
> Several long moments went by before he continued. "Goddamn the press! If you listen to them, you'd think Yeltsin was an incompetent, disloyal boob. The only reason the press have treated him as badly as they have is because he has some rough edges. He doesn't have the grace and ivory-tower polish of Gorbachev." Nixon shuddered with self-recognition. "He moves and inspires the people despite what the Western press says about him."
>
> Yeltsin's defiance fed into his own. "The guy has enormous political appeal. He has the potential to be a great revolutionary leader, charging up the people, his own Silent Majority," he said, making the parallel explicit. "He is very direct. He looks you straight in the eye. He has core convictions that no longer involve communism. He is infinitely better for the United States than Gorbachev. But I don't think he wants Gorbachev's job."
>
> "Do you mean that he doesn't want to lead the Soviet Union, but he may want to lead an independent Russia?" I asked.

"Right, because he knows that there's no future for the Soviet Union. None. . . . If Russia has any future, Yeltsin is it."[55]

Nixon made the point in a meeting with President Bush and in public articles and interviews.

American audiences got a peek at Yeltsin's ability to cut to the chase in the June visit to Washington. At one dinner, he made it about two minutes into his prepared speech and told his interpreter to give it in English. "This cut the delivery time in half, and when it was over the crowd responded with a standing, cheering ovation."[56] Desk analysts for the Central Intelligence Agency began giving Yeltsin respect right at this time. A secret assessment by the Office of Soviet Analysis circulated on June 1 argued that too much attention had been lavished in the government and the press on Yeltsin's quirks, lust for power, relationship with Gorbachev, and tactics—"his larger-than-life persona and remarkable political odyssey invite this." But that was not the whole picture, and it was high time to say so. "Contrary to the stereotype, Yeltsin *does* have goals that he has been consistently pursuing, and strategies for realizing them. These are important not only because they drive his actions, but also because they reflect in broad outline a coherent Russian democratic alternative to the imperial authoritarianism of the traditionalists." The CIA team was especially impressed by Yeltsin's ability to keep up with changes in the Soviet environment and by his "appreciation of the interdependency of goals."[57]

Yeltsin considered his parliamentary position the stepping stone to a Russian presidency. Most of his associates were more interested than he in legislation and were less vociferous on policy toward the Soviet center. Even Vladimir Isakov, the chairman of the Council of the Republic, one of the two halves of the Supreme Soviet—a professor of jurisprudence from Sverdlovsk and a centrist—was upset by his propensity for playing the lone hand. Yeltsin would listen intently to advice, agree in principle, and then act "as if the conversation had never taken place."[58] Comity within the group dissipated in February–March 1991, and agitated sessions of the Supreme Soviet and congress were accompanied by pro-Yeltsin street demonstrations of up to 300,000 people, penned in by soldiers and riot police. Yeltsin's salvation was to induce the legislature to piggyback a question on institution of the office of president onto an all-USSR referendum on the future of the union on March 17. Seventy percent of Russians endorsed the federation and 71 percent an elected Russian presidency. In a masterpiece of brinkmanship, Yeltsin got parliament to schedule the election for June 12, the anniversary of the 1990 sovereignty declaration, before agreeing on presidential powers—something it got to on May 24, with only three weeks to spare. The Communists for Democracy faction headed by Colonel Aleksandr Rutskoi, a mustachioed hero of the Afghan war, provided the requisite congressional votes.

Rutskoi was named Yeltsin's vice-presidential running mate, at Lyudmila Pikhoya's suggestion, and two members of Democratic Russia and the Interregional bloc, Gavriil Popov and Anatolii Sobchak, ran parallel campaigns for mayor of Moscow and Leningrad. Management of the Yeltsin campaign was entrusted to Gennadii Burbulis, an owlish professor of dialectical materialism from Sverdlovsk (born in the oblast town of Pervoural'sk), who was admitted to Yeltsin's circle in 1990 and had hoped to be the vice-presidential nominee. An RSFSR television channel, one of the first inroads in the tussle over sovereignty, went on the air on May 13, in time for the race.

Of the five candidates who vied with Yeltsin in this, his third anti-establishment election in two years, only the former Soviet premier Nikolai Ryzhkov, the nominee of the Russian communists, was a serious contender. The party's beetle-browed leader, Ivan Polozkov, impossible to get elected, would resign his post in August. Yeltsin ducked the all-candidates' debates and did two rambles out of Moscow, formally on parliamentary business, presenting himself as statesmanlike and not grubbing for votes. If Vladimir Zhirinovskii, the windbag Russian nationalist who came in third, is speaking the truth, Gorbachev's office, working through the KGB, implored him to visit the same cities as Yeltsin and covertly gave 3 million rubles (about $2 million) to his vice-presidential candidate, Andrei Zavidiya, to buy his cooperation. But Zavidiya, Zhirinovskii says, did not bring Zhirinovskii in on the scheme and skimmed off 90 percent of the money; Zhirinovskii did not alter his travel plans.[59]

As in 1989 and 1990, an army of amateurish democrats delivered Yeltsin's message. Loosely coordinated by a group around Yeltsin and by Democratic Russia, they printed and photocopied materials, distributed them at Moscow subway stations, and rang doorbells. Retired schoolteachers rode the commuter rails of the capital region and passed Yeltsin fliers out of train windows. The chairman of the pilots' union at Aeroflot, Anatolii Kochur, prevailed upon flight crews to cram bales of broadsheets into cargo bays and get them to activists in the outback. The punchline of the authorized candidate's poster read *Narodnogo deputata v narodnyye prezidenty!*—"People's Deputy for People's President!" The main concern in the Yeltsin camp was that he would not make a majority in the first round and would lose to an anyone-but-Yeltsin candidate in a runoff.

Yeltsin campaigned against Gorbachev and the CPSU, not Ryzhkov or Zhirinovskii. In a firebrand interview on central television, he alluded to Gorbachev's more soothing line in recent weeks as proof that communism, which had made Soviet citizens guinea pigs in a grotesque experiment, was on its last legs:

> As recently as a month ago, he [Gorbachev] was saying everywhere that he is only for socialism, only for socialism, we cannot do otherwise. Just as for over seventy years we have been marching to a bright future, that is how [he says] we will continue, and somehow we will arrive. Our country has not been lucky. . . . It was decided to carry out this Marxist experiment on us—fate pushed us in precisely this direction. Instead of some country in Africa, they began this experiment with us. In the end, we proved that there is no place for this idea. It has simply pushed us off the road the world's civilized countries have taken. This is reflected today, when 40 percent of people are living below the poverty line and . . . in constant humiliation when they receive produce upon the presentation of ration cards. This is a constant humiliation, a reminder every hour that you are a slave in this country.[60]

Support for Yeltsin, polls showed, flagged in late May, then rebounded. He had husbanded his small advertising budget for the home stretch. Come voting day, Wednesday, June 12, the one-man electoral juggernaut received 45,552,041 votes, or 59 percent of the valid ballots cast, to 18 percent for Ryzhkov and 8 percent for Zhirinovskii. He drew best in the Urals, Moscow, Leningrad (which was about to go back to being called St. Petersburg), the urbanized portions of central Russia and Siberia, and the Volga basin; he drew worst in the "red belt" of pro-communist regions on the steppes south of Moscow.[61] Yeltsin's testing of his authority with the demos, as Anatolii Luk'yanov had prophesied, contrasted sharply with Gorbachev's quailing at that test in 1990. You, a Yeltsin ally said to Gorbachev, have been too timorous to try to obtain a mandate from society. Yeltsin dared, and got his agency by being chosen "not in the cloakrooms, not by a narrow circle, but by the people." If the Soviet bosses went on attacking Yeltsin, it would continue to boomerang: "The anti-Yeltsin actions of the bankrupt top echelon have always had effects antithetical to those intended. They have brought forth the people's wrath and elevated his authority."[62]

A gala inaugural was held on July 10 at the Palace of Congresses. Yeltsin seated a Russian Orthodox priest, a rabbi, and a Muslim cleric in the front row as a cue to the television audience that his Russia would be an open-minded place. Patriarch Aleksii II and Oleg Basilashvili, a parliamentary deputy and stage and movie actor from Leningrad, spoke before Yeltsin took the oath of office for a five-year term, with left hand on a copy of the Russian constitution and right hand over his heart. Yeltsin's undertaking as president, he said, beaming, was to transport Russia into the community of nations as "a prosperous, democratic, peace-loving, law-abiding, and sovereign state." He also tried to trim expectations: "The president is not God, he is not a new monarch, he is not an all-powerful worker of miracles, he is a citizen."[63]

Gorbachev said to Shakhnazarov that he had to disabuse Yeltsin of suggestions for projecting the swearing-in onto a jumbo screen on Red Square, firing a twenty-four-gun salute, and taking the oath on the Bible, like an American president. The Soviet president arrived late and spoke briefly. The honoree responded in kind: As Gorbachev reached to shake his hand, Yeltsin took several steps forward and stopped, forcing Gorbachev to come to him. Gorbachev, seeing red at Yeltsin's ambitions, as always, had a new regard for his acumen: "Such . . . a simpleminded yen for the scepter!" he let on to Shakhnazarov. "I am at my wit's end to understand how he combines this with political instinct *[chut'ë]*. God knows, maybe this is his secret, maybe this is why he is forgiven everything. A tsar must conduct himself like a tsar. And that I do not know how to do."[64] After the inauguration, Gorbachev approved rooms in the Kremlin for Yeltsin. They were in Building No. 14, across a cobblestoned square from Gorbachev's lair in Building No. 1.[65]

Gorbachev, having zigged toward the counterreformist pole in 1990, zagged back toward reformism in the spring of 1991. In dread of losing his support in the USSR congress and the Central Committee, of the republics coming to agreement at their own initiative, and of consumer ire at price increases, he restarted the effort to herd the republics together into a union treaty. The "Nine Plus One" talks (nine willing republics and the Soviet government) at the Novo-Ogarëvo state residence west of Moscow, built for Georgii Malenkov as Soviet prime minister in the 1950s, was one more sparring match with Yeltsin and dragged on from April 23 to late July. Gorbachev wanted a federation in which the center retained as many powers as possible.[66] With some sadness, Yeltsin thought the Soviet Union as constituted by Lenin and Stalin was doomed. "I am a Russian," he confided to a French academic of Russian origin in Strasbourg, "and I am not happy with the idea of the collapse of the empire. For me, it is Russia, it is Russian history. But I know it is the end. . . . The only way [forward] is to get rid of this empire as quickly as possible, or to accept the process."[67] He wanted in effect a confederation (although he stuck to the word "federation"), with Russia and the other sovereign republics controlling all taxation and natural resources and delegating a few functions (national security, railroads, the power grid, and atomic energy) to a central authority, which would haggle over its budget with them line by line. Verbal fisticuffs between Yeltsin and Gorbachev on May 24 spotlighted the disagreement over the monetary lifeblood of government:

YELTSIN: On taxes . . . we are thinking of transferring into the federal budget a fixed sum for programs that we are going to implement jointly, or that the union [government] will tackle, including ones for the republics. It will be done by amount and not by percent. That will be it. . . .

GORBACHEV: Hold on. You say it will be by program. But what about permanent functions of the state such as the army or basic scientific research?

YELTSIN: I am thinking of the army, too. We will have a look, so to speak. "Please show us everything" [we will say].

GORBACHEV: Boris Nikolayevich! In this case we will not have a federation. . . .

YELTSIN: We will deposit [the funds] in one bank and hand them over to you.

GORBACHEV: No, no. . . . There needs to be a federal tax.

YELTSIN: Not on every enterprise, no way. We are ruling that out.

GORBACHEV: In this case we will not have a federation.

YELTSIN: Why not? Why not?

GORBACHEV: In this case we will not have a federation.

YELTSIN: That is a federation.

GORBACHEV: We need a federal tax. . . . You want on every question to force us to our knees.

YELTSIN: It is you who wants to force us to our knees.[68]

Gorbachev yielded on taxation after Yeltsin called his bluff on a threat to pull out of Nine Plus One. "Do not," Yeltsin upbraided Gorbachev privately, "take things to the point where we have to decide this question without you."[69] To increase Russian autonomy and defang the CPSU, Yeltsin on July 20 issued Decree No. 14, proscribing any party from having cells or operations within organs of government in the RSFSR. Gorbachev seemed powerless to do anything about it.

A draft treaty for a Union of Sovereign States was initialed by the Novo-Ogarëvo working group on July 23, published on August 15, and its signing fixed for August 20. It largely embodied Russian preferences on taxation, natural resources, and the lesser republics within the RSFSR (they were to sign only as subunits of Russia). The center would still have the power to declare war and manage the military, but even foreign policy and public safety were to be subject to joint jurisdiction. In recognition of Russia's new global stature, President Bush, in Moscow for a summit with Gorbachev, was received by Yeltsin in his new Kremlin office on July 30. To Soviet and foreign correspondents after the meeting, Yeltsin talked up the treaty and the July 20 decree. At the state dinner in the Kremlin, he tried unsuccessfully to upstage Gorbachev by making a beeline for Barbara Bush and escorting her from receiving line to table. Gorbachev also reports Yeltsin pouting over not being seated at the head table at a dinner at Spaso House, the U.S. ambassadorial residence, and pressing a conversation on George Bush.[70] The previous evening, Gorbachev, Yeltsin, and Nursultan Nazarbayev, the party prefect and now president of Kazakhstan, had met at Novo-Ogarëvo and agreed that Nazarbayev would replace Pavlov as prime minister after the treaty signing, the vice presidency would be dissolved, and other heads would roll. The KGB, whose chief, Vladimir Kryuchkov, was one of those to be demoted, bugged their nocturnal conversation. Yeltsin warned Gorbachev that the walls had ears; Gorbachev did not believe him but acknowledged in his memoirs that Yeltsin had it right.[71]

The misbegotten coup d'état of August 19–21, 1991, whisked the rug out from under Gorbachev, the Communist Party, and the Soviet state. It was sprung by the conservatives with whom he had aligned himself in 1990–91 and was timed to forestall the signing of the union treaty. Confining Gorbachev to his summer residence at Foros, Crimea, the eight principals inundated Moscow with armor (about 750 tanks and vehicles) and troops, declared Gennadii Yanayev acting president, and appointed themselves a Public Committee for the State of Emergency, a condition they promulgated for a period of six months. As Yeltsin observed in *Notes of a President*, the committee, or GKChP, was a motley crew. It "had no leader. There was no authoritative person whose opinion would be a watchword and a signal to act."[72] Prime Minister Pavlov found refuge in the bottle; Kryuchkov of the KGB pulled strings behind the scenes; Vice President Yanayev spoke for the GKChP, ashen-faced and with trembling hands. Others represented the higher party apparatus and the military-industrial and agrarian complexes.

The worst oversights were vis-à-vis the born leader who was president of Russia. The fumbling plotters had puzzled at length about Gorbachev but gave little thought to Yeltsin or to his Russian administration. In February 1991, after Yeltsin's public demand for Gorbachev to resign, a KGB colonel contacted Pavel Voshchanov, a journalist who accompanied Yeltsin on the U.S. trip in 1989, to ask for a meeting with Yeltsin to discuss how he and Yanayev could work together "to save the country." Voshchanov took the message to Yeltsin, who said, "Let's see what they are going to do, but we will not have any contact with this hoodlum *[shantrapa]*."[73] The question resurfaced in a conversation on August 7 or 8 between Kryuchkov and the Politburo member and Moscow first secretary, Yurii Prokof'ev, who had delivered a diatribe against Yeltsin at the plenum removing him from the Moscow post in November 1987 and would give the GKChP qualified support. Prokof'ev pushed for a change of heart on Yeltsin: "Now [he told Kryuchkov] the main figure is not Gorbachev, in that Mikhail Sergeyevich has lost all of his authority, but Yeltsin. He is popular and the people support him. This is the figure on whom the problem will hinge." Betting that Yeltsin's authoritarian leanings and the animosity he nursed toward Gorbachev would be enough to make him putty in their hands, Kryuchkov "said roughly this: We will reach an agreement with Yeltsin, we will fix this problem without taking any measures beforehand."[74]

Yeltsin had been to see Nazarbayev for talks in Alma-Ata, Kazakhstan, since August 16. Acting on a premonition, he delayed his return on Sunday, August 18, by four hours (he swam in a mountain stream and attended a concert). He had the pilots land at Kubinka, a military field some miles out of Moscow. Had they put down wheels as scheduled at Vnukovo airport, he said in an interview, he would have been arrested and shot by order of Kryuchkov, and the violence used as cover for a nationwide wave of repression. The claim about a plan to shoot him is not made in Yeltsin's memoir account and seems implausible.[75] A post-coup inquiry turned up evidence that KGB officials intended to divert his aircraft to another landing strip, at Chkalovsk, and to detain him there for a conversation with Defense Minister Dmitrii Yazov and then "negotiations with the Soviet leadership." At Kryuchkov's direction,

Viktor Grushko, his first deputy, chaired a meeting on this stratagem at one P.M. on August 17, in which Deputy Defense Minister Vladislav Achalov made it clear that force would have to be used, but, because of uncertainty about Yeltsin's reaction, was unable to pull the others along. "After the landing [at Chkalovsk], the chief of the airport, on the pretense of delays on the part of those welcoming [the travelers], was to invite B. N. Yeltsin into another room, where Yazov would talk with him. In the course of the meeting, Achalov said that paratroopers and the Alpha Unit [of the KGB] would have to neutralize the guard of the RSFSR president, so as to exclude undesirable excesses such as taking a stand or the use of weapons. Since the participants in the meeting were unable to come to conclusions *about how Yeltsin would react to this and what kinds of actions he would take in response*, no final decision was made." And none would be made.[76]

One of the kingpins of the coup, Oleg Baklanov, notified Gorbachev at Foros on August 18 that they had already arrested Yeltsin, and then modified his story to say they would do so shortly. The available documentation shows Yeltsin to have been high on the general list of seventy persons the GKChP marked for roundup once the tanks went into action. Sixty Alpha rangers were sent in the wee hours of August 19 to the enclosure of RSFSR government dachas in the village of Arkhangel'skoye-2, where Yeltsin slept the night. They had orders to take him alive and hold him on an island at the Zavidovo wildlife reserve ninety miles north of Moscow. Yeltsin was woken up shortly after six in the morning and huddled with his political team, most of whom had been staying at dachas within strolling distance. After first preferring to call a two-hour "precautionary strike" by workers, he moved to more radical tactics. The group put together an anti-coup appeal "To the Citizens of Russia," which Yeltsin's daughters typed up in the dacha kitchen and Ivan Silayev telephoned in to the Russian White House. One of its recommendations was for a general strike of indefinite duration.[77]

Around this time, Kryuchkov revoked the arrest order. He did it upon consultation with Anatolii Luk'yanov, Yeltsin's former dacha mate, who had fallen in with the putsch and promised to get the USSR Supreme Soviet to provide it with legal cover (though not until August 26). "Kryuchkov was impressed by Luk'yanov's advice to take a wait-and-see position, letting Yeltsin 'declare himself' and giving the people to understand that the democratic leader of Russia was against the imposition of order in the country."[78] Shortly afterward, Kryuchkov tried honey rather than vinegar. It did not work: "Yeltsin refuses to cooperate. I spoke with him by telephone. I tried to make him see reason. It was useless."[79] The one general who wanted "measures to extirpate B. N. Yeltsin's group of adventurists" by force was Valentin Varennikov, the commander of Soviet ground forces, and he spent August 19 and 20 in Crimea and Kiev, Ukraine. If Varennikov, who fought in Berlin in 1945 and in Afghanistan in the 1980s, had been in Moscow, military behavior toward Yeltsin might have been more ruthless.[80]

By the time Kryuchkov made news of Yeltsin's obstreperousness known to his co-conspirators, the president of the RSFSR, after discussion in his team of whether to stay in Arkhangel'skoye-2 and the risks of moving, had been allowed to speed off in a car a little after nine A.M., headed to his office at the White House. He put on a bulletproof vest as he left. Naina Yeltsina said it would not be much use, since his head would be unprotected: "And the main thing is the head."[81] His limousine and several accompanying automobiles drove past paratroopers and tanks. Korzhakov's bodyguard detail was armed but under orders not to shoot unless the presidential automobile was hit. Yeltsin did not speak to his family again until he phoned Yelena to wish her a happy birthday on the morning of August 21.

Holed up in the White House, Yeltsin, his government, and the parliamentary chairman pro tem, Ruslan Khasbulatov, demanded Gorbachev's release and coordinated resistance to the putsch and the junta that had mounted it. They propagated their edicts by telephone, fax, and the foreign media, since the Soviet media were closed to them. Yeltsin declared that as president of Russia he was assuming command of all military and police units located in the RSFSR. At half past noon, in gray suit (buttoned at the waist) and tie, he marched onto the White House driveway. He was motivated by curiosity as much as anything and dismissed a warning from Gennadii Burbulis that he would be in danger from snipers, from the bushes or a nearby roof. Four or five aides grabbed at his arm and tried to keep him from going forward. "He was completely fearless—either oblivious of the danger or just thinking it didn't really matter."[82]

A light drizzle was falling. A twelve-wheeled, olive-green T-72 tank, No. 110, from the Taman Motorized Rifle Division, built at the Urals Wagon Works in Sverdlovsk oblast, had just rumbled toward the bottom of the stairs. Yeltsin walked slowly down the steps, grabbed a small Russian flag from a bystander, and stood in front of the machine, intending, he said, to keep it and the three or four additional tanks behind it from coming any closer. For a few seconds, he looked down the barrel of its cannon, "confident that they would not run over a president." Only when the forty-five tons of metal screeched to a halt did it occur to him to heave himself onto the hull, something his training as a tank operator at UPI and his service as party overseer of industry in Sverdlovsk let him know how to do. Once on it, Yeltsin reached into the hatch to shake hands with the driver and gunner and improvised again.[83] Perched on hardware that symbolized Soviet power—and what had been done in its name in Budapest in 1956, in Prague in 1968, and in Kabul in 1979—he pumped his right fist twice. He then read out his appeal to the citizenry, a copy of which he had clutched in his hand as he walked out of the building, unamplified to a knot of television cameras and a sparse audience that grew from about fifty when he began to speak to no more than 150 at the end, as passersby and shoppers from nearby stores came to have a look. Nikolai Vorontsov (the Soviet environment minister), Aleksandr Korzhakov, Gennadii Burbulis, and members of his entourage scampered up the side of the tank as he spoke.

The appeal, rather like Yeltsin's secret speech in 1987, was not particularly eloquent, and it was composed with two other people, Khasbulatov and Silayev. The values it cited were those of the democratic fragment of the fast-dissolving Soviet civilization. Russia's new government, it said, had tried to preserve "the unity of the Soviet Union and the unity of Russia," and it could not accept the illegal and immoral acts of the GKChP, which would "return us to the epoch of the Cold War and the isolation of the Soviet Union from the world community."[84] Yeltsin's most musical moment, to use Anatolii Chernyayev's phrase, was formed less by the words he spoke than by how he spoke them and where.

Within minutes, footage of Yeltsin's stagecraft was transmitted internationally on CNN. Soviet television was allowed to show snippets only, but staffers gave friends in the Western news bureaus tapes they themselves could not broadcast, and copies were sent to the Urals and Siberia. Any Moscow family with a wire antenna could tune in CNN on their home television. Shots of Yeltsin on Tank No. 110 came in a flood when the coup was over. Indigenous viewers saw in them glimmerings of a totemic image from another revolution, tattooed in their heads by the history primers they had read as children—of Lenin at the Finland Station, returning from Swiss exile and holding forth to the Petrograd proletariat from an armored car in April 1917. Immortalized on celluloid from eye level, "Yeltsin's rather awkward bulk makes him appear someone 'larger than life,' his unrefined speaking style 'the voice of the people,' his rather unkempt appearance a sign, not of the confusion of a politician caught by surprise but of a strong leader, righteously indignant and full of selfless resolve."[85]

There were anxious hours still to come. The hoped-for general strike did not happen, although the GKChP was unable to make use of that failure. In the White House, Yeltsin and 300 to 400 followers hunkered down behind sandbags and office furniture, with gas masks and weapons at the ready. Maybe 75,000 people (in the daylight, fewer at night) massed on the streets below.[86] At five P.M. on August 19, he assigned RSFSR Deputy Premier Oleg Lobov, his political client from the Urals, to institute a command center for a "reserve government" at a bomb shelter in Verkhnyaya Sysert, south of Sverdlovsk. Andrei Kozyrev, the hitherto ornamental Russian foreign minister and a fluent speaker of English, was sent to London to lay the groundwork for a government-in-exile.[87] In another decree, Yeltsin reached out to the military, enjoining them not to carry out the orders of the coup makers: "Soldiers, officers, and generals, the clouds of terror and dictatorship are gathering over the whole country. They must not be allowed to bring eternal night."

John Major of Britain was the first of a chain of foreign leaders to telephone with words of support. George H. W. Bush called from the Oval Office the morning of Tuesday, August 20, and for the first time Yeltsin aroused his admiration. "After hearing Yeltsin's voice, Bush began to believe that there might yet be a hero in this drama, one who would actually vanquish the villains—and it was not Gorbachev, but Yeltsin." If he won out over the tanks, the American told Yeltsin, Russia would "pave its way into the civilized community of states."[88] Bush clandestinely ordered U.S. national-security agencies to provide Yeltsin with signals intelligence from intercepts of Soviet military sources, and had a communications specialist from the embassy go the Moscow White House to help the Yeltsin group secure their telephone calls.[89]

That afternoon Yeltsin blazed away at the concourse in front of the White House, this time with loudspeakers to amplify his voice: "You can build a throne out of bayonets, but can you sit on it for long? I am convinced that there is not and will not be any return to the past. . . . Russia will be free!"[90] By telephone and through mediators, he proselytized military officers, after which Generals Yevgenii Shaposhnikov and Pavel Grachëv, the commanders of the Soviet air force and airborne troops, agreed between them to have Shaposhnikov send two jets to strafe military vehicles in the Kremlin if the White House were stormed. The pop groups Helios, Mister Twister, Metallic Corrosion, and Time Machine rocked it up in the square. Poet Yevgenii Yevtushenko did a reading for the crowd, stand-up comedian Gennadii Khazanov performed impersonations of Gorbachev and Yanayev, and the master cellist and conductor Mstislav Rostropovich lionized the opponents of the coup and waved a Kalashnikov rifle. Tension was astronomically high that evening, when soldiers accidentally killed three young male civilians.[91]

Yeltsin was nonplussed that the coup makers did not attack or even seal off the White House: "How could Kryuchkov be so blockheaded as not to understand how dangerous such indecision could be?"[92] The GKChP blinked first. At three in the morning of August 21, Kryuchkov decided not to storm the White House, concluding that the carnage would be politically unmanageable. The blockade was lifted in the afternoon and the troops began to evacuate Moscow. By midnight the putschists were behind bars—arrested by agents of the RSFSR procurator general—and Gorbachev, the emperor who had no clothes, was back from Foros, escorted by Vice President Rutskoi of Russia. Descending the stairs of the plane, Gorbachev thanked Yeltsin and, tone-deaf to the end, spoke of being "an adherent of socialism." On August 24, at the funeral for the three young men who died, Gorbachev was ill at ease, while Yeltsin movingly asked the parents' forgiveness for not saving their sons' lives.

Russia had entered an intermezzo of duopoly, *dvoyevlastiye*, like between the February and October revolutions of 1917. One aspirant, Yeltsin, elected by the people, was ascendant; the other, Gorbachev, chosen by two now lifeless bodies (the Central Committee of the CPSU, which he dissolved on August 24, and the USSR Congress of People's Deputies, which voted to shut itself down on September 5), was descendant.

Capitalizing on the legitimacy gap, Yeltsin compelled Gorbachev to annul his post-coup decrees on leadership of the national-security agencies and appoint men Yeltsin trusted. Gorbachev had made General Mikhail Moiseyev, who was complicit in the plot, acting defense minister on August 21. On August 22 Moiseyev was called to Gorbachev's office and found Yeltsin next to the Soviet president and commander-in-chief. "Explain to him that he is not minister any longer," Yeltsin barked at Gorbachev. "Gorbachev repeated Boris Nikolayevich's words. Moiseyev listened in silence, and off he went." The dovish Shaposhnikov, sight unseen by Yeltsin, was made minister of defense, and Vadim Bakatin, whom Gorbachev had fired as interior minister the winter before, was made chairman of the KGB.[93] On September 1 a Shaposhnikov order cleared by Yeltsin abolished the political directorate of the armed forces, long an implement of party control.

With Gorbachev, Yeltsin went for the jugular in public on Friday, August 23, in the Russian Supreme Soviet. Gorbachev had been requested to make a statement and answer questions from the benches, which he did for ninety minutes. With a national television audience watching, Yeltsin sashayed up to Gorbachev and stuck in his face a transcript by Nikolai Vorontsov showing that most Soviet cabinet members backstabbed Gorbachev at a cabinet meeting on August 19. "Gorbachev kept his dignity when he was alone at the podium. But when Yeltsin came over, the effect was almost as if he crumpled."[94] Yeltsin hectored Gorbachev into reading out quotations from the paper to the lawmakers. That done, Yeltsin asked members, "on a lighter note," to watch him finalize Decree No. 79, suspending the organs of the Russian Communist Party. He scrawled his signature slowly for the delectation of the deputies. They applauded him and heckled the red-faced Gorbachev, who mumbled "Boris Nikolayevich" several times. As an *Izvestiya* reporter noted, in an eerie inversion of the taunting of October–November 1987, Yeltsin, had now selected Gorbachev for the part of "naughty schoolboy."[95]

Brent Scowcroft, viewing the Supreme Soviet scene with President Bush in Kennebunkport, Maine, said it was "all over" for Gorbachev. "Yeltsin's telling him what to do. I don't think Gorbachev understands what happened." Bush concurred: "I'm afraid he may have had it."[96] Scowcroft and Bush were correct. After the overmatch on August 23—Gorbachev called it sadistic in his memoirs—it was anticlimactic the next day when Gorbachev dissolved the Central Committee and resigned as general secretary of the party. Yeltsin's Decree No. 90 on August 25 authorized the RSFSR Council of Ministers to seize all property of the CPSU and its Russian chapter. Yeltsin on August 26 publicly declined Gorbachev's offer to make him a Hero of the Soviet Union. On August 31 *Pravda*, which had remained a much more conservative paper than *Izvestiya*, reprinted an *International Herald Tribune* cartoon of a smiling Yeltsin reaching down to pump the hand of a miniaturized Gorbachev; the tagline read, "Welcome back to power, Mikhail."

The coup could not have been more destabilizing, and politics, economics, and culture converged more than ever on the constitutional question. The union treaty initialed in July was a dead letter. Only six union republics had been prepared to sign it, and, riddled with non sequiturs and ambiguities, it would in any event have been impracticable.[97] As of August 19, two Soviet republics (Lithuania and Georgia) had announced their independence from the USSR. Between August 20 and September 1, nine (Estonia, Latvia, Armenia, Ukraine, Belarus, Moldova, Azerbaijan, Kyrgyzstan, and Uzbekistan) followed their example. Tajikistan was to join the crowd in September, Turkmenistan in October, and Kazakhstan in December.

Gorbachev, his administration comatose (with no prime minister, parliament, budget, or bullion reserves), made a last-ditch effort to forge a treaty of union. The negotiating minuet started again at Novo-Ogarëvo, with the republic leaders sitting as the USSR State Council. Yeltsin was uncheerful about it and deputed two leading Russianists, Gennadii Burbulis and Sergei Shakhrai, to prepare working papers. The line had hardened. Earlier, Russia had been prepared to act as cash cow to the USSR and was "ready to cover any breach . . . even at the cost of its own ruination." After the coup, this was impossible. "The republics had gone their disjunct ways and did not want to return to the old arrangement. The only possibility in these new conditions was an agreement among them in which Gorbachev would act as middleman."[98]

Russia came out for a rump "union of states" or "confederation of states" rather than the "union state" Yeltsin had consented to in July. Gorbachev, who would have taken any form of union with a viable central authority, made the point to the State Council on November 14 that every time he agreed with one of Yeltsin's suggestions Yeltsin would slow down his speech, as if he were asking himself why Gorbachev was acting so agreeably. Yes, Yeltsin said, he was always wary of Gorbachev. Gorbachev "laughed, but without merriment."[99] The talks went on against a backdrop of Russian appropriation of assets from the shell Soviet government. By the late autumn, Gorbachev and his men were accepting receivership as an improvement on insolvency.[100] With Gorbachev caving in to most of Yeltsin's constitutional demands, agreement appeared within reach, yet slipped away at a last Novo-Ogarëvo meeting on November 25. Yeltsin, fresh from a trip to Germany and to Soviet forces there, said he would be prepared to take a confederative agreement to the Russian parliament, only without an irrevocable endorsement from him as president. Gorbachev accused him of weaseling out of commitments. Feeling trapped, Gorbachev said people were whispering that he was a spent force, and the republic leaders seemed to be of the same opinion. In that case, he went on ominously, "Go ahead and agree among yourselves"—something Yeltsin had warned he might do in their tête-à-tête that summer. He would have no part of the "further chaos that would follow from this diffuse position."[101]

Besides the difference over the roles of central and Russian governments, there was another sticking point—the place of Ukraine. It was republic number two of the Soviet Union, with almost 50 million people, and the one for which Russians felt the greatest emotional warmth. On August 24 its parliament had voted for separation from the USSR and set a confirmatory referendum for December 1, to coincide with a presidential election. A real country with its own passports, army, and currency seemed in the offing. "What kind of union would there be without Ukraine?" Yeltsin asked on November 25. "I cannot imagine it." Relations with Kiev could not be sorted out until December at the earliest. Until they were to its satisfaction, any Ukrainian participation would only give feet of clay to a new confederation, since quite likely it would soon have pulled out or set unacceptable terms.[102] Leader Leonid Kravchuk made it clear in comments on November 26 that his reservations were not only about a renewed union but about the Russian entity within it, whose head, Yeltsin, seemed to assume that Ukraine and the others would revolve around it "as if it were the sun."[103] On December 1, 90 percent of the Ukrainian electorate, including a majority of ethnic Russians, who were about one-fifth of the republic's population, voted for independent statehood. Kravchuk was elected president that same day, with 62 percent of the popular vote, and announced he would not negotiate with Gorbachev. Kravchuk and the Ukrainian elite had been encouraged in thinking that secession was a possibility for them by Yeltsin and his Russian elite, and together they were now prepared to drive the final nail in the coffin.[104]

As the November 25 State Council session ended, the new head of state of Belarus, Stanislav Shushkevich, a nuclear physicist whom Yeltsin knew from the Interregional group, invited him to tack onto a planned visit to Minsk some time hunting in Belovezh'e Forest. This was a place where they could talk things over in peace—an old-growth wooded area, the only one surviving in Europe, on the border with Poland, where Warsaw Pact meetings had been held and Khrushchev and Brezhnev had gone shooting. Following the Ukrainian referendum and election, Shushkevich took it upon himself to ask Kravchuk to join them.[105] Kravchuk was the only one of the leaders to do any hunting. Over herbal vodka and supper in the government villa at Viskuli on December 7, they and their advisers (Yeltsin had with him Burbulis, Shakhrai, Kozyrev, his aide Viktor Ilyushin, and Yegor Gaidar, his new deputy premier for economic reform) briefly reviewed the impasse. The Russians favored a trilateral agreement that would end it. Shakhrai, a legal scholar by background, hit upon a juridical device, the argument that the trinity of Slavic republics was qualified to act because they had been high parties to the Bolshevik-engineered treaty in 1922 that formed the USSR. Gaidar handwrote a text late that night. Around four A.M., Kozyrev slid it under the door of the one stenographer present, who was asleep; a cleaning woman picked it up overnight and it had to be retrieved from the trash in the morning and typed up.[106]

When they reconvened after breakfast, Yeltsin unexpectedly made one last stab at salvaging a single state. He had "an assignment from Gorbachev," he said to Kravchuk, to ask whether he would sign the kind of agreement Gorbachev pushed at Novo-Ogarëvo, "if Mikhail Sergeyevich and the others moved to give Ukraine more rights and freedoms." Kravchuk said he might have at some earlier date but could not now, and Yeltsin expressed understanding. They then nailed down the accord outlined by Gaidar.[107] It was signed around one P.M. on Sunday, December 8, Yeltsin and Burbulis doing the honors for Russia. Its fourteen articles recorded the slipping of the Soviet Union under the waves as a fait accompli (it "is ceasing to exist as a subject of international law and a geopolitical reality") and created a Commonwealth of Independent States (CIS), headquartered in Minsk, with limited supranational powers on issues of trade, finance, mobility of persons, and security. Russia, not the CIS, was to be legal successor to the USSR and to its obligations and rights, one of them, it was soon to be revealed, the Soviets' permanent, veto-bearing seat in the United Nations Security Council. Yeltsin phoned George Bush and then USSR Defense Minister Yevgenii Shaposhnikov with the news. "Mr. President," he said to Bush, using Foreign Minister Kozyrev as interpreter, "the Soviet Union is no more." Yeltsin was nervous, giving Bush the impression he was reading from a prepared statement. As host, Shushkevich had the thankless duty of calling Gorbachev, and could not get through to him in the Kremlin until Yeltsin and Bush had rung off. Gorbachev demanded that Yeltsin be put on the line and assailed him for a double-cross and for informing a foreign head of state before the president of the USSR. Yeltsin said Gorbachev had to realize they had no alternative but to make the deal.[108] Yeltsin was apprehensive of some military or KGB group, perhaps with Gorbachev's connivance, taking matters into their own hands. Before going to see Gorbachev on December 9, upon his return from Belarus, he asked him on the telephone whether his security would be guaranteed. Gorbachev said it would be.[109]

The Russian Supreme Soviet ratified the Belovezh'e agreement on December 12, after one hour of deliberation, with a mere six out of 252 deputies voting against and seven abstentions. When Yeltsin received James Baker in the Kremlin on December 16, it was in the St. Catherine's Hall of the Grand Kremlin Palace, with Shaposhnikov at his side. He greeted Baker with the words, "Welcome to this *Russian* building on *Russian* soil." Baker made a point of telling Yeltsin the Americans would "look with disfavor" on any attempt to shame Gorbachev as he left office. "Gorbachev should be treated with respect," Yeltsin replied reassuringly. "It's about time our leaders can be retired with honor."[110]

Eight of the post-Soviet nations joined the CIS at Alma-Ata on December 21. (Estonia, Latvia, and Lithuania never did sign on; Georgia did so in 1993.) Seeing the writing on the wall, Gorbachev on December 23 negotiated a retirement package with Yeltsin and Aleksandr Yakovlev. On Wednesday, December 25, he took leave of the presidency and the Soviet Union on television and gave control of the USSR's 35,000 nuclear weapons to Yeltsin. He described the dismemberment of the USSR as a mistake and a betrayal of a thousand years of Russian history, but accepted that he was unable to prevent it. Thirty-eight minutes after he began, he was done and the hammer-and-sickle was run by hand down the Kremlin flagstaff; five minutes after that, the Russian tricolor was run up to flutter in the hibernal breeze. Gorbachev and Yeltsin bickered down to the wire about the hand-off. They had agreed to meet one-on-one in Gorbachev's study, but Yeltsin, seeing red over parts of the resignation speech that were critical of the republic leaders, demanded he take the nuclear briefcase (the black Samsonite bag containing the authorization codes) in another Kremlin spot. They ended up doing it through the good offices of Shaposhnikov, who received the case from Gorbachev ten minutes after Gorbachev's talk.[111] The USSR had gone the way of the overland empires of the Ottomans and Austro-Hungarians and refracted into fifteen countries.

For Gorbachev, the alternatives had been unpalatable. One was to get Yeltsin to work with him to save the union. Yakovlev plied Gorbachev afain after the coup with the nonstarter idea of Yeltsin as vice president; Georgii Shakhnazarov made several similar proposals. Gorbachev did not move a muscle to pursue them. Another possibility was for Gorbachev to fall on his sword and resign in Yeltsin's favor. Shaposhnikov saw this as desirable and thought it could be followed by USSR-wide elections. The delicate state of civil-military relations kept him from raising it with either Gorbachev or Yeltsin. Gorbachev himself aired the possibility with Gavriil Popov, by now the mayor of Moscow, in late August ("Maybe I should hand everything over to Boris"), and Eduard Shevardnadze spoke with Yeltsin about it around this time. Popov advised against such a choice, thinking Yeltsin as USSR president would drive the non-Russian elites away.[112] Yeltsin heard of this talk but considered it "unserious" and the post-coup Soviet presidency "ephemeral."[113]

Gorbachev's only other option was to reverse the tide by force. This was not in him to do, and his disinclination since 1989 to take responsibility for local tests of strength had made the army officer corps distrustful of his intentions. Any praetorian ambitions the generals might have had were wrung out of them after the coup. In late November the Soviet president fished in his Kremlin office for Shaposhnikov's opinion of a temporary military takeover, to be followed by a return to barracks. The reply was that it would land its authors in jail, upon which Gorbachev replied that his query was only hypothetical. The army did not have the training or equipment for police work, the minister said, and Yeltsin would torpedo any such policy. It could bring August redux or, worse yet, "mountains of corpses and a sea of gore."[114]

Yeltsin, with a steelier spine and far more political capital, had greater choice than Gorbachev did in the matter. It goes without saying that he took power into account, but his actions in late 1991 were not driven by power alone.[115] He came down against even a diluted post-Soviet federation for two reasons. First was his skepticism of the viability of such a construct. Seven union republics (all three in the Baltic, all three in the Caucasus, and the western borderland of Moldova) had boycotted the post-coup talks.[116] The Ukrainians took part in some consultations, but Kravchuk did not darken the door of Novo-Ogarëvo. His refusal to agree was the straw that broke the camel's back.

For Yeltsin, another point, as I see it, was determinative. He opted against a neo-USSR because he was opting *for* a Russian state—self-standing, governable, and capable of modernization and normalization. To put it another way, he opted for nation-building over empire-saving.[117] What he desperately wanted was to leap into post-communism in the protocountry, Russia, that had freely elected him president. The opening move was laid out in the rousing address to the Russian congress on October 28 in which Yeltsin committed Russia to radical economic reform. A liberalization of prices, something Gorbachev had hemmed and hawed about for years, was the key component. The diarist Chernyayev cast a Gorbachevian scowl on Yeltsin's uncouthness but sank it in a panegyric to his call to arms, with an allusion to the French Revolution:

> Yeltsin's report . . . is a breakthrough to a new country, to a new society, although the ideas and concepts behind this very exit were all laid down in the philosophy of Gorbachev-style perestroika. He himself [Gorbachev] was not able to break in good time with his habits, although he more than once confessed, "We are all from the past." I hate to say it, but not everyone has the will to break with this past conclusively and at the right time. . . .
>
> In [Yeltsin's] report it's either win all or lose all. But in Russia that has always been how big things are done. M. S. [Gorbachev] never went fur-

> ther than Mirabeau. This fellow is going all the way to Napoleon, skipping over Danton, Robespierre, Barras, and even the *enragés*.
>
> He has thrown out hope to the people. This is the sign of charisma, for all his gaucheness as a person. As an individual he is all mediocrity and grayness, but as "chieftain" in the current concrete situation he is what is required.
>
> And [Yeltsin] is placing his bets on Russia. I cannot repeat it too often: Gorbachev's historic mistake was that, enfolded in the psychology of "internationalism," he never understood the role of Russia. I feel human sympathy for him. He knows that it is not only senseless right now to oppose Yeltsin. It is simply impossible from the point of view of the country's interests. He has no alternative. . . . The way out lies in an irrational consolidation of the Russians, in the despair that brings people together.[118]

Chernyayev had laid hold of Yeltsin's broader appeal. The Russian leader was forging ahead, not treading water. He was conjuring hope out of despair. Giving up on an obsolete doctrine and the imperial structure it had held up, he was banking on a national community in which people shared material interests and sociocultural affinities. He was passing through a door the star-crossed Gorbachev had jimmied open but could not go through himself. And he was doing it the way he liked, in one stroke. "I have always been inclined toward simple solutions," he was to write in *Presidential Marathon*. "It has always seemed to me that it is much easier to slice through the Gordian knot than to spend years untying it."[119] In 1991 he had the blade in his hands and was not squeamish about using it.

"What if?" analysis holds out myriad counterfactuals for the "thickened history" of 1985 to 1991.[120] Boris Yeltsin was not an uncontainable force. His relations with Gorbachev and Yegor Ligachëv, the authors of his move to Moscow, were guarded at the best of times. Had they any inkling of how he would act, they would have left him in Sverdlovsk. In Moscow, two Soviet prime ministers in a row had misgivings about Yeltsin's ability and malleability; those misgivings were swept under the carpet. Gorbachev could in all probability have kept Yeltsin on board after his mutiny in 1987 or invited him back into the fold at the 1988 party conference; or he could have had the foresight to get Yeltsin out of the country for the 1989 election. It was not too late after the election to genuflect to Yeltsin's popularity by making him head of government. A motivated and more tightly organized CPSU would have blocked the Russian parliament from making Yeltsin its chairman in 1990 and instituting the presidency in 1991. The Five Hundred Days plan offered a sterling but wasted chance to mollify him. Suppler behavior by the Soviet leaders would have aggravated Russians less, and a softer posture on the union treaty would have given Yeltsin incentives to take a compromise position. Averting the opera bouffe of August 1991 would have bought Gorbachev time to try to cook up a hybrid successor regime. And a cutthroat coup d'état instead of a procrastinating one would have resulted in Yeltsin's arrest, in the best of cases, or death in an inferno at the White House, at worst.

Others may have squandered their chances, but not Yeltsin. His criticism of and then defection from Gorbachev, confirmed by Gorbachev's inability to engage him, positioned him as a unique political player. Drawing on currents in the environment and on personal predispositions, Yeltsin refashioned his sense of who he was politically and gravitated to some approximation of a Western paradigm of governance. He milked the opportunities that seismic structural shifts and accident threw his way.

One foot planted in the past and one in the future, Yeltsin was a boss for the bosses, who knew the old ways but looked forward to new ones. For him and the nation, the hard part—to graduate from the simplex of talking about a better country to the complex of building it—was just beginning.

Chapter Nine

A Great Leap Outward

In its last top-of-the-line National Intelligence Estimate on the USSR before its downfall, completed in November 1990, the U.S. Central Intelligence Agency saw "deterioration short of anarchy" as the most likely scenario over the next year, with a probability close to even. Three other scenarios were given chances of one in five or less. They were "anarchy," "military intervention" either as an army coup or at the direction of the civilian leadership, and "light at the end of the tunnel," which would be marked by "substantial progress" toward constructive relationships between the center and the republics, toward "the filling of the political power vacuum by new political institutions and parties," and toward new economic relations based on the market principle.[1] The annus mirabilis 1991 proved the safest prediction wrong: Deterioration short of anarchy was unsustainable. Elements of the second, third, and fourth were all in evidence: There were anarchic outbreaks as governmental control over self-generating processes weakened; the August coup provided military intervention; and, in Russia, the emergence of an embryonic nation state led by Boris Yeltsin pointed to the possibility of light at the end of the tunnel. As the CIA had anticipated in its classified report, "enormous difficulties" in multiple realms would lie ahead under the most bullish of the scenarios, "but a psychological corner would be turned to give the population some hope for a brighter future." Even with such a shift in mass attitudes, economic contraction and constitutional issues, if nothing else, would issue in pressures that "could break any government."[2]

The Yeltsin of 1990–91 was adamant that the days of the Soviet partocracy were numbered, so differing with the allies in intellectual circles, and the observers abroad, who tended to think it would die a dragged-out death. At a clangorous rally on the Moscow Garden Ring in March 1991, Gavriil Popov lectured journalists not to ballyhoo the crisis and to expect the CPSU to hang on into the twenty-first century. Marching at his side, Yeltsin took tart exception: The system was "collapsing of its own weight" and the dénouement would come "very soon."[3] As to the means and timing, he was no more farsighted than the rest. Were Gorbachev to fail or the democrats to be beat out, he held that the populace "would take to the streets and would take their fate into their hands," as it had been in Prague, Bucharest, and other bloc capitals in 1989.[4] Yeltsin was taken unawares by the concatenation of a banana-republic coup and an implosion of the state. "I was in a tense emotional state," he comments of the weeks after August 21, since "the events that had just occurred were so sudden."[5]

Yeltsin all the while regarded winning the game with some trepidation. In *Notes of a President*, he records his response, as parliamentary chairman, to being allocated the White House office of Vitalii Vorotnikov in June 1990. The "seditious thought" that he was about to take charge of Russia, still an undergoverned subunit of the Soviet Union, "frightened" him.[6] On the evening of December 23, 1991, around the Kremlin desk that had been his since July, he gathered cohorts to mark the ironing out of Gorbachev's retirement. Lev Sukhanov, motioning at a wall map of the RSFSR, toasted him with the words, "On this whole territory, there is now nobody above you." "Yes," Yeltsin smiled radiantly, "and for this, life has been worth living!"[7] Four days later he occupied Gorbachev's working office on the third floor of Building No. 1, the triangular, green-domed Senate Palace of tsarist times. Yeltsin's exuberance did not much outlast the bubbles in the drinks. "My rapture," he says about the transfer of authority generally, "was replaced . . . by a bad case of the jitters."[8]

Well might he have been jittery, for he was ill-prepared for victory. It was one thing to appropriate physical trophies and proclaim the goal of changing Russia forever. It was quite another to govern and to flesh out that goal.

Had Yeltsin arrived at Building No. 1 through an unhurried, well-bounded, and educative political contest, he would have had to nominate a shadow cabinet and to propound "profound and affirmative ideas" and "a model of rule," to quote Oleg Poptsov, the editor and cagey observer of the Moscow scene. As it was, the stock advancement from disagreement to opposition and on into the halls of government was fast-forwarded: "The rotten tree of the state broke down, and power and its appurtenances fell at [the opposition's] feet."[9] Yeltsin had shaken its branches and trunk and placed himself to harvest the apples. Except in the broadest brushstrokes, he had not worked through the constitutive choices he would be called upon to make if power were his, all the more so power in a Russian structure not encumbered by the Soviet superstructure.

A flotilla of his aides would conclude in their memoir *The Yeltsin Epoch* that, "not ready for so swift a development of the state of affairs," Yeltsin "entered the genre of improvisation" in 1991.[10] But the novelty was one of degree only. Yeltsin had been improvising brilliantly since 1985: at trying to make perestroika work, challenging Gorbachev, politicking. What distinguished this new situation was that the stakes were higher and the boundaries of the possible laxer than they were in communism's tipping years. Social brakes and buffers had been obliterated. Nothing was sacred and everything of value was up for grabs—even the name of the republic, de-Sovietized and restyled the Russian Federation or Russia on December 25.[11] Yeltsin's message in the 1991 presidential election gave little guidance on what to do next. Russians, Gennadii Burbulis said, voted for Yeltsin in "a purely religious form of protest and hope" and threw in with "a savior," not a reform plan.[12]

Before he was snowed under by events, Mikhail Gorbachev had tried to manage change in the style of a symphony conductor—directing well-primed instrumentalists from fixed, sequent sheet music. Boris Yeltsin conducted a political jazz combo—altering the frequency, duration, and accent of melody lines as he went and open to extemporization by members. The facility for thinking on his feet was part of his political mystique, and his organizational props had been slight, as he relied largely on unsalaried volunteers. "We worked as a team, as a single organism," one of them, Valentina Lantseva, reminisced. "We were fellow fighters, not aides and not hired hands. . . . We worked on ebullience and Russian romanticism."[13]

The amateurism of that innocent time was now an anachronism. President Yeltsin had in his hands the buttons and pedals to all the shambling machinery of government on Russian territory. The communist regime was no longer there as a scapegoat. Was he up to the new assignment? The philosopher Aleksandr Tsipko, a moderate Russian nationalist who wanted to save the USSR, spoke for many when he judged that Yeltsin was not. "I honestly would not want to be in Boris Nikolayevich's shoes," he wrote in *Izvestiya* in October 1991. "Yeltsin the fighter and destroyer is in the past. The time of Yeltsin the creator is upon him." It was, Tsipko said, a terrifying burden that he was slow to face up to. Haunted by the chimera of "a center that no longer exists," Yeltsin would have been content if the old foe were still around to beat up on.[14]

Bringing back the Soviet bugbear was impossible, and it was impossible to get along on differing from Gorbachev, for Gorbachev had been marginalized. Yeltsin forced him to vacate his Moscow apartment and country residence, together with the Kremlin offices, and to scale down his demands for pension and staff, but granted his request to start a Gorbachev Foundation with property deeded by the Russian administration.[15] Gorbachev went on the transatlantic lecture circuit, learned to be a fundraiser (he would even appear in a Pizza Hut commercial in 1997), wrote his memoirs, and established Green Cross International, an environmental organization. He never spoke with Yeltsin after December 23, 1991, and as before looked down on him as a shifty megalomaniac.[16] Yeltsin matched Gorbachev's lack of humility with a lack of magnanimity, making him persona non grata in official Moscow. As Yeltsin planned his first state visit to Washington, D.C., in June 1992, one criterion he gave his hosts for the beyond-the-beltway portion was that it be at a place Gorbachev had never seen—which led him midway across the country to the state of Kansas.[17] (He toured Wichita, rode a farm combine in a wheatfield, and took home a plastic bear filled with Grannie's Homemade Mustard, from a family business in Hillsboro.) In August, convinced that comments by Gorbachev violated a promise made to him in December 1991 of noninterference in politics, Yeltsin had Interior Minister Viktor Yerin carry out a "financial and legal inspection" of the foundation. "Naturally, 'abuses' were uncovered, in particular, participation in trading operations."[18] In September Gorbachev was barred from foreign travel for refusing to testify at the hearing by the new Russian Constitutional Court into the legality of Yeltsin's decrees banning the Communist Party—he would not participate, he said, even if brought into the courtroom in handcuffs. The ban was lifted within weeks, and Gorbachev was fined 100 rubles (the price of a hamburger and cola drink) for contempt of court.[19] Both Gorbachev and Yeltsin eased off, and the dust settled.[20]

If time had passed by the battle with Gorbachev, it had done the same with the levers Yeltsin used to unseat Gorbachev. Foremost among them was the campaign against elite privilege.

In the last few years of the communist regime, Yeltsin lived decently yet not sumptuously, which gave him some standing to cast stones. In June 1991 the vice president–elect, Aleksandr Rutskoi, acting on his wife's counsel, decided Yeltsin needed sartorial upgrade and procured him a smart suit, shoes, and some white shirts with coupons issued to Rutskoi as a military officer. Yeltsin accepted graciously but paid Rutskoi for the apparel.[21] For a barbecue at Arkhangel'skoye-2 the weekend after the defeat of the putsch, press secretary Pavel Voshchanov splurged on a suckling pig he found in a Moscow peasant bazaar. "Naina Iosifovna was touched, because they could not permit themselves this."[22] At their Second Tverskaya-Yamskaya apartment, Naina bid a guest to be careful of the sofa, as the springs poked out through holes and they might rip his trousers: "When Boris Nikolayevich sits on it, first he puts on a little cushion, and then it's okay. Here is a cushion for you."[23]

Once in power, though, Yeltsin came to bask in the same creature comforts as Gorbachev and Leonid Brezhnev before him. He kept his Moscow residential registration at Second Tverskaya-Yamskaya until 1994, when he shifted it to the sixth floor of a new concrete building block on Osennyaya Street, in the Krylatskoye development, on the western outskirts of the capital. Yeltsin saw the building from his limousine and fell in love with it, much to the mystification of his family and of his security detail, who thought it too close to the windows of other houses. They objected, but, recalled his daughter Tatyana, "Papa said we were going to live here, and that was that."[24] Most nights from 1992 through 1996 Yeltsin actually spent at the state dacha Barvikha-4, a three-story river-front mansion in the settlement of Razdory, which was a ten-minute drive farther out the same westward radius from the Kremlin. The army built Barvikha-4 for Gorbachev in Second Empire style and equipped it with the latest communications and security gadgetry. Yeltsin as president took again to hunting, unwinding every several months by shooting deer, stag, wild boar, duck, and wood grouse at the bucolic Zavidovo. He made stops at other provincial retreats left by the Soviets: Valdai, in the northwest near Novgorod, where the big dacha was built for Stalin; Bocharov Ruchei in Sochi, on Russia's semitropical Black Sea coast; Volzhskii Utës, on a crook in the lower Volga; and Shuiskaya Chupa in Kareliya, refurbished with the northernmost roofed tennis court in Europe.[25]

With a bang, the door had shut on Yeltsin's populism. In an interview in retirement, he was unrepentant for using it. "It was necessary to do some undermining, to take things away from the nomenklatura. I did it and I did it correctly. It was not right for the big shots to puff up their privileges that way." But it was "a stage" in his development, he added, and he and Russia outgrew it.[26]

The incongruousness with his recent past required some rationalization. Yeltsin gave it mostly in *Notes of a President.* He had, he says, a brainstorm in 1990, shortly after he was elected speaker of the Russian Supreme Soviet and he asked to be allotted a government dacha at Arkhangel'skoye-2:

> When I was a deputy in the [USSR] Supreme Soviet, I had refused the perks of a chauffeured car and a dacha. I refused to go to a special polyclinic and signed up in my neighborhood one. But now I ran up against the fact that I needed to push for such things and not to reject them. It was not because the leader of Russia needed "privileges" but because he needed normal working conditions, which at that moment he was without. This revelation was so startling that I fell to thinking. Would people understand me correctly? For so many years, I had maligned privileges, and here I was asking for them. Then I decided that the people were as smart as I was. They had realized without me that the struggle was not against the privileges of the [Communist] party; it was against the party's unbridled, all-enveloping power.[27]

And so, once the CPSU was no more, it was appropriate to exchange the unostentatious Arkhangel'skoye-2 for tony Barvikha-4 and Aeroflot for Gorbachev's Ilyushin-62 jetliner, a "ROSSIYA" logo glued to its skin. The replacement for Aleksandr Korzhakov's Niva was a ZIL, and in 1992 a sleek, armor-plated Mercedes limousine from Germany—an "office on wheels," in Yeltsin's words.[28]

Many Russians wondered about the justice of it all. Yurii Burtin, a former dissident active in the shriveling Democratic Russia movement, took aim in an essay in March of 1992 at "the brassiness [that] lets our new leaders take the same offices and drive around in the same luxurious armored limousines that members of the Politburo used to help themselves to."[29] In a television interview in 1993, shot at Gorki-9, an estate where Soviet leaders had lived, El'dar Ryazanov, a director of movie comedies and a Yeltsin supporter, personalized the question. What was it like for someone who had ridden the crest of a moral wave of the downtrodden to glean these benefits, and had he found that power "corrodes the soul"? "Some things inside me have changed," Yeltsin said jumpily, giving Gorki-9 as a barometer: "Earlier, I would never have moved into such a residence. I guess I have come to take a more blasé attitude toward the morality of various privileges than I used to."[30] He squirmed not because his perquisites were so atypical for the leader of a large country but because he had denounced his predecessors for enjoying them and had implied that in power he as people's president would deny himself them.[31]

Of the questions dominating the late Soviet political agenda, the only two that were settled as of the rotation of the Kremlin flags were about the power of the CPSU and the tug-of-war between the center and the union republics. Yeltsin closed out the first with presidential Decree No. 169 on November 6, 1991, a day before the seventy-fourth anniversary of the Bolshevik Revolution. It dismembered the palsied machinery of the party and took possession of its bank accounts, publishing houses, and real estate, from Old Square to the most far-flung Russian villages. The Belovezh'e and Alma-Ata accords and the exit of Gorbachev hardened interrepublic borders into international borders. The purpose of the Commonwealth of Independent States was to accomplish a genteel divorce in a dysfunctional family. With it as cover, Yeltsin took the assets of the KGB in mid-December, and the interrepublic security committee was discharged on January 15, 1992.[32] The commonwealth's charter mission was complete on May 18, 1992, when he gave up on the will-o'-the-wisp of a unified military (joint control over nuclear arms had been agreed at Belovezh'e) and formed national armed forces under Defense Minister Pavel Grachëv. Grachëv oversaw the homecoming of troops from Germany, Poland, Mongolia, Cuba, and the post-Soviet states. All Soviet tactical nukes were in storage in Russia by July 1, 1992, as agreed at Alma-Ata in December 1991; the last strategic warheads from Ukraine, Belarus, and Kazakhstan were transported there by July 1, 1996, after negotiations brokered by the United States. The CIS was up to little else but holding summit meetings and offering a forum for working out bilateral agreements. Yevgenii Shaposhnikov's job, as commander of CIS strategic forces, was to lapse in June 1993.

If the CIS was about tidying up after the past, Yeltsin as leader of the opposition had looked to the future, to the best of his abilities. The prospect he dangled before Russia was a three-pronged de-monopolization—after departing the Communist Party in 1990 he often called it a "de-communization"—comprising democratization, a free-enterprise economy, and territorial devolution. It would, he said, substitute the liberties of a normal life for the regimentation of communism.

At a press conference on September 7, 1991, the first question to Yeltsin, from a French journalist, was what kind of a country Russians lived in and would be living in now that the political logjam had been cleared. Here is what he said:

> I think that the country is now devoid of all "isms." It isn't capitalist, nor communist, nor socialist; it's a country in a transitional period, which wants to proceed along a civilized path, the path along which France, Britain, the United States, Japan, Germany, Spain, and other countries have been and still are proceeding. It's an aspiration to proceed precisely along this path, that is, the de-communization of all aspects of society's life, an aspiration to democracy, furthermore, a market economy, all equal varieties of property, including private property.

A little later, the BBC's world affairs editor, John Simpson, buzzed again to what model Yeltsin had as a goal:

SIMPSON: I want to go back to what Mr. Gorbachev said recently. He was talking about Swedish social democracy; that is his model. What is your model, Yeltsin's model? Perhaps it is the model of François Mitterrand's France, or John Major's Britain, or the United States, or Japan, or Spain, or Germany?

YELTSIN: I would take everything together; I would take the best from each system and introduce it in Russia.

SIMPSON: That is a very politic answer. Mr. Gorbachev said you must have some kind of notion, whether you want to lean to the left, or to the right, to the conservatives, or to the socialists, and so on.

YELTSIN: Well, I have never been a conservative and have no intention of even being a centrist; no, I am still to the left of center; rather, I am for social democracy.

SIMPSON: Or the Swedish model, as Mr. Gorbachev says?

YELTSIN: Well, perhaps not 100 percent. You cannot just take a model and install it ready made. Maybe create a new model, but take something from the Swedish model, and why not take a piece from the Japanese model—an interesting piece—and from the French, too, especially as regards the parliamentary aspect? And in the United States, where they

> have 200 years of democracy . . . they have a definite framework for this democracy, and that's interesting, too. So, in principle, I am in favor of social democracy, but nevertheless, to take the best there really is in these countries.[33]

The statement is indicative of Yeltsin's reasoning as he took the reins. He saw all good things as going together and downplayed trade-offs of one good against another—democracy versus the market, for example. These valued traits he discerned in the long-since developed Western nations and Japan (which he first visited as a Soviet parliamentarian in January 1990), although one country on his A-list, Spain, had transited to political freedom in the 1970s. Yeltsin was fixated not on destination but on *trajectory:* Civilization was a path leading in a particular direction. He did not totally abjure his socialist roots, in that he continued to brand himself a social democrat and to the left of center (left in the common European meaning of the word, indicating attachment to a sizable state role in the economy), a contention he made through the middle and late 1990s in conversations with other politicians and reiterated to me in 2002.[34] And Yeltsin was eclectic—if not to say platitudinous—about his societal models. He considered himself free to cherry-pick, without worrying about coherence in the abstract.

Practically speaking, Yeltsin was satisfied that the first and third elements of his triad, democracy (and its accompanying moral regeneration) and decentralization, had advanced with the shutdown of the CPSU. While there was much unfinished business, principally in devising a democratic and federal constitution for post-communist Russia, it was axiomatic for Yeltsin that, given the assurances he had made and the dismal state of the economy, the most urgent problem was the transition from Marx to market.

Yeltsin had no economic blueprint to pull off the shelf, but he did have thoughts about nongovernmental activity and entrepreneurship to build on. He had long since seen them at work in the interstices of the Soviet planned economy. In Berezniki, while Stalin reigned, his father constructed a private house. As a party boss in Sverdlovsk and Moscow, Yeltsin opposed restrictions on the nonstate sector, favored autonomous work brigades in the state sector, and spoke of the profit motive's effect on economic efficiency in the West.

His ideas about reform while in opposition were initially scattershot and auxiliary to his duel with Gorbachev. The stillborn Five Hundred Days Program encouraged him to think about parameters. That said, Yeltsin never read a page of the two-tome compilation Grigorii Yavlinskii plunked on his desk. He homed in on the political facets—the zippy title and the taut timetable.[35] A law "On Property in the RSFSR," enacted under Yeltsin's legislative gavel in January 1991, after Gorbachev nixed Five Hundred Days, made private ownership a civil right. It was assailed by old-fashioned communists. "For him, the law . . . had greater political than economic significance, and it achieved its purpose."[36]

There were flickers of free-enterprise thinking in Yeltsin's proposal to relegate governmental power from the USSR to Russia and its provinces. It would, he said, unlock social energy suppressed by the leaden hand of the center. In his August 1990 tour, Yeltsin parried demands for instructions and subventions from on high. The beauty of devolution was that local leaders and citizens would have incentives to figure out solutions on their own. In the Arctic coal city of Vorkuta, which had its origins as a Gulag forced-labor camp in the 1930s, he asked miners how they would handle "complete independence." Some were curious about subsidies and guarantees of supplies and distribution. "Yeltsin cut them short: 'No, that's not how it works. Independence is something different. As owners of what you produce, you will have to decide whom you sell to, at what price. All these are your problems. We are not going to feed you anymore.'"[37] At a town meeting on Sakhalin Island, off the Pacific seaboard, a woman wished to know what he would do about the sludge and oil polluting the Naiva River. It was up to them, Yeltsin responded: "You yourselves must put your rivers in order, not Moscow. Our task is to give you independence in solving all kinds of questions, and not to press decisions upon you, to give you the right to settle everything yourselves."[38]

Yeltsin's appetite for change grew as Soviet troubles mounted exponentially. Hard times, he was more willing to assume, made for hard decisions and not for band-aids and stopgaps. Any reform worth its salt needed to come to grips with the deficiencies of the communist paradigm, as he said in a pre-election interview in May 1991:

> My electoral program . . . lays emphasis on radical reforms, above all in the economy. You cannot stretch out the transition to the market and assure people that the more radical the changes are the worse things will be for them. What could be worse than the way we are running around in circles, in fact on a precipice? . . . It seems to me we have to see the big thing here: Partial reforms . . . will destroy us. The people will not stand

> for it. When you hear it said it is logical to extend reforms over a period of years, that is not for us. That is for a society where a fairly good living standard has already been achieved and where the people can wait awhile. In our country, the situation is so critical, and the bureaucratic system so powerful, that we must bring [the reforms] to completion rapidly.[39]

The "big thing" grew out of the art of politics more than the science of economics. Yeltsin's big-bang reform, like the coup de grâce to the USSR, expressed his penchant for dichotomizing choices. He itched to be his own master and not be gulled by erratic partners, as he felt he had been on the Five Hundred Days plan. A precipitous thrust would snap the "hypnosis of words" he so excoriated in Gorbachev. And it would have an ineffable cultural component. Anatolii Chernyayev, we have seen, remarked that in Russia "big things" had always gotten done by the method of "either win all or lose all." In Chernyayev's diary, "either win all or lose all" is rendered as the Russian saw that describes the doughty soldier's choices as *ili grud' v krestakh, ili golova v kustakh:* "Either you come home with medals on your chest or you leave your head in the bushes."[40]

The academics and professionals Yeltsin inducted into his government as the Soviet Union fell apart were in many cases versed in the writings of Western free marketeers like Friedrich von Hayek, Milton Friedman, and Janos Kornai. Others had dirigiste, Keynesian, technocratic, or social-democratic points of view. The reform discussion was outside the ken of an engineer without a liberal arts education, and a political animal to the marrow of his bones. Yeltsin's approach sprang from a visceral intuition about the imperative of change and the general course it should take—not from highbrow theory but not from a whim, either. "I will not pretend to speak about the philosophy of economic reform," he was to write in *Notes of a President.*[41] It did not deter him. Waiting his turn to speak at a 1989 rally in a Moscow park, he had grilled an American correspondent on where he learned about economic affairs. The American in his time worked in a family business and read many books, including the screeds of pre-1917 Russian socialists. "Yeltsin said, 'So neither of us knows about economics!' Then he said, 'We'll find some young guys, there are some young guys who get this stuff.'"[42] There were, and he found them in 1991–92, after several years, as Margaret Thatcher noticed in 1990, of brooding over the scourges of communism.

On his post-communist highway to Damascus, the freedom to which Yeltsin converted was closer to what the political thinker Isaiah Berlin labeled "negative liberty" (freedom *from* hindrance) than to Berlin's "positive liberty" (freedom *to* accomplish some end).[43] For Yeltsin's contemporaries, deliverance from Marxist scripture and Soviet structures took many forms. For him, it was an ease with the market and recoil against the overbearing state. Mikhail Fridman, who became one of Russia's first billionaires as a banker and oilman, makes the point well:

> Yeltsin as an individual who had inner freedom . . . instinctively moved toward the market as the end. That is because . . . as my namesake Milton Friedman says, "Capitalism is freedom.". . . [Yeltsin thought] it was necessary to give people freedom and they would make out well. How exactly to do that he did not know. [But he did know] that it was necessary to free people from control: We were squeezing them dry. He thought that if we let them go they could move heaven and earth. . . . This is the level on which he thought about it. . . . He took a dim view of all these [Soviet] controls. [He felt that] the controllers had long since believed in nothing.[44]

If Yeltsin was a social democrat at all, it was more in the stamp of Tony Blair of Britain, Felipe González of Spain, or Gerhard Schröder of Germany than of the left-wing statists of interwar and postwar Europe. He took it as uncontroversial that Russia could get by only with a just and effective state, but that its state would have the ability to rule and popular support only if it did something to cure Russia's economic disease.

Yeltsin was able to anchor enthusiasm for capsizing Soviet ways in half-buried pieces of his past. In the chapter of *Notes of a President* where he eulogizes Ignatii and Nikolai Yeltsin, he speaks of the windmill, smithy, and land leases they gathered by the sweat of their brow and of the injustice and social disutility of the state expropriating them. He was aware of how Vasilii Starygin fended in exile by selling homemade furniture to local buyers. These kin's only crime was that they held property, were hardworking, and "took many things upon themselves." With its zero-sum thinking, "The Soviet regime liked modest, ordinary folk, people who did not stand out. It did not like and it showed no mercy to the strong, the ingenious, and the lively." Yeltsin's felt mandate, as someone who did stand out, was to undo this mistake and foster an enterprising society in which the writ of the state was circumscribed. For throwing off lassitude, he offered autobiographical role models: the sportsman who trains and betters a rival, as he had on the volleyball court; the public figure who survives after taking an independent stand, as he did in his secret speech in 1987; and the hospital patient who takes the first tottering steps after an operation, as he had after his back surgery in Barcelona in 1990. Russians, he said, needed to cast off their "slavish psychology" and open up space for "people without hangups, intrepid people, of the kind who earlier [in the Soviet period] were simply squelched." The idealized historical reference most on Yeltsin's mind was his thrifty Urals forebears. Russia was giving signs, he wrote, of reemergence of the outlook "of independent peasants *[muzhiki]* who do not wait for another's help, who do not pin their hopes on anyone else . . . [who] scold everyone and stubbornly tend to their own business."[45]

After the 1991 coup, Yeltsin was in no shape psychologically or politically to move into decision gear. He fled Moscow on August 29 for two weeks of sunbathing, swimming, and tennis in the Latvian playground of Jurmala. He was back in town briefly twice, did a peacemaking errand in Armenia, and was then off again to Sochi for another couple of weeks. On September 18, in Moscow, Yeltsin was drained and experienced coronary pain. But on September 25, the day he left for Sochi, Pavel Voshchanov said he "has taken a timeout . . . not for relaxation but so he can in calm surroundings work at his further plans and also on a new book."[46] Yeltsin supporters were stupefied that he had dropped out of sight and at such a juncture could be dabbling in authorship. It was as if Napoleon had repaired to the Riviera to compose poetry after routing the Austrian and Russian armies at Austerlitz, one Democratic Russia parliamentary deputy later said. Gorbachev's advisers thought the Russian leader was playing "a cat-and-mouse game with us," and Gorbachev refused to consider traveling to Sochi to see him ("We have to protect our honor").[47] Yeltsin at Bocharov Ruchei dictated a few paragraphs only of the manuscript, which was to grow into *Notes of a President*, the second volume of his memoirs, and had no interest in playing games with Gorbachev. But his "further plans" could not be put off and were the subject of searing interchanges with members of his team until his return to the capital on October 10.

As the Soviet Union was in extremis and Yeltsin composed himself, Russia's government found itself in turmoil. In July he had asked Gennadii Burbulis, the scholar from Sverdlovsk who had just managed his election campaign, and whom he passed over for Aleksandr Rutskoi as vice president, to be his chief of staff and set up a Presidential Executive Office (Administratsiya Prezidenta) for him. Burbulis balked: He pined to be a grand strategist and not "to work twenty-four hours a day with a card file."[48] Yeltsin contrived the position of state secretary for him, with undefined duties. Rutskoi, elected without a job description, then exhorted Yeltsin to unite the office of vice president with headship of the executive office and to let him be the president's channel to the state apparatus. Yeltsin, saying he had no need of "a commissar," declined.[49] On August 5 he selected as chief of staff his old friend from the Sverdlovsk obkom, Yurii Petrov, who had been Soviet ambassador to Cuba since 1988; Yeltsin had to ask Gorbachev to release him from the post. Petrov reported for duty around noon on August 19, just as the tanks chugged up to the Russian White House. He had no time to introduce himself to Rutskoi, Burbulis, and staff before rushing downstairs to catch Yeltsin making his immortal speech on Tank No. 110.[50]

The ministerial bureaucracy was the main mechanism for carrying out decisions. At its head as prime minister was Ivan Silayev, a "red director"—a widely used term in Russia for the Soviet-era industrial manager, serving at the pleasure of the Communist Party. Silayev, who was Yeltsin's age and had left the besieged White House for his family in August, was in the president's estimation an unsuitable sparkplug for a serious salvage and reform effort. He quit on September 27 to chair an interrepublic economic committee, leaving Oleg Lobov of Sverdlovsk as caretaker Russian premier. The cabinet was rife with jockeying for position; agreements were being signed and disowned and resignations tendered in disgust. The seclusion of the president, one reporter observed, "has produced a crisis of power" and "a conflict of all against all."[51]

For the prime minister's post, Yeltsin looked at first for a "miracle worker" unattached to any program. He offered it in September to Svyatoslav Fëdorov, the proprietor of the USSR's first commercial eye-surgery clinic, who turned it down flat. He had no better luck with Yurii Ryzhov, the rector of the Moscow Aviation Institute, or Mikhail Poltoranin, the editor to whom he had been so close in the Moscow party committee. He then auditioned Yurii Skokov, a conservative industrialist from the military sector, and Grigorii Yavlinskii.[52] In dialogue on beach chairs in Sochi, Burbulis got Yeltsin to look at less familiar names and to link his personnel decision to the reform conundrum. After three days, "Yeltsin understood very well the backlog of problems, the frightening inheritance that had come his way. And so our conversation came down to the hopelessness of surmounting all of this by conventional methods." "It is going to be very sticky," Yeltsin said to him. Burbulis felt "emaciated" by the conversation.[53]

As crafter of the unconventional methods, Burbulis prevailed on the president to turn to Yegor Gaidar, an urbane, moon-faced economist and publicist from the Soviet baby boom—at thirty-five, he was but one year older than Yeltsin's first daughter, Yelena. Born into an establishment family (his father was a navy admiral and both of his grandfathers were famed writers), Gaidar had two graduate degrees in economics, had written for *Pravda* and *Kommunist* (the CPSU's theoretical journal), and directed a research institute. He also had a connection to the city of Sverdlovsk, which had just been renamed Yekaterinburg.[54] Working out of an Arkhangel'skoye-2 dacha, Gaidar and colleagues had drawn up a liberalization proposal more radical than Five Hundred Days and executable in Russia rather than in an undivided Soviet Union.[55] He was asked in the last week of October to return from a lecture booking at Erasmus University, Rotterdam, to meet with Yeltsin. Their interview took all of twenty minutes. The chief "grasped the breathtaking risk connected with the beginning of reforms," yet also "that passivity and dallying would be suicidal." "He seemed geared up to take upon himself political accountability for reforms that would inevitably be punishing, knowing this would add nothing to his popularity."[56] Gaidar agreed to serve in some capacity, although he and his confederates at the dacha rubbed their eyes and "felt as if it were not for real."[57]

Yeltsin tipped his hand publicly on October 28 in a wide-ranging address to the Russian Congress of People's Deputies and the population. "The period of movement by small steps is over," he declared. "We now need a reformist breakthrough. . . . We shall begin, in deeds and not just in words, to pull ourselves out of the morass that is sucking us in deeper and deeper."[58] On November 1 the congress gave him carte blanche to make reforms by decree for twelve months. He was authorized to issue edicts contravening existing laws, reorganize the cabinet without checking with parliament, and appoint heads of provincial administrations. Ruslan Khasbulatov, the new chairman of the Supreme Soviet, shepherded the motion through the assembly. The composition of a reform government was revealed on November 6, the day Yeltsin consigned the CPSU to oblivion. On Burbulis's advice, Yeltsin did the constitutional somersault of naming himself prime minister, averting the need to have anyone else confirmed by parliament. Burbulis was made first deputy premier and Gaidar finance minister and deputy premier for economic policy.[59] To their surprise, Yeltsin left Gaidar and Burbulis alone to nominate the holders of key portfolios. Most were thirty-somethings, up to twenty-five years younger than Yeltsin and Gavriil Popov and the reformists he had known in the Interregional Deputies Group. "Fresh faces were needed to cope with the job. I selected people with a minimum of Soviet baggage, people without mental and ideological blinkers, without a bureaucratic mentality."[60] They passed with flying colors the test he had set in the Moscow party committee in the mid-1980s: readiness to put in insanely long hours at work. Gaidar's days that fall and winter ended at three or four A.M.; eager beavers in his office snatched some slumber on cots or on pillows and blankets spread on the floor.

Political blowups heightened the pressure. One of them led Yeltsin on November 7 to impose martial law in Chechnya, a minority republic in the North Caucasus area of Russia. An air force general, Djokhar Dudayev, had been elected president in the Chechen capital of Grozny and peremptorily declared independence. Yeltsin's show of force, promoted by Vice President Rutskoi, only fanned the flames, and Gorbachev, who still controlled Soviet troops, was opposed. On November 11 the Russian Supreme Soviet voted not to recognize Yeltsin's decree, making it unenforceable. Speaker Ruslan Khasbulatov, an ethnic Chechen, sided with the anti-Yeltsin forces.

For one week of all this Yeltsin was inaccessible to his staff and ministers. Gorbachev, the unsympathetic witness, claims Yeltsin was drunk when they spoke about Chechnya by telephone on November 10. Associates were unsure how much alcohol had to do with it but were disturbed by their leader's unavailability. Either way, the stress of office was giving rise to insalubrious behavior.[61]

The October reform package went under the marquee "shock therapy" (*shokoterapiya* in Russian). The phrase applied to a wider field of action than its original meaning in Latin America and post-communist Eastern Europe, which was the lifting of price controls to halt an inflationary spiral and jumpstart economic growth.[62] Yeltsin, he stated unsentimentally in retirement, aimed at a double-barreled modernizing revolution in economy and by extension in society: "to unloose prices, that is to introduce a real market forcefully and toughly, the way [Russian landlords and peasants] were ordered to plant potatoes under Peter the Great; and, second, to create private property . . . to create a class of owners."[63] Peter had been his paladin since grade school, and Yeltsin was mesmerized by the tsar as enlightened *reformator*—a Russian noun, borrowed from the German, that connotes the likelihood of greater dislocations than the English "reformer." Here was his chance to play Peter, although in a protodemocratic nation: His lords and peasants had the franchise and could topple him at the next election. He knew of Peter's maniacal tendencies, he would concede in 1993 to an interviewer who pointed out that Peter "personally cut off the heads" of his enemies. It was true, Yeltsin said, "but we also have to keep in mind all the things he did for Russia."[64]

Much as summaries—including Yeltsin's wistful retirement speech in December 1999—often refer to the assault as one fast-flying leap, his thinking at the time showed flexibility and realism. Concerning Peter the Great, he writes level-headedly in *Notes of a President* that turning Russians into good Europeans was "an ambitious goal unattainable in one generation." "In a certain sense," the Petrine reforms "have not been completed to this day." "Although we have become Europeans, we have remained ourselves." Every flurry of reform in Russia's past, he said, was followed by a backlash and a rollback. This mold he was determined to break. "The goal I posed for myself was to make reform irrevocable." If there were economic restructuring and "grandiose political changes," the process would be unstoppable and a return of the communists inconceivable: "After us, other people will come who will finish the job off and move the country toward prosperity."[65]

Yeltsin wanted the path chosen to outlive the first burst of change and to outlive him. What he did not want was to take the time to ask the population's approval of his project or to spell out what awaited them. Perhaps, as Yurii Burtin said in 1992, he tended to patronize the people "as one would a child who does not understand his own interests and cannot be allowed to participate in affairs of state."[66] I doubt Yeltsin was as misanthropic as that. As Burtin wrote, condescension toward the population coexisted in the minds of Yeltsin and his men with fear of disorder, a yen to please, and a catering to "the prejudices and the far from admirable feelings of the less conscious strata."[67] Society itself, after generations of communism, was not organized to protect or promote the shared interests of its members, particularly when the patrimonial idols lay broken on the temple floor. The historian Yurii Afanas'ev, formerly co-chairman with Yeltsin of the Interregional group, noted in an essay in the same volume as Burtin's how underdeveloped Russia's civil society was and that political parties, which could now be legally formed, were insubstantial startups: "The absence of large-scale social groups tutored in their own distinct group interests allows the administration of Boris Yeltsin to forget about our current anemic 'multipartyness.'"[68] Most citizens waited for their leader to act and hoped for the best.

Yeltsin's words and his taking on of the premiership left no doubt about who had willed the turnabout in policy. But he held open an escape route. In mid-1992 he was to raise Gaidar in rank to acting prime minister. By the end of 1992, Gaidar and his benefactor from 1991, Burbulis, were both out of government. Yeltsin professed that he always saw the Gaidar-Burbulis grouping as "a kamikaze crew that would step into the line of fire and forge ahead . . . that would go up in flames but remain in history."[69] Did the warriors know they were taking to the sky on a suicide mission? Yeltsin says he never discussed it with them; the head kamikaze says he did. In their get-acquainted meeting, asserts Gaidar in his memoir of the 1990s, he warned Yeltsin that once the most unsavory decisions were behind them the president might have to dismiss the government. Yeltsin "gave me a skeptical smile and waved his arm, as if to say it would not come to that."[70] Either the president was holding his cards close to his vest or, more likely, he was not yet certain how it would all play out.

The decisive break in Yeltsin's October manifesto on reforming the economy, as announced to the Congress of Deputies, was in the realm of prices. Ninety percent of retail prices in Russia, and 80 percent of wholesale prices, were to be freed from state dictate and left to the impersonal forces of supply and demand. Yeltsin dressed down aides when the draft of the speech, in a typing screw-up, omitted the section on price deregulation.[71] Another priority was macroeconomic stabilization through slashing the budget deficit and cutting back on the emission of money and credit. Still another was privatization of state property, to forge "a healthy mixed economy with a strong private sector." Half of all small and medium-sized firms were to be turned over to nonstate owners within six months; large enterprises were going to be refashioned as joint stock corporations, shares in which would later be distributed and sold at supply-and-demand prices. Yeltsin described these actions as proactive and equally as reactive to developments. Members of the nomenklatura had already been sidestepping price controls, trafficking on the black market, and speculating in currency. And they were furtively amassing money and unofficial rights over, and rents from, state property: "Privatization has been going on in Russia for some time, but in a wild . . . and often criminal fashion. Today we need to seize the initiative, and we are intent on doing so."

Yeltsin tended most meticulously in the speech to the politics of the breakthrough. "The experience of global civilization" showed that Russia's plight was "difficult but not hopeless." The nation that overcame Napoleon and Hitler had special reserves that would see it through: "Russia has more than once in its rich history shown that a crucible period is when it is able to mobilize its will and its many powers, talents, and resources in order to lift up and strengthen itself." All could pull together, he said, in the knowledge that relief was in sight. "The uncertainty will be gone and the prognosis will be clear."

When Yeltsin got around to owning up to and distributing the costs of his changes, he was on thin ice. He had been claiming since the 1990 election campaign that he could move Russia toward the market—he did not apply the word *kapitalizm,* so unmusical to Soviet ears, until his second term—without people of ordinary means losing out. In the 1991 presidential campaign, he flailed at Gorbachev for the administered increases in consumer and food prices that April: "They ought not to have begun economic reform by unscrupulously laying all the hardships on the population."[72] Now that he answered for policy, he had to sell belt-tightening. "It will be worse for everyone for approximately a half-year. Then prices will go down, the consumer market will fill with goods, and *by the autumn of 1992* . . . the economy will stabilize and living standards will slowly improve."[73] The one round year seems to have been mostly a figment of his imagination, and was more optimistic than Five Hundred Days, which had posited a two-year stabilization period. Gaidar maintains that two or three years were the minimum needed for growth to return and denies that he misled Yeltsin as to the time needed.[74]

The price reform, postponed two weeks at the request of the Ukrainians and Belarusians, clicked in on January 2, 1992. Budgetary restraint took effect forthwith. On January 29 Yeltsin's Decree No. 65, "On Freedom of Trade," pulled the plug on a state monopoly dating back to the late 1920s. Outside of a few interdicted items like firearms and narcotics, Russians were at liberty to buy and sell anything without asking permission; in effect, exchange had been decriminalized. One of Gaidar's first decisions as deputy premier was to select another youthful economist, Anatolii Chubais from St. Petersburg, as chairman of the State Property Committee and ask him to work out a design for denationalization. Chubais confected a white paper in December 1991, with the preferred formula to transfer assets to "work collectives" (employees and managers) and to call off government output quotas and subsidies. In the first half of 1992, Gosplan, Gosstroi, Goskomtsen (the State Prices Committee), Gossnab (the State Supplies Committee), Gosagroprom (the State Committee for the Agroindustrial Complex), and their ilk were disestablished, while all except for a few of the Soviet industrial ministries were stripped of their command rights and reorganized as holding companies. On August 20, 1992, a year after the 1991 coup d'état, Yeltsin trumpeted a program to call forth "millions of owners rather than a few millionaires" by distributing vouchers citizens could use to purchase equity in 15,000 government-owned companies.

The immediate aftershock of these measures, as is well known, was fearsome. Counter to Yeltsin's rubicund forecast, conditions did not meliorate in the autumn of 1992, or the next year, or the year after that. Consumer prices rose 296 percent in January 1992; inflation hit 2520 percent for the year 1992 and thereby shredded the ruble savings of millions—most of them in Soviet paper printed in the Gorbachev years and stowed under the mattress or in bank accounts because there was nothing in the shops to buy with it. Real national output fell off every single year through 1996 (by 14.5 percent in 1992, 8.7 percent in 1993, 12.7 percent in 1994, 4.1 percent in 1995, and 3.5 percent in 1996), ticked up (by 0.8 percent) in 1997, and fell again (by 4.6 percent) in 1998 to a low point of 40 percent less than it had been in 1989 and 35 percent less than in 1991, the year Yeltsin took office. Fear of layoffs was pervasive in the workforce, as factories were weaned off of state subsidies and contracts and the government budget was squeezed. In 1993 and 1994, the withholding of wage payments and government pensions and allowances became common practice, with the arrears for some extending months and even years.[75] As downturns go, Russia's in the 1990s ranks with the Great Depression of 1929–33 in the United States.

The statistics on gross domestic product and consumer welfare provoked a political firestorm then and cast a pall over later evaluations of the Yeltsin era. They are why no defender of him and his reforms fails to leaven bravos with caveats.[76] Recall that it was *Yeltsin,* as he went on pension in 1999, who vented remorse at having let down the buoyant hopes that Russia could coast from its despotic past to a bountiful future.

Yeltsin's critics in the West, who are legion, rely on the economic and socioeconomic distress of the time to fuel their indictments. One oft-voiced criticism rivets a Burkean animus against social engineering to left-of-center political values. Historian Stephen F. Cohen, for example, argues that Gorbachev had shown Soviet communism to be reformable and that piecemeal adaptation of the old system, statist and respectful of Russian custom, was preferable to throwing caution to the winds. The drive to rebuild Russia from the ground up, abetted by an evangelizing America, was guilty of the "de-modernization" of a great industrial nation: "Never . . . have so many fallen so far."[77] Political scientist Peter Reddaway and Russian coauthor, Dmitri Glinski, agree with Cohen on the noxiousness of the changes of the 1990s (Russia was "slowly succumbing to shock therapy's sequelae while the world watches"), but save their sharpest harpoons for the "market Bolshevik" techniques used to bring them about. Yeltsin and company, in the service of anti-Marxist objectives, were like the Marxist revolutionaries of old in exemplifying "the self-confident, almost messianic vanguard mentality of a self-anointed elite that sees itself entitled to impose 'progress' and 'development' . . . on the 'backward' majority." Shock therapy, they say, was an "administrative revolution from above" comparable to Stalin's collectivization of Soviet agriculture.[78] The titles of the two books—*Failed Crusade: America and the Tragedy of Post-Communist Russia*, by Cohen, and *The Tragedy of Russia's Reforms: Market Bolshevism against Democracy*, by Reddaway and Glinski—give away their contents.

The changes Yeltsin set in train in 1991–92 deserve more nuanced analysis than this. There are several perspectives from which this is true.

One pertains to the circumstances of the reforms. The slump of the 1990s was to be bad but not as bad as frequently depicted, and the government data that track it exclude the illegal and informal sector. Economic shrinkage was ubiquitous in the post-communist space in Eastern Europe and Eurasia. In that the coming apart of the Soviet Union wreaked havoc on supply networks and trade flows among the CIS nations, they were all at a disadvantage compared to their neighbors west of the pre-1991 Soviet border. On output loss, Russia fared perceptibly better than the CIS average, and was not in a league of its own.[79] It did so despite unique handicaps going into the reform maelstrom. Russia was saddled with 80 to 90 percent of the bloated military-industrial complex of the Soviet Union, demand for whose wares tumbled after the Cold War. It would have had an easier time of it had it not agreed to bear all of the USSR's debt, the bulk of it incurred by Gorbachev, and if it had controlled its money supply out of the starting gate and not waited until 1993 or 1994 for the ex-republics to jettison the ruble. Russia would have been much better off if world prices for oil, its most precious natural resource, had not dipped below $20 a barrel for most of the post-Soviet decade. The petrodollars that producers were to be flooded with in the 2000s would have limited the sag in Russian GDP and kept the Yeltsin government out of the red.[80]

Another corrective comes from pondering the Yeltsin revolution in time. The troubles that stimulated his attack on communism did not come out of thin air. Derived from defects hardwired into it by Lenin and Stalin, they heaped up over decades. Well before Yeltsin moved from Sverdlovsk to Moscow in 1985, system decay was manifesting itself in economic decline, social division, and anomie. Once the myopia about these problems was dispelled, large segments of the elite and the population chafed, as they were bound to, at what they took as half-solutions to them. Panglossian assessments of the reformability of the Soviet regime elide this impatience and the rudderless changes and mismanaged mini-reforms that made the everyday life of most Russians bedlam in the perestroika years. Reforming the system from within, as Gorbachev meant to do, was a respectable choice. Heading for the exits was a cleaner and better one.[81]

Economic liberalization fused to political autocracy and a strong state—not to Gorbachev's muzzy humanism—was effected in communist China after the death of Chairman Mao Zedong in 1976. The Soviet Union could possibly have pursued this formula, although it was more industrialized and did not have China's ethnic uniformity and its sea of rural labor. The window of opportunity for adopting a Chinese model was the Kremlin tenure of Yurii Andropov, the righteous former chairman of the KGB, in 1982–84; Andropov was not in power long enough, or definite enough on his policies, to be its guiding spirit. In 1991, after a half-decade of upheaval, atomization of the political class, and state deconstruction, the window was long since closed.[82] Decontrolling prices was the sine qua non for uncorking market forces. When Yeltsin decided to let prices go, Gorbachev, who had refused to drink from this chalice for years, was pleased, one of his aides felt, that Yeltsin "was ready to take upon himself the responsibility for reforms fraught with serious social shocks and to relieve Gorbachev of it."[83] The prime alternative was to recentralize and rebureaucratize the economy, with the option of embarking at a later date on reforms in the mold of Deng Xiaoping. Institutional malaise, the legitimacy deficit, and the nationality problem made such a course impractical without a clampdown that could have rivaled the 1989 massacre in Beijing's Tienanmen Square.[84] The one option not on the table was to do nothing.

Considering the Yeltsin record as de-modernization or a tragedy from start to finish sheds more heat than light. From the vantage of 1992 or 1995, there was little to show statistically for shock therapy. By the day Yeltsin called it quits in 1999, the cradle of state socialism boasted a market economy of sorts. Sixty to 70 percent of material and financial assets, everything from newspaper kiosks to coal mines and aluminum mills, were off the government's books, and most goods and services traded at a going price set by profit-oriented private firms. Anatolii Chubais's privatization had few precedents in Russia, where history and the cultural fiber are congruent with state power, and was the largest divestiture of state resources *anywhere* in history. Inflation was wrestled down into the double digits by 1996, jumped in 1998 when Russia was in financial crisis, and receded to double digits in 1999 and henceforth. Russia by 1999 had a stock exchange (it first appeared in Moscow in 1994), commodity exchanges by the dozen, private banks by the hundred, and scads of business schools. Most pertinent politically, economic growth had resumed, and there has been no stopping it since then. Russia overshot the CIS norm in length of the economic contraction after communism; it undershot it in magnitude of the contraction. With better leadership and better public policy, the economy might have bottomed out several years sooner—on average, output was lowest in the twelve CIS countries in 1996, versus 1998 in Russia—and it might have begun to expand, and the standard of living to improve, several years sooner.

Yeltsin's post-communist reforms transcended the economy. By relaxing the hammerlock of the state on production and distribution, Yeltsin parted with dogma and breathed into being new social categories, and ones that did not necessarily meet with social approval—a propertied middle class, people of means (parodied in the popular culture as the crass "New Russians"), and the super-rich parvenus, "the oligarchs." In daily life, for all the problems, within six months Russia was done with artificial scarcities and the lineups in which the average Soviet adult had wasted one hour per day, waiting to buy sausage or vodka or matches, in 1990. Home ownership went up from 33 percent in 1990 to about 60 percent in 2000. Reform also created political space by enlarging citizens' autonomy, breeding new interests, and making new resources available for acquiring influence in the public domain.[85] And sweeping changes, economic and non-economic, had sweeping implications worldwide as well. Russia, as Yeltsin was to say from every podium offered, no longer had any foundational reason to stand apart from the United States or the Western alliance.

These facts all belie any deep equivalency between Yeltsinism and Bolshevism. Lenin and the revolutionaries of 1917 were violent utopians, hellbent on building a brave new world on universalist precepts inimical to those of the capitalist democracies. On Soviet territory, they were monopolists, centralizers, and annihilators of the tsarist ruling stratum and of lesser social groups, such as the kulaks, whom they saw as uncongenial to the new order.

On the international stage, they were a disruptive force. In sum, the Bolsheviks sought to make a Great Leap Forward, blazing the trail for others to follow. Yeltsin sought a Great Leap Outward. He meant for his de-monopolizing revolution to make Russia more similar to the rest of Europe and mankind by affording it the ABCs of a market economy and of a democratic social and political order, as he conceptualized them. Russia, in his mind's eye, needed "to catch up, to strain every nerve, and to make super efforts *in order to become like the rest*."[86] He parceled out power and had nothing against old-timers from the previous regime going into politics (like Yegor Ligachëv, who was elected to parliament in 1993, and Nikolai Ryzhkov, elected in 1995) or into business. In foreign policy, he was a joiner of transnational organizations and a realistic taker of terms from stronger powers.[87]

In the political realm, Yeltsin after 1991 infracted democratic principles more than once and resorted to military force to quell opponents in 1993 against the Congress of People's Deputies and in 1994 against the separatist rebels in Chechnya. However, there were extenuating circumstances in both these cases, as we shall see. Viktor Sheinis, a distinguished foreign-policy scholar and legislator, who took strong issue with him on specifics, strikes an appropriate balance in his memoirs on the things Yeltsin did right:

> Now that Boris Yeltsin's career is completed and the sternest accusations have been made against him, I would like to underscore something opposite: that the undeniable authoritarianism in his style of behavior and rule had its limits. It was limited by his recognition of certain democratic values, far from all but very important ones, which he did not drink in with his mother's milk but to which, once he had assimilated them, he remained loyal. These would include the right of people to have and express their opinions, freedom of the press and freedom to criticize the government, and the free movement of citizens. Curbs on political pluralism and straightforward suppression of opposition, unless it itself had moved to violent actions, were in a forbidden zone for him. It is impossible not to take into the perspective one other noteworthy factor. From the earliest phase of his ascent to power, starting in 1990, Yeltsin displayed a quality exceptional for a person of his age and circle—an aptitude for educating himself and for intellectual growth.[88]

As president, Yeltsin confined himself by and large to pacific means of realizing his goals. Unlike the Bolsheviks, he did not put his opponents before an execution squad or behind razor wire. He would slough off powers and revenues to the provinces, enlarge media freedoms, and win mass consent through election. For the first sustained period in modern times, Yeltsin's Russia was to be a land without political censors, political exiles, or political prisoners—a museum was built in 1994 at the last camp, Perm-36, which Gorbachev had closed in 1987. Both Peter the Great and the early communists made a cultural revolution in Russia. Peter ordered his subjects to shave their beards, forsake traditional clothing, and take communion once a year. Lenin and Stalin prescribed atheism, discipline on the factory floor, and reverence for the party and backed them up with terror and cradle-to-grave indoctrination. Yeltsin had no stomach for interventions in matters of manners and morals and would continue the trend under perestroika away from state controls over the individual.

A facile parallel with Bolshevism would overrate the mercilessness and consistency of Yeltsin's conduct over the full course of his presidency. Over-rigorous design of the reforms, while sometimes a factor, was to be far from the only cause of the agonies associated with them. Policies that prolonged the needed changes, lacked cohesion, and spared the cost did as much harm, especially but not exclusively in the economic area.[89] As Reddaway and Glinski note—and as flies in the face of the postulate of messianism—Yeltsin and successive subleaders to him adjusted their economic and other policies as they proceeded and seldom behaved as though they had a step-by-step scheme: "Their ruling passion was political pragmatism."[90]

Pragmatism in policy generated neither mere opportunism nor an even flow of decisions. Instead, the reality in the Russia Yeltsin remade was a perplexing blend of types. Reform would be a long footslog—down a winding road, against a headwind. Its political history was studded with acts of statesmanship but also with wasted chances and spells of inaction. As will become apparent in subsequent chapters, when this discombobulated country forged ahead, as it surely did on Yeltsin's watch, it was in fits and starts and not in a steady beat. So it went because of rearing uncertainty, institutional and coalitional politics, and what Oleg Poptsov called "swings in the social temperature." And so it went because of the person whose hand was at the tiller. "Political arrhythmia," as Poptsov colorfully put it, was to be a lasting ingredient of Yeltsin's style as national leader.[91]

CHAPTER TEN

Resistances

Conscious beliefs and intuitions planted Yeltsin's feet on the "civilized path" of radical reformation. They came forth intermingled from disenchantment with communism and a search for a better future. One has to wonder in wide angle why this effort accomplished what it did *and* why it did not accomplish more, and why not less painfully.

Post-communism as a milieu ought to have offered scope for statecraft. Above, a commanding leader promised fundamental change and was liberated from the roles and rules of the now-vanished civilization of the USSR. In so protean a medium, "The room for individual impact—that is, the impact of such things as intelligence, emotions, personality, aggressiveness, skill, timing, connections, and ambitions—is enormous."[1] Yeltsin had all these qualities, from brainpower to timing to ambition. Below, in a time of exigency, a "rescue-hungry people" might have been receptive to charismatic inspiration and guidance.[2] The angst attendant upon the decease of a tyranny, an empire, or a failed social project—and the Soviet Union was all three—should have attracted the populace to a person who acted with dispatch, calmed nerves, and said he knew of a new way. Russia after the convulsions of 1985 to 1991 looked ripe for a season of "extraordinary politics" in which claimants would temper their ordinary demands and think in terms of the common good.[3] The man in the best position to identify the common good and act as rescuer was Boris Yeltsin.

As the post-Soviet reforms got under way, this was the uplifting prospect before him and his colleagues. They faced, Yegor Gaidar has written, incalculable risks but also a freedom of maneuver few governments ever have. The Communist Party, its ideology, and its organizational transmission belts were gone. The army, the KGB, and the military-industrial and agricultural lobbies were paralytic, some of their chiefs moldering in prison for their participation in the August coup. Many Russians who had qualms about Western models held their fire: They were "interested in the most ungrateful [tasks] being undertaken by someone else's hand" so that they could later profit at the reformers' expense.[4]

The scenario of a tabula rasa hanging there, waiting for change to be written on it, was overdone from the beginning. It faded in Yeltsin's first term—in fact, in the initial months of his first term—as resistances to change and to the agents of change multiplied. While no one resistance was an absolute, together they pushed Russia toward compromise though not desertion of the Great Leap Outward. They were twofold: external to Yeltsin, that is, located in his environment of operations; and internal, or dictated by his preferences and his perceptions of where he and Russia stood.

Exogenous constraints started with the fact that Yeltsin was nowhere near the sole winner from the dismemberment of communist authoritarianism. The Soviet collapse unshackled and energized actors who had come out of the woodwork with him and now clamored for their share of the spoils. As standard procedures were overwhelmed, the leader also had trouble employing institutional resources to attain his goals. The consummate resource for any politician in government is the state. In Yeltsin's Russia, indiscipline, uncertainty, and decolonization demoralized and corrupted this resource and converted quotidian chores into an ordeal. The irony was superb. As with transitional leaders in many places and times, it dawned on Yeltsin that "the fluidity of the situation both empowers *and* weakens individuals," hampering satisfaction of the very aspirations the environment has stirred up.[5]

Up to the 1991 watershed, Yeltsin as a communist heretic and then an anti-communist insurgent held a card none of his rivals had—the trust and affection of the powerless. This is not to say they were with him unanimously or unreservedly. In July of that year, the best-known polling organization in the Soviet Union, Yurii Levada's VTsIOM (Center for the Study of Public Opinion), plumbed societal attitudes toward him. Confidence in Yeltsin, the survey showed, was unevenly distributed and was for millions contingent on other considerations. Twenty-nine percent of the interviewees were emotive supporters ("I fully support Yeltsin's views and positions"), while another 11 percent assented "as long as he is leader of the democratic forces" in the country. This core constituency of 40 percent was well short of a majority and nearly 20 percentage points less than his vote total in the June presidential election. Eleven percent of Russians gave Yeltsin the most unfavorable evaluations (they were not supporters of his or would support anyone other than him). Many more than opposed him outright, and almost as many as supported him, gave ambivalent answers. They either were disappointed former aficionados (7 percent), found him unappealing but hopefully "useful to Russia" in the future (16 percent), or supported him "due to the absence of other worthy political figures" (15 percent). Yeltsin had climbed the heights of power only with the consent of a host of crosspressured citizens.[6]

Later studies using the same method traced a hemorrhaging of support. By March 1992, barely two months into his market reforms, the VTsIOM respondents placing Yeltsin in the topmost category had been sliced to 11 percent and his core constituency to 20 percent, or half what it was in July 1991. Those solidly against him were up to 18 percent, and those voicing ambivalence were now a plurality of 37 percent. By January 1993, only 5 percent of Russians were fully with him, 11 percent gave him qualified support, 22 percent were opposed, and a majority, 51 percent, were on the fence.[7]

In political terms, the most shocking thing about shock therapy was that it laid bare the limits of the nationwide consensus. Russians were united on the necessity of doing *something* about the economy and about instability in all things political and constitutional; on *what* was to be done, they were disunited. Bearish economic news and the whittling down of Yeltsin's mass base emboldened elite players who had principled objections to his reform program, or who found it expedient to take up arms. The first yelps of criticism came even before price liberalization took effect, and some were from members of the president's winning coalition, not from unreconstructed communists. Aleksandr Rutskoi, the running mate to Yeltsin a half-year before and now his vice president, spoke against headlong marketization on a tour of Siberian towns in late November 1991. In an interview with the newspaper *Nezavisimaya gazeta* on December 18, he declared that the government had been turned over to amateurs, "lads in pink trunks and yellow boots" who were hurling Russia toward disaster. Ruslan Khasbulatov, just chosen as parliamentary chairman, chimed in several weeks into the new year, and the Supreme Soviet adopted resolutions attacking the government.

In February and March of 1992, as a second planned miniwave of decontrol of prices drew nigh, this one aimed at oil and the energy sector, factory directors and bureaucrats from state industry campaigned to preempt it. Gaidar, elevated to first deputy premier by Yeltsin on March 2, cringed: "Powerful pressure mounted on the president. He was deluged daily by foot-messengers reporting to him what a fearful misadventure, if not perfidy, these monetarists were starting."[8] The Congress of People's Deputies took up the mantra when it convened in April and considered a motion to dismiss four economic ministers. Gaidar took Yeltsin off guard by standing up on April 13 to inform the deputies the entire cabinet was stepping down if the motion passed. Khasbulatov and his legislators did a volte face the next day. Yeltsin wrote in *Notes of a President* that the Gaidar move was unwelcome news to him, but he gave high grades to his understudy's theatrical sense: "Yegor Timurovich grasped the nature of the congress as a political spectacle, a big circus, where only the most unexpected and abrupt thrusts would carry the day."[9] Gaidar recalls that Yeltsin, who was still officially prime minister, "shook his head in pique and doubt yet accepted the decision." Gaidar's sponsor, Gennadii Burbulis, whom Yeltsin demoted in April from first deputy premier without explanation (he stayed on as state secretary), was dubious about the threat. Says Gaidar, "Gennadii Eduardovich, who had worked with Boris Nikolayevich much longer than me and knew him better, understood that our demand was addressed not only to the congress but to the president."[10]

The reprieve lasted only a few weeks. In a preview of what he would do again and again, Yeltsin spoke to Gaidar about introducing armaments specialist Yurii Skokov or Sverdlovsk partocrat Oleg Lobov into the cabinet "for equipoise" *(dlya ravnovesiya)*. The suggestion "was proudly rejected."[11] On May 30, at a Kremlin meeting on energy policy, Yeltsin announced that he was relieving the young minister for the branch, Vladimir Lopukhin, who was in favor of laissez-fire and was one of the four on the congress's blacklist. Writes Yeltsin: "I think back to two faces: one was scarlet, almost vermilion—that was Gaidar; the other was pale as a sheet—that was Lopukhin. It was difficult to look at them."[12] Appointed in Lopukhin's stead and awarded the rank of deputy premier was Viktor Chernomyrdin, an engineer and red director from the Urals; two other experienced managers, Vladimir Shumeiko and Georgii Khizha, were brought in as deputy premiers in mid-June.

Yeltsin did not consult Gaidar on the Lopukhin firing. He knew, Gaidar says, that Gaidar would have resigned if given early warning. Gaidar considered quitting but was talked out of it by friends. The promotion to acting prime minister on June 15 was little solace. Anyone could see he and Burbulis had been taken down a peg.[13] There was further evidence one month later when Yeltsin nominated, and the Supreme Soviet confirmed, Viktor Gerashchenko as chairman of the Central Bank of Russia. Gerashchenko, the last head of the USSR's state bank, was at odds with the Gaidar brain trust's tight-money policy and flooded industry and agriculture with cheap credits. Inflation, having subsided in the spring, took off again that autumn.[14]

When the congress gathered for its winter session (it assembled two or three times a year), Yeltsin's twelve months to make staffing and economic decisions by decree had expired. He asked the deputies to regularize Gaidar's appointment as prime minister, which they refused to do by 486 votes to 467 on December 9, 1992 (the congress had 1,068 members, of whom 252 sat in the Supreme Soviet). Flustered, Yeltsin decided to take his brief to the people. On December 11 he was driven to the AZLK Works, the carmaker in southeast Moscow that manufactured the rattletrap Moskvich. He knew from government documents that Russian workplaces were having hard times:

> But this was all on paper. Here in the immense assembly shop, darkish and slathered in machinery oil, all of the disillusionment and discontent heaped up over the year of reforms poured out. The workers met Yeltsin with a hush. All that rang out were some peals of applause, to which he was completely unaccustomed. There were no cries of acclaim, no supportive posters. The president plainly got skittish. Workers, mute and tense, listened. The concluding words of his speech—"I trust I will have your support"—struck no sparks. The prepackaged resolution was approved, but without any ardor.[15]

Workers bawled that Yeltsin should bury the hatchet with Khasbulatov and reanimate the socialist economy. Only ten or twenty, one observer divined, would have raised their hands for the motion if management and the trade union committee had not cracked the whips. Yeltsin was downcast as he climbed back into his limousine.[16]

AZLK and the dyspepsia of the parliamentarians took the wind out of Yeltsin's sails. He sat down with Khasbulatov and reached a deal on a baroque formula for selecting a prime minister to serve until Russia had a new constitution. The congress on December 14 came up with eighteen candidates; Yeltsin shortened the list to five, and in the process disallowed the favorite of the deputies, Georgii Khizha, an arms manufacturer from St. Petersburg; the congress did a straw poll with three choices per deputy; the president was to make a choice from among the three leading nominees and submit that name for confirmation. Yurii Skokov was the top candidate with 637 votes, followed by Viktor Chernomyrdin with 621 and Gaidar with 400 votes. Chernomyrdin was Yeltsin's pick of the three and was confirmed with 721 votes for.[17] Gaidar, Burbulis, and several other reformists were excluded from the new Council of Ministers. The kamikazes had flamed out—and the commodore who had ordered them into the air stayed at his post.

Yeltsin was gratified in 1991 by Gaidar's minimum of "Soviet baggage." This could not have been said about Chernomyrdin, a jowly veteran of the petroleum industry and the founding head of Gazprom, the state company that took over the assets of the USSR Ministry of the Gas Industry in 1989. Two decades older than Gaidar and only seven years younger than Yeltsin, he was out of Orenburg oblast, the home region of Naina Yeltsina. He had hooked up with Yeltsin when the latter was Sverdlovsk party boss and together they supervised pipeline laying; he was kinder to Yeltsin than most after the rift with Gorbachev.[18] "Viktor Stepanovich and I are united by common views on many things," Yeltsin would say in *Notes of a President,* and were of the same generation. Chernomyrdin had principles but "is not up in the clouds."[19] The earthbound Chernomyrdin was to be an indispensable man, the prime minister for five-plus years, and to win fame equally for his competence, his wiliness, his partiality toward the Gazprom monopoly,[20] and his mangled syntax and diction. Like Yeltsin, he evolved with the times.

The headlines of 1992 illuminated the environmental encumbrances to Yeltsin's reform program in all their abundance. Until he forcibly shut down the Congress of People's Deputies in late 1993 and imposed a presidentialist constitution, an obstructionist legislature lurked over his shoulder and had the legal and often the political force to foil him. But some of his biggest problems were within the amorphous executive branch. It contained a runaway vice president, a chief banker more attuned to parliament than to Yeltsin, and ministers and counselors raring to score points and to draw him into their corner. Large producers in Russia, still the property of the state, entreated for financial assistance. Private business, which was in its infancy, was strong enough in one area, banking, to create a sordid interest-group politics. The banks plumped for, and profited bounteously from, measures to assign them contracts for transferring credits from the central bank to specific firms and sectors, to allow them to pay negative real interest rates to depositors, and to protect them from contributory deposit insurance and foreign competition.[21] Although the populace only looked on from a distance, all principals knew well the peril of social unrest, and grassroots opinion was still viewed by government and opposition as mobilizable.

What was not so apparent in Yeltsin's first year, except to those with inside dope, was the importance of his endogenous thought processes and inhibitions—some of them evincing the Soviet baggage he sought to escape in his advisers, some responding to his reading of popular sentiment. In the springtime flap over bank credits and economic stabilization, to take one example, Gaidar found the president a hard sell on the subject of tight money: "Time after time at meetings between us or sessions of the government, he returned to the question of why we were not increasing the money supply" and thus keeping cash-strapped firms going. "The arguments we advanced did not seem persuasive enough to him anymore."[22] Yeltsin also vetoed Gaidar's call for an instantaneous, Russian-imposed end to the ruble zone in the former USSR. The currency reform occurred only in July 1993.

Yeltsin, rehashing the 1992 Lopukhin story in his memoirs, emphasized that he had his own reasons, and it was not just about pesky parliamentarians or lobbyists:

> The thing is that I myself worked for decades in Soviet economic management. It has no secrets for me. I know just what disorder there is there, what life is really like in factories big and small, what are the best and worst qualities of our directors, workers, and engineers. Despite the fact that I am a builder by profession, which has left its mark on me, I know all about heavy and light industry. In Sverdlovsk I had to be involved in this up to my elbows.
>
> So let's say some elderly industrialist comes to me and says in an agitated voice, "Boris Nikolayevich, I have been working for forty years in the gas industry. Now look at what this Lopukhin is up to, things are going on, here are the statistics to prove it, it is a nightmare, everything is going to hell." What am I going to do? I cannot be indifferent . . . and I feel I have to respond.

Gaidar, Yeltsin elaborated, "was putting the squeeze on me" via Lopukhin to approve liberalized energy prices, and "I considered that we could not adopt so hard a policy."[23]

The jockeying over forming and re-forming the cabinet brought out another phenomenon: Yeltsin's determination as president to have political independence from allies and associates. It applied to the intelligentsia-based movements with which he had made common cause in his tramp to power. Gavriil Popov, who had been elected mayor of Moscow, left city hall in June 1992 to found a private university—Yeltsin named Yurii Luzhkov, a red director and municipal bureaucrat, in his place—and no member of the former Interregional Deputies Group was given a high-level position. Leaders of the related Democratic Russia movement felt that Yeltsin owed them for their help in 1990 and 1991. Lev Ponomarëv and Gleb Yakunin, two of its three co-chairmen, stated publicly that Yeltsin should listen to their recommendations on cabinet positions and appoint members of the organization as his emissaries to the provinces. Ponomarëv and Yakunin invited themselves to Sochi in October 1991, during Yeltsin's sojourn there, and prevailed on him to receive them. The president took notes during the meeting, commended joint action, and did nothing to follow up.[24] Yurii Afanas'ev, the third co-chairman, well known to Yeltsin from the Interregionals, led a faction that was against any collaboration with him. In early 1992 he and ex-dissident Yurii Burtin, ruing "authoritarian degradation" under Yeltsin, walked out of Democratic Russia, which promptly split up into pettifogging sects. Why, Burtin asked, was reform "put in the hands of a bunch of youngsters . . . about whom no one had heard a word a half-year ago?"[25] Yeltsin's attitude is condensed in his memoir putdown of Afanas'ev as a scholastic "eternal oppositionist": "Such people are very necessary, but not in government—somewhere to the side, or on a hilltop where the view is better."[26]

Burbulis, Gaidar, and the mavens of shock therapy, their ties to the older radicals flimsy, learned a little later about Yeltsin chasing his own star. Burbulis unburdened himself in an interview in 2001:

> Soon we felt that the trust that had let us spread our wings, that untied our hands to make decisions and put them into life, had somehow changed into a well-thought-out distancing, into what I would say was the putting of us into orbit *[orbitnost']*. Gradually, the president made over his image from courageous leader of a transformative program into not even a partner but some kind of arbitrator—and he convinced himself that this was the reality. This was the wellspring of his vagueness, of the combinative voting [he encouraged in the Congress of Deputies], of his dangerous

> ambiguity in relation to the intractable [anti-reform] group in the congress, of his reprisals against people on our side. And then we got inconsistency in his ideas, which was tangled up with big blows to Yeltsin's instinct for power. This came out in the incoherence of the reforms. Before you knew it, everything was clear—Polevanov, Soskovets [two relatively conservative officials], and the so-called checks and balances, which bore not only on personnel decisions but on the loss of ideals, the loss of goals and orienting points.[27]

Yeltsin could not get over Burbulis's refusal to serve as presidential chief of staff in 1991 and was ever more of the belief that Burbulis had an allergy to the gritty work of government, whereas the blemish he observed in Gaidar was inexperience and impracticality, not sloth. But the pulling back from the reform maximalists expressed a deeper tendency—in turn an outgrowth of character and habits of Urals self-sufficiency—that would apply to helpmates of sundry orientations. *Everyone* in the game was to be in orbit, and flight plans could be revised on short notice. The conservatives cited by Burbulis as beneficiaries of Yeltsin's decisions help make the point. Vladimir Polevanov, a Siberian provincial leader who was named deputy premier and head of the State Property Committee in November 1994, and who used the appointment to try to undo the privatization of the aluminum industry, lasted only three months and was fired at the demand of Anatolii Chubais. Oleg Soskovets, an ethnic Russian technocrat from Kazakhstan and the last minister of metallurgy of the USSR, was made first deputy premier, the number two to Chernomyrdin, in April 1993. His turn to run afoul of the president came in June 1996, for factional activities in league with Aleksandr Korzhakov.

"Checks and balances" *(sderzhki i protivovesy)*, as the catchphrase went, were built into Yeltsinesque administration from the start, and spanned the bounds between external and internal resistances to purposive change. They would mean that no Kremlin staff and no government, from Gaidar through the premiership of Vladimir Putin in 1999, was homogeneous, and that all of them would present Himalayan challenges of coordination. The president "turned out to have people around him who in terms of their views and approaches would be difficult to call like-minded or brothers-in-arms."[28]

Fractious government contributed to the aforesaid arrhythmia of decision making. However, it did not foreclose an underlying persistence of trajectory, a wobbly equilibrium within a broad band of possibilities. It was stabilized by the solar object—Yeltsin—around which all lesser bodies in the system, planetary and asteroidal, spun. To the extent that the country had a defined course in the 1990s, Viktor Chernomyrdin is surely correct to say that within the structures of government its conservator and guarantor was the president:

> Yeltsin was the flywheel. He could have said, "Hold it, let's go back to where we were," and we would have gone back. His strength was that he understood we had to take *this* path. . . . How to do it was another matter. But to move a whole gigantic country along—do you understand what that is? Yeltsin never faltered, Yeltsin never got distracted by trifles. . . . He had a very powerful intuition in this respect. He made it through it all and led the country through it all.[29]

Yeltsin's subjective resistances to the oversights of reform policy at the micro level were not enough to knock him off his macro course.

Here the vagaries of economic policy in the year or two after the exit of Gaidar are revealing. There was much more continuity substantively, if not stylistically, than Burbulis's elegy would admit. To take the place of Gaidar as minister of finance and deputy premier, Yeltsin hit upon Boris Fëdorov, who was two years younger than Gaidar and had held the job under Ivan Silayev in 1990. Fëdorov tilted against Viktor Gerashchenko and easy money and made some progress on monetary and fiscal restraint in the spring and fall of 1993, twinning with Gaidar when Yeltsin brought him back into the cabinet as deputy premier in September. These gains have been interpreted as evidence of "how much one forceful individual [Fëdorov] in a key post can accomplish in such a volatile situation,"[30] but this disregards the role of a second individual—the Yeltsin who provided Fëdorov with political cover and encouragement. As Fëdorov found his bearings, Yeltsin called him with a tip that Chernomyrdin was preparing a directive on reimposition of curbs on some consumer prices. Fëdorov, with Gaidar's help, sent Yeltsin a memorandum bashing the proposal as inconsistent with marketization. Yeltsin then invited Fëdorov and the prime minister into his office, gave the table a thump, and told Chernomyrdin that if he brought out such an order it would be countermanded by a presidential decree, which he said was ready in the file folder on his desk—a folder that, known to Fëdorov but not to Chernomyrdin, held one sheet of paper, the Fëdorov memo. Chernomyrdin dropped the plan.[31]

In January 1994 Gaidar and Fëdorov resigned from the government for a second time, after a parliamentary election in which liberal candidates were outvoted, and Chernomyrdin gave hints of wage and price controls. But in reality he perpetuated Fëdorov's and Gaidar's policies in 1994 and 1995 and took them further by developing a bond market for government debt. The authors of *The Yeltsin Epoch*, who hold no brief for Chernomyrdin, write of his economic record that, "with less gusto but more reliance on common sense and Russian conditions, [he] basically continued what Gaidar had begun" in 1991–92.[32] This happened not because of Chernomyrdin's priors but because he, like Yeltsin, was learning from changing conditions and because he worked for Yeltsin.

In the final analysis, changing Russia was for Yeltsin about Russians practicing individual self-reliance and collective self-determination and healing themselves as both autonomous and social creatures. The prime service the leader could provide was to loosen the corset of constraints and give them the latitude to think and act without fear of government, of a self-abnegating doctrine, or of one another: "Our ideal is not equality in poverty, self-denial, and envy. We are for people having greater chances to take the bull by the horns, earn good money, and improve their lives."[33]

A corollary to this individualist and restorative idiom was another resistance to radicalism: antipathy to couching social reconstruction as intergroup or interclass warfare, which was how the Bolsheviks had conceived of their cause. And that antipathy deterred Yeltsin from expounding the changes he made as truly revolutionary changes.

When on the Gorbachev team from 1985 to 1987, he disagreed with the general secretary's description of intrasystemic perestroika as a revolution, since Gorbachev was moving too slowly to warrant it. "Revolution" and "revolutionary" then mostly washed out of Yeltsin's vocabulary.[34] Partly this was a tactic to reassure supporters who did not want change to get out of hand. He was alert, as he said in the 1991 election campaign, to the need "not to scare people, since many are afraid of the destruction of that which exists."[35] As president, Yeltsin migrated to the position that he had done Russia a service by *shielding* it from a revolution. He preferred the emollients "radical reforms," "democratic reconstruction," "reformist breakthrough," or, if revolutionary verbiage could not be helped, "quiet revolution" *(tikhaya revolyutsiya)*.[36]

Yeltsin leaned against himself since he was driven to conclude that Russia was susceptible to social upheaval and that any recurrence of the nihilism of the Bolshevik Revolution would be fatal to the country. This is how he phrased it in a speech marking the anniversary of the 1991 coup:

> After the putsch, Russia was in a quandary. The situation was again pushing the country toward revolution. Then, as now, I firmly believed that such a course would be a tremendous political mistake and would be Russia's undoing.
>
> All too well do our people know what a revolution is, how great are its temptations, and how tragic its results. Under Russian conditions, revolution would spin out of control and bring forth colossal antagonisms and conflicts. And then once again we would hear, as Mayakovsky said [in 1918], "You have the floor, comrade Mauser"—only now it would be not a Mauser but a machine gun. Once the storm was unleashed, no one in the country or the world could stop it. . . .
>
> We have chosen the way of reforms and not of revolutionary jolts. Ours is the way of peaceful changes under the control of the state and the president. I consider this our common victory.[37]

To cast change as going forward under the president's control was to cast him in the part of brakeman and regulator—or "arbitrator," as Burbulis put it—as much as locomotive.

As he often did in his memoirs, Yeltsin in *Notes of a President* identified a unique moment when the idea jelled: when he observed Muscovites meting out rough justice in 1991. On the afternoon of Thursday, August 22, he caught a glimpse of the citizens milling around the Central Committee area on Old Square. In a carnival spirit, they broke windows and would have overrun the gates if policemen sent by Mayor Popov had not blocked them. Later that day, the crowd, numbering several tens of thousands, swarmed to the Lubyanka, the headquarters of the KGB, and daubed swastikas and graffiti on the walls; the staff inside had armed themselves and blocked the entranceways and corridors. It was under searchlights that night, in a scene flashed across the globe, that building cranes overseen by Sergei Stankevich and Aleksandr Muzykantskii brought down the iron statue of the founder of the Soviet terror apparatus, Felix Dzerzhinsky, which had stood in the square since 1958.[38]

In this scene, Yeltsin beheld only the apparition of mob rule. "I had visions of the ghost of October—of the pogroms, disorder, looting, constant rallies, and anarchy with which that great revolution began. One wave of the hand, one signature, would have turned August 1991 into October 1917. But I did not do that, and I have no regrets." In Soviet history, the mob was succeeded by the party, which divided society into "the clean and the unclean," he says, and tried to build its new world on the backs of the unclean. Yeltsin in government did not want to sort people or to commandeer the material gains so laboriously accumulated under communist rule. "I saw *continuity* between the society of the Khrushchev-Brezhnev period and the new Russia. It did not enter into my plans to smash and bust up everything as the Bolsheviks did."[39]

The therapeutic take on the post-communist transition and rejection of revolutionism favored another choice—to soft-pedal the retributive side of the change of regime. Yeltsin knew as well as anyone that there was much in the communist past to atone for. In his writings and speeches as president, he decried forced collectivization, the Stalin terror and purges, and the Gulag, as most members of the late Soviet elite had done in the Gorbachev years. Gorbachev in December 1991 gave him the CPSU general secretary's archive, housing the most sensitive papers from the Soviet era. The presidential archive, as it was renamed, threw up new disclosures about atrocities, and some of these he found deflating. Yeltsin was dumbstruck, says head speech writer Lyudmila Pikhoya, at news that Lenin had ordered the execution of 25,000 Russian Orthodox priests in the civil war of 1918 to 1921, and that was only one example.[40]

Yeltsin in his first year in the Kremlin made frequent foreign policy–related use of the archives. In Washington in June 1992, he promised the U.S. Congress information about prisoners of war who might have ended up in Russia after the Korean and Vietnam Wars. Representatives of a Russian-American commission set off to explore the labor camps at Pechora in the northern Urals. "Beamed to television sets around the world, Yeltsin's remarks and the Pechora jaunt served their political purpose," although no actual American prisoners or records of them having been there were found.[41] Vis-à-vis Eastern Europe, the Yeltsin government "proved far more willing to re-evaluate and condemn controversial episodes" in Soviet relations with these countries than Gorbachev had been.[42] Gorbachev had disavowed the 1968 Soviet invasion of Czechoslovakia but never the 1956 intervention in Hungary. In November 1992 Yeltsin handed over to the post-communist government in Budapest a collection of secret materials on 1956, which were later published in Hungarian translation. That same autumn, Rudol'f Pikhoya, the new head of the Russian Archives Committee (and husband of Lyudmila Pikhoya), traveled on Yeltsin's behalf to Warsaw to present the Polish president, Lech Wałesa, with copies of KGB and CPSU files proving culpability at the highest levels in the NKVD's execution of more than 20,000 army officers and other Polish captives near Katyn, Russia, in 1940—files Gorbachev knew of but said did not exist. Yeltsin received journalists from Poland in the Kremlin and termed the shootings "a premeditated and depraved mass murder" at the instigation of "the party of the Bolsheviks." In a visit to Warsaw in August 1993, he went to the city's military cemetery, "knelt before a Polish priest, and kissed the ribbon of a wreath he had laid at the foot of the Katyn cross."[43] Yeltsin also provided to Wałesa the dossier Moscow kept on him when he was leader of the Solidarity labor movement in the 1980s. Similar information was released about the Molotov-Ribbentrop pact of 1939, the disappearance of the Swedish diplomat and wartime saver of Hungarian Jews, Raoul Wallenberg, and the Soviet air force's shooting down of a Korean jetliner in the Far East in 1983.

Within Russia, Yeltsin approached questions of history gingerly. The monstrosity of the Stalinist repressions, he believed, raised concern that rummaging through the files on individuals and abused groups would be injurious to political and social peace. Russians had held back from recrimination and revenge, he told a group of news reporters in July 1992: "And how hard it has been to hold back. . . . Some people were saying, Let us dig away. But, you know, digging things up on the 15 or 20 million who suffered, plus their families, would make society boil with rage."[44] That it might have had the cathartic and prophylactic effect it did in post-communist Eastern Europe was always secondary in Yeltsin's thinking to its destabilizing potential.[45]

Nonetheless, Yeltsin after 1991 did favor the dissemination of knowledge and the righting of wrongs, case by case. Researchers, Russian and foreign, had unexampled access during his presidency to archival information, excepting only top-secret troves such as those of the presidency and security services.[46] Books, memoirs, and documentary films probed the past, and Russian historians rejoined the international scholarly community. General Dmitrii Volkogonov, an orthodox communist turned reformer who served as an aide to Yeltsin until his death in 1995, sprang many materials loose and traced the inhumanity of Soviet communism not to Stalin but to its initiator, Lenin. Yeltsin saw Volkogonov "as a military version of himself—a product and a servant of the old system who had seen the light and was now combating the dark forces of the past."[47] After adoption of a legal framework in October 1991, Yeltsin appointed Aleksandr Yakovlev, the former Central Committee secretary who led a CPSU committee on the depredations of the Stalin period, to chair a blue-ribbon Presidential Commission for the

Rehabilitation of Victims of Political Repression. Some 4.5 million Russians were exonerated over the next ten years, 92 percent of them posthumously. They included kulaks, priests (several hundred thousand of whom were shot or died in captivity), military men, dissidents, and wartime prisoners of the Germans who were sent to Siberia in 1945, some of them sentenced under nonpolitical articles of the criminal code. Yeltsin, in Yakovlev's recollection, "actively supported" his work and signed directives on opening up records and clearing individuals' names prepared for him by the commission. "Of all the requests I brought to him, I do not remember one that he disputed."[48]

What Yeltsin was not prepared for was to come to terms with the communist legacy on a more emblematic level. Some in the dissident counterculture advocated a Nuremberg-type tribunal for surviving malfeasants. But a model for Nazi war criminals in the 1940s was a poor fit with Russian circumstances in the 1990s, since it was predicated on military defeat and the administration of the tribunal, and implementation of its verdicts, by foreign occupiers.[49] In 1992 a group of communists put the Yeltsin government on trial by questioning the constitutionality of the decrees of August and November 1991 that outlawed the CPSU and its Russian offshoot. Sergei Shakhrai represented the government in six months of Constitutional Court hearings, filing thirty-six volumes of evidence to the effect that the ruling party had been so intertwined with the Soviet state and its repressive apparatus that it was undeserving of protection in Russia's democracy. On November 30 a panel of the court—all thirteen members of which had been members of the CPSU—rendered a Solomonic verdict that confirmed the legality of Yeltsin's disassembly of the structures of the old party but said there must be no persecution of individual communists and they must be free to organize a new party if they so wished.[50] A Communist Party of the Russian Federation was established in February 1993 and was to play a significant part in the politics of the decade.

Another formula for de-Sovietizing the state that drew some interest was that of "lustration," a screening of political institutions for former officers of and collaborators with the communist-era security services such as was done in East Germany, Poland, Hungary, and the Czech Republic.[51] Galina Starovoitova, Yeltsin's adviser on nationality issues in 1991–92, was one of the few Russian politicians to come out for a lustration law. A version of her draft statute would have forbidden former apparatchiks in the CPSU from holding political office or teaching positions for five years. Democratic Russia deputies in March 1992 favored a ban on former members of the CPSU who had not turned in their party cards by August 1991. Yeltsin attended the meeting and, with about half of the delegates, left the hall before the vote was taken.[52] Commenting on the approach in 1994, he explicitly linked party and police workers: "The democratic press rebukes me for [the fact that] I preserved the state-security system and did not issue a decree that would debar from work in the state apparatus former officials of the Central Committee of the CPSU, of the party's obkoms, and some would even say of its raikoms [district committees]."[53] Yeltsin could not have been much worried about skeletons in his closet. But he was vexed about the onrush of events possibly getting out of control, and he wanted to keep the substratum of well-trained managers and professionals who, like he, had been part of the Soviet regime. Besides new faces and voices, he wanted "to use in the work of the state experienced implementers and organizers." Although some old hands from the nomenklatura may have "dressed up as democrats," he was more irritated by purely political types from the new wave who "generally did not know how to work."[54]

Yeltsin could have attempted acts of symbolic rectification. For instance, he could have devised holidays and extravaganzas to display solidarity with opposition to the ancien régime and approval of its collapse. He did make a desultory effort to do so in 1992 when he proclaimed June 12, the anniversary of the 1990 sovereignty declaration, Free Russia Day, a nonworking holiday. He largely passed up the opportunity to make the August anniversary of the 1991 coup a commemorative event. After making speeches on the occasion in 1992 and 1993, in 1994 he decreed that August 22 would be State Flag Day, "but did not explain why the [Russian tricolor] flag was the one piece of August to be enshrined or how the day was meant to be marked," and declined to make it a nonworking day.[55] Another decree in 1994 made December 12, as anniversary of the 1993 constitutional referendum, Constitution Day, a nonworking holiday. Like June 12 and August 22, most Russians greeted it with indifference.

Myth making could also have had a physical aspect, as it does in many societies. Yurii Afanas'ev and Yevgenii Yevtushenko lobbied Yeltsin on behalf of the Memorial Society (which Yeltsin had joined in 1988) to make over the KGB headquarters and prison in Lubyanka Square into a museum. Yakovlev favored the construction of a monument to the casualties of Stalinism in front of the building. In October 1990 the Memorial Society had emplaced there an unsculpted stone from one of the northern camps, but the removal of the Dzerzhinsky statue in 1991 created room for something eye-catching. Yeltsin did not warm to these ideas when approached. Yakovlev, he said afterward, should have "squeezed" the president but did not.[56]

Yeltsin was gripped, though, by the reconfiguration of Russia's stellar public space, Red Square. Laid out by Ivan III in the 1490s, it had over the centuries been a place for trade, worship, public gatherings, and executions. The communists made it primarily a parade ground. The square's western margin was converted after 1917 into a necropolis for revolutionaries and Soviet officials and dignitaries. Since 1924 the corpse of Lenin, embalmed in a secret fluid, had been displayed under quartz glass in a mausoleum—of wood until 1930, in salmon-tinted granite and porphyry after then. In 1941, with the Wehrmacht on the approaches to Moscow, it was evacuated to Tyumen, Siberia; it returned to its place of honor after the war's end.[57] Tens of millions of Soviets and foreigners had lined up to file by Lenin, one of them the young Boris Yeltsin in 1953. To the rear of the mausoleum, the bodies and cremated ashes of Stalin (who had lain beside Lenin in the mausoleum until the 1961 CPSU congress ordered him removed), Brezhnev, Andropov, Chernenko, and about four hundred lesser lights lay in and at the foot of the ruddy Kremlin wall. Yeltsin's friend, the stage director Mark Zakharov, suggested as early as 1989, at the first session of the USSR Congress of People's Deputies, that the Lenin mummy be put next to his mother at Volkovo Cemetery in St. Petersburg and the mausoleum and tombs be closed down as "a pagan temple" in the heart of the capital. Democratic Russia embraced the idea after the 1991 coup, when Yeltsin, at the zenith of his popularity, could have made the change with ease. He chose not to respond.

In late 1993, after he defeated the parliamentary opposition, Yeltsin swung to support of the Red Square plan, which resembled reburials in certain other post-communist states.[58] He removed Sentry Post No. 1, the goose-stepping police honor guard, from the crypt on October 5 (in 1997, it was reinstated at the Tomb of the Unknown Soldier on another side of the Kremlin), closed the adjacent Lenin Museum, and decided in principle to move Lenin and the others to the graveyard of the Novodevichii Convent in Moscow—the very place Yeltsin would be buried in 2007. In the coming months, he had a section surveyed at Novodevichii, corresponded through his aide Georgii Satarov with family members, and commissioned public opinion polls. The relatives of foreigners buried in the square—including the only American, the Harvard man and revolutionary John Reed, interred there in 1920—were also approached. Distracted by other problems, though, Yeltsin mothballed the plan. He contented himself for the moment with small acts of de-Leninization—taking down a two-ton Lenin statue in the Kremlin garden and carting Lenin's office in Building No. 1 to Gorki, a Moscow exurb.[59]

With Lenin, 1917, and the building of communism no longer befitting sources of legitimacy, Yeltsin reinstated what he thought the best alternative—imagery of pre-Soviet Russia. On November 30, 1993, he gave official standing to a coat of arms featuring the double-headed eagle of Byzantium and Muscovy. The white, blue, and red Russian flag, originally brought in by Peter the Great as the empire's trade banner but flown by the Romanovs as the state flag from 1883 to 1917, had been in use again from August 1991; a Yeltsin decree made it official on December 11, 1993. The white on top was said to stand for peace and purity, the blue in the middle for steadiness and honor, and the red at the bottom for love and generosity. That same day Yeltsin instituted the "Patriotic Song" by Mikhail Glinka (1804–57) as national anthem, replacing the "Hymn of the USSR" dating from 1944.[60] Beginning with Hero of the Soviet Union, which was replaced by Hero of the Russian Federation in March 1992, he Russified most Soviet awards and medals. Over the years, he also created new honors and brought back some tsarist-period blazonry. By the end of the 1990s, the Russian Federation had as many state awards as the USSR had had. The recommendations were "my favorite documents."[61]

The Kremlin fortress, venerated by Yeltsin as a monument to Russian statehood, received special attention. In late 1992 his office had Boris Ioganson's socialist realist *Lenin's Speech at the Third Congress of the Komsomol*, which had hung over the main staircase of the Grand Kremlin Palace since the 1950s, taken down. It was replaced by a panoramic painting of medieval Russian warriors under Alexander Nevsky of Novgorod fighting on ice against the Teutonic Knights in 1242. The title of the canvas, by Sergei Prisekin, is *Whosoever Shall Come to Us with the Sword Shall Perish by the Sword.*[62] This was but a foretaste: Undeterred by economic stringency, Yeltsin authorized the spending of a king's ransom on reconditioning the main edifices of state on the Kremlin squares.[63] There is a tale making the rounds that he came to the decision after a fireplace in the Green Sitting Room of the Grand Palace disgorged smoke during Bill Clinton's first presidential visit in January 1994.[64] But Yeltsin had signed the first directive about renovations in March 1993, and the project, once started, went on for most of his two terms.

The Red Staircase, which had led into the Faceted Chamber of the Grand Palace, and from whose steps the tsars addressed the people of Moscow on Cathedral Square, was the first piece to be fixed. Stalin had pulled down the staircase in the 1930s and constructed a canteen there. With Patriarch Aleksii, Yeltsin unveiled the replica in September 1994, saying it showed the way to Russians to bring back objects "buried under the former totalitarian regime." Between the fall of 1994 and the spring of 1996, the neoclassic Building No. 1, built by Matvei Kazakov for the Senate in the 1770s and 1780s, was remodeled and modernized. The coordinator of the project, Pavel Borodin, reports that the president pushed for what he thought of as a "stateish" *(derzhavnoye)* look modeled on masterworks of pre-Soviet Russian architecture and especially on Peter the Great's St. Petersburg:

> Boris Nikolayevich played an enormous role in the reconstruction. Do not forget that Yeltsin is a builder and understands a thing or two about such matters. . . .
>
> The president knew what he wanted. We presented him many times with every possible interior, photograph, and suggestion about the reconstruction. He would look at them quietly, and then often he would grin and force us to come up with new ones. When it was September [1994] and we were seeing him for the sixteenth or seventeenth time, he said, "Come on, Pal Palych [Pavel Pavlovich], get your team together and go to St. Petersburg, look at Pavlovsk, Tsarskoye Selo, the Yusupov mansion, the Hermitage, everything they have. Do some sketches, some outlines, a film, look for yourself. Look at what Russian culture really is, at what being a power and being a state is all about. Then bring the whole thing back to me."
>
> Another month of work passed. When we brought him materials for the twenty-first time, he exclaimed, "This is what Russia needs, now go ahead and do it." And the work began on December 1.[65]

His wife, among others, questioned whether the country could afford the reconstruction. But Yeltsin was undaunted. "The country had no money when the Kremlin was built," he said. Someone had to restore it to its former beauty, "and it might as well be me." Russians and foreigners, he let on to Borodin, would be swept up by what was done. "For Boris Nikolayevich this was only a plus: people will remember it two hundred years from now."[66]

Yeltsin was given interim housing in Building No. 14. When he moved back into Building No. 1, new statues by Anatolii Bichukov of four miscellaneous Russian monarchs—the empire builder Peter the Great, the enlightened despot Catherine the Great, the martinet Nicholas I, and the manumitter of the serfs, Alexander II—sat in niches in the walls of the ceremonial office, also called the Oval Hall. There he received guests and foreign leaders under an almond-shaped cupola, with Peter behind his desk. The circular Sverdlov Hall, where Yeltsin had delivered his secret speech to the Central Committee in 1987, was given its original name, Catherine's Hall, and redone in pale blue and gold, with old statuary and reliefs restored and new allegorical sculptures on Russia and Justice by Bichukov.

After the Senate building, it was the turn of the opulent, 700-room Grand Kremlin Palace, erected by Konstantin Ton in the 1830s and 1840s on the initiative of Nicholas I. Yeltsin put out a first decree in 1994 and work began on St. George's Hall, one of its five great vestibules, where Joseph Stalin had erased the tablets with the names of the twenty-five recipients of the Order of St. George, imperial Russia's highest military award. Workers uncovered an infestation of rats, knee-deep water in the cellar, and fissures in the foundation, and had to solidify the base of the building and of the seventeenth-century Terem Palace.

Already in 1994 Yeltsin decided to move on to the St. Andrei's and Alexander Nevsky halls of the Grand Kremlin Palace. In 1932–34, to accommodate the USSR Supreme Soviet and other functions, Stalin had them gutted and unified into an anodyne auditorium adorned with plywood desks and chairs, reinforced-concrete balconies, and a titanic stone Lenin standing behind the platform. The Russian Congress of People's Deputies met here from 1990 until Yeltsin decreed it out of existence in September 1993. Yeltsin was ignorant of the story of the halls until, some weeks after the death blow to parliament, he saw a quaint image of the original rooms in several watercolors by the nineteenth-century artist Konstantin Ukhtomskii. He asked an official what had happened to them and heard that "the Bolsheviks destroyed them." "Yeltsin's face grew dark—seemingly he recalled that here the [congressional] deputies had more than once chastised him and had tried to impeach him [in March 1993]—and he intoned, 'Then we will begin restoring them!'"[67] The decree was issued in January 1996. Yeltsin "studied in fine detail" every sketch considered by the state commission he appointed to oversee, although he left the filigree to them to settle. The commission would meet with him about six times in 1997 alone. His consistent advice was to adhere to Ton's plan.[68] The original halls and their artwork were re-created from drawings and photographs, helped by archival materials Ton had sent to London and finishing details stored in the basement. The nationalist artist Il'ya Glazunov consulted on some lesser rooms and donated several of his paintings. Ninety-nine firms and 2,500 people worked to complete the project.[69]

Yeltsin was to say in *Presidential Marathon* in 2000 that he should have legislated legal and political continuity between post-communist and pre-communist Russia, somehow bypassing the communist era. Going "from 1991 to 1917" would have restored "historical justice" and "historical continuity" and sanctified the liberal values that gained currency in the decades before World War I, when urban business, private farms, free speech, and parliamentarism thrived.[70] But this was never done. Neither mass nor elite opinion was prepared for what could have been a Great Leap Backward with unpredictable and perhaps comic results. The Russia of tsars, onion domes, and Cossacks (and, until 1861, of serfdom) was not a democracy, and territorially and ethnically it was organized as an empire.

Yeltsin's ideological eclecticism and fascination with representations of history made him a practitioner of political bricolage, patchwork that makes a useable past out of whatever fabrics happen to be at the leader's disposal.[71] Just as there was no wholesale assault on the communist order, Yeltsin bridled at a wholesale reconciliation with the imperial order. Five-pointed red stars and other Soviet motifs abounded after 1991, on the Kremlin battlements and all over Russia. Thousands of likenesses of Lenin and streets, squares, and buildings in his name were not touched, even in Moscow.[72] Some cities and city streets were returned to their ancestral appellations, while many others were left alone, at times creating anomalies such as provinces and their formerly eponymous capitals bearing different names. Yeltsin's area of birth was still Sverdlovsk oblast, after the Bolshevik Yakov Sverdlov, even as the city of Sverdlovsk was given back its birth name, Yekaterinburg—and one of the main avenues of Yekaterinburg, leading from downtown out to the former Urals Polytechnic Institute, was still called Lenin Prospect. Yeltsin reached out to post-1917 Russian émigrés in the West in 1992,[73] but no plan to restore their titles and property back in Russia was ever enacted. No agreement was struck on the words to be set to Glinka's nineteenth-century music, so the anthem was a melody without lyrics to which the Russians never took. And aspects of the Soviet experience in which there was popular pride—such as industrialization, wartime victory, and the space program—remained in good odor officially. As a sign, the fiftieth anniversary of victory in the Great Patriotic War in 1995 touched off an orgy of nostalgia and completion of the brutalist war monument on

Moscow's Poklonnaya Hill, whose construction Yeltsin as local party leader had halted the decade before. Yeltsin's government, Mayor Luzhkov, and local communists "all held massive dueling celebrations, blanketing the city in military banners, posters, and other paraphernalia."[74]

Although Yeltsin greeted and forced changes in many Russian institutions, his concern about a loss of control decelerated or halted change in several domains. It influenced him to oppose the eradication of communist-era law codes and regulations, which were considered to be in force unless expressly repealed. To tear up the body of Soviet legislation, and of Russia's prerogatives as juridical heir to the USSR, would in his assessment have brought "so many problems and worries that we were just not prepared to handle at so difficult a time."[75]

In the same spirit, Yeltsin did not wipe out the KGB, the coercive sidearm of the Communist Party, which it was in his power to do in 1991–92. This is not the outcome one might have expected, for, although he had cooperative personal relations with some KGB officers before 1987, in his days in opposition he came to distrust the organization. In 1989 he was one of the few deputies to abstain on the confirmation vote for Vladimir Kryuchkov in the USSR Supreme Soviet, and, says one then volunteer assistant of his, he developed "spy mania" and saw "in every new person a stoolpigeon for the KGB." Asked about a possible recruit, he would tap two fingers on a shoulder, a sign in the USSR for eavesdropping.[76] Yeltsin knew of the KGB's and Kryuchkov's centrality in the 1991 putsch from experience and from the five assorted committees to investigate it, one of which, under Sergei Stepashin, he himself had appointed.

When the committees reported, Yeltsin seemed to lose his zeal for shaking up the organization. Its last Soviet chairman, Vadim Bakatin, says wryly in his memoirs that Yeltsin's men wanted nothing more than "to change the nameplate from 'KGB of the USSR' to 'KGB of the RSFSR.'"[77] This is rather unfair, in that Yeltsin agreed demonstratively with the decision to shut down the Fifth Chief Directorate, which had been in charge of secret informants and hunting dissidents, and to restrict the main body of the agency to counterintelligence and home security. After an experiment with subordinating it to the regular police hierarchy in the Ministry of the Interior (MVD), it was restyled the Ministry of Security in 1992, the Federal Counterintelligence Service or FSK in 1993, and in 1995 the Federal Security Service or FSB. And Yeltsin spun off independent functional units for foreign intelligence, border guards, protection of leaders, and governmental electronic communications. All these components were put on a short political leash, monitored by Yeltsin and reporting to him through discrete channels.

But this was no root-and-branch reform such as had taken down the StB agency in Czechoslovakia and the Stasi in East Germany. There were Russians who were interested on going this route. Gavriil Popov asked Yeltsin in the fall of 1991 to make him chairman of the agency. He wanted, Gennadii Burbulis says, to dig out the roots *(vykorchevyvat')* of the organization—to pare it down, air its secrets, bring its remnants under strict, many-sided civilian control. Yeltsin was unwilling. To Burbulis, he said that the CPSU had been the country's brain and the KGB its spinal cord: "And he clearly did not want to rupture the spinal cord now that the head had been lopped off."[78] Yeltsin kept the spinal cord whole out of fear of multiple threats—to political stability, to democracy, to national unity, and to safekeeping of Russia's weapons of mass destruction.[79]

A last chance at a more intrusive solution was to be missed in 1993–94. Yeltsin felt let down by the Ministry of Security during his 1993 confrontation with parliament (see Chapter 11). The minister, Viktor Barannikov, a favorite of the president's dismissed in August 1993 for corruption, defected to the anti-Yeltsin ultras and headed the shadow security department in Aleksandr Rutskoi's "Provisional Government." On October 4, 1993, the security forces under a new chief, Nikolai Golushko, permitted dozens of deputies and their armed auxiliaries to flee through underground tunnels.[80] In December Yeltsin replaced Golushko with Sergei Stepashin, a former parliamentarian, and issued a statement referring to all changes in the former KGB as having had "a superficial and cosmetic character" with no "strategic concept" behind them.[81] He appointed Oleg Lobov to chair a commission to review the force, making Sergei Kovalëv, a Brezhnev-era political prisoner, a member. Kovalëv asked for but did not receive a list of officers who had gone after dissidents in the past. Lobov "said that Boris Nikolayevich did not have in view any radical changes . . . that we cannot afford to lose professionals."[82] Staff cuts imposed on the FSK were largely reversed by mid-1994. Yeltsin then lapsed back into the confidence that it was enough to subdivide the service—replacing a leviathan with a hydra—place restrictions on surveillance networks, define democratic control as that exercised by him as chief executive, and let sleeping dogs lie. The brotherhood of active and reserve KGB officers, be they engrossed in domestic snooping, foreign spying, or commercial opportunities, persevered. Not until he was a pensioner did Yeltsin confide in Aleksandr

Yakovlev that he had "not thought through everything" about the agency and put too much faith in changing the line of command and leaving the essence of the organization intact.[83]

The last of Yeltsin's inbuilt resistances was to selling Russian society on the general reform course. Truth be told, he was not well equipped congenitally for outreach. By 1991 he had laid aside the harangues of the CPSU boss for question-and-answer volleys, saucy interviews, campaign oratory, and parliamentary interpellation. He treasured parsimony in speech and literature and loved to pull the printout of a talk from his jacket pocket and chuck it sportily in the wastebasket. Nine times out of ten, it was a masquerade: Either he had memorized the talk and would recite it rote, or he had a variation on the original which he then read out. But Yeltsin as president had to address the nation as a whole, and not merely live audiences, and to mate salesmanship with the dignity of a head of state. This meant working through the mass communications media with which Russia had been imbued under the Soviets. Yeltsin fulfilled the role with a sigh. He did not mind *doing* in front of television cameras; *posing* for the blue screen was not his cup of tea.[84] Grouchily, he submitted to pancake makeup, a brittle coiffure (the handicraft of a hairdresser inherited from Gorbachev), and a teleprompter. He would fine-tune speeches with the writers, insisting on brevity, some peppy phrases, and pauses for effect. They would coach him on pronunciation and the purging of Urals localisms—such as his rolling of the letter "r," his flattening of the Russian pronoun *chto* (what) to *shta*, and, in press conferences, his elision of the soft vowel "ye" from the expression for "If you know what I mean" *(Ponimayesh'* became *Ponimash')*.[85]

The problem with Yeltsin as tribune of reform was not that he mishandled any one occasion but that the occasions were intermittent. He did not distill his radical reform into a lapidary phrase such as the New Deal or Great Society. He never related in depth how the economic, social, and political facets of the remaking of Russia cohered. He did not care to take on the task himself and, as Sergei Filatov, his chief of staff after Yurii Petrov, noted, "He was very jealous when others did it."[86]

Yeltsin's disinclination to promote Yeltsinism stemmed from cognitive dissonance over didactic speeches and from the conviction that empty promises had jaded the population and tarnished both true-blue Soviet leaders and Gorbachev's perestroika.[87] Verbal economy was appropriate in the early days, as his first press officer, Valentina Lantseva, recalled: "Compared to the verbose . . . Gorbachev, Boris Nikolayevich was closer to the people in his clumsiness *[neuklyuzhest']* and bear-like quality *[medvezhest']*. He . . . could answer in one word, yes or no. This was very significant to the people."[88] Once the communist regime was dead, though, Russians wanted to be reassured that their sacrifices were not in vain and to be given signposts for the road ahead. These Yeltsin was not the best person to provide. Hearing Marietta Chudakova advise him at a Kremlin meeting in 1994 to tape a televised presentation every two weeks, he clamped his jaw, after the fashion of someone with a toothache.[89] Mark Zakharov, who was at the same meeting, warned of a dearth of ideas and information, which could leave the field to political fanatics and charlatans. Yeltsin countered that any systematic marketing plan would be a warmed-over version of totalitarian brainwashing: "What are you suggesting, that we introduce a ministry of propaganda, like the one under [Joseph] Goebbels?"[90] In his 1994 and 2000 memoir volumes, Yeltsin defended his aversion to any idea of "shimmering heights that must be scaled." No bombast was needed. "Propaganda for the new life is superfluous. *The new life itself* will persuade people that it has become a reality."[91]

One part instinct and one part learning from the Soviet past, this was an exercise in throwing out the baby with the bath water. The defense of post-communist reforms was not doomed to excess any more than elimination of the KGB was doomed to unhinge the body politic. Comparative experience teaches that the political bully pulpit has its uses in democracies and not only in tyrannies. In a free polity, loquacity by leaders can go light years to galvanize citizen opinion behind government programs, shape the public sphere, and delimit the range of voices there.[92] By selling it short, Yeltsin retarded his ability to make his quiet revolution palatable to the newly enfranchised populace and to enliven the debate about where Russia was headed in the long haul.

Chapter Eleven

Falling Apart, Holding Together

When inducted as national leader, Yeltsin intended to stick to economics and treat the structures of government with benign neglect. In retrospect he described this behavior as a mistake: "I probably erred in choosing the economic front as my principal one and leaving governmental reorganization to endless compromises and political games." It put the economic program itself at risk, since, "without political backup, the Gaidar reforms were left hanging in midair."[1] He soon reconsidered: In order to use the state for his ends, he had to hold it together, and in a way that gave him and not others the steering power.[2]

His constitutional options in 1991 were not rosy. An attempt to reorder Russian institutions, at the moment Russia was unscrambling itself from the Soviet Union, was sure to strike many as distracting and incendiary. Yegor Gaidar, for one, was dead set against it. In any such move, Yeltsin would have bumped foreheads with other loci of authority, starting with the Russian Congress of People's Deputies, where his majority was precarious. Even were he somehow to force new parliamentary elections, voters, he admitted later, might not have elected "other, 'good' deputies."[3]

The Soviet reflex was to consign almost any human problem to an administrative department of government. The liberal approach, flaunted by the youthful reformers and by the Western powers and organizations whose advice Yeltsin sought, posited solutions to lie outside of government. Had he acted strictly in this spirit, he would have chopped the post-communist state and pushed it out of the way of nongovernmental actors. Measured by the size of the bureaucracy, this was not quite obtained, as the workforce in the federal, provincial, and municipal governments drifted up by about 10 percent (from 2,682,000 to 2,934,000) between 1992 and 2000.[4] But these figures exclude the host of Soviet factory-level managers who were struck from the rolls during the change to the market. Shock therapy and price decontrol reduced officialdom's directive and regulatory grip on Russian society. And privatization, from the vouchers of 1992–94 to the loans-for-shares initiative of 1995–97, reduced its monopoly over resources.[5] Yeltsin lent support to it at almost every step and believed that when it was over only electric power, atomic energy, the military-industrial complex, and the railroads should be left on the state ledger.[6] In loans-for-shares, first authorized by Decree No. 478 on May 11, 1995, the government turned twelve large properties, mostly with high-value petroleum and mineral assets, over to private banks to manage, in return for forgivable loans from the banks. The banks were allowed to run stock auctions in which they themselves could place bids on the shares deposited with them as collateral for the loans. The auctioneer or an affiliated business won every auction of the state shares—a spectacular act of self-dealing. Formal title to them was reassigned a year later.[7]

The paring in governmental scope, while desirable, raised difficulties. Preeminent among these was the lack of clarity about boundaries between the public and the private realm and about responsibility for seeing to it that the state in its entirety did not go to smithereens. Shifting boundaries meant shifting options for individuals. Consumerism and affluence, forbidden fruit under the communists, were now smiled upon, but the seam between these licit wants and illicit avarice was not well demarcated. The short-range thinking bred by high uncertainty made many officeholders greedy, for feathering one's nest was one way to hedge against an unascertainable future. As the trenchant Oleg Poptsov noted, "When [authority] is transient and when society is poor and has lost all basis for guarantees, the danger rises a hundredfold that someone will take advantage of power in order to live well after a stay in office."[8]

The ambiguity of limits was only the half of it. Emulation of foreign models was the rage in Moscow, and it bled into things political. It could manifest itself in trivialities—such as the electric golf carts purchased for Barvikha-4 after Yeltsin saw George Bush tooling around in one at Camp David in February 1992—but it was not limited to them. Copycat and wishful thinking impelled Yeltsin and his peers toward institutional inventions (a presidency and vice presidency, a constitutional court, and so forth) that often were underspecified and unsynchronized with the surrounding scene. As Yeltsin was to observe mordantly in *Notes of a President*, "there arose beautiful structures and beautiful titles with nothing behind them."[9] Beneath the surface, the very infrastructure of government was buckling. There was marker after marker of it: a doubling in rates of violent crime, to levels comparable to those in Colombia, Jamaica, and Swaziland; spreading corruption, especially after privatization; porous borders; tax evasion by the business class and a yawning budget deficit; a torn social safety net; and demonetization, the flight from the inflation-devalued ruble into dollars, money surrogates, and barter.[10] The army, the crown jewel of Russian governments since Ivan the Terrible, plunged from 2.75 million men under arms in 1992 to a million in 1999; officers and enlisted men huddled in tents after the post–Cold War efflux from Eastern Europe; the pay of a majority of the officer corps was in arrears.[11] And the Communist Party, whose hierarchical apparatus and mass membership base had kept the Soviet state intact, was gone.

Inside the machinery of Russian government, Yeltsin was faced with an enfeeblement of discipline and accountability, as comes out in his anecdote about two reformist members of his first cabinet. Eduard Dneprov, the education minister put into office in 1990, wanted curriculum changes in the schools. He was able to implement some, having had "the luck to work things out under the old regime, when people still listened to the bosses." Academician Andrei Vorob'ëv was commissioned minister of health in late 1991, and made no headway with his advocacy of a role for private physicians and clinics: "Vorob'ëv's system immediately fell into disorganization. No one understood it or wanted to do a thing about it for one reason only—the staff of the ministry had simply ceased to function."[12] For Yeltsin the mutineer, remember, being a steely "boss for the bosses" had been a selling point. Now the compliance of bosses and underbosses was a question mark.

Boris Yeltsin's predicament had an international dimension. Governments the length and breadth of Eurasia faced problems of staggering complexity. In fourteen of the fifteen post-Soviet capitals, there was the silver lining of freedom from foreign—Russian—domination. It was a unity elixir and bought reformers a blame-free startup period. In Moscow, there was no silver lining. The Ukrainians, Kazakhs, and Georgians had attained statehood and membership in the global community. What Yeltsin and the Russians got was less of what they had before—a diminished state struggling to maintain regional influence, let alone the USSR's say in global affairs. About three in four Russian citizens in 1992 accepted the expiration of the Soviet Union as an accomplished fact; two in three were sorry that it had happened.[13] Once the divorce was final, little about it redounded to the political benefit of Yeltsin. "I was convinced," he testifies, "that Russia had to rid itself of its imperial mission." Once nationalized, it "needed a stronger, tougher . . . policy in order not to lose its significance and authority altogether." Greater authority, however, did not come to pass in the post-Soviet space. Yeltsin himself bewailed the hole in the heart of the deposed ruling nation: "We [Russians] seem almost to be embarrassed by the fact that we are so big and incoherent, and we don't know what to do with ourselves. We are tortured by a certain feeling of emptiness."[14] If the end of the Cold War and of the Soviet Union made the United States the solitary superpower, it made Russia the solitary ex-superpower. One had a superiority complex, the other an inferiority complex for which no curative was offered.

Yeltsin was not overdrawing when he said "the specter of discord and civil war" hung over Russia and the ex-USSR in the first half of the 1990s.[15] Gorbachev rates praise for self-restraint and the prevention of a bloodletting. Yeltsin deserves more and has not always received it. The celerity of the parting of the ways after Belovezh'e was preferable many times over to an endeavor to salvage the union state through violence. At home, Yeltsin dampened Russian revanchism, jingoism, and nostalgia for the Soviet Union. In the "Near Abroad," he reached understandings with the majority of the non-Russian fourteen, repatriated troops, did not employ ethnic Russians as a fifth column, and helped float their economies by supplying oil and gas at discounted prices. The most combustive of the potential altercations in the region involved lands over the Russian frontier and populated mostly by ethnic Russians and Russian-speakers, a list that for some nationalists included northern Kazakhstan, Trans-Dniester in Moldova, and the Donbass, Sevastopol and all of the Crimean peninsula, and Odessa area in Ukraine. Yeltsin never pressed claims to these territories. Russia's military involvement as a peacekeeper in three fragile states (Moldova, Georgia, and Tajikistan) shaded over into tampering and patronage of pro-Moscow districts, but these were the aberrations that proved the rule.

Let us not forget Yugoslavia, communism's other multiethnic federation, in those same years. It was a school picnic compared to a possible conflagration in the middle of Eurasia, where the Russians would have been cast as the xenophobic and irredentist Serbs and Yeltsin as Slobodan Milošević. The Russians outnumber the Serbs fifteen to one, and a war of Russians against non-Russians in the former Soviet Union, or of all against all, would have been fought on territory larger than the South American continent and housing millions of soldiers, trainloads of atomic arms (many of them not initially under Moscow's control),[16] and a thousand tons of fissile material. Yeltsin's foreign minister from 1990 to 1996, Andrei Kozyrev, knew the Balkans well and often hashed over with him a Yugoslav scenario for Russia. Gaidar, who had lived in Belgrade as a boy and graduated from secondary school there, had similar conversations with the president.[17] The range of comparisons would include partitions and intercommunal wars in the Indian subcontinent, North Africa, and Indochina. Without hyperbole, the historian Stephen Kotkin underlines what Yeltsin avoided: "The decolonization of Western Europe's *overseas* possessions had been drawn out and bloody. The Soviet land empire . . . could have unleashed a far nastier bloodbath, even an end to the world" through thermonuclear holocaust.[18]

For diplomacy with the world powers, the man from Sverdlovsk was at first woefully unprepared. Kozyrev shopped around in Washington and West European capitals the message that their leaders should personalize their relations with him and appeal to his better instincts.[19] Yeltsin took to addressing his opposite numbers by their first names, often prefaced by "my friend" (my friend George, my friend Bill, my friend Helmut), no easy thing for a stolid Russian male. A mutual admiration society with Robert S. Strauss, the American ambassador to Moscow in 1991–92, helped groom him for the relationship with the United States.[20] Yeltsin was a quick study. On his first official visit to Washington, D.C., he announced in Reaganesque words to a joint session of the U.S. Congress on June 17, 1992, that Russia "has made its final choice in favor of a civilized way of life, common sense, and universal human heritage. . . . Communism has no human face. Freedom and communism are incompatible." Referring to an agreement he and Bush had just concluded to trim nuclear arms by the year 2000, Yeltsin pointedly told Americans that it was in the West's as well as Russia's interest for his Great Leap Outward to succeed: "Today the freedom of America is being upheld in Russia. Should the reforms fail, it will cost hundreds of billions" to mop up.[21]

The hope for a deep partnership with Western governments and institutions, and for buttressing the post-communist Russian state from without, proved evanescent. In 1991–92, as price reform bit and living standards sank, never did the United States, the European Union, or the G-7 really consider forgiveness of Russia's foreign debt—a liability, incurred by the regime the reformers were trying to put behind, whose impact has been compared to that of World War I reparations on Weimar Germany.[22] The U.S. Freedom Support Act, passed in October 1992, earmarked about $400 million for technical and humanitarian assistance to all the post-Soviet countries, a drop in the bucket of need if there ever was one. Under the Clinton administration, American bilateral assistance came to $2,580,500,000. Two-thirds of those dollars were spent in 1994, and Russia's slice of the pie, with no ethnic lobby to fight for it, slouched from more than 60 percent in 1994 to less than 20 percent in 1999.[23] From 1993 to 1999, American aid would come to $2.50 annually per Russian man, woman, and child. It totaled about 1 percent of the U.S. defense budget in the year 1996, or one-quarter of the cost of a single Nimitz-class aircraft carrier—at a time when the evisceration of the Soviet threat let the United States draw down military manpower by 30 percent—and the money flowed primarily to American contractors, not to Russians or Russian organizations. Multilateral assistance siphoned through the World Bank and the International Monetary Fund (the IMF, which Russia joined in June 1992) was larger in volume, yet was belated and took the form of repayable loans. "In spite of requests for support from radical reformers of whose goals it could only approve . . . the Fund was slow in giving meager support on stringent terms."[24] Not inaccurately, Bill Clinton was to adjudge the effort as "a forty-watt bulb in a damned big darkness."[25] In the security sphere, the Cooperative Threat Reduction program (sponsored by Democratic senator Sam Nunn and Republican senator Richard Lugar) funded the decommissioning of nuclear arsenals in Ukraine, Belarus, and Kazakhstan and enhanced the safety of all. In Yeltsin's and Russia's estimation, and in mine, this gain paled before the loss caused by the policy of mechanically expanding the NATO military alliance eastward to take in former republics and dependencies of the USSR but not Russia itself.

At Camp David in 1992, Yeltsin pressed President Bush for reference in the communiqué to Russia and the United States as "allies." Bush refused. For the time being, "transitional language" about "friendship and partnership" would have to suffice.[26] The transitional idiom persisted, even as neocontainment put Yeltsin on the defensive. Western governments never saw Russia's transformation as an urgent task for them and never found or tried terribly hard to find a niche for Russia in a new security architecture for

Europe and Asia. For his part, Yeltsin more than once couched Russia's policy in the ethic of prickly self-reliance that he preached for individuals. In 1991–92, when the case for debt relief was strongest, he did not set about drafting a formal request for it. Meeting Clinton the presidential candidate in June 1992, Yeltsin stressed that Russia was "a great power" and was "not asking for handouts." At the first meeting with Clinton as president, in Vancouver in April 1993, Yeltsin solicited outside help, "but not too much," since a big subsidy would open him to criticism for making Russia dependent on outsiders.[27] In early exchanges, Yeltsin was more than willing to play with Russia someday joining NATO, although, again, his government never articulated it as policy. Yeltsin told Clinton in January 1994 that the post-Soviet countries should enter NATO as a bloc, after an acclimation period, and he repeated this to reporters in August. By December of that same year, as Washington and the alliance moved toward selective admission, Yeltsin informed Vice President Al Gore in Moscow that it would never add up for Russia to join, since it is "very, very big" and NATO "quite small." "Yeltsin put Gore in the bizarre position of trying to persuade him that Russia might actually someday qualify."[28] Future conversations were infrequent and unlinked to current decisions.

Most of the post-communist states in Europe were panting for admission to the European Union more than to NATO. This entryway, too, was closed to Russia and its leader. The union was of the view, as one review of the 1990s put it, that Russia was "simply too big, too complex, and too backward to be considered for EU membership."[29] A ten-year cooperation agreement Yeltsin signed in Corfu's Venetian fort in June 1994 was as close as he got to a meaningful association. Although Russia applied for membership in the Council of Europe, a medium for legal and human rights, and acceded to it and its parliamentary assembly in February 1996, Yeltsin had no strategy for buying into the much more dynamic and rigorous EU.[30]

Domestically, post-Soviet entropy was nowhere more of a threat than in center-periphery relations, the reef on which the USSR's empire of nations had shipwrecked. The showdown between Russia and the Soviet leadership provoked competitive appeasement of the constituent provinces of the Russian Soviet Federative Socialist Republic (RSFSR) and mostly of its republics (known until December 1990 as autonomous Soviet socialist republics), delimited as the homelands of "titular" nationalities such as the Tatars and Bashkirs. Somewhat privileged in communist ethnofederalism, they were the gravest threat to the unity of post-communist Russia. Yeltsin's pronouncement in Kazan about the titulars taking as much autonomy as they could guzzle was an expression of his propensity for decentralization, a jab at Gorbachev in the Russian-Soviet context, and, in the intra-Russian context, an attempt to fight fire with fire and to keep the minorities within whatever state entity survived. While playing to enlightened self-interest, he said geopolitical realities would have to be put on the weigh scales as well. The union republics of the USSR were placed around the Russian lands, but, he noted at Kazan University in 1990, "You [the Tatars] are located in the center of Russia—and you have to think about that."[31] On that same trip, "Yeltsin privately warned local leaders not to go too far in their assertions of local autonomy," U.S. intelligence reported.[32]

The immediate effect of the RSFSR's declaration of sovereignty and the sermon in Kazan was an outpouring from the minorities. Between the Russian parliamentary resolution on June 12, 1990, and Kazan on August 5, North Ossetiya in the North Caucasus was the one republic to declare sovereignty. In the two months after August 5, the legislatures of Tatarstan (formerly Tatariya) and five other republics came forth with resolutions; in the two months after that, ten more, including Bashkortostan (formerly Bashkiriya), followed them; the four remaining did between December 1990 and July 1991.[33] Many centrists and conservatives in the republics bent to agitation by nationalist movements. In Tatarstan, for example, leader Mintimer Shaimiyev, a former CPSU first secretary, had fought against protégés of Yegor Ligachëv in the late 1980s but backed the August 1991 putsch against Gorbachev—and only after its defeat did he defect to the Tatar cause.[34] The radicals in the Ittifaq movement until then wanted Tatarstan reclassified as the sixteenth union republic of the USSR, as Tatar nationalists had favored since the 1920s; after August 1991 they wanted unalloyed independence and held almost daily demonstrations in Kazan to press their claims.[35]

In so unsure an environment, there was no reason a priori why Russia would be vaccinated against the infection that killed off the Soviet Union. Many of its provinces were comparable in magnitude to the smaller of the union republics that hived off in 1991. Wrote Aleksandr Tsipko late that year, "It is difficult to explain to the Ossetins and Chechens," constituent peoples of Russia, "that they have fewer rights than the Moldovans," whose union republic on the Romanian border was making good its exit from the USSR. The fever was contagious, Tsipko observed, as non-republics populated by ethnic Russians now plugged for equality with the minority areas.

Yeltsin "awaits the fate of Gorbachev or of the queen of England, who does not rule anything." Unless a pan-Soviet federation were salvaged, which was soon shown to be impossible, the only way out, he apostrophized, would be for a Russian leader to recentralize and de-democratize: "Under conditions of ongoing disintegration, the pendulum of public attitudes will swing to the other extreme, and this time it is the democrats who will come under fire."[36]

Yeltsin got down to work in 1990 on a "federative treaty," kindred to the never-to-be-consummated union treaty for the USSR, which all of Russia's regions were intended to sign as a reaffirmation. Negotiations were stepped up in the autumn of 1991, with Gennadii Burbulis responsible to the president for protecting the federal government's interests. On March 30, 1992, three texts were contracted in Moscow: for the twenty-one republics, the fifty-seven nonethnic territories (most of them oblasts), and eleven lower-ranking subunits. Yeltsin hailed the treaty as codifying "a prudent balance of interests." At the same time as it "put an end to the ascendancy of the . . . Moscow bureaucracy," it would "defend Russia against chaos, impotence, and an orgy of localism."[37]

The subtreaty for the republics acknowledged republican sovereignty and said they and other ethnic subunits, which had about 17 percent of the total Russian population, would get 50 percent of the seats in the parliamentary upper chamber in a new constitution. Several republics in effect blackmailed Yeltsin to make further concessions. Sakha (Yakutiya), on northeast Siberian permafrost, was given a large portion of the profits from the bankable diamond industry there; Bashkortostan, the most populous republic, got an appendix giving it dispensations. Two republics would not sign on the dotted line at all. Chechnya had declared its independence from Moscow on November 1, 1991. Tatarstan on March 21, 1992, organized a referendum on the proposition that Russia was an abutting state and relations between the two could be set only through state-to-state treaties; 61 percent voted in favor. One of the reasons Burbulis was demoted in April 1992 was that he misgauged the Tatarstan problem and encouraged a referendum on the premise that it would fail. As defeat in the referendum came into view, Yeltsin considered an economic blockade or even military intervention—Shaimiyev says the night before the vote was the scariest of his life. In 1992–93 Chechnya, Tatarstan, Bashkortostan, Sakha, and Tuva led the pack. In varying combinations, republics legislated language laws, skipped Russia-wide referendums, withheld tax payments, and declared republic laws and constitutions preponderate over Russian ones.[38]

Although non-republics could not marshal the fervency of the minority homelands, they noisily aired their concerns and tried to extract benefits from the Kremlin. In the August 1991 power vacuum, Yeltsin appropriated the authority to appoint provincial leaders and presidential representatives in the given region, a power confirmed by parliament in November.[39] He looked the other way at the election of presidents in the republics; Shaimiyev in Tatarstan had been the first, running unopposed in June 1991.[40] The ethnicity-blind oblasts seethed over their second-string status, economically and constitutionally, and wanted to be able to elect their chief executives, most of them now called governors. Yeltsin did not concede this until April 1993, when he permitted votes for governor in eight provinces. Several Russian oblasts tried the nominative cure of declaring themselves republics and ringing up the rights of a Tatarstan or a Tuva. Vologda, north and east of Moscow, was the first to do so, in May 1993. In Sverdlovsk, Yeltsin's stomping ground, where he had made his promotee Eduard Rossel head of the executive after the 1991 putsch, the oblast council ruled to this effect in July 1993 and invited the nearby areas of Chelyabinsk, Kurgan, Orenburg, and Perm to fall in. Projects to create single- or multiprovince republics sprang up in provinces from the Baltic littoral in the northwest to the Volga basin and on to central and east Siberia and Vladivostok.[41]

A second institutional crisis blossomed forth in Moscow, under Yeltsin's nose. It matched his executive branch, beefed up by the creation of the presidency, against the legislative branch he had chaired in 1990–91. Its roots were in the indeterminacy of the rules. The constitution of the RSFSR was chock full of loopholes, having been written under Leonid Brezhnev in 1978 and tinkered with repeatedly. A two-thirds vote in the Congress of People's Deputies was all it took to change the constitution. Several *hundred* amendments carried between 1990 and 1993, and 180 were on the order paper when congress gathered in December 1992; the constitution of the United States, by comparison, has been altered only seventeen times since 1791. Dissentious clauses in the charter garmented the president and the congress with supreme authority in the state. The two branches, independently elected by universal suffrage, had overlapping powers. The Supreme Soviet could strike down a presidential veto by simple majority, and two-thirds of the members of congress could impeach the president if they found he had violated his oath of office. President Yeltsin was in charge of the armed forces but had no right to resolve a deadlock by ending a session of parliament and forcing new elections.[42]

Deadlock was what Yeltsin's Russia had as it entered the reform era. Crosscurrents between organizational and policy issues polarized politics as badly as they had in Gorbachev's Soviet Union. Vice President Aleksandr Rutskoi and many high bureaucrats sided with the foes of Yeltsin in parliament, and the congress was not monolithic, but majority sentiments in the two branches were ever more discrepant. Attempts to craft a post-communist constitution were all for naught, as each camp sought one biased in its favor. On reform issues, the parliamentarists were more statist and the presidentialists much more pro-market. The peculiar two-tier legislature—the RSFSR was the only union republic to mimic the USSR in this regard—added another element. The sessions of the thronging congress, televised live and numbered like unique events, were circus-like. Both the congress and the smaller Supreme Soviet lacked a stable majority, with remnants of the Democratic Russia bloc and the regrouped communist faction having to compete for the affections of small-fry groups.

An enmity between Yeltsin and Ruslan Khasbulatov, who had replaced him as legislative chairman in October 1991, further aggravated the situation. Khasbulatov had more strength on the back benches than the legal scholar Sergei Shakhrai, Yeltsin's first choice for the position. A pipe-smoking professor of international economics from a Moscow institute, Khasbulatov had been elected to represent Groznyi, the Chechen capital. Like Rutskoi, an air-regiment commander in Afghanistan until 1988, Khasbulatov was one of those political figures who had caromed out of obscurity during the transition. Yeltsin made no secret of his view that Khasbulatov and Rutskoi should defer to his lead on policy. He did not ask the counsel of either on the Belovezh'e negotiations, which they heard about from others.[43] But the parliament was a world unto itself in the early 1990s, and showboating and inconsistent voting by the lawmakers provided the chairman "with the ability to manipulate the agenda for his own purposes."[44] He and his presidium emitted hundreds of administrative edicts and formed a guard squad. At the "sixth congress" that refused to confirm Gaidar as prime minister in December 1992, Yeltsin raged that they were thinking not about society or reform but "only about how to dictate their will."[45] After the session, Yeltsin took Khasbulatov off his telephone hotline and had him cut off from information about the president's schedule; not to be outdone, Khasbulatov sent Yeltsin barbed letters and made gratuitous references to his drinking.

Gazing back at it all a decade later, Khasbulatov told me Yeltsin "backed himself and me into a corner" and that, as the junior man (he was born in 1942), he always expected to make the most concessions in any settlement.[46]

Yeltsin did go for total victory in September–October 1993; until then, he was ready to compromise. In December 1992 he proposed a national referendum for January, to ask the population whether they trusted him or the congress and soviet to solve the political crisis. The deputies said no, and the next day Yeltsin, with egg on his face, withdrew the idea.

President and speaker were at each other's throats for the next four months. Khasbulatov drew up plans to send a congress-drafted constitution to a referendum; he threw them over in March. On March 20, determined to play his trump card, public opinion, Yeltsin divulged that he was instituting an undefined "special rule" *(osobyi poryadok upravleniya)* until a referendum on president versus parliament on April 25. Rutskoi balked at countersigning the decree and wrote an open letter to Yeltsin against it. Prime Minister Chernomyrdin desisted from comment until Yeltsin "literally compelled him to declare support,"[47] and the justice minister, Nikolai Fëdorov, resigned.

The congress's riposte was to deliberate impeachment, which had been provided for in the constitutional amendments instituting the presidency in 1991. Meeting Yeltsin, Chernomyrdin, and Valerii Zor'kin, chairman of the Constitutional Court, in the Kremlin on March 24, Khasbulatov gave Yeltsin his conditions for gagging the process: a coalitional government of national accord, restrictions on presidential decrees, recall of Yeltsin's representatives in the provinces, and criminal prosecution of the drafters of the March 20 order. Yeltsin, seeing acceptance as tantamount to straw-man status, rebuffed them.[48] Zor'kin backed Khasbulatov.

Hours before the congressional vote, on the evening of March 28, Yeltsin came before a floodlit rally on the apron of land connecting St. Basil's Cathedral and the Moskva River. His speech drew on principles and personalities, formulating the latter in peppery, testing mode:

> It's been a grueling time since June 12, 1991, grueling in every respect—for you, for the people of Russia, for the president. We have gone onto a completely different road. We have thrown off the yoke of totalitarianism. We have thrown off the yoke of communism. We have taken the path of a civilized country, a civilized democracy. For those whose toes we have stepped on, this is inconvenient.
>
> The national-democrats [Russian ultranationalists] and the has-beens [communists] . . . are going all out in order somehow to destroy Yeltsin—if not to destroy him physically, then to remove him. (Cries from the audience: "We will not allow this!" "Yeltsin, Yeltsin, Yeltsin!")

> I . . . am taken by the simple statement that Varennikov [Valentin Varennikov, the hard-line general in August 1991] has made from Matrosskaya Tishina [prison]: "The only person Gorbachev couldn't handle was Yeltsin."
>
> You know what our congress is like. (Someone cries out, "We know!" A few shouts are heard.) . . . It is not for these six hundred [deputies] to decide Russia's fortunes. I will not yield to them, I will only yield to the people's will. (Cries from the audience, applause. A wave of "Yeltsin, Yeltsin, Yeltsin!")[49]

The voting in the congress was done by hand, anonymously. Yeltsin later said it was low ebb for his eight years as president. "Impeachment was my worst moment. I really suffered through it . . . I sat and waited through it . . . I sat and waited for the votes to be counted."[50] Six hundred and seventeen disaffected deputies voted for the motion, seventy-two short of the 689 needed for the prescribed two-thirds majority. Had it passed, Rutskoi, in the legislators' interpretation, would have taken over as president, in which case the face-off that took place in September would have come six months earlier. According to Aleksandr Korzhakov, the security chiefs had a plan, approved by the president on March 23, to read out a decree dissolving the parliament and to smoke the deputies out by placing canisters of tear gas on the balconies of the hall in the Grand Kremlin Palace.[51]

After the vote, Yeltsin and Khasbulatov agreed that the decree on special rule would be ditched and a four-point referendum to clear the air held on April 25. The four questions would be about (1) trust in Yeltsin, (2) approval of his social and economic policies, and early elections for (3) president and (4) the parliament. Yeltsin campaigned hard for yes votes on questions one, two, and four and a no vote on question three, trying as before to brand Khasbulatov and the congress as ultraconservative, which not all of them were. Khasbulatov struck back by calling Yeltsin a plaything for shadowy power brokers, as Nicholas II and Empress Alexandra had once been for the mystic Grigorii Rasputin. Yeltsin's threats to take decisive action, he said, amounted to "the strong gesture of a weak man" who was "tragically ill-equipped" for his office. "This person degenerated before my very eyes. He stopped being a leader and converted himself into a kind of puppet of those who have been called a 'collective Rasputin' . . . adventurers . . . ignoramuses." Yeltsin's project was to build a "semicolonial regime" in which a "wild, criminal, and semifeudal" capitalism would be in bondage to foreign interests.[52]

When the ballots were tallied on April 25, Yeltsin had prevailed. Fifty-nine percent of Russians expressed trust in him, 53 percent approved of his reforms, those wanting an early presidential election were just short of 50 percent, and 67 percent approved of an early parliamentary election. The results were nonbinding, but the pattern, and the surprising vote on the reform course, in particular, was a moral victory.[53]

Khasbulatov, having said earlier that the initiators of a referendum should resign if they lost out, stayed on. Yeltsin did not press the point and moved at a leisurely general pace, telling Richard Nixon in late April that Khasbulatov and Rutskoi were "midgets" he need not bother with.[54] In May he appointed a 762-member Constitutional Conference to circumvent the constitutional committee under the Supreme Soviet. Yeltsin addressed the conference on June 5, harkening to the tradition of "free Novgorod," whence the Yeltsins had moved to the Urals centuries before, and of Peter the Great and Alexander II. Khasbulatov was drowned out by clangor from the floor and had to recite his remarks from a stairway outside the meeting hall. The conference approved a draft on July 12, though without agreement on the federal system. Khasbulatov and the Supreme Soviet quashed a spate of presidential decrees, and Yeltsin vetoed parliamentary bills. Clashes between them burgeoned on privatization, social policy, and foreign relations. "It was widely assumed in Moscow . . . that another attempt to impeach Yeltsin was imminent and would be launched at the end of September or the beginning of October at the latest."[55]

Yeltsin decided in late summer to lower the boom. Huddling with advisers on August 10, he said that the stalemate on the constitution and on future elections "is pushing us toward the use of force."[56] There was a broad hint on August 31: He flew by helicopter to the army's two armored formations in the Moscow area (the Taman Division and the Kantemirov Tank Division) and to the 106th Airborne Division stationed in Tula, where he rakishly donned a paratrooper's beret. At the Taman garrison, he attended a tank exercise and dined in an officers' mess with Defense Minister Pavel Grachëv; the men drank to his health and gave him a soldierly "Hurrah!" The point was not to check up on the military's loyalty, in which he had complete faith, but to flaunt it before the press and his opponents.[57] In the early days of September, Yeltsin "suspended" Vice President Rutskoi and his Kremlin pass. He also took away Justice Zor'kin's bodyguards and transportation. Zor'kin had been testing the waters for a presidential campaign of his own, on the speculation that Yeltsin would step down as part of a constitutional pact. One of his supporters was Vladimir Lukin, the Russian ambassador to Washington, who was promised the position of foreign minister in a Zor'kin government and who arranged a visit by him to the United States in late summer.[58] Around September 9 Yeltsin gave his aides Viktor Ilyushin and Yurii Baturin some scrabbled notes and told them to prepare a presidential edict. Decree No. 1400 was promulgated on Tuesday, September 21, at eight P.M. Yeltsin shared it with the nation in a telecast. Before recording it, he found some gallows humor in proposing that the Kremlin staff pose with him for a good-bye photograph, since, if he were to fail, "We will sit together [in prison]."[59]

As he did at Belovezh'e Forest, Yeltsin had sliced through a Gordian knot with a freewheeling decision of debatable legality. The unilateralism and extraconstitutionality of his fiat caused him some grief. As he wrote a year later, "Here I was, the first popularly elected president, violating the law—bad law . . . yet law all the same."[60] But Decree No. 1400 stood. Its main articles laid to rest the Congress of People's Deputies and the Supreme Soviet and ordered the election on December 12 of a bicameral Federal Assembly comprising a State Duma (the name Russia's first parliament bore from 1905 to 1917), to represent individuals, and a Federation Council as the upper house, to represent the provinces. The first assembly would sit for a two-year term, and its first item of business would be to adopt a new constitution.

Yeltsin and Khasbulatov had baited and blustered since the winter of 1992–93, and both lowballed the danger of the other party following through. Yeltsin had no detailed battle plan, sure that "political methods" and threats would get the parliamentarians to relent; and Khasbulatov said that "until the last minute, I did not believe he [Yeltsin] would take such a step" (the abolition decree).[61] When the step was upon them, Khasbulatov and the deputies made a last stand. In a midnight session at the White House, the Supreme Soviet passed a resolution to remove Yeltsin from the presidency, which the congress had not done in March. Minutes later, Rutskoi was sworn in. That same night he began appointing ministers of defense, the interior, and security to a provisional government. The congress met on September 23 and passed a skein of measures against Yeltsin and his government, which Khasbulatov now called a "fascist dictatorship" (Rutskoi dubbed Yeltsin Russia's Führer). It also approved capital punishment for failure to carry out the orders of the new government and president.

Frenetic attempts by Zor'kin and Patriarch Aleksii to mediate foundered over the next ten days. At the White House, several hundred hard-line deputies dug in with radical nationalists, racists, and diehard communists. On Sunday, October 3, Yeltsin went briefly to the Kremlin, and on the ride in, "for the first time in my life the thought drilled into my head—had I done the right thing, had there been any other option?"[62] That day, after he returned to Barvikha-4, skirmishes on the streets spun out of control. Yeltsin decreed martial law in Moscow and rushed to the Kremlin as armed fighters, stirred up by Rutskoi, went at the mayor's office and the Ostankino television tower with Molotov cocktails, grenades, and Kalashnikovs. National television screens went blank for several hours. In the black of night, Yeltsin, exasperated that army troops had not penetrated mid-Moscow, as the Defense Ministry said they would, drove to the Russian Pentagon on Arbat Square and, with Viktor Chernomyrdin at his elbow, demanded action by first light. The generals skulked and explained that some of their men had been busy with the fall harvest, leading him to conclude that his military "was being pulled into pieces, and everyone was yanking on his part." A lawful government hung by a thread, "but the army could not defend it: some soldiers were picking potatoes and others did not feel like fighting." Minister Grachëv, who had been hopeful that police forces could manage the disturbances, said he would comply, on the condition that he be given written orders from the commander-in-chief—the kind of explicit authorization Mikhail Gorbachev never brought himself to give in his hour of need. Yeltsin was galled by the request but went back to the Kremlin, signed the order, and sent it to Grachëv by courier. It made all the difference to the officers, who proceeded to discharge their duty.[63]

The dénouement was swift and brutal. Thirteen hundred servicemen flooded inside Moscow's in-city ring road on Monday, October 4. Armored cars scrunched through the barricades in front of the White House at about seven A.M. At 10:00, four T-80 tanks on a bridge over the Moskva broke into a cannonade. "With a thunderous roar that echoed heavily through the nearby streets, the tanks opened fire on the upper floors. . . . Chunks of the marble façade shattered and flew into the air, and the huge clock in the center of the White House froze with its hands at 10:03. Windows were blown out of their frames, and thousands of sheets of paper, flung out of the building, spun slowly in the air like a flock of birds hovering in the sunshine."[64] Yeltsin had warned Khasbulatov to vacate and get to safety before the shooting started. Khasbulatov was not in his tenth-story office when it was one of the first to be slammed by a round. Commandos stormed the structure, emptied it and other occupied buildings, and stamped out the street mayhem.

The footage of tanks lobbing 125-mm. shells over the spot where Yeltsin had peacefully defied the putschists in 1991—upright on a T-72 from the very same Taman Division—and of Khasbulatov and Rutskoi being bused off to Lefortovo prison, was a graphic contrast to happier days. During the victory gathering, Yeltsin was handed Khasbulatov's tobacco pipe; he examined it and dashed it on the floor.[65] The official death toll was 187, none of them elected deputies, and 437 wounded; about three-quarters of the deaths were in and near the White House and about one-quarter at Ostankino.[66] Several anti-government organizations were banned, thirteen communist and rabidly nationalist newspapers were closed down, and editors were told to present articles to censors. After repair of the blast and flame damage by a Turkish contractor, the White House was to go to the Russian government for office space.

The pride and joy of the Yeltsin scheme was the long-awaited post-Soviet constitution to tie the state together and encode the norms of representative government, separation of powers, primacy of the president, and federalism. Its inculcation through even partially democratic means ought to be counted as an achievement, as should the normalization of political life it made possible.

The tactic of having the newly elected Federal Assembly rule on the constitution was as much of a gamble as any Yeltsin made as president, for no one could be sure that it would go over as legitimate, that the assembly would adopt a satisfactory constitution, or that it would approve *any* constitution—if not, he would have lopped off the limb on which they all rested. After the shootout in Moscow, he reconsidered. He decreed on October 15 that the constitution would go to a plebiscite on election day.[67] His Constitutional Conference resumed its labors, and on November 8 Yeltsin approved a draft that largely parroted earlier renderings. Putting it before the electorate was another roll of the dice: What would occur if voters turned thumbs down? For stability's sake, Yeltsin made one more adjustment. On November 6 he rescinded a slapdash pledge he made in September to advance the date of the next presidential election by two years, from the summer of 1996 to the summer of 1994. Even were constitutional ratification and the parliamentary election to come a cropper, he would have a leg to stand on.[68]

The 137-article draft was inserted in national and regional newspapers and affixed in public places. Yeltsin's pitch to the people was binary. It was either him and his constitution or perdition. He promised Russians both democracy and an individuated authority consistent with the needs of reform, with their traditions, and, he said overweeningly in an interview in *Izvestiya*, with their limitations:

> I will not deny that the powers of the president in the draft really are significant. But what else would you want to see? [This is] a country habituated to tsars and chieftains; a country where clear-cut group interests have not developed, where the bearers of them have not been defined, and where normal parties are only beginning to be born; a country where discipline is not great and legal nihilism runs riot. In such a country, do you want to bet only or mostly on a parliament? If you did, within a half-year, if not sooner, people would demand a dictator. I can assure you that such a dictator would be found, and possibly from within that very same parliament. . . .
>
> This is not about Yeltsin but about people being knowledgeable of the need to have an official from whom they can make demands. . . . The president of Russia [in the new constitution] has just as many powers as he needs to carry out his role in reforming the country.[69]

On December 12 the constitutional blueprint was approved by a 58 percent majority. A Constitutional Conference delegate had foreseen that citizens in the plebiscite "will vote for or against the president, and that will be it."[70] This at root is what they did. Fewer than half of the "yes" voters had read the document. More than to constitutional issues, narrowly conceived, most responded to Yeltsin, his market economy, and their like or dislike of the Soviet regime.[71] The constitution went into effect on December 25, two years after the winding down of the Soviet state.

Yeltsin, therefore, got his legal cornerstone, and, imperfectly and inelegantly, the crisis of the state in its white-hot form was allayed.[72] Western specialists, comparing Russia to other post-communist countries, commonly characterize the constitution of 1993 as "superpresidential." Gennadii Zyuganov, the leader of the reborn communists, liked to say it gave the president more powers than the tsar, the Egyptian pharaoh, and a sheikh of Araby put together. A correspondent for the pro-presidential *Izvestiya* asked Yeltsin in November 1993 if he were not laying claim to "almost imperial" powers. An emperor, he replied, would have no need of a constitution, and a tyrant like Stalin would have a merely decorative one. He, Yeltsin, could act only within the law, he was limited to two terms (his second term would be four years, a year less than the first), and parliament could reverse his veto or impeach him.[73]

It was equally true that Yeltsin got most of what he had wished for. Of the ministers in the government, only the prime minister was to be confirmed in office by the Duma. As head of state, the president was going to function as guarantor of the constitutional order, lay down "guidelines" for domestic and foreign policy, and have the power to dissolve the Duma for cause.[74] Two-thirds majorities in both houses of parliament were needed to override a presidential veto, and the president was not compelled to give a reason for using the veto power.[75] Article 90, on the power to issue binding decrees at will, was the benchmark for Yeltsin. In the final draft, he stroked out the caveat that presidential decrees and directives be only "in execution of the powers conferred on him by the constitution of the Russian Federation and by federal laws."[76] The constitution was echoed in the insignia of state—in the Presidential Regiment and Presidential Orchestra (instituted as the Kremlin Regiment and Kremlin Orchestra by Stalin in the 1930s), the chain of office and Presidential Standard, the two presidential yachts, the new Kremlin chinaware (emblazoned with the double-headed eagle in place of the Soviet coat of arms), and the grandiloquent state protocol written up by aide Vladimir Shevchenko, who was one of the few Gorbachev associates Yeltsin kept on.[77]

But the parliamentary election of 1993 did not break Yeltsin's way. On October 18 martial law in the capital and most restrictions on political activity were lifted. While the ban held on three extremist parties and twenty-one persons, Zyuganov's KPRF (Communist Party of the Russian Federation) was reinstated and registered. Half of the Duma's seats were to be filled by national lists and half in territorial districts. Yeltsin stoutly maintained, and with reason, that the ambit of choice in the election was without precedent. "The spectrum of political positions taken by the participants [in the campaign] is uncommonly wide," he said to the Council of Ministers on November 2. "I don't think there has been a thing like it here since the elections to the Constituent Assembly in 1917," before that democratic body's suppression by Lenin and the Bolsheviks.[78] Most forecasts were of a victory for the Russia's Choice movement, the torch carrier for Yeltsin chaired by Yegor Gaidar; also on its slate were Anatolii Chubais and Sergei Filatov, who had replaced Yurii Petrov as head of the executive office of the president. There were predictions that it would get 50 or even 65 percent of the popular vote. But "the party of power" *(partiya vlasti)*, as it was known, never got a Yeltsin endorsement and did not prevent other reformist politicians, including cabinet members, from entering the contest under different banners. Prime Minister Chernomyrdin admonished his ministers to campaign only "outside of working hours."[79] On December 12 the Russia's Choice list ran a dispiriting second in the national poll, with 16 percent of the votes, and came in with sixty-five deputies out of 450. Many reformist votes were diverted to the smaller parties headed by Grigorii Yavlinskii, Sergei Shakhrai, and Anatolii Sobchak of St. Petersburg. The party-list vote was won by the misnamed Liberal Democratic Party of Russia of the flamboyant Vladimir Zhirinovskii, whose message was one of chauvinism and inchoate protest; the LDPR took 23 percent of the ballots cast and finished with sixty-four deputies. The neocommunist KPRF was third, with 12 percent of the national vote and forty-one seats, and five lesser parties were also seated. Ivan Rybkin of the Agrarian Party, a moderate leftist offshoot of the KPRF, was made speaker of the Duma in January.

The constitution did not give Yeltsin the dictatorial "throne of bayonets" he had charged the GKChP with wanting to construct in 1991. Aleksei Kazannik, the Siberian lawyer who in 1989 gave up his seat in the USSR Supreme Soviet to Yeltsin, accepted appointment as procurator general of Russia on October 3, 1993, promised by the president that he could go ahead with investigations with "a maximum of legality" and "a maximum of humanitarianism."[80] Yeltsin then demanded that he press murder and complicity charges against some of the jailed perpetrators, which Kazannik would not do, saying the evidence of homicidal intent was lacking and the worst they could be indicted for was "organizing mass disorder." Kazannik also told Yeltsin that he was considering prosecution of executive-branch officials for failing to negotiate in good faith with the opposition, and he was to say later that he might have indicted Defense Minister Grachëv and Interior Minister Viktor Yerin.[81] One of the Duma's first legislative acts, on February 23, 1994, was to pass, by 252 votes to sixty-seven, a bill of amnesty for Rutskoi, Khasbulatov, and the Supreme Soviet leaders, and some supporters, sixteen people in all. Yeltsin, who fervently dissented from the motion, ordered Kazannik not to comply. Kazannik, finding the Duma's decision profligate but constitutional (under Article 103), informed Yeltsin he would carry out the decision and then leave office. "Don't dare do it," Yeltsin threw back at him.[82] Kazannik did dare. On February 26 the prisoners were freed and Kazannik resigned. Clenching his teeth, Yeltsin did not pursue the matter further.

All members of the 1990–93 Supreme Soviet were permitted to keep the housing that had been assigned them. Khasbulatov, for example, retained the oversize apartment on Shchusev Street in central Moscow once occupied by Brezhnev and reverted to his professorship at the Plekhanov

Economics Institute.[83] Rutskoi organized a new political party called Derzhava, or Great Power. Even Viktor Barannikov, the former security minister who deserted to the opposition, was treated with kid gloves.[84] The February 23 law amnestied the organizers of the 1991 coup attempt, and not only Yeltsin's opponents from 1993. They had gone to trial in April 1993, but the proceedings had been delayed and no judgment yet given. Only General Varennikov, the most radical of the GKChP conspirators, who refused to accept the amnesty, was not released. He stood trial and was acquitted by the military panel of the Russian Supreme Court on August 11, 1994. Varennikov was to be elected to the Duma in 1995, as a communist, and to chair its committee on veterans' affairs. Other political enemies of Yeltsin from bygone days, such as Yegor Ligachëv, also sat in the Dumas formed in 1993 and 1995.[85]

Parliament, limited in the oversight function, still had the power of the purse, and that gave it bargaining chips with relation to the budget and to fiscal and macroeconomic policy. And it had the power to legislate, which it soon did with far greater productivity than analyses treating it as a fig leaf would imply. It adopted only six laws in 1994; in 1995, despite the continued lack of a stable majority, it adopted thirty-seven; in the first half of 1996, after another parliamentary election, it adopted eight.[86] Yeltsin still had to resort freely to the decree power, though somewhat less frequently than before the constitutional reform. In 1992 and 1993, he had published an average of twenty-four rule-making decrees per month. They were to average seventeen per month in 1994 and twenty per month in 1995.[87]

Constitutional gridlock in 1993 gave Yeltsin both the necessity and the chance to rejig relations with the subunits of the federation. As before, the ethnic enclaves were the nub of the problem. In the April referendum, the governments of two of the twenty-one republics, Chechnya and Tatarstan, refused to participate, and in twelve republics confidence in the president was lower than 50 percent. (In the sixty-eight non-republics, Yeltsin stacked up majority support in fifty-four.) Yeltsin left no stone unturned in trying to secure provincial support. On August 12–14 he met in conclave in Petrozavodsk, Kareliya, with the heads of the republics and representatives of eight interregional associations, treating them to a full-day sail in a presidential yacht on Lake Onega. Yeltsin's proposal to co-opt all of the regional leaders into his Federation Council irked republic leaders who preferred special treatment.

In many places, Decree No. 1400 met with a glacial reception. Several dozen provincial legislatures, among them those in twelve of the nineteen republics with functioning assemblies, passed motions of solidarity with Khasbulatov and Rutskoi. Yeltsin retaliated on October 9 and 12 by disbanding all of the non-republic soviets, ordering the election of more compact assemblies between December 1993 and June 1994, and advising the republics to do the same. The governors and republic presidents were less incautious than the legislators. Fifteen of them indicated hesitancy about Decree No. 1400. Four governors opposed it fervidly, and Yeltsin gave them the axe. A fifth case was Sverdlovsk oblast's Eduard Rossel, who did not support Khasbulatov but proclaimed his Urals Republic on November 1. Yeltsin abolished the republic on November 9 and dismissed Rossel on November 10. Of the presidents of the existing ethnic republics, Kirsan Ilyumzhinov of Kalmykiya, in the North Caucasus, joined the defenders of the blockaded White House and issued anti-Yeltsin declarations. Once the parliamentarist forces had been subdued, Ilyumzhinov "capitulated and made the rather remarkable proposal to eliminate Kalmykiya's status as a . . . republic . . . [and] abolish its constitution." Yeltsin allowed him to stay in his post, only much more compliant with Moscow than before.[88]

The constitutional plebiscite on December 12 seemed at first to portend more fireworks. Majorities went against the presidential draft in eight republics and ten other regions. The 1993 conjuncture, however, was a bottoming out for Yeltsin and the federal administration. The masterstroke for recovery was his consolidation of power at the center, which showed regional leaders, to put it crudely, who was king of the mountain. On the local scene, aping Moscow, the republic presidents emerged more potent than their legislatures. The muting of political competition made them better able to withstand nationalist pressures, and these pressures simmered down. "Yeltsin's centralization of power altered Russia's entire institutional environment, shifting power from republican parliaments to executives and eliminating the massive central state weakness that had made possible republican challenges to federal sovereignty in the early 1990s."[89] There was similar momentum in the non-republics. Yeltsin felt strong enough in November 1993 to disclaim the line in the federative treaty of 1992 that would have given the ethnic reserves half of the seats in the upper house. The new Federation Council gave all territories two places apiece. Yeltsin further lessened the inequality between the republics and the non-republics by consenting to gubernatorial elections in selected oblasts and making them universal practice in December 1995. After two years in which Federation Council members were elected, it was agreed at the end of 1995 that each province's two seats would be assigned ex officio to its head executive and legislator, bringing the regional leaders into the central political establishment.[90]

The innovation in relations between center and periphery was Yeltsin's espousal of custom-built power-sharing "treaties" with many of the provinces. This was not a new concept: He had lofted it on the same 1990 sortie to Tatarstan when he urged it to take all the sovereignty it needed.[91] The first bilateral treaty was struck, appropriately, with Mintimer Shaimiyev of Tatarstan on February 15, 1994. Yeltsin traveled to the republic in May. He made appearances at the spruced-up Kazan kremlin, the Mardzhani mosque, an Orthodox church, several factories and farms, a children's hospital, and a press conference. "They beat me up and denigrated me for the treaty with Tatarstan," he said, standing beside Shaimiyev, "but nonetheless I have been proven right. . . . Tatarstan has taken as many powers under the treaty as it can. The rest that remain with the federal government are enough to satisfy us."[92]

Neighboring Bashkortostan and Kabardino-Balkariya in the North Caucasus came to understandings with Moscow later in 1994, four republics did in 1995, two in 1996, and, after Yeltsin's second inauguration, one in 1997 and one in 1998. In 1995 Yeltsin was to extend the practice to nonethnic provinces, with Viktor Chernomyrdin's native Orenburg and Yeltsin's Sverdlovsk first. Eventually forty-seven of eighty-nine federal subunits were to have their treaties. The sweeteners were mostly economic—provisions allowing signatories to hold some federal taxes collected locally, for instance, or giving them a fixed share of revenues from sale of oil and other natural resources—but some ancillary agreements touched on environmental issues, conscription, and linguistic policy. Yeltsin held the signings in the gilded and chandeliered St. George's Hall, the most resplendent in the Grand Kremlin Palace: It measures 13,500 square feet, and has a fifty-seven-foot-high ceiling. It did not go unnoticed that the statues on the eighteen monumental pylons, by the nineteenth-century sculptor Ivan Vitali, stood for regions ingested by the Russian state from the 1400s to the 1800s. It was the room Gorbachev had reserved for the signing ceremony for the USSR union treaty in August 1991.

The Russian "parade of treaties" was a consensual and eminently defensible means of keeping the federation together. Through them, Yeltsin traded concessions to particularistic interests for recommitment to the federation and to his policies. The first several were the most generous. Beginning with Sakha in June 1995, "style and content shifts from a recognition of distinctiveness to agreement to conformity with established rules and jurisdictions."[93] Aspects of the agreements breached the 1993 constitution and federal statutes. Moscow winked at these and other constitutional transgressions, notably by the republics—a policy that was to be reversed in the next decade.[94]

Yeltsin also took a hands-off stance toward regional development, enjoining local leaders to solve their problems self-reliantly with minimal tutorship from Moscow: "We have said to the Russian republics, territories, and oblasts, Moscow is not going to give you commands anymore. Your fate is in your hands."[95] He acknowledged that the provinces' revenues would swell in relation to central revenues (they went from 41 percent of the Russian total in 1990 to 62 percent in 1998) and that interregional inequalities unacceptable under Soviet rule would emerge. The squeaky wheel was oiled, in that regions that voted against Yeltsin and his allies or that were hard hit by strikes and social unrest were given financial transfers and tax breaks.[96] The logic again was that of tacit reciprocity of support:

> In exchange for loyalty or even for neutrality, Boris Yeltsin often gave the governors a free hand, not hindering those who carried out reforms, others who imitated them, or a third group who, as the adage went, wanted "to uphold the gains of socialism in one oblast" [a joking reference to Stalin's catchword of "Socialism in One Country"]. Not infrequently in the arguments of the federal government with the regions, the president took the part of the latter and would come out as the lobbyist of several of them, supporting their requests for supplementary budget allocations for this or that purpose—which badly nettled the reformers in the cabinet. Most often Yeltsin preferred to distance himself from these questions, considering that life itself would show who was right. Mind you, he took an understanding attitude when the government used unorthodox methods of influencing the regions, such as reallocation of financial resources. He would look at such methods in the context of preserving the balance. Knowing from his own experience how heavy was the burden of leaders on the spot, he in any case saw to it that some limit in the relations between the center and the regional leaders was not crossed.[97]

Immanent in the principle that regional leaders would not serve anymore at Yeltsin's pleasure was sufferance of incorrigible communists and of politicians with whom he had been at loggerheads, such as Eduard Rossel (returned to power by the Sverdlovsk electorate in August 1995) and, more dramatically, Aleksandr Rutskoi (elected governor in Kursk in October 1996). He was willing to let bygones be bygones: "I forget such things. It is better for the health."[98] With the more obliging provincial barons, Yeltsin cultivated human ties. He kept in contact with officials he had known through the nomenklatura or in the USSR and RSFSR parliaments, and went on a charm offensive with others. Anatolii Korabel'shchikov, a trusted aide out of the CPSU apparatus, was his contact man for the regions and had unrestricted entrée to him on his provincial tours. Yeltsin invited groups of fifteen to twenty governors to his ABTs compound on Varga Street in southwest Moscow (taken from the KGB in 1991) for discussion and a dinner. A select few were fêted in the Kremlin or at Zavidovo and were telephoned to consult on decrees and political trends. The pleiad of regional leaders with whom the president had a confidential relationship took in Dmitrii Ayatskov (of Saratov), Vladimir Chub (Rostov), Nikolai Fëdorov (Chuvashiyia), Anatolii Guvzhin (Astrakhan), Viktor Ishayev (Khabarovsk), Nikolai Merkushkin (Mordoviya), Boris Nemtsov (Nizhnii Novgorod), Mikhail Prusak (Novgorod), Mintimer Shaimiyev (Tatarstan), Anatolii Sobchak (St. Petersburg), Yegor Stroyev (Orël), and Konstantin Titov (Samara).[99] With one of the youngest and the brightest of them, Nemtsov—born in 1959, trained as a nuclear physicist, and the leader of an environmental protest movement before Yeltsin appointed him governor in 1991—Yeltsin developed a father-son relationship. To a local audience in August 1994, Yeltsin said he could see Nemtsov as the worthiest successor to himself as president. The central media picked up the statement.[100]

"The danger of Russia falling apart has passed," Yeltsin stated boisterously the same month as the lovefest with Nemtsov. "This does not mean," he said in qualification of his good cheer, "that all difficulties are behind us."[101] Little did he know that he was about to get into a fratricidal war that bore out this admonitory note.

Chechnya, a swatch of North Caucasus uplands fringed on the north by plain, had as many grievances against the Russian state as any region. Its people, incorporated into the empire against their will in the nineteenth century, raised revolts against tsars and commissars. From 1944 to 1956, they lived in exile in Central Asia and Siberia, having been deported by Stalin on the charge of sympathizing with the German invaders. Although their troubles were not unique,[102] their sense of deprivation and an ingrained willingness to take up arms were a flammable combination. The Chechens follow Sunni Islam and are organized into clans that drive off higher authority, be it Russian or Chechen.

The Brezhnev-era leadership of the republic was not changed until June 1989, when Moscow replaced an ethnic Russian first secretary with Doku Zavgayev, a Chechen partocrat. Nationalist and reformist ferment flared in 1990, and that November republic sovereignty was duly declared. The next month Djokhar Dudayev was chosen to chair a national congress, an alternative legislature working in collaboration with street-level activists. In August–September 1991 his congress and paramilitary overthrew Zavgayev, with some loss of life, and on October 27 Dudayev was elected president in a procedurally flawed contest. On November 1 he declared Chechnya fully independent of the Soviet Union and the RSFSR. The Moscow authorities fled the territory and left behind thousands of heavy weapons—the only province of Russia where they did so.

The proximate cause of the Chechen horror show was leadership failure. An air-force officer by profession, Dudayev was the first ethnic Chechen to make general in the Soviet military and had commanded six thousand men in a strategic bomber wing in Estonia—a force that in the event of war with NATO would have rained nuclear bombs on Western Europe. Except for a few weeks in babyhood, he had never lived in Chechnya until 1991. Between him and Yeltsin there were certain parallels: The two were model servants of the former regime, broke with it, and succeeded politically as populists. But there the similarities ended. Where Yeltsin was a risk-taker who knew his limits, Dudayev was a narcissist influenced by the Chechen mountaineers' cult of the *jiggit*, the madcap or knight who proves himself in armed forays and lives on in heroic songs if he falls on the battlefield.[103] And Dudayev was more beguiled by the trappings of power than by its utilization—"much more interested in the idea of calling Chechnya independent than in the practicality of making that idea work."[104] He had a weakness for cinematic costumes and pageantry. Of a commemoration in Grozny where Dudayev took the platform in a leather trench coat, epaulets, and jackboots, one observer writes that "he looked like nothing so much as a bad copy of Charlie Chaplin's Little Dictator, toothbrush mustache included."[105] Unlike Mintimer Shaimiyev, who flirted with separatism and then did a workable deal for his republic under the Russian tent, Dudayev scorned the via media and a Tatarstan-type accommodation. As was once said of Yasser Arafat, he rarely lost an opportunity to lose an opportunity. Dudayev's Chechnya was an economic basket case, at the mercy of political cliques, smugglers, counterfeiters, local mobsters, and Russian businessmen and officials who valued it as a haven and transit point. Between 1992 and 1994, nearly 200,000 people, or one-fifth of the population, left the republic as refugees; most were ethnic Russians.

Yeltsin was not at the top of his game, either. It was he who had said the minorities should take all the sovereignty they could swallow, and here was a minority that said it wanted every last crumb. As Aleksandr Tsipko had pointed out, it was no walkover to explain to the Chechens or anyone in their position that they had no title to the independence that the fifteen union republics of the USSR—one of them Russia—asserted in 1991. In 1995, when the war was in full swing, Yeltsin was to imply that there was a limit the Chechens should have known not to cross: "I have said, 'Take as much sovereignty as you can.' But a very profound meaning sits within this word 'can.' As much as you can—meaning, Don't take more than you can. And if you do, you will crack up, like Chechnya did."[106] After the fact, the Chechens' crackup was instructive to the others, but at the time it was not foreseen.

Racked by indecision, Yeltsin entrusted policy on Chechnya to a revolving carousel of advisory groups. The attitude stiffened after Vladimir Zhirinovskii led the polls in the December 1993 parliamentary election. The sole Chechen with authority in the Russia-wide political arena was Ruslan Khasbulatov. Released from prison under the amnesty, he set up shop in the Chechen village of Tolstoy-Yurt in March of 1994 and offered his good offices as a broker. Yeltsin, however, warned his former adversary off, thus ruling out of court one potentially nonviolent outcome.[107]

A flag-waving group headed by Nikolai Yegorov, the former governor of Krasnodar province, led in defining Kremlin policy once he was appointed minister of nationality and regional affairs in May 1994. Attempts to arrange a meeting between Dudayev and Yeltsin were to no avail. "Beside the powerful historical and sociopolitical currents, the Chechen conflict . . . was decisively rooted in personal and emotional influences that cannot be explained in the usual categories of positivist causality."[108] Yeltsin informed Shaimiyev in the early summer that he was thinking about a meeting; he hardened his position when, apparently in reaction to an assassination attempt, Dudayev contemned him on Russian television as an unfit leader and a dipsomaniac. Yeltsin as a result "crossed Dudayev off the list of . . . politicians with whom it was permissible in any way to communicate and raised him to the rank of a primary enemy."[109] The patience of Job would have been required to work things out with Dudayev, and that was a quality

Boris Yeltsin lacked. Dudayev gave journalists a glimpse of the patience needed at press conferences called to publicize the Chechens' policy. The pattern was that he would lead off with a rational statement. "Then, however, he would rapidly degenerate into hysterical insults and . . . philosophical, racial, and historical speculations, almost as if possessed by some evil demon." Anatol Lieven, the Briton who made this observation, also recalls Dudayev in interviews before the war ranting at Yeltsin and the Russians as Nazis, totalitarian, satanic.[110]

What made the case for a military response irresistible was the shared hubris of assuming that the army was capable of prevailing in a surgical strike. The Defense Ministry questioned only the feasibility of doing it rashly and in mid-winter. Pavel Grachëv believed the republic could be secured in ten days, and showed Yeltsin and Chernomyrdin on a map how the advance would go.[111] Oleg Lobov, the Sverdlovsk apparatchik who by this time was secretary of the Security Council, the coordinating body for national security (rather like the National Security Council in Washington, D.C.), is reported to have boasted to a lawmaker in November 1994 that there would be "a small, victorious war" in Chechnya, which would "raise the president's ratings" as, he said, the U.S. intervention in Haiti had helped Bill Clinton's.[112] Lobov in an interview with me in 2002 said he never made the statement, while confirming that he had thought the war would go more swimmingly than it did.[113] As for Yeltsin, although there is no evidence that he linked Chechnya to his approval ratings, he had a pollyannaish view of Russian military capabilities and was now of the opinion that independence for a Chechen statelet would be "the beginning of the breakup of the country."[114]

The Kremlin first attempted covert action to overthrow Dudayev in league with local anti-government militias. When this did not work, Yeltsin had his Security Council sanction a military operation. On November 30 he signed Decree No. 2137 authorizing the army and the MVD to "restore constitutional order" in Chechnya. Three columns of troops and armor tore across the provincial border on December 11. On December 31, without proper intelligence or infantry cover, tanks entered Grozny, which the tsar's Terek Cossacks had founded as a fortress in 1818. Chechen squads mowed down many of the crews and hid in housing and office buildings. Russian guns and airstrikes within weeks made a moonscape out of the city and created a humanitarian catastrophe. The Russian contingent numbered 40,000 by January 1995 and 70,000 by February. By some estimates, 25,000 civilians and

1,500 Russian troops had died by April 1995. As early as January 4, Yeltsin was demanding to know at a Kremlin meeting why so many had been killed in the blitzkrieg. "Russia at this moment," he was to write in his memoirs, "parted with one more exceptionally dubious but fond illusion—about the might of our army . . . about its indomitability."[115] He and the country had paid a prohibitive price for the illusion and for being drawn into what he confessed in 1996 had been "the most botched war in the history of Russia."[116]

Chechnya has been called Yeltsin's Bay of Pigs, Vietnam, or Iraq. It was a sorrier trial in one sense—its firsthand feedback into national life and politics. The butchery and squalor seen on the television news were not in some distant land but in a corner of Russia. The vox populi turned against the war in the spring of 1995, even as federal battalions chased the Chechen warriors out of the urban areas and into the hills. But on June 14, 1995, Shamil Basayev, a former firefighter, computer salesman, and airplane hijacker—who claimed he had been in the crowd defending Yeltsin at the Russian White House in August 1991—opened up a home front using the foreign weapon of terrorism. Basayev and his gunmen drove three trucks untouched into Budënnovsk, Stavropol province, and took 1,400 patients, medical personnel, and others hostage in a hospital, demanding a Russian pullout from Chechnya. Yeltsin ill-advisedly took off for a meeting of the G-7 in Halifax, Canada, leaving Viktor Chernomyrdin to negotiate with Basayev (and save lives) for two days of the crisis. By the time it was over on June 18, 126 townspeople had been executed or killed in the crossfire and the Chechens had escaped. On June 21 the Duma for the first and only time voted (by 241 votes to seventy-two) no-confidence in Yeltsin's government, after which he fired the Stavropol governor and three cabinet members: Interior Minister Yerin, Minister of Nationality and Regional Affairs Yegorov, and the head of the security service, Sergei Stepashin.

The military thrust in Chechnya wound down after Budënnovsk. On July 30 Moscow signed a protocol with the guerrillas calling for a cease-fire, a disarming of the Chechen formations, and a drawdown of army units. In late 1995 it went through the motions of returning Doku Zavgayev as head of the republic and staging an election. But militants in the countryside continued to ambush the federal forces and their local clients, kidnapping and piracy went on unabated, and few weapons were turned in. Dudayev's death in April 1996 had little effect on the Russians' growing yearning for a way out. The presidential election of the summer of 1996 (see Chapter 14) was to force the issue.

If any consolation is to be taken from the Chechen fiasco, it is that Yeltsin did not put it to use to asphyxiate debate or political liberties. He pats himself on the back in *Presidential Marathon:* "If during those . . . critical days we had gone for extraordinary measures and had limited freedom of speech, a split would have been unavoidable" between state and society.[117] It is no idle boast. At one of the low points of his administration, struggling to keep the state together with the bluntest of instruments, he could have attacked democratic freedoms in the name of protecting the state, but elected not to.

Chapter Twelve

Boris Agonistes

If there is an enduring truism about Boris Yeltsin, it is that he had a colorful personality—a juicy or succulent personality *(sochnaya lichnost')* is another idiom one hears Russians use. It was the stuff of countless news stories in his years in power and suffuses the Yeltsin legend.

Human personalities are elusive. The out-of-the-ordinary individual may outdo the ordinary in erecting "identity shields" to mask what is beneath the skin.[1] Yeltsin's carapace as national leader was unusually impenetrable. It differed in degree if not in kind from the reserve he maintained in Sverdlovsk, where he had found himself on familiar and stable terrain. Yeltsin seemed to bring to the metropole a fear of giving himself away, as Sergei Filatov, his chief of staff for three years, says—an unease "that someone would half-open a nook of his personal, secret life or read his inmost thoughts." Vyacheslav Kostikov, his spokesman from 1992 to 1995, gives up in his memoir on jamming him into a master formula or sobriquet: "In reality, no one knows Yeltsin, and he does nothing to bring clarity to his self-portrait." A member of the Kremlin press pool remembers Yeltsin as "the substantiation of power on two legs"; what went on inside his head flummoxed her to the end.[2]

The swashbuckler Man on the Tank from 1991 remains the culminating image of Yeltsin for the ages. Going from maverick to master, he began to project other, competing images. And some of them—lashing out at former parliamentary colleagues in 1992 and 1993, brandishing the notorious conductor's baton in Berlin in 1994, looking wan after heart attacks in 1995—spoke of disquiet and even anguish. But these were not the only juices that flowed, which makes it important to eschew clichés and pop psychology and establish, as best one can, the actual balance among them. If the private man had not been predictive of the public man, one might not care. Here we can rest easy. As milestone events of Yeltsin's first presidential term go to show, his interior landscape, inscrutable as it was, was highly relevant to his choices and to the fingerprints he left as leader.

Events were overtaking two of Yeltsin's life scripts as the curtain lifted on the post-communist era. He had long since sloughed off his sense of political duty to the Soviet Union. His residual sense of filial duty ended on March 21, 1993, with the death of his mother from heart failure. Klavdiya Vasil'evna was eighty-five and had been staying with the Moscow Yeltsins for some months. The evening before, as the raucous conflict with the Supreme Soviet heated up, she took in the television news with them, bussed her son, and said to him, "That's my boy, Borya," as she went back to her bedroom. This was the last he heard from her. She was given an Orthodox burial at Kuntsevo Cemetery, with several priests and a choir. Yeltsin held a clod of frozen earth in his hand for some minutes before tossing it on the casket.[3]

The rebellion scenario now read like diaries stored in a dusty attic. In the August coup, Oleg Poptsov had marveled at his capability for overturning the status quo: "The framework of power has to be adjusted to him. A person with a cunning, deep-set capacity for mutiny, he can smash this framework in a single minute."[4] The framework of power had been not only adjusted to Yeltsin but harnessed to him. There was no one left to rebel against.

Yeltsin never discarded his testing script, with its tinges of strength and competency. At his desk, he used trite policy details as tests. A topnotch speed reader—aided by a pencil, he ran his eye along the diagonal of the page, from upper left to lower right—he would memorize factoids and passages from official documents and retrieve them in discussions weeks or months later, tickled when he could recite the exact page number. Away from the office, exercise and sport remained the main devices. For old times' sake, Yeltsin might still do a walrus swim in a frigid river or lake. Aleksandr Korzhakov reports one on the Moskva River on a March day in the early 1990s, with ice floes bobbing. Whenever possible, Yeltsin capped a steam bath with a plunge into a snowbank or freezing water; he would submerse himself in the water, ticking off the seconds, for two full minutes, longer than most men half his age could stand the temperature and the oxygen deprivation.[5] With volleyball behind him, Yeltsin had taken up tennis, the racket sport that also has a serve-and-volley structure, while working at Gosstroi. He played it in pairs and had a booming serve, although he was lumbering on his feet and rallied poorly with his mutilated left hand. Shamil Tarpishchev, the professional captain of the Russian national team, was his personal coach, and found him no more genial in the face of a loss than his Sverdlovsk volleyball mates had. One time Tarpishchev thought it would be amusing to offer to play doubles against Yeltsin and Korzhakov by pairing with Yeltsin's grandson Boris, and to neutralize his advantage by handcuffing himself to young Boris. The manacled Tarpishchev and Boris, Jr., won the first set. "I looked over and the president was exerting himself and glowering at Borya and me. We threw the second set and got out of there."[6]

As in almost any leadership career, success was still the script of the most import to Yeltsin. Richard Nixon, who met with him in 1991, 1992, and 1993, saw in Yeltsin "a relentless inner drive that propelled him to the top," rather like Nixon, who was also raised poor, made it almost to the top in the United States, was set back, and clawed his way back up Everest.[7] If getting to be "first" motivated Yeltsin in the good old days, staying first motivated him now, and that was no easier a task, for one had to pedal like mad in this environment just to stand still. And building a better way of life, as he was to say in his retirement speech, was proving to be "excruciatingly difficult" and "exceptionally complicated," and that realization was never out of his mind. He had always been hard on himself. As his daughter Tatyana said in an interview, "Even when he had made some kind of speech and I would say, 'Papa, that went fantastically,' or he had pulled off some kind of deal very well, he would say, 'No, nonetheless I could have done it better.' . . . Even when something came out very well, he was always dissatisfied to some extent."[8] Now he seemed to be such more often and more thoroughly. In one of his several televised dialogues with the president in 1993, the filmmaker El'dar Ryazanov inquired if he was satisfied with his work. Yeltsin's stygian response prefigured his 1999 valedictory: "I am rarely satisfied with my work. . . . I am satisfied with my work 5 to 10 percent of the time and 90 percent of the time I am dissatisfied. I am *constantly dissatisfied* with my work, and that is a frightful thing."[9]

At the middle of the heaving sea that was Boris Yeltsin's life in his presidential years there sat an atoll of domestic tranquility. As he had except at UPI and in his first year as an engineer, he based himself in, and drew succor from, a traditional household—"a patriarchal Urals family" arrayed around "a supreme authority, the grandfather."[10] Yelena Okulova and her husband and children (a boy, Ivan, was born in the late 1990s) had an apartment midtown and then in the Krylatskoye block, a floor below the in-laws' pied-à-terre. Yeltsin's second daughter, Tatyana, and her family resided in Boris and Naina's home, dividing their time between Moscow and Barvikha-4. She went from the military institute to a position in the Dawn of the Urals Bank, a small firm based in Perm, in 1994, and then onto maternity leave when her second son, Gleb, was born in August 1995. (Tatyana's first son, Boris, studied at Winchester, an English boarding school, from 1996 to 1998.) The Dyachenkos and Okulovs had dachas of their own. Callers at the Yeltsin home often remarked on the prevalence of females, children, bicycles, and toys.

While Boris Nikolayevich may have been the patriarch, the stabilizer in the family unit was its warmhearted, retiring, and boundlessly patient matriarch. Now a homemaker full-time, she devoted herself to a demanding spouse. Naina Iosifovna, an aide of hers, Natal'ya Konstantinova, observed in a memoir, "carries her husband like a crystal vase," seeing him through toil and trouble.[11] She overcame the claustrophobia about vehicles and airplane cabins that she had been subject to in Sverdlovsk. In 1993, after eight years in the capital, she declared that she did not yet feel "at home" there and spent long hours on the telephone with friends and kin in Yekaterinburg and Orenburg. "Life here has not treated us kindly," she said to Ryazanov. "They have poured so much filth on us. In my entire life before, I never had even one drop of this."[12] Her widowed mother, Mariya Girina, lived in Yekaterinburg; she was buried in Shirokorechenskoye Cemetery next to Yeltsin's father in 1994. Naina attended religious services with greater regularity in the 1990s and hung several painted icons on the walls of Barvikha-4. Without fanfare, she took up small-scale philanthropy. She sponsored maternity homes, pediatric hospitals, and orphanages and arranged food and medical aid for elderly female stars of the Soviet stage and screen who had fallen upon hard times. Boris did not make a habit of discussing politics with her, but they consulted on the personal fallout of political matters and she had a voice on staff she saw daily (such as drivers, cooks, and photographers). "Without her," he confided mawkishly but truthfully, "I would never have borne up under so many political storms . . . not in 1987, not in 1991, not later."[13]

Boris and Naina Yeltsin "generally do not worry about material things," as Konstantinova wrote.[14] Although it would be absurd to say he was against the good life, Yeltsin did not go into post-communist politics, and did not stay in it, for mercenary purposes. Had he so wished, he could have left the government and ridden the new free-enterprise economy to riches. He continued to be partial to plain Russian food. In Paris on an official visit in February 1992, Foreign Minister Andrei Kozyrev invited him to dine in one of the city's three-star restaurants, where he could try out nouvelle cuisine concoctions. Leaving Kozyrev to go out on the town, Yeltsin stayed behind at the embassy and had the kitchen cook him meat patties and potatoes.[15]

President Yeltsin handed Naina his pay envelope every Friday, as he had in Sverdlovsk, and she gave him back an allowance. He was at a loss about consumer prices, did not recognize ruble notes by denomination, did not have credit cards, and needed to be shown how to swipe a debit card at one of the automated teller machines that were cropping up in Moscow.[16] His ruble salary was worth five hundred to a thousand dollars a month, varying with the exchange rate. Extra income came from several hundred thousand dollars in book royalties, mostly from his second memoir volume, *Notes of a President*, published in Russian and many foreign languages in 1994. Upon retirement, the couple owned, he said in *Presidential Marathon*, a 1995 BMW automobile (7-series), home furnishings, and personal articles (he listed guns, tennis rackets, costume jewelry, and electronics); they held no stocks, bonds, or foreign bank accounts.[17]

If Yeltsin came into any bonanza, it was in the real estate market. The presidential manse at Barvikha-4 (and Gorki-9, where the family lived in the second term) was under what is today the Federal Protection Service or FSO, known up to 1991 as the Ninth Directorate of the KGB. The house was never Yeltsin's personal property, his to sell for monetary benefit or to transmit to heirs. On two lesser holdings, the English edition of *Presidential Marathon* mistranslates Yeltsin. "I own some real estate jointly with my wife," it says, referring to the Krylatskoye flat and a 4,900-square-foot dacha on ten acres in Odintsovo district, a few miles from Barvikha-4.[18] In this context, the verb *vladeyu* means "dispose of," "have occupancy of," or "have exclusive use of." Neither the apartment nor the Yeltsin dacha, which is in the Gorki-10 compound, was owned by Boris and Naina. Both were on the books of the Presidential Business Department, another arm of the government. Under Russian legislation dating to 1991, the Yeltsins could have privatized the Krylatskoye unit by filling out a few forms but, unlike some neighbors, did not. The Gorki-10 getaway was built in 1995–96 by troops from the protection service, on the grounds that it needed to be a secure site. Yeltsin paid for the materials himself out of book revenues and, ignorant about prices, was so mortified by the cost that he considered giving up on the project. Only in 2006–7, making use of a Putin–period law on vacation homes, did he privatize the Gorki-10 dacha. It must be worth some millions of dollars, and represents Yeltsin's main financial gain—a second-order, delayed (he took ownership just before his death), and legal effect.[19]

With the signal exception of his drinking, Yeltsin as president retained the tastes and mannerisms of his stiff-necked Urals ancestors. He did not use tobacco and would not abide it around him. On one presidential visit to Germany, seated at a dinner next to Chancellor Helmut Kohl's wife, Hannelore, he removed a cigarette from her fingers and stubbed it out in an ashtray.[20] Unlike Gorbachev, who cursed like a trooper, Yeltsin did not use profanity and forbade it in his hearing: He first came to question his selection of Aleksandr Rutskoi as vice president in 1991 when Rutskoi and his wife, Lyudmila, used expletives at the post-election victory party.[21] Yeltsin threw no tantrums and almost never raised his voice. He spoke to officials, again in contrast to Gorbachev, in given name and patronymic, not given name only or diminutive, and in the decorous second person plural. This applied even to his sidekick Korzhakov, whom he hailed as Aleksandr Vasil'evich unless they had been speaking one-on-one for a time, when he might say Aleksandr or, infrequently, Sasha.[22] Yeltsin still had his shoes buffed to a gossamer sheen and in gaps in the conversation would scan them for scuffs. The wardrobe was updated some: He switched from Russian to more debonair foreign-tailored suits and footwear and brought in tuxedos and black ties for formal Kremlin affairs, for the first time since Lenin.[23]

In addressing the core features of Yeltsin's personality, we must address the incongruities raised in the Introduction to this volume. In human relations, many contemporaries saw in him a mating of antipodes: He was at once too forward and too mistrustful, too brash and too wary. And his mood presented sharp contrasts over time. Some moments found him the epitome of energy and activism; at others, he was unexpressive and withdrawn. These divergences were a joint product of the mercurial setting and of Yeltsin's idiosyncrasies.

He had always kept an affective distance from almost all professional and political collaborators. The trait was probably handed down from the Urals village. A Butka acquaintance who had known Nikolai Yeltsin told a journalist, "Boris Nikolayevich . . . had an attitude that if he developed a friendship with someone, that would mean that he couldn't demand as much from them. So he kept everyone at an arm's length. He was just like his father."[24] The dog-eat-dog medium of the CPSU apparatus reinforced this attitude. As Sverdlovsk party boss, Yeltsin did not camouflage it. At his elk and duck shoots, "He relaxed in the outdoors and permitted himself to greet [people] in hail-fellow-well-met fashion. All the same, he always kept his detachment."[25] About his years in the obkom and after that the Moscow party committee, Yeltsin said, "Number ones as a rule have no close friends. There arises a complex of insularity, and your caution in communicating with others grows. All of this in time made its appearance in me—unreachability, a nervousness about socializing with new acquaintances."[26] Another person might have responded by reaching out *to* like spirits and not to recoil *from* them. Not Yeltsin: In him, being number one bred Chekhovian solitude. And it did so with greater intensity once he was leader of all Russia, in conditions of uncertainty and flux.

Yeltsin did open himself up to close connections with the odd foreigner. One was Robert S. Strauss, the last U.S. ambassador to the Soviet Union and the first to Russia. "He neither liked nor trusted most people," Strauss recalled years later, "but he did me." Strauss could only explain it in terms of fellowship—each saw the "twinkle" in the other—and by the facts that they were of the same generation and Strauss did not want anything of him.[27] Yeltsin's making friends with Helmut Kohl, the first world leader he called on in 1991, and with President Jiang Zemin of China, would be other examples. All three are of Yeltsin's age group or older (Strauss was born in 1918, Kohl in 1930, and Jiang in 1926).[28]

Symptomatic of the very different pattern with Russians, where the tie was severed when suspicions set in, was the relationship with Gennadii Burbulis (born in 1945), the ex-academic from Sverdlovsk who had Yeltsin's ear at the beginning of his administration. After they got to know one another in the Soviet parliament, Burbulis was right-hand man to Yeltsin in the Russian congress, ran his 1991 election campaign, was the first choice to establish his presidential office (an invitation he foolhardily declined), advised on the recruitment of Yegor Gaidar, and was given the titles of first deputy premier and state secretary. Before 1992 was rung out, as we have seen, Burbulis and Yeltsin were estranged. There was an interpersonal dynamic as well as a political one:

> I won't hide the fact that at a certain point I began to feel an impalpable, cumulative fatigue. I got tired of seeing the same face every day in my office, at meetings and receptions, at the dacha, on the tennis court, in the

> steambath. It is possible and necessary for someone to try to influence the president—to get things done, to carry through on one's ideas. But there has to be some limit. As freely as Gennadii Burbulis had walked into any meeting he felt like, he started coming to see me in person all the time. He overstepped some boundary in our personal relations. Well, it happens.[29]

Yeltsin's one intimate friendship of any duration with a public figure was with Aleksandr Korzhakov, the beefy security officer whom he made head of the Kremlin's praetorian guard. Through the first half of the 1990s, they were inseparable: They commuted, worked, broke bread, played games, and vacationed in one another's company. On a visit to the republic of Sakha, Yeltsin accidentally nicked Korzhakov with a knife he had received as a gift; at Yeltsin's suggestion, Korzhakov reciprocated and they mingled their blood. They repeated the rite several years later in Moscow.[30] In 1994, hearing from Yeltsin his fears about surgery for a deviated septum in his nose—a condition Korzhakov also had—Korzhakov volunteered to have his operation first, "as a guinea pig." He did, and Yeltsin repeated the procedure later that year.[31] Korzhakov had his in-town apartment in the Krylatskoye building, on the sixth floor next door to the Yeltsins, and was apportioned a dacha plot in Gorki-10, again next to Yeltsin. When travel forced Yeltsin to miss the wedding of Korzhakov's daughter Galina in 1994, the family repeated it upon his return. In 1995 Korzhakov was godfather to Yeltsin's fourth grandchild, Gleb Dyachenko.

In *Notes of a President*, published in 1994, Yeltsin wrote that Korzhakov's position "forces him to be next to me twenty-four hours a day."[32] But it was his disposition, and its fit with Yeltsin's, that won the president over. They were, in Russian argot, *tovarishchi*, comrades, of the nonpolitical variety, who had achieved sympathy and trust. They shared plebeian origins—Korzhakov, born in 1950, was the son of a Moscow textile worker and lived until age seven in a flyblown barracks—although Yeltsin was considerably better educated. Comradeship, political as well as nonpolitical, was mostly a manly phenomenon in the Soviet Union, going back to the Bolsheviks, and so it was with Yeltsin and Korzhakov.[33] Korzhakov was Yeltsin's drinking companion, safety blanket, and confessor. Yeltsin in his book remembered unwinding at the Korzhakov cottage when he was out of favor with the Politburo. "We did not stay in the house but bivouacked beside it, angled for fish, went for a dip in the creek." As head of state, he still relied on Korzhakov: "Korzhakov never leaves my side, and when we are traveling we sit up at night unless we are asleep. He is a very decent, shrewd, strong, and courageous person, although outwardly he seems quite simple."[34] While Naina Yeltsina always had her doubts about Korzhakov, she considered him "almost a member of our family." She once asked his wife, Irina, over a meal if he would ever give away confidences. Irina said the Korzhakovs loved the Yeltsins so much that they would take their secrets to the grave, and Korzhakov repeated these words.[35]

However, Yeltsin wearied of Korzhakov and Korzhakov of him: Twenty-four hours a day of togetherness was too much. The age difference mattered more as Yeltsin's health declined, and Korzhakov alarmed Yeltsin by expanding his Kremlin role into all-round aide-de-camp and gatekeeper. The blood brothers parted over Korzhakov's affiliation with the clique of high-level conservatives who favored postponement of the 1996 presidential election and who scuffled with liberals for control of the electoral campaign. A funding scandal on June 20, 1996, in between the two rounds of the voting, was the final insult. Yeltsin was to fire Korzhakov for insubordination, saying he and his group "took much for themselves and gave little." The jilted retainer, who was not offered another job, made the separation irreparable by publishing a vengeful memoir, *Boris Yeltsin: From Dawn to Dusk*, brimming with unflattering stories and photos of Yeltsin with tousled hair, in baggy swim trunks, or with glass, fishing rod, or rifle in hand. Yeltsin thenceforth considered Korzhakov a traitor to him, and with some reason: For bodyguards, like clergy, valets, and physicians, circumspection is the golden rule. Yeltsin was never to exchange a word with him again. To Korzhakov, Yeltsin was the traitor. In a letter on June 22, 1996, he said the people would hold the dismissal against Yeltsin: "They take everything at face value and are coming to the judgment, 'He betrayed his own and now he will betray us.'" Korzhakov quotes Irina as saying she saw "the smile of Judas" on Yeltsin's face when he spoke on television about the firing.[36]

Students of human nature more astute than Burbulis and Korzhakov were alive to the risks in overfamiliarity with number one or in giving him the sense that he was in someone's debt. Viktor Chernomyrdin, Russia's prime minister from 1992 to 1998 (and born in 1938), went to Zavidovo and had some holiday meals with the president, yet knew enough to respect his wish for autonomy: "Even when we were hunting together, I never allowed myself to try to make use of the proximity. . . . I saw that anyone who did, ha-ha, would end up [paying the price]."[37]

More polar to the Yeltsin presidency than his hot-and-cold relations with people is the question of phasing and consistency over time. In the organization of his everyday docket, he was as ever a stickler for promptness. Family members teased by getting him to guess the time of day without checking his watch—and usually he could do it down to the minute, he says. Yeltsin valued protocol officer Vladimir Shevchenko for his good judgment and for being "fanatically punctual," and said to Aleksandr Rutskoi that one reason for picking him as running mate was his military devotion to schedule.[38] A subordinate a minute late for an appointment would find Yeltsin tapping his foot irascibly. At Russian-American summits, he was irked by the tardy Bill Clinton. The only times Yeltsin was late for organized events were when he wanted to indicate displeasure. An example would be the 1991 negotiations at Novo-Ogarëvo, before and after the August coup, at which he often arrived after Gorbachev had called the meeting to order.

Fastidiousness about the hands of the clock makes it all the more noticeable that in the sweep of the process of national reconstruction Yeltsin displayed his marked political arrhythmia. In the event-packed first term, he often wove puzzlingly between assertive activism and sluggish quiescence.

Where did this cadence come from? A plethora of answers rooted in external factors—none of them particularly believable—have been floated. Several acquaintances have seen a similarity to Russia's national mascot, the brown bear, which hibernates in winter and prowls the forest in the warm weather.[39] Gaidar saw Yeltsin as a latter-day Il'ya Muromets, the knight-errant of Slavic folk poems.[40] Lame since his youth, Il'ya is restored to health by two psalm-singing pilgrims and gallops off to smite evil serpents and barbarian hordes. Every Russian schoolchild knows the tale; it is commemorated in paintings, in a symphony by Reinhold Glière, in the name of the country's first bomber aircraft (built in World War I by Igor Sikorsky), and in Aleksandr Ptushko's film from the 1950s, the first widescreen movie made in the USSR. In a more real-life vein, Mikhail Gorbachev has pointed to Yeltsin's career in the Soviet construction industry, with its ethos of "storming" and "hurry up and finish" after intervals of idleness.[41]

These zoological, folkloric, and occupational analogies do not hit the bull's-eye. Yes, Yeltsin might have been said to be ursine in visual aspect and gait, but any parallel across species can be no more than lightheartedly allegorical, and his highs and lows did not issue forth in the seasonality of a hibernating mammal. The mythic Il'ya Muromets roused himself from his pallet only once, at the age of thirty-three, and never revisited it. Soviet civil engineers, unlike Yeltsin as president, functioned in an orderly temporal framework laid down by the monthly, quarterly, and yearly planning calendars. And, since Russian politicians with this professional past differed in their styles and predilections, labor in construction could not have been determinant.[42]

Others, meanwhile, have looked to Yeltsin's psyche for a totally internal explanation—less than compellingly, in my view. Gorbachev, while citing Yeltsin's background in the construction industry, has also belabored him for an innate preference for confrontation. "In his human qualities," Gorbachev claims in his memoirs, "he was better suited to an epoch of Sturm und Drang" than to "normal work." "He contains a volcanic mixture and is capable only of destruction."[43] Gorbachev and some Moscow pundits have also insinuated that Yeltsin stirred tumult so as to rouse himself to action and look the hero while he was at it. The charge that Yeltsin was a purely destructive factor is a red herring, inconsistent with many chapters in his life. Yeltsin denied that he manufactured artificial emergencies: The obstacles to easy accomplishment "have always found me," and not he them.[44]

The Moscow psychologist Oleg Davydov finds Yeltsin's rebuttal flawed because it deals only with the conscious incitement of crisis and not with the subconscious. Yeltsin's bent for getting into tight spots was subliminal, Davydov thinks, and was matched by an almost mystical belief in his ability to escape unscathed. Yeltsin, he said, governed himself from adolescence onward by means of a distinctive "three-step": He bumbles into peril by acting preemptively; the misstep sets off a crisis; through an exercise of will, and with a pinch of good fortune, he saves the day. As a homely early case, Davydov cites Yeltsin's and his school chums' quest for the headwaters of the Yaiva River after ninth grade; the start of economic shock therapy is a politicized case from the 1990s.[45] Davydov's thesis is way too rigid and is circular as well: Yeltsin's motivation is inferred from his behavior, and then used to account for that same behavior. What can be said is that, whether or not danger sought him out, it not uncommonly found in Yeltsin a willing accessory.

There is no shortage of other conjectures about the alternating moods of Yeltsin. One or two journalists have said he had the mental affliction cyclothymia, a class of bipolar or manic-depression disorder. Patients with this condition experience swings from elated to somber.[46] However, no clinician who examined Yeltsin, or any other, has ever indicated such a diagnosis. Normal onset of cyclothymia is in the teens or early twenties, for which Yeltsin's biography provides zero evidence, and the moods of patients oscillate furiously, in a matter of days, which his are not known to have done. Yeltsin's temper when on the knife's edge is typically described as self-controlled and collected, not euphoric. A good specimen would be the events of September–October 1993, in the heat of the battle with the Congress of Deputies. A general who was present at one of his garrison visits before September 21 found him energetic, focused, and "going deep into every word" the officers said. Speaking on the telephone to President Clinton right after his edict, Yeltsin was "pumped and combative" yet on task. The evening of October 3, as street battles raged in Moscow, he was not equal to addressing the population on television. By the early morning hours of October 4, though, as he awaited his climactic predawn meeting with the army command, he had the sang-froid to take to a sofa in his office suite for a two-hour snooze.[47]

Yeltsin's red-letter actions as leader were most often taken in spasms of effort and in crises he had a part in stimulating. His pugnacity was a given, and had been since Berezniki. "I am not the type," he had exclaimed at the Higher Komsomol School in 1988, "to take the easier or more pleasing course, to go by the satiny paved road rather than the rough footpath" (see Chapter 7). The novelty here was that the Moscow pressure cooker and the pluralism and quicksilver quality of transitional politics supplied him with incomparably more make-or-break *situations* in which it could be activated.

Yeltsin and people who knew him in the 1990s often linked his flair for rising to the occasion with his athletic experience, even though he and they well knew that governing a country is infinitely more complicated than batting a ball about with a small number of players and fixed rules. One might see it as a crossbreed of Yeltsin's success and testing scripts—improving his record while proving himself. Yeltsin was likeliest to see a political challenge as in scale to his talents when its magnitude was great and the chips were down. He took for granted that he could meet the challenge and others would not.

Yeltsin's tennis teacher and friend until 1996, Shamil Tarpishchev, recalls that on the court his understudy "rallied his nervous system" and went all-out only at the breakpoint in a game, when the server risks losing his serve and the opposing player or team stands to go back on offense. "He was the same in politics," Tarpishchev notes. "The direr the situation, the more he concentrated."[48] About his decision to go outside and face the crowd and the tanks on August 19, 1991, Yeltsin once observed, "I sorted everything out. I am an athlete and I know very well how it happens. All of a sudden, you are jarred and feel that the game is on, that you can boldly take the initiative into your hands."[49] He approached in the same frame of mind shock therapy in 1992, the 1993 conflict with parliament, Chechnya in 1994, and eventually his reelection campaign in 1996. El'dar Ryazanov interrogated him, weeks after the bombardment of the White House, about his métier being do-or-die situations. "Yes," Yeltsin responded, "I know myself too well not to agree with this. . . . I constantly have to keep myself in fighting trim. . . . Even in sport, when I played volleyball in my student years . . . you would not see much of me in the main part of the game. . . . *But if the match is on the line I am able to work miracles.*"[50] In suspenseful situations, Yeltsin's habit was to ratchet up the sense of crisis, and ergo the demand for decisive action to defuse it, by playing wait-and-see as long as he could. It was in his nature, as his former aides put it well, "to bide his time as things percolated, until the situation presented a danger to him and his power"—until the match was on the line.[51] Procrastinating up to the split second his intuition whispered was the right one, it was then into the breach, the adrenalin surging.

"Am I a strong or a weak person?" Yeltsin asked in *Notes of a President.* "In exigent situations, I am usually strong. In routine situations, I am sometimes limp." There are also "times when I do not look like the Yeltsin people have grown used to seeing," including times when "I fly off the handle in stupid ways, like a child."[52]

Yeltsinesque torpor was of two basal types, although the line smudged some. The first, and the easier to grasp, was the emotional blowback from failure. Several of the traumas that actuated such feelings during perestroika have been discussed in earlier chapters: the overload of governing the capital city, the secret speech, the attacks on him during his political resurrection. The psychodrama continued after 1991. In writing of it in *Notes,* he started with economic shock therapy:

> The first one who was in for shock, and repeatedly—with pained reactions, having to strain every resource—was me, the president. Enervating bouts of depression, agonizing reflections late at night, insomnia and headaches, despair at the grimy and impoverished look of Moscow and other Russian cities, the criticism that billowed out every day in the newspapers and on the television screen, the badgering at sessions of the congress, the weight of the decisions made, the people close to me who did not support me when I needed it, who did not hold up, who deceived me—all this I had to brook.[53]

Yeltsin reacted in pain to the general flow of negative news and to specific events. In the spring of 1992, he was despondent for weeks over the unexpectedly high rate of inflation and the nonarrival of recovery in production. Bad tidings in the economy were a constant during his first term, but the degree of awfulness varied, with "Black Tuesday"—October 11, 1994, when the ruble lost one-quarter of its value in a single day—taking the cake. As an afterclap of Black Tuesday, the Duma initiated but did not approve a vote of no-confidence in the government.

The constitutional turbulence of 1992–93 afforded a series of precipitating events. The blows of Ruslan Khasbulatov and the deputies at the congress in December 1992 produced, Yeltsin recalls, "a relapse of the psychological wretchedness" that had plagued him when he was demoted by Gorbachev.[54] He was wretched enough to think of ending it all. On December 9, 1992, the day the congress refused to accede to Gaidar as prime minister, he came home to Barvikha-4 "in a complete trance" and locked himself in the steambath. There he was lost in "very bad" thoughts (Yeltsin's phrase, from *Notes*) until Korzhakov broke into the bath and took him to his wife. "I was just in time," Korzhakov asserts, "to stop him from taking the ultimate step"—connecting the dots, that step would have been killing himself through scalding and suffocation in the steam. Korzhakov, who depicted the rescue in his anti-Yeltsin memoir, is a hostile witness. It is instructive, though, that Yeltsin's wording implies he was in truth suicidal and that he did not contest Korzhakov's account in *Presidential Marathon* in 2000. This affair is thus a far cry from the feigned suicide attempt of November 9, 1987.[55] A week after locking himself in the steambath, Yeltsin was in a blue funk while on a visit to China and broke the trip off with a complaint of numbness in his extremities. Korzhakov blithely mentioned to him that Franklin Roosevelt ran the U.S. government from a wheelchair.[56]

Yeltsin recovered from this low-water mark, but as parliament moved toward impeachment in the spring of 1993 he "fell into a depression," Korzhakov reports, and began to lose the thread of conversations. His mother's death, a week before the March 28 vote on the resolution, intensified the gloom. Security Minister Viktor Barannikov had made him a birthday present of an imported handgun and a carton of ammunition, which Yeltsin stashed in an office cabinet. Alerted by an informant, Korzhakov had one of the Kremlin chefs boil the cartridges in water to disable them. Days before the roll was called, Yeltsin, with Korzhakov and two other officials looking on, took out the pistol, cocked it, and threatened to shoot himself. He let himself be talked out of pulling the trigger, unaware that the bullets had been doctored. Korzhakov says he eventually removed the firing pin.[57]

Chechnya brought further torture the next year. The president "was greatly afflicted by the tragedy" of the storming of Grozny, which began on December 31, 1994. For several days he cut himself off from the telephone and refused to receive even Korzhakov.[58] A secondary effect of the intervention was the breakdown in relations with political liberals who had once been at his side. When Yelena Bonner criticized Yeltsin for his praise of Defense Minister Grachëv, Naina Yeltsina, with whom she had maintained social contact since Andrei Sakharov's death, phoned to give her a tearful talking to, and the two stopped speaking.[59] A schism broke out in the pro-reform Russia's Choice movement, where Yegor Gaidar came out against the war while Boris Fëdorov, the former finance minister, left the organization in search of a more "patriotic" one. Yeltsin had arrived at "almost complete political isolation" because of the war and other issues. "I could no longer feel the support of those with whom I had begun my political career."[60] The hostage-taking at Budënnovsk, introducing Russia at large to terrorism, sent him into a tailspin in June 1995. He announced to a meeting of the advisory Security Council on June 30 that he planned to resign the presidency, since he had initiated an unsuccessful war. Council members asked him not to, and he withdrew the threat. "I don't think this was play-acting on Yeltsin's part," writes Yevgenii Primakov, who attended as director of Russian foreign intelligence. "He suffered over everything connected with Chechnya."[61]

Yeltsin was in good company. Among modern leaders whose biographies were studied by the psychiatrist Arnold M. Ludwig, the lifetime rate for episodes of depression or melancholia lasting several weeks or more is 14 percent (as compared to 6 percent in the population of the United States), and under a more catholic definition would be about 30 percent. Ludwig found visionary statesmen who try to reshape society, and politicians whose power is crumbling, to be most susceptible to the problem.[62]

Yeltsin, however, was also prone to a second type of withdrawal that is not well captured by the usual typology. It came, ironically, in the backwash of heady victory as opposed to jarring defeat.

Late Soviet occurrences of this complex—his flight from Moscow after the 1989 and 1990 elections and the 1991 putsch—have been discussed in earlier chapters. The pattern reared its head again in the first several months of 1992, when Yeltsin left Gaidar and the cabinet to prosecute economic reform with little guidance from him. In 1993, after the successful referendum of April 25, Yeltsin was dilatory in following up and took a long summer holiday at Valdai. After he did take decisive steps against the parliament in September–October, he honored a promise to pay a visit to Tokyo, worked on the constitution for several weeks, and then was hard for most of his ministers and staffers to reach until after the December election and plebiscite. The pressure of those months "was so powerful that I still do not understand how my organism got through it, how it coped," Yeltsin recollects.[63]

With his presidentialist constitution, and hence his supremacy in Russian politics, in the bag, one might have predicted that Yeltsin would be in a glowing frame of mind in 1994. His mood, though, was indolent for the first half of the year. Write his former aides, "The presidential timetable for that year logs Yeltsin's numerous and often lengthy absences, attesting to the fact that he was going through a protracted crisis." He took two weeks in Sochi in March and did not travel publicly in the provinces until his visit to Kazan at the end of May. His annual list of presidential objectives was finalized only in late April, when he initialed it but declined to set priorities among them. A staff memorandum attributed falling approval ratings to "the president's passivity and lack of clarity over goals and policy."[64]

These events are harder to make sense of than the straightforwardly dysphoric episodes in the first category. Why would Yeltsin's very triumphs, the thrashing of his political rivals, weigh on him? There was, first, an exhaustion factor. When I questioned him about it in 2002, Yeltsin acknowledged it as a form of letdown *(spad)* or breather *(peredyshka)*, not of depression *(depressiya)*, and as a natural way for him to unwind after the battle.[65] It is an admissible point. Even revolutionaries and warriors need a vacation every now and then, and Yeltsin after a victory was usually languid and distracted rather than morose. At his hideaways, he would make himself unavailable by telephone and spent much of the time in the fresh air.

Considerations other than fatigue were involved. Draining as his Nietzschean moments were, Yeltsin felt in his element in them. When they had passed, he sagged. He was hardly the only leader to have had that tendency: Witness the Duke of Wellington's famous statement the day after Waterloo in 1815 that, "Nothing except a battle lost can be half as melancholy as a battle won." What's more, a post-crisis hiatus, as Aleksandr Muzykantskii observed of Yeltsin's victory in the 1989 USSR election (see Chapter 7), put the onus on potential allies to come to him with proposals for joint action and gave him the opportunity to look them over. Most important, Yeltsin needed an intermission after a victory because it gave him the chance to consider his options. His moratorium after the attempted coup in 1991 was one of the more fruitful ones. The rolling time-outs in 1993 and 1994 were accompanied by reflection on the future.

There were reasons tangible and intangible why winning was less fun after 1991. The battles won were more ambiguous, for one thing. In the transitional setting, even the alpha leader did not have an inexhaustible storehouse of political capital, and advances could come at a terrible price. Progress achieved put him up foursquare against a fresh set of choices, often more troubling than the last. In the summer of 1993, for example, after Yeltsin had won the April referendum, he backed out of meetings with officeholders, literati, and journalists. It was quite plain to press secretary Vyacheslav Kostikov that the president was shunning contact because he lacked the answers to some of the questions he knew were to be flung at him. Kostikov found the indisposition more pronounced in 1994. Even though the new constitution made Yeltsin's legal position airtight, Kostikov got used to coming across the superpresident seated pensively at a bare desk. Yeltsin, Kostikov felt, "found himself without his internal pivot" as he came to understand that solutions to Russia's key reform problems would take five, ten, or more years to resolve. The political system he had constructed left him and only him to answer for problems. "It was my impression," says Kostikov, "that Yeltsin was getting lost as he faced up to the magnitude of the responsibilities he had arrogated to himself in his constitution."[66] Meantime, personnel turnover and defections had deprived Yeltsin of the most creative minds from his first months in government. Many decisions could be shunted to the trustworthy Chernomyrdin, but the prime minister was not an ideas man, and Yeltsin knew it. What discommoded him the most, as his ghostwriter Valentin Yumashev has noted, was "not psychological loneliness but intellectual loneliness." "He had begun to feel, I don't know what to do and I don't have people around who can supply me with ideas that I can go forward with."[67]

One should not imagine that Yeltsin's depressions and intermissions, in all their multifariousness, went on uninterruptedly from his first to his second inauguration. One by one, he kicked them off. He returned from Sochi to appoint Gaidar and decree shock therapy in 1991; he adjusted the market reforms and accepted Chernomyrdin as his head of government in 1992; he upended the Supreme Soviet and imposed his constitution in 1993; he resumed traveling and politicking and eased Viktor Gerashchenko out of the central bank after Black Tuesday, in 1994, and that same year he picked up the tempo of privatization; he moved crabwise toward negotiations with the Chechen rebels in 1995; in 1996 he decided to run for a second term. The point is not that he failed to accomplish these things but that he did it in a stuttering fashion, which often dragged out the length of time required and intruded on the building of political coalitions to accomplish the task.

The parsing of Yeltsin's psychodynamics would be incomplete without reference to the substance with which his name is most often linked—alcohol.

Until the second half of the 1980s, drinking had a subsidiary function in his life. For the next ten years, until he had to give it up, it loomed larger and took a toll politically, physically, and reputationally.

Although doctors noted at the time that Yeltsin's consumption increased when he moved to Moscow, and although there were some signs of it interfering with decision making, until 1991 he kept it under control. A Democratic Russia activist who saw him fifty to sixty times between 1989 and the end of 1992 never observed him affected by alcohol. Jack Matlock, the second-to-last U.S. ambassador to the USSR, saw him have drinks but never too many; his successor, Robert Strauss, reports the same. Aleksandr Korzhakov, whose exceedingly unfavorable memoir about Yeltsin, published in 1997, has served as a main source about Yeltsin's drinking, says that when Yeltsin was chairman of the Russian parliament and under constant watch by the KGB, in 1990–91, he drank relatively little. At Yeltsin's sixtieth birthday party in February 1991, at a children's camp near Moscow, he sipped champagne with merrymakers and was the last to retire from the campfire.[68]

But the rules changed once the Kremlin was his. Korzhakov saw to it that the trunk of the presidential limousine held a satchel containing drinks, shot glasses, and appetizers, renewed daily. Yeltsin's levels of use, family members testify, went up steadily from 1991 through 1994. His mother's death removed a watchful parent who had always looked askance at personal excess.[69] Yeltsin switched in 1993 from brandy to Gzhel'ka and grass-flavored Tarkhun vodka; he also liked a cocktail of champagne laced with cognac. Vodka, removed by Gorbachev and Yegor Ligachëv from the Kremlin menu in 1985, was reintroduced in 1993. Yeltsin's afternoon tennis matches would often lead to the sauna and then to a meal rife with toasts. Nips were common at his private luncheons, and Yeltsin squirreled away a rainy-day supply in his office suite.

Foreign partners had to work around Yeltsin's habit. When Bill Clinton got him on the telephone several days after Clinton was inaugurated in January 1993, Yeltsin's speech was slurred and "he seemed barely listening to what Clinton had to say," after which Clinton chuckled that he was "a candidate for tough love, if ever I heard one." Clinton was to have about fifty phone conversations with Yeltsin over the seven years. To be on the safe side, his aides placed most calls before the dinner hour in Moscow.[70] At his first summit meeting with Clinton in Vancouver on April 3–4, 1993, Yeltsin tossed back drinks on the warm-up day, and Secretary of State Warren Christopher and other American officials began the unbecoming practice of keeping a tally.[71] First Lady Hillary Rodham Clinton, often seated next to Yeltsin at official banquets, found him "delightful company" and that, "as is often apparent, he enjoys a drink or two." On the Clintons' first official visit to Moscow, Yeltsin provided a running commentary on the food and drink, "informing me in all seriousness that red wine protected Russian sailors on nuclear-powered submarines from the ill effects of strontium 90."[72]

Domestic players were more aware of the syndrome. On April 22, 1993, three days before the national referendum on approval of his policies, Yeltsin made a scheduled appearance at a large rally and rock singalong next to St. Basil's Cathedral. He was far from sober, and Yelena Bonner took the microphone away.[73] Yeltsin did not drink alone, a saving grace that may have kept him from worse problems. But drinking with confederates in the first half of the 1990s often closed him off from them, rather than open him up. He would sometimes fall silent, in his "sleeping crocodile" pose, as some called it, while continuing to watch the company. At one such event, a minister of the government offered a lewd bottoms-up. Warned that Yeltsin would not stand for such talk, he made a comment about the chief not hearing. The next morning, Yeltsin signed a decree dismissing the minister, who never reclaimed so high a post.[74]

Yeltsin's overindulgence was elevated from an open secret to a public issue in 1994. On August 31 he was in Berlin to represent the country at ceremonies with Chancellor Kohl to mark the departure of Russian forces from the former East Germany. He had gotten a head start the night before by bending elbows at the hotel with Defense Minister Pavel Grachëv. On that day, in baking heat, he imbibed enthusiastically. After lunch, on the square in front of the High Renaissance city Rathaus, where a brass band from the local police was serenading the troops with march music, Yeltsin motioned for the stick from the conductor. Bent at the waist, he woozily stabbed the air with it for several minutes as the band played on gallantly. Minutes later, he took up a microphone to lead the assembled Russians through unmelodious couplets from the folk song "Kalinka-Malinka" (Juniper-Raspberry), concluding with a whoop, a thumb-up sign, and kisses blown to the tittering crowd.[75]

Yeltsin's political advisers, a gaggle of whom were there, considered resignation and decided against it. Kostikov inserted vocal articles about the pratfall in Berlin into his daily media reviews. Yeltsin knit his brows upon seeing the material but did not comment. They then tried to convince Korzhakov to level with Yeltsin. He declined, saying he had tried to reason with Yeltsin in the past, but suggested they write the president a letter, something assistant

Viktor Ilyushin, who had worked with him since the 1970s, at first opposed as counterproductive. The supercautious Ilyushin came around, and Kostikov cobbled together a collective letter. It was signed by seven people: Kostikov; Ilyushin, who gave it a final edit; Korzhakov and his colleague from the security services, Mikhail Barsukov; Vladimir Shevchenko, the long-suffering chief of presidential protocol; speechwriter Lyudmila Pikhoya; and Dmitrii Ryurikov, Yeltsin's foreign-policy assistant. Korzhakov delivered the missive by hand on September 10, on a presidential flight to Sochi. The document—wags in the press, which got wind of it, named it "The Letter of the Aides to Their Sultan," after a nineteenth-century painting by Il'ya Repin—took the president to task for his hermetic tendencies; his complacency and "tsarist" airs; his aversion to planning, which left too many decisions to hang on "irrational factors, chance, and even caprice"; and his separation from past and prospective allies. The authors did not trace all or most of Yeltsin's problems to alcohol. But, using code to spare his feelings, they stated clearly that in their estimation his dependency—"the well-known Russian vice"—was dragging him down. The signals he had sent in Berlin were "impossible to ignore and difficult to correct." He needed, they said, "to reassess once and for all your attitude toward your health and your harmful habits," halt "unexpected disappearances and periods of rehabilitation," and find ways of decompressing other than "athletics followed by a banquet." No ruler of Russia before or since has seen the likes of it.[76]

Yeltsin sulked. He would not shake hands with the messengers for weeks, excluded several of them from a trip to London and Washington, and did not speak to Pikhoya for six months. Kostikov in November was to be handed the honeyed exile of the Russian ambassadorship to the Vatican. Walking the beach in Sochi in mid-September, Yeltsin meditated on his behavior and, he says, made a resolution "to revive [his] strength" and set limits.[77] So the message was in a way received, although the incidents, including documented ones abroad, did not stop.[78]

Yeltsin had progressed from convivial social drinking to drinking with abandon as a balm for a battered ego—to lighten the weight of the world in a period of extreme personal tension. Only in *Presidential Marathon*, the memoir volume published after his retirement, did Yeltsin begin to concede what had happened: "At a certain time, I sensed that alcohol is a means that rapidly relieves stress." In Berlin he had been beset by the emotion of the moment and by the onerousness of his office. "The load eased after several glasses, and then, in that light-headed condition, it was possible for me to conduct an orchestra." Yeltsin wrote it up with a self-pitying slap at those who harped on the theme: "If it was not the blasted alcohol, it would have been something else, they would found some other vulnerable point."[79]

Drinking in moderation and on his own time might have been good for Yeltsin's mental health and equanimity. Drinking immoderately and on the government's time was a self-inflicted wound that brought no good to anyone. While he must bear responsibility, it is only fair to observe that others tolerated and even condoned his behavior. Naina Yeltsina did her best to restrain her husband and chided associates who did not. She and her daughters blamed Aleksandr Korzhakov for feeding the alcohol habit so as to maintain his personal access to the president. By 1995 Naina was avoiding social contact with Korzhakov for this reason.[80] Korzhakov denies the charge, and is half-right in doing so. As the authors of *The Yeltsin Epoch* point out, he "knew how to 'regulate the process'" and could be either an enabler or a restrainer. And Korzhakov was but one of those around Yeltsin who saw benefit to them in lifting a glass with the president. For the Berlin incident, the inciter was Pavel Grachëv: "Every shot of vodka taken with Yeltsin was like a star on his general's epaulets."[81]

The "letter to the sultan" was better late than never. But Yeltsin and Russia would have been better served if more people had taken a stand, earlier, and put their positions on the line if that was what it took. Even the Berlin signatories did not have the temerity to speak to him about their handiwork. Yeltsin asked Pikhoya why she signed the letter but had not once brought up the issue in person. "There are situations," she said sotto voce, "where it is easier to write than to speak."[82] This was one of them. "I was not going to make excuses for myself in front of my assistants," Yeltsin says of the epistle. "I doubt whether any of them would have been able to help me. The distance between us was too great."[83] The author of that distance was Boris Yeltsin, whose personality cowed those who might have helped.

Yeltsin was not the first modern statesman to have a soft spot for Bacchus. One study of modern rulers estimates 15 percent of them abused alcohol at one time or another, or about the same proportion as in the American population.[84] Kemal Atatürk of Turkey and Winston Churchill, to mention two great leaders, ingested potables in quantities that would put Yeltsin to shame.[85] No sensible historian would reduce Atatürk's or Churchill's career to his drinking escapades. None should do that to Yeltsin's, either.

Yeltsin opponents and haters sometimes tried to link his alcohol use to political outcomes. Gorbachev complained to his staff in November 1991 that Gennadii Burbulis and Yeltsin's entourage were plying Yeltsin with liquor to get him to concur in their separatist designs and that there was a danger he would be a "blind pawn" of others.[86] There is no credible evidence of this ever being the case. Foreign partners found Boris Yeltsin's drinking to be irrelevant, other than in distracting him and lengthening the communications and negotiations. At the Vancouver meeting with President Clinton in 1993, Yeltsin's conduct on the first evening "didn't seem to impair his performance the next morning. The summit was a success."[87] In domestic politics, none of Yeltsin's crucial actions in his first term, before he swore off drinking, happened because of alcohol or under the influence of alcohol.

But drinking was detrimental to the Yeltsin presidency through more roundabout routes. In the early 1990s, the Russians forgave it, seeing it as secondary to his crusade to improve their lives, and in some cases thinking it connoted soulfulness and the release of inhibitions. When his quiet revolution went sour, it was taken as validation of egocentrism and transmogrified into a political liability.[88] It sparked rumors of misbehavior even when there was none, something he resented but was helpless to counter. It disrupted his schedule and his accessibility to interlocutors. In July 1993 Ruslan Khasbulatov arranged for President Nursultan Nazarbayev of Kazakhstan to visit to mediate the affray between Yeltsin and the Supreme Soviet. A meeting was arranged for the ABTs guesthouse. Yeltsin was not adequate to the task and Nazarbayev had to leave without seeing him. Khasbulatov blamed "the forces behind" Yeltsin for wrecking the plan.[89] Lower-ranking political tasks, such as press briefings, were shortchanged as the tennis/steambath/dining cycle waxed in importance. But the greatest harm was that done to Yeltsin's health.

His medical issues, and his tendency not to look after them, dated back decades. The tonsil infection and rheumatic fever at UPI, when Yeltsin refused the bed rest prescribed, foretold a tendency to slight doctor's orders, on the assumption that exercise and self-command would see him through. "I take risks with my health," he said in one of his books, "because I rely heavily on my body's [strength]. I do not always take special care of myself."[90] In June 1992 he had his first comprehensive physical examination since 1987. A bulletin signed by a consilium of five doctors pronounced his health good and noted "the staying power of the patient."[91] Yeltsin's complaints over the next several years were mostly minor, in particular, backache (for which he had an arthroscopic procedure in September 1993), sciatic inflammation of nerves in the legs, and the nasal condition. But his haggard visage and no-shows fueled often scurrilous speculation. The movie director El'dar Ryazanov, who interviewed him in April 1993 and in two sessions in November, found him changed over the seven months. Courtly in April, Yeltsin was perspiring, puffy-eyed, and "programmed" in November and lugged "an enormous burden of guilt" over political developments. Midway through the first November session, he had to interrupt it for a catnap, informing Ryazanov that he was now in the habit of sleeping in the daytime.[92] By 1994 Moscow insiders were using the alias *Dedushka*—Grandpa, or the Old Man—in chitchat about him.

It emerged that the principal problem was cardiovascular illness. Yeltsin is known to have experienced angina pectoris, ascribable to ischemic deterioration of blood flow to the heart, in September–October 1991, January 1992, and September 1994. On the last occasion, on September 30, 1994, he ruffled diplomatic feathers when he was a no-show for a meeting with the Irish prime minister, Albert Reynolds, at an airport layover in Shannon. After Berlin, one month before, the world press ascribed it to drinking, which had indeed triggered the incident. First Deputy Premier Oleg Soskovets greeted Reynolds in Yeltsin's place. Yeltsin apologized to Reynolds on October 6, saying he had overslept. He was sensitive to those who made fun of his excuse.[93] In 1995 his symptoms reached life-threatening dimensions in a rapid-fire sequence of three heart attacks in six months: the first two (on July 10 and October 26) reported in the Russian media, the third (in late December) unreported.[94] He was laid up after each in the TsKB, the government's premier hospital, in southwest Moscow, spending a total of six weeks there and seven in the sanatorium at Barvikha. At the TsKB in October–November, he for the first time did government business out of a hospital bed for a considerable period. From now on, there would be an ambulance in his motorcade.

Aging, the wear and tear of a lifetime, the high-fat diet common in Russia and the former Soviet Union, and the acute pressures of governing in a decade of troubles made Yeltsin an excellent candidate for the disease. His burning of the candle at both ends made him even more vulnerable. Although he cut back his alcohol intake after Berlin, he was not consistently abstinent. The day of his first coronary, says Korzhakov, he had marked Mikhail Barsukov's appointment as chief of the Federal Security Service, part of the post-Budënnovsk purge, by sharing two liters of sugary Cointreau liqueur with Barsukov.[95] Yevgenii Chazov, the former health minister and head of Russia's best cardiology hospital, and a consultant on the Yeltsin case, says the patient's willfulness helped bring on the next crisis. "He decided to show that all the prattle about the state of his health was groundless and took to his previous way of life. He went to Sochi, played tennis, and did some drinking. Of course, it all ended sadly." The October attack came right after Yeltsin deplaned in Moscow from a trip to the United States. Only following it did he behave more carefully, writes Chazov, although he would not agree to the diagnostic angiogram urged by the Kremlin doctors. The circumstances of the December coronary seem to have been similar to those of the first two.[96] In 1996, as he ran to defend his presidential position against the communists, he was more careful.[97]

Much as he might have wanted it under wraps, Yeltsin, not so different from the Samson Agonistes pushing the grain mill in John Milton's verse, played out his torments in public view. This was because Russia's press was freer and livelier in the 1990s than in any other period of the nation's history. Censorship had been abolished by Soviet legislation in June 1990. Two of the three authors of that law, Yurii Baturin and Mikhail Fedotov, were to hold senior positions after 1991. The constitution of 1993 affirmed the ban on censorship, and in the drafting sessions Yeltsin agreed to language that strengthened it.[98]

The media frankness about Yeltsin's derelictions and peccadillos was unprecedented for a Russian leader. Yeltsin did not cotton to criticism of his person, or of his policies, and had no shortage of opportunities to throttle it. His refusal to take them is traceable to principle, psychology, and realism. After communism, he accepted the need for a modern country to have an inquisitive and contentious press. "Criticism is a necessary thing," he declaimed in 1992. "If we do not take part in criticism today, we will fall into the same swamp in which we wallowed for decades." Suppression of it would also be a confession of pusillanimity: "If a statesman or leader or president goes about squeezing the press, this means he is weak-kneed. A strong leader will not squeeze the press, even if it criticizes him."[99] Once in a great while, he had to be reminded this was so. He asked press secretary Kostikov in 1994 if he could not do something about the withering stories carried by Kostikov's friend Igor Golembiovskii, the editor of *Izvestiya*. Kostikov replied that he could take care of the problem if Yeltsin arranged to give him "the powers of Suslov"—Mikhail Suslov, the intransigent overseer of ideology in Leonid Brezhnev's Politburo. Yeltsin left it at that and based his press strategy on carrots more than sticks.[100] His first-term press secretaries, all of them professional journalists, helped him cajole political reporters and commentators; Gorbachev had talked only to the editors-in-chief. Yeltsin could name the anchors on the national television news programs (although he watched only excerpts from the evening news spliced together by staff), the main correspondents for the several Russian wire services, and half of the roughly twenty print journalists in the "Kremlin pool" started by Kostikov in 1994. While formal press conferences were rare, he made himself available to reporters for weekly off-the-record briefings and conversed quietly with them at pro-forma events, such as the accreditation of ambassadors.

In the television market, the population's primary source of political information, Yeltsin inherited two state-owned national networks, Ostankino (Channel 1) from the Soviet government, and Russian Television or RTR (Channel 2), created in 1991. He did not shrink from using the personnel weapon, firing Ostankino director Yegor Yakovlev in November 1992 and the chairman of Channel 2, Oleg Poptsov, in February 1996.[101] Editorial autonomy on state television was greater than in the Soviet era, by virtue of drift and division in the executive branch as well as legal guarantees and ethical scruples.[102] Yeltsin's biggest gift to pluralism on television was his agreement to the establishment of a full-service private network, NTV. Headed by Igor Malashenko, a former Central Committee deskman, and owned by Vladimir Gusinskii, one of the first of the oligarchs, it aimed for white-collar, urban viewers and soon distinguished itself by hard-hitting reportage of Moscow political scandals and the war in Chechnya. It went on the air October 10, 1993, the week after the shelling of parliament.[103]

A landmark was NTV's launch of the hilarious weekly satire *Kukly* (Puppets) in November 1994. In it, life-sized rubber dolls of politicians acted out skits that were often based on literary or film classics. The puppets did not have fixed roles but rotated through a repertoire. The creators had some doubts about the propriety of deriding the president of the country. It did not take long to resolve them. Like the man-woman Margaret Thatcher in *Spitting Image*, the British prototype, so Boriska, a gimpy, apple-cheeked double of Boris Yeltsin, was the drawing card in *Kukly*. Aleksandr Korzhakov, unprompted by Yeltsin, tried several acts of intimidation against NTV in the winter of 1994–95. He and his government ally Oleg Soskovets demanded that Gusinskii scrap *Kukly*, which he would not do.[104] In June 1995 Procurator General Aleksei Il'yushenko indicted the show for slander. The provocation was a burlesque, "The Lower Depths"—its title taken from Maxim Gorky's 1902 drama—that showed Yeltsin and Prime Minister

Chernomyrdin as besotted vagrants panning for loose change in post–shock therapy Russia, with Korzhakov as a wailing babe in Yeltsin's arms. The criminal charge was dropped in October 1995 and *Kukly* went its merry way. Two other episodes—"Feast in the Time of Plague" (about revelers in a miserable land, the title taken from a poem by Pushkin) and a Winnie-the-Pooh piece that showed Yeltsin as the teddy bear with fluff in his head—were quashed by NTV as too salty. One hundred and fifty others were aired unamended. Boriska was in about two-thirds of them.[105]

For head writer Viktor Shenderovich, Yeltsin was the caricaturist's dream. He evoked the coroneted tragic heroes of William Shakespeare and the protagonists of the Russian playwright Alexander Ostrovsky (1823–60), who were merchants or clerks in patriarchal families, living lives of contradiction and futility. Shenderovich's favorite was the first sketch he wrote in January 1995. It limned Yeltsin as a Hamlet torn by warring impulses. Boriska, the orotund voice supplied by actor Sergei Bezrukov, was "unsure if he is a tsar or a democratic president," asking whether to lock up his opposition or promulgate liberal reforms. He was "many-threaded . . . willful and capricious but conscientious for all that . . . lonely . . . never knowing what he is going to do tomorrow."[106] One of the wickedest of the *Kukly* spoofs, in early 1996, cast Yeltsin as the director of a surgical clinic. In a play on the word *operatsiya*, operation, it slammed both the Russian military action in Chechnya and economic shock therapy. Boriska explains to visiting journalists that he was elected head surgeon five years before "by a democratic assembly of the seriously ill." He and his staff are all ignoramuses, but not to worry. "Lack of expertise and lack of nimbleness," he says, "can be offset by power of the will and devotedness to the reforms." "So what is the main thing" at the clinic? the narrator asks. "The main thing is to convince everyone that you are head surgeon. Once you have convinced them, you can cut away at anything you want and have nothing to fear."[107]

Most of the *Kukly* skits were friendlier to Yeltsin than this—Shenderovich, Malashenko, and Gusinskii all counted themselves supporters of the president—and interlarded praise, disapproval, and puzzlement. Besides the accursed Hamlet, Faust, and Othello (Mayor Yurii Luzhkov of Moscow, with whom Yeltsin had feuded, was the inconstant Desdemona), the latex Yeltsin was God (gazing down smugly at Russia from the empyrean), Robinson Crusoe, a woebegone Don Quixote, Louis XIII, Priam of Troy, the Grand Inquisitor, a sultan closeted with his servants and ambassadors, the winner in a cheesy game show, the custodian of a Soviet communal apartment, a fireman, a Russian motorist bribing his way through a safety check, a Mafioso, a superannuated hospital patient padding around in his pajamas, and Caligula bullying senators to confirm one of his racehorses as consul of Rome—among others.[108]

Some of the more memorable *Kukly* offerings painted Yeltsin as a man molded by his time and place no less than a molder of them. In a 1995 sketch modeled on the children's fantasies of Grigorii Oster, Boriska looks raffishly in the mirror and says to himself:

> *If you become president*
> *Of a surprising country,*
> *You will never be surprised*
> *By anything, you see!*
> *Here two times two makes thirty-eight,*
> *And the compass points to the east;*
> *Here princesses are made from frogs,*
> *And soup from axes.*
> *The Turks [Turkish construction workers] are in GUM*
> *[the big Moscow department store]*
> *And the Urks [goblins] are in the Duma,*
> *And the communists believe in Christ.*
> *And that, you see,*
> *Is why reform doesn't work!*
> *You can sign as many decrees as you like*
> *And damn the consequences—*
> *It doesn't matter because here in Russia*
> *No one carries them out!*
> *And if you want things to get better,*
> *They will get a thousand times worse.*
> *Here it is not so good to govern honorably—*
> *People won't understand.*
> *Generally, I can't believe*
> *What a weird country this is.*
> *Luckily, I have five more years*
> *To figure out what's going on.*[109]

The conclusion is that the problem with the times lay not only with the man at the top but with the Russian disarray, which he had internalized and which had helped sweep him to power. Yeltsin may not have laughed at the charade—he watched *Kukly* only several times and decided it was not for him.[110] He did, though, get out of the way of others laughing. In a country where politics were more associated with tears, this was something to be grateful for.

Chapter Thirteen

Governing the State

Weekdays and most Saturdays through 1996, President Yeltsin got up at five A.M., did his ablutions, breakfasted, eyeballed briefs and a press digest, and was on the job by 8:30. From Barvikha-4 he commuted five miles eastward on the Rublëvo-Uspenskoye Highway and through the pine-forested corridor along the Moskva River where the Soviet upper crust had their dachas and the New Russians were beginning to put up more commodious dwellings. In Moscow, his car whisked him inbound on "the government route" *(pravitel'stvennaya trassa)* for official limousines and cavalcades, down Kutuzov Prospect and Novyi Arbat Street, and up a ramp into the Kremlin through the Borovitskii Gate.[1]

Writ small, Boris Yeltsin's workplace was the vaulted, wainscoted office in Building No. 1, handed over to him by Gorbachev in 1991. As a personal touch, he had the desk decorated with a lamp and writing set made of turquoise-hued Urals malachite.[2] He described the room in retirement in hushed tones and in the present tense. To the left as he occupies his chair is the console through which he can dial any member of his government on a hotline. The wood surface before him he knows like the back of his hand. If one file folder is awry, "I experience an unaccountable irritation."[3] The shipshape folders, readied before his arrival by his head of chancery, Valerii Semenchenko, are color-coded: In the red ones, to the side of the control panel, lie decrees, letters, and papers that are to be read and signed at once; in the white, in the center, there is lesser correspondence needing his attention; and in the green folders, on the right, he finds laws voted by parliament and requests for clemency.

As Yeltsin's loving account conveys, his workplace writ large was the executive branch of the state. The white folders, on which he makes a checkmark as he riffles through them, were a porthole:

> They contain the entire life of the state—of the state as a vehicle, if you will, with a steering mechanism, an engine, and moving parts. From these white folders, you can understand how the vehicle works, whether the engine knocks, whether the wheels are falling off. They hold documents from various agencies and ministries, all of them awaiting my agreement. . . . Hidden behind each line is the intricate web of public administration. . . . The contents of these white folders, out of sight of the public, constitute the inner workings of our gargantuan state.

The green folders captivate him least, since they mostly originate in the legislature. The papers in the red folders, holding draft edicts, are the business end of government:

> When a decree comes out of a folder, someone is dismissed or appointed. If it stays in the folder, the decision is shelved. Sometimes several people wait for these decrees and sometimes the whole country. . . . And [they are] not only about hiring and firing. . . . One thing I know for certain is that what sits in [these folders] today will be the main event tomorrow. . . . If a muddleheaded or ill-thought-out decision is found there, something is wrong with the system and with the mechanism for making decisions, and something is wrong inside of me.[4]

Like so much in Russia after communism, this was a habitat in transition—partly continuous with the past, partly reformed, partly in disrepair. Yeltsin was required by circumstances to devote inordinate effort to keeping his state vital, to ensuring that the wheels did not fall off or the engine freeze up. But he also wanted to steer the vehicle to make his anti-revolutionary revolution. And this was an exercise that stretched him as few others did. The pulverizing effects of the Soviet collapse had made the post-communist state an object to *be* governed and not only a subject *of* governance. Yeltsin was a wizard at exerting personal control over the machine. He was less proficient at using it to effect social change.

Yeltsin cadged many particulars of formal institutional design from abroad.[5] His model of leadership after communism, however, was a homegrown syncretism of ingredients shaped as much by usage and improvisation as by laws and organization charts. It borrowed from three wells of inspiration.

The first and for Yeltsin the definitive source was his sense of historical mission, which linked up with his success script and expansive sense of self. A presidential form of government, he exclaimed at his first inauguration, had resonance in a country whose populace had always been voiceless. By aggregating political power and personifying it in a freely chosen individual, presidentialism would engender "a voluntary interdependence" between leader and led, as there never was under the tsars or the Communist Party. His election was a wager on reform: "The citizens . . . have selected not only a personality but the road down which Russia is to go . . . the road of democracy, reforms, and rebirth of human dignity."[6]

When Yeltsin spoke of carrying out the mandate, he frequently dramatized himself in the third person. His October 1991 speech previewing shock therapy is a top-flight example. Russia and its leader, he said, were at a branching point where a choice about trajectory had to be made. "Your president" had already chosen. "I have never sought out easy paths, but I can see with clarity that the coming months will be the most difficult for me. If I have your support and faith, I am ready to travel this road with you to the end."[7] A strong head of state would proceed down the chosen highway in lockstep with his fellow travelers in society. Their support, given in a democratic election, raised him above all other servants of the state and gave him the cape of legitimacy, as it had in his battle with Mikhail Gorbachev and the CPSU.

Some inspiration flowed, counterintuitively, from a second source: Russia's monarchic heritage. Yeltsin as a reincarnation of the tsar was a recurrent motif in the discourse of the 1990s, as it once was for Stalin.[8] Gorbachev, we have seen, attributed to his nemesis the ability "to conduct himself like a tsar," a knack Gorbachev knew he could not equal. Some scholars have referred to Yeltsin pejoratively as "Tsar Boris" and an "elected monarch" ringed by courtiers and lackeys.[9] Some Yeltsin supporters at the time put a positive spin on the royalist argot. Boris Nemtsov, the reformist governor of Nizhnii Novgorod (Gorky from 1932 to 1990), who was to move to Moscow in Yeltsin's second term, was the leading popularizer. He sketched the myth in expansive and flexible strokes:

> Yeltsin is a true Russian tsar. That is what he is about, with all the pluses and minuses, with all his recklessness and sprees, with his decisiveness and courage, and the odd time with his bashfulness. Unlike the "bad" Russian tsars, Yeltsin is a "good" Russian tsar and a completely forgiving person. For all that, his physique plays a role: he is such an enormous peasant and from the Urals.
>
> Naturally, all kinds of intrigues wind around him, and many people try to get something for themselves out of their closeness to him. But he is an unselfish person, of that I am certain.
>
> He is a lord of the manor *[barin]*, sure, yet not the kind who bathes in luxury. I think luxury is of little appeal to him. He is the tsar, and first and last he feels responsibility for what is going on. He takes to heart, though very much in his peculiar way, goings-on in the country.

Nemtsov recalled Yeltsin's pyrotechnics in August 1991, which he witnessed from the plaza of the Russian White House: "He leaped up on the tank. Everyone held him in honor and was covered in goose pimples. 'This is the kind of tsar we have [they thought], a president who is afraid of nothing.'" Nemtsov went on to describe a Yeltsin excursion to Nizhnii Novgorod in early 1992, when Nemtsov was presidential envoy. He and the city mayor were "spellbound" as Yeltsin castigated a factory manager for the inedible food in the workers' canteen and then told Nemtsov to fire the director of a grocery store for overpricing butter—the destatization of retail prices on January 2, by presidential rescript, notwithstanding. "It all brought to mind the actions of a tsar who puts things in order when he drops in on one of his patrimonial estates."[10]

Nemtsov was cavalier in his historiography: No factual tsar hailed from a peasant hut or the Urals. If utterances like his had little to offer as doctrine, they did conform to canonical themes in Russian political culture. In particular, they consorted with the timeless idea of the nation's leader as a father figure both authoritative and possessing the common touch. Yeltsin as president looked the part, up to a point. Like a storybook tsar, he asserted the right, when justice and raison d'état prescribed, to buck parchment rules (by pardoning reprobates), bureaucratic formalities (by short-circuiting the chain of command), and precedent (by countermanding decrees he had authored). With citizens and midlevel officials, his bearing was regal—posture straight, chin held high, gestures spare, manner of speech magisterial.[11]

Yeltsin's take on president-as-tsar was mixed. He did speak openly about his admiration for Peter the Great and made several public references to himself as Boris I.[12] The word was sometimes used nonchalantly in family circles.[13] In closeted settings, he a few times donned the mantle, as when, on a state visit to Sweden, he ribbed King Carl Gustav about the lengthiness of the seven-course palace banquet. "The king answered, 'You have to understand, Mr. President, that we have a certain ritual here, and it has been observed since the thirteenth century.' And Yeltsin replied jovially, 'Listen, you are a king and I am a tsar, and you tell me the two of us cannot solve such a problem?'" Carl Gustav had the wait staff speed up the feast.[14] On occasions, Yeltsin would toss out the trope of the tsar to reprimand employees. He once chastised a cheeky press secretary with the words, "Go and do what the tsar has ordered."[15] And the figure of speech in which he and members of his staff belittled matters not worth his personal attention was that they were "not the tsar's business" *(ne tsarskoye delo)*.

Yeltsin in the end recognized that the partial democratization of Russia made it impolitic to apply monarchism literally. As he knew, the plasticity that was the great boon of the monarchial legend was its great bane as well. Elected monarchy is an oxymoron. Kings are chosen on the hereditary principle from a royal caste, train for the throne from birth, and sit on it until death. Yeltsin was elected to a fixed term and knew that he would have to leave his post. In an exchange with me about the subject, he saw no way to conciliate tsardom with democracy: "How can a tsar lead in a democratic society? There are certain democratic institutions through which you have to act."[16] When subalterns pressed him too hard to address a ticklish issue, he was known to turn them aside with the question, "What do you think I am, a tsar?"

A third template for directorship of the post-communist state came from Russia's recent national past, the Soviet period, and from Yeltsin's personal past. The reflex here was to the CPSU boss he was in Sverdlovsk and Moscow.

Like the provincial party prefect of yore, Yeltsin as president felt qualified, when the spirit moved him, to intervene on any issue. His onetime economic adviser Aleksandr Livshits testifies he had "the mentality of the obkom first secretary" in assuming "the right and the duty to make decisions about urgent questions then and there."[17] The interventions that counted most, as in the Soviet system, were those given verbally. The richly experienced Viktor Chernomyrdin knew the norm: "The verbal assignments the premier received [from Yeltsin] . . . were carried out strictly, which cannot be said about decrees or even the written assignments of the president. That is to say, as things had been signified in the [party] apparatus, words spoken orally outranked pieces of paper."[18] As in the Sverdlovsk obkom and the Moscow gorkom, Yeltsin did not sweat the small stuff of public policy, the technicalities of administration, and the legal niceties, all of which were best farmed out to specialists. He "understood the limits of what he understood," Yegor Gaidar has said.[19] He would "'grab' a question on the wing . . . get a feel for problems without subjecting them to long and detailed study," to cite Boris Fëdorov, who held several economic portfolios in the first term.[20] Like the party secretary, Yeltsin in the Kremlin wanted to leave his door open to petitioners and not filter the upbound flow of information and advice. To quote Livshits again, "For him to say to people who made overtures to him that he had to check with Livshits or [Georgii] Satarov [another Kremlin aide] was as good as saying he did not have *vlast'* [power], and that was something he could never admit."[21]

Yeltsin also bore a resemblance to a CPSU first secretary in swinging the big stick of control over cadres.[22] Anyone was expendable if he connived against the president, was flagrantly inefficient, or if Yeltsin had simply had his fill of him or wanted to reshuffle his team. Upon removal, an official would not normally be granted an audience to hear why. He could consider himself lucky if he got a telephone call giving him the news and wishing him well, and luckier still if Yeltsin found him a new position.[23] On average, deputy premiers in Yeltsin's first term lasted sixteen months; ordinary members of the Council of Ministers lasted twenty-three months. By the time he faced re-election in 1996, Yeltsin was on his seventh finance minister, his sixth minister of economics and trade, his fifth minister of regional development, and his fourth ministers of agriculture and energy. In the national-security realm, he had one defense minister and two foreign ministers in term one, but three chairmen of the Security Council, four heads of state security, and four interior ministers.[24]

Yeltsin, like many partocrats in their day, turned courtesies and picayune favors to his advantage. He did it not only to build personal fealty, as had been the practice in Soviet days, but to paper over cracks in the post-Soviet institutional edifice. During the strife with Ruslan Khasbulatov and the Supreme Soviet, he played this card adroitly, especially with holdovers from the communist establishment:

> Having all that experience in the nomenklatura, Yeltsin appreciated that if former communists, even those numbered among his most ferocious opponents, could be "affectionately" brought nearer to the president's chair, then their communist radicalism might blow off like smoke. Be-

> sides "political goodies," Yeltsin made skillful and maybe cynical use of pittances—a prestigious position, an apartment, a dacha, medical care in the Central Clinical [Kremlin] Hospital, a car. In a quid pro quo for political loyalty, he could tolerate and forgive a great deal, foremost with the regional leaders. Many leaders of the [parliamentary] opposition and opposition deputies were seduced in the same way and at the requisite moment ended up as "clients" of the president.[25]

Parliament at first had an independent apparatus for granting supplies and perquisites to members, as did the prime minister's office and the judiciary. In November 1993, a month after coming down on the parliamentary rebels, Yeltsin centralized the servicing of the federal government under one roof, a unified Presidential Business Department with more than 30,000 employees. The Fourth Chief Directorate of the old Soviet Ministry of Health, of which he had been so critical when in opposition, had been under presidential control since 1991. It was renamed the department's Government Medical Center.[26] Yeltsin selected Pavel Borodin, a Siberian city mayor championed by Aleksandr Korzhakov, to head the department and exhorted him to "feed the administration [executive office] and the government well."[27] The department's budgetary demands "grew in geometrical progression" the moment Borodin was appointed, says Boris Fëdorov, the finance minister in 1993.[28] The Kremlin quartermaster also showed great inventiveness in giving his unit a market aspect—primarily to finance operations and special projects such as the Kremlin reconstruction, although many suspected it was also to provide emoluments to officials. The business department not only operated facilities taken from its Soviet antecedents (such as office and apartment buildings, the TsKB and other clinics, hotels, farms, construction organizations, and ateliers) but diversified its funding by going into for-profit healthcare, banking, commercial real estate, and oil exports.[29] Borodin spent the next six years on Yeltsin's behalf meting out perks—offices, apartments and dachas, travel and vacation vouchers, hospital stays, and even books and cellphones—to lawmakers, bureaucrats, and judges.

Borodin—known to one and all as Pal Palych, a contraction of his first name and patronymic—was a bon vivant and reputed to be the best joke-teller in the government, able to hold his ground with professional comedians. He emceed many presidential lunches and dinners and was the only official permitted to tell gags at them. The function of the Ministry of Privileges, as the press christened his agency, was no laughing matter. For the good of Yeltsin and democracy, it systematized service provision for the elite on a scale surpassing Soviet precedent. The soil was fertile: Housing and other goods and services were starting to be distributed commercially in Russia; state officials could not afford the best of them on their wages; and any revision of individual status still required a sheaf of permissions. "Goodies" that could be granted could also be withheld. When Yeltsin wanted to turn up the political heat on the Duma in the summer of 1995 and the spring of 1996, deputies were put on notice that, were the Duma to be dissolved, they would lose their offices and attendants, franking privileges, and VIP apartments in Moscow.

None of this establishes that Yeltsin governed as a CPSU secretary reborn, pure and simple. Regional party bosses until the 1980s, while all-powerful in their fiefdoms, reported to the general secretary, and that was a party role Yeltsin had never filled. Yeltsin as president took orders from no one and owed his post to the electorate. His refusal to be over-absorbed in detail was a character trait over and above what he learned in his party career. Some of the administrative levers associated with the Soviet partocracy, such as the personnel weapon and administration of perks, have been found in other times and places—for example, in the heyday of machine politics in big American cities. The Soviet formula was an alloy of machine techniques with the police state, the planned economy, and communist ideology, and those combinatory variables were absent after 1991. Yeltsin either would not or could not lock up dissidents, censor the press, or take 99.99 percent of the votes in a single-candidate election, and he had no hard-and-fast ideology and no propaganda mechanism at his fingertips. In the privileges area, he stayed aloof from the dross of Pavel Borodin's decisions.[30] The operation was constrained by a body of legislation on official benefits and by muckraking journalism, neither of them operative under the communist regime. Only when a good was in very short stock and the queue was long—state dachas are the best example—did Borodin and his office have much of an ability to play favorites.[31] Once out of government service in the 1990s, most at the level of government minister, presidential adviser, or provincial governor were left to their own devices, without a helping or a hindering hand from Building No. 1.

The historicist, monarchial, and apparatchik paradigms all underplay the gnarly complexity of Yeltsin's part in governing the state. Of the three, the first, with its sense of mission, is closest to his self-conception. But how effective was the Yeltsin recipe of governance in practice? As an oppositionist, he had presented himself as an improvement on Gorbachev, whose means of rule were rusting out. In power, he rammed through a constitution vesting him with the prerogatives he had lacked until then. The optimist would have forecast that state behavior in the new Russia would be more proactive and coherent than in the old, and it was some of the time but not consistently so. Presidential leadership was constrained by the disorganization of Yeltsin's surroundings and by institutional counterweights. It was further influenced by his *own* conception of politics in an era of transition.

The results were there to see inside his organizational home, the executive branch in Moscow. Yeltsin was as well-spoken as anybody on the pathologies of government after communism. He titled his maiden state-of-the-country address to parliament in 1994 "On Strengthening the Russian State." It began with "the gap between constitutional principles and the real practice" of rule. Russia had repudiated autocracy but not found a workable replacement, and this was undermining the whole course of reform:

> Having relinquished the command principle of governing, the state has not fully assimilated the law-based principle. This has brought forth such menacing phenomena as . . . an efflorescence of bureaucratism, which stifles the growth of new economic relations, . . . the inclusion of part of the bureaucracy on various levels in the political struggle, which leads to the sabotage of state decisions . . . the imbuing of the state and municipal apparatus with corruption . . . a low level of discipline in implementation . . . lack of coordination in the work of the ministries and departments. . . . Here we must confess openly that democratic principles and the organizations of government are more and more being discredited. A negative image of democracy is being formed, as a lethargic and amorphous system of power that gives little to the majority of people and defends above all its own corporate interests. Russian society has attained freedom, but does not yet feel democracy as a system of state power that is both strong and accountable before the nation.[32]

The Yeltsin constitution of 1993 cleared up the struggle between the executive and the legislative wings. Other than excising the vice presidency, which Aleksandr Rutskoi had made a base for attacking the president, it did little to bring order to the executive. One option would have been to snuff out its structural duality. Gennadii Burbulis had wanted to scrap the office of prime minister and make the president a U.S.-type chief executive, with agency heads reporting to him and forming a presidential cabinet. He saw Yeltsin's combination of the posts of president and premier in the autumn of 1991 as a first step toward realizing his goal. Initially open to the suggestion, Yeltsin was unalterably against it by mid-1992, wanting someone else do the legwork on reform and be a lightning rod. As Burbulis put it in an interview, "The president's path [Yeltsin thought] would be the main source of will on questions of direction. The difficulties, pain, and burdensome decisions at any given moment would be undertaken by others, who could be removed [if they failed]."[33] The new constitution reaffirmed the separation between a popularly elected president and a prime minister confirmed by parliament and in day-to-day charge of the civilian bureaucracy and the budget. The arrangement resembled the Gaullist Fifth Republic in France. In a way, it also honored the Soviet legacy: For most of the communist period, different individuals served as general secretary of the Communist Party and chairman of the USSR government, with the former, like the post-Soviet Russian president, very much in the driver's seat.

The dispersive undercurrents within the state apparatus were never enough to prod Yeltsin into radical action. The bureaucracy, no longer the handmaiden of the CPSU apparatus, and with its economic monopoly burst by market reform, seemed to him a headless monster and not an immediate threat. Making it less corrupt and more responsive were desirable objectives but low on his to-do list. A ranking official who was caught red-handed peddling influence stood to be fired. In August 1993, for example, Yeltsin released Viktor Barannikov, the minister of security, for taking bribes. Barannikov then switched sides in the constitutional dogfight and was arrested after the October violence. In November 1994 Yeltsin removed Deputy Defense Minister Matvei Burlakov, who had been accused in the press of profiteering from the evacuation of troops from Germany, but the general was never prosecuted. On systemic graft, kickbacks, and falsification, Yeltsin promulgated ameliorative decrees to little effect. To the demand of Grigorii Yavlinskii, the leader of the liberal Yabloko Party, that he make a full-scale attack on corruption as a condition of Yavlinskii supporting him in the 1996 presidential election, Yeltsin came back with a shrug of the shoulders: "So what can I do about it? This is Russia, after all."[34]

Boris Yeltsin as decision maker should be measured by an appropriate yardstick. Innovative statesmen in democracies or half-democracies do not address the dilemmas of the day singlehandedly. They identify problems, stir the pot, and begin to act. When followers join in, it may mainly serve the leader's requirements and ramify his influence; empower followers to mold the relationship, so that leaders wind up following the followers; or mutually empower, as it was with Franklin Roosevelt and the New Deal coalition in the United States in the 1930s. The most successful leaders respond to the material and psychic needs of followers and motivate them to invest in the shared cause and to help fix its terms.[35]

The early Yeltsin fostered mutual empowerment with acolytes on the street and in the halls of power. Once in the Kremlin, he still did, only with the difference that his empowerment of others tended to be ambiguous and, one could say, schizoid—the authorization of persons with multiple outlooks to speak and act in his name, either serially or simultaneously. The president's team was deficient in teamwork.

Captaincy of the team was not up for debate. An underperforming player might be slighted for months before Yeltsin let him go. In July 1994, aboard a steamship on the Yenisei River in Siberia with the governor of Krasnoyarsk province, Valerii Zubov, Yeltsin was out of sorts at japes made by press secretary Vyacheslav Kostikov and ordered him thrown into the drink, fully clothed. Pavel Borodin rescued Kostikov with only his self-regard harmed.[36] Foreign Minister Andrei Kozyrev was on the receiving end in 1995. Yeltsin complained of him at press conferences in July and September. When they traveled to the United States in October, the Americans were astonished to see Kozyrev disembark the presidential airplane in New York through a rear door. He was assigned to the hindmost car in the motorcade and forbidden to accompany Yeltsin to the United Nations, after which he "went forlornly off to his hotel."[37] In January 1996 Yeltsin replaced Kozyrev with Yevgenii Primakov.

In meetings scheduled for briefing purposes, Yeltsin never tipped off the questions he would ask of the reporting official. No exception was made for his Tuesday A.M. update from the prime minister, the number two in the Russian state. "Prompting would not have corresponded to the style of Boris Yeltsin. He wanted the weekly performance to have some suspense about it, something unexpected for the prime minister. The latter, of course, was not overjoyed."[38] The prime minister had the same right to ask questions as the president, and Yeltsin had no interest in seeing them before the meeting. In one-on-one meetings the president initiated, he would call for a summary of the recommended course, then ask to hear in a nutshell which pieces of it were *spornyi*, debatable—likely to cause implementation and political problems. If the discussion had been initiated by a subordinate, it was not unusual for Yeltsin to stare poker-faced for most of the encounter. I heard in interviews that the guest often felt as if trapped in a magnetic field, or like a rabbit in the gaze of a boa constrictor that could strike without warning. Kostikov convincingly attributes Yeltsin's silence at many meetings to his work in the CPSU apparatus, "when you could pay with your career for a careless word or an overly frank glance," as well as to an instinct to protect yourself from people "who are prepared to change their opinion depending on the eyebrow movements of a powerful person."[39] But there was personal style at work, too. Yeltsin reflected on it in the last volume of his memoirs: "In conversation, I love sharp turns, gaps, and unexpected transitions. I hold to my own rhythm and cannot stand stupid monotony."[40]

At meetings with many policymakers present, Yeltsin kept them on their toes by arbitrarily assigning seats at the table and sometimes changing the order at the last second, moving them toward or away from his chair. If he had already made a decision on an issue, he might hear out advice on how to do it better but hated to be contradicted. Were he to revise a position, it was by stealing the critic's thunder without explicitly endorsing the critique: He "came out in public support of the stand he had previously spurned, without naming names."[41] During a discussion he thought unproductive, Yeltsin could vacate the room to stunning effect, leaving the others to cool their heels for twenty or thirty minutes. The signing of a memorandum or position paper—though not of a decree or law, which would have undergone laborious review—could evoke "the Yeltsin pause." The president would take up to sixty seconds to reread the text word for word, pan over the spectators, and then roll up his shirt sleeve and scratch out his signature with a fountain pen. There were days when Yeltsin, pen uncapped, spied a problem in the document and discarded it. The sponsors would go scurrying for cover, and Yeltsin would take the unsigned document away with him.

Another expression of this same approach was Yeltsin's acting as a court of appeal for suppliants. It was a partial continuation both of his populism, which implied listening to voices from below, and of his CPSU bossism, which gave the chief the right to settle disputes over resources. Yeltsin acted in this mode with the greatest frequency in his first several years in the Kremlin. "Witnesses say," wrote one political journalist, "that from morning to evening Yeltsin's reception area is under attack by foot-messengers and applicants with draft decrees in their pockets." Since there were many more requests than Yeltsin could give thoughtful consideration to, the process let well-placed bureaucrats decide whom to give "access to the body" (Yeltsin's) and which edicts to give priority to, with no one looking out for coherency and comprehensibility. "They commission expert reviews of the drafts and assess their results. They 'report' drafts for [the president's] signature, correcting the texts by their lights. As a result, today's decrees often contradict yesterday's decrees and the-day-before-yesterday's."[42]

Mindful of the danger, managers on the Kremlin staff tried throughout the first term to rationalize the process by restricting access to Yeltsin by suitors for loans, subventions, and pork-barrel projects. Decree No. 226 in February 1995, written by Aleksandr Livshits and Anatolii Chubais, lifted the bar by requiring that any presidential decision touching on the budget kitty first be authorized by the Council of Ministers. Yeltsin found ways around this rigmarole, mostly by issuing offhand rulings. The Presidential Business Department and the Center for Presidential Priorities, headed by Nikolai Malyshev, provided convenient off-the-books funds, and provincial governors could always be enmeshed in the same spirit. Yevgenii Yasin, Yeltsin's economics minister in 1995, shortly after adoption of Decree No. 226, protested a promise to extend financial credits for retooling to the Krasnodar Automotive Works. Yeltsin remonstrated, "And who is president of Russia? They have told me you are a saboteur, and now that is obvious. I gave you an instruction. How to carry it out is your problem." A loophole was eventually found and the loan funded.[43]

The phenomenon was larger than Yeltsin. It was rooted also in the governing cohort he assembled, which sector by sector and across them all was fractious and fluctuating. Why so? Some of it was out of Yeltsin's hands, in that he had to split the difference over personnel and policy with other forces in the political system. Inside the executive, the CPSU horse collar was not succeeded by the norms of rule of law and collective responsibility that prevail in the cabinets and bureaucracies of established democracies. Faced with uncertainty, government bureaus strove for autarky, and jurisdictional boundaries among them, not crisp to begin with, were imprecise in the extreme—"everyone was interested in everything."[44] The legislature was another serious constraint on Yeltsin. The Congress of People's Deputies was the main factor behind the removal of economic liberals like Yegor Gaidar and the promotion of more conservative figures like Viktor Chernomyrdin. Although the State Duma had fewer powers than the congress, Yeltsin continued to make concessions, "willing to sacrifice . . . executive officials at critical junctures in order to placate a parliament that was hostile to zealous reformers."[45] This happened after both the 1993 and the 1995 Duma elections. Gaidar left the government for the second time after the first; Chubais and Foreign Minister Kozyrev were among those demoted after the second.

But Yeltsin and his preferences were also centrally involved in building disunity into the executive. For one thing, he liked to take his chances with individuals whose egos were as strong as his. He several times told Chubais that "he really liked working with bright people and even with people brighter than he."[46] He would never select a collaborator who was after his throne or discourteous toward him. Within those doughy limits, personal qualities weighed almost as much as opinions. Policy intellectuals and semi-intellectuals, red directors from the planned economy, ex-apparatchiks, journalists, security officers, oligarchs and their tagalongs—Yeltsin found room for all of them under his institutional big tent. Were someone not to work out, he would be handed his walking papers, and that would be that.

Yeltsin, furthermore, custom-built some positions for individuals whose contribution or company he valued, and when he did so he gave scant thought to the whole chessboard. In 1990–91, still head of the RSFSR parliament, he designated a Supreme Economic Council as a consolation prize for Mikhail Bocharov, who had been a candidate for prime minister; Bocharov quit after failing for five months to get an appointment with him to discuss the council's program.[47] Yeltsin in 1990 gave Gennadii Burbulis the title of "authorized representative of the chairman of the Supreme Soviet"; in 1991–92 it was "state secretary of Russia." Undefined in legislation, both offices amounted to carrying out those tasks Yeltsin commissioned him to do.[48] For almost a year in 1992–93, the government had two press agencies, one headed by his former Moscow workfellow Mikhail Poltoranin and the other by the jurist and journalist Mikhail Fedotov. This situation was the upshot of Yeltsin's desire to protect Poltoranin from the Supreme Soviet and of some prevarication on relations between the state and the mass media.[49] From 1992 to 1994, Shamil Tarpishchev, the skipper of the Russian tennis team and Yeltsin's coach and doubles partner, served as presidential "adviser for sports and physical culture" and had a Kremlin office.

Yeltsin's creed of personal independence inclined him against micromanagement of bench members' discharge of their duties. He would speak briefly with a new appointee, ask him to check in on issues of principle only, and leave him to go to it. Presidential assistants submitted weekly reports of one or two pages; most others turned to him only on time-urgent matters and only with short messages.[50] This did not mean that the appointee could breathe easily, for the president's eye was peeled: "Although Yeltsin rarely gave concrete assignments to workers in his apparatus, he watched carefully to see how self-reliant and energetic these workers were and rewarded such self-reliance."[51] Self-reliance was no salvation if political breakers were encountered, and it was secondary to presidential wishes, if and when these could be ascertained. The most benignant outcome would be like that accomplished by Viktor Chernomyrdin: "He [Yeltsin] did not interfere in my work . . . or in what the government was supposed to do. But I did not do anything without clearing the basic questions with him."[52] Any number of others did not thread the needle as adeptly.

A panoply of points of view nearby had additional utility for Yeltsin. In an overloaded and underpowered state, redundancy and rapid turnover provided some protection against local failure: If the first underboss and his outfit let you down, the second or third might be better. This is how Oleg Poptsov explains the anomaly of Russia having several armies and quasi-armies (the military, MVD, border guards, railway troops, and so on) when it could not really afford one of them. "It is all for the same reason: because of hesitation, because of uncertainty. If one does not come to your defense, you can always call on another."[53] In a fractionated society, it was apropos, the president felt, that the executive and not just the legislature contain representatives of the fractions. "I had to go this way," Yeltsin explained to me in 2001. "It should have been so. The situation [at the top] mirrored the interplay of forces in the country."[54] The Yeltsinesque system of checks and balances was there less to shield society from state encroachment, as *The Federalist Papers* told Americans how to do in the 1780s, than to sub for a stunted civil society, shield the sovereign from state dysfunction, and facilitate divide-and-rule in the innards of the government.

In economic policy, even as he gave the liberals license to marketize and privatize, Yeltsin was determined to find a place in his government for more conservative voices from the Soviet industrial conglomerate, and was unapologetic about the conflicting signals it sent about his policy and the standing of the prime minister. Red director Yurii Skokov, whose specialty had been power systems for spacecraft, was first deputy premier in 1990–91, secretary of a presidential board on federalism in 1991–92, and secretary of the president's Security Council in 1992–93. He was a backstairs negotiator with the putschists in August 1991 and was distinguished by a go-slow economic policy and political ambition. Wrote Yeltsin:

> Skokov is an intelligent man, that is the first thing you have to say, and a very closed one. [Ivan] Silayev . . . and Gaidar . . . felt a latent threat coming from Skokov and argued with me about him.

> What was the role of Skokov in Yeltsin's ingroup? It was a reasonable question. Skokov was really my "shadow" prime minister. . . . I understood that his general political position, in economics above all, was quite different from mine and from the positions of Gaidar and Burbulis. His double-dealing always concerned my supporters. But I thought that if a person understood that it was necessary in today's Russia to work for a strong government and not against it, then what was wrong with that? Let the shadow premier . . . urge on the real prime minister.[55]

Yeltsin lost faith in Skokov and fired him only when he dissented from Kremlin policy toward the parliament in the spring of 1993.

Chernomyrdin, who got the prime minister's job in December 1992, would not have lasted for almost two-thirds of the Yeltsin presidency if he had not been forbearing toward his leader's juggling of people and interests and had not displayed some of the same aptitude himself. The construction organizer Oleg Lobov, from Sverdlovsk, acquired some of Skokov's and Deputy Premier Georgii Khizha's military-industrial responsibilities and fought to decelerate the privatization program. Lobov wrote several memorandums to this effect to Yeltsin: "He never expressed dissatisfaction about what I wrote. He never said I was not right. No, he was surprised that my memos were not moving forward or being looked into."[56] Metallurgist Oleg Soskovets was named the ranking of the deputy premiers in the autumn of 1993, answering for heavy industry and the defense complex and chairing the cabinet's committee on daily "operational questions." He lobbied unabashedly for state credits, bailouts, and tariff barriers and, through Korzhakov, had a privileged relationship with Yeltsin. He was a thorn in Chernomyrdin's side until his dismissal in June 1996.[57]

President Yeltsin was not unobservant of the hazards of his polycentric modus operandi. Beginning in 1991, he deployed several safeguards to prevent balkanization from degenerating into chaos. One of those was to declare proprietary rights over the ultrasensitive precinct of national security and foreign policy and put it out of bounds to all but him and the agency heads. Yeltsin met one-on-one weekly with his foreign minister, spy chief, and police ministers and shut the prime minister and most of the Kremlin staff out of those colloquies.

Another low-cost response was to infiltrate protégés from earlier in his career into strategic positions, as Soviet party bosses had always done. Because

Yeltsin's term as head of the Moscow party organization had been so brief and doleful, few products of it worked in his presidential office. The main exceptions were Viktor Ilyushin (who started with him in Sverdlovsk), Valerii Semenchenko, and Mikhail Poltoranin. The best pool Yeltsin had at his disposal was the "Sverdlovsk diaspora," the old-boy network whence he drew his chief of staff from 1991 to 1993 (Yurii Petrov), his senior presidential assistant from 1991 to 1996 (Ilyushin), the head of the Kremlin business department before Pavel Borodin (Fëdor Morshchakov), and a representative in the Council of Ministers and Security Council (the peripatetic Oleg Lobov).[58] Gennadii Burbulis, head speech writer Lyudmila Pikhoya, and her colleague Aleksandr Il'in were Sverdlovskers but low-ranking members of the professoriate—advantageously for them, at Yeltsin's alma mater, UPI.[59] "You feel more confident, you feel certain warmth, among people from your area *[zemlyaki]*," says Pikhoya.[60] Yeltsin's reliance on people from his province of birth, though, was quite limited, since he wanted to avoid charges of cronyism and to be free to recruit outside the group. Burbulis left office by the end of 1992, Petrov by early 1993, and the others followed. No new Sverdlovskers were brought into the administration after then.

A related habit for Yeltsin was to find new favorites. These might be all-round comrades and purveyors of good cheer with whom he had *ryumochnyye otnosheniya* (shot-glass relations); examples would be Soskovets or Vladimir Shumeiko, a first deputy premier in 1992–93 and chairman of the Federation Council in 1994–95. Or they might be Young Turks who pushed reforms—like Anatolii Chubais, Boris Fëdorov, and Sergei Shakhrai. As a show of favor, Yeltsin several times followed up on a Fëdorov complaint by telephoning Chernomyrdin, with Fëdorov seated in the office. Fëdorov saw it a sign of confidence when Yeltsin did not tell Chernomyrdin that Fëdorov was there and made gargoyle faces at him during the conversation.[61]

A corrective to personalization and governmental disconnectedness would have been a collegial entity for sharing information, arbitrating conflicts, and inculcating common purpose. Yeltsin was stubbornly against such a linchpin—as should come as no shock, given his individualism and his intuitive approach to political action. Acquaintance with the communist era's plenteous underbrush of committees, bureaus, and secretariats seems to have helped sour him on communal decision making. This aversion shows the selectiveness of his attitude toward the Soviet legacy.

During the seven months in 1991–92 when Yeltsin did double duty as prime minister, it was up to him to chair sessions of the Council of Ministers.

He had nothing but distaste for the unwieldy council and the eye-glazing detail that marked its meetings. Several months of watching him sleepwalk through the proceedings won Burbulis and Gaidar over to two events per week—a working session on Tuesdays over sandwiches and tea, which Yeltsin did not attend, and one with him on Thursdays, to approve the decisions made on Tuesday. Yeltsin was relieved to make Burbulis and, after the spring of 1992, Gaidar his proxy for cabinet paperwork.[62] The Yeltsin constitution gave the president the right, which he wrote into the draft, to chair any sitting of the Council of Ministers. He did it once in a blue moon after 1993 (and only twice in the second term), and then it was mostly to make announcements for the television cameras. Size and practice disqualified the Council of Ministers as a serious decision maker, as was the case with its Soviet predecessor. The fifty or sixty officials in attendance sat in rows facing forward, like pupils in a classroom. All remarks were made from a microphone and lectern at the front of the hall. Votes were almost never taken.

A more propitious attempt to rejoin the threads was the Russian State Council of 1991–92. The council was born in July 1991 as the brainchild of Burbulis and a subset of the Westernizing intellectuals who had congregated around Yeltsin during his drive for power. They wanted a summit-level panel that would deliberate direction and priorities and not bog down in detail. Members were to have entrée to the president as individuals; as a group, they were to sit down with him in the chair to consider the big picture. Burbulis intended to make the State Council the modernizing center of policy making and to have its role as clearing house for ideas given constitutional sanction. The council was "to work out for the head of state questions about the country's development overall and gather under its roof people of the same turn of mind who were scattered around other structures."[63]

The core members of the State Council were Burbulis and five "state counselors" whom Yeltsin made responsible for reform sectors: Yekaterina Lakhova (women's and social issues), Sergei Shakhrai (legal affairs), Yurii Skokov (defense), Sergei Stankevich (politics), and Galina Starovoitova (nationalities). Burbulis, Shakhrai, Stankevich, and Starovoitova were progressive academics; Lakhova, a pediatrician from Sverdlovsk, was a political centrist; Skokov was a secretive conservative. Added to them were five cabinet ministers of liberal outlook.[64] Yegor Gaidar and Vice President Rutskoi, fearful of exclusion, asked for the right to participate as well. Burbulis, who had begged off the job of organizing Yeltsin's presidential office, was not the optimal salesman for the council. Yurii Petrov, Viktor Ilyushin, and the veterans of the CPSU apparatus to whom Yeltsin had turned for assistance gave it a chilly reception, as did ministers and parliamentarians who stood to give up powers.[65]

The backbiting would have been extraneous unless Yeltsin had the reservations he did. They went back to the rationale for the State Council, which, as Stankevich was later to say frankly, was "to make up for [Yeltsin's] shortcomings" and for his "inadequate vision of the future."[66] Getting his back up at the tutorship, Yeltsin waffled. He would not commit to a firm schedule or appoint more counselors, and missed most of the early sessions. This left Burbulis to lead them, which it was hard to do when political heavyweights sat around the table. Yeltsin took offense at press reports that the council would elevate the tone of government and that Burbulis was his "gray cardinal," pulling wires from backstage: "This, of course, was balderdash. For there to be a 'cardinal,' the person in the president's chair would have had to be spineless, soft, and apathetic," adjectives inapplicable to the first president of Russia.[67] The State Council convened about twice a month until Yeltsin abolished it in May 1992. Of the counselors, now "presidential advisers," Shakhrai made a good career as a government minister, Lakhova entered electoral politics, and Skokov stayed on in the Security Council Yeltsin established by decree in April 1992. Burbulis and Starovoitova walked the plank in November 1992 and Stankevich, after losing his Kremlin office and hotline connection to the president, in December 1993.[68] A Presidential Council, chaired by Yeltsin, continued to function throughout his first term as an unpaid sounding board for thirty or so opinion makers and an audition chamber for future aides.

From time to time, journalists and analysts would proclaim that some other body was succeeding where the State Council had not. Invariably, speculation about the latest candidate petered out. Modest requests by staffers for small-group meetings with the president were laughed off. At the reception for Yeltsin's sixty-third birthday in 1994, assistant Georgii Satarov saluted him and said it would be good if all his aides sat down with him once a week. Yeltsin said no: "Why is this necessary? After all, each of you can come to see me and chat. What do you want to do, bring back the Politburo?"[69]

Yeltsin put higher stock in two other ways of mitigating the unruliness of the executive branch. The first was the extramural hobnobbing that he had practiced in the Sverdlovsk committee of the CPSU. An aspect of it was the new apartment house in Krylatskoye, which the Yeltsins made their legal Moscow domicile in 1994. Chernomyrdin, Korzhakov, Gaidar, Borodin, and Yurii Luzhkov were among the tenants who danced to a live orchestra at the housewarming. The building was a poor stimulant of friendly feelings, since the family rarely overnighted in their flat and those registered there, like them, lived mostly at country homes. Those who stayed behind avoided their neighbors due to political disagreements and to a psychological reaction against being cooped up in the same company.[70]

Yeltsin sank more effort into an association named the Presidential Club. It was established in June 1993 in a facility taken over from the CPSU Central Committee at 42 Kosygin Street, on the Sparrow (formerly Lenin) Hills. Yeltsin got the idea, through Korzhakov and Shamil Tarpishchev, from the Il'inka Sports Club attached to the Council of Ministers. The plant combined a sports complex (covered tennis courts, a swimming pool, a weight room) with lounges, a restaurant, and a movie theater. Yeltsin played doubles tennis at the club with Tarpishchev twice a week and others when possible. His most rollicking steambath parties and dinners were held there, and some political scuttlebutt was digested with the meals and drinks. Yeltsin was president of his club, which was to be for "people who are close in spirit and in views, who like one another, and who want to see one another regularly."[71]

The generic resemblance to Urals precedent cloaked dissimilarities. Kosygin Street was far plusher than anything in the hinterland. Tennis, the main athletic pursuit, had snob appeal—it was not part of the Soviet sports machine until the 1980s—and, in singles and doubles, was less cooperative than the volleyball favored in Sverdlovsk. Yeltsin as regional boss had enrolled party workers in his volleyball league inclusively, but the Moscow lodge was exclusive. Entrants were issued cards and paid token dues; cursing was forbidden; enrollment was capped at 100 members; recruits were approved by Yeltsin in annual batches. It was not enough for the candidates to like one another: *The president* had to like them. A spot on the members' directory was a mark of honor, which did not always fit with protocol position. Vice President Rutskoi, for example, was out, as were the head of the president's staff (Sergei Filatov), all of Yeltsin's liberal advisers, the mayor of Moscow (Yurii Luzhkov), and the chief of foreign intelligence (Yevgenii Primakov); for some reason, Yeltsin wanted at first to bar Prime Minister Chernomyrdin, then allowed him in.[72] But Yeltsin's senior aide (Viktor Ilyushin), who was equal to Filatov in status, was clubbable, and was joined by the head of the Presidential Business Department (Pavel Borodin), the ghostwriter of Yeltsin's memoirs (Valentin Yumashev), the commander of the palace guard (Korzhakov) and top security officers, several elite intellectuals (Mark Zakharov and Yurii Ryzhov), and two comedians (Gennadii Khazanov and Mikhail Zadornov). An invitation into the club could recognize newly won standing. In 1994, for instance, businessman Boris Berezovskii, industrialist Vladimir Kadannikov (whose factory made the cars marketed by Berezovskii's main business, Logovaz), and Ivan Rybkin, the new speaker of the State Duma, were asked to join. At his induction, in June, Berezovskii was in bandages for injuries suffered in an assassination attempt the week before.[73] The organizers had planned to add a substantial number of figures from business and the arts but found limited interest in those they approached, and some of those who did accept came to the place only once. It was, in the end, "a club of chiefs," in the words of Yumashev, and the membership was never over sixty.[74]

More than all these mechanisms, Yeltsin relied on top-down administrative resources to supply policy input, check on underlings, and impose his decisions. The instrument was the Presidential Executive Office created by Yurii Petrov and modeled in part on the Central Committee Secretariat. Petrov wanted it to have the planning and monitoring capacity of the high party apparatus in its prime, without it getting mired in operations, and to this end did not give it divisions for sectors of the economy, such as Yeltsin knew so well from an earlier life. Much of Petrov's time went to the organizational tangles brought on by the change in regime, including the appropriation of the property of the CPSU, and he was struck by how little sway he had over the provinces—the obkoms and gorkoms were as extinct as the Central Committee—and over his boss.[75] The intelligentsia-based Democratic Russia movement, with Gennadii Burbulis's support, attacked Petrov in early 1992 as a symbol of nomenklatura revanche. He in April offered his resignation, which Yeltsin refused to accept. Petrov lost Yeltsin's support in December 1992 when he dickered with communist legislators about his being selected as prime minister.[76] In January 1993 the president supplanted Petrov with Sergei Filatov, a bookish Moscow academic and a vice speaker of the Congress of Deputies. Although Yeltsin was to slight Filatov in *Presidential Marathon* for having "turned the executive office into some sort of research institute on the problems of democracy in Russia,"[77] staff strength grew under his aegis from about 400 to the level of about 2,000 office workers. That is higher than the circa 1,500 in the American White House staff (the U.S. population is more than twice Russia's) and much more than the several hundred in the Élysée Palace in France, which, like Russia, has a dual executive.[78]

Petrov and then Filatov had some substantive impact on policy, but had to compete for Yeltsin's ear with a squadron of policy experts reporting to him through separate ganglia. In 1993 Yeltsin began to appoint thematic presidential assistants *(pomoshchniki)*, who were either former party or state placemen of a technocratic stripe or Moscow intellectuals, mostly of a democratic orientation. In the group of about twelve assistants, Anatolii Korabel'shchikov (who managed relations with the provinces) and Dmitrii Ryurikov (a professional diplomat who coordinated foreign policy) were the most prominent representatives of the first category; Yurii Baturin (assistant for national security), Georgii Satarov (domestic politics), and Aleksandr Livshits (economics) were the most prominent from the second category.[79] These individuals, a generation younger than the president, were required to communicate with him not through Filatov but through Viktor Ilyushin, the tight-lipped apparatchik from Sverdlovsk who was responsible for blocking out Yeltsin's workday. Filatov, Ilyushin, and their respective groupings were rivals from the start. This was no accident. "For a long time, the president's apparatus had two leaders. . . . The president saw the contradictions but did nothing to efface them. . . . Often Yeltsin even encouraged antagonism between parts of his executive office and between individuals. It seemed to him that this would make it easier to control things and avert any one person increasing his influence unduly."[80]

There was another generator of dissonance: Aleksandr Korzhakov and the Presidential Security Service. The service was founded in 1990 as a small bodyguard for Yeltsin as parliamentary chairman. Upgraded in 1992, it was on paper part of the Main Protection Directorate (previously the Ninth Directorate of the KGB), but that agency was headed by Mikhail Barsukov, a brother officer Korzhakov had known since 1979, whose son was married to Korzhakov's daughter, and who was willing to give him autonomy. Korzhakov freely admits in his memoirs that he was given to role expansion even in the first leg of his service to Yeltsin, in the Moscow party committee from 1985 to 1987.[81] In national government, his star soared after the principal security forces flubbed the operation against parliament in October 1993. Yeltsin took to calling the service his "mini-KGB" and acceded to Korzhakov's demand for status parity with Filatov and Ilyushin, enlargement of the service—it went from 250 men in September 1991 to 829 by June 1996—and improvement of their pay, housing conditions, and weaponry. Korzhakov convinced Yeltsin that, beyond keeping him safe, the service would fight corruption in the Kremlin and in the bowels of the bureaucracy.[82]

Armed with an unpublished presidential decree dated November 11, 1993, Korzhakov tapped telephones and fed Yeltsin dossiers of surreptitiously gathered compromising material *(kompromat)* on officials. Filatov, a target, sounded off in the press about Korzhakov turning the executive office into "a team of stoolpigeons."[83] Yeltsin, he said in an interview, "began to toss [Korzhakov's] letters back to him," but they kept coming, and some were directed to Prime Minister Chernomyrdin and other cabinet ministers.[84] Unfazed, Korzhakov formed an in-house "analytical center" that made proposals on a wide range of public issues and badmouthed market reforms. Beginning in 1994, he wrote sharp letters on economic and other policy problems unrelated to his job description, not only to Yeltsin but to high-ranking leaders, including Chernomyrdin, and leaked information about his views to the media.[85] By this time, Korzhakov was also a force in personnel decisions. Pavel Borodin and First Deputy Premier Soskovets were friends and allies of his, and in his last year in the Kremlin he had the principal say over the designation of a chief of the FSB (Barsukov), procurator general (Yurii Skuratov), and press secretary to Yeltsin (Sergei Medvedev).[86] In January 1996 he engineered the replacement of Filatov by Nikolai Yegorov, the former governor of Krasnodar province, a hard-liner on Chechnya (who had been demoted from a ministerial position after Budënnovsk), and a man of "haughty manners and a slighting attitude toward those occupying more modest posts than he in the hierarchy of state service."[87] Korzhakov pressed Yeltsin to make Soskovets prime minister in Chernomyrdin's place.[88] And in the early months of 1996, he and Soskovets controlled the organization of Yeltsin's campaign for re-election (see Chapter 14).

Yeltsin was later driven to lament the wideness of Korzhakov's reach:

> Korzhakov came to influence the appointment of people in the government, in the executive office, and in the power [security] ministries. . . . With every passing month and year, the political role of the . . . guard service . . . and concretely of Korzhakov grew. Korzhakov fought tooth and nail with everyone who did not submit to him and anyone he considered "alien." He interfered in the work of my secretariat and violated established procedures to bring his own documents to me. He fought with Filatov and Ilyushin and tried through Oleg Soskovets to have a say in the country's economic policy. . . . I take full responsibility for his unbelievable rise and his deserved fall. It was my mistake, and I had to pay for it.[89]

Yeltsin came to this wisdom in the rearview mirror. During his first term, though, it was his indulgence of Korzhakov that taught the Moscow high and mighty that the ex-watchman was a man to be feared and propitiated. Korzhakov family celebrations, such as his daughter's nuptials and his twenty-fifth wedding anniversary, became must-show events. Prime Minister

Chernomyrdin gave the newlyweds a handsome china set. When Yeltsin dropped in on the silver anniversary party, Chernomyrdin, if Korzhakov can be believed, pouted because he had not been invited.[90] Korzhakov's public reputation shot to rarefied heights. To go by the experts' poll published monthly in newspaper *Nezavisimaya gazeta*, beginning in late 1994, he was ranked among the ten most powerful political figures in the country. In November 1995 he placed *fourth*, behind no one but the president, the prime minister, and Mayor Luzhkov; in January 1996 he was fourth again, trailing only Yeltsin, Gennadii Zyuganov (the communist leader, who was about to run for president against Yeltsin), and Chernomyrdin.

The subdivision of executive authority between president and prime minister was sanctioned by Russia's constitution and laws. It created, as Yeltsin observed in 1994 in *Notes of a President*, "a second center of power" within the state—existing on the sufferance of the first center yet still formidable—and this did not disturb him.[91] To curb centrifugal tendencies in the formal structures of the state and to make decisions as he saw fit, Yeltsin had recourse to informal and personalistic means, some of them concocted anew, some of them out of the Soviet or pre-Soviet Russian armory. In *Midnight Diaries*, published in 2000, Yeltsin looked back at the Kremlin of the early and middle 1990s and remarked that it harbored a multiplicity of "informal leaders" and "centers of power" pushing in contradictory directions.[92] The institutional remedy for polycentric government, Yeltsin's shop within the executive branch, was itself wantonly polycentric—more tower of Babel than beacon of strength.

This outcome was reached with Yeltsin's cooperation. It was a fine example of a paradox of post-communism, as dissected by the sociologist Alena Ledeneva—"that informal practices are important because of their ability to compensate for defects in the formal order while simultaneously undermining it." This contradiction, Ledeneva adds, "serves to explain why things in Russia are never quite as bad or as good as they seem."[93] Governing the state from 1991 to 1996 the way he did allowed Yeltsin to maintain his power within it and avail himself of diverse talent and knowledge. He orchestrated a leader-centered ruling coalition by cowing and cajoling political and bureaucratic actors into compliance, playing potential rivals off against one another, and accepting—even glorying in—compromise and ambiguity in policy. That same mix of tactics, however, came at a price. It left the program for transforming Russia less integrated in its content, and jerkier in its phasing, than it ought to have been.

Chapter Fourteen

Reconnecting

The replenishment of his electoral mandate in June–July 1996 was a peerless ordering moment in the Yeltsin presidency. Holding an election for chief executive on track and in more or less competitive fashion affirmed the post-communist regime and its reliance on popular consent. Yeltsin's 1996 victory must rate with the 1991 putsch as his magic hour as practitioner of mass politics. It gave him a fresh lease on political life and another crack at governing, at heavy cost to his health. It prevented neo-communists from retaking power and undoing some or all of the changes of the preceding decade. And it pulled new participants, and new techniques for exercising influence, onto Russia's civil stage.

It was not predetermined that Yeltsin would be a candidate for re-election upon expiration of his five-year term. He told Aleksandr Korzhakov in the spring of 1992 that he would "not be able to bear up under a second term" and needed to find a successor, and in May he said in a press interview that there was "a limit to a person's physical and other abilities" and his first term would be his last.[1] Richard Nixon, dropping in on him in June 1992, called his disclaimer a fiendishly clever strategy—"a masterstroke" that transmitted his fearlessness as a reformer "and would be to Yeltsin's advantage even should he eventually decide to run again." Yeltsin gave a knowing smile and said that "of course" he would benefit politically; how he would was impossible to make out.[2] He commented to Bill Clinton, still a U.S. presidential candidate, in Washington that same month that taking himself out of the running had already had "an important psychological impact" and that people appreciated "that I'm not fighting to stay in office but to ensure that the reforms become irreversible."[3]

Yeltsin soon second-guessed the decision. He declared, the week after dissolving the Supreme Soviet in September 1993, that he would be willing to proceed with a presidential election, and to be a candidate, in the summer of 1994—a statement he revoked just as suddenly that November. In March 1994, when an article in *Izvestiya* maintained that he would participate in the next election "only in his capacity as a voter," Yeltsin had his press secretary persuade the paper to print a new article saying he was agnostic about standing. Later in 1994 there was a different iron in the fire: the idea of postponing, in the interests of political stability, the Duma election slated for 1995 and/or the presidential election slated for 1996. Gennadii Burbulis, no longer a member of the government but still influential in the liberal beau monde, wanted Yeltsin to extend his term by decree for two years and not to seek re-election. Although these and related proposals bristled with constitutional complications, Yeltsin was content to leave them in play. Aides were kept in the dark about his true intent but formed the impression by the summer of 1994 that the president meant to run, be it in 1996 or 1998, and they should begin to clear the decks. This was also the burden of remarks he made to staffers in 1995.[4]

Reconnecting with the electorate was going to take some doing. Entranced by the Kremlin and high politics, Yeltsin had long since let his reputation as "people's president" lose its luster. To be sure, he continued to escape Moscow and accept bread and salt, the customary token of Russian hospitality, in the provinces. A hobby project of his in 1992–93 was to circuit through every subunit of the federation. He dug in against staffers who urged him to prioritize the populous regions and align his peregrinations with the Moscow political calendar.[5] When out in the field, he could still gladhand with the best of them. Unlike Gorbachev, who invariably initiated group conversations, Yeltsin's way was to wait for someone else to lead off and to make a retort, and one that frequently contained a nonverbal element. In May 1992, for example, he held court at the Omsk Oil Refinery in west Siberia. Hearing out one disgruntled worker, Yeltsin gave him a light slap on the forehead and cried "Mosquito!" after which the two men swapped jokes. To the refinery employees, it was a playful and egalitarian gesture.[6] In June 1994 Yeltsin descended on Kyzyl, the capital of Tuva, the mountain republic of shamanistic and Buddhist heritage on the border with Mongolia. Decked out in the national costume at a concert by Kongar-ool Ondar, Tuva's renowned throat singer, he mounted the stage, hummed along, and quaffed *arakar,* a potent beverage from fermented goat's milk.[7]

Russians after 1991 rarely accorded Yeltsin an abusive reception. Correspondents in the advance party would see the eyes of local residents light up when the president's blue Mi-8 chopper landed on the tarmac, especially if he shushed his bodyguards and waded into the throng: "We would stand around [beforehand] and ask people what they made of Yeltsin. They would do nothing but denounce him something fierce: 'As soon as he gets here we are going to tear him to shreds,' that type of thing. Then Yeltsin showed up, perhaps not in the best of form, and did a walkabout. And suddenly these very same people would be saying, 'Oh, Boris Nikolayevich, may you be healthy, you are one of us.'"[8] These swooning scenes speak volumes about the Russian tradition of deference to leaders. Members of the crowd often came up and asked Yeltsin to intercede on a family or community problem; adjutants took down the requests and referred them to central or local functionaries.

Nonetheless, as the first term wore on, Yeltsin communed person-to-person with his fellow citizens less and less. Security tightened during the 1993 constitutional conflict and when the Chechen war made him an assassination target. Some governors discouraged him from making appearances when in their regions. A tour in the spring of 1995 was aborted after one stop because of lack of interest in the events.[9] Yeltsin's extemporaneous contacts with the masses, the press corps noticed, were getting to be more perfunctory. "He preferred to go up to the crowd, slap it on the back . . . and get away," is how Tatyana Malkina, a beat reporter for the newspaper *Segodnya,* recalls it. Yeltsin, she said, was losing sight of "people" *(lyudi)* and starting to see only "the people" *(narod).*[10]

As the 1995–96 election season approached, it was equally apparent that Yeltsin lacked a key resource that leaders and aspiring leaders have in the retail politics of mature democracies: an effective party. Post-Soviet Russia was a petri dish for political parties and protoparties (there were 273 of them registered in 1995), and they were found in every ideological hue, from fascist to feminist. Quality, admittedly, did not match quantity, and many of these organizations were jerry-built, personality-driven, and transient.[11] Nonetheless, a party or mass movement of his own would have given Yeltsin a chance to advance positions, build organizational capacity in the parliamentary election arena, and utilize them in a presidential campaign.

There had been no want of schemes for hatching a Yeltsin party. Early on in his administration, advisers Gennadii Burbulis, Sergei Stankevich, and Galina Starovoitova pushed a broad-based national party—an August Bloc, they suggested calling it, in honor of the turning back of the coup. In March 1992 Yeltsin received the representatives of several dozen liberal organizations and said he was for creation of a pro-reform Assembly of Russian Citizens. All that came from it was a charter meeting in April, chaired by Burbulis. The plan revived in June 1992 as an Association in Support of Democracy and Reforms, bracketing forty-three reformist groups. In consultations, Yeltsin gave it his imprimatur, said that in principle he might lead it, and even expressed a preference for a name with the words "people's" or "democratic" in it. This endeavor, too, trailed off into nothingness. Then, after the April 1993 referendum, Burbulis and Stankevich thought they had won Yeltsin over to an overarching League of the Twenty-Fifth of April or an April Alliance in the same mold. All over again, they were unable to get him to act.[12]

Russia's Choice in the 1993 Duma election was a Yeltsin-friendly electoral formation that did get into the air. Without his assistance, it gathered together government ministers and reformist intellectuals, all in the hopes of a symbiosis with their hero: "Our bloc makes no bones about who is its leader—it is President Boris Nikolayevich Yeltsin."[13] Yeltsin indicated to Yegor Gaidar, who headed up the list of candidates, that he would throw his weight behind them. On his journey to Japan in October, he promised Gaidar to address the bloc's convention and back its list. But he never did. Pouring all of his energies into making and ratifying the constitution, Yeltsin determined at the eleventh hour not to attend the meeting, withheld sanction, and did not take issue when cabinet minister Sergei Shakhrai formed a separate electoral list, the Party of Russian Unity and Accord. A planned post-Tokyo meeting with Russia's Choice panjandrums became a presidential soliloquy on Asian affairs.[14] Gaidar estimates that a Yeltsin statement would have swung 10 percent of the vote to Russia's Choice and made it the undisputed winner of the election.[15]

Sergei Filatov, Yeltsin's chief of staff, was behind the next party-building maneuver in 1994 and into 1995. He and Aleksandr Yakovlev founded a Russian Party of Social Democracy, dedicated to democratic values and a mixed economy, and registered it in February 1995. Filatov and Yakovlev felt they had a commitment from Yeltsin to help it with financing, back it in the next Duma election, and chair it after that.[16] Despite assurances, Yeltsin went off on a tangent. Prodded by Shakhrai, the spoiler from 1993, he gave license for not one but two pro-presidential electoral groupings. Our Home Is Russia, headed by Viktor Chernomyrdin, who had sat out the 1993 election, was right-of-center programmatically (right in the sense of favoring the market over government control); the bloc struck by Ivan Rybkin, the Duma speaker, was left-of-center (left in the sense of partiality for government direction over the market). On April 25, 1995, Yeltsin jumped the gun to unveil plans for the two blocs to journalists and to blubber that they would stride coordinately in "two columns," implying that they were apologists for the status quo. After that, he did not bestir himself to help either organization, although he did go on television on December 15 to speak out against the command economy and plans to restore the Soviet Union. Rybkin assumed he was at liberty to rebuke the prime minister and the government, only to find that, whenever he did, Chernomyrdin complained to him and Yeltsin; he also was strapped for campaign funds.[17] On election day, December 17, Rybkin scraped together 1 percent of the popular vote. Our Home Is Russia far exceeded him in resources and had thirty-six governors on its national list, yet Yeltsin made slighting comments about its drawing power and it was not able to claim that it spoke for the president. Chernomyrdin noted both these points to Korzhakov. "I said to him right away [after Yeltsin made his comments in September], 'Boris Nikolayevich, this is not my personal initiative only, it is necessary to all of us.'" Yeltsin was unmoved. "And then the governors would ask me, 'Are you together or not together?' I would say, 'What are you talking about, why don't you want to understand?' [And they would reply], 'We're not able to figure it out, and that is it.'"[18] On December 17 Our Home Is Russia finished with a puny 10 percent. The winner in the popular vote (with 23 percent) and in seats was the Communist Party of the Russian Federation, the KPRF, which was ferally opposed to Yeltsin.

Why all the bobbing and weaving on affiliation with a party? Yeltsin did not offer a reason during his years as president. In an interview in the privacy of retirement, he offered this comment:

> The CPSU had left a belch in the air. I had an extreme reaction against the word "party," an allergy against all of this stuff. So I had no wish to join any party and I did not join one, and I am not a member of any party today. . . . I had a very negative attitude toward [the creation of] a unifying party. . . . [I felt I should] be above the interests of any party. I was the president. He should respect every registered party and every tendency in

> society; he should help them and listen to them. That is it. If I had been a member of one of the parties, I would have had to concern myself with lobbying for that party. That would have been incorrect. . . . I did not want to give up on this preference of mine, that was a credo for me. . . . The president should be above all these things.[19]

Having chafed at the ruling party in the past, Yeltsin was pleased to be unbound from it and from anything that reeked of its subservient culture. For the present, he considered the president to be above the fray and representative of the whole nation, very much in the spirit of his constitution. The not caring to "lobby" for any organization was what registered most in the political elite. As one former activist in the Interregional group observed, from the turn of the 1990s onward Yeltsin "did not want any structure that might force upon him the necessity to coordinate his decisions with others."[20] From this perspective, a party was harmful less for constraining followers than for constraining *the leader*. Yeltsin had seen Gorbachev labor to steer both the CPSU and the Soviet state, while he as an oppositionist had flexibility after he walked out of the party in 1990. He was not sure how agreeable Russia's untrammeled political elite would be to reimposition of partisan discipline in any form. And he knew that party organizations in open or semi-open political systems provide opportunities for subleaders to excel, and that subleaders can become rivals to the alpha leader if his grip slackens. In 1995 Yeltsin desired Our Home Is Russia to do well in the Duma campaign but not so well as to make Chernomyrdin a credible pretender to the presidential suite. Chernomyrdin would say in an interview that Yeltsin's Kremlin entourage "feared that Chernomyrdin would get too strong, with 1996 coming up."[21] It would not have taken such a position without the president knowing.

Yeltsin's allergic reaction to the party form was in keeping with his style of acting and governing—visceral and charismatic rather than cerebral and institutional. As with his reluctance to act as propagandist for Russia's transformation, he was overcompensating for aspects of the totalitarian past. At times when he saw salvation in hooking up directly with the people, a permanent party machine might have posed hurdles. But a party can work for a leader and a cause: by supplying a brand with which citizens can identify, sharing responsibility for making choices in government, and acting as a repository of ideas. With no party at his side, Yeltsin, as Oleg Poptsov wrote, had difficulty answering the question, "Who is the president with?"[22] Charles de Gaulle in France, who had slighted the Fourth Republic as a "regime of parties" that divided society, came to see the merits of an integrating, pro-presidential quasi-party, the Union for the New Republic, in his Fifth Republic. Yeltsin never drew the same conclusion in Russia.

And who was with Yeltsin as the 1996 election train pulled out of the station? Public opinion surveys in 1995 showed not very many unqualified supporters remained and that as few as 5 percent of citizens had the firm intent of voting for him if he were to run.[23] Observers frequently gave him no chance of prevailing and forecast a sweep by Gennadii Zyuganov of the KPRF. Yegor Gaidar was typical in a statement in February: "No matter how you arrange the possible coalitions, it is hard to imagine that the president will win."[24] But the polls also showed that a goodly portion of the electorate was undecided and that the attitude of roughly 40 percent of Russians was ambivalent: They were disappointed in Yeltsin but not unalterably against, they hoped he might do better in the future, or they preferred him to the available alternatives, as the best of a bad lot. These numbers, and the two-stage electoral format, which would allow a candidate into a runoff round, were one to be needed, with well under half of the votes, held open the possibility that Yeltsin would be able to turn things around on the campaign trail.[25]

Yeltsin firmed up his choice to seek a second term in late December 1995, a month in which his political allies suffered defeat in the parliamentary election and he endured his third coronary in a half-year. Naina Yeltsina and their daughters were moved to tears by the very suggestion. Physicians had reported that the rigors of an electioneering marathon might kill him or shorten his life and leave him incapacitated.[26] Not for the first time, Yeltsin overrode family and medical science.

His motivations, as always, were a jumble. In political terms, the neo-communists he so detested were now the main enemy and would gain the most from a failure to stand and fight: "The idea that I myself would facilitate the communists coming to power was more than I could bear."[27] In personal terms, the stacking of the deck against him made the challenge seem especially worthwhile. As he met staff after New Year's to inform them of his decision, he took umbrage at reports that pollsters hired by the Kremlin found his popularity at a record low: "I am being stuffed to the gills with sociology, but I myself know sociology better than the whole lot of you."[28] His memoir self-portrait of those weeks might be captioned "King Lear Makes a Comeback." "My whole life was buffeted by all manner of storms and winds," he wrote. "I was on my feet but almost knocked over by the gusts." His health was bad, power was slipping through his fingers, trusted comrades were letting him down, and the people would not forgive him for shock therapy and Chechnya. "It appeared as if all was lost. But this was one of those moments when a sort of clarity comes over me. With a clear head, I said to myself, 'If I run in this election I am going to win it without any doubt.' This I knew with certitude, regardless of all the forecasts, all the polls. . . . Most likely, I was saved by my imperishable passion and my will to resist."[29] Yegor Gaidar in his memoirs was to call up a Russian cultural trope: "Our Il'ya Muromets had finally roused himself."[30]

Yeltsin left Moscow's Vnukovo field on February 15 to make the official announcement in old Urals haunts. Aides and ministers had been summoned to the airport. "With his storied stare, he looked around at all the functionaries there to send him off and asked with great sincerity, 'So tell me, do you think it's not worth it for me to get mixed up in this business?' And the answer that rang out was, of course, a simultaneous chorus of voices: 'How can you say such a thing, Boris Nikolayevich, what is this all about? You must!'" "If I must, then I must," Yeltsin replied.[31] His speech in Yekaterinburg was in the same Youth Palace where he had dialogue with local students as first secretary of the Sverdlovsk obkom fifteen years before. Battling laryngitis, he portrayed himself as ready to learn from his mistakes but not to turn back the clock: "I am for reforms but not at any price. I am for a correction in course but not a return to the past. I am for basing Russian politics not on utopia and dogmas but on practical utility." He struck an inclusive note, suggesting that he shared the people's concerns about the road taken since 1991, yet reproved reactionaries who rejected the trajectory. "We," he proclaimed, "are stronger than those who for all these years have put a spoke in the wheel and have impeded our motion toward a great and free Russia. . . . We are stronger than our own disappointments and doubts. We are tired out but we are together, and we will win."[32]

The "we" at the head of the uphill effort was an open-ended category. On January 15 Yeltsin put Oleg Soskovets, the powerful first deputy premier and friend of Aleksandr Korzhakov, in charge of his re-election headquarters. In the past year, Yeltsin had spoken several times to Soskovets of the possibility of Soskovets in due course succeeding him as president. What with Soskovets's high position in Moscow, this talk was bound to be taken more seriously than the fleeting conversation he had with Boris Nemtsov in Nizhnii Novgorod in 1994. Yeltsin now conceived of the assignment as a tryout: "I saw it this way: If Oleg Nikolayevich had political ambitions, let him display them. Let him show what kind of politician he was and what kind of political will he possessed, and then we would see."[33] Loading up the nascent campaign with a secondary objective was a mistake Yeltsin would soon regret. The drive to gather signatures for his nomination papers (one million were required by the 1995 law on presidential elections) was badly bungled. Railway and metallurgical workers were instructed by government officials to sign nominating petitions before collecting their pay at the wicket, and some governors were ordered to deliver signatures on quota.

Around February 1, Yeltsin asked his daughter Tatyana Dyachenko, age thirty-six, to sit in on meetings of the Soskovets group. Other than transcribing speeches and canvassing in his early campaigns, this was her first involvement in her father's politics. She was smart and resolute like her father but soft-spoken and unassuming like her mother. She had felt unfulfilled in the defense-related institute where she had worked for a decade and where she turned down a suggestion in the mid-1980s that she join the Communist Party (she said she did not know enough about politics and did not consider herself "worthy"), and in the bank where she was on staff in 1994–95: "My character is such that I for some reason tend to have inflated expectations of myself. And then it seems that each time I do not quite live up to them."[34] This time she was willing to heed her father's request.

Dyachenko was soon saying to Yeltsin that something was out of whack with the Soskovets effort.[35] But at first nothing much came of her efforts. It was then that Yeltsin's need to reconnect with the mass electorate intersected with the process of connecting differently with players at the elite level. Come what may, he had to empower a functional campaign staff and to appease other public politicians. A new presence in post-communist politics—the leaders of the nonstate business class that was beginning to amass fabulous wealth in the market economy—showed both tasks in a new light.

The Russian moguls were mostly in their thirties and forties, had been nobodies under Soviet power, and until the year before Yeltsin's re-election were mostly financiers who made money out of currency speculation, arbitrage, handling governmental deposits, and buying high-interest state debt. On August 31, 1995, Yeltsin had his first meeting with a group of them, about reserve requirements and other banking issues, and referred to the banks as having a political role. "Russian bankers," he told ten representatives, "take part in the country's political life. . . . The banks, like all of Russia, are learning democracy."[36] The loans-for-shares auctions in November–December 1995 allowed the more conspicuous of "the oligarchs," as they were now known, to reposition as captains of industry. Initially dreamt up by Vladimir Potanin of Oneximbank, this privatization scheme was backed by Chubais but also by Kremlin conservatives like Soskovets, who was the one to get Yeltsin's signature on it.[37] At bargain-basement prices, Potanin picked up Norilsk Nickel, the world's number one smelter of palladium and nickel, and he, Mikhail Khodorkovskii of Menatep, and Boris Berezovskii acquired the oil giants Sidanco, Yukos, and Sibneft. Two oligarchs also had extensive media interests and were bound to figure in the 1996 campaign: Vladimir Gusinskii of Most Bank was de jure the proprietor of NTV television; his rival Berezovskii had been de facto the moneyman behind the ORT network (formerly Ostankino) since 1994. Relations between Gusinskii and Berezovskii had always been testy, but they were willing in 1996 to set differences aside in order to protect their gains.

The one business figure on the Soskovets board was the hyperactive Berezovskii. He more than any of his colleagues was out to build status and influence in the political realm, to which end he had added to his portfolio the quality newspaper *Nezavisimaya gazeta*, the TV-6 entertainment network, and a one-third share in the Ogonëk publishing house. He had frequently offered advice, solicited and unsolicited, to Soskovets and Korzhakov, and lobbied for advantage. His path had crossed Yeltsin's in November or December 1993, when he and Vladimir Kadannikov volunteered to underwrite publication under the Ogonëk imprint of the Russian edition of volume two of Yeltsin's memoirs, in which Yeltsin was advanced 10 percent against the domestic royalties. Berezovskii first shook the president's hand when he went to his office to sign the contract. (The foreign rights, which brought in four or five times the revenue, were handled by the British literary agent Andrew Nurnberg.) In 1994 he was the first businessman to join the Presidential Club.[38] Berezovskii also knew Tatyana Dyachenko, though not yet much less cursorily than he knew her father. Korzhakov was to write in his 1997 memoir that at some time in 1994 or 1995 Berezovskii made her a present of two cars: a Russian-made Niva wagon and a Chevrolet Blazer. The claim was claptrap and is controverted by both Dyachenko and Berezovskii.[39] But the two were acquainted and had as a friend in common Valentin Yumashev, who had prepared both volumes of Yeltsin's memoirs for publication. In his professional life, Yumashev was deputy editor of *Ogonëk* magazine from 1991 to 1995 and director general of the Ogonëk company in 1995–96.[40]

It took only several meetings of the Soskovets group for Berezovskii to conclude that not all was well. From February 2 to 5, he and seventy other Russian capitalists and officials attended the World Economic Forum in Davos, Switzerland, where they were upset by the polite reception given to Gennadii Zyuganov, who had a bulge over Yeltsin in the polls. At Berezovskii's suggestion, Viktor Ilyushin arranged for Yeltsin to host an unpublicized Kremlin luncheon for six businessmen—Berezovskii, Gusinskii, Khodorkovskii, Potanin, Aleksandr Smolenskii of SBS-Agro Bank, and Vladimir Vinogradov of Inkombank—and Chubais, who had been Yeltsin's deputy for privatization until Yeltsin threw him to the wolves in January as a result of the Duma election. The meal was held about a fortnight after the Davos forum, in Shrovetide on the Russian calendar, and the chef served traditional fare for the season: pancakes with garnishes and drinks.[41] Yeltsin had thought the diners wanted to speak with him about campaign finance, since "they had nowhere to go and would have to support me," but the conversation was about the hopelessness of the Soviet-style effort under Soskovets. "I had not expected such tough talk," he was to write in *Presidential Marathon*.[42] Gusinskii and Chubais held nothing back. "Boris Nikolayevich," Chubais stated, "your popularity rating is zero." As usual when he was confronted by unlovely news, the meeting was marked by a long silence from the chair. One of the visitors, Khodorkovskii, thought "the tsar was thinking about whether to send of us all to the execution block"; another, Smolenskii, said in 2003 that "the pause was so loud that I hear it to this day."[43] The frank comments gave every appearance of shaking Yeltsin out of his apathy. Hesitating to catch his breath, he asked what they recommended. He promised after forty minutes of discussion to think about ways to energize the campaign and to involve Chubais and associates of big business in it. Berezovskii stayed to chat with Yeltsin briefly after the group dispersed.[44]

It is important to realize, though, that the dialogue with the magnates had no immediate effect.[45] Almost a month after the Kremlin meeting, on March 14, Yeltsin's political assistant, Georgii Satarov, and a group of consultants sent him a blistering memorandum noting that the campaign was still a shambles:

> [Soskovets] is not a specialist on public politics or electoral technologies, as immediately revealed itself. But this has not been offset by the possible merits on which you apparently were counting.
>
> Soskovets has displayed no organizational ability: The headquarters has not yet begun to work normally. He is unable to make contact with people who have a different point of view but are necessary to the campaign. His

> influence on the regional leadership has been exercised through vulgar and vain officiousness, which not only compromises you as president but turns off possible allies. The same methods are being employed, with the same result, with government agencies and with representatives of the mass media and of commercial and banking circles. The weirdest thing is that Soskovets has not resolved the problem of mobilizing in a short span of time the financial resources needed to wage the campaign. . . . More than a month has been lost.

Satarov urged Yeltsin to redo the organization while there was still time.[46]

I have no doubt that Yeltsin did not reorganize in February for a reason—because he had not yet resolved the bedrock dilemma of whether there should be a presidential election *at all.* The detonator here was a nonbinding resolution by the newly elected State Duma on March 15, 1996, to renounce the Supreme Soviet vote of December 12, 1991, on the Belovezh'e accord. Sponsored by the KPRF caucus and passed by a majority of 250 to ninety-eight, the vote asserted in effect that the Soviet Union and the legislation undergirding it still had legal force. Yeltsin reacted with indignation to an "attempt to liquidate our statehood" that "casts doubt on the legitimacy" of the new Russia and its political system.[47] Within twenty-four hours, the Korzhakov-Soskovets group, fearing a loss to the communists in the forthcoming election and sensing an opportunity to prevail in the palace struggle—where Korzhakov had not yet persuaded Yeltsin to make Soskovets prime minister and thus to put him in the line of succession—had come up with a proposal to postpone the presidential election until 1998, ban the KPRF, and shut down the Duma so as to rule by executive decree for the two years. The proposal took the postponement project entertained by Moscow democrats in 1994–95 and linked it to radically anti-democratic ends.[48]

Yeltsin at first bought into the idea. On the morning of March 17, he ordered his aides to draft implementing directives and law-enforcement officers to make operational plans. There were, even so, dissenting voices, and Yeltsin did not shut them out. Viktor Ilyushin, four of Yeltsin's liberal assistants, and Sergei Shakhrai said in a memorandum that they could not write a general decree because they could come up with no legal basis for it. Were one to be written and signed, they warned, Russia could be in for a civil war.[49] Anatolii Kulikov, the MVD minister who had led the ministry's troops in Chechnya in 1994–95, rallied the procurator general, Yurii Skuratov, and the chairman of the Constitutional Court, Vladimir Tumanov, to come out against the decision as unworkable, in part because his best soldiers were still embroiled in the North Caucasus. They saw him together in his office: "The president was really and truly glum. His complexion was sallow, he was ungracious. . . . He especially disliked that we had come as a threesome." "Minister, I am dissatisfied with you," Yeltsin spluttered. "A decree will follow shortly. Leave and prepare to implement it." Kulikov and two officers secured a second Kremlin meeting, at six A.M. sharp on Monday, March 18. Yeltsin was in a darker mood than the day before and would not shake hands with them; Kulikov could see on the presidential desk an unsigned decree dismissing him. Repeating that Yeltsin had no constitutional or moral case, he added that there was no evidence the army would back the president, and that the communists would go underground as martyrs for principle. "Yeltsin interrupted me and said, 'This is my affair and not yours.'" When Kulikov hung in, Yeltsin reminded him that "you are sitting in my office" and rebuked him for speaking on others' behalf. But the minister stuck to his guns, and Yeltsin showed signs of fickleness and allowed that the communists might have to be turned back "in stages."[50] President Clinton, alerted by Yegor Gaidar (who sent a message through Ambassador Thomas Pickering), had written Yeltsin a private letter about the need to hold the election on timetable.[51] Chernomyrdin and Yurii Luzhkov of Moscow were against the project as well.

But the greatest influences, according to Yeltsin, were not Kulikov or Clinton and not the oligarchs, with whom he had been out of contact. They were Tatyana Dyachenko and Anatolii Chubais. Tatyana secured an appointment with Yeltsin for Chubais, also on March 18, and Chubais for the one and only time in his years with Yeltsin raised the volume of his voice in protest. The one-hour meeting, Yeltsin said in his memoirs, made him feel "ashamed before those who had trusted me." He got in a poke at Chubais in the conversation—"You also made plenty of mistakes in privatization," he said. But he heeded the advice and that day dropped his ill-considered plan.[52] Blessedly for Russia and for his reputation, he had come to his senses—for which those who tar him with neo-Bolshevism give him not a granule of thanks. "The president," Kulikov writes accurately, "was wise enough to overstep himself and his character. He understood that the undertaking could end tragically and that some people were trying to use him."[53]

On March 19, the day after finally giving the election a green light, Yeltsin appointed a new campaign council, chaired by himself, with Viktor Chernomyrdin as deputy chairman. But his most consequential decision was to impanel an "analytical group" under Chubais, who had agreed to it at a rendezvous with the oligarchs in Berezovskii's Logovaz Club—an ideal place, Berezovskii chortled, because no one could bug it with listening devices except him. Chubais accepted several million dollars up front for campaign expenses, from which he was to deduct a monthly salary of $60,000. True to form, Yeltsin did not do away with the Soskovets grouping, whose senior members joined the council and which continued to occupy offices on a different floor of the Presidential Hotel. The nomination formalities, completed by April 5, were dealt with by an All-Russian Movement for Public Support of the President, an ecumenical front of 250 preexisting organizations headed up by Sergei Filatov, Yeltsin's former chief of staff. It stayed around to liaise with regional and local leaders, while another organization still, People's House, made connections to citizen groups and was the unofficial disburser of campaign funds.

The nerve center was the Chubais workshop, which, beginning about April 1, met five or six days a week, two to three hours at a time. Yeltsin sat in on a half-dozen of its meetings, although, knowing his aversion to collective decision making, members mostly went to see him singly or in pairs. The group took in the pollster Aleksandr Oslon, of the Public Opinion Foundation; Valentin Yumashev; presidential assistants Ilyushin and Satarov; Vasilii Shakhnovskii, chief of staff to Mayor Luzhkov; Igor Malashenko, the president of NTV, and Sergei Zverev, an executive in Media-Most, NTV's corporate parent; and Sergei Shakhrai, once deputy premier and now a Duma deputy. The tenth member was Tatyana Dyachenko. Casually dressed and in flowing bangs, she was never far from Yeltsin's side between then and the July runoff. She carried messages back and forth and advised on his grooming and the staging of campaign appearances. "On everything else," says an eyewitness, "she felt herself unprepared."[54]

Aleksandr Korzhakov, stung by Yeltsin's change of heart, traduced the new team and continued his efforts to abort the election, holding exploratory talks with Chernomyrdin, the KPRF leadership, and others. On April 16, in a lengthy meeting with the prime minister at the Presidential Club, he flattered Chernomyrdin and poked fun at the Chubais group (they were wet-behind-the-ears pupils and laboratory assistants), savaged Viktor Ilyushin for defecting to them ("Viktor has no ideas of his own"), and said the vote, if held, was winnable by only a few percentage points and would thus be illegitimate. Apparently getting some sympathy from Chernomyrdin, Korzhakov said again that the presidential election should be postponed by two years and, in a new kink, that the neo-communists should be brought into a coalition government to rule until then. "The chief himself will be against this idea," Korzhakov quotes himself as saying about Yeltsin, "but he can be broken."[55] In late April, in Khabarovsk, Korzhakov pulled aside Naina Yeltsina and asked her to deliver a letter to the chief. She was reluctant, since she stayed out of decisions of state, but gave Yeltsin the letter at Barvikha-4 upon their return. It touched on the election and argued that there was an urgent need to appoint Oleg Soskovets prime minister. Yeltsin read it and threw it in the wastebasket, an angry look on his face.[56] On May 5 Korzhakov, who rarely spoke with journalists, brazenly called in a press interview for a two-year deferral of the vote for stability's sake. The next day, with a beatific-looking Korzhakov behind him, Yeltsin informed the press that the election would be held without fail and that he had ordered his chief bodyguard "not to meddle in politics." "I trust in the wisdom of the Russian voters," he said. "That's why the election will be held in the time determined by the constitution."[57]

Yeltsin took some time to make his peace with the re-election assignment and with having to ask the people on bended knee for what he had come to see as rightfully his, so unlike the cakewalks of 1989, 1990, and 1991. By the time he made his first forays into the heartland, he had modified his posture. What tipped him were recognition of the novelty of the quest, the alacrity of the Chubais group, and the clicking in of his personal testing script: "He caught fire. . . . He assimilated it as a new game for himself. . . . He was the ideal candidate. It had all begun to be attractive to him. He could not get enough of it."[58]

The principal adversary was Gennadii Zyuganov, who had chaired the KPRF since its founding in 1993. Zyuganov, a propaganda specialist in his home province of Orël and in Moscow before 1991, epitomized the gray apparatchik who had kept faith with state socialism. Presenting himself as the voice of "responsible opposition" and of "popular-patriotic forces" that went beyond his party, he charged that Yeltsin had not kept a single promise since he beat out Nikolai Ryzhkov for the presidency five years before. He advocated constitutional changes to strengthen parliament and reintroduce the office of vice president (Yeltsin's former vice president, Aleksandr Rutskoi, supported Zyuganov), appointment of a medical commission to review the health of leaders (an obvious dig at Yeltsin), settlement of back wages, measures "to guarantee all citizens the right to labor, leisure, housing, free education and medical care, and a worthy old age," and a review of privatization policy.[59]

The two principal combatants were joined by a piebald field of eight lesser contestants. Two were put forward by political parties that had standing in the Duma: Vladimir Zhirinovskii, the publicity hound and head of the scrappily imperialist LDPR; and Grigorii Yavlinskii of the liberal Yabloko Party, an economist by training and one of the authors of the Five Hundred Days Program in 1990. The semiforgotten Mikhail Gorbachev chose to run for the office that Yeltsin had used to destroy his power base, describing himself as Russia's candidate of "consolidation." The most serious of the independent candidates was Aleksandr Lebed, a gravel-voiced professional soldier from the Soviet military's airborne branch who had retired from the service as a two-star general in 1995. Lebed's defense of the Slavic minorities in post-Soviet Moldova, as commander of the Russian Fourteenth Army there, gave him cachet with nationalists, and his platform emphasized law and order. The four remaining candidates ran as personalities, although nominated by tiny political organizations: Vladimir Bryntsalov, a businessman who had made millions in the pharmaceuticals industry; Svyatoslav Fëdorov, the eye surgeon whom Yeltsin had tried to make prime minister in 1991; Martin Shakkum, a think-tank scholar; and Yurii Vlasov, once a world-champion weightlifter and now a Duma deputy and Russian chauvinist.[60]

Yeltsin and his administration did nothing to impede the registration of other candidates but did try hard to persuade several of them to drop out in his favor or at a minimum not to come together into a potential "third force" in the campaign. The priorities were Lebed, whose curt, masculine deportment was selling well,[61] and Yavlinskii. Since Yeltsin knew from polls that Lebed would draw first-round votes away from Zyuganov, the objective was to gain his cooperation in the two-candidate runoff, Zyuganov against Yeltsin, that was expected to follow. Lebed initiated the contact secretly and met in April with Aleksandr Korzhakov. Korzhakov offered him command of Russian airborne forces, saying he did not know enough about the economy to succeed in politics, and Lebed declined, with the statement, "I know my price."[62] Lebed called on Yeltsin in the Kremlin on May 2 and the negotiations restarted. Within several weeks, the general agreed to throw his support to the president in the second round; he would get an infusion of campaign funds in the first round and appointment as minister of defense after it.[63] Aleksandr Oslon's research showed Yavlinskii as competing for votes with Yeltsin, not Zyuganov, and suggested that his supporters would migrate naturally to Yeltsin in the second round, so it was desirable to knock him out of round one. Negotiations through intermediaries began in January, and Yavlinskii met with Yeltsin on May 5 and 16. The older man "entreated, browbeat, pressured, and buttered up" the younger to throw in the towel and accept the position of first deputy premier; Yavlinskii demanded the dismissal of Chernomyrdin and other points Yeltsin found unacceptable. "I would not have withdrawn, either," Yeltsin told him as he showed him to the door in Building No. 1 on May 16.[64]

Bare-knuckle tactics were deployed in other areas, too. Chernomyrdin assigned a deputy premier, Yurii Yarov, to work daily with the campaign staff and see to it that the federal bureaucracy used "administrative levers" as best it could to the president's gain. Sergei Shakhrai handled relations with the governors and republic presidents, most of whom swung into line.[65] The Kremlin collected explicit endorsements, among them from dignitaries (such as Yegor Gaidar) who had split with Yeltsin, and unformalized support from the Russian Orthodox Church and the military hierarchy. The mass media, and especially the three national television channels, on which paid advertising for the candidates opened on May 14, were of special concern. The ORT and RTR networks were owned by the state; NTV was privately owned and had been very critical of the war in Chechnya, but it broadcast on sufferance of Yeltsin's government. And yet, coercion was not the primary reason the media sided with Yeltsin in 1996. Since the alternatives appeared to boil down to him or a return of the communists who had censored the press for seventy years, it seemed to most journalists and media managers, as Igor Malashenko put it, that "damaging" as it might have been for the press to take sides in a political conflict, its corporate self-interest meant it "did not have any choice" in the matter. Malashenko remained as president of NTV while moonlighting as Yeltsin's chief media adviser. Although he considered resigning or going on leave from the network, "I believed this would have been just cant, because everybody in Russia would know that this is not the United States, that my position in the [NTV] group would be the same."[66] Between mid-May and mid-June, 55 percent of all campaign stories on ORT's nightly prime-time news mentioned Yeltsin, compared to 35 percent mentions for Zyuganov; on NTV's program, it was 59 percent and 34 percent.[67]

None of these methods, however, was enough to dictate victory. Yeltsin was not able to oust Yavlinskii, and the backing from Lebed would take effect only in a runoff round. The electronic and print media had been skewed toward Our Home Is Russia in 1995, and that had not done the party or Chernomyrdin much good.[68] A great many citizens distrusted the news media and did not believe them to be even-handed; almost 40 percent of Russians had questions about coverage of the 1995 Duma campaign and more than 50 percent about the 1996 presidential campaign.[69] Even with the media elite's bias toward Yeltsin, the flow of information and advocacy that got through to individual voters was quite large and diverse. Paid ads aside, a lottery gave all candidates eight free ten-minute slots on national television. As of the beginning of June, a non-trivial 45 percent of the population had been exposed to Zyuganov campaign materials on television, on the radio, or in print in the preceding week; for Yeltsin, it was 58 percent.[70] And news bulletins, particularly on NTV, offered substantial reportage on opposition candidates (mostly by replaying their words) and on issues, such as economic difficulties and Yeltsin's health, that were inconvenient for the president.[71]

From his single-digit popularity in January, Yeltsin rebounded to a plurality of the votes in June and a second-round majority in July. In Aleksandr Oslon's first systematic poll of the electorate on March 1, 13 percent of Russians intending to vote in the first round preferred Yeltsin and 19 percent Zyuganov. Over the course of March and April, Yeltsin's anticipated vote share doubled while Zyuganov's only edged up. The first Oslon poll to show Yeltsin ahead of Zyuganov, by 23 percent to 22 percent, was on April 13, but they were tied on April 20 and again on May 4. On May 11 Yeltsin nosed ahead by 4 points, by 28 percent to 24 percent, and he never looked back after that. By June 11, 36 percent of citizens intended to vote for him and Zyuganov's expected share had dipped to 18 percent.[72] The spread narrowed some by election day, but any way you look at it was a blockbuster recovery. And it was achieved in all demographic subgroups, be they by age, community size and location, gender, or social class.[73]

One device whereby Yeltsin could overcome his initial deficit in public opinion was to employ incumbency to bolster his image, shape the campaign agenda, and offer amends for the deficiencies of the previous five years. Even before declaring his candidacy, he issued the first of a string of edicts directing material assistance to target groups. On January 25 he decreed a 50 percent increase in payments to recipients of old-age, survivor, and invalid pensions above the minimum pension. Another decree raised grants for students in universities and institutes by 20 percent. On February 1 he ordered stricter schedules for payment of wages to public-sector workers, including the military and police. Orders to clear up arrears in the non-state sector were given the next week.

The foreign-policy realm offered opportunities for reputation building. Bill Clinton had agreed in 1995 to hold off on NATO enlargement until after the election, responding to Yeltsin's plea that "my position heading into 1996 is not exactly brilliant."[74] Chancellor Helmut Kohl of Germany visited Yeltsin on February 20, four days after his statement of candidacy, and pronounced him "the best president for Russia." Kohl, it is claimed, offered Yeltsin political asylum in Germany should he lose the election, a suggestion Yeltsin found insulting.[75] In March the IMF unveiled a $10.2 billion loan to the Russian government, the second-largest it had ever made. On April 2 Yeltsin signed an agreement with President Aleksandr Lukashenko of Belarus to create a "community" of the post-Soviet neighbors. The document opened, he said, "a qualitatively new stage in the history of our two brotherly peoples." National television broadcast the Kremlin event live. On April 20 the G-7 leaders were in town for a joint meeting with Russia, chaired by Yeltsin, on nuclear security. It was done, according to President Clinton's deputy secretary of state, Strobe Talbott, "for no other purpose than to give Yeltsin a pre-election boost." A meeting at Spaso House with opposition candidates was on Clinton's itinerary. "It's okay to shake hands with Zyuganov, Bill," Yeltsin said, "but don't kiss him."[76] Summiteers Clinton, Jacques Chirac of France, and Ryutaro Hashimoto of Japan stayed on an extra day for bilateral talks and photo ops. Several days later Yeltsin was off to China for a state visit. On May 16 UN Secretary General Boutros Boutros Ghali helpfully paid his respects in Moscow, and on May 17 a summit of CIS leaders did the same. James D. Wolfensohn of the World Bank stopped by the Kremlin on May 23 to announce a $500 million project for the coal industry. "The timing of the loan is purely coincidental," he said with a straight face. "But I was happy to do it in support of the government's reform efforts."[77]

A security issue of domestic scope where again incumbency could be applied was the quagmire in Chechnya. With one eye on the opinion polls, Yeltsin on March 31 announced a presidential "peace initiative" designed by his adviser Emil Pain, still claiming there could be no direct negotiations with the separatist president, Djokhar Dudayev. The killing of Dudayev on April 21 (he was hit by a Russian missile while talking on a satellite phone to a member of the State Duma) removed that obstacle, and Yeltsin signaled he was willing to meet the new Chechen leadership. On May 27 a deputation of five fighters, flown to Moscow with their bodyguards in a presidential aircraft, was ushered into a Kremlin office. Swiss diplomat Tim Guldimann of the Organization for Security and Cooperation in Europe attended to help mediate. Zelimkhan Yandarbiyev, the leader of the team—a former poet and children's author, he was attired in green battle fatigues and a *papakha,* the Chechens' tall, flat-topped lambskin hat—argued with Yeltsin about seating order, with Yeltsin insisting he be at the head of the table. Yandarbiyev said he might have to pull out of the talks. Yeltsin first told the guards to seal the doors, then asked Guldimann to take his place and sat down across from the Chechen. Yeltsin next sought to gain the upper hand by acting the part of the masterful host. "As an experienced administrator, he knew that in such cases it is best to obtain a psychological advantage over the opposing side. The quickest way to get it is to find a pretense for an earboxing. 'I do not understand,' he said in an ice-cold voice. 'Nobody has ever had the nerve to be late for a meeting with me. You got here late. I could have scrapped our meeting if I felt like it.' Yandarbiyev shook and made apologies."[78] After the conclusion of their conversation, Chernomyrdin stepped in to work out an agreement with Yandarbiyev on a truce in the war, effective midnight May 31, to be followed by an exchange of prisoners and negotiations for a peace settlement. Off-camera, Yeltsin growled that if the Chechens did not honor their commitments, "We know how to find everyone who has signed this document."[79]

The next day Yeltsin flew to Grozny, pushing aside a warning by officers from the security services, whom he called cowards, that Shamil Basayev's hawkish group was going to assassinate him by shooting down the presidential helicopter with a U.S.-made Stinger missile. To preempt objections from Naina, he told her he was going to spend the day in the Kremlin. He was accompanied by Governor Boris Nemtsov of Nizhnii Novgorod, who a few months before had presented him with a million signatures from the Volga area protesting the war.[80] Yeltsin signed two ancillary decrees in the republic, one of them on the steel frame of an armored personnel carrier. Every minute of his six hours there was mined for visuals and sound bites for the final weeks of the election campaign. Aleksandr Oslon's interviewers found in early June that two-thirds of the electorate approved of Yeltsin's peace initiative.[81]

The second way Yeltsin promoted his candidacy was to bifurcate the electorate around the paradigmatic question of choice of regime and to give the vote the properties of a referendum, in all but name, on communism versus democracy. This was the question Yeltsin had posed with such science during his rise to power, only augmented now with the prospect that any attempt to restore communism would put Russia through one more revolution.

Yeltsin's experience in the Kremlin, reasoned a confidential analysis for the campaign in April, should be made to count in his favor, and it should be coupled with the point that "nothing except instability and unpredictability can be expected" from the other candidates.[82] In 1995 and early 1996, another memorandum laid out in May, Russians mostly asked who should answer for the country's plight. "But with the approach of the election the question, 'Who is guilty?' began to be replaced by the question, 'What will it be like after the election?' For the majority of the population, the future election is connected with the choice of *the lesser of two evils.* The main motive here is turning out to be to escape shakeups after the election."[83]

The self-criticism in Yeltsin's rhetoric was an invitation to opponents and doubters to cross the line into his camp. Mistakes had been made in the design of the reforms, he said on April 6. "We from the very beginning undervalued the importance of constant dialogue with citizens." Many Russians had not yet benefited from the post-communist changes, he conceded, and there had arisen "parasitic capital," which concentrated on the division of property rather than economic growth. But it would be very different in a second Yeltsin term. Russia, he stated, would have a 5 percent economic growth rate within two or three years, and the fruits would be spread around more fairly.[84]

Television ads to expand on Yeltsin's speeches were prepared by Video International, Russia's largest TV advertising agency, with advice from the U.S. public-relations firm Ogilvy and Mather—whose 1996 clients included Dresdner Bank, American Express, Unilever, and Telefonica—and from other American and British consultants. Forty-five short ads on the theme "I Believe, I Love, I Hope" ran two or three per evening. Laymen selected to represent a type (farmer, doctor, housewife, athlete, student, and so forth) spoke soothingly about the future in store if Yeltsin got his second mandate. In one of the first to air, a World War II veteran "looks straight into the camera and says wistfully, 'I just want my children and grandchildren to finally savor the fruits of the victory we fought for and that they didn't let us enjoy.' 'They' is a not-so-subliminal reference to communists."[85] A related series of "Choose or Lose" clips and rock concerts were aimed at getting younger citizens to turn out to vote. At the same time, anticommunist videos, posters, and billboards represented the Soviet regime in a harsh light, through representations of labor camps, bare store shelves, and overage Politburo members reviewing parades on Lenin's tomb. Borderline demagogic as the line was, it served Yeltsin's electoral purpose admirably. Of men and women who preferred the post-Soviet political system, almost 70 percent backed Yeltsin on June 16 and fewer than 10 percent voted for Zyuganov; among backers of the Soviet polity, the proportions were reversed.[86]

A third vote-getting technique was hinged on Boris Yeltsin's persona. The candidate in this mode would be presented as a father figure, rugged and knowing but also suffering and recovering with his people. A gauzy "Vote with Your Heart" ad series was unrolled in May, after extensive survey and focus-group research. As Yeltsin noted in a memoir, "Humble people were shown speaking on the television screen what they thought of me. . . . Interest in the president's personality rose. The people were surprised and started thinking . . . [and] woke up. . . . 'Look at the new Yeltsin [they said], he has come alive, he is up to something, so maybe we should bet on him again!'"[87] In the closing days of the campaign, an ad was aired showing Yeltsin musing about his youth and his courtship of Naina Yeltsina, to the accompaniment of schmaltzy music. To improve her husband's image, Naina gave press interviews about their children, grandchildren, and family life. A mass-distributed photo album and documentary film shots showed the president bone tired, elated, and frustrated and pictured his thumbless left hand, which he normally did his best to conceal.

This strand of the re-election campaign must be judged a qualified success. In-depth survey data from the summer of 1996 show majorities reckoning Yeltsin to be intelligent and possessed of a vision of Russia's future, while opinion on his strength and trustworthiness split evenly. On one character trait, though, Yeltsin continued to get consistently critical assessments. That trait was empathy, where respondents were asked if Yeltsin "really cares about people like you." Only one person in four agreed with that statement, and responses were closely correlated with economic assessments.[88] That explains the seriousness with which the Yeltsin campaign took its fourth objective—to find ways to bring him down from his lordly perch to relate to Russia's transitional citizens as human beings.

The greening of Yeltsin could be attempted through the electronic advertising blitz and through creative use of incumbency. In the latter capacity, Yeltsin played Santa Claus for a solid half-year, ladling out material and symbolic largesse to well-selected segments of the populace. The economic payout was brought about by administrative discipline and legerdemain, use of foreign credits, and borrowing against future revenues. In January, February, and March, Yeltsin signed seven or eight decrees per month allocating concrete benefits to particular constituencies; the number hit twenty-two in April and thirty-four in May and the first two weeks of June.[89] Although many of his acts of generosity were in response to requests, "Often Yeltsin was the inspirer of the decrees, which . . . grew copiously in the election season. He felt an especially sharp need for them in May. Getting his assistants together, he would demand from them 'fresh ideas for decrees.'"[90]

Responding to Yeltsin's January and February directives and to dogged pressure from the government and the presidential executive office, back wages in the nonstate sector were paid up by early April; in the state sector, a large improvement was made by early May. National-level initiatives in social spending raised pensions for war veterans and other elders, allowances for single mothers and diabetics, and salaries and summer pay for teachers and scientists; ordered restitution for bank depositors whose savings were made worthless by hyperinflation in 1992; and instituted a loan program for house builders. Other decrees singled out aerospace contractors, the agrarian complex, and small businesses. In the symbolic domain, there was something for almost everybody. Several decrees recognized the rights of Cossack communities shattered by the communists. In April Yeltsin ruled that a Soviet-style red banner (adorned with a gold star in place of the communist hammer-and-sickle) would fly alongside the Russian tricolor at patriotic observances, while having the Presidential Regiment fitted out in splendid new dress uniforms recalling the tsar's guard force before 1917.[91] In a sop to youth, he decreed on May 16 that Russia would have an all-volunteer army and conscription would be ended by 2000.

The biggest contribution of Igor Malashenko was to convince Yeltsin of the need for direct communication with the public. This was a way to both go beyond mediated contact and supply raw material for circulation in the mass media. In one of their first meetings, Malashenko told Yeltsin the story of how George H. W. Bush had profited politically from his dropping in at a New Jersey flag factory during the 1988 campaign against Michael Dukakis. Yeltsin needed scenes like that, Malashenko said, and would have to generate one headline per day that could be associated with him personally. "He grasped it at once," Malashenko recalled. "I never had a reason to complain because, although his health was waning, he did incredible things. He made news every day."[92] It took several weeks for Yeltsin to grasp that he had to make contact locally and in the flesh. He wended his way through the Belgorod area south of Moscow in the first week of April and then through

Krasnodar and Budënnovsk, the site of the 1995 terror incident, in mid-April. In Krasnodar Yeltsin stood behind a line of guards, with silent people kept at a distance. Malashenko and Chubais showed him photographs of the scene and contrasted it to his barnstorming in 1989–91. On his next field trip, to Khabarovsk in the Russian Far East (where he dropped in on his way to Beijing), Yeltsin hoofed it into the crowd and "it produced a whole different image."[93]

May 3 found Yeltsin in Yaroslavl, on the Volga north of Moscow. The next week he alighted in Volgograd and Astrakhan on the lower Volga, and the week after that in central Siberia. The northern reaches of European Russia and the Urals followed at the end of May, and then came Tver, Kazan, two jaunts into the North Caucasus, west Siberia, Nizhnii Novgorod and the middle Volga, St. Petersburg, and, for a curtain call, Yekaterinburg on June 14. On May 9, for Victory Day over Nazi Germany, Yeltsin addressed the parade in Moscow's Red Square. He then jetted to Volgograd, the former Stalingrad, to speak a second time at Mamayev Kurgan, the tumulus looking out over the Volga that bears a towering statue of Mother Russia. It was dusk, and people lit candles and flashlights. Press secretary Sergei Medvedev stood next to him: "I could sense that he was stirred up, as if by the common breathing of thousands of people. He had with him some prepared materials but threw them away and spoke effusively. . . . The people accepted him and cried out. . . . It was as if the air was electric, and he could feel it."[94] The kinder, gentler Yeltsin jested with well-wishers and asked if they had questions for him, kissed ladies' hands, and laid wreaths at statues and war memorials. Cordless microphone in hand, he forged through town squares, cathedrals, produce markets, army barracks, pig farms, fish hatcheries, foundries, and coal mines. During an interlude by musicians in Ufa on May 30, he did the twist: "Quite a plucky little twist it was, too, complete with swaying hips, flapping elbows, and upper teeth bared over lower lip. The 10,000 kids . . . went wild." After Yeltsin waved and left the stage, Andrei Makarevich, lead singer of the rock group Time Machine, which had been kept off the radio under Brezhnev (and which performed before the Moscow White House in August 1991), urged them to vote for Yeltsin "so Time Machine can keep on playing."[95] On June 10 at a concert by the pop singer Yevgenii Osin in a stadium in Rostov, on the Don River, Yeltsin called on the standing-room-only audience to "vote as you should" so they could all "live in a free Russia," and then doffed his suit jacket and boogie-woogied with Osin and two miniskirted female vocalists.

No campaign event was complete without gifts large and small. The aim was to give a foretaste of the eventual benefits of reform and to underline the candidate's responsiveness. As each day on the hustings was planned out the evening before, staffers asked *Chto podarim zavtra?*—"What shall we hand out tomorrow?"[96] The city of Yaroslavl provided a typical backcloth, as the *New York Times* correspondent described:

> President Boris N. Yeltsin was in a beneficent, spendthrift mood on the campaign trail today. He promised a Tatar leader he met on the street $50,000 to open a new Muslim cultural center here. He visited a convent of the Russian Orthodox Church and gave $10,000 from the treasury to help cover the nuns' housekeeping costs. . . . He even vowed to have a telephone installed for a woman who complained that she had been waiting for telephone service for eight years. . . .
>
> But it was at an afternoon encounter with more than thirty local officials, factory directors, and local newspaper editors that Mr. Yeltsin disclosed the risks he is prepared to take in his effort to remain in the Kremlin. . . . Several local officials stood up to complain that taxes were strangling their companies and factories. They begged Mr. Yeltsin to restore a tax break that was introduced in 1994 to help ailing industries burdened by tax debts. . . . Under pressure from the IMF, the Russian government phased out the loophole last year. . . .
>
> [Vladimir] Panskov, the finance minister [of Russia] argued against the loophole] in the middle of the meeting. . . .
>
> Mr. Yeltsin turned to his audience. "The government is definitely against this," he said. "Can any of you, specialists, economists, think of another way out?"
>
> When they cried "No!" Mr. Yeltsin turned back to his finance minister, who stood waiting, wearing a pained expression. "Before the election," the president instructed him with a smile, "let's submit a decree."
>
> Everyone in the room applauded except Mr. Panskov.[97]

In the Siberian center of Krasnoyarsk on May 17, Yeltsin jibed to residents that he had thrown a coin into the Yenisei River for luck, "but you should not think that this will be the end of my financial help to the Krasnoyarsk region."[98] On a stopover at the White Sea port of Arkhangelsk on May 24, he proclaimed that he had arrived "with full pockets." "Today a little money will be coming into Arkhangelsk oblast."[99] Having announced grants to local building projects there, he belted along to a meet-and-run in Vorkuta, a coal-mining center near the mouth of the Ob, where he committed to assistance for the construction of retirement homes in the south, a 50 percent reduction in rail tariffs on coal from the area—and, to miner Lidiya Denisyuk, whom he encountered underground, a Zhiguli car for her disadvantaged family.[100] In Chechnya on May 28 with Boris Nemtsov, he asked the governor to deliver Gazelle trucks and Volga cars to Chechen farmers from the GAZ plant in Nizhnii Novgorod. In Ufa on May 30, Yeltsin marked the beginning of preparatory construction work for its new subway. In Kazan on June 9, wearing a *tyuboteika,* a needlepointed Tatar skullcap, he promised to finance a subway; city and republic had been pushing for one since 1983. Elsewhere, the handouts included tractors and combines for kolkhozes, discounts on electricity costs, forgiveness of municipal debts, funds for reconstructing and enlarging libraries and clinics, and power-sharing pacts with governors and republic presidents (twelve of these were finalized during the campaign).

Promises made on the stump would be promises to keep afterward. The unrealism of some of those offered in 1996 was not lost on the craftsmen. They chose to subordinate this point to the realpolitik of winning in the here and now. The populist decree on ending the military draft by 2000 was a case in point. To write it, Yeltsin had to overrule the generals and his national security adviser, Yurii Baturin, who counseled that out of practical considerations the draft could not be dispensed with before 2005. Baturin refused to sign off on the draft edict, whereupon Nikolai Yegorov, the president's new chief of staff—a conservative with good ties to the army—telephoned to say it would go ahead without him. "Now it is necessary to win the election, and after that we will look into it."[101] Russia today still has conscription.

Yeltsin's last election campaign was a catch-all campaign. Vitalii Tret'yakov, the editor-in-chief of *Nezavisimaya gazeta,* saw in his plan of attack the philosophy of Luka, the picaresque codger in the play *The Lower Depths,* by Maxim Gorky. "Ni odna blokha ne plokha," Luka quipped to his fellow boarding-house residents—"Every flea is a good flea," as they are all dark in color and they all know how to jump. "Yeltsin-Luka lets everyone gallop away" to their heart's content, editorialized Tret'yakov; mixing metaphors, he added that the Yeltsin team had vacuumed up everyone else's ideas and taken "one million positions on one hundred questions." He was being somewhat unkind, for Yeltsin was consistent on some higher-order political questions, such as whether or not to let the communists return, while picking his openings on many lower-order questions. But Tret'yakov also noted that to Yeltsin's million positions his opponents had been "unable to counterpoise clear and legible positions on even ten key problems."[102]

Tret'yakov's editorial came out on May 7. Seventy-five million participating voters had their say on Sunday, June 16. Yeltsin took 26,665,495 votes. It was some 19 million fewer than he had received in 1991 but still put him in first place, with 36 percent of the ballots. Zyuganov had 32 percent, Lebed 15 percent, Yavlinskii 7 percent, and Zhirinovskii 6 percent. Everyone else trailed with less than 1 percent. In his final indignity at Yeltsin's hands, Mikhail Gorbachev took one-half of 1 percent—386,069 votes. While bleeding strength compared to 1991 in every macroregion of Russia, Yeltsin carried forty-six of the provinces and Zyuganov forty-three. Yeltsin did better than average in the northern and northwestern sections of European Russia, Moscow, the Urals, and Siberia; he was weakest in the red belt south of Moscow and in the North Caucasus.

And so Yeltsin and Zyuganov found themselves in a sudden-death second round, with voting to occur on Wednesday, July 3, a workday. The strategy of the Yeltsin camp, aided by the electoral format, was simple—to distill everything to the toggle choice of forward on the historical continuum or backward. At the level of tactics, it dichotomized the decision as expertly as a fisherman filleting a trout. The choice could not be clearer, he stated on June 17. "Either back, to revolutions and turmoil, or ahead, to stability and prosperity."[103] National television obliged by airing documentaries about the Gulag, the hounding of dissidents, and economic stagnation under the Soviets.[104]

Two political melodramas unfolded overtly in the seventeen days between ballots. On June 18, as agreed in May, the third-finishing Aleksandr Lebed issued a statement endorsing Yeltsin. The price had gone up, as he was offered and accepted the position of secretary of the Security Council and assistant to the president for national security. Yeltsin relatedly dismissed his defense minister, Pavel Grachëv, who had once been Lebed's commanding officer, and replaced him several weeks later with Igor Rodionov, an older general in whom Lebed had confidence. On June 20 a funding scandal pushed relations between Yeltsin and the clique around Aleksandr Korzhakov to the breaking point. The day before, officers in Korzhakov's guard service had arrested Sergei Lisovskii and Arkadii Yevstaf'ev, two staffers to the Chubais team, on the steps of the White House and confiscated a half-million dollars in cash that was part of the funding stream for the campaign. When Chubais and Tatyana Dyachenko intervened, Yeltsin fired Korzhakov, Oleg Soskovets, and Mikhail Barsukov, a move that accented his decisiveness and innovativeness.[105]

Another drama, playing out covertly, was about the incumbent's medical condition, which had been abraded by stress, travel, and twelve-hour workdays. On June 23, midway between the two halves of the election, Yeltsin was hit with chest pains while on a whistle stop in Russia's Baltic enclave of Kaliningrad. On June 26, resting at Barvikha-4, he was stricken with a fourth heart attack. His presiding physician, Anatolii Grigor'ev, was in the room and revived and medicated him. The seizure was kept secret and Yeltsin's disappearance written off to a head cold. NTV's president, Igor Malashenko, knew Yeltsin was in a bad way, if not the details, yet kept information about his condition out of the news. As he told me, he would have preferred "the corpse of Yeltsin" to Zyuganov alive.[106] On June 28 Yeltsin somehow bulled ahead with a meeting with Lebed on Chechnya. The klieg lights were shining and television cameras were whirring, but the scene was staged by staffers in a room of the Barvikha sanatorium, with them and the medical attendants edited out of the videotape.[107] All campaign appearances were canceled. Viktor Chernomyrdin read out a greeting to several thousand farm workers in the Kremlin Palace of Congresses, who had gathered to hear the president. It did not sit well, and by Chubais's estimate Yeltsin was losing 1 or 2 percentage points in the polls every day.[108] On July 3 it was all Yeltsin could do to take several steps with his wife and hand in a ballot slip at the polling station located in the sanatorium.

Irrespective of the fears, voting in the runoff went very much as planned. Yeltsin received 40,208,384 votes, about five million fewer than in 1991 but enough to outpoll Zyuganov by 54 percent to 41 percent. He carried fifty-seven of eighty-nine provinces, bettering his 1991 numbers in scattered oblasts and a number of the minority republics, losing strength in the red belt and the Muslim republics of the North Caucasus, and holding his own elsewhere. In between rounds, Yeltsin's share of the popular vote went up 19 percentage points and Zyuganov's by only 8 points. Division around the question of returning to communism or escaping it was more complete than in the opening round: 90-plus percent of those who favored the new political system voted for Yeltsin; 80 percent of those who wanted to re-create the communist system went for Zyuganov. Healthy majorities of the first-round supporters of the non-communist candidates other than Zhirinovskii went for the president now that their top choices were out of the game: 57 percent of the Lebed voters, 67 percent of Yavlinskii voters, 30 percent of Zhirinovskii voters, and 57 percent of those who had voted for the lightweight candidates.[109]

Yeltsin had rejuvenated himself politically just as he was failing corporeally. He entered his second term as Russia's leader under contradictory stars, one of them encouraging and the other pointing in a discouraging direction. The night of July 3, family and friends gave him teary hugs and flowers. He had accomplished "a fantastic, surprising victory." He wished he could dance a jig, and one suspects he would not have been averse to some liquid refreshment, but these were beyond him: "I lay in my hospital bed and gazed tensely at the ceiling."[110] Right he was to be tense. The game hereafter was about Yeltsin trying to resume Russia's progress while grappling with grievous physical limitations and with power parameters that had changed subtly and unsubtly from those of his first term.

Chapter Fifteen

Autumn of a President

President Yeltsin's fourth proven heart attack, on June 26, 1996, was the most invasive to date and came on the heels of indication after indication that he was at the end of his rope.[1] The consilium of ten physicians watching over him during the campaign had sent a letter to Aleksandr Korzhakov on May 20 warning of "changes of a negative character" in his state of health, the result of "the mounting burdens on him, physically and emotionally," and of his sleep allotment dwindling to three or four hours a night. "Such a work regimen poses a real threat to the health *and life* of the president." The Yeltsins were apprised of the findings, although Korzhakov inexplicably withheld the letter.[2] El'dar Ryazanov, filming a conversation for broadcast, found Yeltsin on June 2 "a whole other man" than the last time they spoke, in November 1993: sallow-complected, careworn, and churlish. Had a rival obtained the unedited footage of the interview, Ryazanov is sure Yeltsin would never have been re-elected. "When I left, I was disheartened. I thought to myself, My God, if he wins, in whose hands will Russia find itself?"[3] He still voted for Yeltsin.

The second inauguration, on August 9, was low-key, in contrast to July 1991. Plans for another inaugural address went by the boards. The event was moved indoors into the Kremlin Palace of Congresses instead of Cathedral Square, in the sunlight. Onstage, looking pudgy but frail, Yeltsin swore the oath in forty-five seconds, his hand on a bound copy of the constitution and his eyes on a teleprompter primed to help him notice the pauses. The speaker of the upper house of parliament, Yegor Stroyev, slipped the presidential chain of office around his neck.[4] It was done within sixteen minutes:

> Knowing his condition, Boris Yeltsin was extremely nervous. But once awareness set in that it was all behind him, that he been installed in office again, it was as if he had gotten a second wind. After the official ceremony, attendees at the state reception were surprised to see quite a different person. He entered the hall briskly, made a brief but animated toast, and even chatted up several guests. After about a half hour, he left. It was obvious to everyone who witnessed the official start to Yeltsin's second presidential term that the ill-health of the leader was now a basic factor in Russian politics.[5]

On July 16 Yeltsin appointed Anatolii Chubais, his campaign mastermind, as presidential chief of staff, sending Nikolai Yegorov, a political soulmate of the demoted Korzhakov, back to Krasnodar as governor.[6] The press dubbed Chubais Russia's "regent." For prime minister, Yeltsin stayed with the old pro Viktor Chernomyrdin, whom the State Duma confirmed uncomplainingly on August 10.

The theme of the next half year was apolitical—Yeltsin's fight for elementary survival and recovery. Injections of a clot-dissolving drug eased unstable angina in July. After the induction, a battery of tests, beginning with the coronary angiogram he had refused in 1995 (an X-ray of the heart arteries, using iodized liquid), was done at the Moscow Cardiology Center. German surgeons tapped by Helmut Kohl advised from afar that the Russians consider an arterial bypass and have it done abroad. The conferences with the family were awkward, as Yevgenii Chazov, the director of the Moscow center, was the one who, as USSR health minister, had supervised Yeltsin's care on behalf of the Politburo after the 1987 secret speech. Some of the medicos feared Yeltsin would not withstand a multiple bypass operation and were hopeful he could get away with balloon angioplasty. Chazov thought the risk was "colossal" but Yeltsin had to chance it.[7] The blood ejection fraction from the left ventricle, a standard index of operating efficiency, was 22 percent; a healthy person's is 55 to 75 percent. Without an intervention, Chazov and his deputies gauged the life expectancy of someone with these symptoms to be one and a half to two years. The choice, they told the family, was either bypass surgery or curtailment of Yeltsin's activities to several

Exchanging pens with George H. W. Bush after initialing a strategic arms pact, Washington, June 17, 1992. (DMITRII DONSKOI.)

Members of Yeltsin's governing team, autumn 1992. Left to right: Yegor Gaidar, acting prime minister; Yurii Skokov, secretary of the Security Council; Vice President Aleksandr Rutskoi; Aleksandr Korzhakov, chief of the Presidential Security Service. (DMITRII DONSKOI.)

With Ruslan Khasbulatov, chairman of the Supreme Soviet, in 1992. (DMITRII DONSKOI.)

With long-serving Prime Minister Viktor Chernomyrdin, January 1996. (AP IMAGES.)

Wielding the tennis racket, June 1992. (DMITRII DONSKOI.)

With his mother, early 1990s. (YELTSIN FAMILY ARCHIVE.)

A quiet moment with Naina in Sochi, summer 1994. (DMITRII DONSKOI.)

With Chancellor Helmut Kohl on the Berlin visit during which he attempted to conduct a police band, August 31, 1994. (AP IMAGES/JOCKEL FINCK.)

Walking beside the Kremlin wall in May 1995 with three of his most influential ministers. Left to right: Interior Minister Viktor Yerin; First Deputy Premier Oleg Soskovets; Defense Minister Pavel Grachëv. Aleksandr Korzhakov can be seen in the background. At right is Vladimir Shevchenko, chief of presidential protocol. (Dmitrii Donskoi.)

The Russian White House billowing smoke after army tanks shell it on order from Yeltsin, October 4, 1993. (AP Images/Alexander Zemlianichenko.)

Negotiating with Chechen rebels, May 27, 1996. With Yeltsin, left to right: Viktor Chernomyrdin; Doku Zavgayev, head of the pro-Moscow administration in Chechnya; Tim Guldimann of the Organization for Security and Cooperation in Europe; Zelimkhan Yandarbiyev, head of the Chechen delegation. (AP Images/Yuri Kadobnov.)

Signing a cease-fire decree on an armored vehicle in Grozny, May 28, 1996. Yeltsin's national security adviser, Yurii Baturin, is second from the left. Interior Minister Anatolii Kulikov (in the beret) is two persons behind. (DMITRII DONSKOI.)

Comforting an elderly woman at a campaign stop in the Klyaz'ma district near Moscow, May 1996. (DMITRII DONSKOI.)

Shaking it up with rock singer Yevgenii Osin at an election rally in Rostov, June 10, 1996. (AP IMAGES/ALEXANDER ZEMLIANICHENKO.)

Embracing the crowd in downtown Kazan, June 9, 1996. Tatarstan's president, Mintimer Shaimiyev, a key Yeltsin ally, is third from right. (RIA-NOVOSTI/ VLADIMIR RODIONOV.)

With Viktor Chernomyrdin and Chernomyrdin's new first deputies, Anatolii Chubais (left) and Boris Nemtsov, after a cabinet shuffle, March 26, 1997. (AP Images.)

Words to the wise from his daughter and adviser, Tatyana Dyachenko, June 1997. (Corbis/Shone Vlastimir Nesic.)

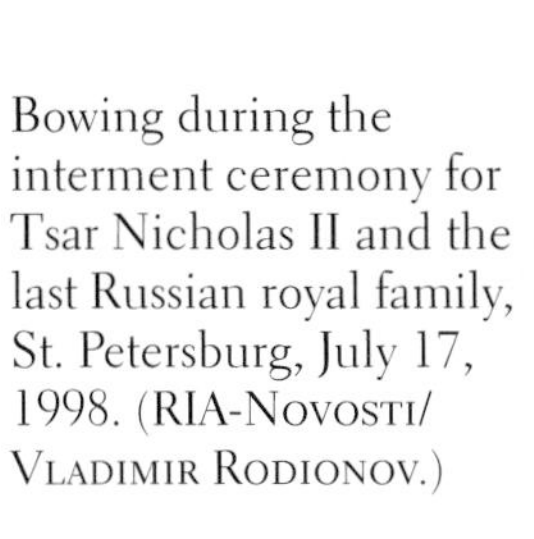

Bowing during the interment ceremony for Tsar Nicholas II and the last Russian royal family, St. Petersburg, July 17, 1998. (RIA-Novosti/Vladimir Rodionov.)

With business oligarchs, September 15, 1997. Left to right: Mikhail Khodorkovskii, Vladimir Gusinskii, Aleksandr Smolenskii, Vladimir Potanin, Vladimir Vinogradov, Mikhail Fridman. Yeltsin's chief of staff, Valentin Yumashev, is beside him. (AP IMAGES.)

Boris Berezovskii, November 1997. (AP IMAGES/MISHA JAPARIDZE.)

Prime Minister Sergei Kiriyenko, July 1998. (AP IMAGES/MISHA JAPARIDZE.)

With Prime Minister Yevgenii Primakov and the presidential chief of staff, Nikolai Bordyuzha, February 1999. (AP Images.)

Sergei Stepashin, Yeltsin's second-last prime minister, June 1999. (AP Images/ Mikhail Metzel.)

With Vladimir Putin at his presidential inauguration, May 7, 2000. (AP Images/Alexander Zemlianichenko.)

Cheering the Russian team's victory over France in the Fed Cup women's tennis tournament, Moscow, November 28, 2004. (AP Images/Mikhail Metzel.)

A celebratory toast with Vladimir Putin, Lyudmila Putina, and Bill Clinton at Yeltsin's seventy-fifth birthday, St. George's Hall, the Kremlin, February 1, 2006. (Yeltsin family archive.)

Yeltsin's coffin being carried out of the Cathedral of Christ the Savior, April 25, 2007. (RIA-Novosti/Mikhail Klimentyev.)

Boris Yeltsin: The Man Who Broke Through the Wall, by the MishMash Project (Mikhail Leikin and Mariya Miturich-Khlebnikova), a semifinalist in the Yeltsin memorial competition, August–October 2007. (Courtesy of the MishMash Project.)

hours a day and an end to most exertion and travel—diminution from governing president to a figurehead.

Yeltsin was apprehensive of the dangers of open-heart surgery and the loss of control it would entail. His daughter Tatyana took Sergei Parkhomenko, the editor of the newsmagazine *Itogi*, into her confidence. In late August she came into possession of a draft of an article *Itogi* was about to print on the pros and cons of an operation; she thought it would help ease his fears, provided she and her mother could share it with him before publication. Parkhomenko delayed the piece by one week and was rewarded with a written interview with the president. Prime Minister Chernomyrdin, a former heart patient, also sang the therapy's praises to Yeltsin.[8]

Sifting through the not very good alternatives, Yeltsin decided to go under the knife. He revealed to Russian television on September 5 that he had a sick heart and would submit to an unspecified procedure at the end of the month, and in Moscow: "The president is supposed to have operations at home [in Russia]." In that he had been noncommittal in his last meeting with the doctors, his statement was to them "like a thunderclap in an unclouded sky"—a vintage Yeltsin surprise.[9]

Acting in character, Yeltsin put a brave face on the situation to *Itogi* and posed it as a test of his abilities and self-command: "Some say to me, Take care of yourself, don't go to any special difficulty, spare yourself. But I can't spare myself! A president should not allow himself this. . . . Russians didn't vote for me so that I would spare myself."[10] If consenting to the surgery could be rationalized as an affirmative act, it was also a blow to Yeltsin's ego, as he was to admit in his memoirs:

> For so many years, I had kept the sensation of myself as a ten-year-old boy: I can do absolutely anything! That is right, absolutely anything! I could climb a tree or float on a raft down the river. I could hike across the taiga. I could go days on end without sleeping or spend hours in the steambath. I could defeat any opponent. You name it, I could do it. But a person's omnipotence can disappear in a flash. Someone else—the doctors, destiny—acquires power over his body. [I asked myself] was this new "I" needed by his loved ones? Was he needed by the country as a whole?[11]

He was admitted to the TsKB, the central Kremlin hospital, on September 12. The Yeltsins took Chazov's advice to bring in a group of consultants from Methodist Hospital in Houston, Texas, headed by the pioneering cardiac surgeon Michael E. DeBakey, whose professional contacts with Soviet and Russian peers went back to the 1950s. The Americans came to the conclusion that his heart was failing and the bypass operation was the patient's only hope. DeBakey delivered his verdict on September 25. He informed Yeltsin the bypass should let him live comfortably for ten to fifteen years. "I'll do what you say if you can put me back in my office," Yeltsin replied, which DeBakey told him was doable.[12]

Yeltsin took a month more to lose weight, overcome transient anemia from gastrointestinal bleeding, and improve his thyroid function. Reconciled to his fate, he was wheeled into the cardiology center's operating theater at seven A.M. on November 5. Before going under, he temporarily ceded his constitutional powers, among them those of commander-in-chief of the armed forces, to Chernomyrdin.[13] The twelve-member operating team was led by Renat Akchurin, who had spent a sabbatical in Houston and was Chernomyrdin's surgeon in 1992. DeBakey, four American colleagues, and two Germans watched them on closed-circuit television from an adjoining room, with devices for ventricular assistance at the ready if needed. Yeltsin's chest was opened and portions of his left internal mammary artery and saphenous vein were transferred to form five grafts on the heart. The painstaking work took seven hours. For sixty-eight minutes, heartbeat was stopped and his blood was circulated by a heart-lung machine. The muscle restarted on its own without chemical stimulation.[14]

The operation was a lifesaver. Yeltsin's coronary ejection fraction rose to 50 percent, still subnormal but not menacing. In gratitude, he was to have the Presidential Business Department quietly allocate larger apartments to Akchurin and six anesthesiologists and nurses.[15] But rehabilitation was long and uncertain. Yeltsin was taken off the ventilator on November 6 and initialed a decree taking authority back from Chernomyrdin, twenty-three hours after giving it away. He pestered the doctors into moving him on November 8 to the TsKB, where the VIP suite had secure communication lines. On November 20, the sutures removed, he was allowed a stroll in the hospital park. The yard "was dank, quiet, and cold. I went slowly along the path and looked at the brown leaves and the November sky. It was autumn, the autumn of a president."[16] On November 22 he was taken to the Barvikha sanatorium to rest.

Yeltsin went home on December 4. Home until 2001 was not Barvikha-4, which came under renovation that summer, but Gorki-9, a state dacha in Usovo, just upriver on the Moskva. (The household kept the apartment in Krylatskoye as a Moscow address, but Yeltsin seems not to have stayed one night there in his second term.) His medical condition would force him to spend far more time at Gorki-9 than he had at Barvikha-4. The house had been built in the late 1920s for Lenin's successor as chairman of the Soviet government, Aleksei Rykov; it was Vyacheslav Molotov's country place for twenty-five years and Nikita Khrushchev's from 1958 to 1964. After then, it was used mostly as a governmental guest manor. Gorki-9 was nondescript, with narrow Grecian columns in front and a hotel-style layout; long corridors on two floors opened left and right onto small rooms. It was rather dilapidated; in 2000 part of the second-floor ceiling was to fall in.[17] To regain his strength, Yeltsin perambulated the extensive grounds where Khrushchev, who fancied himself an agriculture expert, had in his day planted vegetables, flowers, and berries. Khrushchev liked the path around the property because it was level, and this no doubt was an attraction to Yeltsin.[18]

Yeltsin was restricted to thirty minutes of business conversation daily, signing decrees and bills (a facsimile signature was used for protocol decisions), and meeting several times weekly with Chubais.[19] On December 23 he finally made it to his Kremlin desk for an hour or two. He was on top of the world. "I had a palpable sensation of impatience, a desire to work. . . . I was another person. I could deal with any problem."[20] On December 31 he attended the mayor's annual tree-trimming party in the Kremlin. Several days later he went to a steambath. It had not been properly heated, and he caught cold. He was hospitalized on January 7 with double pneumonia and could not drag himself back to the office until the last week of the month. One of his first foreign visitors, on February 21, was the new U.S. secretary of state, Madeleine Albright. She found him "like a figure made of wax," his face pasty and his body "startlingly thin" (he was sixty pounds lighter than at his inauguration). Nonetheless, "Yeltsin's voice was strong and his blue eyes sparkled."[21]

Healthwise, 1997 was the best year of Yeltsin's second term. He made rapid strides that spring. Foreign statesmen saw it in Paris on May 27, at the signing of the "founding act" that formalized Russia's begrudging acceptance of the eastward expansion of the NATO bloc. In the grand ballroom of the Élysée Palace, he gave an earthy reminder of the Yeltsin of old:

> When Yeltsin joined the sixteen allied leaders and [Secretary General] Javier Solana at the podium, he behaved as though he were a famous comic

> actor listening to testimonials before accepting a lifetime achievement award: He knew that the occasion required solemnity, but he couldn't help giving the fans a little of what they'd come to expect from him. Yeltsin's expression kept changing. One minute he was beaming with pleasure as the other dignitaries, one by one, praised his statesmanship as well as his credentials as a reformer and democrat; the next he was screwing up his face in exaggerated concentration on the weightiness of the moment. When it came time for him to sign the Founding Act, he took a huge breath, wrote his name with a flourish, then gave Solana a bear hug and a big kiss on both cheeks.[22]

Yeltsin was in similarly fine fettle at the G-8 meeting in Denver in June, when the G-7 club of industrial powers was enlarged to include Russia. On his summer vacation at Shuiskaya Chupa and Volzhskii Utës in July and August, which Russian television cameras were allowed to show, he was tanned and relaxed. He did not have another setback until December, when he had to be treated for a respiratory infection.

Memories of the cover-up of his June 1996 heart attack and of his long nonappearance at the Kremlin were fresh, though, and more than anything explain the subsidence of Yeltsin's approval ratings to the depths they had hit before the 1996 campaign.[23] Aleksandr Korzhakov, elected to the Duma in a February by-election, came out with his voyeuristic book about Yeltsin in August 1997; it gave details on his health problems and first-term drinking extravagances.[24] Armchair diagnoses of some untreatable condition circulated in the press and the Moscow rumor mill—that he suffered from Alzheimer's, diabetes, Parkinson's, dropsy, a brain tumor, or cirrhosis of the liver. All were false, but suspicions lingered. Aleksandr Salii, a KPRF legislator, claimed in June to have evidence that Yeltsin was so far gone that a body double had been standing in for him, and demanded that the procurator general's office investigate. This featherbrained line of questioning would go on for years, reaching a low point in a potboiler published in 2005 whose thesis was that Yeltsin died during a heart-transplant operation in 1996, before the election, and was replaced by an imposter on the payroll of the CIA.[25]

The fact remained that Yeltsin was getting on in years, was in compromised general health, and was prone to emergencies and indispositions, which were to recur with greater frequency and harshness in 1998 and 1999. He put back on most of the girth he lost in 1996. The last flecks of gray in his mane had given over to snowy white and his voice had deepened from baritone to a raspy bass. His walk was stiff. Staff plotted itineraries at home and overseas that got around high staircases; three or four doctors, one of them a cardiologist, flew with him on all his foreign travels (this practice was begun in the first term); a larger medical area was built into the new presidential jet, an Ilyushin-96, delivered in 1996.[26] By this age, political leaders in societies with far higher levels of well-being and healthcare than post-Soviet Russia may be hard-pressed to discharge their duties. Yeltsin had marked his sixty-sixth birthday shortly before returning to the Kremlin in 1997, which made him one year older than Dwight Eisenhower when he was felled by his big heart attack in 1955—and only one year younger than Yeltsin's father when he had a devastating stroke in 1973.

Gone were the swagger and stamina that had been Yeltsin trademarks in Berezniki, Sverdlovsk, and Moscow. His beloved tennis and cold-water swims had to be put aside, and there were no more road shows or boogeying à la Ufa or Rostov.[27] He was left with tame leisure pursuits like swimming, in heated pools, trout fishing, driving powerboats and snowmobiles, and billiards, in which he could still run the table and shoot from behind his back. And he was somewhat more given to verbal faux pas and dizzy spells. In Paris for the NATO confab in May 1997, for example, he proclaimed that Russian forces were going to take the nuclear warheads off their strategic missiles; they were not, and aides spent the rest of the meeting doing damage control. His visit to Stockholm in December 1997 brought stray claims about nuclear weapons and momentary confusion about whether he was in Sweden or Finland. A highlight of his call on Pope John Paul II in February 1998 was his declaration during a Vatican banquet of his "undying love for Rome, Italy, and Italian women." Yeltsin referred to glitches like these by the abstruse Russian word *zagogulina*, which stands for "curlicue," "squiggle," or "bit of mischief." The mishaps sometimes had a physical aspect. At a news conference at Stockholm city hall, for instance, his knees buckled and press secretary Sergei Yastrzhembskii had to prop him up, "trying to make it appear as if he were handing Yeltsin some important pieces of paper."[28]

Russian journalists reported these occurrences in gory detail, as they had every right to. Memories were short, for there had been malapropisms when Yeltsin was healthy, too, and some observers had thought them endearing at the time (and this is not to mention those made over the years by leaders in other countries—think no further than the forty-third president of the United States).[29] The misstatements and also the stumbles were interpreted much less charitably in the altered Russian context.

Anxiety over the condition of his circulatory system persisted after the operation. Yeltsin was bothered by insomnia, as before 1996, and used prescription sleeping pills. He took analgesics for pain in his back and asked doctors whether the pangs were connected with his heart condition; the doctors said they were not. Conspiracy buffs hypothesized that illness excused Yeltsin from answering tough questions about policy and was helpful as a loyalty test, in clarifying who was willing to stand by him and who was not.[30] Maybe there was something to these theories, but Yeltsin on any given day was more apt to feel caged in by his limitations. Family members say that the one great regret of his second term was the failure to recover bodily vigor, as he had trusted he would when he consented to the surgery.

Yeltsin's medical situation necessitated a substantial reduction in his time at official workplaces. He was still an early bird (rising for a freezing shower at five A.M.), but many days he stayed at home and his spokesmen told the media he was "working with documents." When he did come to the office, it was usually at 9:00 or 9:30, and stays after the midday meal around two P.M. were the exception rather than the rule. In January, February, and March of 1998, for instance, Yeltsin lasted after four P.M. on only seven or eight days; on two of them, it was for state dinners (for the king of Belgium and the Ukrainian president). The correspondent who disinterred this information titled her exposé "Yeltsin in Gorki." Russian readers would have seen the double entendre. Gorki (not to be confused with Gorki-9 or Gorki-10) is a former nobleman's estate south and west of Moscow where Vladimir Lenin lived as an invalid from his cerebral hemorrhage in May 1922 to his death in January 1924. A photo of a sunken-eyed Lenin in a rattan wheelchair, a blanket draped over his knees, was reprinted in many Soviet history texts.[31]

While it was patent that Yeltsin was not his former self, some of the coverage of his condition was misleading. He was acutely ill in hospital eight times between November 1996 and December 1999, and while on vacation he was out of touch with most staff for one or two weeks a year. The rest of the time, if and when his departure from the Kremlin was on the early side, he would indeed work "with documents" at Gorki-9. Yeltsin went on long, restful vacations, true, but so do many other world leaders with fewer health concerns. Ronald Reagan, for example, took 436 vacation days in eight years, or an average of fifty-five days a year, spending many of them at his ranch in Santa Barbara, California. George W. Bush had taken 418 days by mid-2007, or sixty-four a year, mostly in Crawford, Texas, and President Eisenhower is said to have spent 222 days playing golf in Augusta, Georgia.[32] Yeltsin's vacation time after 1996 was of the order of thirty or forty days a year. When in the country near Moscow, he made more use of the telephone than in the past. Politicos and bureaucrats were expected to come to him when invited, which a handful were on most workdays. Unlike Lenin in the 1920s, he was not dying, was not a shut-in, and had not lost cognitive capacity.[33]

The bottom line politically was that when the second-term Yeltsin rationed his effort and expended it purposefully, he *still* had the last word in national affairs. As it was put by Sergei Stepashin, who filled a number of positions in the second administration and was his next-to-last prime minister, Yeltsin made "all decisions about goals and strategy" in his government.[34]

One fortuitous byproduct of worsened health was that it prompted a near cessation of Yeltsin's drinking. Consuming alcohol in volume, daily or almost daily, stopped for him in 1996. The craving diminished greatly during his reclusiveness before and after surgery. Self-preservation supplied the most hardheaded of motives: Akchurin and Chazov told him bluntly that not to give the habit up would be the death of him, and Yeltsin took their word for it. He was instructed to hold himself to a glassful of wine a day—advice he followed to the letter, he wrote in *Presidential Marathon*.[35] The fall of Aleksandr Korzhakov and the faction around him removed the small-group medium in which Yeltsin had found drinking most congenial. Naina Yeltsina's say over his diet and routine increased markedly. For state receptions and dinners, the family had the Kremlin kitchen lay in red wine adulterated with colored water, specially prepared for the president's table. On social occasions, according to his daughter Tatyana, he might allow himself one, two, or, rarely, three glasses of dry red wine or champagne, but he knew when to stop.[36] These restraints seem to have been breached on a limited number of occasions, although even domestic and foreign observers who record them note the contrast with the first term.[37] Alcohol had ceased to be the part of Yeltsin's life that it was in the first half of the 1990s, and no longer figured significantly in his relations with others.

More's the pity that he received no political dividends from this sobriety. Most Russians did not know his conduct had changed, and most analysts of those years write as if it had not. Yeltsin's privacy fetish and embarrassment over past miscues deterred him from providing any kind of explanation. It would have been undignified, as he put it in his final memoir volume, to "beat my breast" about the issue, and many would never have taken his word for it anyway.[38] He was in a when-did-you-stop-beating-your-wife trap: He could not say he had licked the vice without admitting he had it in the first place, which he was not willing to do until after retirement. Without a signal from him, no one in the government or the Kremlin could talk about the subject, and the press corps, for its part, considered it taboo.

Another change for the better was in psychological humor. The truncated second term was on the whole, his daughter said in an interview, "a calmer period" mentally for Yeltsin than the first.[39] He was less subject than back in the day to the mood swings between sleeping giant and snarling tiger. Physical debilitation precluded the spikes of supercharged effort, and the letdowns in their wake, that punctuated the first term: "I had endured a lot and, you could say, I had returned from the dead. I could not solve problems as I used to, by mustering all my physical strength and charging head-on into frontal clashes. That wasn't for me anymore."[40] Objectively, Russia's "reformist breakthrough," as Yeltsin termed it in October 1991, was behind him. The foundations of a post-communist order had been laid, for better or worse, and his re-election ruled out a communist restoration for now. Although there would be political exigencies—the 1998 financial crash and the 1999 attempt to impeach him stand out—nothing would measure up to the initiation of shock therapy, the constitutional donnybrook of 1993, the first Chechen war, or the 1996 election. About his own role, Yeltsin seems to have been more philosophical following his second inauguration, more accepting that his main work was done and judgment of it would be up to history. And, in his presidential autumn, the end of his time at the top, and the transfer of power to friend or foe, were on the horizon. Someone else would soon be opening the color-coded files in Building No. 1.

From the summer of 1996 to the spring of 1997, Yeltsin's leadership was in reactive mode. Besides weathering his parlous recovery and enforced leave, he was limited to tying up loose ends from the campaign. Promises that were affordable or whose costs could be deferred until better times were satisfying to return to. Small-change works projects and giveaways authorized during the campaign went ahead, at considerable expense to the budget. The cities of Ufa and Kazan used federal and provincial resources to start tunneling their subways in 1997; they opened to riders in 2004 and 2005 and are supposed to be under construction until the year 2040.

Cleaning up unpaid wages and social allowances was like rolling a boulder up a steep hill again and again. To give the government the wherewithal to make good on claims, Yeltsin in October 1996 appointed a Temporary Extraordinary Commission for Strengthening Tax and Budgetary Discipline. Chaired by the prime minister, it went colloquially by the name VChK, a contraction of three of the Cyrillic letters in its tongue-twisting title—the very same acronym as the first version of the Soviet secret police in 1917, and taken as instilling the Kremlin's seriousness of purpose. Yeltsin thought the problem well on the way to solution until he met with the commission in January 1997 and learned there was no timetable for catching up in the state sector. He threatened to issue a decree mandating full back payment of pensions by April 1 and then settled grumpily for a July 1 deadline.[41] There was no fix by July 1. Only strenuous effort got the total nonpayments in the economy by year's end down to the level of about $8 billion where they had stood in January, and they were to rise in the first half of 1998. Individuals and Russian families made adjustments on their own, as well as they could.[42]

The most urgent item on the presidential agenda was Chechnya, where fighting had resumed right after the electoral runoff. On August 6, 1996, Chechen units commanded by Aslan Maskhadov attacked Grozny. The Russians under Konstantin Pulikovskii counterattacked, and the city was ablaze as Yeltsin took his oath of office. On August 11 he made Aleksandr Lebed, the electoral rival whom he had brought into his administration in between rounds of the election, his personal envoy to the republic and ordered him to hammer out an agreement that would honor his pledge to put a stop to the war and bring the boys home. With General Pulikovskii's troops encircled and running short of supplies, Lebed and Maskhadov signed an armistice at Khasavyurt, Dagestan, on August 30. Yeltsin may have been able to push around the Chechen delegation in the Kremlin in May; on the field of battle, the superior morale and mobility of the rebels gave them the edge over the Russian conscripts. Khasavyurt deferred determination of the province's final status until 2001 and made provision for the exodus of all army and MVD forces. Yeltsin and Maskhadov, by then the elected president of Chechnya, would formalize the agreement as a treaty on May 12, 1997. The Chechens had won de facto recognition, the expunging of all Muscovite influence, and a promise of economic aid. Yeltsin had bought peace, at a heavy price but one that public opinion at the time wanted paid.

Dissension over Chechnya between Lebed and Anatolii Kulikov, the free-spoken interior minister who had helped talk Yeltsin out of canceling the presidential election, and who was on close terms with Prime Minister Chernomyrdin, broke into the open in September 1996. Kulikov, not without reason, felt the Khasavyurt terms were ambiguous and that it was only a matter of time before the war restarted. Lebed further antagonized him by reproving the MVD troops under Kulikov's command and, says Kulikov, by scheming to institute a "Russian Legion," a crack military force that would report to Lebed as national security adviser and would be reinforced by 1,500 Chechen guerrillas. Anatolii Chubais publicly backed Kulikov and drew counterfire from Lebed.[43]

As Yeltsin saw it, the general in mufti was after bigger game than Kulikov or Chubais. It was no coincidence that Lebed had picked this moment to strut his stuff: "All that went on in the Kremlin during those months was closely connected with one specific circumstance—my illness." Yeltsin disliked Lebed's pugilism about everything under the sun and, worse, his transparent attempt to come across as the alternative to an infirm civilian leader: "With his demeanor, he was trying to show that the president is doing badly and I, the general-politician, am ready to take his place . . . [and] I alone know how to communicate with the people at this trying moment." The last straw was when Lebed had the impertinence to call on September 28 for the president to step down from office until he was fully recovered from surgery. Yeltsin stayed his hand for several weeks because, interestingly, Lebed "someways reminded me of myself, only in caricatured form."[44] On October 17 Yeltsin came out of preoperative quarantine to fire Lebed and found the strength to shoot a clip about the decision for the evening news, in which he compared Lebed, not to himself, but to another politicized general, Aleksandr Korzhakov.[45] Lebed had made it through nearly four months on the job. As was his way, Yeltsin did not further punish the defrocked comrade. Lebed spent the coming year networking and raising funds; in May 1998 he won election as governor of the Siberian province of Krasnoyarsk.

A further spinoff from the just-concluded presidential campaign was the accord reached with Aleksandr Lukashenko in April 1996 to form an interstate community between Russia and Belarus. Details were left to be negotiated. As Yeltsin convalesced that first winter, Dmitrii Ryurikov, his presidential assistant for foreign policy, worked out a treaty of "union," a deeper association than Yeltsin had in mind. Like Lebed, Ryurikov, confident he was free to act, got too far ahead of himself. He had the document approved by the Belarusians and by Gennadii Seleznëv, the communist speaker of the Russian State Duma, and, before sharing it with his boss, informed the press that Yeltsin had agreed. The draft treaty would have fathered a bicameral union parliament (with equal representation for Belarus, a nation of 10 million, and Russia, with more than 140 million), a rotating presidency, and a ratification referendum within three months. Its neo-Soviet and pan-Slavic harmonics pleased Lukashenko, as did the possibility of a political presence within Russia, where he had built a provincial following since taking over in Minsk in 1994. Yeltsin was not a bit pleased. The draft was impossible to reconcile with his constitution (it would bring into being a second legislature and budget and open up bothersome questions about the federal structure), and sharing executive powers with anyone else was the farthest thing from his mind. It would have midwifed "a new country," he told his chief of staff, Valentin Yumashev, and he had done that once before in the 1990s.[46] On April 4, 1997, Yeltsin unceremoniously dismissed Ryurikov, who was soon appointed ambassador to Uzbekistan. A vague and saccharine agreement was agreed to and signed by the two presidents in the Kremlin on May 23.

The final case of overreach by a refractory subordinate came again from the field of national security. In July 1996 Yeltsin, having let Pavel Grachëv go with the Korzhakov-Soskovets group, appointed Igor Rodionov his second minister of defense at the strenuous recommendation of Aleksandr Lebed. Rodionov was a four-star Soviet general whose career had been wrecked when soldiers under his command killed twenty civilian protestors in Tbilisi, Georgia, in 1989. Since then he had been commandant of the General Staff Academy and branched into military doctrine and organization, which is what won Lebed's respect. Yeltsin asked Rodionov to come up with a design for "military reform"; the desiderata were a gradual switch from conscript to professional troops (as Yeltsin had agreed to do during the election campaign), holding the line on defense spending, and development of airborne and mobile forces. Instead, Rodionov sat tight on conscription, clamored for a budget increase, and tried to transfer airborne regiments to the infantry. Yeltsin was most affronted by Rodionov's speeches and media leaks, feeling they were intended to put pressure on him through popular opinion, and by what he saw as the minister's going back on his word to do army reform on a shoestring.

In September 1996, in an effort to limit Lebed's influence as secretary of the Security Council, Yeltsin created a separate consultative board, the Defense Council, which he put under Yurii Baturin's management as executive secretary. It was the Defense Council that Yeltsin chose as the place to clear the air on May 22, 1997. The scene in the General Staff's white marble quarters on Arbat Square has been set down by Baturin and his coauthors of *The Yeltsin Epoch:*

> Yeltsin . . . was cold, stern, and forbidding. He said hello and gave the floor to the minister.
>
> "You have fifteen minutes for your report."

"Fifteen minutes is insufficient," replied the minister.

"Fifteen minutes," the president snapped.

"If we want to talk seriously about reform, I need fifty minutes," Rodionov stated.

"We are losing time, let us begin." Yeltsin's voice was getting sterner.

"In that case, I refuse to make my report," the minister declared.

Yeltsin called on [General Viktor] Samsonov: "Chief of the General Staff, please go ahead."

"I also refuse."

"Igor Sergeyevich Sergeyev," the president said, misstating the patronymic of the commander-in-chief of the Strategic Rocket Forces (which is Dmitriyevich).

Sergeyev stood up and, thinking he was supposed to report, moved toward the desk where the president was sitting.

"Hold on," said Yeltsin, stopping him. "Will you take on the duties of minister of defense?"

"Very good, sir!" Sergeyev retorted curtly.

"Viktor Stepanovich Chechevatov," the president went on in the same self-assured voice. For some time, he had known and respected this general, who had gone up the service ladder to commander of [the Far Eastern] Military District; in the summer of 1996, Yeltsin had received him in the Kremlin as a candidate for defense minister. "Do you agree to take the position of chief of the General Staff?"

"If you don't mind, Boris Nikolayevich, I would like a private word with you when the session of the Defense Council is over, and I will give you an answer then."

"Fine, sit down."

The president turned to the secretary of the Defense Council [Yurii Baturin], seated at his left hand, and uttered a single word: "Decrees."

Baturin left to phone the State Legal Directorate, which was responsible for composing presidential decrees. While Yeltsin was delivering an irate and not exactly fair speech berating the generals, several alternative draft decrees were brought over from the directorate—alternatives, since there was no clarity about the chief of the General Staff. Having had his say, the president headed off to the defense minister's office for the talk with Chechevatov. All of a sudden, on his way there, he handed his aide a form on which he had written, "Call in [Anatolii] Kvashnin [the commander of the North Caucasus Military District] for a chat." Yeltsin had made up his mind that Chechevatov was not to be chief of the General Staff. If he had not agreed to the offer right away, so be it. The president does not offer twice. He almost never made exceptions to this rule of his.

Soon [on May 23] Anatolii Kvashnin was appointed chief of the General Staff. And Yeltsin was to work well with the new defense minister, Igor Sergeyev, and always respected him greatly.[47]

Yeltsin had evidently all but made up his mind to dismiss Rodionov before the meeting. The flow of it confirmed his decision and then had unexpected knock-on effects in the General Staff.[48]

Out of uniform, Rodionov turned to forming a lobby organization for retired officers; in 1999 he was elected to the Duma on the KPRF ticket. Like Lebed and Ryurikov, he may have had reasons to feel abused on the substance of policy, and he and Samsonov (and the poor Chechevatov) had more reason than the others to dislike the way they were disciplined.[49] All, however, had brought this penalty on their own heads by misreading Yeltsin and poaching on presidential turf. As the saying goes, when the cat's away, the mice will play. The cat was back from limbo, though not for too long.

Right after his second-round victory over Gennadii Zyuganov, Yeltsin tested the turbid waters of cultural and symbolic politics. Speaking laboredly at a reception for several hundred campaign workers on July 12, 1996, and presenting them with wristwatches as souvenirs, Sverdlovsk-style, he thanked them for their assistance and asked them not to twiddle their thumbs now that the election had been won. The new Russia, he said, in contradistinction to the tsarist empire and the Soviet Union, lacked a "national idea" or "national ideology," "and that is too bad." He asked them to give it some thought and promised to ask for a report by one year later, saying it would come in handy then or when his successor was elected in 2000.[50] Yeltsin appointed an advisory committee chaired by his Kremlin assistant for political affairs, Georgii Satarov, and the government newspaper *Rossiiskaya gazeta* offered 10 million rubles (about $2,000) to the reader who produced the best essay on the topic, in seven pages or less.

The project fizzled on the launching pad. Satarov denied that Yeltsin meant to enact some Soviet-type ruling doctrine. No, what was being proposed was a consensual process to discover an idea that already existed in the minds of Russians, as opposed to inflicting one on them: "A national idea cannot be imposed by the state but should come from the bottom up. The president is not saying, 'I'm going to give you a national idea.' On the contrary, he is asking, 'Go out and find it.'"[51] *Rossiiskaya gazeta* made a preliminary award in January 1997 to Gurii Sudakov, a philologist from Vologda province, for an essay on "principles of Russianness," by which time it was apparent that the exercise would be about navel-gazing and vaporous futurology. The newspaper never did decide on a grand winner and discontinued the essays in mid-1997. To the panel, Satarov commended as a model postwar West Germany, where an economic miracle was complemented by an outlook of "national penitence" after Nazi totalitarianism. Few members agreed, and the group was no better positioned to enunciate a nonexistent societal consensus than Yeltsin or Satarov would have been on his own. On the anniversary of its establishment, Satarov published an anthology of papers of liberal and centrist coloration. He then called it a day, and the commission fell into disuse.[52]

Yeltsin, knee-high in other concerns, did not weigh in and ignored his one-year target date. It is unlikely he could have salvaged much from the process, since it flew in the face of his own efforts to debunk Marxism-Leninism and of the very concept of "propaganda for the new life." Intellectual critics of the idea of a national idea sounded like no one more than Boris Yeltsin. "It is intolerable to cultivate and instill in public consciousness something that has not formed spontaneously," one of them wrote. "The banefulness of such experiments was evidenced by the socialist system," which had a moral that reminded him of an alcohol-free wedding "where mineral water sits on the table and under the table they are pouring liquor." Were post-communist Russia to be capable of working out a unifying idea at all, it could not possibly be done in one year or in several, and the hardships of daily life put no one in the mood for trying: "Ideologies come and go, but people always want to eat."[53] Yeltsin's silence in the face of these strictures tells me that he came to realize he quite agreed with them.

If he felt free to orphan his national-idea initiative, Yeltsin did not wash his hands of myth making and the reckoning with the past. In his first official act after reclaiming statutory powers on November 6, 1996, he signed a decree renaming November 7, the celebration of the Bolshevik Revolution, as the Day of Reconciliation and Accord, and unveiling a Year of Reconciliation to last until the following November. The edict was composed by Kremlin staff under Anatolii Chubais, who was of the belief that the vehement anti-communism of the re-election campaign had to be muzzled and that it was more important to get the KPRF-controlled Duma to approve progressive economic legislation than to refight 1917 or 1991 ad infinitum. Yeltsin supporters who were more interested in political change, like Satarov, were against the renaming but lost the argument.[54] The pronouncement might be interpreted as an enhancement of pluralism or, alternatively, "as profoundly uncritical, in the sense that it embraced all perspectives on the past without acknowledging the contradictions inherent in different views."[55] It was, as a matter of fact, a smidgen of both, and Yeltsin's ambivalence on historical questions continued throughout his second term.

One piece of the past where his views evolved only slowly concerned Mikhail Gorbachev, the last head of the Soviet state. Yeltsin stroked Gorbachev's name off the guest list for his second inauguration and made it hard for associates to maintain friendly relations with him. The president of Kyrgyzstan in Central Asia, Askar Akayev, bid welcome to Gorbachev in his capital, Bishkek, and honored him at a public event in July 1997. Yeltsin, a friend since they were deputies in the Soviet congress in 1989–90, refused to shake Akayev's hand for the next year, asking him at one point, "Askar, how could you?" He did not apologize to Akayev until 2004.[56] Yeltsin did relax the hostility some by inviting Gorbachev to attend a number of state functions in 1997, 1998, and 1999, but Gorbachev never accepted.[57] When Raisa Gorbacheva took ill and died of leukemia in a German clinic in September 1999, Yeltsin sent condolences and had a government airplane return her body to Moscow for burial. Naina Yeltsina consoled Gorbachev at the graveside service. Boris Yeltsin did not attend.

The second-term Yeltsin did continue to rehabilitate visual markers of pre-Soviet Russia. The biggest architectural project was the restoration of the Grand Kremlin Palace, a building to which few Russians ever gain entry. It was reopened in June 1999. Several blocks away, workmen constructed a carbon copy of the Cathedral of Christ the Savior, designed by Konstantin Ton as the largest church in Russia, which Stalin had dynamited in 1931. Yeltsin gave it his approval and laid the keystone, but the moving spirit, and the one to profit politically, was Yurii Luzhkov, the mayor of Moscow.

An issue that would not go away was what to do with the body of Lenin in his shrine on Red Square. Yeltsin's stance was a reprise of his first-term position. In May 1997 several aides gave him a plan for raising the issue afresh and bringing it to a "revolutionary resolution." He agreed to the advice and to recast it as an ethical choice, and requested Patriarch Aleksii in a private audience to get the Orthodox hierarchy behind it.[58] Aleksii, with some reluctance, spoke out directly and through lesser clergy, pointing out that prisoners had once been executed in Red Square and that it was now being used for rock concerts, and so was unsuitable to be a graveyard. On June 6 Yeltsin poured fat on the fire at a meeting in the Russian Museum, St. Petersburg. While Lenin and communism were part of the tapestry of Russian history, it was indecent, he said, for any person not to be buried in the ground. That autumn he called for a national referendum to settle the question: "Let the people decide whether to give him a Christian burial or to leave things the way they are." The president did, though, deviate from the depoliticization line, saying with some relish that the communists would be opposed: "The communists, of course, will fight it. No need to worry, I know all about struggling with them."[59] Polls in 1997 showed Russian popular opinion to be evenly divided, but the numbers fluctuated over the next two years.[60] And the intensity of feeling was greater among the enemies of reinterment, who took their cues from the KPRF and from the closest relative of Lenin's to survive, his niece Olga Ul'yanova.[61] Some threatened to use lawsuits, protest, and even violence to prevent the mausoleum from being emptied.

As had happened before 1996, Yeltsin was unwilling to chance it. "There was not enough time" to prepare Russia for the move, he said in an interview in 2002, and the social tension raised by holding the referendum or moving Lenin without a vote would have been intolerably high. He pointed out that those still queuing to view the body were mostly pensioners who were raised in Soviet days to revere the founder—"and it is hard to accuse them of anything."[62]

A second entombment issue had more of a connection with Yeltsin's previous life. This one was settled positively, though not without soul-searching and disagreement. The mortal remains in question were those of Russia's last monarch and his family, executed by Bolshevik riflemen in Yekaterinburg in 1918. The skulls and bones of Nicholas II, his German-born spouse (Alexandra), three of their five children (Olga, Tatyana, and Anastasia), and four royal attendants (a cook, two servants, and a physician) had been exhumed in 1991 from the unmarked forest grave at the village of Koptyaki, north of Yekaterinburg. Yeltsin knew the story only too well, as he had supervised the demolition of the place of their deaths, Ipat'ev House, while Sverdlovsk CPSU boss in 1977. Remorse at his part in the drama gave it an immediacy that the Lenin-in-Red-Square soap opera did not have.[63] DNA analysis at the Yekaterinburg morgue by Russian, American, and British laboratories had verified the identities. Predictably, the KPRF, which no longer excused the killings but considered the Romanovs parasites, came out against the project. What was unexpected was that the communists' political bedfellow was the Orthodox Church. Aleksii II met with Yeltsin twice, in May and June, to express opposition to the burial and spoke out openly against it. He and the Holy Synod thought the DNA evidence less than ironclad, and the relics were under discussion between them and the Russian Orthodox Church Abroad, a diaspora organization with which the in-country hierarchy was to reintegrate in 2007.[64]

Yeltsin, in short, faced more by way of elite resistance to relocating the Romanovs than to doing the same with Lenin. But this time he was willing to use his plenary powers to steamroller it and follow his conscience, and without much head-scratching about mass reaction—Kremlin pollsters seem not to have surveyed the population. It was decided in February 1998 to lay the royals to rest in the chapel of the Peter and Paul Fortress in St. Petersburg. The stout-walled fort on the bank of the Neva had been the burial place for all tsars from Peter the Great in 1725 to Alexander III, Nicholas's father, in 1894. Yeltsin, having said he would not attend out of deference to the patriarch, changed his mind twenty-four hours before the observance—setting himself up once again to catch his political competition short. Foreign ambassadors, who had planned to stay away unless Yeltsin came, had to make plans on a few hours' notice. Aleksii boycotted, as did communist spokesmen and Yurii Luzhkov, who was mad that the city of Moscow was not the site.[65] The reburial took place on July 17, 1998, the eightieth anniversary of the murders. A church choir sang and twelve white-robed priests and deacons officiated without mentioning the deceased's names. After the coffins were lowered into a crypt under the floor, more than fifty members of the Romanov family who had flown in for the occasion threw fistfuls of sand on them. Yeltsin said the final rites were an act of atonement and not of vengeance. "The gunning down of the Romanov family was the result of the implacable schism within Russian society into one's own and the others." Those who put them to death and those "who justified [this crime] for decades"—and the former first secretary in Sverdlovsk was surely one of them—were equally at fault. "We are all guilty. . . . The burial of the remains . . . is a symbol of the unity of the people and an expiation of our common guilt."[66] A commemoration service was held the same day on the vacant Yekaterinburg lot where Ipat'ev House had stood. A five-cupola Church on the Spilt Blood was to be built as a memorial on the site and consecrated in 2003.

The second Yeltsin administration resembled the first in that the daily grind was about down-to-earth issues of power and policy, especially economic policy, and not primarily about ideas and symbols. Its rhetorical beginning was

Yeltsin's annual address to parliament on March 6, 1997, his first presentation after returning to work. Wanting to get off to a fast start and not to have the scene stolen by Duma deputies, his staff worked with a director of stage plays, Iosif Raikhel'gauz, to plot and rehearse his every step and word on the Kremlin stage. Lights were dimmed in the hall before the president and the chairmen of the two chambers entered from the wings, with a break before Yeltsin's appearance to draw the crowd's attention. Were legislators to try to make statements at the end of the speech (none did), Raikhel'gauz was poised to pipe the national anthem over the loudspeakers to drown them out. He also had a teleprompter installed, which Yeltsin ordered removed.[67]

The talk itself was as alarmist as some of Yeltsin's jeremiads against the Soviet regime a decade before, only now the choler was directed at *his* government. Russia was carrying, he said, "a heavy load of problems," and there had been no improvement to speak of since the election: "Spinelessness and indifference, unaccountability and incompetence in addressing public issues—this is how Russian government is being assessed today. And one has to confess that this is correct." Although the state was supposed "to soften the inevitable costs of the transformations" which Russia was in the throes of, "we have not done that." Yeltsin in 1991 spoke of the transition being about finding and adhering to the pathway leading toward world civilization. He now chose a less cheery metaphor. It was as if Russia after communism was in a river whose fast-flowing waters run crosswise to the line of advance. The boat was "stuck halfway" in this uninviting and unforgiving stream. "We have shoved off from the near shore but continue to flounder midstream in a current of problems [that] carries us along and keeps us from making it to the far shore."[68]

Yeltsin did not put forth a spic-and-span approach or methodology for resuming the passage from one shore to the other. The emphasis was on two more measured points. The first was the need to reinvigorate economic reform through a stronger effort to draw the line between the public and the private arenas. Over the five years since the introduction of shock therapy, "the state has not mastered effective methods for regulating the market" and was standing in the way of a resumption of growth. Government, the president complained, "interferes in the economy in areas where it should not be doing that, and in places where it should be doing something it is inactive." The second moral of the March 6 speech was that national government had to put its own house in order. The executive branch needed fundamental reform and to learn how to coordinate its efforts within a range of duties narrowed down from the all-embracing socialist state. Without that, it would continue to act like a fire brigade, rushing from one minicrisis to the next.[69]

The end to the Kremlin tenure of Aleksandr Korzhakov in June 1996 convinced Yeltsin to tame the sulfurous discord within the Presidential Executive Office. Korzhakov's mini-KGB lost its surveillance rights and was folded into the larger body (headed by Mikhail Barsukov until he went down with Korzhakov) henceforth known as the Federal Protection Service. It steered clear of high politics for the rest of the 1990s. The crash-and-burn of Aleksandr Lebed in October quickly removed another threat to amity in the executive.[70]

Yeltsin brought Anatolii Chubais into the Kremlin establishment in July 1996 so as to give it a long-needed overhaul. The first Yeltsin lieutenant to carry a laptop computer, Chubais wasted no time weeding out parallel subunits and positions, centralizing decision making, and imposing a managerial style with a stricter division of labor and command hierarchy. The supernumerary post of senior assistant, held until the election by Viktor Ilyushin, was done away with. All aides now reported to the president through the one chief of staff and his deputies. The pre-1996 presidential assistants, most of them intellectuals by background, were allowed to stay with pruned responsibilities. The new crowd had less experience in academe and more in public administration, communications, and, in some cases, private business.[71]

This change came at the expense not only of the infighting of earlier days but of their restless energy. The old crowd did not take kindly to it. As a group of them were to write in 2001, "The time had passed when Yeltsin needed 'eggheads' to help him figure out pieces of 'the transition to democracy.' . . . Now the inconveniences presented by independent people outweighed their merits."[72] The eggheads left one at a time, the last departures being in mid-1998. At least one of the separations took a strange turn. Yurii Baturin, who had been the presidential assistant for legal and security policy, made inquiries about satisfying his life's dream of training as a cosmonaut. Yeltsin heard of it, said all was well, and then fired him on August 28, 1997. Rushing back to Moscow from vacation, Baturin received a handshake, a two-minute audience, and an autographed photo portrait. Unhindered by Yeltsin, he was accepted into the space program in September and flew on two space missions.[73] The duplicative Defense Council he had run for a year was abolished soon after.

Besides policy implementation, Yeltsin's reshaped team immersed itself in public relations, the art that had allowed him to keep his job in the 1996 election. The Chubais "analytical group" was continued after inauguration as a session on "political planning" that met every Friday at ten A.M. and was chaired at first by Maksim Boiko, a Chubais deputy.[74] Yeltsin agreed to give a weekly address to maintain contact with the electors. The chosen medium was national radio, which was judged friendlier than television and better at masking his infirmities. Ten-minute chats, taped on Fridays, went on the air every Saturday morning until the summer of 1998.

A regular in the Friday group was Valentin Yumashev, the Urals-born journalist and editor, amanuensis for the Yeltsin memoirs, and friend of the family. At age thirty-nine, he was made head of the executive office on March 11, 1997, in place of Chubais, who went to the government chambers in the White House. Yumashev stuck in the main to the Chubais mold, although, with no governmental experience, he had nothing like Chubais's political heft.

Another member of the coterie was Tatyana Dyachenko, who had no formal role in government after the 1996 campaign. When Yeltsin returned to work in 1997, he realized that he wanted her involvement, yet was ill-positioned to ask for it since he had always segregated home from work and had censured Gorbachev for nepotism in making his wife a public figure. He recalled hearing that Claude Chirac, the daughter of President Chirac of France, had been a special adviser to her father since 1994. He asked the Chiracs to receive Tatyana and explain how the arrangement worked. She went to Paris and was satisfied, and on June 30, 1997, Yeltsin had Yumashev name her to the Kremlin staff and assign her an office on the presidential floor of Building No. 1. It was explained that she would be his image adviser *(sovetnik po imidzhu)*.[75] Her alliance with Yumashev was close and at this point political and platonic only. They would marry in 2001, after Yeltsin and the two of them were out of politics.

Dyachenko's meteoric rise, her familial relationship with the chief, and his frequent nonattendance stoked the impression that she filled a void and was a major power in Russian politics. In the savants' ratings of influence carried monthly by *Nezavisimaya gazeta*, she showed up in the top twenty-five in September 1996 and in the top ten in July 1997, where she remained until the end of 1999. She was to be ranked as high as third in the nation in June, October, and November of 1999.

That Dyachenko was a significant presence is beyond doubt. She busied herself with much more than Yeltsin's image, as she traveled with him, made the odd foray to the provinces as his surrogate, sat in on staff meetings, edited speeches, and was the back-channel communications conduit to him. Her main role, she said in an interview, "was that I could tell Papa certain unpleasant things, which for other people, you see, it was not so comfortable to do. . . . I was better able to find the right moment and the necessary words." But the understanding between father and daughter was that in general she was to express opinions only on matters that he broached to her or that flowed from assignments she had been tending to at his request. She had no right to raise questions about personnel unless invited and never weighed in on security-related issues. She did not make public statements or deal with journalists. Neither did she possess anything like the standard bureaucratic toolkit. She had only one aide and no authority whatsoever to sign directive documents or commit government funds.[76] Unlike Boris Yeltsin and her older sister, and like her mother, Tatyana did not have much talent for organization or time management.[77] And, in the grand scheme of things, she did not have a political agenda or preferences of her own. Dyachenko was no vizier, and there never was a Dyachenko program or strategy autonomous of Yeltsin's.

Yeltsin's iffy health necessarily affected decision making in other regards. Yurii Yarov, who supplanted Ilyushin as superintendent of his schedule, cut back on meetings, which made for glancing contact with some of his officials and next to none with others. Early in the 1990s, Yeltsin had hosted up to twenty visitors a day to his study, and a prime minister, first deputy premier, or foreign minister could count on running into him five days a week. After 1996, only his chief of staff and press secretary (and Dyachenko) were in daily touch and the names on his calendar for weekly or biweekly meetings were down to a half dozen. The Kremlin's lead speech writer, Lyudmila Pikhoya, who huddled with Yeltsin once or twice a day in the first term, usually at her initiative, was seeing him once or twice a month, and communicating with him mostly on the telephone hotline, when she departed in the late 1990s.[78] As the press reported, formal Kremlin briefings were quite often canceled. In the first three months of 1998, Yeltsin called off nine of his scheduled get-togethers with Chernomyrdin and met only once in his office with the foreign minister, twice with the minister of the interior, three times with the head of the FSB (Federal Security Service), four times with the defense minister, and not once with the chief of foreign intelligence.[79] What the press rarely divulged was that many of these meetings were held at Gorki-9, Zavidovo, a vacation spot, or, if Yeltsin was under the weather, in the Barvikha sanatorium or even in hospital. Failing that, telephone calls replaced face-to-face conversations. With top functionaries, Yeltsin clung religiously to the weekly reports in whatever form was available.[80] The further down the line an official was, the more likely he was to have phone contact only. That was tolerable for workers who knew the boss well but not for new recruits, some of whom were never to have a single substantive talk with him. Yeltsin's travel outside of Moscow was also restricted, and provincial leaders found it much harder to get in the door than before, although some did manage to take appeals to him to reverse decisions made by other federal officials. Nonstaff advisers, who had intermittent access in the first term, had little in the second. Yeltsin's Presidential Council, though never disbanded, was not to meet after February of 1996.

The mooted "fundamental reform" of the state was explored but never brought to life. Kremlin assistants Mikhail Krasnov and Georgii Satarov got Yeltsin to write the commitment into his March 1997 address to parliament. Although they preferred a reform that encompassed rule-of-law questions and the judiciary, the task was narrowed to the executive branch. By August 1997 Krasnov had produced three drafts of a conceptual document, and by March of 1998 twelve. The thrust was to simplify the bureaucratic estate, make it less opaque, and institute a merit-based, Western-style civil service. Yeltsin was agreeable but unprepared to invest in the project. Yumashev did not make it a high priority, either. In the summer of 1998, as economic and political problems accumulated (see Chapter 16), the report was quietly tabled and Krasnov left office.[81]

The ouster of Lebed, Ryurikov, and Defense Minister Rodionov showed that Yeltsin kept the capacity to make mincemeat out of any lesser official who dared provoke him. The passage of time did not tranquilize the governing stratum. Far from slowing down, the revolving door for officials swung faster in the second term than in the first. Deputy premiers served for an average of eight months in the second term, compared to sixteen months in the first; for other government ministers, the drop was to fifteen months in the second term from twenty-three months in the first term. Of the informal coordination mechanisms on which Yeltsin placed some reliance in 1991–96, several were inapplicable after 1996. The extramural fraternization withered as tennis matches, collective soaks in the steambath, and like pursuits became but a pleasant memory. The Presidential Club ceased to function; in 1997 the buildings on the Sparrow Hills were turned over to receptions and conferences. The inflow of trusted townsmen from Sverdlovsk also dried up. Those associates Yeltsin valued most had made their contribution and gone on to other things, and he did not want to be identified with a territorial subgroup.[82] Yeltsin was as antipathetic as ever to collegial procedures for bringing about more coherent governance. Interior Minister Kulikov proposed to him twice that a new State Council be created, "with the powers of the Politburo," partly to correct for Yeltsin's physical incapacity. He says he explained to Yeltsin, "One head is good but ten are better!" The president indicated sympathy but did not reply when Kulikov sent him a memorandum elaborating on the idea.[83]

Even as he went along with the limited cleanup Chubais promoted, there was something in Yeltsin that made him continue to abhor an overly systematic, impersonal approach to governing Russia. Sergei Kiriyenko, who was first deputy minister and then minister of fuel and energy for a year until taking over the prime ministership in the spring of 1998, remembered the attitude well from the safaris outside of Moscow on which he accompanied the president:

> Boris Nikolayevich, who . . . had such a feeling for power, did not very much like to take the hierarchy into account. . . . He vented a sort of internal democratism. If he had decrees or decisions to sign, he was likely to do it on a tractor or on a tank or, I don't know, on the tire of a bus or at a mill or factory. This was not just public relations, it was a reflection of his heart and soul, of protest again the hated bureaucratic machine of Soviet times. His directives were never written so as to encourage the implementers to maneuver or palm things off. But everybody wanted to palm [costs] off anyway. . . . This is what got us into the nonsense of [granting favors] that were not in the interests of the state. [Yeltsin would tell us that] there was a promise; it had to be discharged right away or on a three-day deadline, and so on. After the fact, it was very hard to persuade him that the supplicant—for example, the governor who sent him a letter in which he lied barefacedly about being owed subsidies from the budget—should have his ears boxed. This was very tough. . . . It was like getting him to part with a dear toy. . . . My feeling was less that he had trouble letting go of financial questions per se than that he was irked that, "Heck, everything is already decided," and he was unable to take care of problems expeditiously. He seemed to think, "Here we go again with all this bureaucracy, studying and checking everything. I don't give a fig; you people aren't able to decide anything."[84]

Heart and soul, the late Yeltsin still believed in his right to make decisions on the go. No amount of organizational streamlining could have gotten him to give it up.

A few changes were made in the Council of Ministers after the confirmation of Viktor Chernomyrdin by the Duma in August 1996. Vladimir Potanin, appointed first deputy premier for macroeconomics at Chubais's behest, was the first private businessman to take high political office. Boris Berezovskii was the second when he was made deputy secretary of the Security Council in October. Chernomyrdin brought in miscellaneous red directors, and Viktor Ilyushin and Aleksandr Livshits moved over from the executive office. The cabinet was adrift, disparate, and, in Yeltsin's view, "not capable of resolving the country's slew of economic and social problems."[85]

Only on March 17, 1997, did he intervene to replace Potanin with Anatolii Chubais and to recruit Boris Nemtsov, the photogenic governor of Nizhnii Novgorod province and longtime favorite of his, to work alongside Chubais as first deputy prime minister. Chubais (forty-two years old) and Nemtsov (thirty-eight) in turn selected like-minded members of their generation for many of the economic and social portfolios. The press labeled them the young reformers, and it was hard not to see echoes of the Gaidar team of the early 1990s.

There was, though, one difference: Yegor Gaidar as acting prime minister ran the show in the Council of Ministers in 1992; in 1997 Yeltsin would not take Chernomyrdin out of the premier's chair and award it to one of the up-and-comers. It would be another year before he would, and the delay cost them and him dearly. In his memoirs, Yeltsin defended the combination as a way to harness the talents of both sides: "to get [Chernomyrdin] going" by flanking him with "two young and in a good way pushy and aggressive" deputies who would keep him under "high tension and steady, positive pressure."[86] The arrangement was too byzantine by half. Having learned his lesson and excluded antagonistic factions from his Kremlin sanctum, Yeltsin consciously wove them *into* the machinery of the government. Chernomyrdin still worked quite amicably with Chubais. He did not warm to Nemtsov and required constant reassurance from Yeltsin that his job was not in jeopardy. A specific source of tension was policy toward Gazprom, the hugely profitable gas producer Chernomyrdin had founded. Nemtsov supervised the energy sector and headed the energy ministry until November 1997, and made attempts to limit Gazprom's operational autonomy. He also scuppered a deal under which the Gazprom president, a Chernomyrdin man named Rem Vyakhirev, would have acquired a large block of the company's shares for a few million dollars. Nemtsov came to rue that he had not held out for the retirement of Chernomyrdin, and the hoopla he generated—such as his campaign to have bureaucrats driven only in Russian-made limousines—led Yeltsin to suspect he was not prime-ministerial or presidential timber. Chubais had the aptitude for the premier's job but was not willing to ride roughshod over Chernomyrdin to get it, and in any event would have had difficulty gaining a majority in the Duma.[87]

Yeltsin got a kick out of demonstrating to the young reformers he had taken under his wing—and perhaps to himself—mastery of the Soviet functionaries who still predominated in the federal and regional governments. Mayor Luzhkov, long in disagreement with Chubais on privatization, decided to show his annoyance by fouling up Nemtsov's registration for residency in Moscow, a communist-period formality still required in the capital and routinely expedited for newcomers at his level. Making small talk with Nemtsov, Yeltsin repeatedly asked him if the registration had gone through. Told that it had not, he at some point, with Nemtsov sitting there, picked up his hotline telephone, clicked the Luzhkov button, and without a how-do-you-do or explanation boomed, "You are behaving pettily, Yurii Mikhailovich!" and hung up. Nemtsov was befuddled: How would Luzhkov know what Yeltsin was talking about? Luzhkov was "a Soviet boss," Yeltsin said. Leave him be, "young fellow": Luzhkov would call the duty officer, ask who was in the president's office, and do what was expected. Nemtsov's registration went through the next morning. But Yeltsin did not identify completely with the Chubais-Nemtsov faction, as his clinging to Chernomyrdin showed. In one conversation, something in Nemtsov's manner irritated him and Yeltsin accused him and Chubais of laughing at him behind his back and believing "that I don't understand anything." "Keep in mind," Yeltsin said to Nemtsov, "that I am the president and you are simply boyars" (the nobles of Muscovy to Yeltsin's tsar). "Yes, you are smart and you are educated, but all you are is boyars. I am not afraid of you. It is you who should be afraid of me."[88]

All these intramural frictions make it impressive to a double degree that the young reformers, with a pat on the head from Yeltsin, put forward a program for reforming the Russian reforms and made a start on implementing it. The timing was auspicious in one regard: The decline in the country's economic output had halted, and it experienced a boomlet of 0.8 percent growth in 1997. Its stock market was the best-performing in the world in percentage gains from the summer of 1996 through 1997. The benchmark RTS (Russian Trading System) index of publicly traded stocks, set at 100 on

September 1, 1995, and having lost value in late 1995 and early 1996 in anticipation of a communist election victory (it reached a low point of 67 in March 1996), rose to 201 points by the end of 1996 and to a peak of 572 on October 6, 1997. In January 1998 the government redenominated the ruble, lopping three zeros off the old notes, in a sign of confidence that inflation had been conquered. It was understood on all sides that a new round of changes to build on these gains could not be accomplished by executive edict. After issuing a high of thirty-eight decrees per month in 1996, many of them election-related, Yeltsin lowered his monthly output to sixteen in 1997, eighteen in 1998, and twelve in 1999, well below the pace of his first term.[89] The volume of legislation was up at that same time, and it was laws, adopted by the federal parliament and approved by the president, that Russia required to underpin its market economy.

The progress made was skimpy, for one simple political reason—lack of support in the legislature elected in December 1995. An attempt to tie old-age pensions to workers' lifetime earnings rather than rely exclusively on the public purse, on the model of a number of Latin American countries, was debated by the Duma in 1997, then taken out of consideration by the government in July 1998, when it was apparent that it would not pass. A new tax code had been under discussion since 1995. It was with difficulty that Yeltsin got the leftist and nationalist majority to approve a first part, setting out general principles and duties, in July 1998; the remaining parts had to await a new president and a new Duma. Yeltsin was especially eager to get through the legislative pipeline a framework that would permit the commercial sale of rural land and knock down barriers to private farming. A conservative land code drafted by socialistic deputies from the Agrarian Party passed the two houses of parliament in 1997 but was blocked by a presidential veto that July. Yeltsin emceed a forum on the statute with lawmakers and interested parties in December. "Life itself" and the failures of collectivized agriculture had put the question on the agenda, he said, and he was prepared to accept restrictions on the resale of land and a ban on foreign ownership.[90] The compromise bill that emerged fell one vote short of the majority needed for adoption in the State Duma on July 16, 1998. This proposal, too, was in abeyance until 2000.[91]

In the first leg of Yeltsin's second term, the most portentous event in Russia's evolving political economy was, on the face of it, one of the more esoteric. On July 25, 1997, the government entertained bids for a 25 percent share in

Svyazinvest, a company formed in 1994 to hold the assets of regional telecommunications firms. Chubais and Nemtsov organized the equity sale to revive the privatization process and to help with the budget deficit, and did it in such a way as to prevent the pitfalls of loans-for-shares. Bids were submitted to a state auctioneer (the property ministry), and they were sealed, making collusion difficult. Nemtsov wanted the new rules to signal a break with what he called "bandit capitalism"; although Chubais did not use this phrase, he agreed with the sentiment and with the criticism of the corruption bred by the loans-for-shares mechanism. Two groups entered bids, one led by Vladimir Gusinskii of NTV and one by Vladimir Potanin, now back in the private sector. Potanin, who partnered with American trader George Soros, was victorious with an offer of $1.87 billion; Gusinskii bid $116 million less and lost.

That would have been the end of it were it not for the refusal of Gusinskii, "blinded by greed and wounded pride,"[92] to accept the result. He had not participated in loans-for-shares, unlike Potanin, and felt it was his turn at the trough; being in the media business, he saw Svyazinvest as a natural fit. Boris Berezovskii, whom Potanin had outmaneuvered to get control of Norilsk Nickel in 1995, was barred as an officeholder from formal involvement, yet took part informally as an impassioned ally of Gusinskii. Berezovskii and Gusinskii had their press and television outlets vilify Potanin, the auction, and the integrity of the public servants, chiefly Chubais, who stood by it.

Much ink was expended in the late 1990s on the thesis that Russian big business had "captured" the post-communist state and subordinated it to its purposes.[93] The Svyazinvest fiasco, and Yeltsin's role in it, suggests the outcome was more complex than that.

In their several prior encounters with the president, the moguls gathered the impression that he was well disposed toward them. Yeltsin, Mikhail Khodorkovskii said in an interview in 2001, looked upon the oligarchs the way CPSU bosses used to see members of the Komsomol—as individuals of a different generation, with strange opinions, perhaps, but on the right track and "following the defined rules of the game." Mikhail Fridman of Alpha Group felt Yeltsin regarded them as "the product of his hands" and as "one of the instruments for realizing his plans," and that he was sure "that all he needed to do was snap a finger and we would do what he said." To Potanin, Yeltsin's attitude was akin to that of a headmaster toward star athletes who sometimes break windows in the schoolyard: He approved of their talents more than he disapproved of their hooliganism. Yeltsin's tsarist self-regard and playacting, all report, inoculated him against envy of their money and influence, and he was untouched by the anti-Semitism common in the old CPSU apparat (many of the most successful businessmen were of Jewish origin).[94] As it had been with other players, Yeltsin badly wanted not to appear beholden to the nouveau riche. He needed prodding to accept their help in 1996, and they would have donated almost any sum to fund his campaign if ordered to do so. Had he wished, Yeltsin without question could have financed his campaign from state coffers.[95] After the election, he had no patience with warnings that the oligarchs were capable of causing him trouble. When he recruited Nemtsov from Nizhnii Novgorod, Nemtsov shared with him the perception that they were beginning to behave as if Yeltsin no longer counted. "Nonsense," Yeltsin replied. "That is what they think."[96]

Yeltsin received intelligence about the budding conflict over Svyazinvest and had Yumashev confer with Potanin and Gusinskii before July 25. Yumashev's recommendation was that they divide the company down the middle—a notion hard to reconcile with the principle of market competition—but Chubais would not hear of it. One week after the auction, Berezovskii took advantage of a phone call Tatyana Dyachenko made to him on another matter to bend her ear on the injustice of the result.[97] He addressed her in the second person singular and struck a cloying tone which she did not reciprocate.[98] Dyachenko sounded politely receptive, although she did have doubts about Gusinskii's belligerency. "Some kind of compromise" should be found on the case, she said, and on the whole the rules should require "normal competition" for state assets. Tatyana did not indicate her father's opinion and Berezovskii did not ask her to influence it. When he opined that the minister for privatization, Al'fred Kokh, should be dismissed, she replied that would be up to Chubais, who supervised his department. Berezovskii went on to put in a good word for another cause close to his heart (and wallet)—a general amnesty for back taxes owing, with "a normal tax regime" instituted only after previous illegality had been forgiven. "Let me tell you with certainty," he said knowingly, "no one [in Russia] has filed an honest tax return, except for the president, naturally." Dyachenko took exception. Her entire family had paid all its taxes; a free ride for tax delinquents would be unfair to the upstanding majority of Russians; and, by some formula or another, business should pick up more of the tab for government.[99] Berezovskii signed off by telling her he had been talking with "Valya" (Yumashev) and giving her his cell phone number. She had to ask him what codes to use to dial. The conversation demonstrated that the country's best-known businessman had access to the president's daughter and adviser in 1997, but also that they were not close and she had a mind of her own.

Whatever Dyachenko may have preferred, Yeltsin was opposed to reconsideration of the Svyazinvest auction, as Gusinskii and Berezovskii were demanding, but made oracular comments that sounded more critical of Potanin and his government backers than of the sore losers. He did not want to meet with the parties. Yumashev brought him around after an alarming article in the Berezovskii-owned *Nezavisimaya gazeta* painted Chubais as power-mad, Potanin as in cahoots with him, and the two of them as conspiring to find a "Trojan horse" candidate for president in 2000; in the interim, they meant to castrate Yeltsin politically, and would be much more devious at doing so than Aleksandr Korzhakov and Oleg Soskovets before them, who could not see "beyond the tennis court and the steambath" (no compliment to the president who whiled away so many hours with them in those locations).[100] Potanin's *Russkii telegraf* and *Izvestiya*, which his conglomerate partly owned, replied in a like manner.

On September 15, in the Oval Hall of Building No. 1, Yeltsin hosted the third of his four roundtables with high-flying businessmen. At the table with him and Yumashev were five of the six (Gusinskii, Khodorkovskii, Potanin, Aleksandr Smolenskii, and Vladimir Vinogradov) who had conferred with Yeltsin in February 1996 (see Chapter 14), plus Fridman as a substitute for Berezovskii. Yeltsin maintained neutrality between Gusinskii and Potanin but tested Potanin with a barb about how much government money (from taxes and customs duties) he had on deposit in his bank. Hearing that, Potanin feared the Svyazinvest auction was going to be overturned. Then Yeltsin pulled back. Potanin was at once relieved and let down: "Essentially, [Yeltsin] said, 'Guys, I have had a look at you, and in principle I remind you that I am the chief here, so everybody should go ahead and live in friendship!' But nobody was arguing with him about whether he was the chief. The chief is the chief. How were we to live from now on, and by what rules? He didn't explain anything about the rules." Yeltsin was to recount in his memoirs that he could tell as the conference broke up that no good would come of it. He does not say why. Be it out of fatigue, confusion of the oligarchs with state employees whose standing depended completely on him, or some other cause, Yeltsin had failed to lay down the law.[101]

For the Svyazinvest combatants, the only law for the moment was the law of the jungle. President and government did not act to change the auction result. After another six weeks of mudslinging, Yeltsin on November 4 agreed to a proposal by Chubais and Nemtsov to remove Berezovskii from his position in the Security Council. The decisive consideration was conflict of interest: He was mixing business and politics. Yeltsin was disgusted with Berezovskii and made a show of firing him by minor executive order *(rasporyazheniye)* rather than full-dress presidential decree *(ukaz)*.[102] On November 12 Berezovskii and Gusinskii struck back by releasing "kompromat," compromising material put together by their corporate security branches, to the effect that Chubais and four of his young reformers had accepted honorariums of $90,000 each for a not-yet-written book on the history of Russian privatization. The money had come from a firm that was soon to be purchased by Potanin. Within days, Yeltsin felt compelled to dismiss all of the coauthors except Chubais, who had to relinquish his second cabinet title, as minister of finance, on November 20.[103] Nemtsov was also lowered a notch, losing his second position as minister of fuel and energy to Sergei Kiriyenko. After that, writes Yeltsin, "My meetings with Chubais became much less frequent."[104] Nemtsov noticed the same, as he dropped from two audiences a week to one every several weeks.

The Svyazinvest imbroglio turned into a loss maker for all, and not least of all for Boris Yeltsin. On business's role in the new politics, he had to concede after the fact that he "did not immediately grasp the scale of this phenomenon and all the dangers it posed."[105] The winners of the auction did not make money from it, and George Soros sold his stake in 2004 at a loss. The oligarchs as a group also lost and were revealed, not as omnipotent, but as selfish and even rapacious and as politically inept—disunified, shortsighted, overplaying their hands. The scandal would have echo effects for years to come. After the 1996 election, it had been understood in all quarters that the cream of Russian business and the Yeltsin government, to quote Nemtsov, were "in the same boat."[106] The question was now not only about who had captured whom but about whether *anyone* would be moving the boat forward, and toward what destination. In certain regards, as the *Washington Post*'s David Hoffman has written, the business elite and Westernizing politicians, with Yeltsin looking on at a regal remove, had been functioning as a comfortable club. When the members came to blows over one obscure company, "the club of tycoons and reformers began to fall apart."[107]

Chapter Sixteen

Endgame

The effective length of Yeltsin's second presidential term was less than half of the first. Constitutionally limited to four years, it got off to a late start owing to the heart operation and was foreshortened by early retirement in December of 1999. Indeed, the nomination of Vladimir Putin as prime minister and heir apparent put him partway out the door that August. If the front half of term two was about taking power back, the back half was about letting go of power and, in so doing, not rubbing out everything he had tried to achieve. His behavior at the time, ridiculed by some contemporaries as impulsive and unserious, accomplished his short-term goals, against the odds. The long-term effects are still being acted out and debated today.

The Yeltsin endgame began in earnest with his government. He first gave thought to revamping it in November–December 1997. The brunt of his disaffection was borne by the man who had been his prime minister since 1992. While Viktor Chernomyrdin and his ever-changing roster of ministers had rendered faithful service, they, in Yeltsin's estimation, were not up to the task of bringing about sustainable development in a marketized economy. The strength of Chernomyrdin, Yeltsin set down in *Presidential Marathon*, was his "exceptional capacity for compromises. . . . But that was also the problem. The main compromise Chernomyrdin 'sat on' all these years was . . . between market relations and the Soviet directors' corps," a bargain from which Russia had to move on. Yeltsin, moreover, was looking ahead to the making of the next president, a prize Chernomyrdin had lately grown hopeful of attaining. Yeltsin was sure that his love for "the commonplaces of cautious administration" and the masses' weariness of "the same old faces" in politics would make him unelectable when the next presidential campaign rolled around. Chernomyrdin would have to make way for someone younger, more resolute, and with "another view of the world" in his head.[1]

Testimony on all sides makes it plain how greatly Yeltsin at the conclusion of his career relied on personnel renewal within the executive branch as the key to presidential leadership. In the role of political impresario, he was to gloat in 2000, he and no one else had populated Russia's blank public stage. "By giving a politician the chance to occupy the premier's or a vice premier's seat, I instantly made him famous, his actions significant, and his personage notable." Yeltsin acknowledged that this role flourished out of necessity: "I sometimes think I had simply no other way to bring new people into politics," and through them new ideas and approaches.[2]

There was no other way because Yeltsin's energies were depleted and his charisma blotted, and because of his past choices. He had refused to create a political party that would furnish a Yeltsinist organizational framework for those seeking office and a Yeltsinist conceptual framework for those holding it. A last gasp at drawing him into partisanship occurred right after the 1996 election. Georgii Satarov sent him a memorandum in July about a new party of power that he would head and that would subsume Chernomyrdin's Our Home Is Russia and a raft of centrist and liberal organizations. It would consolidate the new political system and "the pro-system political elite." The sketch interested him, Yeltsin assured Satarov. But he was unfit and awaiting coronary surgery, and took no steps to implement after the operation.[3]

Yeltsin met with contenders for prime minister under "various pretexts," on the lookout for a technocrat free of "debts and obligations to his party or his section of the political elite." This ruled out party heads and power brokers, national and subnational. The search narrowed to three members of Chernomyrdin's latest cabinet, another person who held economic positions earlier in the decade, the director of the central bank, and a former commander of Russian border troops.[4] As lists go, it was an obscure one, and only one on it (the former minister, Boris Fëdorov) had ever run for election or worked in a party. Two ministers were excluded for closeness to the sectors they controlled; Fëdorov was "too politicized and ambitious"; the banker, Sergei

Dubinin, and the military officer, Andrei Nikolayev, were quick-tempered and unsteady.[5] Yeltsin's later conduct makes the otherwise unmemorable Nikolayev noteworthy. Yeltsin knew and respected him in Sverdlovsk and was full of praise for him in the border-guards job, which he left in December 1997 after squabbles with other security officials. That the general was a candidate at all shows that the soldierly style was exercising an appeal to Yeltsin well before the rise of Putin.[6]

By a process of elimination, Yeltsin went to the sixth name on his list. Sergei Kiriyenko, a protégé of Boris Nemtsov in Nizhnii Novgorod, had worked in the Komsomol, commercial banking, and oil refining; he relocated to Moscow with Nemtsov in the spring of 1997 and made energy minister in November. He was by far the youngest on the short list, at age thirty-five, and had a mild manner and a decidedly boyish appearance. Yeltsin valued his business experience and restrained articulateness, yet conceded there was "something of the honor-roll graduate student" to him.[7] The two first met on the 1994 layover in Nizhnii at which Yeltsin spoke improvidently of Nemtsov as his successor. In early March 1998, Kiriyenko handed Yeltsin a clipped report about streamlining the Russian coal industry; Yeltsin liked it and Kiriyenko's "youthful maximalism" on market principles.[8] More than Chubais and Nemtsov in 1997, Kiriyenko was Yeltsin's second-term Yegor Gaidar, the well-connected wunderkind who would accelerate change as the agent of an impatient president.[9]

Yeltsin precluded doing in 1998 what he suspected he should have done in 1997: put the seasoned young reformers around Chubais in unqualified control of the government. Svyazinvest had cheapened the stock of Chubais and Nemtsov, who had far more hands-on experience of government and elite folkways than Kiriyenko. Practiced junior members of the team, untouched by the incident, were available for promotion. Yeltsin knew whom he wanted, and it was Kiriyenko. First thing on March 23, 1998, he informed Chernomyrdin. Kiriyenko took on the nomination and Yeltsin signed the papers making him acting prime minister. Yeltsin, according to Kiriyenko, shed a tear when he briefed him on the exchange with Chernomyrdin.[10]

The nominee had to be confirmed by an absolute majority of 226 votes in the State Duma. The deputies were of no mind to oblige. The constitution's Article 111 stated that if they rejected the president three times in the two weeks allowed, he was to disband the house and call a parliamentary election. Were there to be an initial turndown, it did not lay down whether he was free to resubmit the name of his preferred candidate. After Kiriyenko took only 143 votes on April 10, Yeltsin unflinchingly asserted that right and renominated him; in the second ballot, on April 17, Kiriyenko sank to 115 votes. Yeltsin pulled out all the stops on a third try. He hosted a roundtable for politicians in Catherine's Hall of Kremlin Building No. 1, importuned leaders of the Duma factions, and got the Federation Council to sanction Kiriyenko. Vladimir Zhirinovskii of the nationalistic LDPR, with the third largest bloc of Duma votes, swung them to Yeltsin and Kiriyenko—to ensure political stability, he said ("A bad government is better than no government"), and for pecuniary benefit, it was widely believed.[11] Nikolai Ryzhkov, Yeltsin's old foe and now the kingpin of a small socialistic caucus, helped by rationalizing a positive vote as a strike "against the destruction of the Duma." The Duma speaker, Gennadii Seleznëv of the KPRF, came out solidly in the affirmative and warned that dissolving the Duma for the first time ever would endanger the unity of Russia. "The president," he said for good measure, "is tightening the screws on us and we have no alternative."[12] Seleznëv got the chamber to conduct the third ballot anonymously, enabling many communists and others to elude party discipline. Unpopular though Yeltsin was, he was able to play on fears by rank-and-file deputies that in a new election they might not secure nominations and seats, would have to campaign without their Duma office base, and would be blamed for economic side effects. As icing on the cake, Yeltsin went on television to say he had asked Pavel Borodin of the Presidential Business Department "to tend to the deputies' problems" if they took a "constructive" approach to the confirmation vote—the problems being those of housing and perks. "One can only guess whether this should have been understood as responding to their material needs or as classic bribery."[13]

The Duma knuckled under on April 24. When the division bells rang, 251 deputies voted to confirm Kiriyenko as head of government.[14] Yeltsin showed him around his new office in the Russian White House. For them both, it was all downhill from here.

Yeltsin could not resist the temptation to make a few balancing ministerial changes, notably the removal of Chubais and of Anatolii Kulikov, the relatively conservative interior minister, and to insist that his ex-favorite Boris Nemtsov be retained as a deputy prime minister. That done, he gave Kiriyenko as much latitude in selecting cabinet members and defining program initiatives as Gaidar and Gennadii Burbulis had enjoyed in 1991–92. Passionately wanting him to succeed, Yeltsin conferred with Kiriyenko in the Kremlin or at Gorki-9 two or three days a week until his summer break.[15] Vigorous young ministers took over finance (Mikhail Zadornov),[16] economic coordination (Viktor Khristenko), tax collection (Boris Fëdorov), and labor (Oksana Dmitriyeva). Draft bills on economic liberalization were submitted to the Duma. In May Kiriyenko and Yeltsin's chief of staff, Valentin Yumashev, seconded by Tatyana Dyachenko, asked Yeltsin to dismiss Pavel Borodin and get to the bottom of allegations of corruption in the Kremlin business directorate, and they had him almost sold on the idea. After a heart-to-heart with Borodin, the president ordered him to institute competitive bidding for future contracts but kept him in the job.[17]

If Kiriyenko had some of the properties of the right man to reform the reforms, the timing was wrong and it would be all he could do to tranquilize a volatile situation. The deus ex machina was a downturn in the overheated economies of southeast and east Asia, hit in 1997 by falling commodity prices and runs on the local currencies. Contagion from the "Asian flu" gave Russia financial sniffles in October–November. Government intervention to shore up the ruble did not restore full confidence, as is demonstrated by the slide in the RTS stock index from its high of 572 points on October 6 to 397 points on December 31.[18] Economic uncertainty played into Yeltsin's agonizing over Chernomyrdin: He was unhappy with the prime minister's inability to answer pointed questions about finances, and conveyed this to insiders.[19] By March, observers were beginning to see an Asian-style crisis as in the making. In the second week of May, as the world price of crude oil fell to $12 a barrel (it had been $26 in January 1997) and the RTS average careened toward 200 points, the press predicted an imminent devaluation of the ruble. Yeltsin, with Kiriyenko and Dubinin, could have acted then to give in to the inevitable and cushion the effects. But the new cabinet was "terrified" by the prospect and of its political consequences.[20] When no one acted, speculation reached a fever pitch. Defense of the ruble cost an estimated $4 billion per month in reserves that summer, bringing hard-currency and gold reserves down to less than $15 billion.

The pain would have been less were it not for a domestic background factor—the fiscal overexposure of the government. Yeltsin stated later that he had shone a flashlight on the problem at a meeting of the Council of Ministers in December 1997. "I said [to Chernomyrdin and the ministers], 'You always explain everything in terms of the world financial crisis. Sure, the financial hurricane has not spared Russia and it did not originate in Moscow. But there is another aspect to the problem: the deplorable state of the Russian budget. And here you have no one to blame but yourselves.'"[21] What Yeltsin did not say was that the red ink in the budget was something for which he *himself* had no small part of the responsibility.

The condition was chronic and dated back to the macroeconomic stabilization program of 1992 to 1995. Soviet-era social guarantees having been liquidated, Yeltsin did not want to antagonize the population further by cutting back on social allowances and services, or to alienate public-sector workers by doing away with their jobs or not paying their wages. As Aleksandr Livshits, his assistant for economics, put it, the president "felt there were limits to ordinary people's patience" and "was afraid of a social explosion" if living standards deteriorated without relief.[22] An attempt in May 1997 to sequester unfunded items in the federal budget was dropped after several months, and then revived without lasting success in 1998. On the revenue side, the weak post-communist state struggled to collect taxes, often accepting nonpayment, promissory notes, or goods in kind in lieu of money. Anxious not to drive firms into layoffs or bankruptcy, it instructed Gazprom and the electric grid to follow its lead and did not force them to honor their debts to the government. The 1996 election campaign engendered a new round of promises for bailouts and special projects and more unwillingness to squeeze out additional revenues. Post-election endeavors to increase tax yields cut little ice, as we saw in Chapter 15. A federal deficit that was reduced from 10 percent of GDP in 1994 to 5 percent in 1995 was back to 8 percent in 1997, only 1 percent less than tax revenues in total—meaning that the government of Russia was spending almost two rubles for every one it took in. As a non-inflationary tool to finance the deficit, it relied on treasury bills known as GKOs (the acronym for State Short-Term Obligations), distinguished by their ultrahigh yields and fast maturity. The GKOs were purchased by domestic banks and by nonresident portfolio investors, who in 1996 acquired the right to convert their earnings to hard currency at will. The public borrowing required to float the GKOs produced a major overvaluation of the currency.[23]

Soft oil prices, capital managers' aversion to country risk, fear of a global recession, and the ensuing hike in interest rates made the mountain of state debt untenable. In Ponzi fashion, the Ministry of Finance begat ever more GKOs to cover the shortfall and boosted the annual yield from 18 percent in July 1997 to 65 percent in June 1998 and 170 percent in mid-August. Russia went further out on a limb by issuing several billion dollars in Eurobonds and making cash loans that would have to be repaid in dollars. Interest payments on the debt, which were 17 percent of the budget in January 1998, gobbled up 34 percent by July of 1998.[24] The RTS stock index went down in tandem to 135 points in early July, on its way to a low of 38 points on October 2, 1998—seven cents on the dollar for those who bought in at the high one year before.

Yeltsin's infant government had limited options. Kiriyenko got Boris Nemtsov to meet with coal miners who were on strike over unpaid wages and blockading the Trans-Siberian Railroad; the pledge to redress their grievances added to the government's obligations. Dubinin and the Central Bank of Russia pressed what monetary buttons they had. With Anatolii Chubais as head negotiator, Russia talked with the IMF about disbursement of a tranche from earlier loans and about new credits. The $5 billion of a $14.8 billion rescue package to make it to Moscow in August disappeared without a trace.[25] Boris Fëdorov proposed a cut in tax rates tied to a crackdown on tax debtors, targeting the 1,000 wealthiest Russians. In July, as an olive branch to the communists in parliament, Yeltsin appointed Yurii Maslyukov, a defense industrialist, former Politburo member, and KPRF lawmaker, as minister of industry and trade. But efforts to get the Duma to pass an austerity program fell flat. Refusing to trim spending, reduce subsidies, or introduce a sales tax and other new charges, legislators adjourned for a summer recess.

Yeltsin issued pronouncement after pronouncement about budget discipline, but did not swear off using the power of the purse, albeit a nearly empty purse, to please constituents. In late June he passed a day in Kostroma, on the Volga River two provinces northeast of Moscow, with local managers, students, and peasants:

> Yeltsin was in good cheer and a curious mood. At the Karayevo State Breeding Farm—the enterprise is famous for its thoroughbred cows and has forty Heroes of Socialist Labor on its staff—the president tortured the director with questions about forage, calving, and cleaning out manure. At a certain moment, Yeltsin even got angry: "You are not answering me concretely! What is it, do you think the president understands something about politics but nothing about cows?" Then Yeltsin fell head over heels for the Russian flax [grown and processed in the region]. After comely young Kostroma women showed him the newest fashions at a linen mill, the president took out his fountain pen and, right there on a wall poster, labeled "Government Support for Russian Flax," he wrote, "There is going to be a decree! Yeltsin."[26]

As part of the consultations, Yeltsin had his fourth meeting with the oligarchs, ten of them, on June 2. Bankers Mikhail Fridman, Vladimir Gusinskii, Mikhail Khodorkovskii, Vladimir Potanin, and Aleksandr Smolenskii had been at previous gatherings; Vitalii Malkin of the Russian Credit Bank joined them; and four industrialists were added—Chubais, wearing his hat as head of electricity wholesaler YeES (the position he was given when he left the cabinet in March), Vagit Alekperov of Lukoil, Vladimir Bogdanov of the Surgutneftegaz oil and gas company, and Rem Vyakhirev of Gazprom. Kiriyenko sat in, unlike Chernomyrdin, who had not been present at the meetings in 1995, 1996, and 1997. Yeltsin described the state of affairs as ominous and enjoined the moguls to pay their taxes, keep their money in Russia, and keep faith in his government. He asked what they most needed from him; Fridman replied that it was stability. Perhaps, Yeltsin volunteered, I will make an announcement that Kiriyenko will chair the Council of Ministers until 2000.[27] No such announcement came forth, which was not lost on Kiriyenko. The prime minister met separately on June 16 and 18 with most of the June 2 participants, and his spokesmen said leading capitalists and state officials would form a joint Council for Mutual Economic Assistance. But Yeltsin did not express an opinion. The attempt to give business-government cooperation a formal cast died on the drawing board.

Yeltsin claimed on several occasions that the emergency had passed, even as he spoke more frankly with his subordinates. On August 13 the *Financial Times* of London printed a letter from U.S. financier George Soros about Russia being at "the terminal phase" of a "meltdown" of its financial markets. He recommended a prompt devaluation of 15 to 25 percent and turning over management of the ruble to an expert currency board. At the request of Kiriyenko, his economic team, and Valentin Yumashev, Yeltsin made one last demurral. On August 14, in Novgorod, he stated "firmly and concisely" that there would be no devaluation. Kiriyenko, Yumashev, Chubais, and Dubinin (accompanied by Yegor Gaidar) went to Zavidovo two days later to tell him the game was up. Yeltsin concurred and, as was typical of his style, asked them to spare him the fine print. "The head of government started describing the details, but I stopped him. Even without them, it was clear that the government, and all of us along with it, had become hostages to fate. . . . 'Go ahead,' I said. 'Do take emergency measures.'"[28]

On August 17 Russia let the exchange rate float, defaulted on its treasury bills and bonds, and imposed a ninety-day moratorium on payments to foreign creditors. In two frantic weeks, the ruble lost half of its exchange value, going from 6.3 to the U.S. dollar to 9.3; it was to plummet to 21 to the dollar by September 21. GKOs were reduced to all but worthless scraps of paper. The three-month moratorium favored Russians over foreigners without keeping hundreds of the banks from going under in a triage process that stretched into 1999. Citizens queued at tellers' windows to withdraw their deposits. Prognoses of economic and social breakdown swamped the domestic and world media.[29]

Political change came inexorably in the wake of the financial bulletins. The alternatives facing Yeltsin, as one writer put it in September, were "the bad, the atrocious, and the bloodcurdling."[30] The leftist and nationalist majority in the Duma, and especially the far-left communists, were out for nothing less than the president's head. On August 21 the house met and passed a nonbinding resolution calling on him to step down, with 248 votes for and just thirty-two against. Opinion makers had been scoping out an abdication in earnest since early summer, some pitching ideas for institutional innovations that might grease the skids. In an essay in *Nezavisimaya gazeta* on July 10, the sagacious Vitalii Tret'yakov pointed the finger at Yeltsin and his loyalists for following an "ostrich policy." Without a change of course, Russia was in for popular insurrection, a coup d'état, or civil war; if the last were to break out, the country would come under foreign military occupation, since the world could not abide the breakup of a former superpower with a nuclear arsenal and ten atomic power stations. To stave off a cataclysm, Russia, he said, needed to hold special legislative and presidential elections within three months. The Federal Assembly should establish a Provisional State Council consisting of main ministers, parliamentary leaders, party heads, and representatives of Russia's macroregions and trade unions. Yeltsin was to be barred from chairing the council and to be a member only if he consented in writing not to stand for another term in the extraordinary election for president. To head the council, Tret'yakov suggested Foreign Minister Yevgenii Primakov; he also recommended that Viktor Chernomyrdin be returned as the caretaker prime minister for the interregnum.[31]

Tret'yakov was right in the presentiment that there would be a shakeup and that Chernomyrdin and Primakov would be players in it. The Provisional State Council, though, was too contorted an idea to fly.[32] And Tret'yakov miscalculated about the president. Yeltsin did not consider renouncing power in 1998, to a Supreme Council or anybody else, despite repeated testimony in the press that he was on the verge of doing so.[33]

Yeltsin notified Kiriyenko on August 22 that his premiership was done, after four months. The choice to replace him was the amazing one foreseen by Tret'yakov in July— Chernomyrdin, the same veteran of the red directors' club whom Yeltsin had deposed in March. As he made the offer to Chernomyrdin in his Kremlin office on August 23, Yeltsin made a fulsome apology for the past spring and offered to repeat it on the airwaves. Chernomyrdin said the confidential amends were sufficient. It was made clear in this meeting and others that Yeltsin expected Chernomyrdin to sit until 2000 and to run for president then with his support. Yeltsin was more acceptant of Chernomyrdin's return than excited by it.[34] He divulged his decision in a televised speech the next day. "Today we need the people who are usually called 'heavyweights.' In my view, the experience and weight of Chernomyrdin are needed." Yeltsin drew a link to the succession question, saying the reinstatement would help assure "continuity in power in 2000" and that human qualities such as Chernomyrdin's "will be the decisive argument in the presidential elections."

The Duma would have none of it. In the first round of the voting, on August 31, only ninety-four deputies voted for the former and acting prime minister, worse than Kiriyenko had fared in April. Meeting on September 2 with Bill Clinton, in Moscow to show the flag, Yeltsin was truculent. He was not afraid to provoke a system-wide crisis if the Duma would not confirm his nominee: "Yeltsin seemed ready for that, even to welcome it. He could use his presidential powers, he said, to 'wreck the Communist Party once and for all.' The communists 'have committed plenty of sins in the past. I could make a list of those sins and take it to the Ministry of Justice and prosecute them.' Clasping his hands and gritting his teeth, he added, 'I could really put the squeeze on them.'"[35] But Yeltsin also shared with the Americans that he was debating alternatives, and Chernomyrdin knew it full well.[36] Doubts only grew when, upon resubmission, Chernomyrdin could garner no more than 138 votes. While this was more than Kiriyenko received in the second round in April, the climate of opinion was different: Gennadii Seleznëv would not arrange a secret ballot; the communist caucus stuck to its guns; the Federation Council was not on board; Yeltsin and Chernomyrdin were damaged goods. There was also a constitutional complication. The communists were preparing to introduce a bill to impeach Yeltsin. Under Article 109, the president was not empowered to dissolve the Duma and force a new parliamentary election if an article of impeachment had passed the lower house. Had Yeltsin persisted, militant KPRF deputies had a chance to tie his hands by railroading through an impeachment bill before the nomination of Chernomyrdin came to a vote.

Yeltsin now executed another U-turn: As in December 1992 with Chernomyrdin, he agreed to a compromise candidate. Yevgenii Primakov, two years older than Yeltsin (and thirty-three years older than Kiriyenko), had been Russia's spymaster and latterly its minister of foreign affairs. Before that he was a journalist, academic, and nonvoting member of the Gorbachev Politburo, always working hand in glove with the security services. Primakov was portly, avuncular in comportment, and center-left in his politics. He wanted a broad-based government, heightened state regulation of the market, and a more muscular foreign policy, all of which fit better with what parliament and the populace wanted than Chernomyrdin or Kiriyenko had. Primakov needed to be talked into taking the position of prime minister. After three meetings with Yeltsin and many more with staffers, he acquiesced on September 10. The nomination sailed through the Duma on September 11, with 317 votes in favor to sixty-three against.

Yeltsin's back-to-back reversals, in a setting of economic distress, led some to the surmise that his star had set irretrievably. "The Yeltsin factor, with his . . . utter unpredictability in the struggle for personal power, has departed for all time from Russian politics," Tret'yakov submitted in *Nezavisimaya gazeta* the morning after the Primakov confirmation. "In the larger scheme of things, politician Yeltsin no longer exists"; all that was left now was "citizen Yeltsin," yesterday's man. He had failed to "appoint" an heir, Tret'yakov continued, and would be unable to appoint one in future.[37]

But Yeltsin was not yet ready to fade from the scene, and he was not bereft of political resources, as would be evident in 1999. What Tret'yakov's diagnosis also overlooked was that the Primakov solution was in some ways a blessing in disguise for Yeltsin. Defeat in a third Duma ballot, if that was the alternative, held more dangers for him than it did for the communist-led opposition, which most likely would have come back from an election strengthened. Yurii Luzhkov of Moscow was a much-bruited option for prime minister in September. Put off by his ambition and forwardness, Yeltsin was passionately against the candidacy and sacked several close aides for pushing it.[38] Had a Chernomyrdin restoration come about, it would have been a standing reproach to Yeltsin for his poor judgment in ousting him earlier. Unlike Primakov, Chernomyrdin had open presidential aspirations that Yeltsin would need to manage. Chernomyrdin had reason to feel aggrieved at Yeltsin's treatment of him and to reckon that he could feed off it politically.[39]

And parliamentary approval for Chernomyrdin would have come at the price of a huge power-sharing concession, to be in effect until 2000. During the negotiations Yeltsin had offered to waive his right to dissolve the legislature (it would waive its right to vote no-confidence) and to give it a veto over the appointment of deputy premiers, the minister of finance, and the heads of the force agencies. Gennadii Zyuganov renounced the pact on August 30, thinking there were more concessions to wring out of Yeltsin.[40] Yeltsin took it off the table when he submitted Primakov's name, leaving him able in future to put his new prime minister through the same meat grinder he subjected Chernomyrdin and Kiriyenko to in 1998.

Primakov, most importantly, was in a position to pursue the needed course correction with far more credibility than Chernomyrdin. Talk of a constitutional revision to dilute Yeltsin's presidential powers withered on the vine in October. Yeltsin was prepared to give Primakov as much autonomy to select collaborators as the young liberals Gaidar and Kiriyenko had in their time. Primakov filled many positions in his White House apparat with reserve intelligence officers. In staffing the cabinet, he would say in a memoir, "The president and his entourage . . . desisted from imposing . . . particular people on me."[41] As his first deputy premier for economic affairs, he lined up the communist and dirigiste Yurii Maslyukov.[42] At Primakov's urging, Viktor Gerashchenko, evicted from the position by Yeltsin in 1994, came back on September 12 to chair the central bank.

Primakov on the whole was a moderate and pragmatic prime minister. He ran for Yeltsin what was essentially a coalition government. Fourteen of thirty-one cabinet members, among them reformists like Finance Minister Zadornov, were carried over from Kiriyenko, and he blended in leftists, centrists, and clients of Luzhkov and other politicos. Primakov and his ministers employed administrative levers to put failed banks into receivership, slow capital flight, and force the payment of some back wages to civil servants and the disgruntled miners.[43] The budget they submitted had a deficit of only 3 percent of GDP. Primakov and Gerashchenko financed the deficit that remained through the printing press, thereby ramping up inflation to 84 percent in 1998 (from 11 percent in 1997) while short-circuiting the ruinous lending cycle. The feeble economic growth of 1997 yielded to still another slump in output, by 4.9 percent in 1998, but the bottom did not drop out of the system, as had been feared. Primakov, in Yeltsin's assessment, "chose the perfect intonation" to reassure the nation. "With his confident unhurriedness, Yevgenii Maksimovich managed . . . to convince almost everybody that things would calm down."[44]

Counter to the doomsday talk, the Russian economy after those first jumpy weeks commenced a dramatic upturn that has continued to this day. There were signs as early as October and November of 1998. The annual figures for 1999 were music to Yeltsin's ears—5.4 percent growth and inflation under 40 percent. The seemingly disastrous decision to mark down the currency ended up being a revitalizing tonic. The devalued ruble made petroleum and other exports more affordable to external buyers and formed a nontariff barrier against imports, which sparked a recovery in the domestic supply of food, apparel, and consumer durables. Shut out of international capital markets, Russia was at last pressed to harden its state budget and restructure the sovereign debt. Crisis let these revisions, undoable in normal times, be imposed and locked in against regression. In the worldwide economic environment, trends turned in Russia's favor for the first time since the 1980s. Most critically, oil prices more than doubled between 1998 and 2000. That surge, compounded by an increase in production and exports, tripled revenues from the oil and gas trade, which in turn restored liquidity to cash-starved commerce and put an end to the demonetization and nonpayment syndromes.[45]

In his survey of the financial collapse in *Presidential Marathon,* Yeltsin revisited the therapeutic imagery he had applied to shock therapy six or seven years beforehand. "A political crisis," he wrote, "is a temporary phenomenon and is even useful in a way. I know from my life that the organism uses a crisis to overcome an illness, renew itself, and return to its customary, healthy state."[46] The passing of the great panic of 1998, however, was not followed by a revival of Boris Yeltsin's fortunes. Instead, he was increasingly beleaguered and preoccupied by finding a way out of the jam he was in.

One reason this was so was that the economic turnaround seemed fragile and did not improve the well-being of the average Russian family for some time to come. Per-capita income and consumption reached pre-crash levels only in 2001, by which time Yeltsin was in retirement.

A more immediate problem was with the president's personal health and ability, actual and perceived, to do his job. Yeltsin maintained mental equilibrium after the blur of events in August–September, largely out of relief that things were not worse and that Primakov had taken the bit between his teeth. It was his physical condition that worsened noticeably. One month after Primakov's installation, Yeltsin's occasional appearances at the Kremlin were being played up by the Russian media as "breaking news." On a visit to Kazakhstan and Uzbekistan in the second week of October, he had coughing spells, several times lost his footing, and returned to Moscow early.[47] He checked into the Barvikha sanatorium at the end of October, went on a three-week layoff attributed by his staff to exhaustion, and was admitted to the TsKB on November 23 with double pneumonia, staying there for better than two weeks. On January 17, 1999, he was hospitalized with a bleeding stomach ulcer. He emerged from the sanatorium in early February to fly to the funeral of King Hussein of Jordan, where Primakov had been announced as Russia's representative. His doctors were unconditionally against the expedition. "No one understands me," Yeltsin declared to his staff, ordering a six A.M. departure for the presidential plane.[48] He was on the ground in Amman for only six hours.

The ulcer flared up again in late February. Yeltsin was readmitted for three weeks in hospital and sanatorium. The *Izvestiya* columnist Maksim Sokolov floridly summed up the contrast with Yeltsin in his prime: "The material out of which nature made Yeltsin is the wood from which kings are carved. Yeltsin's and all Russia's misfortune is that nine years of transitional burdens have managed to chew this wood into dust."[49] Attendees at the G-8 meeting in Cologne in June 1999, where Yeltsin dropped in on the final day, found that he "looked like a battered statue that might topple over at any moment."[50] After an even-keeled summer, he was in hospital for several days in October 1999 for influenza and laryngitis and, following a short visit to Istanbul—his last as president—went through it all over again in November and early December, for pneumonia.

The decline in Yeltsin's health provoked repeated pleas in parliament and the media for him to resign. Some went so far as to appeal to Naina Yeltsina and the family to intercede to put a stop to the "public spectacle" of him "dying away" in office—unsolicited advice that the Yeltsins found deeply wounding.[51]

There were multitudinous markers of poorer political health after August 1998—poorer than Yeltsin had ever been in as national leader. Public-relations and policy-planning endeavors begun in 1996–97 were inaudibly abandoned. The Friday brainstorming group did not convene after the 1998 crisis. The Saturday radio chats were canceled rather than having to make amends each time for "the disaster of the week."[52] In the monthly ratings of influence in *Nezavisimaya gazeta* for October, the superpresident, Yeltsin, was put in third place, below Prime Minister Primakov and Mayor Luzhkov; he remained there until the February 1999 poll, when he was back in second place, with Primakov still in first.[53] A corruption scandal broke out early in

1999 around the Swiss construction company Mabetex. Prosecutors in Switzerland alleged that it had paid kickbacks to Pavel Borodin and other high-level officials to secure the main contract for the reconstruction of Building No. 1, in Yeltsin's first term. The procurator general, Yurii Skuratov, who had long been estranged from Yeltsin's administration, launched an internal investigation. It eventually was claimed that the owner of Mabetex, Kosovar-Albanian businessman Behgjet Pacolli, had transferred a million dollars to a Hungarian bank account for President Yeltsin, supplied him and his two daughters with credit cards, and paid for expensive purchases through them. Guilt or innocence is impossible to ascertain with certainty, owing to the secrecy surrounding all these transactions, but the finger pointing at the Yeltsin family lacks credence and none of the charges was ever proved. Still, the affair was of sufficient magnitude for Yeltsin to mention it on the telephone with President Clinton in September 1999.[54]

Proof of an embattled presidency could not be missed in various areas. In center-periphery relations, provincial governors were among those who summoned Yeltsin to cede power during and after the 1998 crisis, and there was a spike in regional noncompliance with central laws and policy at this same time. Chechnya, brutalized by the war of 1994 to 1996, remained an open sore. Leader Aslan Maskhadov proved incapable of reining in gangsters, terrorists, and Islamic fundamentalists; dealings with Moscow became tenser by the month.[55] Foreign policy had its own frustrations, as Yeltsin could not stop NATO from retaliating against Serbia for its repression of rebel forces and civilians in Kosovo. An air war against the Serbs began on March 24, 1999, leading Russia to freeze relations with the alliance.

Yeltsin's hesitancy showed in the pattern of executive appointments. More than in unsettled periods in the past, he was prepared to select helpers who would score points for him with audiences that found him deficient. On Yumashev's suggestion, Yeltsin on December 7, 1998, named career KGB officer Nikolai Bordyuzha to replace Yumashev as chief of the Kremlin administration. Bordyuzha retained the position of secretary of the Security Council that he had held since September. Yeltsin wrote afterward that he had doubts about Bordyuzha; they were only partly offset by assurances that at the beginning he would clear all big decisions with Yumashev. But Yeltsin swallowed his doubts, hoping the choice would send the message that he still meant business. His office "needed some force behind it, at least for show." Let the opposition shout at him as much as they wanted. "It would be harder to do that when next to the president there stands the figure of a colonel general who simultaneously holds two of the principal positions in the state." Yeltsin likened the decision to castling (*rokirovka* in Russian), the chess move that shelters the king beside a rook, away from the middle of the board.[56]

Yeltsin saw himself as taking cover in a storm. Contemporary analysts often concluded, though, that he had made the more drastic step of surrendering control to a collectivity termed, in the parlance of this period, "the Family" *(Sem'ya)*. The Family, so it was said, consisted of relatives of the president, high state officials, selected financiers, and hangers-on; at its hub were Tatyana Dyachenko, Valentin Yumashev, and especially Boris Berezovskii. The unspoken reference was to the Sicilian Cosa Nostra or the clan of Suharto, the corrupt president of Indonesia forced out of office in May 1998. The group was portrayed as bound together by consanguinity and marriage, frequent socializing, shared economic interests, and Berezovskii's powers of persuasion. And it was Russia's real government. "Few people do not know," journalist Yelena Dikun wrote breathlessly in 1999, "that the Family rules our country. In the popular mind, it is the highest institution of power—higher than the president himself."[57] The picture of an unassailable cabal, with a chief executive, unwell, acting as its stooge, has been a part of the conventional wisdom about the Yeltsin era.

Fragments of this image had cropped up before. Ruslan Khasbulatov, remember, had attacked Yeltsin in 1993 for surrounding himself with a "collective Rasputin." Other fragments did not necessarily have sinister connotations. It was no revelation that the president would take counsel from his chief of staff, which Yumashev was until the end of 1998, or from a daughter whom he had appointed a Kremlin adviser and who lived under the same roof as he. The economic and non-economic ties that purportedly bound the Family together vary from one story to another; the evidence for them is uneven and in some cases missing entirely.[58] Leonid Dyachenko, the then-husband of Tatyana, took up oil trading in the mid-1990s for a firm called Belka; a Belka specialty was the sale of products from a Siberian refinery run by Sibneft, the petroleum company owned by Berezovskii and his partner Roman Abramovich. But the information about his business operations is inconclusive, and no one has suggested that Yeltsin knew much about them or that Leonid had any great affinity for or competence in politics.[59] Meanwhile, in the spring of 1997, Valerii Okulov, Yeltsin's other son-in-law, was made director general of Aeroflot, a blue-chip company in which Berezovskii also had a stake. Within a year, he started to purge Berezovskii allies from the board and to cut the financial apron strings to the oligarch—for which Berezovskii sharply criticized him.

Narratives of the Family in action exaggerate the power and unity of its putative members, including Berezovskii—who missed no chance to toot his own horn. Sibneft, Berezovskii's acquisition through loans-for-shares, was Russia's sixth or seventh largest oil company. Some of the other oligarchs got choicer industrial assets, and Berezovskii lost out to Vladimir Potanin on Norilsk Nickel, which he very much wanted to take over in 1995. Berezovskii and Vladimir Gusinskii were bested in the Svyazinvest battle of 1997; in May 1998 Berezovskii was prevented from merging Sibneft with fellow oligarch Mikhail Khodorkovskii's company, Yukos. In the political sphere, Berezovskii after the 1996 election had his ups and downs. Yeltsin took away his position in the Security Council in November 1997. In April 1998 Berezovskii bounced back as executive secretary of the Commonwealth of Independent States, for which he had lobbied extensively with the CIS presidents; Yeltsin had him stripped of that post in March 1999, following a criminal inquiry into embezzlement at Aeroflot. On some questions on which he took a position, Berezovskii came out on the winning side; on others, he found himself on the losing side.[60]

As for Yeltsin, it is apparent that he had not the slightest fondness for Berezovskii. "I never liked and I do not like Boris Abramovich," he wrote in *Presidential Marathon*, where he skewered Berezovskii's overconfident manner, his "scandalous reputation," and "the fact that he was ascribed a special influence on the Kremlin that he never had." He valued Berezovskii as an ally on an issue-by-issue basis, one who was talented and energetic if "painful" to work with. What pained Yeltsin most was the combination of personas Berezovskii presented. He posed as the offstage kingmaker and the intimate of the present king, the very point that was infuriating about Gennadii Burbulis in the early 1990s. Then again, on the issues of the day Berezovskii expounded loudly and demandingly, often reaping more publicity than members of the elected government and, on some points, than the president. To continue with the section in *Marathon*:

> In people's eyes, Berezovskii was my constant shadow. "The hand of Berezovskii" was seen behind the Kremlin's every decision. Whatever I did and whomever I appointed or dismissed, they always said the same thing: "Berezovskii!" And who was creating this mysterious halo, this reputation

> of the éminence grise? Why, it was Berezovskii himself. . . . Every time the situation heated up, Berezovskii would go on television and say, "For my part, I am dead set against this. . . . I believe that . . . I am certain that . . ." He always got a lot of airtime. And the people would think: This is who is really governing the country.[61]

So far as the actuality and not the myth of influence goes, it bears mentioning that Yeltsin as president had only several direct conversations all told with Berezovskii. He did not give the tycoon telephone access; in fact, the two never seem to have spoken on the phone. Nor was Berezovskii ever once invited into the Yeltsins' home or to an out-of-Moscow residence like Zavidovo or Bocharov Ruchei.[62] Their dialogues were purely business. "I felt that Yeltsin was not fond of me personally," Berezovskii said in an interview in 2002; "he did hear out what I had to say and took it seriously."[63] But listening was not the same as agreeing, on either one's part. When Berezovskii saw it as in his interest, he was not afraid to come out against the government line (as on Svyazinvest in 1997) or even to have his newspaper, *Nezavisimaya gazeta*, in 1998 predict devaluation of the ruble and question the fitness of Yeltsin to finish out his term. At a press conference in September 1999, Berezovskii spoke disparagingly of Yeltsin's lack of a master plan and his "abominable" cadres decisions.[64]

What, then, of an oblique connection to Yeltsin? Berezovskii got together with Tatyana Dyachenko once every two or three months in the late 1990s. With adversaries, he found it useful to brag that he played Svengali to the unsophisticated daughter of the president and had psychological sway over her.[65] Asked in 2002 whether she was his gateway to number one, he was much more guarded. This would be "a worse than mistaken judgment," he replied. "I was well acquainted with her, but mark my words: Tatyana is in the same genetic mold as Boris Nikolayevich. And Tatyana also kept her distance *[tozhe derzhala distantsiyu]*. It was as if she constantly felt that she was the daughter of the president." Tatyana acknowledged that she thought well of Berezovskii's intellect and drive but at the same time related to him with "great caution," as she was unsure of his motives and did not want to favor or be seen as favoring one particular plutocrat. Chief of Staff Yumashev, who had worked with Berezovskii in the publishing industry, was friendlier. "A lot of what I wanted to say to Boris Nikolayevich," Berezovskii has stated, "I said to Yumashev."[66] And yet, Yumashev's primary loyalty was unambiguously to Yeltsin, and he and Berezovskii were not on the same wavelength on every issue. To give one example, Yumashev and Dyachenko, fearing that Berezovskii would be deadweight on Yeltsin, both opposed his appointment to the CIS position in 1998 and favored his removal from it in 1999. To give another, in March 1999 the Yeltsins and Yumashev were reliably reported to be livid at stories in the press that Berezovskii was using one of his companies to record their cell phone calls and that Dyachenko was financially dependent on him.[67] In other words, mutual wariness between Berezovskii and the other two set the tone within the threesome as much as mutual appreciation.

As he did repeatedly in his first term as president, Yeltsin in his second term sent out mixed signals about whether he intended to seek another. He and aides talked both sides of the question. He mostly said he had no interest in a third term; they tended to qualify his disclaimers and say nothing should be ruled out. The State Duma asked the Constitutional Court in October 1997 to review the question of his eligibility to seek another four years. Although Article 81 of the basic law prescribed that no one could hold the office for more than two consecutive terms, lawyers for Yeltsin reasoned that, since he had been elected to one term before the constitution was ratified, he was eligible to stand again. On November 5, 1998, the justices ruled in favor of the Duma brief. There was "an absence of uncertainty" on the merits, they said. Yeltsin had begun a second term in 1996 and had no right to stand for re-election when it ended in the summer of 2000. That was fine by Yeltsin, since "I long ago answered for myself the main question—about the fact that in 2000 I will not participate in the presidential election."[68]

The issue of a third term was more theoretical than practical. Yeltsin had made a solemn vow to his wife that the 1996 campaign would be his last and never once indicated that he would go back on it.[69] His infirmity, the many setbacks of the second term, and his unremittingly low scores in the opinion polls only reinforced the case. As long as Yeltsin remained Yeltsin, there was always the chance he would reconsider. It lingered until the very end. In mid-December 1999, two weeks before the handover to Putin, Yeltsin staggered his long-serving head of protocol, Vladimir Shevchenko, with the question, "What do you think? Should I or shouldn't I go for a third term?" Shevchenko believes the query was part of the process of Yeltsin accommodating himself to the loss of power and that by then his mind was made up.[70] No one can be sure. After the Constitutional Court judgment, the only way to cling to power would have been something like what Korzhakov and his sympathizers favored in 1996—martial law, postponement of the mandated presidential election, a suspension of the Duma and of many liberties, and the rest. Yeltsin's physical and political weaknesses being what they were, it was an all but impossible scenario. The premise for Yeltsin, his family, and his political team was, therefore, that he would retire, and a new president would put on the chain of office, in July 2000, four years after his second inauguration.

Until then, Yeltsin was going to have his hands full. The harbingers of post-crisis normalization did not assuage the oppositionists who favored his impeachment, as had been tried without success in 1993. Article 93 of the new constitution set an obstacle course for those who would depose the president more difficult to traverse than the one in place in 1993. The only lawful justification was guilt of "high treason or another grave crime." Upon motion of one-third of the Duma deputies, the chamber was to appoint a special committee to investigate presidential conduct; two-thirds of the deputies in the Duma had to vote in favor of any motion to remove; the Supreme Court had to certify the criminality of the president's actions and the Constitutional Court to confirm the procedural regularity of the proceedings; and then the Federation Council, composed of regional leaders, needed to concur.

The Duma struck an impeachment committee in May 1998. It reported out a first charge on September 7. By February 1999 Yeltsin had been arraigned on five counts: for destroying the USSR by signing the Belovezh'e accord; abetting murder during the crackdown on the congress and Supreme Soviet in 1993; exceeding his powers by taking up arms in Chechnya; deliberately ruining the army; and bringing about "the genocide of the Russian people." On May 13 and 14 Viktor Ilyukhin of the KPRF, a procurator by profession, read out the charges to the whole Duma and made a pitch for a yes vote. During hearings on the genocide charge, Ilyukhin had "stunned many . . . by declaring . . . that fewer Russians would have perished under Yeltsin's rule had the president not surrounded himself with Jewish advisers."[71] The accusations were mostly about Yeltsin's first term, ignoring the facts that the legislature had approved the Belovezh'e agreement, that Russians had elected him to a second term, and that the Duma derived its own legitimacy from the referendum that approved the Yeltsin constitution in 1993. In his defense, the most that liberal and centrist deputies were willing to do was plead that a bad status quo would get worse if parliament acted rashly. Impeachment "may lead to complete chaos," one said. "Have we not had enough foolhardiness from the president? Do we want to add a parliamentary contribution to the destabilization of Russian democracy?" The constitution, he added, did not provide for the dethroning of the head of state "for weakness and incapacity as such. . . . And this is only fair. The country should have the president it has elected," unless he has perpetrated high crimes, and not the trumped-up offenses listed in the indictment.[72]

Just as the impeachment motions were coming to a vote, Yeltsin, written off for dead only months before, grabbed hold of the initiative. Keeping the Duma in his sights, he began in March and April to make the most of a weak hand. In foreign policy, Yeltsin appointed Viktor Chernomyrdin as his personal envoy on the Yugoslav crisis, sent several warships into the Mediterranean, and offered in a telephone conversation with Bill Clinton, in a shocker even for Yeltsin, to meet him for negotiations aboard a Russian submarine he would send specially for the occasion; the Americans passed on the invitation.[73] Once the NATO bombing campaign got the Serbs to agree to terms in June, Yeltsin approved the dispatch of two hundred Russian troops from Bosnia to establish a presence in Kosovo. It was Moscow's only unilateral use of force in Europe since the Cold War and caused a deep division on the NATO side between Wesley Clark, the American supreme commander, who wanted to block the Russians, and Michael Jackson, the British officer in command on the ground, who was alarmed by the risks of trying. "I'm not going to start World War III for you," Jackson told Clark.[74]

In domestic politics, Yeltsin on March 19 fired his KGB-reared chief of staff, Nikolai Bordyuzha, and appointed Aleksandr Voloshin, a civilian with business experience, some of it with Berezovskii. The Kremlin inner circle had found Bordyuzha unresponsive to political concerns and readier to listen to Primakov than to the president. Bordyuzha had tried to get Yurii Skuratov, the procurator, to resign. Skuratov at first agreed, only to rescind his agreement and then to have the Federation Council refuse on three occasions to exercise its constitutional right to approve his removal. The Kremlin's response was to deploy kompromat of the tawdriest sort: It authorized the showing on Russian television of a videotape showing the procurator in bed with two prostitutes. On April 2 Yeltsin suspended Skuratov from his duties. Although Skuratov was not properly dismissed for another year, he was locked out of his office and unable to carry out further inquiries.[75]

Tension between Yeltsin and his prime minister mounted over the winter of 1998–99. The specifics mattered less than the overall point that the president was coming to the conclusion that their continued cohabitation was no longer in his interest. Primakov posed an opposite political problem to the one posed by Chernomyrdin a year before. The Russian public was tired of Chernomyrdin and blamed him for governmental failures; it warmed to Primakov and gave him credit for recent successes. Polls in early spring showed that two-thirds of the electorate approved of his work as head of government, that he was trusted by more Russians than any other leader, and that he was being put in the category of potential president. Given Primakov's age and socialistic proclivities, that was not an outcome Yeltsin could live with. He was nervous that Primakov, while not disloyal to him, could be a focal point for dissent and opposition if he chose to speak out on policy differences from inside the establishment, not unlike Yeltsin had in 1987.[76]

Yeltsin waited for his moment, one of the very last he was to have in the political arena, and acted. Some on his staff wanted to wait until the impeachment vote was held before handling the Primakov problem, reasoning that a dismissal would increase the chances of impeachment going through. Yeltsin saw it differently in part due to a technical point: He knew that the adoption of even one impeachment motion would take away the weapon of threatening to dissolve the Duma in the case of a disagreement over chairmanship of the government. But the essence of his thinking was intuitive, as it had been so many times before. "A sharp, unexpected, aggressive move," he wrote about the choice, "always knocks your opponent off his feet and disarms him, especially if it appears absolutely illogical and unpredictable. I was convinced of this more than once over the course of my presidential career."[77] The "utter unpredictability" that Vitalii Tret'yakov wrote off the preceding summer was not yet gone from the scene.

Yeltsin had been sending out hints that he was restless with Primakov and had someone else in mind to put in his place. That someone was Sergei Stepashin, the easygoing interior minister, with a background in police administration, whom Yeltsin had known since 1990. Stepashin, generally viewed as a liberal but uninvolved in electoral politics, headed a string of law and order–related ministries (security, justice, and interior), recovering from his loss of the directorship of the FSB (Federal Security Service) as a result of the Budënnovsk terror incident of 1995. On April 27 Yeltsin appointed him first deputy premier.[78] On May 12, three days *before* the scheduled Duma vote on impeachment, Yeltsin dismissed Primakov and named Stepashin acting prime minister. Commentators were incredulous that Yeltsin had done it again. For the third time in fourteen months, he had made a splashy move to "deflect the country from discussing the president's inadequacy for his job" or so it was seen.[79]

The Duma roll calls on impeachment were carried live on television. A Lenin double paraded in front of the entranceway, flanked by died-in-the-wool communists with placards denouncing "Führer Boriska." Many of the witnesses invited to testify at the two days of committee-of-the-whole hearings failed to show. Fire-breathing rhetoric did not carry over into coherent legislative action on the part of the opposition, and Yeltsin's representatives craftily played on divisions among the parliamentarians. Two hundred and ninety-four deputies voted on May 15 for at least one of the five motions, but no individual motion received that many. The Chechnya resolution got 283 ayes, or seventeen fewer than required; the motion on the 1993 events got 263, that on the Belovezh'e accord 241, that on the army 240, and that on genocide 238. The Chechnya motion, which was championed by the reformist Yabloko Party, was seen as the only one having a realistic chance of passing. A number of legislators who were willing to vote yes on another motion abstained or spoiled ballots on Chechnya. The LDPR refused to let its deputies participate at all; Yabloko ended up allowing its members to vote their conscience (nine of them voted against the Chechnya resolution); and a small caucus of regional representatives asked their members to lodge one positive vote each.[80]

Yeltsin had gambled and won on impeachment. Sergei Stepashin needed only one ballot to win Duma confirmation on May 19, with 301 votes in favor, almost as many as Primakov took in 1998.

Was the endgame without larger purpose, a contest entered into for the sheer pleasure of it? Yeltsin's delight in dealing and playing the cards is undeniable and is confirmed in the chapter in *Presidential Marathon* about the summer of 1999, one titled "Prime Ministerial Poker." There Yeltsin recounted a double ruse. Shortly before sending Stepashin's name to the Duma, and knowing full well that he was going to do so, he phoned Speaker Seleznëv to say that he was nominating somebody else entirely—Nikolai Aksënenko, the Russian minister of railways. Tall, burly, and Siberian-born, Aksënenko had worked his whole life in the transport system. In Yumashev's words, he "reminded Yeltsin of himself in his days as a builder of apartment houses in Sverdlovsk."[81] He was one of the candidates Yeltsin had considered for premier in the spring of 1998 and had scant backing on the Duma benches. Yeltsin says at one point that the Aksënenko feint had the tactical motivation of making Stepashin look good by contrast. But he also paints it as an enjoyable test in its own right: "I liked the way I had ginned up intrigue around Aksënenko. It was a nice little bit of mischief [*zagogulina*]."[82] Minutes after Seleznëv passed on word about

Aksënenko to the members, the envelope containing Yeltsin's letter of nomination for Stepashin was delivered to him. Seleznëv voiced annoyance and helplessness at the trickery: "The president has five Fridays in his week."[83]

If Yeltsin's memoir is to be believed, a second deception, on the strategic and not merely the tactical plane, lay behind the shenanigans of May 12. He meant to execute a final change in headship of the government, in favor of a dark horse, Vladimir Putin. He had decided to make Putin not only prime minister but his successor as leader of Russia—metaphorically, "to transfer to him Monomakh's Cap," the fur-trimmed crown of gold worn by the rulers of medieval Moscow. But the time was not yet right. Only the impending electoral struggle, in late 1999 over parliament and in 2000 over the presidency, would give Putin the chance to shine. For two or three months, Stepashin was to be the placeholder. The whole scheme had to remain Yeltsin's secret, not known to Putin himself, to the Duma, to Stepashin, or even to Tatyana Dyachenko and his close advisers. "I did not want the public to get too used to Putin in those lazy summer months. This mystery, the suddenness of it all, could not be allowed to evaporate. It would be so important for the elections, this factor of the expectations aroused by a potent new politician."[84]

Not every piece of this tale is a true guide to what happened in 1999. The ill-fated Stepashin's stretch of time in the Russian White House was pure "torture." He called the president on the telephone every day, wanting him "to feel something from me in a purely psychological way," but never felt appreciated in return. He is convinced that Yeltsin very nearly made up his mind to appoint Aksënenko in May and that Aksënenko, not Putin, was at first the intended beneficiary of the shell game. He has no explanation for why Aksënenko lost out to Putin.[85] Valentin Yumashev, Yeltsin's confidant and, after retirement, his son-in-law, is convinced Aksënenko was never really in the running and that Yeltsin left open the possibility that Stepashin would be the chosen one. Yeltsin abandoned Stepashin when he was wishy-washy in the face of the two big crises of the summer of 1999—a renewal of violence in the North Caucasus and the attempt by a coalition of anti-Kremlin elites to field a winning slate for the Duma election—and when Stepashin did not deal firmly with lobbyists for governmental favors, passing on some of the pressure to Yeltsin himself.[86]

So why did the needle spin around to Vladimir Vladimirovich Putin? Yeltsin had time and again shown a partiality for younger politicians. Putin, though, was older than many earlier favorites and, at forty-seven, was the very same age as Stepashin. Putin's St. Petersburg roots could hardly have been decisive; Yeltsin had no network in Russia's second city, and Chubais and Stepashin, among others, were also from there. In personal style, Putin was in some regards the un-Yeltsin—medium in height, trim, imperturbable, abstemious—but there were plenty of individuals out there who were different from Yeltsin. It has been suggested that Yeltsin chose Putin because Boris Berezovskii or some other master manipulator put him up to it, or because Putin had a unique ability to protect Yeltsin and his family from prosecution after his retirement. Neither of these interpretations holds water, either. There is no evidence that Berezovskii or anyone like him advocated Putin. My guess is that Berezovskii's support, had it been extended and had Yeltsin known of it, would for Yeltsin have been the kiss of death to any candidate.[87] Any senior politician Yeltsin would have considered, not only Putin, would have been happy to extend him the limited immunity Putin was to give him (not him and his family) by decree on December 31, and any presidential edict of this sort could subsequently have been superseded by legislation. Yeltsin never negotiated over immunity or any aspect of the Putin decree, which was finalized only in the hours after his resignation.[88]

Presidential Marathon drops a key clue to Putin's appeal to Yeltsin when it harks back to the decision, which he soon repudiated, to make Nikolai Bordyuzha Kremlin chief of staff in 1998. "I was already coming to feel that society needed some new quality in the state, a steel backbone that would strengthen the political structure of authority. We needed a person who was *thinking, democratic, and innovative yet steadfast in the military manner.* The next year such a person did appear. . . . Putin."[89] Putin acquired the military manner while serving sixteen years in the foreign intelligence wing of the Soviet KGB. His democratic and pro-market qualifications, such as they were, were earned in the first half of the 1990s, when he was lieutenant to Anatolii Sobchak, the liberal mayor of St. Petersburg, and was in charge of attracting foreign investment to the city. After Sobchak was voted out of office in 1996, Putin came to Moscow and worked in successively more responsible positions under Borodin, Chubais, and Yumashev. On July 25, 1998, Yeltsin appointed him director of the FSB, over the heads of hundreds of more senior operatives. Putin soon showed his reliability behind the scenes by suppressing talk among disgruntled army officers of a coup against the civilian government.[90] In March 1999 he made a public display of loyalty to the president by standing up for the authenticity of the scandalous charges against Procurator General Skuratov. Right after that, he was given the additional post of secretary of the Security Council.

On August 9, 1999, Yeltsin revealed that he had once again fired his prime minister and nominated a replacement. Whereas he had given Chernomyrdin a backhanded endorsement for president in August 1998, and had never linked any of his other changes in the premier's chair to the succession, this time he explicitly put forward Putin as his designated heir. Putin, Yeltsin said, was capable of "consolidating society" and seeing to "the continuation of reforms in Russia" after him.

The whole plan would have been scuttled if the votes to confirm could not be found in the Duma. Two hundred and thirty-three were found in the first round, on August 16, and Putin was duly installed. It is worth noting that this was only seven votes more than the 226 required and was substantially less than the support given to Primakov, Stepashin, and even Sergei Kiriyenko on his third try. The KPRF caucus could have blocked Yeltsin and Putin if it had been united on the issue. It was disunited, and, like so many other actors, did not foresee the mallet blow that Putin was to strike against its interests.[91]

After August 16, there was but one potential impediment to the transfer of Monomakh's Cap to Putin—the attitude of his patron in the Kremlin. Although Yeltsin in his retrospective memoir account treated the choice of Putin as hard and fast, in real time it was more tentative than that. In an interview with journalists shortly after the fact, Putin reported that in their conversation about the premiership Yeltsin was vague about the future: "He did not use the word 'successor.' Yeltsin spoke about 'a prime minister with prospects' [*s perspektivoi*] and said that if all went well he considered this [the presidency] to be possible."[92] In his public statement on August 9, Yeltsin reminded Russians that there was to be a presidential election in less than a year. Over that time, he was persuaded that Putin as prime minister would do "very useful things for the country," which would allow citizens to evaluate his "professional and human qualities" for themselves. "I have confidence in him. But I want everyone who in July 2000 will go to the voting stations and make their choice to also be sure. I think this will be enough time for him to show himself."[93]

What would happen if Putin faltered, the new man failed to catch fire with the public, and, by Yeltsin's definition, his qualities proved inadequate for leading Russia into the twenty-first century? One must assume that, if time allowed, the president would not have hesitated to act again. Having done in four prime ministers in seventeen months, what was to stop him from doing it to a fifth? Putin was the latest in a long line of army- and police-related functionaries to have captured his imagination. The line stretches back through Stepashin, Bordyuzha, and Nikolayev to Lebed, Korzhakov, and Rutskoi. In every other case, Yeltsin sooner or later lost faith in the man with the military manner. In the appropriate circumstances, he might well have done so for this understudy, too.

Russia's new prime minister did not falter, he did catch fire with the public, and the president did not reassess his vote of confidence. The politics of the four months following the August breakpoint belong more to the rising Putin era than to the fading Yeltsin one. Boris Yeltsin chose for himself the lame-duck status that pundits a year earlier saw as being inflicted on him by other people and by conditions. Putin as premier made almost no personnel changes, concentrating on mobilizing resources to deal with a pair of ripening crises.

The first of these was a deadly threat to the shaky peace in the North Caucasus, Russia's most unruly area. On August 7, following several months of infiltrating villages, a force of 2,000 Chechnya-based guerrillas crossed into Dagestan, the multiethnic republic within Russia separating the Chechen lands from the western shore of the Caspian Sea. They proclaimed an independent Islamic Republic of Dagestan, with the desperado Shamil Basayev as its leader, on August 10. In early September, as the Russians were counterattacking in Dagestan, Moscow and two southern towns were rocked by nighttime terror bombings of apartment houses. Three hundred civilians were killed and the FSB blamed the violence on pro-Chechen fanatics. Putin was convinced that failure to respond would be the death knell for the country: "My evaluation of the situation in August, when the bandits attacked Dagestan, was that if we did not stop it immediately Russia as a state in its current sense was finished. . . . We were threatened by the Yugoslaviazation of Russia."[94] Russian tanks and troops entered Chechnya in early October and fought their way across the Terek River toward Grozny; they seized the city on February 2, 2000, and pushed on into the southern high country.

Putin asked Yeltsin to entrust day-to-day coordination of the military effort to him. Yeltsin "did not hesitate to support him," the first time he had delegated so many of his national-security powers.[95] Putin's forceful prosecution of the war, and his verbal jabs at the rebels, had speedy impact on public opinion. He won further respect for announcing increases in pension payments from the federal budget, something the incipient economic recovery enabled. His approval ratings skyrocketed, and so did the number prepared to vote for him in a presidential election. If in August 1999 some 2 percent of prospective voters said they would cast their ballots for Putin, by September that was 4 percent and in October it jumped to 21 percent, overtaking Yevgenii Primakov and Gennadii Zyuganov. In November Putin's forecast vote share had doubled to 45 percent; by the time of the election to the State Duma, on December 19, it stood at 51 percent.[96]

With Yeltsin's encouragement, Putin also intervened in the Duma campaign, the second critical event that autumn. The favorite in the election had been the alliance patched together over the preceding year by Yurii Luzhkov. It took final shape in August as the Fatherland–All Russia Bloc, with the widely esteemed Primakov heading its electoral slate. The bloc was center-left and nationalistic in policy orientation and included many of Russia's most powerful regional chiefs. With the involvement of Vladimir Gusinskii and the NTV television network, its materials depicted the central government and "the Family" around Yeltsin as corrupt and devoid of ideas. The burden of fending off Fatherland–All Russia was assumed by a pro-Kremlin coalition called Unity, which took shape only in September. Led by Sergei Shoigu, the minister for emergency management in all cabinets going back to 1990, Unity put forward a hazy program that mixed liberal ideas with populism, patriotism, and national unity. Berezovskii-controlled ORT television promoted Unity, sparred with Gusinskii and NTV, and attacked Fatherland–All Russia.

Unity's logo was a stylized drawing of a forest bear, the universal symbol of Russia. It is also the animal to which Boris Yeltsin had often been compared, but that was as close as Unity got to linking itself to the president. Yeltsin cool-headedly accepted the need for a firewall between them. After the initial discussions, "I very quickly ceased to have anything to do with this work. It was clear to me . . . that the party of social optimism should not be associated in the consciousness of the voters with my name. . . . It did not bother me that Unity distanced itself from me."[97] The movement was eager to associate itself with the Russian leader whose political coattails were now the longest—Putin. On November 24 Putin stated that "as a citizen" he was going to vote for the Unity bloc. "Our goal is to create a pro-Putin majority in the State Duma," Unity blared the next week. "Unity supports Putin, and Putin relies on Unity." Although Unity did not win a majority outright, it routed Fatherland–All Russia, with the Putin sound bite counting for as much as half of its vote share, and came a close second to the KPRF in the national vote. It was soon able to build a working parliamentary majority, something Yeltsin never had as president.

Yeltsin had one more trick up his sleeve. In black and white, Article 92 of the 1993 constitution gave a mechanism that permitted him to control the timing and atmospherics of his exit and to smooth the handover of power. It stipulated that, in the event of a presidential resignation, the prime minister automatically became "acting president" and there was to be a national election of a permanent head of state within ninety days. Anticipating a favorable outcome in the scheduled Duma election, Yeltsin came to the decision to invoke Article 92 the week before it. He brought Putin up to date on his plans at Gorki-9 on December 14, and Putin gave his assent, although Putin thought Yeltsin had in mind retirement in the spring of 2000, not before the end of the year. Putin expressed reluctance about his readiness for the job, to which Yeltsin answered that he, too, came to Moscow with "other plans," and learned about national leadership only by doing it. On December 28 Yeltsin instructed Aleksandr Voloshin, the head of his executive office, to work out a resignation decree and other administrative arrangements and asked former head Yumashev to draft a retirement speech, so as to keep it secret from the regular speech writers. Yeltsin broke the news to his daughter Tatyana the evening of December 28 and to his wife the morning of his resignation.[98]

December 31, the final date of the millennium, was chosen as the leave-taking date for its symbolic value, as the end of one unit of history and the start of another. Yeltsin's grim-faced address, a classic of ceremonial rhetoric, had as its centerpiece a poignant apology. He had told Yumashev to include in the speech a passage about the sufferings of the population in the 1990s and his regrets for them. The speech as delivered requested the Russian people's forgiveness "for not making many of your and my dreams come true," faulting the speaker's performance and the naïveté of the dreams in whose name he attempted his anti-revolutionary revolution. "I did all I could," Yeltsin said.

Decree No. 1761, his last, took effect at twelve noon sharp. Around one P.M., citizen Yeltsin returned to the president's office from the farewell lunch and toasts. An adjutant slipped on his overcoat. As they waited for the private elevator of Building No. 1, he presented Putin with the fat fountain pen with which he had signed decrees and laws. He put on his sable hat at the front door. "Take care of Russia," he said to Putin as the flashbulbs popped. He walked to the car in a light snowfall and was gone out the Kremlin gates.

Chapter Seventeen

Aftermath

Boris Yeltsin's expectations for life after power were uneven. He looked forward to the peace and quiet but "had no illusions." "People were not going to love or worship me. I even had some doubts. If . . . I made a public appearance or went to the theater, would they jeer at me?" What would become of him "when the old Russian tradition requires that all misfortunes and sins are heaped upon the departed chief"?[1]

The remaining stages of the handover of power went by without a hitch. Vladimir Putin, acting president since December 31, was elected president on March 26, 2000, in the first round of voting, without really campaigning for the job. He was sworn in on May 7. Yeltsin, standing beside him in the renovated Grand Kremlin Palace, gave remarks in which he repeated the injunction to take good care of Russia. He delivered them "slowly and with one pause so long that a handful in the audience applauded, thinking the speech was over."[2] When he was done, Putin spoke as president and the shift from one leader to the next was complete.

Yeltsin's days now centered on his country residence—Gorki-9 in the first year, the more pleasant Barvikha-4 for the duration. The feared personal indignities did not come about. He was never jeered at or made a spectacle of. No one went after him for his actions in government or tried to do him harm through his family.

Aside from the evils avoided, retirement brought with it two good things, in particular. For one, it did wonders for Yeltsin's physical condition. "Immediately after my departure from the post of president, an enormous, unbelievably heavy load fell from my shoulders and I began to breathe easy"; "the constant pressure that . . . saps the health of the strongest organism" was behind him.[3] Health problems did nag at Yeltsin. He submitted to surgery for eye cataracts in 2000 and 2005. He came down with double pneumonia in January–February 2001 and spent his seventieth birthday in the hospital. In December 2001 he had an angioplasty at the German Heart Center in Berlin. A virus kept him away from Putin's second inauguration in May 2004. Except for the bout with pneumonia—when the doctors warned the family he might have only days to live—these were pinpricks compared to what he endured from 1996 through 1999.[4] Yeltsin still awoke at dawn.[5] Under Naina Yeltsina's watchful eye, he trimmed his waistline, ate a wholesome diet, and kept his drinking to a minimum. His overall condition took a turn for the better in 2002. Acquaintances thought he looked ten years younger.

The other great bonus from relinquishing office was the time and freedom to pursue interests he had long put on the back burner. Yeltsin saw a fair amount of his old Sverdlovsk friends and in May 2005 hosted a fiftieth reunion of his UPI class at a mountain spa in Kislovodsk. Of high-ranking coworkers from his presidential years, he renewed acquaintances with almost every one from whom he had parted amicably and with many from whom he had not—Aleksandr Korzhakov being the outstanding exception.

Yeltsin's deepest interest was in a family circle that continued to swell. His daughter Tatyana, who ceased all political activity, married Valentin Yumashev in 2001 and bore Yeltsin his sixth grandchild, Mariya. Tatyana Yumasheva moved out of Boris and Naina's home, but she and Yelena Okulova came around to see their father almost every day. The marriage of Yumashev's daughter, Polina, to aluminum magnate Oleg Deripaska, one of the richest men in Russia, assured that segment of the Yeltsin clan financial security.[6] A first great-grandchild, a boy, had been born in late 1999; a second and third, also boys, arrived in 2005 and 2006.[7] In September 2006, Boris, Naina, and brood celebrated the couple's golden wedding anniversary.

The biggest claim on Yeltsin's leisure hours was reading. He had the children's nursery on the first floor of Barvikha-4 converted into a library with a writing desk and armchair. Tatyana had a box of about a dozen books delivered to him each week. They were put on a sorting table and stored on floor-to-ceiling shelves only when he was through with them. With a target of three hundred pages a day, Yeltsin plowed through memoirs, biographies, historical novels, foreign literature in translation, detective and spy thrillers, science fiction, military history, and the poetry of Pushkin. He read the multivolume works of the great Russian historians Nikolai Karamzin (1766–1826), Nikolai Kostomarov (1817–85), Sergei Solov'ëv (1820–79), and Vasilii Klyuchevskii (1841–1911). When I last conversed with him, in 2002, he had just finished a number of classic and recently released books about Peter the Great. He was appalled by the evidence of his hero's cruelty and imbalanced mind: "I have come to view him with great realism, although I remain a defender of Peter."[8]

Yeltsin on pension went for a walk and a swim in the pool daily and hunted at Zavidovo several times a year. Unable to take to the tennis court, he played it vicariously by being an ardent fan of the professional game. He attended every big match in Moscow and rented a satellite dish that pulled in broadcasts from every continent—he sometimes watched them live at all hours of the night. Another luxury within reach was extensive travel. In addition to domestic destinations across Russia and the former Soviet Union, he and Naina paid visits to Israel, Germany, China, Japan, France, Britain, Norway, Alaska, Ireland, and Italy. He was in Paris on December, 1, 2002, when Russia won its first major team trophy in tennis, the Davis Cup. Snatching victory from the jaws of defeat, Yeltsin-style, Mikhail Youzhny came back from a two-set deficit to edge a French player in the deciding match. "Yeltsin sat in the VIP box along with French President Jacques Chirac during the entire three-day encounter, cheering wildly at every winning point for Russia. In the most dramatic moments of the tie [on December 1], Yeltsin, the self-proclaimed team mascot, punched the air in delight. The moment Youzhny clinched the title, Yeltsin climbed over a courtside barrier to bearhug him and the rest of the squad."[9] He made it to Paris again for the French Open in June 2004, to Wimbledon on the same trip, and back to the French Open in June 2006.

Whereas private life after power had many joys, Yeltsin had to withdraw from the public realm, and this process brought the sting of disappointment as well as relief that somebody else was making the decisions. On January 10, 2000, back from an excursion to Jerusalem and Bethlehem, Yeltsin opened the door of his study at Gorki-9 and found the desk empty of papers. The handset of the secured government telephone line had no dial tone. "There was absolutely nothing for me to do in this office. I sat in the chair for a time and then picked up and left." The phone connection was quickly re-established—the interruption had been a technical hiccup—but for some days Yeltsin experienced "an engulfing emptiness." He had been a boss at one level or another since the 1950s and had held senior political positions since the 1970s. Now a psychological adjustment was needed. He would have to accept that he was not in charge of anything outside the grounds of his home, and even they belonged to the state. While people might come to him with questions and comments, he had to "contain my . . . leader's reflex" and get used to expressing no more than an opinion.[10] In a press interview a year after bowing out, he conceded that he was sometimes subject to melancholy *(toska)*. "It happens. After all, I have been used to a stormy life, to seething effort." What did he do when he felt that way? asked the correspondent. "Then I struggle with myself," Yeltsin replied.[11]

Unlike Mikhail Gorbachev, who after his involuntary retreat set up a large philanthropic foundation and gave numerous lectures, Yeltsin chose to keep out of the public eye. He abstained from formal speeches in Russia and abroad and gave only about ten newspaper and television interviews in seven years. A Yeltsin Foundation was established in November 2000, with his daughter Tatyana as president and headquartered in a modest building across the Moskva River from the Kremlin. It concentrated on nonpolitical, youth-oriented work, spending several million dollars a year. Among the beneficiaries were the village school in Butka, the Pushkin School in Berezniki, and Urals State Technical University (the former UPI) in Yekaterinburg. There were national programs for sick children, young athletes, and tennis and volleyball tournaments in the hinterland. The organization opened a Urals branch in Yekaterinburg in 2006.[12] A presidential library, announced by the Kremlin as a government project in 2000, was funded only after his death in 2007—in the form of a library named after Yeltsin in St. Petersburg, dedicated to the history of the Russian state. Yeltsin dictated and edited *Presidential Marathon,* the third installment of his memoirs, in the months after stepping down. It came out at the end of 2000. All invitations to write more were turned down. "To be honest," he said in 2006, "I am in no mood to try to recollect events from ten or fifteen years ago. What is the sense in digging up the past?"[13]

The new head of state treated Yeltsin with respect, if not affection or deference. On June 12, 2001, the tenth anniversary of his election as president, Putin made Yeltsin the first Russian recipient of the Order for Services to the Fatherland, First Grade (established by Yeltsin in 1994), and pinned the badge on his lapel at a Kremlin reception. In Yeltsin's first year out of office, the two met, usually at his residence, an average of once a month. The meetings were sometimes arranged at his initiative and sometimes at Putin's. "A new president," Yeltsin professed, "*is obliged* to periodically hear out the opinions of his predecessor." He was content on the whole with Putin, but "I tell him frankly about his mistakes and . . . that he has to live up to people's hopes."[14]

Yeltsin let loose with some of his opinions in the open. In August 2000, when Putin was slow to interrupt a vacation and respond to the sinking of the Russian nuclear submarine *Kursk,* Yeltsin made it known that Putin had been insensitive. That December he took Putin to task for siding with parliamentarians who wanted to bring back the musical score of the pre-1991 Soviet anthem, with updated lyrics. "For me, the old hymn has only one association—the [Communist Party] congresses and party conferences at which the power of the party bureaucrats was confirmed and strengthened." Yeltsin scoffed at Putin's report that Russian athletes at the Summer Olympics in Sydney were not inspired by the nineteenth-century Glinka melody that Yeltsin instituted as the national anthem in 1993, and to which words had not yet been set. The athletes would adapt to whatever music the country required, Yeltsin said, and in any case they were young people who looked "to the future and not to the past." On symbolic matters, he continued, "The president should not blindly follow the people's mood; on the contrary, it is up to him to actively influence it."[15] Three weeks after Yeltsin spoke out, Putin signed the anthem bill into law.[16]

Putin in power at first combined economic liberalism with vigorous and often brutal prosecution of the second Chechen war and a moderate tightening of political controls. Yeltsin was in full agreement with the economic changes, which were mostly designed and implemented by younger technocrats whom he had promoted in his second term, and were pushed through the Duma by Putin's coalition there.[17] For the first wave of political changes, he expressed "restrained support." They included new central levers over the regions and a squeeze on the more forward of the oligarchs, prompting both Vladimir Gusinskii and Boris Berezovskii to flee the country in 2001.[18] Yeltsin was fully behind the drive for a military solution in Chechnya. Most of the surviving warlords from 1994 to 1996 were killed in the Russian operation, and he came to believe he had erred when he ended that first conflict on the separatists' terms.[19]

With the passage of time, though, the authoritarian flavor of many of Putin's choices in the political arena, made and executed in concert with fellow products of the security services, was increasingly at odds with Yeltsin's more liberal outlook.[20] A tender point was the curbing of media autonomy, starting with Gusinskii's NTV network and ORT, which had been in Berezovskii's orbit. Gusinskii and Berezovskii defended their assets more out of financial interests and power concerns than out of democratic principle,[21] but the net effect was the narrowing of the sphere in which officialdom's behavior could be held up to scrutiny. In March 2002 Yeltsin gave his consent to a suggestion by Boris Nemtsov that he chair a new supervisory board for TV-6, a small for-profit channel, previously owned by Berezovskii, that had begun to carry news programming and to which some of the journalists from NTV migrated when Gusinskii and Igor Malashenko were ousted there. Putin heard of it and insisted that Yeltsin pull out of the arrangement before it could be announced.[22]

The Putin administration crossed a threshold in October 2003 with the arrest of billionaire businessman Mikhail Khodorkovskii. He was put on trial for fraud and tax evasion and sentenced in 2005 to nine years in a Siberian prison camp; his oil company, Yukos, was broken up and the pieces acquired by state-dominated firms. The affair was motivated in part by Khodorkovskii's political independence. In September 2004 Putin took advantage of a horrific hostage-taking by Chechen and pro-Chechen guerrillas in the town of Beslan, North Ossetiya, to introduce legislation ending the popular election of oblast and republic leaders and authorizing him in effect to select them from above. The Beslan tragedy and the fall of a pro-Moscow government in neighboring Ukraine in December 2004 were also followed by the imposition of stiffer restrictions on opposition groups, human-rights activists, and nongovernmental organizations. Yeltsin disapproved of these retrograde changes and others. As Yegor Gaidar, who had several searching conversations with him, summarized it the week of Yeltsin's death, Yeltsin "was very disconcerted by much of what was going on in Russian politics."[23]

The Yeltsin-Putin relationship inevitably deteriorated under these strains. Their face-to-face meetings became less frequent in 2001, occurring only every second or third month. The first three years, the Yeltsin and Putin families had a social gathering on New Year's Eve to mark the anniversary of the transfer of power; there was none in December 2003 or any subsequent year. From late 2002 on, the leaders visited only on Yeltsin's birthday and for chats on protocol occasions. They did not talk substance until two confidential conversations they had in Yeltsin's final months.[24]

When I had a chance to ask Putin in September 2007 how it had been between them, the first thing he volunteered was that they had seen little of one another in recent years. His attitude was courteous and correct but markedly cool. Yeltsin, he said, had been satisfied with the "general course"; they were at variance on "particular problems."[25]

Yeltsin, although he was more displeased with the particulars than before, was also more discreet in passing judgment on them. One reason this was so was that Putin took care not to go at him ad hominem and even to praise him on occasion for liberating Russians from the dead hand of the communist past. Yeltsin continued to trust Putin's good intentions. If the new president was acting in error, time would heal the wounds. But the key basis for Yeltsin's acquiescence was situational realism. It derived from the weariness with politics that had led him to leave the Kremlin ahead of schedule, his candid acknowledgment in 1999 that he had let many Russians down, the recognition that it was he who put Putin on the throne and that he bore a certain moral responsibility for Putin's behavior, and a practical awareness of the limits of his influence as ex-president. The economic boom and the perception that order had been restored made Putin, year in and year out, as popular as Yeltsin had been during his romance with the electorate in 1990–91. He swept the 2004 presidential election with 70 percent of the popular vote, double what Yeltsin took in the first round of his 1996 reelection bid. Putin was not an easy leader to challenge.

The constraints that kept Yeltsin on the sidelines came through in his interview with Kirill Dybskii of *Itogi* magazine in January 2006:

DYBSKII: Does everything in current Russian politics suit you?

YELTSIN: I always have reproofs to make. It would be strange if I didn't. But the main thing is the strategic course, and I support it and consider it the right one.

DYBSKII: But how about tactical differences?

YELTSIN: I don't discuss these in the press. I can talk about them one on one with Vladimir Vladimirovich, but in public, as they say in the West, no comment. Don't forget, I'm not a public politician any more.

DYBSKII: But knowledgeable people say it is impossible to get out of politics entirely.

YELTSIN: Perhaps [you can keep at it] if you have the force of will and the brains. But you need to figure out that there is a time to leave, to make way for the young, to stop interfering. Of course, in my inner thoughts I constantly analyze what is going on in the country and try to guess what I would have done in this or that context. But here's where I have to stop myself and say, "Hold on! Today the president of the country is named Putin and not Yeltsin. . . ." I hope I had the intelligence and the self-mastery to depart the proper way. So you're not going to hear any critical comments from me. Why sow discord? This is of no use to the country or its leader. I am the one who put Putin forward and I ought to support him. . . .

DYBSKII: But it used to be that you criticized openly. For example, you complained about the new Russian anthem and said it was just the old Soviet one dressed up.

YELTSIN: I grumbled a little, and then I calmed down. And what came of it? The anthem stayed in place.[26]

Matters of state were forgotten when Yeltsin on February 1, 2006, accepted Putin's hospitality for a seventy-fifth birthday party in the Kremlin palace. It was his last hurrah before a political audience. Bill Clinton, Helmut Kohl, Patriarch Aleksii II, and Mstislav Rostropovich, and all of Yeltsin's prime ministers headed the guest list of three hundred. They were treated to champagne and canapés in Alexander Nevsky Hall, chamber music in St. Andrei's Hall, and a dinner of pheasant, sturgeon, and veal in St. George's Hall. He had been a free man since 2000, Yeltsin said in his toast to the company, and would not trade it for anything. For the first time in a thousand years a past leader of Russia "did not have his head chopped off" and got to enjoy an evening in his honor in the Kremlin. During the response toasts, he sat with a microphone in hand, "like at a production meeting," prepared "to give a piece of his mind to subordinates," which he did several times. Viktor Chernomyrdin drew the loudest applause. Yeltsin had been hard to work with and was no angel, "But angels are not able to govern the state."[27]

Yeltsin liked to tell his wife and children that he intended to see one hundred but might be willing to settle for eighty-five. As he grew old, he grew more introspective, and as he did he gave considerable thought to spiritual issues. There was abundant media speculation in Russia in 2007 that he had undergone a religious re-conversion and died a devout Orthodox Christian. It was whetted by the church funeral he received, by word that he had gone on a trip to the biblical Holy Land weeks before his fatal illness, and by the Patriarch's statement at the fortieth-day rite, on June 1, that Yeltsin in recent times had journeyed from atheism to being a believer *(veruyushchii)*.

It is clear that Yeltsin's curiosity about, and regard for, religion revived during and after the collapse of communism. When he and Billy Graham spent an hour together in Moscow in July 1991, it was with pride that he said his grandchildren all wore crucifixes around their necks. "I could tell," Graham recalled, "that he was growing in his sympathetic attitude toward the church and toward the gospel."[28] Yeltsin attended services on holidays from the late 1980s onward; during them, he would make an offering, light a votive candle, and cross himself in the Orthodox fashion, right shoulder before the left. At his mother's funeral in 1993, he is said to have queried one of the priests about the afterlife.[29] His attention to religious themes appears to have increased after 2000. In an interview in 2006, he for the only time in public referred to God as a presence and to himself as having a soul: "For me, God is the creature who knows what goes on in my soul. He sees within me that which no one else sees. And I want to believe God sees that my thoughts have been clean."[30] In late March and early April of 2007, he traveled to Jordan, which he had seen once before, on government business, in 1999. He and Naina stayed at a Dead Sea resort and took a drive one day to the River Jordan. Yeltsin waded in and washed his face in the waters of the river, close by the place Jesus is thought to have been baptized. The couple, in Naina's words, "warmly addressed God" by voicing words of prayer together.[31]

Despite these incidents, Yeltsin, like most Russians, did not worship weekly, did not pray regularly or keep the Lenten fast, and did not delve in any detail into church teachings. He was drawn mostly in a general, cultural sense to the faith of his parents and grandparents. He did take comfort, however, from what he knew of it, and showed so in gestures that the communist of the 1960s, 1970s, and 1980s would never have made.

The beginning of the end for Yeltsin was the fall he took on the bathroom floor of a hotel suite in Sardinia on September 7, 2005. He fractured his left thigh bone up near the hip and had to have surgery on the joint upon his return to Moscow. He was on crutches for several months and walked with a limp after that. Less mobile than before, he exercised less and put on weight. He began to feel a malaise in the autumn of 2006. His perennial aide, Vladimir Shevchenko, noticed that winter that he was "more inside himself." "He was thinking things over, taking them to heart, reconsidering."[32]

Yeltsin caught a head cold in Jordan that did not respond to rest. Shortly after getting back to Moscow, on April 11, 2007, he was admitted to the Central Clinical Hospital. He persuaded the doctors to discharge him after two days. On April 16 he was readmitted with an upper respiratory infection and symptoms of failure of the heart, lungs, and internal organs. He and his wife fully expected him to recover: He had been sicker than this in 2001 and had pulled through. He laid plans that weekend to be given his release early the coming week. About eight A.M. on Monday, April 23, Naina spoke to his adjutant by phone and said she would come in to help him wash up and shave. At 8:20 Yeltsin's eyes went blank. She was told and rushed to the hospital. He was in intensive care, in a coma, when she made it there. Naina covered him with a shawl and sprinkled him with water she had taken from the Jordan.[33] His pulse stopped at 3:45 P.M.

Neither the family nor the government had made funeral plans. That evening Putin announced a day of national mourning for the Wednesday. He proposed through his office and through the Patriarch an Orthodox service and accompanying state honors, with burial in Novodevichii Cemetery. Naina gladly accepted. Overnight Tuesday the body lay in state under the golden dome of the neo-Byzantine Cathedral of Christ the Savior, destroyed by Stalin in the 1930s and rebuilt from scratch in the 1990s. There had been no time to take down the banners from Easter, April 8. Yeltsin's Soviet-era and post-Soviet medals were on view on a velvet cushion. Twenty-five thousand people filed briskly by the open oak casket, draped in the Russian tricolor. The morning of Wednesday, April 25, the family was comforted by Putin, by former Yeltsin associates, by foreign statesmen (Clinton and Kohl again, George H. W. Bush, Lech Wałesa, a total of thirty-five sitting and former national leaders), and by UPI classmates. The most surprising to find among the mourners was Yeltsin's archrival, Gorbachev. Their paths had not crossed since December 1991. Gorbachev "stood there downcast and suddenly looked much older. It was evident that he was suffering in ways that few in the hall were. Together with the life of Boris Yeltsin, a piece of his own life had been torn away."[34] Naina thanked him for coming and wished him well.

Twenty white-robed clergy chanted the requiem mass at midday. A hearse took the coffin in procession from the cathedral to Novodevichii and an armored vehicle pulled it through the gates on a gun carriage. Behind the red walls, Yeltsin's widow tucked a white handkerchief inside the casket and took her leave.[35] It was lowered into one of the last plots left in the congested graveyard, where Nikita Khrushchev, alone of the Soviet leaders, and Yeltsin's favorite writer, Anton Chekhov, lie and where he had planned to put Lenin. Three cannons fired a salvo and a band played the new-old national anthem.

Coda

Legacies of an Event-Shaping Man

What makes a political leader interesting is not necessarily what makes him influential. Reactions to his personality and to its unfolding over a life span will always be subjective. When it comes to the actor's influence, it has to be gauged on two dimensions, the empirical and the normative. The key empirical question is about facts—how much of a difference the man made. The key normative question is about values—whether the difference was for good or for evil.

Immediate responses to Boris Yeltsin's passing in 2007 are illustrative. The day of his funeral, KPRF deputies refused to stand for a minute of silence in the Duma. One of them joked bitterly that a stake of ash wood should be hammered into his grave, as if he were a vampire. The communists were in no doubt that Yeltsin's influence had been overpowering. The source of their fury was the sentiment that communism's and the Soviet Union's demise was a crime for which he ought to be condemned.[1]

It would have done Yeltsin's heart good to hear Anatolii Chubais, his associate in many projects, reach for precedents: "If you try to understand who in the history of Russia measures up to Boris Nikolayevich in the sum of what he did, perhaps [you would look to] Peter the Great. Or maybe it would be Lenin and Stalin combined, only each of them had a minus sign and [Yeltsin] had a plus sign."[2] Chubais thus rated Yeltsin high on both the empirical and the normative scales.

At the memorial banquet in the Kremlin, Vladimir Putin preferred in his eulogy to link Yeltsin's life with freedom: "It is the rare person who is given the destiny to become free himself and at the same time to carry millions along behind him, and to inspire truly historic changes in his homeland

and transform the world."[3] Putin's eloquent words make you wonder what he meant by freedom, given his labors since 1999 to retrench the liberties Yeltsin had helped install. One suspects they were propaganda for his approach no less than a heartfelt attempt to honor Yeltsin.

For one more assessment, we may turn to Viktor Shenderovich, the head writer of *Kukly,* the television satire that tirelessly parodied Yeltsin from 1994 to 1999. His tribute was emotional and poetic. Yeltsin, Shenderovich wrote, did many things right and many things wrong, but he apologized for his mistakes at the end of the day and he surrendered power, as no tsar or general secretary had ever done. The sincerity of his confession mitigated the mistakes. "He asked our forgiveness—so let's forgive him!" Shenderovich's Yeltsin was, quite like the Yeltsin of this volume, a paradox:

> He was someone out of [the nineteenth-century writers Alexander] Ostrovsky and [Nikolai] Leskov, with [Mikhail] Saltykov-Shchedrin and Dostoevsky thrown in. He was large-scale, authentic, perpetually breaking out of bounds, not susceptible to simple description. Everything he did, he did himself. His victories and his disasters were all in his own hand and were a match for his personality—enormous. . . . He had character enough for a whole army division. Fate broke itself against this flint many times. But he would not have been Russian if he was not capable of self-destruction. And he never would have been first secretary of the Sverdlovsk obkom of the CPSU if he did not know how to step all over people. He was of one bone and one flesh with the nomenklatura and of one bone and one flesh with the people.

On the benevolent side, Shenderovich offered a selective comparison with Yeltsin's handpicked successor. In the days Yeltsin came under fire for his missteps, he tolerated the flak. Putin, whose subordinates had *Kukly* yanked from the airwaves in 2002, did not, and therein lay a difference that gave "some basis for talking about the scope of [Yeltsin's] personality."[4]

If assessments of a historical figure, especially on the normative plane, often diverge, attempts to come to closure by appealing to the person himself or to the court of public opinion are unlikely to be satisfactory. Out of power, Yeltsin, in this instance, simultaneously stood by his record and conceded some veracity to the charge that he failed to bring about the speedy improvement he had promised. While still in office, he could display a sense of humor about the partial and discordant results he was getting. At a Kremlin luncheon in the mid-1990s, John Major asked him to describe the state of Russia in one word. "Good," Yeltsin said. Major was flabbergasted, since he had the impression the place was going to the dogs. The Briton next asked him to give his diagnosis in two words. "Not good," Yeltsin replied drolly.[5]

The populace, who in Yeltsin's second term and into his retirement years were inclined to appraise him unkindly, have drifted toward a similar ambivalence. In April 2000 the Public Opinion Foundation asked a representative sample of voting-age adults whether Yeltsin had played a positive or negative role in Russian history. Only 18 percent saw him in a positive light, while 68 percent were negative and 14 percent could not answer. Shortly after Yeltsin's death, the poll was repeated. By this time, favorable and unfavorable readings had equalized, as 40 percent of respondents believed Yeltsin's contribution was positive, 41 percent saw it as negative, and 19 percent were unable to say. Positive reviews in 2007 were 13 percentage points ahead of negatives among respondents who fully trusted President Putin, presumably reflecting Putin's gracious send-off as well as Yeltsin having been his patron. The gap was 10 to 12 points among persons thirty-five or younger, university graduates, and residents of the big cities.[6] These are kinder results than polls have revealed for the contemporary reputation of Mikhail Gorbachev.[7]

Soviet communism died not even twenty years ago. Most would agree that ultimate perspective on Yeltsin and his role will be more attainable when a generation or two has passed than it is at present. The best we can do right now is come up with the first, rough draft. I put one forward in full recognition of Yeltsin's many paradoxes and imperfections. His paradoxes do not rule out a verdict, and his imperfections do not rule out a positive one.

It is helpful in summing up Yeltsin's record to revisit a thought-provoking treatise about "the hero in history" penned in the 1940s by the philosopher Sidney Hook. Hook discriminated between two types of hero, the "eventful man," the pale imitation, and the "event-making man," the hero deserving of the name. Both come along at "forking points of history" that are admissive of alternative solutions to human problems. The eventful man happens to be in the right spot at the right time and commits a trite act that pushes the players down one avenue and not another. The event-making man—Hook adduced as examples Caesar, Cromwell, Napoleon, and Lenin—encounters a fork in the road and "also helps, so to speak, to create it." The event maker goes beyond choosing the one tine of the fork; his qualities of intelligence, will, and temperament boost its odds of success.[8]

From his entry into the Soviet industrial establishment in the 1950s through to his appointment as Communist Party prefect of the city of Moscow in the 1980s, Yeltsin was either a historically irrelevant man or at very most an eventful man, confined by structures and routines that gave room for innovation only at the margin. The case for him as a hero in history, therefore, is going to be proved or disproved with reference to the event-packed years 1985 to 1999.

How would we know an event-making man if we saw one? Five tests are applicable to Yeltsin or any other candidate.

The first asks whether the leader in question has what Erik Erikson in *Gandhi's Truth* called the capacity "to step out of line" and to address the central issues of the day in a fresh way. This happens, as Erikson wrote, only when there is "a confluence [between] a deeply personal need and a national trend," the product of which, in a certain period of the person's life, is a "locomotor drivenness" to effect change.[9]

Yeltsin stayed in line well into middle age. In the late 1980s and early 1990s, however, stirred by inner testing and rebellion scripts and by changes in the social environment, he broke stride and linked his personal journey to larger trends. In so doing, Yeltsin turned political disgrace into vindication and parlayed vindication into political realignment and victory. His gift was not originality or profundity of thought but the ability to translate abstractions into the idiom of ordinary people. From knee-jerk populism he moved to adopt a program for de-monopolization through democratization, market reform, and territorial devolution that addressed main issues of the day, and in such a way as to stay a half-step ahead of his rivals.[10] It earned him the opportunity to preside over the birth of a nation and an attempt to construct a bold new future for it.

A second criterion for identifying an event-making man is the faculty of "political judgment," as Isaiah Berlin succinctly labeled it. Political judgment has to do with grasping a political situation in its totality, synthesizing the whole out of discrete facts and imponderables, and discriminating "what matters from the rest." Berlin drew an analogy with the motorist coming up to a rickety-looking bridge. The driver with road judgment, without ever learning about how to engineer piers, struts, or ties, senses through a "semi-instinctive skill" whether or not the bridge will bear the weight of his vehicle.[11] In public affairs, it takes a leader of political judgment to *see* Hook's fork in the road for what it is, and not to overlook or misconstrue it.

Yeltsin incontrovertibly possessed political judgment. It was based primarily on the instinctive aptitude that Berlin put accent on. Intuition, not grand theory, whispered in his ear in 1986–87 that Gorbachev's gradualist program was falling short. We saw in Chapter 8 that Gorbachev concluded about Yeltsin's feel for the situation and for his commanding role in it that "A tsar must conduct himself like a tsar." Gorbachev could not take charge with that kind of force; Yeltsin could and did. An inner voice led him to conclude in 1991–92 that a Great Leap Outward was indispensable to compel the new Russia into step with a rapidly evolving world. It convinced him to go for the brass ring in the constitutional conflict of 1992–93 and to throw himself into the presidential race of 1996. After re-election and medical intervention, it led him to try to reform the reforms and, when that did not work, to try to salvage them. While nothing like infallible, Yeltsin's political judgment repeatedly showed itself to be superior to that of his adversaries, from Gorbachev through Ruslan Khasbulatov, Gennadii Zyuganov, and Yurii Luzhkov.

The third test to pose of a potentially great leader is to see if he demonstrates a talent for identifying and tapping into new sources of political power. For example, Robert Caro in his epic study of Lyndon Johnson finds that as majority leader of the U.S. Senate in the 1950s he "looked for power in places where no previous [holder of that office] had thought to look for it—and he found it. And he created new powers, employing a startling ingenuity and imagination to transform parliamentary techniques . . . transforming them so completely that they became in effect new techniques and mechanisms."[12] Johnson on Capitol Hill leveraged, adjusted, and manipulated procedural rules. Other effective leaders have acted as entrepreneurs in markets wider than the institutions in which they are based.

By this yardstick, Yeltsin fares no less well. Unlike Gorbachev, he had the ingenuity and imagination in the perestroika period to realize that people power, as channeled in competitive elections, would trump administrative power and build legitimacy. He used symbolic acts, such as his demand for rehabilitation at the Nineteenth CPSU Conference in 1988 and his magical moment on Tank No. 110 in 1991, to craft and project an image that towered over all others. Enough remained of his legitimacy and his image to save him in 1996 and, combined with the powers of the presidency, as ratified in the 1993 constitutional referendum, to tide him over the recurrent crises of the late 1990s.

A fourth and related criterion is about the short-term impact of the leader's decisions during his time in the driver's seat. Were his decisions while in a position of authority consequential or not? The easiest event for which to give an unqualified yes would be Yeltsin's rallying of opposition to the attempted coup d'état of August 1991. Sergei Stankevich, the historian who was a democratic legislator and Yeltsin adviser until the mid-1990s, believes Yeltsin's charisma counted for more than all other proximate causes combined. The Yeltsin factor, by Stankevich's estimate, had 60 percent of the causal power in August. Guesswork the number may be, but it is suggestive guesswork. If it were 50 percent or 40 percent or 30 percent, it would still have been an awe-inspiring effect.[13] The 1987 secret speech and the 1991 theater on the tank had powerful multiplier effects and reverberated in the system for years.

Countless other well-placed observers bear witness to the same for Yeltsin's two terms as president. To quote but one of them, Anatolii Kulikov, who commanded Russian forces in Chechnya and headed the Interior Ministry for three years, and who finds fault with much of Yeltsin's behavior:

> There is one thing you cannot deny him, and that is that over the course of an entire decade he remained the central figure in the country's political life. Let's not kid ourselves. Boris Yeltsin—whether you are talking about the late Yeltsin or the early Yeltsin, good or bad, take your pick—not only loved to dominate but knew how to dominate the people around him. His character, his political calculations, and his energy and initiative were *the causes of the majority of the huge events of this swift-flowing Yeltsin epoch*. . . . His words and actions have left footprints on the fate of every Russian.[14]

Many of Yeltsin's key decisions, in areas as diverse as shock therapy, rehabilitation of Stalin's victims, and the interment of the Romanovs, were affirmative, about making something desirable happen. But some of his most important choices and impacts were preventive, about keeping something undesirable from happening.[15] His anti-putsch actions in August 1991 are one obvious example. A no less telling one is his multifaceted management of center-periphery and majority-minority relations and his efforts to avert what could have been a vortex of territorial and ethnic hatreds on an order of magnitude ghastlier than in Yugoslavia.

This claim about causal impact must, of course, be qualified in sundry ways. As we have seen, Yeltsin was never the only mover, only the most potent one. His anti-revolutionary revolution was inadequately conceptualized and inadequately explained to the population. The economic changes that were its focus were too slow to bear fruit, partly because they were compromised by the voracity of the winners and governmental appeasement of the losers. Some of the mechanisms devised, such as loans-for-shares, were seriously flawed. In his first term, Yeltsin neglected his allies, caroused too much and had psychological ups and downs, made strategic decisions arrhythmically, and overdid divide-and-rule. In his second term, these proclivities were in check. But, with his health impaired and his liabilities on the increase, his grip on the system he had forged slackened. The boss for the bosses now took evasive action as often as forward thrusts. His influence, though, was always far greater than anyone else's, as his imposition of Putin in 1999 showed.

There is a fifth test to apply to the would-be hero in history. It concerns the forward projection of influence, *after* he has exited the scene. How consequential are the departing leader's decisions in the middle term? Do they constrain his successor or successors five to ten years out?

If we disentangle change in Russia's mixed, post-Soviet economy from political change, it is striking how indicators have reversed in the second decade after communism. Ten years ago, the Yeltsin presidency was limping to its end and Russia was bankrupt. Today the country prospers, in "a remarkable trajectory no less exceptional than that of post–World War II Germany or Japan."[16] Output has surged by 7 percent a year, disposable income is up by 11 percent a year, foreign currency reserves stand at $450 billion, and the RTS stock index has topped 2,000 points, or fifty to sixty times the all-time low in 1998. The lines for matches, kettles, and caramels that Yeltsin had to act contrite for in Sverdlovsk in the 1980s are as quaintly remote from present-day experience as the early five-year plans.

Politically, on the other hand, we see a different picture. Russia under Yeltsin could be classified as "feckless pluralism," less than a fully articulated democracy. The regime was characterized by the presence of considerable political freedoms and of electoral contestation, although democratic practices were shallowly rooted and there was widespread mistrust of the government. Yeltsin in his valedictory speech on December 31, 1999, proclaimed that, as he had hoped in the early 1990s, change was irreversible and Russia would "proceed only forward" from now on. If the forecast holds up reasonably well in the economy, it does not in politics, where the nation has in many regards gone backward. Russia now has a "dominant-power politics" in which there is "a limited but still real political space" and some electoral competition, and yet a single power grouping, the one hinged on Putin, "dominates the system in such a way that there seems to be little possibility of alternation of power in the foreseeable future."[17]

This does not mean all hope for democracy is lost. At the social base, the modernization of Russia proceeds apace. The unshackling of the individual, begun under Gorbachev and intensified under Yeltsin, has positioned its citizens well to partake in innovations in communications that give them more autonomous access to information. At the end of 2007, some 29 million Russians, or one-fifth of the population, used the Internet with some frequency, as compared to 5.7 million in 1999, and Russia had the fastest-growing Internet community in Europe. There were 3.1 million blogs in Russia in 2007. In a country of 142 million people, cell phones numbered more than 100 million. About 3 million Russians traveled abroad that year, with passports available for the asking and the costs affordable to more and more members of the new middle class.

Developments signify that Russians treasure their personal independence but place a lower premium on political openness and accountability. In 1999, pulling off an extrication from peril worthy of Houdini and designating as his heir a KGB man through and through, Yeltsin's vaunted intuition let him down, so far as political if not economic and social variables go. Putin has exploited the superpresidential constitution Yeltsin made and the base in public opinion Yeltsin taught him how to cultivate.[18] Yeltsin unquestionably would have reversed the decision later if given the chance, sending Putin the way of Silayev, Gaidar, Chernomyrdin, Kiriyenko, Primakov, and Stepashin. But pensioned-off leaders do not get second chances on such matters, as he was aware. Putin's political system, a dispassionate British scholar notes, retains "the potential for renewed democratic advance."[19] Assuming that is so, it will be up people other than Yeltsin to realize that potential.

It is vital, again, to keep in mind the full range of counterfactual alternatives to what has happened. Neo-Soviet impulses in Russia and the post-Soviet space would have been much harder to contain if Yeltsin had not dissolved the CPSU and the Soviet Union in 1991. Thanks to him, the barrier to re-monopolization is high, and tens of millions of others are lucky that it is.

I conclude that Boris Yeltsin, although he managed to do much more with the cards dealt him than the ho-hum eventful man, impinged rather less and in a less linear manner than Hook's event-making man. To talk of the agent purposefully sculpting events is to cast the role in more architectonic terms than suit Yeltsin. Revising Hook somewhat, I envisage him as an event-shaping man, an intuitivist planted in intermediate ground between event making and eventfulness. The event-shaping man recognizes the fork in the historical road, shakes up the status quo, and bumps things off their familiar track. His inbuilt qualities magnify his influence, as do ambient tendencies and ripple effects. Concurrently, these same factors limit his ability to direct and to consolidate the changes he touches off, so that he comes up short of fulfilling promises and short of making his solutions stick. The event-shaping man kicks history's wheels into motion, yes, but not invariably as he intends or as the situation requires.

In August 2007, Art4.ru, a private art gallery in the Moscow business district, organized an unofficial competition to design a monument to commemorate Boris Yeltsin. Nothing like the contest would have been conceivable in Soviet days. It received more than a hundred submissions from professional and amateur sculptors and graphic artists. Several dozen mockups were put on display at the gallery and on its website. The public was allowed to vote in person or electronically on five finalists selected by an expert jury. According to the coordinator, the entries fell into three categories. There were figural likenesses in the old socialist realist style. These were quickly discarded, as were "the bitter, sarcastic parodies, mostly from people who had fallen on bad luck in the 1990s and wanted to blame Yeltsin. . . . Then there were some really interesting pieces—very different from each other—that show a complicated picture of Yeltsin's legacy."[20] The best of them captured significant and not always harmonious aspects of the historical Yeltsin.

The winner announced in October, by Dmitrii Kavarga, was a chaotic mass of dark metal with white figurines hanging upside-down from flat surfaces within it. One figure, Yeltsin, stands upright on top, which "emphasizes the force Yeltsin's person had in a period of instability."[21] Another highly plastic scheme, by Yuliya Gukova, portrayed a rough-surfaced wall with a large crack, and out of the wall Yeltsin's face, hands, and feet protrude. Its message was that Yeltsin was an inalienable part of the social reality he was trying to change. "With incredible, ox-like stubbornness, Yeltsin is turning the wall out of which he has grown and into which he has implanted himself. The wall turns just as the country's history turned, and the crack is not only a yawning break in the wall but in him, too."[22] The runner-up, by Rostan Tavasiyev, was a fanciful image of Yeltsin as a toy rabbit at the foot of a wobbling stele, at the top of which sits a porcelain vase—all set against the backdrop of the Lubyanka, the KGB/FSB's headquarters. Yeltsin here is a balancer instead of a dominator or sufferer. "Why the bunny?" the artist asked in his description. "Because there was no one else to do it. Maybe it was he who tipped it over or maybe he just happened to be near when the column started to fall."[23]

My favorite composition was not in the final group, and so I was not able to cast a ballot for it when I dropped by the gallery in September. It was by Mikhail Leikin and Mariya Miturich-Khlebnikova, who collaborate under the name MishMash Project, and was titled *Boris Yeltsin: The Man Who Broke Through the Wall.* It features a stainless steel wall painted bright red. On one side a runner carpet, also in red, leads to a gap in the wall. The gap traces a life-size figure of Yeltsin, including hairdo and misshapen left hand. Yeltsin here is not a prisoner of the wall: He has punched right through it and left the scene. But attendees at the exhibit are to have a choice, rather as Yeltsin's real-life legacy has given them a choice. "The viewer himself can go through the breach and feel its real human dimensions, compare them with his own and feel the toughness of the wall's metal. He can return to the past along the carpeted path. . . . [Alternatively] the exit of the viewer out of the red zone is the path that Yeltsin traveled."[24] No future is foreclosed. The citizen can go through the wall either way, forward or backward.

Acknowledgments

The spark for this book was struck in a multi-sided conversation I had with several Russian friends and acquaintances toward the end of 1999. The idea was that a group of scholars and public-policy analysts would meet with Boris Yeltsin, who was still president of the country, and, after his expected retirement, possibly organize a collective study of his presidency. The participants in that discussion were Sergei Grigoriev, Mikhail Shvydkoi, Dmitrii Yakushkin, and Valentin Yumashev. No sooner had we had our chat than Yeltsin had quit office, and, for a variety of reasons, the original impulse to begin the study was lost. My conversation mates, however, proved willing to cooperate with my launching a one-man project, which came to encompass the full course of Yeltsin's life. In researching and writing the book, I amassed all manner of debts to informants and information brokers. I trust they will not need to be reminded, however, that all responsibility for its line of argument and its flaws lies with me.

Interviews with players in, and close observers of, the story were key sources from the beginning. Individuals who provided specific bits of evidence used in the text are cited in the endnotes. I also had benefit of the knowledge and insights of Yevgeniya Al'bats, Anders Åslund, Pilar Bonet, Maksim Boiko, Vladimir Bykodorov, Dmitrii Donskoi, Mikhail Fedotov, Chrystia Freeland, Leonid Gozman, Kirill Ignat'ev, Irina Il'ina, Andrei Illarionov, Sergei Karaganov, Sergei Khrushchev, Yurii Kir'yakov, Paul Klebnikov, Al'fred Kokh, Pavel Kuznetsov, Yurii Levada, Viktor Manyukhin, Vladimir Mau, Garri Minkh, Vyacheslav Nikonov, Pavel Palazchenko, Nikolai Petrov, Oleg Rumyantsev, Vladimir Semënov, Lilia Shevtsova, Andrei Shleifer, Aleksandr Shokhin, Andrei Shtorkh, Vladimir Shumeiko,

Nadezhda Smirnova, Boris Smolenitskii, Dmitrii Trenin, Dmitrii Vasil'ev, Aleksei Venediktov, Vladimir Vlasov, and Grace Kennan Warnecke.

I am particularly grateful to those individuals, mostly Russians, who opened other people's doors to me—this in a climate in which imparting sensitive information to foreign specialists is not always welcomed by the authorities. Valentin Yumashev and Tatyana Yumasheva arranged for me to see Boris Yeltsin and Naina Yeltsina. They also made themselves available for interviews and follow-up exchanges on numerous points of fact and interpretation, and Tatyana located and shared revealing photographs from the family's private collection. Sergei Grigoriev in particular put himself out to facilitate meetings in Moscow, especially in the first two years. Yevgeniya Al'bats, plying her very different network, also spared no effort. Thanks in this regard go also to Dmitrii Bakatin, Vladimir Bokser, Valerii Bortsov, James Collins, Leonid Dobrokhotov, Mikhail Fedotov, Leonid Gozman, Sergei Kolesnikov, Mikhail Margelov, Michael McFaul, Vitalii Nasedkin, Aleksandr Popov, Vladimir Shevchenko, Olga Sidorovich, and Vladimir Voronkov. When midway through the project I ran into certain travel difficulties, crucial interventions were made by several Russians and Americans whose names will go unmentioned for now.

A number of colleagues were good enough to go over draft text. Elise Giuliano, Marshall Goldman, Thane Gustafson, Mark Kramer, Alena Ledeneva, Thomas Simons, and Gwendolyn Stewart were beady-eyed readers of an early version of the entire book. I was especially influenced by the close comments of Jonathan Sanders, for whom many years ago I wrote my first (quite awful) paper on Yeltsin, and who gave me dozens of valuable leads, and by William Taubman, who convinced me to take the time needed to bring the two halves of the volume into harmony. Nanci Adler, Elena Campbell, John Dunn, Yoshiko Herrera, Edward Keenan, Gijs Kessler, Eva Maeder, Terry Martin, Olga Nikonova, Sarah Oates, Thomas Remington, Roman Szporluk, and Lynne Viola guided me to published and unpublished sources. Stephen White let me use the interview with Yakov Ryabov that is part of his oral history project at the University of Glasgow. Leon Aron shared important printed material that I was unable to locate on my own. Mark Kramer has my gratitude for identifying and retrieving key documents from the Communist Party archives and related troves. Yevgenii Kiselëv and Irena Lesnevskaya made available unique videotapes from the 1990s, and Aleksandr Oslon did the same with previously confidential polling data from the 1996 presidential election campaign. In Yekaterinburg, Anatolii Kirillov and Galina Stepanova were generous with their time, contacts, and expertise. In Berezniki, Aleksandr Abramov, Aleksandr Kerimov, Oleg Kotelnikov, and Natalya Kuznetsova were hospitable and informative. Aleksei Litvin, Dane Ponte, and Artur Yusupov helped me obtain information about Yeltsin's childhood years in Kazan.

Masha Hedberg was my research assistant at Harvard for the two make-or-break years of the project and could not have done a better job. She accompanied me to the Urals in 2005 for a journey made productive by her tenacity. At the Davis Center for Russian and Eurasian Studies, Maria Altamore, Sarah Failla, Melissa Griggs, Helen Grigoriev, Ann Sjostedt, Penelope Skalnik, Lisbeth Tarlow, and Patricia Vio gave me unflagging administrative support. Masha Tarasova in Moscow patched through dozens of communications and shored up logistics. The Davis Center, the Government Department, the Faculty of Arts and Sciences, and the Harvard Academy for International and Area Studies underwrote travel and other expenses.

My wife, Pat, kept the home fires burning and was the first to see and apply pencil to rough drafts.

Wesley Neff placed the project with Basic Books. At Basic, Lara Heimert was wise and patient in equal measure, and Norman MacAfee expertly edited the manuscript into shape on a tight schedule.

Notes

Introduction

1. The lunch with a few ministers and aides began at 11:30. But the television in the dining room did not work, and so at noon the group briefly repaired to the nearby office of Yeltsin's daughter Tatyana Dyachenko to watch the speech. The legal transfer of powers to Putin as acting president took effect at that very minute.

2. The Russian Orthodox Church still uses the Julian calendar introduced by Julius Caesar in 46 B.C. It currently lags thirteen days behind the more accurate Gregorian calendar in use in the West since 1582 A.D., and so Russian Christmas falls on January 7. The Soviet government introduced the Gregorian calendar for secular purposes in 1918.

3. This was the ruling party's name as of 1952, before which it was the All-Russian Communist Party and the Bolshevik Party.

4. "Boris Yel'tsin: glavnoye delo svoyei zhizni ya sdelal" (Boris Yeltsin: I have done with the main business of my life), *Nezavisimaya gazeta*, January 6, 2000.

5. Ibid.

6. Sergei Roy, review of Leon Aron, *Yeltsin: A Revolutionary Life* (New York: St. Martin's, 2000), in *Moscow Times*, January 22, 2000. Aron's book, elegantly written and uniformly praiseful, is the most informative on Yeltsin's life by a Westerner. Several of the better books were put out by journalists at the turn of the 1990s: John Morrison, *Boris Yeltsin: From Bolshevik to Democrat* (New York: Dutton, 1991); and Vladimir Solovyov and Elena Klepikova, *Boris Yeltsin: A Political Biography*, trans. David Gurevich (New York: Putnam's, 1992). George W. Breslauer's fine scholarly monograph *Gorbachev and Yeltsin as Leaders* (Cambridge: Cambridge University Press, 2002) compares how Yeltsin and Gorbachev "built authority" in the 1980s and 1990s, with Gorbachev's predecessors as Soviet general secretary as the benchmark, and offers insights into Yeltsin's "patriarchal" aspect. Further enlightenment comes from Gwendolyn Elizabeth Stewart, "SIC TRANSIT: Democratization, *Suverenizatsiia*, and Boris Yeltsin in the Breakup of the Soviet Union" (Ph.D. diss., Harvard University, 1995); and Jerrold M. Post, "Boris Yeltsin: Against the Grain,"

Problems of Post-Communism 43 (January–February 1996), 58–62. Stewart observed Yeltsin as a photojournalist, and Post is a psychiatrist who has profiled foreign leaders for the U.S. government.

7. Sergei Markedonov, "Boris Yel'tsin: eskiz istoricheskogo portreta" (Boris Yeltsin: outline of a historical portrait), http://polit.ru/author/2006/02/01/eltsyn_75.

8. A recent tour of the genre describes the English as historically more "biography-obsessed" than Americans, but adds that the celebrity culture of the United States partly compensates (James Atlas, "My Subject Myself," *New York Times Book Review*, October 9, 2005). See also Lewis J. Edinger, "Political Science and Political Biography: Reflections on the Study of Leadership," *Journal of Politics* 26 (May 1964), 423–39. Russia scores far below both Britain and America in acceptance of biography.

9. The best-known biographical project in the country is the series "Lives of Outstanding People," put out by the Molodaya Gvardiya publishing house in Moscow. Its almost 1,200 titles cover cultural as well as political and military figures, in Russia and abroad. Unfathomably, there is no Yeltsin title in the series. The collective memoir by nine former aides, Yu. M. Baturin et al., *Epokha Yel'tsina: ocherki politicheskoi istorii* (The Yeltsin epoch: essays in political history) (Moscow: VAGRIUS, 2001), is the best book about Yeltsin in power in any language. But the points of view of individual contributors are not identified, and it just scratches the surface of Yeltsin's personality and decision-making processes. The journalist and editor Vitalii Tret'yakov, who was one of the first to comment on the Yeltsin phenomenon, and to do so favorably, wrote most of an unfavorable biography of him in 1998–99. Tiring, he said, of "the banality of the theme and of the main hero of the book," he did not finish it. Vitalii Tret'yakov, "Sverdlovskii vyskochka" (Sverdlovsk upstart), part 1, *Politicheskii klass*, February 2006, 36. Selections from the manuscript, which takes Yeltsin to 1989 only, were published in the February through August issues of this magazine.

10. "Authors are wary of tackling [the issue] precisely because Yeltsin has played a huge and overpowering role in the birth of the new Russia." Peter Rutland, "The Boris Yeltsin of History," *Demokratizatsiya/Democratization* 6 (Fall 1998), 692.

11. A search of books for sale at www.amazon.com, using the person's name and "biography" as keywords, on November 15, 2007, turned up 2,904 titles about Washington, 2,202 about Lincoln, 1,009 about Churchill, and 975 about Hitler.

12. Boris Yel'tsin, *Prezidentskii marafon* (Presidential marathon) (Moscow: AST, 2000), 420. This book appeared in English as *Midnight Diaries.* Unless specially noted, I will quote the Russian originals of Yeltsin's memoirs and cite them by their Russian titles—translating those titles, in the body of the text, into English. English- and Russian-language texts of all three books are now available at the Yeltsin Foundation website: http://yeltsin.ru/yeltsin/books.

13. Oleg Poptsov, *Khronika vremën "Tsarya Borisa"* (Chronicle of the times of "Tsar Boris") (Moscow: Sovershenno sekretno, 1995), 218.

14. Kenneth Jowitt, *New World Disorder: The Leninist Extinction* (Berkeley: University of California Press, 1992), 260.

15. Mikhail Gorbachev, *Zhizn' i reformy* (Life and reforms), 2 vols. (Moscow: Novosti, 1995), 1:281.

16. Dmitry Mikheyev, *Russia Transformed* (Indianapolis: Hudson Institute, 1996), 48.

17. Boris Nikol'skii, *Kremlëvskiye mirazhi* (Kremlin mirages) (St. Petersburg: Neva, 2001), 124.

18. Stephen Hanson, "The Dilemmas of Russia's Anti-Revolutionary Revolution," *Current History* 100 (October 2001), 331.

19. Strobe Talbott, *The Russia Hand: A Memoir of Presidential Diplomacy* (New York: Random House, 2002), 285. Clinton made the remark to U.S. officials traveling with him to meet Yeltsin in Moscow in the summer of 1998.

20. Sergei Filatov, *Sovershenno nesekretno* (Top nonsecret) (Moscow: VAGRIUS, 2000), 418–19.

21. Aleksandr Yakovlev, *Sumerki* (Dusk) (Moscow: Materik, 2003), 644 (italics added).

22. Talbott, *Russia Hand,* 185. Foreigners were not the only ones to spy these incongruities. A presidential press secretary was led to conclude Yeltsin was "warring against himself" (Vyacheslav Kostikov, *Roman s prezidentom: zapiski press-sekretarya* [Romance with a president: notes of a press secretary] [Moscow: VAGRIUS, 1997], 313). See also the general discussion in Lilia Shevtsova, *Yeltsin's Russia: Myths and Reality* (Washington, D.C.: Carnegie Endowment for International Peace, 1999).

23. Here I follow Clayton Roberts, who defines a historical interpretation as "an abbreviation of a complete explanation" and "an assertion that some variable or number of variables are the most important causal agencies in a particular historical development." Roberts, *The Logic of Historical Explanation* (University Park: Pennsylvania State University Press, 1996), 242, 245.

24. I have the dubious honor of being one of the first to do so, in Timothy J. Colton, "Moscow Politics and the Yeltsin Affair," *Harriman Institute Forum* 1 (June 1988), 1–8.

25. Indicative of the latter is the claim by Solovyov and Klepikova, written in the last months of 1991 (*Boris Yeltsin,* 23): "Boris Yeltsin's historical mission has been completed. The titanic role he played was a destructive one; we are not sure he has enough strength for constructive activity."

26. As characterized, critically, by Andrei Shleifer and Daniel Treisman, "A Normal Country," *Foreign Affairs* 83 (March–April 2004), 20.

27. Michael R. Beschloss and Strobe Talbott, *At the Highest Levels: The Inside Story of the End of the Cold War* (Boston: Little, Brown, 1993), 349.

28. Peter Reddaway and Dmitri Glinski, *The Tragedy of Russia's Reforms: Market Bolshevism against Democracy* (Washington, D.C.: U.S. Institute of Peace, 2001),

32. For a forceful summary, see Dusko Doder, "Russia's Potemkin Leader," *The Nation*, January 29, 2001. A noxious specimen of what can only be called hate journalism, published after Yeltsin's death in 2007, is Matt Taibbi, "The Low Post: Death of a Drunk," http://www.rollingstone.com/politics/story/14272792.

29. I speak of a positive assessment beyond the empathy that usually goes with the writing of a life: "No honest biographer—as opposed to the propagandist or the avowed debunker—can long remain in company and consort with a subject and avoid at least a touch of empathy. Empathy . . . is the biographer's spark of creation." Frank E. Vandiver, "Biography as an Agent of Humanism," in James F. Veninga, ed., *The Biographer's Gift: Life Histories and Humanism* (College Station: Texas A&M University Press, 1983), 16–17.

30. Viktor Shenderovich, *Kukly* (Puppets) (Moscow: VAGRIUS, 1996), 35–36.

31. Frank Vandiver's term, from "Biography as an Agent of Humanism," 16.

Chapter One

1. A. K. Matveyev, *Geograficheskiye nazvaniya Urala* (Geographic names of the Urals) (Sverdlovsk: Sredne-Ural'skoye knizhnoye izdatel'stvo, 1980), 49–50. It has also been suggested that the name comes from *budka*, the term for a sentry box such as European settlers in the area would have set up, and slang for toilet stall. There is an eponymous Butka Lake southeast of the village of Butka and a Butka River (a creek, really) that flows into the Belyakovka from the right. But the lake is not connected to either river, and the conflux of the Butka and Belyakovka rivers is about twelve miles downstream of the village on the Belyakovka.

2. I. Butakov, "Butke—300 let" (Butka is 300 years old), *Ural'skii rabochii*, November 3, 1976.

3. See A. A. Kondrashenkov, *Krest'yane Zaural'ya v XVII–XVIII vekakh* (The peasants of the Trans-Urals in the seventeenth and eighteenth centuries) (Chelyabinsk: Yuzhno-Ural'skoye knizhnoye izdatel'stvo, 1966), 30, 53; "Iz istorii Butki" (From Butka's history), http://rx9cfs.narod.ru/butka/7.html; and "Rodnomy selu Yel'tsina ispolnilos' 325 let" (Yeltsin's native village is 325 years old), http:/txt.newsru.com/russia/03nov2001/butka.html.

4. See on this point Peter Kolchin, *Unfree Labor: American Slavery and Russian Serfdom* (Cambridge, Mass.: Harvard University Press, 1987). Eighty percent of rural dwellers in the Urals on the eve of emancipation were state peasants. There were urban serfs in the Urals, attached to mines and factories.

5. Vasilii Nemirovich-Danchenko, *Kama i Ural (ocherki i vpechatleniya)* (The Kama and the Urals [Essays and impressions]) (St. Petersburg: Tipografiya A. S. Suvorina, 1890), 551.

6. V. P. Semënov-Tyan-Shyanskii, *Rossiya: polnoye geograficheskoye opisaniye nashego otechestva* (Russia: a complete geographic description of our fatherland), 11 vols. (St. Petersburg: Devrien, 1899–1914), 5:170.

7. Michael Cherniavsky, "The Old Believers and the New Religion," *Slavic Review* 25 (March 1966), 24. See also Roy R. Robson, *Old Believers in Modern Russia* (DeKalb: Northern Illinois University Press, 1995); and Georg Bernhard Michels, *At War with the Church: Religious Dissent in Seventeenth-Century Russia* (Stanford: Stanford University Press, 1999). Most Old Believers lived deep in the interior, but there were also concentrations, particularly of merchants, in the big cities. One-third of the population of Yekaterinburg in the mid-eighteenth century was Old Believer. The rural sectarians tended to be more radical in their beliefs than the urban, who were usually willing to say prayers for the tsar.

8. The Russian historian Rudol'f Pikhoya, quoted in Pilar Bonet, "Nevozmozhnaya Rossiya: Boris Yel'tsin, provintsial v Kremle" (The impossible Russia: Boris Yeltsin, a provincial in the Kremlin), *Ural*, April 1994, 15. This valuable study was first published in Spanish as *La Rusia Imposible: Boris Yeltsin, un provinciano en el Kremlin* (Madrid: El Paìs, S.A./Aguilar, S.A., 1994).

9. *Ocherki istorii staroobryadchestva Urala i sopredel'nykh territorii* (Essays on the history of the Old Believers of the Urals and abutting territories) (Yekaterinburg: Izdatel'stvo Ural'skogo gosudarstvennogo universiteta, 2000), 85. The 1897 census (which I consulted in the original) counted 23,762 Old Believers in Shadrinsk district, or 8 percent of the population. Experts have generally felt that official statistics underestimated the number of Old Believers.

10. The census of 1897 said 780 of the 825 lawful residents of Butka were Orthodox. Most of the remaining forty-five would have been Old Believers, and undoubtedly quite a few of the 780 had mixed beliefs. Seventeen residents of Basmanovo and 105 in Talitsa were unaccounted for in the same way. In Butkinskoozërskaya village, at the terminus of the Butka River, the census recorded 162 of 914 persons as Old Believers.

11. Irina Bobrova, "Boris bol'shoi, yemu vidnei" (Boris is a big shot, he knows better), *Moskovskii komsomolets*, January 31, 2007, reports that approximately 1,000 people bearing the name live in today's Sverdlovsk and Perm provinces.

12. Students of twentieth-century cinema will recognize the name from the characters Aleksei and Fëdor Basmanov in Sergei Eisenstein's Soviet film classic, *Ivan the Terrible*, released in parts in 1944 and 1958. Aleksei is a lieutenant of Tsar Ivan. His only son, Fëdor, is the bloodthirsty founder of the Oprichnina, Ivan's palace guard.

13. D. A. Panov, *Opyt pokolennoi rospisi roda Yel'tsinykh* (An experiment in doing a genealogy of the Yeltsin clan) (Perm: Assotsiatsiya genealogov-lyubitelei, 1992), and Panov's work at http://www.vgd.ru/Ye, give years of birth and death for all male heads of the Yeltsin family prior to Yekim, and only a year of birth for him. At that point, the well runs dry because of changes in record keeping under the Soviet regime.

14. Ivan Yeltsin (1794–1825) was a nephew of Savva. He returned to Basmanovo from the army and fathered two children. After his death, his widow, Marfa, had seven more sons and daughters by another man.

15. For Boris Yeltsin's grandparents on both sides, I rely on a personal communication from his daughter Tatyana Yumasheva dated March 4, 2005, which collated information from family sources, and on interviews with Stanislav Glebov, a distant cousin, in Butka and Serafima Gomzikova, Boris's first cousin, in Basmanovo (both on September 11, 2005). Yumasheva appears in the pages of this book mostly as Tatyana Dyachenko, her married name when her father was president. The family has no record of Anna Dmitreyevna's maiden name. Dmitrii Panov was unable to find even her given name and patronymic for his genealogy. Ignatii is sometimes referred to as Ignat Yeltsin.

16. Pilar Bonet and Rudol'f Pikhoya have speculated about Yeltsin's Old Believer roots. Klavdiya Yeltsina, his mother, spoke of them before her death in 1993: Alya Tanachëva, a Sverdlovsk political activist who befriended her, interview with the author (June 22, 2004). Surviving members of the family cannot confirm Klavdiya's assertion and say that, if there were Old Believer roots, they were deep in the family's past.

17. Klavdiya Yeltsina in the 1950s, as recalled by Naina Yeltsina, second interview with the author (September 18, 2007).

18. Yumasheva communication; police file on Nikolai Yeltsin compiled before his arrest in 1934, as given in A. L. Litvin, *Yel'tsiny v Kazani* (The Yeltsins in Kazan) (Kazan: Aibat, 2004), 28–29.

19. Excerpted in Igor Neverov, "Otets prezidenta" (The president's father), fragment of an unpublished manuscript by Neverov, *Nikomu ne otdam svoyu biografiyu* (We won't give anyone our biography), 1998; copy provided to the author in September 2005 by the Museum of History and Art, Berezniki, Russia.

20. Or so local residents told a foreign correspondent in the 1990s: Matt Taibbi, "Butka: Boris Yeltsin, Revisited," http://exile.ru/105/yeltsin. Nikolai and Taisiya Bersenëva romanced before her marriage and resumed the relationship after five years.

21. Izabella Verbova, "Za tysyachi kilometrov ot Belogo doma" (Thousands of kilometers from the White House), *Vechernyaya Moskva*, October 2, 1991.

22. Yumasheva communication. The phrase about the Yeltsins' golden hands is in Verbova, "Za tysyachi kilometrov," and was repeated in my interview with Serafima Gomzikova. Klavdiya's ancestors up to her parents' generation can be located at www.vgd.ru/S.

23. For a claim that Boris Yeltsin was born in Basmanovo and not Butka, see Natal'ya Zenova, "Mesto rozhdeniya prezidenta izmenit' nel'zya" (You cannot change a president's place of birth), *Obshchaya gazeta*, April 30, 1997. Yeltsin hotly denied it and said he had "all the documentation" to prove he was born in Butka. Boris Yeltsin, second interview with the author (February 9, 2002).

24. Boris Yel'tsin, *Ispoved' na zadannuyu temu* (Confession on an assigned theme) (Moscow: PIK, 1990), 18. This volume was published in English as *Against the Grain*. A relative said sixty years afterward (Bonet, "Nevozmozhnaya Rossiya,"

15) that the story about the font is apocryphal and Yeltsin was baptized at home, the Butka church having been closed. Yeltsin's report that the church was being made to serve the surrounding villages, and that baptisms were being held there only one day a month, suggests the closing of places of worship was under way. His description educes a long-standing Russian image of the intoxicated rural clergyman, going back at least as far as Vasilii Perov's 1861 painting *Easter Procession in a Village.*

25. Bobrova, "Boris bol'shoi," reports incorrectly that Yeltsin's birthplace was demolished some time ago. Stanislav Glebov gave me the address in 2005, and several residents of the street confirmed that this was the place. The household took in Ignatii and Anna Yeltsin, their four sons, the wives of the three oldest sons, and, it seems, three grandchildren. Ignatii's daughter, Mariya, had married one Yakov Gomzikov in the early 1920s and remained in Basmanovo.

26. Leonid Brezhnev, *Vospominaniya* (Memoirs) (Moscow: Politizdat, 1983), 27. There were more than 1,300 peasant uprisings and mass protests in the Soviet Union in 1929 and the early 1930s. Fifty-two occurred in the Urals in only the first three months of 1930. I. S. Ogonovskaya et al., *Istoriya Urala s drevneishikh vremën do nashikh dnei* (History of the Urals from ancient times to our day) (Yekaterinburg: Sokrat, 2003), 346.

27. T. I. Slavko, *Kulatskaya ssylka na Urale, 1930–1936* (The banishment of the kulaks in the Urals, 1930–36) (Moscow: Mosgorarkhiv, 1995), 33; Ogonovskaya et al., *Istoriya Urala*, 348.

28. The bell tower fell to the ground at one point. After communism, in 1993, the church was reconsecrated; a temporary tower was built in the yard and five bells purchased. Boris Yeltsin as president (personally or via a government grant, it is not clear) made a contribution to restoration (Bobrova, "Boris bol'shoi"). A gutting and reconstruction funded by local businessmen began in 2005. The church in Basmanovo, dating from 1860, was torn down in the 1930s and never replaced. The location is still a debris-strewn vacant lot. Orthodox services are held in the village in a home chapel.

29. On cannibalism, Pëtr Porotnikov, a regional official who grew up in Butka, interview with the author (September 10, 2004). See the reference to the phenomenon in Ogonovskaya et al., *Istoriya Urala*, 347.

30. *Raskulachivaniye* (dekulakization) was a pre-existing Russian word adapted to a new purpose. Derived from *kulak,* whose original meaning was "fist," it denoted the relaxing of the fingers in a clenched fist. In the context of Stalinist class warfare, it signified the draining away of the wealth of the village elite, the heartless kulaks.

31. References to Yel'tsin, *Ispoved'*, 18–19, 20, 26, 144.

32. Andrei Goryun, *Boris Yel'tsin: svet i teni* (Boris Yeltsin: light and shadows), 2 vols. (Sverdlovsk: Klip, 1991), 1:5–6.

33. See John Morrison, *Boris Yeltsin: From Bolshevik to Democrat* (New York: Dutton, 1991), 32–33; Vladimir Solovyov and Elena Klepikova, *Boris Yeltsin: A Political Biography*, trans. David Gurevich (New York: Putnam's, 1992), 116–18; Timothy J.

Colton, "Boris Yeltsin: Russia's All-Thumbs Democrat," in Colton and Robert C. Tucker, eds., *Patterns in Post-Soviet Leadership* (Boulder: Westview, 1995), 50–51, 71; Dmitry Mikheyev, *Russia Transformed* (Indianapolis: Hudson Institute, 1996), 49–51; and Leon Aron, *Yeltsin: A Revolutionary Life* (New York: St. Martin's, 2000), chap. 1, which has rather more up-to-date information than the others about Nikolai Yeltsin. Mikheyev mistakenly refers (51) to Yeltsin's childhood as "difficult but devoid of atrocities and destruction."

34. For background, see Golfo Alexopolous, *Stalin's Outcasts: Aliens, Citizens, and the Soviet State, 1926–1936* (Ithaca: Cornell University Press, 2003). In the cities, the disenfranchised were denied ration cards, which did not apply in the countryside.

35. A. I. Bedel' and T. I. Slavko, eds., *Sud'ba raskulachennykh spetspereselentsev na Urale, 1930–1936 gg.* (The fate of the dekulakized special migrants in the Urals, 1930–36) (Yekaterinburg: Izdatel'stvo Ural'skogo gosudarstvennogo universiteta, 1994), 14.

36. Gomzikova interview. Serafima Gomzikova, who was a young girl in 1930, recalled the scene. Her parents' house was confiscated and local communists demanded that her father divorce her mother, Mariya (Ignatii's only daughter), which he refused to do. If Anna Yeltsina's name has been left out of previous accounts, the very existence of Mariya, who died in the 1950s, has not registered. Serafima is her surviving daughter.

37. Statistics in Viktor Danilov et al., eds., *Tragediya sovetskoi derevni: kollektivizatsiya i raskulachivaniye; dokumenty i materialy, 1927–1939* (The tragedy of the Soviet village: collectivization and dekulakization; documents and materials, 1927–39), 5 vols. (Moscow: ROSSPEN, 2000), 2:745; and Slavko, *Kulatskaya ssylka*, 73. The peak number, about 484,000, was reached in early 1932; by a year from then, it was down to 366,000, mostly because of deaths (33,000) and flight (97,000). For perspective, see James R. Harris, "The Growth of the Gulag: Forced Labor in the Urals Region, 1929–31," *Russian Review* 56 (April 1997), 265–80; Judith Pallot, "Russia's Penal Peripheries: Space, Place, and Penalty in Soviet and Post-Soviet Russia," *Transactions of the Institute of British Geographers* 30 (March 2005), 98–112; and Lynne Viola, *The Unknown Gulag: The Lost World of Stalin's Special Settlements* (New York: Oxford University Press, 2007). As Viola shows, the regional administration was originally against central efforts to make the Urals the prime locale for deportees from all over the Soviet Union.

38. The Basmanovo council's report on the family to the police in Kazan, in connection with the case against Ignatii's son Nikolai, said Yeltsin senior was "on the run" *(v begakh)*. The report was sent in February 1934. Litvin, *Yel'tsiny v Kazani*, 29.

39. The age limit is noted in Slavko, *Kulatskaya ssylka*, 64.

40. Family details taken from Yumasheva communication. The severity of the restrictions suggests some unusual police animus toward the Yeltsins. Second-category kulaks were supposed to get shipment of thirty poods (about a half-ton) of baggage per family member. Slavko, *Kulatskaya ssylka*, 80.

41. Ogonovskaya et al., *Istoriya Urala*, 340.

42. Slavko, *Kulatskaya ssylka*, 94–95.

43. The town took its name when founded in the 1890s from Nadezhda (Hope) Polovtsova, the owner of the local iron mine and the wife of a personal aide to the tsar. From 1934 to 1937, it was called Kabakovsk, after Ivan Kabakov, the first secretary of the Communist Party committee of Sverdlovsk province—the job to be held by Boris Yeltsin from 1976 to 1985. When Kabakov was purged in 1937, Kabakovsk reverted to Nadezhdinsk. In 1939 it was named after Anatolii Serov, a Soviet aviator and hero of the Spanish Civil War.

44. No one can be sure today, but the likely trigger for Ignatii's blindness was a stroke. His son Nikolai, Boris's father, was to die of stroke in the 1970s.

45. Yumasheva communication. Taibbi, in his unpublished "Butka," is the only analyst to have suggested that Yeltsin's maternal grandfather was sent to the north. He tracked down no other details.

46. Second Yeltsin interview. The only way to reach Serov, just 130 miles northeast of Berezniki as the crow flies, was a laborious U-shaped train route, taking two days of travel.

47. About 70,000 banished peasants in the Urals were called up into the army during the war and qualified for release that way. Others were allowed to leave in dribs and drabs before the war. By January 1946 the number of peasant exiles in the Urals was down to 138,000 and by January 1954 it was less than 10,000. By that last date, though, the total number of banished people in all categories in the Soviet Union as a whole was still very high—2,720,000. Slavko, *Kulatskaya ssylka*, 145–46.

48. Details again from Yumasheva communication.

49. Neverov, "Otets prezidenta."

50. Yel'tsin, *Ispoved'*, 18–19, describes Nikolai as present for his baptism. He could not possibly have remembered who attended, but it is a fair guess that Klavdiya would have let it be known if Nikolai had missed the event. A Spanish journalist heard from Yeltsin relations in 1991 that Nikolai around this time worked on the construction of the Butka-Talitsa road (Bonet, "Nevozmozhnaya Rossiya," 16), but the project went on from 1934 to 1936, so the timing seems off. It is possible that another one of the brothers worked on the road.

51. Klavdiya Yeltsina told an American visitor in 1991 that the three of them did exactly that (she used the name Serov for their destination). Gwendolyn Elizabeth Stewart, "SIC TRANSIT: Democratization, *Suverenizatsiia*, and Boris Yeltsin in the Breakup of the Soviet Union" (Ph.D. diss., Harvard University, 1995), 78–79.

52. Eventually known as the Gorbunov Works, the plant was over the years to make reconnaissance planes, Blackjack strategic bombers, and civil airliners. The nearby Kazan Helicopter Works built the Mi-8 helicopter that Boris Yeltsin flew as president of post-Soviet Russia.

53. This was his claim in his 1950s autobiography: Neverov, "Otets prezidenta."

54. This is by later assertion of Klavdiya Yeltsina (Goryun, *Boris Yel'tsin*, 1:5). The trips ended, she said, when her brother-in-law Ivan left Butka for Berezniki, which was in 1935.

55. Litvin, *Yel'tsiny v Kazani,* 26. Litvin dug out Nikolai's OGPU file from the Kazan archive of the KGB and gave it to Boris Yeltsin, who included excerpts in his second book of memoirs. The file also provided information on the dekulakization of Ignatii. English-language readers can find some details in Boris Yeltsin, *The Struggle for Russia,* trans. Catherine A. Fitzpatrick (New York: Times Books, 1994), 94–98, which translates Boris Yel'tsin, *Zapiski prezidenta* (Notes of a president) (Moscow: Ogonëk, 1994), 121–25.

56. The secret police arrested 4,721 people in Tatariya in 1931 and shot 252 of them. None of the 887 arrested in 1934 was shot. In the last four months of 1937, some 4,750 individuals were arrested and 2,510 of them shot. Altogether, from 1929 through 1938 more than 20,000 were arrested in the republic and about 4,000 were executed. Litvin, *Yel'tsiny v Kazani,* 18, 47, 49–50.

57. Ibid., 27.

58. Ibid., 38.

59. This is also the take of Boris Yeltsin's daughter Tatyana Yumasheva, who perused the OGPU dossier in 1993. "He was not expressing insolent ideas," she said of her grandfather. "He never spoke that way. He was simply trying to get them [his crewmen] to work, and they wanted to react for themselves." Remarks by Yumasheva during second Yeltsin interview.

60. Litvin, *Yel'tsiny v Kazani,* 45.

61. Yel'tsin, *Zapiski,* 124.

62. Rimma Akhmirova, "Prezidenta nyanchil tovarishch Sukhov" (Comrade Sukhov took care of the president), *Komsomol'skaya pravda,* September 4, 1999; and, for Klavdiya's literacy class, Stewart, "SIC TRANSIT," 79.

63. The only public reference Yeltsin ever made to kindergarten in Kazan was on his last visit there, in 2006. Vera Postnova, "Yel'tsin nazval Shaimiyeva samym-samym" (Yeltsin called Shaimiyev the best of the best), *Nezavisimaya gazeta,* June 26, 2006. But family members say he spoke of the kindergarten with them as well.

64. Litvin, *Yel'tsiny v Kazani,* 88.

65. Ibid., 55.

66. His autobiographical statement from the 1950s (in Neverov, "Otets prezidenta") said that in 1936 or 1937 he was discharged from work "and left the third year of the tekhnikum by my own wish." But the statement did not mention his arrest or time served in Gulag, so this information is of questionable value.

67. Akhmirova, "Prezidenta nyanchil tovarishch Sukhov"; and Yevgenii Ukhov, "Imennaya 'dvushka'" (An inscribed "two-roomer"), *Trud,* April 25, 2007.

68. Historical sketch of the city at http://www.berezniki.ru/topic/gorod. The Gulag directorate allocated 4,000 convicts to the Berezniki camp in 1929. The writer Varlam Shalamov, one of the prisoners, said in his memoirs it had 10,000 workers in 1930. Vladimir Mikhailyuk, *Ne odin pud soli: Berezniki v sud'be Rossii* (Not one pood of salt: Berezniki in the fate of Russia) (Perm: Pushka, 1997), 238–40. The Vishera camp itself began as a branch of the detention camp at Solovki monastery,

on an island in the White Sea, set up in 1921. It peaked at 37,800 inmates in 1931 and was closed in July 1934. A lumbering camp was opened at Nyrob, on a branch of the Kama north of Vishera, in 1945 and held 24,800 prisoners as of 1952.

69. The family details here come from Tatyana Yumasheva. On Nikolai Yeltsin's rehabilitation (and Andrian's, also posthumously), see Litvin, *Yel'tsiny v Kazani*, 60.

70. Yeltsin's handwritten self-description when he was admitted to the party, in 1961, said he moved with his parents to Kazan in 1935 and to Berezniki in 1937. It is reproduced in Grigorii Kaëta, *Boris Yel'tsin: Ural'skii period zhizni* (Boris Yeltsin: the Urals period of his life) (Yekaterinburg: TsDOOSO, 1996), 32. Later essays in the archive gave other dates but always referred to Kazan.

71. Valentin Yumashev, who as a journalist helped Yeltsin edit tape recordings into the first volume (and later volumes) of his memoirs, was not aware that the family had lived in Kazan, although he doubts Yeltsin (who became his father-in-law in 2001) made a conscious effort to suppress this fact. In *Ispoved'*, 19, Yeltsin said the family went straight from Butka to Berezniki when his father heard there was work at the potash combine, and that they took a horse and cart to the train station, disposing of surplus belongings as they went. Either he was being mendacious—and I cannot begin to think why he would—or his memory was playing tricks on him. The family moved to Berezniki from Kazan, not from Butka, and Kazan is a large city with its own station. It is highly unlikely Yeltsin was describing their departure from Butka to Kazan in 1932, when he was twenty-two months old.

72. Sixty years later, Yeltsin still wanted to prove (*Zapiski*, 123) that his father was not a bad hat in Kazan: "By the way, the [OGPU] file contains no especially pointed statements on my father's part. His brother and the other 'participants' did most of the talking." In his second interview with me, he stressed that Ignatii and Anna Yeltsin, before being expropriated in 1930, were in accordance with the law because they did not hire wage labor. "They were hard workers. They walked behind the wood plow and the metal plow, they did the work themselves, without hired laborers, they worked on their own in the village, as a family."

73. Glebov interview.

74. Yel'tsin, *Zapiski*, 124; second Yeltsin interview.

75. As already indicated, the statement (in Neverov, "Otets prezidenta") had him spending 1930 to 1932 in Nadezhdinsk and 1932 to 1936 in Kazan, carpentering at Works No. 124 and studying in the tekhnikum. It then has him departing for Berezniki in 1937, leaving only one year unaccounted for.

76. Goryun, *Boris Yel'tsin*, 1:5.

77. Second Yeltsin interview.

78. This sentence appears only in the English-language edition of the memoir (Yeltsin, *Struggle for Russia*, 98), not in the Russian original.

79. Ogonovskaya et al., *Istoriya Urala*, 354, where it is noted that, of the 8 million residents of the Urals, 900,000 were convicted of crimes in the 1930s, many of them of a political nature. Stalinist fears of sedition from without were not entirely based

on fantasy. There were in fact attempts by émigrés and others to smuggle anti-Soviet materials into the country, the main effect of which was to intensify police attacks on real and imagined oppositionists.

80. Source: the Perm branch of the Memorial Society. See http://www.pmem.ru/index.php?mode=rpm&exmod=rpm/12, which has a list of the 6,553 known victims.

Chapter Two

1. Vasilii Nemirovich-Danchenko, *Kama i Ural (ocherki i vpechatleniya)* (The Kama and the Urals [Essays and impressions]) (St. Petersburg: Tipografiya A. S. Suvorina, 1890), 170–71.

2. Figure on blood diseases from Murray Feshbach and Alfred Friendly, Jr., *Ecocide in the USSR: Health and Nature under Siege* (New York: Basic Books, 1992), 101. Chemical-weapons making and pollution in Berezniki are documented at http://www.pollutedplaces.org/region/e_europe/russia/berez.shtml; http://www.ourplanet.com/imgversn/86/sakan.html; http://neespi.gsfc.nasa.gov/science/NEESPI_SP_chapters/SB_Appendix_Ch_3.pdf; and http://www.fco.gov.uk/Files/kfile/russiaenviro.pdf.

3. M. M. Zagorul'ko, ed., *Voyennoplennyye v SSSR, 1939–1956: dokumenty i materialy* (Prisoners of war in the USSR, 1939–56: documents and materials) (Moscow: Logos, 2000), 104, 112; Obshchestvo "Memorial" and Gosudarstvennyi Arkhiv Rossiiskoi Federatsii, *Sistema ispravitel'no-trudovykh lagerei v SSSR, 1923–1940: spravochnik* (The USSR's system of corrective-labor camps, 1923–40: a reference book) (Moscow: Zven'ya: 1998), 275–76, 291–92, 451–52, 456–57, 491–92, 493–94, 514. A detailed map of Gulag in the Perm area is available at http://pmem.ru/rpm/map/Rus06.htm. Gulag inmates in the Urals totaled 330,000 in 1938, excluding the 530,000 exiles in special settlements and not confined to camps. At war's end, there were about 300,000 German POWs in camps in Sverdlovsk province alone.

4. In Molotov province as a whole in 1940–41, convict crews came to 30 percent of the total industrial labor force. Ol'ga Malova, "Gulag Permskoi oblasti" (The Gulag of Perm oblast), http://perm.psu.ru/school136/1945/antifashist/newspaper/malova.htm. But Gulag labor was concentrated in the Berezniki and Vishera areas, where its proportion was considerably higher.

5. This was so even in the largest Soviet cities. See David L. Hoffman, *Peasant Metropolis: Social Identities in Moscow, 1929–1941* (Ithaca: Cornell University Press, 1994).

6. Larisa Korzhavkina, *Berezniki* (Berezniki) (Perm: Permskoye knizhnoye izdatel'stvo, 2002), 76–77.

7. Boris Yel'tsin, *Ispoved' na zadannuyu temu* (Confession on an assigned theme) (Moscow: PIK, 1990), 20. Yeltsin told an interviewer in the 1990s that a sixth person, a male Kazakh worker, shared the barracks room with them for some time during the war. *Den' v sem'e prezidenta* (A day in the president's family), inter-

views of the Yeltsin family by El'dar Ryazanov on REN-TV, April 20, 1993 (videotape supplied by Irena Lesnevskaya). Polya's name is not given in Yeltsin's memoirs, but his mother mentioned it to acquaintances later.

8. Klavdiya Pashikhina, interview with the author (September 7, 2005). House, barracks, and fields were located just west and just east of where today's Berezniki Street meets Five-Year-Plan Street.

9. Details on the house from author's second interview with Naina Yeltsina (September 18, 2007). She says conversations in the 1950s suggested that the family had lived in a small rented house for a short time before moving into their private home.

10. Igor Neverov, "Otets prezidenta" (The president's father), fragment of an unpublished manuscript by Neverov, "Nikomu ne otdam svoyu biografiyu" (We won't give anyone our biography), 1998 (copy given to the author in September 2005 by the Museum of History and Art, Berezniki); and Naina Yeltsina, personal communication to the author, July 29, 2007. Mrs. Yeltsin checked the particulars with Boris Yeltsin's brother and sister.

11. Igor Neverov, interviewed in *Prezident vseya Rusi* (The president of all Russia), documentary film by Yevgenii Kiselëv, 1999–2000 (copy supplied by Kiselëv), 4 parts, part 1.

12. Tatyana Yumasheva, personal communication to the author, March 4, 2005. In Butka Nikolai was to supplement his pension by working part-time for a Talitsa-based building organization. One of his projects was to supervise construction of a new village school.

13. The quotation and the description of Klavdiya's hidden icon are from *Muzhskoi razgovor* (Male conversation), interview of Yeltsin by El'dar Ryazanov on REN-TV, November 7, 1993 (videotape supplied by Irena Lesnevskaya). Other details from the author's interviews.

14. Yeltsin said shamefacedly in 1993 *(Muzhskoi razgovor)* that he chided his mother for praying in the 1960s, after he joined the Communist Party, but she ignored him.

15. Izabella Verbova, "Za tysyachi kilometrov ot Belogo doma" (Thousands of kilometers from the White House), *Vechernyaya Moskva*, October 2, 1991.

16. Details from ibid., and my interviews with Sergei Molchanov (September 8, 2005) and Klavdiya Pashikhina.

17. Boris Yeltsin, second interview with the author (February 9, 2002).

18. Yel'tsin, *Ispoved'*, 20, 26.

19. "Boris Yel'tsin: ya khotel, chtoby lyudi byli svobodny" (Boris Yeltsin: I wanted people to be free), *Izvestiya*, February 1, 2006.

20. Yel'tsin, *Ispoved'*, 20. The drinking was a delicate subject in the family. One relative who knew Nikolai well in Butka in the 1960s said in an interview that he hid bottles of vodka from his wife in the cellar of their house.

21. "In a way they were a match: if the father was a sadist, then the son showed an early masochistic bent." Vladimir Solovyov and Elena Klepikova, *Boris Yeltsin: A*

Political Biography, trans. David Gurevich (New York: Putnam's, 1992), 120; also 128–29, where it is claimed he showed the same attitude at college in Sverdlovsk. Cf. Oleg Davydov, "Prezidentskii kolovorot" (Presidential brace), in A. N. Starkov, ed., *Rossiiskaya elita: psikhologicheskiye portrety* (The Russian elite: psychological portraits) (Moscow: Ladomir, 2000), 81–92, for an Oedipal interpretation.

22. Verbova, "Za tysyachi kilometrov."

23. Oksana Bartsits, "Shkol'nyye gody Borisa Yel'tsina" (The school years of Boris Yeltsin), http://www.aif.ru/online/sv/1181/11_01.

24. Yel'tsin, *Ispoved'*, 20. This picture is supported by workmates. See in particular Neverov, "Otets prezidenta," which mentions Nikolai trying to invent a machine for unloading railroad freight cars.

25. Yeltsina communication.

26. Zhdanov does mention (Bartsits, "Shkol'nyye gody Borisa Yel'tsina") a friendship at School No. 95 with one Svetlana Zhemchuzhnikova, an evacuee from Leningrad, "very pretty" and somewhat of a tomboy. When she broke her leg in an accident, Boris talked his pals into visiting her at home.

27. Stalin made most Soviet schools single-sex schools during and after the war; they reverted to coeducation in 1954.

28. See Michael Ellman and S. Maksudov, "Soviets Deaths in the Great Patriotic War: A Note," *Europe-Asia Studies* 46 (July 1994), 671–80; and more generally on gender roles Lynne Attwood, *The New Soviet Man and Woman: Sex-Role Socialization in the USSR* (Bloomington: Indiana University Press, 1990).

29. Quotation from Boris Yel'tsin, *Zapiski prezidenta* (Notes of a president) (Moscow: Ogonëk, 1994), 155.

30. I use scripts in the sense that some biographers use phrases such as inner myths and private self-concepts. See James E. Veninga, "Biography: Self and Sacred Canopy," in Veninga, ed., *The Biographer's Gift: Life Histories and Humanism* (College Station: Texas A&M University Press, 1983), 59–79; and Leon Edel, *Writing Lives: Principia Biographia* (New York: Norton, 1984), 159–73.

31. Bartsits, "Shkol'nyye gody." Details about the schools come from my interviews with Sergei Molchanov and with Viktor Tsipushtanov (September 8, 2005).

32. Indicative are the food supplies allocated to the town of Solikamsk, just up the Kama, for the year 1938. For each resident, they provided 1.1 kilograms of meat (less than 2½ pounds), 2.4 kilos of sausage, 3.9 kilos of fish, one jar of preserves, 100 grams of cheese, and 2.6 kilos of macaroni. The worst years were 1932–33, when rationing was in effect and the Urals norms for urban laborers were a pound of bread or bread surrogate, a pound of potatoes, and a glass of milk per day. I. S. Ogonovskaya et al., *Istoriya Urala s drevneishikh vremën do nashikh dnei* (History of the Urals from ancient times to our day) (Yekaterinburg: Sokrat, 2003), 341.

33. Andrei Goryun, *Boris Yel'tsin: svet i teni* (Boris Yeltsin: light and shadows), 2 vols. (Sverdlovsk: Klip, 1991), 1:8. Yeltsin's daughter Tatyana does not find the story of the siblings being sent to the restaurant a credible one, and surmises that Goryun misunderstood Klavdiya Yeltsina in their interview. Tatyana heard many stories

about hardship from her grandparents but never this one. Asking neighbors for help would have been much more acceptable conduct. Tatyana Yumasheva, second interview with the author (September 11, 2006). Since Valentina Yeltsina was born only in 1944, she could not have been active in the search for food during the war years.

34. Yel'tsin, *Ispoved'*, 21. The hay mowing was one of many behavioral ties to village life. Fifty years later, as president of Russia, Yeltsin still owned two scythes *(Den' v sem'e prezidenta)*.

35. Verbova, "Za tysyachi kilometrov."

36. See Erik H. Erikson, *Gandhi's Truth: On the Origins of Militant Nonviolence* (New York: Norton, 1969), 125. I learned about Nikolai's mistreatment of his wife from a number of interviews. Tatyana Yumasheva, his granddaughter, confirmed it in my second interview with her.

37. Second Yeltsin interview.

38. Irina Bobrova, "Boris bol'shoi, yemu vidnei" (Boris is a big shot, he knows better), *Moskovskii komsomolets,* January 31, 2007. *Moskovskii komsomolets* has over the years made it a specialty to present unflattering and often untrue information about Boris Yeltsin and his family. In this case, the sentiment expressed by Boris Andrianovich seems to have been accurately reported.

39. Goryun, *Boris Yel'tsin,* 1:6.

40. Neverov, "Otets prezidenta," says Nikolai's personnel file contained references to twenty-eight official punishments he had meted out to workers under his supervision—for poor bricklaying, negligence, and falsifying records. But, "He was always orderly and smart in his appearance, and I cannot remember him ever raising his voice or losing his temper." Neverov says, without providing details, that he and Nikolai were both disciplined in January 1961 for exceeding the wage fund.

41. Second Yeltsin interview.

42. Yeltsin's participation in approved youth activities was strongly borne out in my interview with Sergei Molchanov: "Yeltsin was in the active group." He took part in Komsomol meetings, asked questions, and made comments.

43. Quotation from Yel'tsin, *Ispoved'*, 24. Materials in the museum of the Pushkin School, to which Yeltsin transferred in 1945, show that thirteen of twenty-three who finished the school in June 1941 (including two girls) went straight to the army from their graduation ball. Three teachers also shipped out.

44. Quotation from second Yeltsin interview. His interest and the notebooks are reported in Goryun, *Boris Yel'tsin,* 1:7, from a conversation with Mikhail Yeltsin. None of this ever made Boris Yeltsin a great expert on the history of the revolution. When an American journalist tried in the late 1980s to engage him in conversation about the Mensheviks and other non-Bolshevik factions, Yeltsin was not familiar with the groups and the names of their leaders. Jonathan Sanders, interview with the author (January 21, 2004).

45. Lewis Siegelbaum and Andrei Sokolov, *Stalinism as a Way of Life: A Narrative in Documents* (New Haven: Yale University Press, 2000), 374 (italics added).

46. Boris Yeltsin, third interview with the author (September 12, 2002). Aleksei Tolstoy (1883–1945), a distant cousin of Leo Tolstoy, published his novel in three parts between 1929 and 1945. Yeltsin may also have been familiar with the 1910 silent-film classic *Peter the Great*, directed by Vasilii Goncharov, which was often shown in Soviet cinemas with the Petrov movie. His admiration for Peter put him at odds with the Old Believer tradition, in which Russia's first emperor was seen as the Antichrist.

47. Yel'tsin, *Ispoved'*, 21.

48. Bartsits, "Shkol'nyye gody."

49. Goryun, *Boris Yel'tsin*, 1:8.

50. Verbova, "Za tysyachi kilometrov."

51. In "Istoriya shkoly No. 1" (History of School No. 1), typescript, museum of Pushkin School, 9.

52. Unpublished bulletin for class reunion by Tatyana Babiyan, in the school museum.

53. Facts and figures from the school museum and the Berezniki Museum of the History of Education.

54. Quotation from Molchanov interview. Khonina is the only teacher Yeltsin gave by name in *Ispoved'* (23), where he called her a "marvelous" mentor.

55. School records, including Yeltsin's school-leaving certificate *(attestat zrelosti)*. Soviet schools at the time assigned daily and weekly grades in each subject, which were then aggregated into quarterly and full-year grades. Khonina's log for 1947–48, ninth grade for Yeltsin, contains a fair number of one-day and one-week 3s, but none lower than that. The log for 1948–49 was destroyed in a basement flood at the school. Yeltsin (*Ispoved'*, 25–26) misremembered his last year's grades, saying he received only two 4s and got 5s in the rest.

56. Tsipushtanov interview.

57. Molchanov interview. The railway school, as was not uncommon in the Soviet provinces, had no athletics. "The teacher would lead out the class single file into the corridor for 'free calisthenics.' You would wave your hands, and that was the whole sports program." Bartsits, "Shkol'nyye gody."

58. Ol'ga Yevtyukhova and Yelena Zaitseva, "Rovesniki moi" (They were the same age as me), 1999 essay in the Pushkin School museum.

59. "Istoriya shkoly No. 1," 9.

60. Aleksandr Abramov, the current Pushkin headmaster, showed me the 1948 directive in my interview with him (September 8, 2005). The class photograph and notes about future occupations are in the archive of the Berezniki Museum of History and Art.

61. Second Yeltsin interview.

62. Marietta Chudakova, interview with the author (April 14, 2003).

63. Yel'tsin, *Ispoved'*, 21–26. His book dates most of these incidents, but not the one with the grenades, where the source is Goryun, *Boris Yel'tsin*, 1:8.

64. Second Yeltsin interview; Molchanov interview. The bath was of the "black" variety, in which smoke from the fire escapes the steam room through a hole in the ceiling. (In a Russian "white" steambath, such as Boris Yeltsin built in his family's yard, smoke exits through a stovepipe.) In *Ispoved'*, 24, Yeltsin mentions long rural hikes and a climb up the Denezhkin Stone, a scenic Urals massif north of Berezniki.

65. Yel'tsin, *Ispoved'*, 22.

66. Alya Tanachëva, interview with the author (June 22, 2004).

67. Yel'tsin, *Ispoved'*, 22–23.

68. Ibid., 25. When he fought the school's decision on tenth-grade registration, he repeated the cycle: "The path was already familiar." He was by then known to some city officials because of his success as an athlete.

69. Bartsits, "Shkol'nyye gody."

70. Interviews with Abramov (jump out of the window) and Pashikhina (needles on the teacher's chair).

71. Molchanov interview. Molchanov was an unusually reliable source, since, he said, he never read Yeltsin's published account. In his memoirs, Yeltsin's memories of his years at the Pushkin School are generally clearer than those of School No. 95. His studies at Pushkin were less remote in time and the school is still a going concern, whereas School No. 95 was converted into a trade school in 1964 and shut down in 1971 (a fragment of the building remains). Yeltsin, by this time Communist Party boss of Sverdlovsk province, sent a sculpture of semiprecious Urals stone for the fiftieth anniversary of the Pushkin School in 1982. He had planned to attend the celebration but could not because his opposite number in Perm, Boris Konoplëv, would not make the time to accompany him, as protocol required. His gift for the sixtieth anniversary in 1992, on display in the school museum in 2005, was a book inscribed "With thanks for the foundation." In the 1990s Yeltsin had discretionary funds from the president's office donated to the schools for repairs and renovations. His foundation also provided assistance to the school after his retirement.

72. His school-leaving certificate dates his entry to the school in 1945, without giving the month.

73. Zhdanov remembers nothing about pupils being required to collect scraps for the teacher's pig or about Yeltsin attacking her at a public ceremony. When he read these things in Yeltsin's memoirs, "I even wanted to phone him up and ask, 'Where did you come up with that?'" Bartsits, "Shkol'nyye gody." Conversion of the three secondary schools in town into single-sex schools was completed only in 1946, but in 1945, when Yeltsin transferred, the Pushkin School was already the only one to admit boys.

74. Interviews with Stanislav Glebov (September 11, 2005) and Abramov. Yarns pop up every now and then about Yeltsin doing some dastardly deed around this time. One of the silliest is to the effect that in the hand-grenade incident he threw the weapon at a group of his friends and killed two of them. It can be found in Yurii Mukhin's screed *Kod Yel'tsina* (The Yeltsin code) (Moscow: Yauza, 2005), 51.

75. The family's pain is undeniable. Gorbachev did not speak about it publicly until 1990. Both of his grandfathers were arrested in the 1930s, his paternal grandfather (who joined the kolkhoz only in 1935) spent a year in Siberia, and several relatives died in the collectivization-induced famine. Grandfather Gopkalo, arrested in 1937, was released in 1938 and restored as a party member and as head of the kolkhoz. Raisa Gorbacheva's maternal grandfather was shot in 1937. See Mikhail Gorbachev, *Zhizn' i reformy* (Life and reforms), 2 vols. (Moscow: Novosti, 1995), 1:31–58.

76. The essay is not mentioned in Gorbachev's memoirs but came out in a discussion in the Politburo in 1986. Gorbachev told his colleagues (including Yeltsin) that he preferred to have someone else meet with Stalin's daughter, Svetlana Alliluyeva, who had defected to the West in 1967, returned to the USSR in 1984, and now sought permission to leave again (which she eventually received). Offended by letters in which she criticized her father, Gorbachev said, "If you ask me, it is necessary to place a high value on Stalin, Stalingrad, et cetera. I myself am from such a family. My grandfather wrecked his health [building the kolkhoz]. My mother and her four sisters were from an impoverished family. I received a medal for a composition on the theme, 'Stalin Is Our Glory, Stalin Is the Delight of Our Youth.'" Politburo transcript for March 20, 1986, in Volkogonov Archive (Project on Cold War Studies, Davis Center for Russian and Eurasian Studies, Harvard University), 41. "Stalin Is Our Glory, Stalin Is the Delight of Our Youth" was the title of a prewar song by Matvei Blanter and Aleksei Surkov.

77. Interviewed by a journalist in 2000 (see http://www.achievement.org/autodoc/page/gor0int-1), Gorbachev recalled that "the party's slogans appealed to me, they made quite an impression on me. It was very seductive, very attractive, and I took it all on faith."

78. Molchanov interview.

79. Arnold M. Ludwig, *King of the Mountain: The Nature of Political Leadership* (Lexington: University Press of Kentucky, 2002), 448. Thirty-two percent of the leaders in Ludwig's sample were outgoing in the group and 29 percent were solitary. Again, Yeltsin manifested both of these traits at different times. Yeltsin's avid readership of books was shared by 39 percent of Ludwig's subjects, but his athletic skills by only 15 percent, his very close relationship with his mother by 11 percent, and his at times hostile relationship with his father by 21 percent.

80. Yel'tsin, *Zapiski*, 155.

81. Quotations from Yel'tsin, *Ispoved'*, 26; and Tanachëva interview.

Chapter Three

1. A mining institute opened in Molotov (Perm) in 1953 and was upgraded to a polytechnic in 1960. According to a passage in Yeltsin's first memoir book not printed in the Russian edition, he saw the new campus of Moscow State University on the Lenin Hills while on his first visit to Moscow in the summer of 1953, shortly after Gulag laborers completed it. He was taken by the magnificence of the build-

ings and regretted that he had not applied for admission in 1949. But then he thought to himself he probably would have failed the entrance test and, as the Russian proverb goes, "Better a sparrow in the hand than a blue titmouse in the sky." Nikolai Zen'kovich, *Boris Yel'tsin: raznyye zhizni* (Boris Yeltsin: various lives), 2 vols. (Moscow: OLMA, 2001), 1:27–28 (quoting from the Norwegian-language edition of *Ispoved' na zadannuyu temu*).

2. Perm was founded in the same year as Yekaterinburg, 1723, but was the only large Russian city other than St. Petersburg to be laid out rectilinearly. It had more cultural and educational institutions than Yekaterinburg and was made capital of the Urals region in 1781. During the revolution and civil war, Perm was more supportive of the White forces.

3. James R. Harris, *The Great Urals: Regionalism and the Evolution of the Soviet System* (Ithaca: Cornell University Press, 1999).

4. Leonid Brezhnev, *Vospominaniya* (Memoirs) (Moscow: Politizdat, 1983), 29.

5. A partial list of evacuated plants may be found at http://www2.warwick.ac.uk/fac/soc/economics/staff/faculty/harrison/vpk/history/part1/list.txt.

6. Sheila Fitzpatrick, "A Closed City and Its Secret Archives: Notes on a Journey to the Urals," *Journal of Modern History* 62 (December 1990), 776.

7. The *American Jewish Handbook* for 1980 was to estimate the Jewish population of Sverdlovsk that year to be 40,000. The 1989 census officially recorded 14,300 persons of Jewish nationality in Sverdlovsk oblast, fifth place in the Russian republic of the USSR. (Jewish was listed as nationality—that is, ethnicity—on Soviet passports.) Due mostly to emigration, the number declined to 6,900 in 2002, when it was fourth in the country.

8. The institute began as part of the new Urals State University in 1920 and for most of the time from 1925 to 1948 was called the Urals Industrial Institute. Its construction division, formed in 1929, functioned as a separate institute from 1934 to 1948. UPI was to be renamed Urals State Technical University (UGTU) in 1992 and now has 23,000 students.

9. *Stroitel'nyi fakul'tet UGTU–UPI: istoriya, sovremennost'* (The construction division of UGTU–UPI: history and current situation) (Yekaterinburg: Real-Media, 2004), 12–20.

10. Yakov Ol'kov, interview with the author (September 12, 2004). In Sverdlovsk Germans built a firemen's school, the central stadium, and housing, paved roads, and refaced city hall. The last prisoners were returned in 1955.

11. The claim about reading German with a dictionary is in "Lichnyi listok po uchëtu kadrov" (Personal certificate for the register of cadres) for Boris Nikolayevich Yeltsin, dated June 16, 1975; in TsDOOSO (Documentation Center for the Public Organizations of Sverdlovsk Oblast, Yekaterinburg), fund *(fond)* 4, register *(opis')* 116, file *(delo)* 283, 4. The Documentation Center is the official title of the Sverdlovsk archive of the CPSU. According to a usually reliable source, a Russian journalist who covered him as president in the 1990s, Yeltsin was unable to distinguish the languages at that time. See Boris Grishchenko, *Postoronnyi v Kremle: reportazhi iz "osoboi zony"*

(A stranger in the Kremlin: reportage from "the special zone") (Moscow: VAGRIUS, 2004), 159–60.

12. Lidiya Solomoniya, interview with the author (September 11, 2004); Aleksandr Yuzefovich, *Komanda molodosti nashei: zapiski stroitelya* (Team of our youth: notes of a builder) (Perm: Fond podderzhki pervogo Prezidenta Rossii, 1997), 35, 49. Yakov Sverdlov, who died in 1919, was Jewish, but officials never got around to changing the name of the city in the late Stalin period. It persisted until September 1991, when Sverdlovsk reverted to the original Yekaterinburg; the province is still called Sverdlovsk oblast. In July 1957 three Sverdlovskers, already expelled from the party, were arrested for distributing anti-Semitic letters; they were released in 1964. One of their proposals was that the city be renamed. See V. A. Kozlov and S. V. Mironenko, eds., *58-10: nadzornyye proizvodstva Prokuratury SSSR po delam ob antisovetskoi agitatsii i propagande (Mart 1953–1991), annotirovannyi katalog* (Article 58, section 10: the supervisory files of the USSR Procuracy about cases of anti-Soviet agitation and propaganda [March 1953–1991], an annotated catalogue) (Moscow: Mezhdunarodnyi fond "Demokratiya," 1999), 345.

13. Kozlov and Mironenko, *58-10*, 41. Okulov was arrested on March 5, 1953, as Stalin lay dying in Moscow.

14. A. Ye. Pavlova, a Yeltsin classmate, is quoted in a recent book of reminiscences: "We were inculcated with faith in Stalin. We deified him from afar. When he spoke on the radio, we would run to listen—on our own, no one had to force us to do it. And, when he died, we cried out loud. It seemed to us that all was lost and nothing good would happen in future." Vladimir Sutyrin, "Boris Yel'tsin i Ural'skii politekhnicheskii" (Boris Yeltsin and UPI), http://www.ural-yeltsin.ru/knigi/knigi_elcina/document427.

15. Details from Andrei Goryun, *Boris Yel'tsin: svet i teni* (Boris Yeltsin: light and shadows), 2 vols. (Sverdlovsk: Klip, 1991), 1:8–10; Irina Bobrova, "Yel'tsiny tozhe plachut" (The Yeltsins also cry), *Moskovskii komsomolets*, February 18, 2000; and Ol'kov and Solomoniya interviews.

16. Anatolii Yuzhaninov, quoted in Anna Veligzhanina, "Pervaya lyubov' Borisa Yel'tsina" (Boris Yeltsin's first love), *Komsomol'skaya pravda*, April 26, 2007. Yerina and Ustinov moved back to Berezniki and soon divorced.

17. Sutyrin, "Boris Yel'tsin i Ural'skii politekhnicheskii."

18. Naina Yeltsina, second interview with the author (September 18, 2007); Bobrova, "Yel'tsiny tozhe plachut." Naina was born in the village of Titovka, outside Orenburg, but grew up in the city. She also spent some of her childhood in Kazakhstan, the nearest republic in Central Asia.

19. Sutyrin, "Boris Yel'tsin i Ural'skii politekhnicheskii."

20. Boris Yel'tsin, *Zapiski prezidenta* (Notes of a president) (Moscow: Ogonëk, 1994), 252. The dance lessons are described in Natal'ya Konstantinova, *Zhenskii vzglyad na kremlëvskuyu zhizn'* (A woman's view of Kremlin life) (Moscow: Geleos, 1999), 105.

21. Goryun, *Boris Yel'tsin*, 1:9.

22. Interview with Ol'kov, who also described Yeltsin participating in polite petitions to the rectorate about students' workload. On the petitions, see also Vladimir Solovyov and Elena Klepikova, *Boris Yeltsin: A Political Biography*, trans. David Gurevich (New York: Putnam's, 1992), 127–28.

23. "Otduvalsya v dekanate za Borisa tozhe" (I answered at the dean's office for Boris, too), http://gazeta.ru/politics/yeltsin/1621092.shtml.

24. Boris Yel'tsin, *Ispoved' na zadannuyu temu* (Confession on an assigned theme) (Moscow: PIK, 1990), 29; Sutyrin, "Boris Yel'tsin i Ural'skii politekhnicheskii." Rogitskii headed the department until 1965. The official history of the construction division (*Stroitel'nyi fakul'tet UGTU–UPI*, 21) describes him as a gifted engineer and a humane teacher, but also absent-minded.

25. On the UPI Komsomol committee, Galina Stepanova of the Sverdlovsk/Yekaterinburg Communist Party archive, interview with the author (September 7, 2004). In his second interview with me (February 9, 2002), Yeltsin volunteered that he avoided participation: "In general I was a leader, a guide. But not in the Pioneers and Komsomol. I was little concerned with that."

26. Yel'tsin, *Ispoved'*, 23.

27. Ol'kov interview. Even in Berezniki, Yeltsin had the best spike on his school team.

28. Yel'tsin, *Ispoved'*, 29–30; Sutyrin, "Boris Yel'tsin i Ural'skii politekhnicheskii."

29. Yel'tsin, *Ispoved'*, 29.

30. The principal's order discharging Yeltsin is dated March 27, 1952; he applied for re-admission on August 30; the request was granted in mid-September. See Leon Aron, *Yeltsin: A Revolutionary Life* (New York: St. Martin's, 2000), 17.

31. Ol'kov interview.

32. Ibid.; *Stroitel'nyi fakul'tet UGTU–UPI*, 21.

33. Ol'kov interview.

34. Yel'tsin, *Ispoved'*, 27. In 2006, while on a visit to Kazan, Yeltsin referred to one such incident. He said it happened in Kazan and he told the police he was going to see his aunt; he spent some time in the brig. Anna Akhmadeyeva, "Boris Yel'tsin priznalsya v lyubvi k Kazani" (Boris Yeltsin professed his love for Kazan), http://www.viperson.ru/wind.php?ID=276299&soch=1.

35. Yel'tsin, *Ispoved'*, 29. The Norwegian version of the memoir recounts further risky ventures in Moscow, including a party with female students and a brawl with criminals. See Zen'kovich, *Boris Yel'tsin*, 1:27–30.

36. Aleksandr Kil'chevskii, interviewed in *Prezident vseya Rusi* (The president of all Russia), documentary film by Yevgenii Kiselëv, 1999–2000 (copy supplied by Kiselëv), 4 parts, part 1. Yeltsin in retirement referred to a similar-sounding incident with the team in Kazan. He said he "fell in love with some paintings" at an exhibition, missed the train, and then got to Tbilisi in a freight train. Akhmadeyeva, "Boris Yel'tsin."

37. Quotation from Yel'tsin, *Ispoved'*, 29 (italics added). Coach Kil'chevskii, though, interviewed by Kiselëv almost forty years later, still remembered Yeltsin's summer outing with deep disapproval.

38. N. A. Vilesova, quoted in Sutyrin, "Boris Yel'tsin i Ural'skii politekhnicheskii."

39. Yel'tsin, *Ispoved'*, 30. The certificate for the diploma project, dating his defense on June 20, 1955, was on exhibit in the school's museum when I was there in 2005, and the description shows it was a design for a bucket line. Next to the document in the display case was a wood abacus of the kind a UPI student in the 1950s would have used to do the math.

40. Three schemes that Yeltsin drew for the bucket line towers are stored in the institute's archive (copy shared with the author by Sergei Skrobov of Yekaterinburg). One of them is an ink sketch of a lattice steel pylon, 325 feet high, that bears some likeness to a tower for a television transmitter. It is possible that while dictating his memoirs Yeltsin was forgetful of the original project, saw a copy of the sketch, and mistook it for a television tower.

41. Local mountaineers began to scale the tower's exterior wall with their climbing gear, which could take hours or even days. Several people staged parachute jumps from the platform. After two accidental deaths and one suicide, city workers in 1998 cut off the outside ladder and welded the entrance door shut. See http://tau.ur.ru/tower/etower.asp.

42. See, for example, Zen'kovich, *Boris Yel'tsin*, 1:36; and Vitalii Tret'yakov, "Sverdlovskii vyskochka" (Sverdlovsk upstart), part 2, *Politicheskii klass*, March 2006, 85.

43. Yel'tsin, *Ispoved'*, 35.

44. Blair A. Ruble, "From *Khrushchëby* to *Korobki*," in William Craft Brumfield and Blair A. Ruble, eds., *Russian Housing in the Modern Age: Design and Social History* (Cambridge: Cambridge University Press, 1993), 232–70.

45. Second Yeltsina interview. Yeltsin's career moves are conveniently summarized in handwriting in his "Lichnyi listok," 4.

46. Yel'tsin, *Zapiski*, 269.

47. Yel'tsin, *Ispoved'*, 74. Yeltsin was so sure their second child would be a boy that he had already purchased a blue blanket and a toy truck. "Yelena Yel'tsina chut' ne zadushila sestru v koryte" (Yelena Yeltsina almost smothered her sister in the trough), http://www.allrus.info/obj/main.php?ID=217454&arc_new=1.

48. Second Yeltsina interview and author's third interview with Tatyana Yumasheva (January 25, 2007).

49. Most details about housing are taken from ibid. The point about the shared washing machine is from an interview with Lyudmila Chinyakova in *Prezident vseya Rusi*, part 2.

50. Interview on Ekho Moskvy radio, March 1, 1997, http://echo.msk.ru/guests/1775. In several other interviews, Naina said she always knotted Boris's necktie and that he never learned how to do it himself. This was an overstatement. Boris may have preferred to let his wife knot his tie at breakfast, but he knew how to do so himself.

51. Yel'tsin, *Ispoved'*, 74. The story of the school diaries, attributed to Naina Yeltsina, is in Vladimir Mezentsev, "Okruzhentsy" (Entourage), part 3, *Rabochaya tribuna*, March 28, 1995.

52. "Naina Yel'tsina: Boris Nikolayevich na menya vorchit, a mne nravitsya . . ." (Naina Yeltsina: Boris Nikolayevich grumbles, but that is fine with me), *Komsomol'skaya pravda,* February 2, 2006; and "Naina Yel'tsina: ya nikogda ne vmeshivalas' v dela svoyego muzha" (Naina Yeltsina: I never interfered in my husband's business), *Izvestiya,* June 28, 1996.

53. Third Yumasheva interview.

54. Yel'tsin, *Zapiski,* 251.

55. Al'bert Tsioma, a Butka neighbor of the neighbors, interview with the author (September 11, 2005). Butka's population got to about 3,500 in the 1970s and about 4,000 today. Basmanovo leveled out at less than 2,000.

56. Yel'tsin, *Ispoved',* 40–41.

57. Boris Yeltsin, second interview with the author (February 9, 2002).

58. A good control group would be the 115 regional CPSU leaders selected full or candidate members of the party Central Committee with Yeltsin in 1981. Their average age of admission to the CPSU was 24.5. Specialists in ideological and control functions had joined earlier (at an average age of 22.5), but even among those whose careers were mostly in the economic realm, like Yeltsin, the average was 25.6. Only four of the 115 were admitted at an older age than he—two who were thirty-one and two who were thirty-two. Calculated from biographies in the 1981 yearbook of the *Bol'shaya sovetskaya entsiklopediya* (Great Soviet encyclopedia).

59. "In 1956 the party authorities were shaken by the bold statements by students in a number of Sverdlovsk institutions, demanding 'freedom to criticize,' 'free speech,' and democracy. Harsh measures were taken against them." Several were put on trial and sent off to labor camps or psychiatric prisons. A Sverdlovsk group favoring an anti-communist revolution, headed by factory technician L. G. Shefer, was broken up in April 1963. A. D. Kirillov and N. N. Popov, *Ural: vek dvadtsatyi* (The Urals: the twentieth century) (Yekaterinburg: Ural'skii rabochii, 2000), 175–76; Kozlov and Mironenko, *58-10,* 631.

60. Goryun, *Boris Yel'tsin,* 1:6.

61. Yel'tsin, *Ispoved',* 43.

62. Leon Aron, who interviewed some coworkers, goes into informative detail on such practices (*Yeltsin,* chap. 2). See also Stewart, "SIC TRANSIT," 87–95.

63. Goryun, *Boris Yel'tsin,* 1:11.

64. Svetlana Zinov'eva, quoted in Vadim Lipatnikov, "Boris Yel'tsin i DSK" (Boris Yeltsin and the DSK), http://www.ural-yeltsin.ru/knigi/knigi_elcina/document639.

65. On the model brigade, see Goryun, *Boris Yel'tsin,* 1:11; Yel'tsin, *Ispoved',* 42–43; and Zen'kovich, *Boris Yel'tsin,* 1:40. Aron (*Yeltsin,* 36–37) views the incident in a more favorable light.

66. Yel'tsin, *Ispoved',* 43.

67. Aron, *Yeltsin,* 40.

68. The fullest account is in Yakov Ryabov, *Moi XX vek: zapiski byvshego sekretarya TsK KPSS* (My 20th century: notes of a former secretary of the Central Committee of

the CPSU) (Moscow: Russkii biograficheskii institut, 2000), 33. The reprimand is at TsDOOSO, fund 161, register 39, file 9, 22–24.

69. Ryabov, *Moi XX vek*, 32.

70. See Goryun, *Boris Yel'tsin*, 1:11.

71. Third Yumasheva interview. It must be said that for all of Yeltsin's life some people saw him in such terms as well.

72. Andrei Karaulov, *Vokrug Kremlya: kniga politicheskikh dialogov* (Around the Kremlin: a book of political dialogues) (Moscow: Novosti, 1990), 98.

73. Yakov Ryabov, interview in files of Central Committee Interview Project, University of Glasgow (transcript supplied by Stephen White). He recalled discussing the need to replace Nikolayev with Brezhnev and Ivan Kapitonov of the Secretariat, but did not mention Kirilenko.

74. Oleg Podberëzin, formerly a Sverdlovsk party worker, interview with the author (September 9, 2004). Ryabov had been appointed party secretary of the turbine works in 1958 and of a district of Sverdlovsk city in 1960. He was active in Komsomol affairs from 1946 to the mid-1950s.

75. TsDOOSO, fund 4, register 116, file 283, 14.

76. Yel'tsin, *Ispoved'*, 44. As documented in the archive, he was "elected" to the Chkalov district soviet in 1963, the Sverdlovsk city soviet in 1965, and the city committee of the party in 1966. Once on the obkom staff, he joined the soviet and party committee of the oblast.

77. Ryabov, *Moi XX vek*, 34–35.

78. Ibid., 35.

79. Yel'tsin, *Ispoved'*, 44.

80. Yel'tsin, *Zapiski*, 253.

81. Yel'tsin, *Ispoved'*, 41.

82. Oleg Lobov, interview with the author (May 29, 2002).

83. Ryabov, *Moi XX vek*, 35.

84. Aron, *Yeltsin*, 43–44.

85. Ryabov, *Moi XX vek*, 38.

86. Details on motivations here from Ryabov interview (University of Glasgow).

87. Ryabov, *Moi XX vek*, 40.

88. In ibid., 40–41, Ryabov reprints a five-point summary from his diary of a conversation in June 1976 in which he let into Yeltsin for sharply worded instructions, superciliousness, disrespect for fellow communists ("including members of the bureau of the obkom"), and taking criticism as an insult. Every time they had such a conversation, Ryabov says, Yeltsin protested that his rudeness was only out of zeal to get the job done and promised to be more correct in future. "This way Boris won me over and calmed me."

89. Ryabov interview (University of Glasgow).

90. I heard about Ponomarëv's attempt from a then member of the bureau who wishes to go unnamed. Confirmation of the Bobykin-Yeltsin rivalry may be found in the memoir by Viktor Manyukhin, a contemporary of Yeltsin's in the Sverdlovsk party apparatus: *Pryzhok nazad: o Yel'tsine i o drugikh* (Backward leap: about Yeltsin

and others) (Yekaterinburg: Pakrus, 2002), 34–35. Some bureau members certainly preferred Yeltsin. Ryabov (interview, University of Glasgow) identifies Korovin, secretary N. M. Dudkin, the commander of the local military district, and the trade-union chief as in favor and says that even in 1975 "several secretaries" preferred that Yeltsin be made second secretary, over Korovin's head.

91. Ryabov, *Moi XX vek*, 54–55; Yel'tsin, *Ispoved'*, 48–49. Yeltsin mentions Ryabov attending some of the meetings, but breathes not a word of his sponsorship.

92. Yel'tsin, *Ispoved'*, 49–50.

Chapter Four

1. "Law-and-order prefects" and "developmental prefects" (below) are taken from Jerry F. Hough, *The Soviet Prefects: The Local Party Organs in Industrial Decision-Making* (Cambridge, Mass.: Harvard University Press, 1969), 5.

2. The instructions, signed by Yeltsin in November 1981 and stamped "Top Secret," are in TsDOOSO (Documentation Center for the Public Organizations of Sverdlovsk Oblast, Yekaterinburg), fund 4, register 100, file 119, 135–36. On Yeltsin and Kornilov, see Viktor Manyukhin, *Pryzhok nazad: o Yel'tsine i o drugikh* (Backward leap: about Yeltsin and others) (Yekaterinburg: Pakrus, 2002), 71–73.

3. Boris Yel'tsin, *Ispoved' na zadannuyu temu* (Confession on an assigned theme) (Moscow: PIK, 1990), 60.

4. That figure, coming to 32.5 percent of industrial employment in the oblast, was inferred from classified data for 1985. It does not include personnel in R&D or defense-related tasks done in plants subordinated to civilian ministries (Uralmash, for example). Brenda Horrigan, "How Many People Worked in the Soviet Defense Industry?" *RFE/RL Research Report* 1 (August 21, 1992), 33–39.

5. On Compound No. 19, see Anthony Rimmington, "From Military to Industrial Complex? The Conversion of Biological Weapons Facilities in the Russian Federation," *Contemporary Security Policy* 17 (April 1996), 81–112; Jeanne Guillemin, *Anthrax: The Investigation of a Deadly Outbreak* (Berkeley: University of California Press, 1999); and Ken Alibek, with Stephen Handelman, *Biohazard: The Chilling True Story of the Largest Covert Biological Weapons Program in the World* (New York: Random House, 1999), chap. 7. Some analysts have charged the United States with making as much use of Japanese technology as the Soviets did. See Sheldon H. Harris, *Factories of Death: Japanese Biological Warfare, 1932–45, and the American Cover-Up*, rev. ed. (London: Routledge, 2002).

6. A. D. Kirillov and N. N. Popov, *Ural: vek dvadtsatyi* (The Urals: the twentieth century) (Yekaterinburg: Ural'skii rabochii, 2000), 180.

7. Yel'tsin, *Ispoved'*, 55.

8. Bobykin was transferred to a Central Committee department in 1978. He returned to Sverdlovsk as obkom first secretary in June 1988, when Yeltsin was in political disfavor, and was removed in February 1990.

9. Manyukhin, *Pryzhok*, 32.

10. Grigorii Kaëta, who at this point was an official in the obkom's propaganda department, interview with the author (September 9, 2004). Mekhrentsev, a war veteran, had been a party member since 1946. He was a deputy in the Supreme Soviet and had been awarded two Orders of Lenin and a USSR State Prize. He died in January 1985 at the age of sixty and rated an obituary in *Pravda*. Yeltsin was one of the officials who signed it, as a mark of respect. Mekhrentsev's replacement as chairman of the province's government was Oleg Lobov.

11. Manyukhin, *Pryzhok*, 37–39.

12. This last phenomenon is reported in Kaleriya Shadrina, "Yel'tsin byl krut: soratniki perezhidali yego gnev v spetsbol'nitse" (Yeltsin was gruff: his brothers-in-arms thought about his anger in the special hospital), *Komsomol'skaya pravda*, November 25, 1997.

13. Pilar Bonet, "Nevozmozhnaya Rossiya: Boris Yel'tsin, provintsial v Kremle" (The impossible Russia: Boris Yeltsin, a provincial in the Kremlin), *Ural*, April 1994, 100. This incident seems to have happened in 1984.

14. Rossel, interviewed in *Prezident vseya Rusi* (The president of all Russia), documentary film by Yevgenii Kiselëv, 1999–2000 (copy supplied by Kiselëv), 4 parts, part 1. Rossel was appointed head of a more important building organization in 1981 and deputy head of the construction directorate for the oblast in 1983.

15. The case was initially a disappearance, with no one knowing what had become of Titov. His body was found outside of town several months later, with the pistol next to it. The KGB eventually ruled the death a suicide and a personal affair with no political aspect. Source: interviews with former obkom officials.

16. Viktor Chernomyrdin, interview with the author (September 15, 2000).

17. Interview with Ryabov, Central Committee Interview Project, University of Glasgow (transcript supplied by Stephen White). Ryabov went so far as to say in this interview that Yeltsin "was fully under my influence" in the late 1970s.

18. What Ryabov said in Nizhnii Tagil, after being asked about Brezhnev, was that the Politburo and Secretariat were quite capable of "covering for an ailing leader." The incident is described in Yakov Ryabov, *Moi XX vek: zapiski byvshego sekretarya TsK KPSS* (My 20th century: notes of a former secretary of the Central Committee of the CPSU) (Moscow: Russkii biograficheskii institut, 2000), 129–30. He mentioned Kornilov's likely role only in the University of Glasgow interview. In 1971 Ryabov had pushed for serial production of the T-72 main battle tank in Nizhnii Tagil; Ustinov preferred a model made in Kharkov, Ukraine. Brezhnev eventually settled the matter in Ryabov's and Sverdlovsk's favor.

19. Manyukhin, *Pryzhok*, 175.

20. Alibek, *Biohazard*, 79. Stalin appointed Ustinov, born in 1908, as minister (people's commissar) of the armaments industry in 1941, and he had been in high positions ever since.

21. "Boris Yel'tsin: ya ne skryvayu trudnostei i khochu, chtoby narod eto ponimal" (Boris Yeltsin: I do not conceal the difficulties and want the people to understand that), *Komsomol'skaya pravda*, May 27, 1992.

22. Some Western Kremlinologists interpreted Ryabov's demotion as a reflection of a decrease in the Moscow standing of Kirilenko. I see no direct connection, but Ryabov's account makes it clear that the incident made Kirilenko nervous. "I sat there with Kirilenko and could feel his perplexity and feeling of helplessness. I quietened him down and stated that I would not stir up a scandal in the Politburo and would make a worthy statement. He thanked me and we said good-bye until the session of the Politburo." Ryabov, *Moi XX vek*, 130.

23. Manyukhin, *Pryzhok*, 51–52.

24. Andrei Goryun, *Boris Yel'tsin: svet i teni* (Boris Yeltsin: light and shadows), 2 vols. (Sverdlovsk: Klip, 1991), 1:14. There is no independent confirmation of Yeltsin's opposition to the Brezhnev museum. Brezhnev's daughter, Galina, was born in Sverdlovsk, and in 1999 his grandson Andrei ran unsuccessfully for governor of the province.

25. There is careful analysis in Aron, *Yeltsin*, 58, 73–75.

26. Nikolai Tselishchev, a Sverdlovsk propaganda official at the time, interview with the author (June 23, 2004); Manyukhin, *Pryzhok*, 133–34.

27. Aron, *Yeltsin*, 45–46.

28. Press reports say the apartment sold for $200,000 in 2003 and has a net living area (not counting halls, kitchen, and bathroom) of about 1,800 square feet. I visited a unit of identical layout in the building in June 2004. By way of comparison, the *median* size of a single-family, detached house in the United States was 1,858 square feet in 2005, and of a house built between 2000 and 2005 it was 2,258 square feet.

29. The tower, promoted by Ryabov and sanctioned by Prime Minister Aleksei Kosygin, was completed in 1980, but construction defects kept it from opening for two years. Yeltsin had supervised the first stages of the project. As first secretary, he was able to blame others for its problems.

30. Bonet, "Nevozmozhnaya Rossiya," 45–47, profiles Hospital No. 2, which went from 100 staff members in 1970 to 750 in 1979. The listening devices are described in Irina Bobrova, "Yel'tsiny tozhe plachut" (The Yeltsins also cry), *Moskovskii komsomolets*, February 18, 2000.

31. On obkom promotion of volleyball courts, see Bonet, "Nevozmozhnaya Rossiya," 82. Of the four former participants in the officials' volleyball games with whom I spoke, none was critical. I was shown around the area and the now moldering Dacha No. 1 in September 2004.

32. Oleg Lobov, interview with the author (May 29, 2002).

33. Yeltsin later told associates he had seen the gun in a shop while heading an official delegation to Prague, but did not have the money to pay for it. Morshchakov took up a collection from the delegates, bought the weapon, and presented it to him as they boarded the return flight to the USSR. See the account by Aleksandr Korzhakov in Aleksandr Khinshtein, *Yel'tsin, Kreml', istoriya bolezni* (Yeltsin, the Kremlin, the history of an illness) (Moscow: OLMA, 2006), 65.

34. Manyukhin, *Pryzhok*, 177. Manyukhin claims Yeltsin demanded the right of first shot at the elk, but Yeltsin writes of the hunters waiting in a row for the quarry to

spring, at spots paced off from the nearest hunter, with the man closest to the animal getting the shot. Boris Yel'tsin, *Prezidentskii marafon* (Presidential marathon) (Moscow: AST, 2000), 347.

35. Vladimir Mezentsev, "Okruzhentsy" (Entourage), part 8, *Rabochaya tribuna*, April 5, 1995.

36. Manyukhin, *Pryzhok*, 67.

37. Ryabov, *Moi XX vek*, 45.

38. Source: a witness to the episode who prefers to remain anonymous. Yeltsin refers in his memoirs to a visit by another KGB deputy chairman, Vladimir Pirozhkov.

39. Summaries of these cases are in V. A. Kozlov and S. V. Mironenko, eds., *58-10: nadzornyye proizvodstva Prokuratury SSSR po delam ob antisovetskoi agitatsii i propagande (Mart 1953–1991), annotirovannyi katalog* (Article 58, section 10: the supervisory files of the USSR Procuracy about cases of anti-Soviet agitation and propaganda [March 1953–1991], an annotated catalogue) (Moscow: Mezhdunarodnyi fond "Demokratiya," 1999), 720–21, 769–70, 792, 782. The Andropov memorandum may be found at http://psi.ece.jhu.edu/~kaplan/IRUSS/BUK/GBARC/pdfs/sovter74/kgb70-10.pdf.

40. The victims were sprayed with gunfire and bayoneted. Some had to be finished off with a shot to the head because precious stones sewn into their clothing deflected the blows. Yakov Yurovskii, the chief executioner and a party member since 1905, was guilt-stricken after the killings. The story is told in Mark D. Steinberg and Vladimir M. Khrustalëv, *The Fall of the Romanovs: Political Dreams and Personal Struggles in a Time of Revolution* (New Haven: Yale University Press, 1995).

41. The Andropov memo and Politburo resolution, as well as Yeltsin's speculation that the timing was connected with the anniversary of the coronation, are in Yel'tsin, *Marafon*, 330–31. Yeltsin does not explain why the demolition did not occur in 1975, and Ryabov makes no mention of any aspect of it in his memoirs.

42. Manyukhin, *Pryzhok*, 124–25.

43. The restrictions on plays and films are found at TsDOOSO, fund 4, register 107, file 118, 96. This was in addition to the filtering done by the Moscow authorities. The play, *Dear Yelena Sergeyevna*, by Lyudmila Razumovskaya, is about secondary-school graduates who, at their mathematics teacher's birthday party, beseech her to change their grades and threaten to rape one of their number in the process. The play was censured by the Central Committee Secretariat in April 1983. It was made into a successful Soviet film by director El'dar Ryazanov in 1988. Bonet, "Nevozmozhnaya Rossiya," 103, describes the measures on photocopiers.

44. Bonet, "Nevozmozhnaya Rossiya," 84.

45. Valentin Luk'yanin, interview with the author (September 9, 2004). The Nikonov text had been cleared by the local censor assigned to the magazine. This scandal, together with an earlier case where the errant writer was Konstantin Lagunov, is thoroughly discussed in Aron, *Yeltsin*, 118–25.

46. Matt Taibbi, "Butka: Boris Yeltsin, Revisited," http://exile.ru/105/yeltsin.

47. Quotation from Bobrova, "Yel'tsiny tozhe plachut." Boris Yeltsin is said to have ordered Mikhail to tear down a toolshed on his out-of-town garden plot because it exceeded the state norm by a tiny amount. But after their mother's death he did set Mikhail up in a studio apartment in the VIP complex by the Town Pond.

48. Irina Bobrova, "Boris bol'shoi, yemu vidnei" (Boris is a big shot, he knows better), *Moskovskii komsomolets*, January 31, 2007, says on the basis of inquiries in Berezniki that one of the sources of tension between Valentina and her husband, Oleg, was his belief that her brother could help them out in life. "Oleg Yakovlevich constantly reproached his wife for the fact that she felt shy about asking [Boris] for material assistance."

49. Details from Bobrova, "Yel'tsiny tozhe plachut"; Natal'ya Konstantinova, *Zhenskii vzglyad na kremlëvskuyu zhizn'* (A woman's view of Kremlin life) (Moscow: Geleos, 1999), 171–83; and various interviews.

50. Vladimir Solovyov and Elena Klepikova, *Boris Yeltsin: A Political Biography*, trans. David Gurevich (New York: Putnam's, 1992), 84–85; Gwendolyn Elizabeth Stewart, "SIC TRANSIT: Democratization, *Suverenizatsiia*, and Boris Yeltsin in the Breakup of the Soviet Union" (Ph.D. diss., Harvard University, 1995), 95.

51. Shadrina, "Yel'tsin byl krut."

52. Manyukhin, *Pryzhok*, 220. In a 1996 campaign document, Yeltsin is quoted as saying the prediction was made by an astrologer and for the year 1983. *Prezident Yel'tsin: 100 voprosov i otvetov* (President Yeltsin: 100 questions and answers) (Moscow: Obshcherossiiskoye dvizheniye obshchestvennoi podderzhki B. N. Yel'tsina, 1996), 78.

53. Galina Stepanova, party archivist, interview with the author (September 7, 2004).

54. Manyukhin, *Pryzhok*, 207.

55. Quotation from Tat'yana D'yachenko, "Yesli by papa ne stal prezidentom . . ." (If papa had not become president), *Ogonëk*, October 23, 2000. Other details from Yel'tsin, *Marafon*, 337; Bobrova, "Yel'tsiny tozhe plachut"; and interviews. For background on blat, see Alena Ledeneva, *Russia's Economy of Favors: Blat, Networking, and Informal Exchanges* (Cambridge: Cambridge University Press, 1998). There is nothing about his daughters' failed first marriages in Yeltsin's memoirs. It was a painful subject, although Yeltsin welcomed his new sons-in-law and embraced the children from the second marriages. Tatyana married for a third time in 2001.

56. When the boy was born, Boris Nikolayevich pressed Khairullin to have him bear the Yeltsin surname. Khairullin has said in press interviews that he agreed with reluctance but on the understanding that a second child would have his family name.

57. Andrei Karaulov, *Vokrug Kremlya: kniga politicheskikh dialogov* (Around the Kremlin: a book of political dialogues) (Moscow: Novosti, 1990), 103.

58. Naina Yeltsina, personal communication to the author (July 29, 2007).

59. Yel'tsin, *Marafon*, 331.

60. The idiom "compliant activism" was struck to describe aspects of grassroots politics in the Brezhnev era. See Donna Bahry, "Politics, Generations, and Change

in the USSR," in James R. Millar, ed., *Politics, Work, and Daily Life in the USSR* (Cambridge: Cambridge University Press, 1987), 76–84.

61. TsDOOSO, fund 4, register 101, file 105, 73. At the same time, Yeltsin took a firm line against forms of private enterprise that contravened Soviet laws and mores. For example, he condemned the informal sale of radio receivers and spare parts, which might allow citizens to listen to foreign broadcasters like the BBC or Voice of America (with the local favorite, Willis Conover's jazz hour).

62. Aron, *Yeltsin*, 66.

63. B. N. Yel'tsin, *Srednii Ural: rubezhi sozidaniya* (The middle Urals: milestones of creation) (Sverdlovsk: Sredne-Ural'skoye knizhnoye izdatel'stsvo, 1981), 83, mentions Uralmash, the Kalinin Works, and others making washing machines, kitchen dishware, lightbulbs, vacuum cleaners, and baby carriages. The obkom drew 600 factories into a plan to increase output of consumer goods in the province by 50 percent in the 1981–85 five-year plan.

64. Yel'tsin, *Zapiski*, 251.

65. Manyukhin, *Pryzhok*, 30, 84.

66. Boris Yeltsin, third interview with the author (September 12, 2002); and Yurii Petrov, second interview (February 1, 2002). According to Naina Yeltsina (second interview with the author, September 18, 2007), Boris already owned a considerable number of books when they married in 1955, and they installed a bookshelf before having the chance to acquire any furniture. He did more reading when in construction than when in the party apparatus, but the reading never stopped. Visitors to the Yeltsins in Moscow in the late 1980s were taken with his collection, which sat in the entrance hall to their apartment on the same unpainted plank shelves as in Sverdlovsk.

67. Third Yeltsin interview and comments by Naina Yeltsina during the interview.

68. Goryun, *Boris Yel'tsin*, 2:20–21. Goryun dates the trip in 1968, after Yeltsin transferred to party work. Yeltsin, in his CPSU membership file (TsDOOSO, fund 4, register 116, file 283, 5, 300), says it was in May 1966, when he was still director of the housing combine. The file shows him taking ten foreign trips before his transfer to Moscow in 1985. Four of these were vacations and six were on business. Six of the ten trips were to Soviet-bloc countries (Bulgaria twice, Czechoslovakia twice, Rumania, and Cuba) and four were to Western countries (France in 1966 and 1974, Sweden and Finland in 1971, and West Germany in 1984). Altogether he had spent three to four weeks in the West.

69. Transcript of interview with Mike Wallace for CBS News's *60 Minutes* show of October 6, 2000 (made available by Jonathan Sanders); this piece was not broadcast. In *Zapiski*, 250–51, Yeltsin mentions Naina bringing him news about shortages from conversations at the office and visits to the food market.

70. Yel'tsin, *Ispoved'*, 64.

71. Lidiya Solomoniya, interview with the author (September 11, 2004).

72. Lobov interview.

73. Vladimir Polozhentsev, "Privet, pribaltiitsy!" (Greetings, people from the Baltic), http://podolsk-news.ru/stat/elcin.php. This interview was given in July 1988 but never published. The Russian is idiomatic and not the easiest to translate: *brezhnevskaya sistema postoyanno sverbela v mozgu, i vnutri ya vsegda nës kakoi-to vnutrennii uprëk.*

74. Karaulov, *Vokrug Kremlya*, 111.

75. Sergei Ryzhenkov and Galina Lyukhterkhandt-Mikhaleva, *Politika i kul'tura v rossiiskoi provintsii: Novgorodskaya, Voronezhskaya, Saratovskaya, Sverdlovskaya oblasti* (Politics and culture in the Russian provinces: Novgorod, Voronezh, Saratov, and Sverdlovsk oblasts) (Moscow: Letnii sad, 2001), 161. On the UPI group, see Bonet, "Nevozmozhnaya Rossiya," 123. After the singer Yulii Kim gave an unauthorized concert at UPI in the late 1970s, a music club at the institute was closed and the teacher who invited him was fired. See also Anita Seth, "Molodëzh' i politika: vozmozhnosti i predely studencheskoi samodeyatel'nosti na vostoke Rossii (1961–1991 gg.) (Youth and politics: the possibilities and limits of student amateurism in the east of Russia [1961–91]), *Kritika* 7 (Winter 2006), 153–57.

76. TsDOOSO, fund 4, register 100, file 116, 119.

77. Sverdlovsk's was the fifth subway to be started in the USSR's Russian republic. Yeltsin's conversation with Brezhnev is described in *Ispoved'*, 54. But Kirilenko played a key role before then in getting the Soviet railways minister, Ivan Pavlovskii, to agree in a single telephone conversation. Although he misnamed the project—calling it the *metr* (meter) rather than *metro* (subway)—Uncle Andrei came through for Sverdlovsk. Manyukhin, *Pryzhok*, 130.

78. Second Petrov interview. Overcentralization was also rampant within the CPSU. Lobov, Yeltsin's second secretary from 1982 to 1985, had to ask the Central Committee to let him add a cleaning lady to his staff chart (Bonet, "Nevozmozhnaya Rossiya," 41).

79. Terry Martin, *The Affirmative Action Empire: Nations and Nationalism in the Soviet Union, 1923–1939* (Ithaca: Cornell University Press, 2001), 395.

80. Second Yeltsin interview.

81. Comments by Naina Yeltsina during third Yeltsin interview.

82. Second Petrov interview. On the pursuit of regional autonomy, see James R. Harris, *The Great Urals: Regionalism and the Evolution of the Soviet System* (Ithaca: Cornell University Press, 1999); and Yoshiko M. Herrera, *Imagined Economies: The Sources of Russian Regionalism* (Cambridge: Cambridge University Press, 2005).

83. See on this point Alexei Yurchak, *Everything Was Forever, Until It Was No More: The Last Soviet Generation* (Princeton: Princeton University Press, 2006), 54–59.

84. There is film of the ceremony in *Prezident vseya Rusi*, part 1.

85. Bonet, "Nevozmozhnaya Rossiya," 78.

86. Rossel, interviewed in *Prezident vseya Rusi*, part 1. According to what Yeltsin told Rossel, he and Brezhnev met on work matters on Yeltsin's birthday—it would

have had to be February 1, 1977, his forty-sixth—and an aide informed the general secretary of the birthday. Brezhnev gave him the watch at that point. The funny thing is that Brezhnev had a reputation among foreign diplomats for asking if he could trade *their* watches for one of his, usually a mass-produced Soviet model.

87. Second Yeltsina interview.

88. Kaëta interview.

89. Manyukhin, *Pryzhok*, 50.

90. Kaëta interview. Beside the public-relations and morale-building side of these forays, Yeltsin could have a soft heart for those in need. Kaëta remembered an episode in the town of Severoural'sk when Yeltsin was approached by a female construction worker with four children, who said she was unable to feed her family on her wages. Yeltsin volunteered in front of the group to give her 100 rubles a month from his own salary. Kaëta doubted the woman ever received any of this cash, but suspected that Yeltsin found some other way to help her out.

91. Plans for the meeting with the students are contained in TsDOOSO, fund 4, register 100, file 275, and the questions and answers are in file 116 (quotation about capitalist competition at 136). Aron, *Yeltsin*, 87–92, gives a good account of the meeting.

92. Yel'tsin, *Srednii Ural*, 101–2; Aron, *Yeltsin*, 78–80.

93. TsDOOSO, fund 4, register 101, file 106, 3.

94. Ibid., register 107, file 118, 101.

95. Ibid., 37–42.

96. Ibid., register 101, file 105, 116.

97. Anatolii Kirillov, interview with the author (June 21, 2004).

98. Ryabov, *Moi XX vek*, 56.

99. Yel'tsin, *Ispoved'*, 53.

100. Ibid., 22.

101. Second Yeltsin interview. Compare to Yel'tsin, *Ispoved'*, 53: "We found ourselves working, practically speaking, in almost total self-reliance [*samostoyatel'nost'*]."

Chapter Five

1. Boris Yel'tsin, *Ispoved' na zadannuyu temu* (Confession on an assigned theme) (Moscow: PIK, 1990), 67–69.

2. Yakov Ryabov, *Moi XX vek: zapiski byvshego sekretarya TsK KPSS* (My 20th century: notes of a former secretary of the Central Committee of the CPSU) (Moscow: Russkii biograficheskii institut, 2000), 37–38. Ryabov mentions Yeltsin fielding suggestions to become secretary of the party obkom of Kostroma province and, in Moscow, deputy head of Gosstroi, the State Construction Committee. The second organization is where Yeltsin was to be sent after his break with Gorbachev in 1987.

3. Interview with Yakov Ryabov, Central Committee Interview Project, University of Glasgow (transcript supplied by Stephen White).

4. Calculated from lists at http://www.worldstatesmen.org/RussSFSR_admin.html. We have only years of birth, not exact dates, for most of the secretaries. Five of the 1976 first secretaries had been born in 1931, the same year as Yeltsin.

5. "Vstrecha v VKSh, 12 noyabrya 1988 goda s 14 do 18 chasov" (Meeting in the Higher Komsomol School, November 12, 1988, from 2:00 P.M. to 6:00 P.M.), in RGANI (Russian State Archive of Contemporary History, Moscow) (microform in Harvard College Library), fund 89, register 8, file 29, 41. Yeltsin said in this presentation that the two met twice, but it was unclear whether that was twice overall or twice during Andropov's general secretaryship. My suspicion is that it was the former. Assuming they conferred after the anthrax incident in 1979, they likely had one meeting while Andropov was Soviet leader.

6. Ye. K. Ligachëv, *Predosterezheniye* (Warning) (Moscow: Pravda International, 1998), 410.

7. Arkadii Vol'skii, interview with the author (June 13, 2000); Ligachëv, *Predosterezheniye*, 410.

8. Mikhail Gorbachev, *Zhizn' i reformy* (Life and reforms), 2 vols. (Moscow: Novosti, 1995), 1:291–92. As he often does, Gorbachev imputes to third parties the gossip about Yeltsin drinking, in this case "the observation" that he left a Supreme Soviet session on somebody's arm. "Many people were upset—what was it? Well-wishers offered assurances that nothing special had occurred, it was just a little rise in his blood pressure. But [Sverdlovsk] natives smirked: This happens with our first secretary; sometimes he overdoes it a bit."

9. Aleksandr Budberg, "Proigravshii pobeditel': Mikhailu Gorbachevu—75" (Losing victor: Mikhail Gorbachev at 75), *Moskovskii komsomolets*, March 3, 2006.

10. Yel'tsin, *Ispoved'*, 67. While Yeltsin says he took "one or two seconds" to say no to Dolgikh, he also relates that he barely slept a wink that night and expected to hear from someone else shortly.

11. Tatyana Yumasheva, first interview with the author (July 15, 2001). When Tatyana first moved to Moscow in 1977, the only family friend her parents had there was one female classmate from UPI, who lived in a communal apartment. Boris Yel'tsin, *Prezidentskii marafon* (Presidential marathon) (Moscow: AST, 2000), 337.

12. Yeltsin's favorite folk song was "Ural'skaya ryabinushka" (Urals Mountain Ash). In his third book of memoirs (*Marafon*, 183), Yeltsin mentioned his preference as a young man for the lilting compositions of Isaak Dunayevskii (1900–55), Mark Fradkin (1914–90), who was mainly a writer of movie scores, and the much decorated Aleksandra Pakhmutova (1929–), who was said to be Leonid Brezhnev's favorite songwriter. The English translation of Yeltsin's memoir, perhaps trying to make him look hipper, drops Pakhmutova from the listing and adds guitar-strumming troubadours Bulat Okudzhava (1924–97) and Yurii Vizbor (1934–84).

13. See Yel'tsin, *Ispoved'*, 56–58. Vitalii Tret'yakov, "Sverdlovskii vyskochka" (Sverdlovsk upstart), part 3, *Politicheskii klass*, April 2006, 87, points out a "comradely" tradition in the Politburo of addressing one another as *ty*. Yeltsin was not aware

of it and never ascribed this tendency to any member of the inner elite other than Gorbachev.

14. Grigorii Kaëta, a member of the bureau at the time, interview with the author (September 9, 2004).

15. Yel'tsin, *Ispoved'*, 71.

16. Ryabov, *Moi XX vek*, 56.

17. The city of Tomsk is 1,100 miles east of Yekaterinburg (Sverdlovsk) and, like it, was closed to foreigners until 1990. This was because of secrecy surrounding the Tomsk-7 chemical combine, the USSR's largest complex for producing weapons-grade plutonium.

18. Viktor Manyukhin, *Pryzhok nazad: o Yel'tsine i o drugikh* (Backward leap: about Yeltsin and others) (Yekaterinburg: Pakrus, 2002), 54–56.

19. Kaëta interview.

20. Pilar Bonet, "Nevozmozhnaya Rossiya: Boris Yel'tsin, provintsial v Kremle" (The impossible Russia: Boris Yeltsin, a provincial in the Kremlin), *Ural*, April 1994, 105–6.

21. Stanislav Alekseyev, a party propagandist in Sverdlovsk at the time, interview with the author (June 24, 2004).

22. Manyukhin, Yeltsin's last second secretary in Sverdlovsk, says (*Pryzhok*, 56) that Ligachëv at some point told Yeltsin he was going to be made a Central Committee secretary, and that Gorbachev forced the appointment to be made at the department level.

23. Gorbachev writes in *Zhizn' i reformy*, 1:292, that, when the Politburo resolution appointing Yeltsin to the construction department was being drafted, the two had "a short conversation" in his office. "It has not stuck in my memory," he adds snootily.

24. Kaëta interview.

25. Gorbachev, *Zhizn' i reformy*, 1:292.

26. Yelena's husband, Valerii Okulov, was reassigned to overseas Aeroflot flights, a nice promotion. Following Boris Yeltsin's demotion in 1987, Okulov was not allowed to fly at all for three years.

27. Politburo transcript for June 29, 1985, in APRF (Archive of the President of the Russian Federation, Moscow), fund 3, register 3194, file 22, 8–9. I do not know why Tikhonov should have been so unimpressed. In the first volume of his memoirs (*Ispoved'*, 54–55), Yeltsin states that as Sverdlovsk leader he had "normal, businesslike" relations with Tikhonov from 1980 to 1985. It could be that Tikhonov's ire was directed at Gorbachev as much as at Yeltsin.

28. He was never anyone's deputy and had no desire to be one now, Yeltsin wrote in *Ispoved'*, 70. The first assertion is only partly true. He had never carried the precise title of deputy (*zamestitel'*), but as head engineer of two construction concerns in the early 1960s he reported to the director. And from 1968 to 1975, as head of the construction department of the Sverdlovsk obkom, he answered to the first secretary through one of the secretaries—just as it was with Dolgikh in the Central Commit-

tee apparatus from April to July 1985. In ibid., 110, Yeltsin asserts that Dolgikh, finding him "sometimes too emotional," tried to block his promotion to Central Committee secretary at the Politburo meeting of June 29. The transcript of the meeting, however, shows Dolgikh as supporting the decision. Yeltsin also reports that he and Dolgikh served together amicably after that, which does seem to have been the case. Dolgikh was ousted from the Politburo and Secretariat in September 1988.

29. Gorbachev, *Zhizn' i reformy,*1:292.

30. Yel'tsin, *Ispoved'*, 82–83.

31. Manyukhin, *Pryzhok*, 59–60. On the other hand, Yakov Ryabov spoke to Yeltsin about the Moscow job and found him to be unenthusiastic. Ryabov interview (University of Glasgow).

32. Politburo transcript for December 23, 1985, in Volkogonov Archive (Project on Cold War Studies, Davis Center for Russian and Eurasian Studies, Harvard University), 1–3.

33. The Politburo had nineteen full and candidate members as of February 1986. Yeltsin was one of only nine full-time party apparatchiks in the group. He continued to attend the Secretariat's weekly meetings.

34. See Timothy J. Colton, *Moscow: Governing the Socialist Metropolis* (Cambridge, Mass.: Harvard University Press, 1995), 384–92, 428–29, 567–72; and Viktor Grishin, *Ot Khrushcheva do Gorbacheva: memuary* (From Khrushchev to Gorbachev: memoirs) (Moscow: ASPOL, 1996), 292–320.

35. Nikolai Ryzhkov, interview with the author (September 21, 2001). In *Ispoved'*, 54, Yeltsin says he and Ryzhkov were acquaintances *(znakomyye)* in Sverdlovsk and that when Ryzhkov was named prime minister he tried "not to abuse" their relationship. Naina Yeltsina was cool toward Ryzhkov and felt his rapid rise had gone to his head.

36. Ryzhkov interview. Most of these details are omitted in his published account: N. I. Ryzhkov, *Desyat' let velikikh potryasenii* (Ten years of great shocks) (Moscow: Kniga, Prosveshcheniye, Miloserdiye, 1995), 139. Ryzhkov told me he was sure the Politburo would have ratified the appointment even if he had opposed it.

37. Yel'tsin, *Ispoved'*, 83.

38. Yurii Prokof'ev, *Do i posle zapreta KPSS: pervyi sekretar' MGK KPSS vspominayet* (Before and after the ban on the CPSU: a first secretary of the Moscow gorkom remembers) (Moscow: Algoritm, 2005), 71.

39. Anatolii Luk'yanov, interview with the author (January 24, 2001).

40. Ye. I. Chazov, *Rok* (Fate) (Moscow: Geotar-Med, 2001), 86–88.

41. Luk'yanov interview.

42. Aleksei Shcherbinin, a professor at Tomsk State University, interview with the author (February 24, 2006).

43. Aleksandr Korzhakov, *Boris Yel'tsin: ot rassveta do zakata* (Boris Yeltsin: from dawn to dusk) (Moscow: Interbuk, 1997), 52. Korzhakov also writes that Yeltsin "worshiped" Gorbachev at the beginning, which is an exaggeration.

44. "Otchët Moskovskogo gorodskogo komiteta KPSS" (Report of the Moscow city committee of the CPSU), *Moskovskaya pravda*, January 25, 1986.

45. Grishin, *Ot Khrushcheva do Gorbacheva*, 298–99.

46. Yel'tsin, *Ispoved'*, 84.

47. A. S. Chernyayev, *Shest' let s Gorbachevym* (Six years with Gorbachev) (Moscow: Progress, 1993), 63–64. This valuable memoir is available in English as Anatoly S. Chernyaev, *My Six Years with Gorbachev*, trans. Robert D. English and Elizabeth Tucker (University Park: Pennsylvania State University Press, 2000).

48. *XXVII s"ezd Kommunisticheskoi partii Sovetskogo Soyuza: stenograficheskii otchët* (The 27th congress of the Communist Party of the Soviet Union: stenographic record) (Moscow: Politizdat, 1986), 140–42. The references to officials' privileges were purged from the chronicle in the next day's *Pravda* but, as quoted here, appeared in the final transcript of the congress.

49. "Vypiska iz vystupleniya t. Yel'tsina B. N. 11 aprelya s. g. pered propagandistami g. Moskvy" (Extract from the statement of comrade B. N. Yeltsin on April 11, 1986, before Moscow propagandists), Radio Free Europe/Radio Liberty, *Materialy samizdata*, July 18, 1986, 3.

50. Yel'tsin, *Ispoved'*, 85; Valerii Saikin, interview with the author (June 15, 2001).

51. Prokof'ev, *Do i posle zapreta KPSS*, 64.

52. Lobbying the center is described in V. I. Vorotnikov, *A bylo eto tak: iz dnevnika chlena Politbyuro TsK KPSS* (But this is how it was: from the diary of a member of the Politburo of the CPSU) (Moscow: Sovet veteranov knigoizdaniya, 1995), 84; and "Kak reshalsya v Moskve prodovol'stvennyi vopros" (How the food question was resolved in Moscow), *Izvestiya TsK KPSS*, December 1990, 125.

53. On October 23, 1986, for example, the Politburo discussed Soviet bread shortages. Yeltsin observed that bakers—his mother's occupation in Kazan in the 1930s—were not being trained in Moscow. Andrei Gromyko demanded to know why the Politburo was discussing so picayune a matter and asked rhetorically if it was supposed to answer for the supply of *lapti* (handwoven bast shoes). Gorbachev expostulated that, if such resolutions were to be adopted, at the urging of Yeltsin or anyone, the Soviet military would have to be engaged, "so as to deal with this at the point of the gun." *V Politbyuro TsK KPSS* . . . (In the Politburo of the CPSU) (Moscow: Gorbachev-Fond, 2006), 92.

54. Saikin interview.

55. Korzhakov, *Boris Yel'tsin*, 54–58.

56. Vitalii Tret'yakov, "Fenomen Yel'tsina" (The Yeltsin phenomenon), *Moskovskiye novosti*, April 16, 1989.

57. "Vypiska iz vystupleniya," 7–8. George W. Breslauer, *Gorbachev and Yeltsin as Leaders* (Cambridge: Cambridge University Press, 2002), detects similarities with the populism of Nikita Khrushchev a generation before. There were some commonalities, but Khrushchev was a much less radical agent of change than either Yeltsin or Gorbachev. The definitive study is William Taubman, *Khrushchev: The Man and His Era* (New York: Norton, 2003).

58. Vladimir Mezentsev, "Okruzhentsy" (Entourage), part 2, *Rabochaya tribuna*, March 25, 1995.

59. According to Jonathan Sanders, the Moscow-based staffer who worked with producer Susan Zirinsky, "I pointed out that we were sending one of our most respected correspondents to do the interview, someone who was a veteran of the Nixon White House and was personally quite interested in him [Yeltsin]. At this point, the ever clever Ms. Zirinsky pulled out a glossy eight-by-ten photo of Diane Sawyer and said this was the star who would be doing the interview. Now, remember what the Soviet anchorwoman looked like in the mid-1980s? Remember how much [Richard] Nixon was respected? And remember how much Boris Nikolayevich understood intuitively about the power of the media? So we did the interview." Sanders, personal communication to the author (October 9, 2005).

60. "Pribavlyat' oboroty perestroiki" (Quicken the pace of perestroika), *Moskovskaya pravda*, April 4, 1987.

61. Colton, *Moscow*, 576.

62. Gavriil Popov, interview with the author (June 1, 2001).

63. "Vypiska iz vystupleniya," 5; "Mera perestroiki—konkretnyye dela" (The measure of perestroika is concrete affairs), *Moskovskaya pravda*, March 30, 1986.

64. Andrei Karaulov, *Vokrug Kremlya: kniga politicheskikh dialogov* (Around the Kremlin: a book of political dialogues) (Moscow: Novosti, 1990), 96.

65. Tret'yakov, "Sverdlovskii vyskochka," part 3, 86–91. Aleksei Stakhanov was a miner in the Donbass area of Ukraine who in 1935 set a USSR record for digging coal on his shift. The Stakhanovite movement was organized to imitate his fervor. It experienced a revival in 1988, eleven years after Stakhanov's death.

66. "Vypiska iz vystupleniya," 3.

67. The resolution was about services in one of Moscow's municipal districts. Two deputies voted against it and three against proposed amendments. Press reports did not mention Yeltsin's role, which I learned about in my interview with Arkadii Murashov (September 13, 2000).

68. On the flavor of these hothouse organizations, see Judith B. Sedaitis and Jim Butterfield, eds., *Neformaly: Civil Society in the USSR* (New York: U.S. Helsinki Watch Committee, 1990). A then-deputy of Saikin's reports that Yeltsin telephoned Gorbachev for advice before meeting the Pamyat group. Prokof'ev, *Do i posle zapreta KPSS*, 186–88.

69. Speech to Central Committee, January 27, 1987, in RGANI, fund 2, register 5, file 34, 73.

70. Gorbachev, *Zhizn' i reformy*, 1:310, 371 (italics added).

71. Korzhakov writes (*Boris Yel'tsin*, 61) that during the Georgia visit Yeltsin played with his security detail and staff every day, starting the first morning at five A.M. They then invited the local champions, who for one of their matches engaged a professional athlete. The Muscovites still won.

72. Boris Yel'tsin, *Zapiski prezidenta* (Notes of a president) (Moscow: Ogonëk, 1994), 270.

73. Yel'tsin, *Ispoved'*, 95.

74. Korzhakov, *Boris Yel'tsin*, 58.

75. Ibid., 55. Korzhakov, though of proletarian origin, exemplified Muscovite condescension when describing in his book (50) Yeltsin's musical activities: "Yeltsin was born in the village of Butka, and there it was a prestigious thing to play on the spoons." In an interview in 1989 (Karaulov, *Vokrug Kremlya*, 100), Yeltsin was still thin-skinned about Sverdlovsk, saying it was "not on the periphery" and that it had more to teach the rest of Russia than to learn from it.

76. "Vypiska iz vystupleniya," 5; Yel'tsin, *Ispoved'*, 90; "Deputaty predlagayut, kritikuyut, sovetuyut" (The deputies recommend, criticize, and advise), *Moskovskaya pravda*, March 15, 1987.

77. Tret'yakov claims to have heard from former subordinates of Yeltsin that some of the questions at encounters like this were planted by organizers and that Yeltsin prepared his answers in advance. Tret'yakov, "Sverdlovskii vyskochka," part 4, *Politicheskii klass*, May 2006, 103.

78. "Vypiska iz vystupleniya," 7, 9–10. Yeltsin instituted the changes in the workday immediately after taking office. Prokof'ev, *Do i posle zapreta KPSS*, 63.

79. Erik H. Erikson, *Young Man Luther: A Study in Psychoanalysis and History* (New York: Norton, 1962), 155–56.

Chapter Six

1. Boris Yel'tsin, *Ispoved' na zadannuyu temu* (Confession on an assigned theme) (Moscow: PIK, 1990), 116. Gorbachev, too, reports in his memoirs being unhappy with the unsociability of official Moscow. But he was much better acquainted than Yeltsin with its ways. He spent five years at university in Moscow, and general secretaries and Politburo members often holidayed or took the cure at the mineral-springs resorts of Stavropol Province.

2. Ibid., 69, 115–16, 119. The inconsistencies in Yeltsin's discussion of his housing and perks are brought out in Vitalii Tret'yakov, "Sverdlovskii vyskochka" (Sverdlovsk upstart), part 3, *Politicheskii klass*, April 2006, 82–84, 88–90. Tret'yakov maintains that Gorbachev's former dacha was posher than what Yeltsin had the right to and this created nervousness on his part. There may be some exaggeration in the Yeltsin account. A former chief of Kremlin protocol notes, for example, that candidate members of the Politburo were entitled to two cooks, not three, and that their monthly food allowance was half that of full members. Vladimir Shevchenko, *Povsednevnaya zhizn' Kremlya pri prezidentakh* (The everyday life of the Kremlin under the presidents) (Moscow: Molodaya gvardiya, 2004), 124.

3. *Den' v sem'e prezidenta* (A day in the president's family), interview with El'dar Ryazanov on REN-TV, April 20, 1993 (videotape supplied by Irena Lesnevskaya).

4. Tret'yakov, "Sverdlovskii vyskochka," part 3, 90.

5. Vladimir Voronin, a city hall functionary at the time, interview with the author (June 15, 2001).

6. Boris Yeltsin, third interview with the author (September 12, 2002).

7. Author's first interview with Aleksandr Yakovlev (June 9, 2000) and interviews with Arkadii Vol'skii (June 13, 2000) and Anatolii Luk'yanov (January 24, 2001). Several individuals who attended the October 1987 plenum of the Central Committee told me Yeltsin mentioned Raisa there, and the claim is made in Aleksandr Yakovlev, *Sumerki* (Dusk) (Moscow: Materik, 2003), 405. Aside from Yeltsin's memory, the published transcript and unpublished archival materials, which I have examined, confute this.

8. Jack F. Matlock, Jr., *Autopsy on an Empire* (New York: Random House, 1995), 223. At a public meeting in May 1990, someone passed Yeltsin a note asking if he thought Soviet television spent too much time on Raisa. He replied that he thought it did. "I spoke to Gorbachev about this. He was insulted." Vladimir Mezentsev, "Okruzhentsy" (Entourage), part 3, *Rabochaya tribuna*, March 28, 1995.

9. Third Yeltsin interview.

10. Matlock, *Autopsy on an Empire*, 112, citing a conversation with Afanas'ev.

11. Grishin was already a candidate member of the Politburo when given the Moscow position in June 1967 and had to wait four years, until the 1971 party congress, before getting his full member's seat. Yeltsin's expectations are recounted in Viktor Manyukhin, *Pryzhok nazad: o Yel'tsine i o drugikh* (Backward leap: about Yeltsin and others) (Yekaterinburg: Pakrus, 2002), 59–60.

12. Mikhail Gorbachev, *Zhizn' i reformy* (Life and reforms), 2 vols. (Moscow: Novosti, 1995), 1:370–71.

13. Oksana Khimich, "Otchim perestroiki" (Stepfather of perestroika), *Moskovskii komsomolets*, April 22, 2005.

14. Yel'tsin, *Ispoved'*, 95–96. His views on the tenacity of opposition to reform evolved rapidly. In April 1986 he discounted as "completely incorrect" the judgment "that the party has somehow cut itself off from the people." "Vypiska iz vystupleniya t. Yel'tsina B. N. 11 aprelya s. g. pered propagandistami g. Moskvy" (Extract from the statement of comrade B. N. Yeltsin on April 11, 1986, before Moscow propagandists), Radio Free Europe/Radio Liberty, *Materialy samizdata*, July 18, 1986, 7.

15. Politburo transcript for January 19, 1987, in AGF (Gorbachev Foundation Archive, Moscow), KDPP (Kollektsiya "Kak 'delalas" politika perestroiki" [The collection "How the policy of perestroika 'was made'"]), 6 vols., 2:21–46; quotations here at 32–35, 44–46.

16. The transcript records a break in the discussion after Yeltsin's remarks but gives no details. Yeltsin in his memoirs (*Ispoved'*, 97) described Gorbachev walking out of a Politburo meeting on his account, but misremembered it as occurring in October 1987.

17. In a never-printed interview in July 1988, Yeltsin said there had been an element of competition with Gorbachev in making his Moscow personnel changes. He added that he wished there had been time to do more and that additional district party secretaries were on his list to be removed. Vladimir Polozhentsev, "Privet, pribaltiitsy!" (Greetings, people from the Baltic), http://podolsk-news.ru/stat/elcin.php.

18. Yel'tsin, *Ispoved'*, 11, 97–98.

19. V. I. Vorotnikov, *A bylo eto tak: iz dnevnika chlena Politbyuro TsK KPSS* (But this is how it was: from the diary of a member of the Politburo of the CPSU) (Moscow: Sovet veteranov knigoizdaniya, 1995), 123. For more on Gorbachev's reaction, see Vadim Medvedev, *V komande Gorbacheva: vzglyad iznutri* (In the Gorbachev team: a view from within) (Moscow: Bylina, 1994), 45–47; and V. I. Boldin, *Krusheniye p'edestala: shtrikhi k portretu M. S. Gorbacheva* (Smashing the pedestal: strokes of a portrait of M. S. Gorbachev) (Moscow: Respublika, 1995), 326. George W. Breslauer, *Gorbachev and Yeltsin as Leaders* (Cambridge: Cambridge University Press, 2002), 117, surmises that Yeltsin was unhappy that Gorbachev settled for a closing resolution by the January plenum of the Central Committee that was less radical than Yeltsin preferred. It is a good point, but the Politburo records show the men were in conflict before the committee convened.

20. Vorotnikov, *A bylo eto tak*, 123.

21. Yel'tsin, *Ispoved'*, 11–12.

22. Politburo transcripts, March 24, 1987 (AGF, KDPP, 2:154–55); April 23, 1987 (ibid., 241–42); April 30, 1987 (ibid., 264); May 14, 1987 (ibid., 305, 317–18); September 28, (ibid., 539).

23. Gorbachev, *Zhizn' i reformy*, 1:368.

24. Politburo transcript, October 15, 1987, in Volkogonov Archive (Project on Cold War Studies, Davis Center for Russian and Eurasian Studies, Harvard University). All quotations here are at 138–40.

25. Vladimir Gubarev, "Akademik Gennadii Mesyats: beregite intellekt" (Academician Gennadii Mesyats: conserve your intellect), *Gudok*, October 12, 2005.

26. Yeltsin, however, did manage to keep Ligachëv's men at bay most of the time. At the plenum of the city committee that removed Yeltsin from his job in November 1987, one member of the bureau, N. Ye. Kislova, noted that Central Committee workers had not recently dropped in on bureau meetings and that she could not remember an instance of a formal visit by a central CPSU official even at the level of subdepartment head. "Energichno vesti perestroiku" (Energetically carry out perestroika), *Pravda*, November 13, 1987.

27. Speech to Central Committee, June 25, 1987, in RGANI (Russian State Archive of Contemporary History, Moscow) (microform in Harvard College Library), fund 2, register 5, file 58, 33–34.

28. Nikolai Ryzhkov, interview with the author (September 21, 2001).

29. Mikhail Poltoranin, interview with the author (July 11, 2001).

30. Yakovlev, *Sumerki*, 407. Plans for such a site were discussed at the August meeting of informal organizations, which Yeltsin had authorized. One delegate proposed it be located in the Arbat area, in downtown Moscow. A district-level Communist Party official in attendance opposed the idea: "Why does the Party need a Hyde Park at which it will be permitted to speak out on equal terms with you?" John B. Dunlop, *The Rise of Russia and the Fall of the Soviet Empire* (Princeton: Princeton University Press, 1993), 74.

31. Politburo transcript, September 10, 1987 (AGF, KDPP, 2:507–8).

32. Ye. I. Chazov, *Rok* (Fate) (Moscow: Geotar-Med, 2001), 218–19.

33. Valerii Saikin, interview with the author (June 15, 2001).

34. Naina Yeltsina, second interview with the author (September 18, 2007).

35. All quotations from the letter are taken from Yel'tsin, *Ispoved'*, 8–11 (italics added). An English translation, leaving out some details, is in Boris Yeltsin, *Against the Grain: An Autobiography*, trans. Michael Glenny (New York: Summit Books, 1990), 178–81.

36. Gorbachev made his claim to the CPSU conference in the summer of 1988, and Yeltsin made his in *Ispoved'*. The aide who was with Gorbachev during the phone call says Gorbachev told him after putting down the phone that Yeltsin "agreed he would not get nervous before the holidays," which suggests partial acquiescence in Gorbachev's preferred timing. A. S. Chernyayev, *Shest' let s Gorbachevym* (Six years with Gorbachev) (Moscow: Progress, 1993), 175.

37. See *Ispoved'*, 13–14. Yeltsin did not bring up this point in our 2002 interview about these events.

38. Poltoranin interview.

39. Third Yeltsin interview.

40. At the October plenum, Gorbachev leveled the charge that Yeltsin had used this and similar meetings "to find accomplices" *(naiti yedinomyshlennikov)*, but did not claim that Yeltsin had contacted Central Committee members in between plenums. "Plenum TsK KPSS—oktyabr' 1987 goda (stenograficheskii otchët)" (The CPSU Central Committee plenum of October 1987 [stenographic record]), *Izvestiya TsK KPSS*, February 1989, 284. To me, Yeltsin said flatly that he did not speak to potential supporters, in person or by telephone, before the plenum.

41. Third Yeltsin interview.

42. The first interpretation of Gorbachev's motives is stressed in the eyewitness account by the then-first deputy head of the party's international department. Karen Brutents, *Nesbyvsheyesya: neravnodushnyye zametki o perestroike* (It never came true: engaged notes about perestroika) (Moscow: Mezhdunarodnyye otnosheniya, 2005), 100–101. The second is favored by then-Politburo member Vitalii Vorotnikov, in *A bylo eto tak*, 169–70. Tret'yakov offers a variation on Brutents's thesis, that Gorbachev had already decided to discharge Yeltsin and wanted him to fire at party conservatives on the way out the door. See Vitalii Tret'yakov, "Sverdlovskii vyskochka," part 5, *Politicheskii klass*, June 2006, 99–100.

43. Vorotnikov, *A bylo eto tak*, 169.

44. Gorbachev, *Zhizn' i reformy*, 1:372.

45. In his diary of events, Anatolii Chernyayev had already likened Yeltsin's address before the Moscow city conference of the CPSU, in January 1986, to the Khrushchev speech (Chernyayev, *Shest' let*, 63). But I think the October 1987 speech fits the bill much better. It had incomparably more impact, and the 1986 speech was not secret.

46. All quotations from Yel'tsin, *Ispoved'*, 131–33.

47. The previous spring, the Moscow gorkom and government, wanting to economize on land and labor, had resolved to trim institutes from 1,041 to 1,002. When Yeltsin addressed the Central Committee, seven institutes had been liquidated and fifty-three new ones created, taking the total to 1,087, or 4 percent more than when the campaign started.

48. The phrase "cult of personality" *(kul't lichnosti)* was censored out of the official transcript released in 1989 but is present in Yeltsin's rendering of the speech in *Ispoved'*, 132. The official record from 1989 does, though, contain the *critique* by Gorbachev of Yeltsin's use of the unprintable phrase.

49. Yel'tsin, *Ispoved'*, 133.

50. Third Yeltsin interview.

51. Chernyayev, *Shest' let*, 177.

52. I have long thought of Yeltsin's manner as feline. I am indebted to Jonathan Sanders for suggesting Gorbachev's as canine.

53. Yel'tsin, *Ispoved'*, 22. These words are omitted from the English-language edition of the memoir.

54. Boldin, *Krusheniye p'edestala*, 328.

55. "Plenum TsK," 241.

56. Vorotnikov, *A bylo eto tak*, 170, records this aspect of the scene with clarity.

57. Ryzhkov interview.

58. Yakovlev, *Sumerki*, 406.

59. "Plenum TsK," 257. Yakovlev's soft criticism of Yeltsin was for "conservatism"—which he made, he says (*Sumerki*, 405–6) to throw conservatives off the scent and ease their alarm at the moderate changes Gorbachev was committed to making.

60. "Plenum TsK," 242–43.

61. In a mirror image of the collective attitude toward him, Yeltsin in his account of the day (*Ispoved'*, 135–36) refused to give the speakers he knew well credit for any but the most ignoble motives. "We had worked together side by side and, it would seem, eaten a pood of salt together. But each one was thinking of himself and considered this a chance to earn a few points for good behavior."

62. "Plenum TsK," 251–52 (Konoplëv), 253–54 (Ryabov). Yeltsin was especially unkind to Ryabov in his memoir, saying he spoke "to lay down some path for himself upward, if not for his future [assignments] then at least for his pension" (*Ispoved'*, 135). Yeltsin saw Ryabov when he visited France in May 1990. On the Aeroflot flight back to Moscow, he asked Ryabov, in full hearing of others, why he said what he did in 1987. Ryabov answered that he had nothing to be sorry for and was sticking to his opinion. Pilar Bonet, "Nevozmozhnaya Rossiya: Boris Yel'tsin, provintsial v Kremle" (The impossible Russia: Boris Yeltsin, a provincial in the Kremlin), *Ural*, April 1994, 25.

63. "Plenum TsK," 254–57 (Ryzhkov), 262–63 (Yakovlev), 273–76 (Solomentsev), 259 (Vorotnikov), 261–62 (Chebrikov).

64. Ibid., 280 (Gorbachev and Yeltsin), 249 (Vladimir Mesyats on immaturity), 265 (Shevardnadze), 245 (Shalayev), 244 (Manyakin), 280 (Gorbachev).

65. Ibid., 279–81. That Gorbachev was open to compromise is the interpretation of Politburo member Vorotnikov (*A bylo eto tak,* 169) and, without comment on the penalty to be paid, of Gorbachev himself (*Zhizn' i reformy,* 1:373).

66. Politburo transcript, October 31, 1987 (AGF, KDPP, 2:648–49).

67. Details here from Aleksandr Kapto, *Na perekrëstkakh zhizni: politicheskiye memuary* (At life's crossroads: political memoirs) (Moscow: Sotsial'no-politicheskii zhurnal, 1996), 185–87; Vorotnikov, *A bylo eto tak,* 173–74; and Gorbachev, *Zhizn' i reformy,* 1:373.

68. "Plenum TsK," 286.

69. Chernyayev, *Shest' let,* 176–78.

70. Third Yeltsin interview.

71. Matlock, *Autopsy on an Empire,* 116.

72. Yel'tsin, *Ispoved',* 138. The medical evidence is given in Gorbachev, *Zhizn' i reformy,* 1:374; and Chazov, *Rok,* 221–23. Both are unfriendly witnesses, but Chazov is no better disposed toward Gorbachev than toward Yeltsin. The reliable Vorotnikov attests (*A bylo eto tak,* 174–75) that Gorbachev shared the facts of the slashing incident with members of the Politburo on November 9 and that Viktor Chebrikov of the KGB verified them. According to Chazov, Yeltsin offered the doctors the far-fetched explanation that he cut himself accidentally when leaning on the scissors. Gorbachev repeats this story and another Yeltsin is said to have told about being knifed by an assailant on the street.

73. Interviews with Aleksandr Korzhakov (January 28, 2002) and Valentina Lantseva (July 9, 2001).

74. Chazov, *Rok,* 225.

75. Third Yeltsin interview and comments by Naina Yeltsina during it.

76. Although the Leningrad group did not want to come into conflict with the Soviet center, members of it advocated creation of a Russian branch of the Communist Party, and some advocated transfer of the capital of the RSFSR to Leningrad. See David Brandenberger, "Stalin, the Leningrad Affair, and the Limits of Postwar Russocentrism," *Russian Review* 63 (April 2004), 241–55.

77. Aleksandr Korzhakov, *Boris Yel'tsin: ot rassveta do zakata* (Boris Yeltsin: from dawn to dusk) (Moscow: Interbuk, 1997), 65; Chazov, *Rok,* 224–25; Boris Yel'tsin, *Prezidentskii marafon* (Presidential marathon) (Moscow: AST, 2000), 53.

78. Mikhail Poltoranin, interviewed in *Prezident vseya Rusi* (The president of all Russia), documentary film by Yevgenii Kiselëv, 1999–2000 (copy supplied by Kiselëv), 4 parts, part 2.

79. All quotations from "Energichno vesti perestroiku."

80. Yurii Belyakov, the second secretary, and Yurii Karabasov, the gorkom's secretary for ideological matters, also spoke, and were less forgiving than Nizovtseva. All three secretaries stressed the costs to them and to the Moscow organization of

Yeltsin's refusal to consult them before making his attack. Belyakov, whom Yeltsin recruited from Sverdlovsk, did credit him for his hard work and leadership, but this, Belyakov said, made the boss's change of position even harder to take. And Yeltsin's name was now being used by "dubious elements," at home and abroad, to stir up scandal.

81. Comment by Naina Yeltsina during my third interview with Boris Yeltsin: "They all said, 'Well, the system made us cripples,' that is, they all considered this [the attack] incorrect."

82. Poltoranin in *Prezident vseya Rusi.* Gorbachev's actions are not mentioned in the official account. He said in his memoirs (*Zhizn' i reformy,* 1:375) that some of the speeches at the plenum had left him with a bad taste in his mouth. He also commended Yeltsin for taking the punishment and behaving "like a man."

83. Poltoranin in *Prezident vseya Rusi.* Before that, Gorbachev evidently came over and comforted him.

84. Second Yeltsina interview.

85. Poltoranin interview.

Chapter Seven

1. Boris Yel'tsin, *Ispoved' na zadannuyu temu* (Confession on an assigned theme) (Moscow: PIK, 1990), 142–43.

2. Erik H. Erikson, *Young Man Luther: A Study in Psychoanalysis and History* (New York: Norton, 1962), 100–101.

3. A first-mover advantage is that achieved by the first firm to offer a new product or service, or by the first player to enter into some other kind of competition for resources. There is considerable controversy over the magnitude of the advantage in specific contexts. See Herbert Gintis, *Game Theory Evolving: A Problem-Centered Introduction to Modeling Strategic Behavior* (Princeton: Princeton University Press, 2000); and Martin J. Osborne, *An Introduction to Game Theory* (New York: Oxford University Press, 2004).

4. Yu, M. Baturin et al., *Epokha Yel'tsina: ocherki politicheskoi istorii* (The Yeltsin epoch: essays in political history) (Moscow: VAGRIUS, 2001), 53. On the forgeries, petitions, and rallies, see also Andrei Goryun, *Boris Yel'tsin: svet i teni* (Boris Yeltsin: light and shadows), 2 vols. (Sverdlovsk: Klip, 1991), 2:7; Nikolai Zen'kovich, *Boris Yel'tsin: raznyye zhizni* (Boris Yeltsin: various lives), 2 vols. (Moscow: OLMA, 2001), 1:336–37; Leon Aron, *Yeltsin: A Revolutionary Life* (New York: St. Martin's, 2000), 220–22; and Lev Osterman, *Intelligentsiya i vlast' v Rossii, 1985–1996 gg.* (The intelligentsia and power in Russia, 1985–96) (Moscow: Monolit, 2000), 31.

5. Mikhail Poltoranin, interviewed in *Prezident vseya Rusi* (The president of all Russia), documentary film by Yevgenii Kiselëv, 1999–2000 (copy supplied by Kiselëv), 4 parts, part 2; and Poltoranin, interview with the author (July 11, 2001).

6. A. S. Chernyayev, *Shest' let s Gorbachevym* (Six years with Gorbachev) (Moscow: Progress, 1993), 175.

7. This point is made in Vitalii Tret'yakov, "Sverdlovskii vyskochka" (Sverdlovsk upstart), part 7, *Politicheskii klass*, August 2006, 103.

8. See Yegor Gaidar, *Gibel' imperii: uroki dlya sovremennoi Rossii* (Death of an empire: lessons for contemporary Russia) (Moscow: ROSSPEN, 2006), 190–97. Gaidar traces the revenue crunch to Saudi Arabia's decision in 1981, in exchange for American military backing, to boost its oil output and thereby restrain global prices. As he shows, Soviet specialists were well apprised of this trend.

9. Aleksandr Kapto, *Na perekrëstkakh zhizni: politicheskiye memuary* (At life's crossroads: political memoirs) (Moscow: Sotsial'no-politicheskii zhurnal, 1996), 192.

10. Razin, called Russia's Robin Hood by some, was quartered alive in Red Square in 1671, by order of Tsar Aleksei Mikhailovich. Catherine the Great had Pugachëv beheaded in the same place in 1775. Pugachëv's uprising began in the southern Urals and got as far as the town of Zlatoust, about 300 miles from Butka.

11.Yel'tsin, *Ispoved'*, 140; Mikhail Gorbachev, *Zhizn' i reformy* (Life and reforms), 2 vols. (Moscow: Novosti, 1995), 1:374–75.

12. Gorbachev recounted his comment to Yeltsin in response to a question from the author during a visit to the Gorbachev Foundation by a Harvard University study group, September 11, 2002.

13. In 1960 the Kremlin transferred Molotov to Vienna as ambassador to the International Atomic Energy Agency. It recalled him in 1961 and excluded him from the party. His ally, Georgii Malenkov, another former prime minister, was given internal exile as director of a hydroelectric station near Ust-Kamenogorsk, in northern Kazakhstan. "He and his wife were removed from the train twenty-five miles west of Ust-Kamenogorsk (lest he receive a warm greeting there) and driven directly to the tiny settlement of Albaketka, where they lived in a small dark house until the summer of 1958. At that point . . . Khrushchev dumped him even deeper into exile in the town of Ekibastuz, where police observed every move, shadowed his children when they came to visit, and even stole his party card and then accused him of losing it so as to threaten him with expulsion from the party." Lazar Kaganovich, a confederate of Molotov and Malenkov, was sent to manage a potash plant in Solikamsk, in Perm oblast just north of Berezniki. William Taubman, *Khrushchev: The Man and His Era* (New York: Norton, 2003), 369.

14. Boris Yeltsin, third interview with the author (September 12, 2002).

15. Gorbachev, *Zhizn' i reformy*,1:374–75.

16. Yel'tsin, *Ispoved'*, 140–41.

17. Georgii Shakhnazarov, interview with the author (January 29, 2001). Jerry F. Hough, *Democratization and Revolution in the USSR, 1985–1991* (Washington, D.C.: Brookings, 1997), 326, also plays up the overconfidence variable.

18. Mikhail Shneider, quoted in Michael E. Urban, "Boris El'tsin, Democratic Russia, and the Campaign for the Russian Presidency," *Soviet Studies* 44 (March–April 1992), 190.

19. Assignment of the KGB to monitor Yeltsin is described in the memoir by Gorbachev's former chief of staff: V. I. Boldin, *Krusheniye p'edestala: shtrikhi k portretu M. S. Gorbacheva* (Smashing the pedestal: strokes of a portrait of M. S. Gorbachev) (Moscow: Respublika, 1995), 334. I heard of details in interviews.

20. Aleksandr Muzykantskii, interview with the author (May 30, 2001).

21. The only place I have been able to find this memo is in Aleksandr Khinshtein, *Yel'tsin, Kreml', istoriya bolezni* (Yeltsin, the Kremlin, the history of an illness) (Moscow: OLMA, 2006), 527–58. It was never sent to Ryzhkov.

22. Quotation from "Vstrecha v VKSh, 12 noyabrya 1988 goda s 14 do 18 chasov" (Meeting in the Higher Komsomol School, November 12, 1988, from 2:00 P.M. to 6:00 P.M.), in RGANI (Russian State Archive of Contemporary History, Moscow) (microform in Harvard College Library), fund 89, register 8, file 29, 5.

23. Lev Sukhanov, *Tri goda s Yel'tsinym: zapiski pervogo pomoshchnika* (Three years with Yeltsin: notes of his first assistant) (Riga: Vaga, 1992), 40.

24. Yel'tsin, *Ispoved'*, 143; Boris Yel'tsin, *Zapiski prezidenta* (Notes of a president) (Moscow: Ogonëk, 1994), 31.

25. Aleksandr Korzhakov, *Boris Yel'tsin: ot rassveta do zakata* (Boris Yeltsin: from dawn to dusk) (Moscow: Interbuk, 1997), 152.

26. M. S. Solomentsev, *Veryu v Rossiyu* (I believe in Russia) (Moscow: Molodaya gvardiya, 2003), 510.

27. Yel'tsin, *Ispoved'*, 151–57; "Vstrecha v VKSh," 27; Boldin, *Krusheniye p'edestala*, 335–36. KGB guards tried unsuccessfully to lure Yeltsin into the vestibule behind the stage, with the aim, one supposes, of cutting off his appeal to the audience and perhaps of preventing him from speaking.

28. Quotations from *XIX Vsesoyuznaya konferentsiya Kommunisticheskoi partii Sovetskogo Soyuza: stenograficheskii otchët* (The 19th conference of the Communist Party of the Soviet Union: stenographic record), 2 vols. (Moscow: Politizdat, 1988), 2:56–61.

29. Vitalii Tret'yakov, "Sverdlovskii vyskochka," part 6, *Politicheskii klass*, July 2006, 106.

30. Chernyayev, *Shest' let*, 218–19. Zaikov's involvement is described in Yurii Prokof'ev, *Do i posle zapreta KPSS: pervyi sekretar' MGK KPSS vspominayet* (Before and after the ban on the CPSU: a first secretary of the Moscow gorkom remembers) (Moscow: Algoritm, 2005), 209–10. Ligachëv's statement about Yeltsin being wrong was omitted from the official transcript of the conference.

31. Sukhanov, *Tri goda*, 57.

32. Yel'tsin, *Ispoved'*, 166–67. On the letters and telegrams, see also the testimony of a journalist who saw stacks of them in a side office at Gosstroi: Vladimir Polozhentsev, "Privet, pribaltiitsy!" (Greetings, people from the Baltic), http://podolsk-news.ru/stat/elcin.php.

33. Ivan Sukhomlin in Khinshtein, *Yel'tsin, Kreml', istoriya bolezni*, 136–37.

34. Memorial was founded in 1987. The Nineteenth Conference had agreed to the idea of the monument, but Memorial soon broadened its agenda to human

rights in general. Yeltsin attended one meeting of the board and communicated with Memorial leaders. Nanci Adler, *Victims of Soviet Terror: The Story of the Memorial Movement* (Westport, Conn.: Praeger, 1993), 54–67; and personal communication to the author (November 13, 2006).

35. Jonathan Sanders, interview with the author (January 21, 2004).

36. Sukhanov, *Tri goda*, 71–73.

37. "Vstrecha v VKSh," 66–67.

38. Aleksei Yemel'yanov in L. N. Dobrokhotov, ed., *Gorbachev–Yel'tsin: 1,500 dnei politicheskogo protivostoyaniya* (Gorbachev–Yeltsin: 1,500 days of political conflict) (Moscow: TERRA, 1992), 338.

39. See on this process Alexei Yurchak, *Everything Was Forever, Until It Was No More: The Last Soviet Generation* (Princeton: Princeton University Press, 2006), 291–96.

40. "Vstrecha v VKSh," 56.

41. Pavel Voshchanov, "Ne zabudem o cheloveke" (Let us not forget about the person), *Komsomol'skaya pravda*, December 31, 1988.

42. Naina Yeltsina, first interview with the author (February 9, 2002).

43. "Vstrecha v VKSh," 56.

44. See the perceptive discussion in Vitalii Tret'yakov, "Sverdlovskii vyskochka," part 5, *Politicheskii klass*, June 2006, 104–5. So as not to provoke Gorbachev, Yeltsin avoided using the Russian word for oppositionist, *oppozitsioner*. At dinner with the American ambassador as late as June of 1989, "there was not the slightest hint that Yeltsin thought of himself in competition with Gorbachev." Jack F. Matlock, Jr., *Autopsy on an Empire* (New York: Random House, 1995), 223.

45. Georgii Shakhnazarov, *S vozhdyami i bez nikh* (With leaders and without them) (Moscow: VAGRIUS, 2001), 365.

46. Sukhanov, *Tri goda*, 68.

47. "Vstrecha v VKSh," 28–29.

48. The archival transcript of the January plenum duly records Yeltsin's historic abstention. In March dozens of negative votes were cast as Gorbachev led the members through the list of official nominees, one at a time. The number but not the identities of the nays was noted in each case. Yeltsin said in public that he was one of the seventy-eight in March to vote against sending Ligachëv to the congress, which was by far the largest number of nay votes. Since Yeltsin's disgrace in October 1987, the Central Committee had convened in February, May, July, and November of 1988, and on each occasion he added his vote to the unanimous support for motions from the leadership.

49. Boldin, *Krusheniye p'edestala*, 339.

50. Yel'tsin, *Ispoved'*, 16–17. Valentin Yumashev, then a young journalist who had made the acquaintance of Yeltsin and his family, recalls that Yeltsin in the autumn of 1988 never displayed any doubt that he would run for the congress. Yumashev, first interview with the author (February 4, 2002).

51. Muzykantskii interview.

52. David Remnick, "Boris Yeltsin, Adding Punch to Soviet Politics," *The Washington Post*, February 18, 1989.

53. Author's interviews with Valerii Bortsov (June 11, 2001) and Valentina Lantseva (July 9, 2001).

54. On this important group, see Marc Garcelon, "The Estate of Change: The Specialist Rebellion and the Democratic Movement in Moscow, 1989–1991," *Theory and Society* 26 (February 1997), 55–56.

55. Bill Keller, "Soviet Maverick Is Charging Dirty Tricks in Election Drive," *New York Times*, March 19, 1989.

56. Yeltsin had addressed Ipat'ev House, and admitted to his role in the destruction of the landmark, at the Higher Komsomol School in November 1988. He said more in the first volume of his memoirs, published in 1990.

57. Vitalii Tret'yakov, "Fenomen Yel'tsina" (The Yeltsin phenomenon), *Moskovskiye novosti*, April 16, 1989.

58. Michael McFaul, *Russia's Unfinished Revolution: Political Change from Gorbachev to Putin* (Ithaca: Cornell University Press, 2001), 70–71; Brendan Kiernan and Joseph Aistrup, "The 1989 Elections to the Congress of People's Deputies in Moscow," *Soviet Studies* 43 (November–December 1991), 1051–52; Sergei Stankevich, interview with the author (May 29, 2001).

59. V. A. Kolosov, N. V. Petrov, and L. V. Smirnyagin, *Vesna 89: geografiya i anatomiya parlamentskikh vyborov* (Spring of 1989: the geography and anatomy of the parliamentary elections) (Moscow: Progress, 1990), 225.

60. Ibid., 218–20.

61. Matlock, *Autopsy on an Empire*, 210.

62. All quotations from Tret'yakov, "Fenomen Yel'tsina" (italics added).

63. Muzykantskii interview. In Yeltsin's absence, reformist candidates distributed materials playing up their links with him.

64. Yel'tsin, *Ispoved'*, 170; *V Politbyuro TsK KPSS* . . . (In the Politburo of the CPSU) (Moscow: Gorbachev-Fond, 2006), 482. Ligachëv told the Politburo he would be happy to speak out against Yeltsin at the party plenum or the congress, but other members counseled against it. Gorbachev sounded nervous about a confrontation.

65. *V Politbyuro TsK KPSS*, 489.

66. On the agreement by Yeltsin's unnamed representative, see Sukhanov, *Tri goda*, 84. Vitalii Tret'yakov, who has excellent sources of information, is convinced Yeltsin all the while hoped to challenge Gorbachev for the position. Tret'yakov, "Sverdlovskii vyskochka," part 7, 106–9.

67. Popov describes his intervention, without mentioning Gorbachev's waffling, in *Snova v oppozitsii* (In opposition again) (Moscow: Galaktika, 1994), 66. The other details are in Alexei Kazannik, "Boris Yeltsin: From Triumph to Fall," *Moscow News*, June 2, 2004.

68. As an alternative, Gorbachev offered him the chair of the People's Control Committee of the USSR, a monitoring organization most reformers considered superfluous. It would have required Yeltsin to give up his parliamentary seat. He de-

clined, preferring, Gorbachev says, "to take upon himself the functions of leader of the opposition in the parliament" (Gorbachev, *Zhizn' i reformy*, 1:458). The job went to Yeltsin's former Sverdlovsk colleague, Gennadii Kolbin.

69. Andrei Karaulov, *Vokrug Kremlya: kniga politicheskikh dialogov* (Around the Kremlin: a book of political dialogues), 114–15. Another mark of the committee's low status was that until December 1989 its offices were in the Moskva Hotel, not in a government building.

70. Vladimir Mezentsev, "Okruzhentsy" (Entourage), part 3, *Rabochaya tribuna*, March 28, 1995.

71. "Yeltsin Discusses Candidacy, Issues, Rivals," FBIS-SOV-91-110 (June 7, 1991), 61.

72. Andrei Sakharov, *Gor'kii, Moskva, daleye vezde* (Gorky, Moscow, after that everywhere) (New York: Izdatel'stvo imeni Chekhova, 1990), 169. Sakharov (170–71) writes of Yeltsin hogging the microphone at a rally organized by the dissident group Moscow Tribune.

73. Edward Kline, interview with the author (February 15, 2007). Sakharov told Kline he only had one serious conversation with Yeltsin.

74. Shapovalenko in August 1991 was to be designated presidential representative to Orenburg oblast. He was one of only three presidential representatives in the provinces to survive Yeltsin's two terms. Pëtr Akonov, "Sud'ba komissarov" (Fate of the commissars), *Izvestiya*, August 23, 2001.

75. Viktor Sheinis, *Vzlët i padeniye parlamenta: perelomnyye gody v rossiiskoi politike, 1985–1993* (The rise and fall of parliament: years of change in Russian politics, 1985–93) (Moscow: Moskovskii Tsentr Karnegi, Fond INDEM, 2005), 229–31. Yeltsin's cause was also strongly supported by the environmentalist Aleksei Yablokov and by Il'ya Zaslavskii, an advocate for the disabled.

76. Yevgenii Savast'yanov, a Sakharov camp follower who attended the Interregional meetings, interview with the author (June 9, 2000). Also Bortsov and Lantseva interviews and interviews with Yelena Bonner, Sakharov's widow (March 13, 2001), Mikhail Poltoranin (July 11, 2001), and Gavriil Popov (June 1, 2001).

77. Arkadii Murashov, interview with the author (September 13, 2000). Yeltsin complained openly about the group's disorganization and "endless meetings and consultations." "Yeltsin Interviewed by *Sovetskaya molodëzh'*," FBIS-SOV-90-021 (January 31, 1990), 73).

78. In addition to those mentioned in the text, Stankevich interview and interviews with Yurii Ryzhov (June 7, 2000) and Mark Zakharov (June 4, 2002).

79. Popov interview.

80. Yeltsin expressed approval of foreign investment in the USSR but, just weeks before the fall of the Berlin Wall, also gave a favorable assessment of economic change in East Germany. To a young Harvard economist at the meeting, Yeltsin showed "all the dissatisfaction with the sclerotic Soviet system but no clue about any market anything." Lawrence H. Summers, interview with the author (November 25, 2005).

81. Dan Quayle, *Standing Firm: A Vice-Presidential Memoir* (New York: HarperCollins, 1994), 170.

82. Michael R. Beschloss and Strobe Talbott, *At the Highest Levels: The Inside Story of the End of the Cold War* (Boston: Little, Brown, 1993), 104–5. See also George Bush and Brent Scowcroft, *A World Transformed* (New York: Knopf, 1998), 142–43.

83. Sukhanov, *Tri goda*, 99.

84. Yeltsin and his party did not always see American reality for what it was. For example, he came to the conclusion that homelessness was not a major problem in New York, and one member of the Russian group declared that the homeless were on the streets not because they had nowhere to sleep but because they wanted the authorities to give them plots of land on which they could build houses. Ibid., 100–101.

85. Ibid., 149, 153. I learned of Yeltsin's upset on the bus from Wesley Neff of the Leigh Bureau, who witnessed it. Excerpts from the Randall's video are in *Prezident vseya Rusi*, part 2.

86. Sukhanov, *Tri goda*, 150.

87. Boris Nemtsov, first interview with the author (October 17, 2000). Yeltsin was "shocked" when he described the Houston store to Naina upon his return. She underwent a similar shock a few months later during a private visit to the Netherlands. In November 1991, when she accompanied Yeltsin on his first foreign visit as Russian president to Germany, the wife of the mayor of Cologne took her shopping for shoes and on a walk through the city market. Thinking of Moscow's bare shelves, "I was ashamed. I had worked my whole life, we had wanted to make life better, and we had not done anything. I wanted to hide somewhere." Naina Yeltsina, second interview with the author (September 18, 2007).

88. Yel'tsin, *Zapiski*, 181.

89. James MacGregor Burns, *Transforming Leadership: A New Pursuit of Happiness* (New York: Atlantic Monthly Press, 2003), 166.

90. Gaidar, *Gibel' imperii*.

91. See especially Archie Brown, "Gorbachev, Lenin, and the Break with Leninism," *Demokratizatsiya/Democratization* 15 (Spring 2007), 230–44.

92. I owe the sequence frown-doubt-assent to Steven Englund, *Napoleon: A Political Life* (New York: Scribner, 2004), 38. On the ambiguous attitudes of younger Soviets, see Yurchak, *Everything Was Forever.*

93. "Yeltsin Airs Plans for Deputies Elections," FBIS-SOV-9-021 (January 31, 1990), 69. In this context, Yeltsin meant "leftward" to connote openness to change, and not to a greater state role in the economy, as the word tends to mean in the West. In the 1990s Russian understandings of left-right terminology came into better conformity with foreign ones.

94. In John B. Dunlop, *The Rise of Russia and the Fall of the Soviet Empire* (Princeton: Princeton University Press, 1993), 49–50. Yeltsin first indicated he

thought of himself as a social democrat on a visit to Greece the month before. John Morrison, *Boris Yeltsin: From Bolshevik to Democrat* (New York: Dutton, 1991), 108.

95. The decision was made a few days after Korzhakov celebrated Yeltsin's fifty-eighth birthday with him. "The bosses especially did not like the toasts I raised to Boris Nikolayevich. Fallen leaders of the Communist Party, it turns out, are not supposed to have any prospects for the future." Korzhakov, *Boris Yel'tsin*, 69. Viktor Suzdalev, another of Yeltsin's three guards from 1985 to 1987, was removed for the same offense. Yurii Kozhukhov, the head bodyguard, was demoted by the KGB after November 1987 but dropped contact with Yeltsin.

96. Aleksandr Korzhakov, *Boris Yel'tsin: ot rassveta do zakata; posleslovïye* (Boris Yeltsin: from dawn to dusk; epilogue) (Moscow: Detektiv-press, 2004), 517–18. He relates that the machine was at idle as the driver talked to the driver of a Zhiguli car through the car window. "It became clear later" that the passenger had a damaged spinal disk and bruised kidneys, "after which he was very ill for a long time." Korzhakov says he and a neighbor, businessman Vladimir Vinogradov, helped with medical expenses and paid for the funeral, since the unnamed victim "had no close relatives." Korzhakov writes that Yeltsin never inquired about the man's condition, and does not mention having volunteered information about it to his boss. Yeltsin family members say the Korzhakov volume was the first they had heard of the matter.

97. A lurid book written with Korzhakov's cooperation replays many of his stories about Yeltsin, but not this one. The book also makes extensive use of KGB files. See Khinshtein, *Yel'tsin, Kreml', istoriya bolezni.*

98. Robert S. Strauss, interview with the author (January 9, 2006).

99. Viktor Yaroshenko, *Yel'tsin: ya otvechu za vsë* (Yeltsin: I will answer for everything) (Moscow: Vokrug sveta, 1997), 20.

100. Sukhanov, *Tri goda*, 174.

101. See on the coverage Leon Aron, *Yeltsin: A Revolutionary Life* (New York: St. Martin's, 2000), 341–50; and Yaroshenko, *Yel'tsin*, 29–61.Wesley Neff, who accompanied Yeltsin on the trip, says he most nights had no more than one or two drinks and was never inebriated. Yaroshenko, a USSR deputy who accompanied him, recalls (*Yel'tsin*, 21) that Yeltsin was insulted when he found his New York hotel room stocked with many bottles of liquor, saying this showed how some Americans extended "hospitality to a 'Russian peasant.'"

102. "Yeltsin Interviewed," 77.

103. Vadim Bakatin, interview with the author (May 29, 2002). Bakatin was to be head of the KGB in the autumn of 1991 and may have had access to files about the incident there. Rumor has long had it that Yeltsin went to see the Bashilovs' chambermaid. The woman, Yelena Stepanova, denies any relationship and says KGB officers told her he met someone and then ended up in a ditch on the property. Anna Veligzhanina, "Yel'tsin padal s mosta ot lyubvi?" (Did Yeltsin fall from the bridge out of love?), *Komsomol'skaya pravda*, November 21, 2004. Several persons close to Yeltsin at the time believe he engineered the occasion as a publicity stunt.

104. Mezentsev, "Okruzhentsy," part 3.

105. At an interview with a journalist on October 21, Yeltsin was "in a fantastic mood." Andrei Karaulov, *Chastushki* (Humorous verses) (Moscow: Sovershenno sekretno, 1998), 169.

Chapter Eight

1. George W. Breslauer, *Gorbachev and Yeltsin as Leaders* (Cambridge: Cambridge University Press, 2002), 125. As Breslauer shows, polarization was Gorbachev's worst fear, because of his personality and his reading of historical experiences such as the destruction of reform communism in Czechoslovakia in 1968. As for Yeltsin, his power-seeking is difficult to comb out from his substantive goals. The study that most accentuates his drive for power is Jerry F. Hough, *Democratization and Revolution in the USSR, 1985–1991* (Washington, D.C.: Brookings, 1997). Even it must concede (340) that Yeltsin also had transformative aims.

2. Lev Sukhanov, *Tri goda s Yel'tsinym: zapiski pervogo pomoshchnika* (Three years with Yeltsin: notes of his first assistant) (Riga: Vaga, 1992), 241.

3. Yu, M. Baturin et al., *Epokha Yel'tsina: ocherki politicheskoi istorii* (The Yeltsin epoch: essays in political history) (Moscow: VAGRIUS, 2001), 78.

4. Lyudmila Pikhoya, interview with the author (September 26, 2001). Kharin died in 1992, but Il'in stayed with Yeltsin until 1998 and Pikhoya until 1999.

5. Michael McFaul, *Russia's Unfinished Revolution: Political Change from Gorbachev to Putin* (Ithaca: Cornell University Press, 2001), 81.

6. V. I. Vorotnikov, *A bylo eto tak: iz dnevnika chlena Politbyuro TsK KPSS* (But this is how it was: from the diary of a member of the Politburo of the CPSU) (Moscow: Sovet veteranov knigoizdaniya, 1995), 342–43, 348, 362–63.

7. The book was widely distributed in other Soviet republics. The CPSU first secretary in Ukraine, Vladimir Ivashko, told the Politburo it had made Ukrainian coal miners question their party dues: "The miners say, Why should we pay money so that someone else can live in luxury?" Politburo transcript, April 9, 1990 (Volkogonov Archive, Project on Cold War Studies, Davis Center for Russian and Eurasian Studies, Harvard University), 356.

8. "Yeltsin's RSFSR Election Platform Outlined," FBIS-SOV-90-045 (March 7, 1990), 108–9; L. N. Dobrokhotov, ed., *Gorbachev–Yel'tsin: 1,500 dnei politicheskogo protivostoyaniya* (Gorbachev–Yeltsin: 1,500 days of political conflict) (Moscow: TERRA, 1992), 173 (italics added).

9. For example, in January 1990, Yeltsin, building on discussions in the Sverdlovsk years, advocated the creation of seven "Russian republics" within the RSFSR, which apparently would have been controlled by ethnic Russians and would have been equal in powers to, but much larger than, the non-Russian republics. He repudiated this formula for confusion and conflict in August 1990. In an equally problematic statement, he said to the Russian congress in May 1990 that

he favored "the sovereignty of the raion [district] soviet," which would have subjected Russia and its provinces to centrifugal forces at the most local level. He never repeated the phrase. See V. T. Loginov, ed., *Soyuz mozhno bylo sokhranit'* (The union could have been saved), rev. ed. (Moscow: AST, 2007), 135, 156, 166.

10. Vyacheslav Terekhov, interview with the author (June 5, 2001). It is a confused comment, for in the Bible Jesus goes to the hill of Golgotha to be crucified. Yeltsin believed that in the forthcoming struggle it was his opponents who would lose out.

11. Politburo transcript, March 7, 1990 (Volkogonov Archive), 356.

12. Polling figures are given in John B. Dunlop, *The Rise of Russia and the Fall of the Soviet Empire* (Princeton: Princeton University Press, 1993), 28–29; Archie Brown, *The Gorbachev Factor* (Oxford: Oxford University Press, 1996), 203, 270–71; and Matthew Wyman, *Public Opinion in Postcommunist Russia* (New York: St. Martin's, 1997), 85.

13. Politburo transcript, March 22, 1990 (Volkogonov Archive), 219; Sergei Filatov, *Sovershenno nesekretno* (Top nonsecret) (Moscow: VAGRIUS, 2000), 40–41.

14. Politburo transcript, March 22, 1990, 207–8.

15. In Loginov, *Soyuz mozhno bylo sokhranit'*, 147–48.

16. Boris Yel'tsin, *Zapiski prezidenta* (Notes of a president) (Moscow: Ogonëk, 1994), 175; Margaret Thatcher, *The Downing Street Years* (London: HarperCollins, 1993), 803–4.

17. Journalist Vladimir Mezentsev, interview with the author (September 26, 2001). Mezentsev had worked for Yeltsin until just before the event and was present at it.

18. Georgii Shakhnazarov, *S vozhdyami i bez nikh* (With leaders and without them) (Moscow: VAGRIUS, 2001), 367.

19. Vladimir Mezentsev, "Okruzhentsy" (Encourage), part 9, *Rabochaya tribuna*, April 7, 1995.

20. Nuisance candidates took thirty-two votes in the first round and eleven in the third. The remaining deputies not included in the totals here crossed off the names of all the candidates entered.

21. Aleksandr Budberg, "Proigravshii pobeditel': Mikhailu Gorbachevu—75" (Losing victor: Mikhail Gorbachev at 75), *Moskovskii komsomolets*, March 3, 2006.

22. Korzhakov, Yeltsin's bodyguard and confidant, had had his wages covered by three business cooperatives. Lantseva, his main press spokesman until July 1991, first received a salary in February 1991. Neither Lantseva nor Bortsov, who wrote speeches for Yeltsin until 1995, had Moscow residency until 1991. Author's interviews with Lantseva (July 9, 2001), Bortsov (June 11, 2001), and Mezentsev. See also Vladimir Mezentsev, "Okruzhentsy," part 3, *Rabochaya tribuna*, March 28, 1995.

23. Mikhail Bocharov, interview with the author (October 19, 2000).

24. The delegates "took into account that if they voted for [Lobov] it would be a kind of linkup between the party and Yeltsin." Yurii Prokof'ev, *Do i posle zapreta*

KPSS: pervyi sekretar' MGK KPSS vspominayet (Before and after the ban on the CPSU: a first secretary of the Moscow gorkom remembers) (Moscow: Algoritm, 2005), 218.

25. *XXVIII s"ezd Kommunisticheskoi partii Sovetskogo Soyuza: stenograficheskii otchët* (The 28th congress of the Communist Party of the Soviet Union: stenographic record), 2 vols. (Moscow: Politizdat, 1991), 1:472–75.

26. Author's interviews with Gavriil Popov (June 1, 2001) and Sergei Stankevich (May 29, 2001).

27. Baturin et al., *Epokha,* 93. See also Sukhanov, *Tri goda,* 338–39.

28. An early draft of the announcement called on legislative leaders and President Gorbachev to follow his example. A copy, with corrections in Yeltsin's handwriting, is in Aleksandr Khinshtein, *Yel'tsin, Kreml', istoriya bolezni* (Yeltsin, the Kremlin, the history of an illness) (Moscow: OLMA, 2006), 543; it was obtained from the widow of Lev Sukhanov.

29. Viktor Sheinis, *Vzlët i padeniye parlamenta: perelomnyye gody v rossiiskoi politike, 1985–1993* (The rise and fall of parliament: years of change in Russian politics, 1985–93) (Moscow: Moskovskii Tsentr Karnegi, Fond INDEM, 2005), 357.

30. Naina Yeltsina, personal communication to the author (July 29, 2007).

31. Anatolii Chernyayev, *1991 god: dnevnik pomoshchnika Prezidenta SSSR* (The year 1991: diary of an assistant to the president of the USSR) (Moscow: TERRA, 1997), 37.

32. Politburo transcript, May 3, 1990 (Volkogonov Archive), 516, 533.

33. *Pervyi s"ezd narodnykh deputatov SSSR, 25 maya–9 iyunya 1989 g.: stenograficheskii otchët* (The first congress of people's deputies of the USSR, May 25–June 9, 1989: stenographic record), 6 vols. (Moscow: Izdaniye Verkhovnogo Soveta SSSR, 1989), 2:48.

34. Hough, *Democratization and Revolution,* 385. On this general issue, see also Edward W. Walker, *Dissolution: Sovereignty and the Breakup of the Soviet Union* (Lanham, Md.: Rowman and Littlefield, 2003).

35. Most accounts leave out this last detail. The congress in fact rejected an amendment that would have had the declaration of primacy click in immediately. Gwendolyn Elizabeth Stewart, "SIC TRANSIT: Democratization, *Suverenizatsiia,* and Boris Yeltsin in the Breakup of the Soviet Union" (Ph.D. diss., Harvard University, 1995), 272–73. Once the provision was in effect, though, it was reminiscent of the theory of nullification put forth to defend states' rights in the United States by John C. Calhoun in the 1820s and 1830s.

36. Boris Yeltsin, first interview with the author (July 15, 2001).

37. Ivan Silayev, interview with the author (January 25, 2001). Agreements were reached with Lithuania in the Baltic and Kyrgyzstan in Central Asia, but the general arrangement stayed put.

38. Bill Keller, "Boris Yeltsin Taking Power," *New York Times,* September 23, 1990.

39. "Trusy Yel'tsina" (Yeltsin's trunks), http://www.channel4.ru/content/200205/10/112.trus.html.

40. A. L. Litvin, *Yel'tsiny v Kazani* (The Yeltsins in Kazan) (Kazan: Aibat, 2004), 70–71; Loginov, *Soyuz mozhno bylo sokhranit'*, 165–66.

41. "Yeltsin Continues Russian Tour to Bashkir ASSR," FBIS-SOV-90-156 (August 13, 1990), 82.

42. Dobrokhotov, *Gorbachev–Yel'tsin*, 198.

43. Ibid., 194.

44. Shakhnazarov, *S vozhdyami i bez nikh*, 373; Aleksandr Yakovlev, first interview with the author (June 9, 2000). Yakovlev said that with him Gorbachev was at first somewhat receptive to the vice-presidential initiative, but went solidly against it after discussion with Politburo members.

45. Boris Yeltsin, second interview with the author (February 9, 2002).

46. At the Politburo meeting hours after Yeltsin attacked Gorbachev, the Kremlin chief of staff, Valerii Boldin, said it was time "to part with illusions with relation to Yeltsin. . . . He will never work together with us. He is a not entirely healthy person and sees himself only in confrontation." Prime Minister Ryzhkov concurred, saying Yeltsin was only interested in power and would not rest until he had Gorbachev's job. *V Politbyuro TsK KPSS* . . . (In the Politburo of the CPSU) (Moscow: Gorbachev-Fond, 2006), 618–19.

47. Yelena Bonner, interview with the author (March 13, 2001). Yeltsin made the comment as Bonner stood with him on the balcony of the Russian White House, at the conclusion of the putsch of August 1991. She had told him several months before that Gorbachev had made him look foolish over the Five Hundred Days plan.

48. Vyacheslav Chornovil, "Yel'tsin vnis duzhe konstruktyvnyi moment u politychnu real'nist' v Ukraini" (Yeltsin injected a very constructive note into Ukrainian political reality), *Za vil'nu Ukrainu* (Ukrainian-language newspaper, L'viv), November 23, 1990; reference supplied by Roman Szporluk. Despite the implicit recognition of the border, Chornovil did say Yeltsin's attitude toward the Crimea issue gave him some concern.

49. Chernyayev, *1991 god*, 76.

50. Karen Brutents, *Nesbyvsheyesya: neravnodushnyye zametki o perestroike* (It never came true: engaged notes about perestroika) (Moscow: Mezhdunarodnyye otnosheniya, 2005), 108.

51. Jack F. Matlock, Jr., *Autopsy on an Empire* (New York: Random House, 1995), 488.

52. Yeltsin was invited to Strasbourg by the International Politics Forum, a Paris-based organization linked to European Christian Democratic parties. When he arrived, he mistook dignitaries at the airport, waiting for another visitor, for a welcoming group for him. The city mayor, Cathérine Trautman, recognized the situation for what it was and organized a dinner the next day with local officials and businessmen. "These people were impressed by him for presenting so dignified a face." Yeltsin flew out of Strasbourg when it became clear he would not be allowed to participate in the assembly's deliberations. Hélène Carrère d'Encausse, French scholar and parliamentarian, interview with the author (September 11, 2007).

53. John Morrison, *Boris Yeltsin: From Bolshevik to Democrat* (New York: Dutton, 1991), 252.

54. Dmitri K. Simes, *After the Collapse: Russia Seeks Its Place as a Great Power* (New York: Simon and Schuster, 1999), 89.

55. Monica Crowley, *Nixon in Winter* (New York: Random House, 1998), 43. Nixon said to another associate (Simes, *After the Collapse*, 89) that in American terms Gorbachev was "Wall Street" but Yeltsin was "Main Street." In his last book (*Beyond Peace* [New York: Random House, 1994], 45), Nixon said Gorbachev was better suited to "drawing rooms" and Yeltsin to "family rooms."

56. Dan Quayle, *Standing Firm: A Vice-Presidential Memoir* (New York: Harper-Collins, 1994), 171.

57. CIA, Directorate of Intelligence, "Yeltsin's Political Objectives," SOV 91-10026X (June 1991), 1, 7; declassified version obtained at http://www.foia.cia.gov .browse_docs.asp? On interdependency, the report acknowledged Yeltsin's "awareness of the multistranded interweaving of goals and analysis." He understood, for example, that, "One cannot promote Russian welfare without (a) dropping the burden of empire, (b) marketizing the economy, and (c) cutting military expenditures." He realized that, "One cannot marketize if one does not (a) dismantle the Stalinist system and create a climate of legality, (b) cut back the military-industrial complex, (c) resolve societal problems peacefully, and (d) gain Western economic collaboration." And it had sunk in that, "One cannot achieve nonviolent solutions to societal problems without (a) eliminating totalitarian structures, (b) gaining voluntary resolution of ethnic conflicts, and (c) improving living standards."

58. Vladimir Isakov, interview with the author (June 4, 2001). For details, see V. B. Isakov, *Predsedatel' Soveta Respubliki: parlamentskiye dnevniki, 1990–1991* (Chairman of the Council of the Republic: parliamentary diaries, 1990–91) (Moscow: Paleya, 1996).

59. Vladimir Zhirinovskii, interview with the author (January 22, 2002). On CPSU and KGB backing for the formation of Zhirinovskii's party, and the financial sum provided, see Aleksandr Yakovlev, *Sumerki* (Dusk) (Moscow: Materik, 2003), 574–75.

60. "Yeltsin Gives Speech in Moscow," FBIS-SOV-91-106 (June 3, 1991), 75.

61. On spatial distribution of the vote, see Gavin Helf, "All the Russias: Center, Core, and Periphery in Soviet and Post-Soviet Russia" (Ph.D. diss., University of California at Berkeley, 1994); and Scott Gehlbach, "Shifting Electoral Geography in Russia's 1991 and 1996 Presidential Elections," *Post-Soviet Geography and Economics* 5 (July–August 2000), 379–87.

62. Aleksei Yemel'yanov in Dobrokhotov, *Gorbachev–Yel'tsin*, 339.

63. "My mozhem byt' tvërdo uvereny: Rossiya vozroditsya" (We can be certain that Russia will be reborn), *Izvestiya*, July 10, 1991.

64. Filatov, *Sovershenno nesekretno*, 84–87; Baturin et al., *Epokha*, 122; Shakhnazarov, *S vozhdyami i bez nikh*, 377.

65. Of the two main office buildings in the Kremlin, No. 14, dating from the 1930s, when Stalin razed a monastery, a convent, and a small palace to make room for it, was much the inferior, although Brezhnev had his office there. Building No. 1, completed in 1790, housed the imperial Senate before 1917 and was mostly for the USSR Council of Ministers after 1917.

66. Gorbachev at first tried to work on a new union treaty in negotiations within USSR institutions. His switch in April to negotiations among and with the Soviet republics was a sign of how much his position had weakened, and opened him up to pressure for concessions on issue after issue. Philip G. Roeder, *Where Nation-States Come From: Institutional Change in the Age of Nationalism* (Princeton: Princeton University Press, 2007), 178–80.

67. Carrère d'Encausse interview. Revisiting the inter-republic negotiations of the winter before, and anticipating the agreement struck in December 1991, Yeltsin specifically raised with Carrère d'Encausse the possibility of a voluntary "commonwealth" of the three Slavic republics of the USSR—Russia, Ukraine, and Belarus.

68. Baturin et al., *Epokha*, 135, 137.

69. V. I. Boldin, *Krusheniye p'edestala: shtrikhi k portretu M. S. Gorbacheva* (Smashing the pedestal: strokes of a portrait of M. S. Gorbachev) (Moscow: Respublika, 1995), 403.

70. See Michael R. Beschloss and Strobe Talbott, *At the Highest Levels: The Inside Story of the End of the Cold War* (Boston: Little, Brown, 1993), 412–13; Stewart, "SIC TRANSIT," 361–62; and Mikhail Gorbachev, *Zhizn' i reformy* (Life and reforms), 2 vols. (Moscow: Novosti, 1995), 2:308.

71. Boris Yel'tsin, *Zapiski prezidenta* (Notes of a president) (Moscow: Ogonëk, 1994), 54–56; Gorbachev, *Zhizn' i reformy*, 2:556–57.

72. Yel'tsin, *Zapiski*, 96.

73. Voshchanov, interviewed in *Prezident vseya Rusi* (The president of all Russia), documentary film by Yevgenii Kiselëv, 1999–2000 (copy supplied by Kiselëv), 4 parts, part 3. Gorbachev reports the overture in his memoirs (*Zhizn' i reformy*, 2:555) and criticizes Yeltsin for not informing him about it. "Most likely he held it in reserve, never knowing when it might come in handy."

74. Prokof'ev, *Do i posle zapreta KPSS*, 244. A number of well-informed Muscovites have told me they are sure that Kryuchkov and the plotters briefed Yeltsin on their plan. No evidence has ever been brought forward. Ruslan Khasbulatov, the acting chairman of the Russian parliament at the time, and later to be a blood enemy of Yeltsin's, was one of the first to see him the morning of August 19, and he reports that Yeltsin was "flabby and prostrate" at the news of the coup, which can only mean that he had been given no warning. R. I. Khasbulatov, *Velikaya Rossiiskaya tragediya* (Great Russian tragedy), 2 vols. (Moscow: SIMS, 1994), 1:161.

75. Boris Yeltsin, third interview with the author (September 12, 2002), in which he told me about the Kubinka landing. In *Zapiski*, 73, he wrote that he landed at Vnukovo, not Kubinka. He also stated there (71) that the putschists considered having

his plane shot down. Sukhanov, *Tri goda,* 15, says the same. These details will not be clarified until independent researchers get access to the archives concerned.

76. V. G. Stepankov and Ye. K. Lisov, *Kremlëvskii zagovor* (Kremlin plot) (Moscow: Ogonëk, 1992), 119–21; "GKChP: protsess, kotoryi ne poshël" (The GKChP: the process which never got going), part 4, *Novaya gazeta,* August 13, 2001 (italics added).

77. Viktor Yaroshenko, *Yel'tsin: ya otvechu za vsë* (Yeltsin: I will answer for everything) (Moscow: Vokrug sveta, 1997), 131–32.

78. Stepankov and Lisov, *Kremlëvskii zagovor,* 121. The plotters' plans for Yeltsin's detention at Arkhangel'skoye-2 are described in ibid., 117–25, 156–57, 160–61, 165–66. In *Zapiski,* 97–98, Yeltsin recounts another telephone conversation with Kryuchkov, taken at Yeltsin's initiative from the Russian White House. And Vadim Bakatin, who headed the KGB in the fall of 1991, adds that there was dissension among the Alpha commanders over whether to arrest Yeltsin: *Izbavleniye ot KGB* (Deliverance from the KGB) (Moscow: Novosti, 1992), 20–21.

79. Stepankov and Lisov, *Kremlëvskii zagovor,* 123.

80. See Brian D. Taylor, *Politics and the Russian Army: Civil-Military Relations, 1689–2000* (Cambridge: Cambridge University Press, 2003), 241–42. Several Russian sources add that at the meeting at which Kryuchkov revealed Yeltsin's non-cooperation, Oleg Baklanov, the party overseer of the military-industrial complex and one of the GKChP octet, scribbled a note to himself saying, "Seize B. N. [Boris Nikolayevich]."

81. Yel'tsin, *Zapiski,* 68. As Yeltsin's grandchildren prepared to leave the dacha with Naina a little later, his daughters warned them to take to the floor of the car if firing broke out, at which point his ten-year-old grandson asked if they would be shot directly in the head. *Den' v sem'e prezidenta* (A day in the president's family), interviews of the Yeltsin family by El'dar Ryazanov on REN-TV, April 20, 1993 (videotape supplied by Irena Lesnevskaya).

82. Gennadii Burbulis, "Prezident ot prirody" (A president by nature), *Moskovskiye novosti,* January 27, 2006; and quotation from Mary Dejevsky, a British journalist who was on the spot, interview with the author (September 14, 2007).

83. The quotation and details of his decision are taken from my third Yeltsin interview. Khasbulatov has written (*Velikaya Rossiiskaya tragediya,* 1:163) that he and others persuaded Yeltsin to get up on the tank, but Yeltsin's account contradicts this. Viktor Yaroshenko, a Yeltsin adviser who was present, has said Yeltsin may have seen a young man lie down on the ground in front of another tank minutes before, and the man's bravery may have influenced him. Friends pulled the man from the path of Tank No. 112 with a split-second to spare. The scene and Yaroshenko's comments are captured in *Prezident vseya Rusi,* part 3.

84. The appeal and other major documents from August 1991 can be found at http://old.russ.ru/antolog/1991/putch11.htm.

85. Victoria E. Bonnell and Gregory Freidin, "*Televorot:* The Role of Television Coverage in Russia's August 1991 Coup," in Nancy Condee, ed., *Soviet Hieroglyph-*

ics: Visual Culture in Late Twentieth-Century Russia (Bloomington: Indiana University Press, 1995), 32.

86. That was the peak crowd at the White House. But there were about 200,000 pro-Yeltsin demonstrators on August 20 at Moscow city hall on Tverskaya Street, where the police and military presence was slighter, and significant demonstrations were mounted at many Russian and Soviet cities. See Harley Balzer, "Ordinary Russians? Rethinking August 1991," *Demokratizatsiya/Democratization* 13 (Spring 2005), 193–218.

87. When the unassuming Lobov addressed a rally in Sverdlovsk, the commander of the local military district threatened to lock him up. Lobov then warned that he would call a general strike. The standoff was averted by the collapse of the coup. Oleg Lobov, interview with the author (May 29, 2002).

88. Beschloss and Talbott, *At the Highest Levels*, 434; Yel'tsin, *Zapiski*, 172. Richard Nixon thought Bush's praise of Yeltsin grudging and that the putsch had shown that Bush had been "wrong all along" about the relative merits of Gorbachev and Yeltsin. Crowley, *Nixon in Winter*, 64.

89. John B. Dunlop, "The August 1991 Coup and Its Impact on Soviet Politics," *Journal of Cold War Studies* 5 (Winter 2003), 112–13. Bush's decision and the "bitter protests" of the National Security Agency were first reported in Seymour M. Hersh, "The Wild East," *Atlantic Monthly*, June 1994. Testified one U.S. official, "We told Yeltsin in real time what the communications were. . . . We monitor every major command, and we handed it to Yeltsin on a platter." The NSA's concern was about disclosure of American monitoring capabilities. President Bush decided, properly, that helping Yeltsin at a turning point was a more important stake.

90. "Throne out of bayonets" was an expression of the English theologian William R. Inge (1860–1954). I do not know how Yeltsin came across it.

91. The Yeltsin speech and the comments about the Kremlin are in Stepankov and Lisov, *Kremlëvskii zagovor*, 163–64, 179. In his interview with me (May 22, 2000), Shaposhnikov said he prepared a written order on shooting up the Kremlin and discussed implementation with local officers.

92. Yel'tsin, *Zapiski*, 114.

93. Quotation from Aleksandr Korzhakov, *Boris Yel'tsin: ot rassveta do zakata* (Boris Yeltsin: from dawn to dusk) (Moscow: Interbuk, 1997), 115–16. See also Robert V. Barylski, *The Soldier in Russian Politics: Duty, Dictatorship, and Democracy Under Gorbachev and Yeltsin* (New Brunswick: Transaction, 1998), 131–34. Yeltsin had known Bakatin, the former party boss of Kirov province, for some time and had considered him as a vice-presidential running mate. But he never met Shaposhnikov before demanding that Gorbachev appoint him—they had spoken by telephone only. Author's interviews with Bakatin (May 29, 2002) and Shaposhnikov.

94. Dejevsky interview.

95. I. Karpenko and G. Shipit'ko, "Kak prezident derzhal otvet pered rossiiskimi deputatami" (How the president answered the Russian deputies), *Izvestiya*, August 24, 1991.

96. Beschloss and Talbott, *At the Highest Levels*, 438.

97. See on this point Mark R. Beissinger, *Nationalist Mobilization and the Collapse of the Soviet State* (Cambridge: Cambridge University Press, 2002), 423–25.

98. As paraphrased by Gorbachev's chief negotiator, Shakhnazarov (*S vozhdyami i bez nikh*, 462).

99. Yurii Baturin, "Kak razvalili SSSR 15 let nazad" (How they pulled down the USSR fifteen years ago), *Moskovskiye novosti*, December 8, 2006; Baturin, "Pochemu 25 noyabrya 1991 goda tak i ne sostoyalos' parafirovaniye Soyuznogo dogovora" (Why the union treaty was not initialed on November 25, 1991), *Novaya gazeta*, December 12, 2006.

100. Bakatin, *Izbavleniye ot KGB*, 223, describes meeting with Yeltsin in early December to ask for cash to pay the KGB's bills until the end of the year.

101. Baturin et al., *Epokha*, 167. Gorbachev did not give up entirely on November 25. At the press conference, skipped by all of the republic leaders, he expressed the hope that a treaty would be signed on December 20.

102. Transcript in *V Politbyuro TsK KPSS*, 724–28.

103. Quoted in Roeder, *Where Nation-States Come From*, 185.

104. Kravchuk told Richard Nixon in 1993 "that Boris Yeltsin's drive for Russian sovereignty led him to believe for the first time that secession from the USSR was a credible option for Ukraine." Simes, *After the Collapse*, 55.

105. In an account published in 1994, Kravchuk claimed that he first thought of the meeting and sold Shushkevich on the idea. Shushkevich has consistently claimed authorship, and Yeltsin always agreed. See Loginov, *Soyuz mozhno bylo sokhranit'*, 432–45. A quirky line in Shushkevich's biography was that he taught Lee Harvey Oswald Russian in 1960–61 while chief engineer at a Minsk electronics plant.

106. Stanislav Shushkevich, interview with the author (April 17, 2000); Jan Maksymiuk, "Leaders Recall Dissolution of USSR," http://www.ukrweekly.com/Archive/2001/520104.shtml. Yegor Gaidar, *Dni porazhenii i pobed* (Days of defeats and victories) (Moscow: VAGRIUS, 1996), 149, says the source of the confusion was that Kozyrev put the draft under the wrong door.

107. Leonid Kravchuk, "Kogda Belovezhskiye soglasheniya byli podpisany, Yel'tsin pozvonil Bushu" (When the Belovezh'e accord was signed, Yeltsin phoned Bush), http://president.org.ur/news/news-140783.

108. Details from ibid.; Leonid Kravchuk, "Nekontroliruyemyi raspad SSSR privël by k millionam zhertv" (An uncontrolled dissolution of the USSR would have led to millions of casualties), http://news.bigmir.net/article/worldaboutukraine/724174; Bush and Scowcroft, *World Transformed*, 554–55; and Gorbachev, *Zhizn' i reformy*, 2:601.

109. Gorbachev, *Zhizn' i reformy*, 2:600.

110. James A. Baker, *The Politics of Diplomacy: Revolution, War, and Peace, 1989–1992* (New York: Putnam's, 1995), 569–70 (italics added); Strobe Talbott, "America Abroad," *Time*, October 26, 1992.

111. Andrei Grachëv, *Dal'she bez menya: ukhod prezidenta* (Go ahead without me: the exit of a president) (Moscow: Progress, 1994), 247–48; Shaposhnikov inter-

view. There were reports after the August coup that Gorbachev was consulting Yeltsin on control of the nuclear force. Dunlop, *Rise of Russia*, 269.

112. Aleksandr Yakovlev, second interview with the author (March 29, 2004); Shakhnazarov, Popov, and Shaposhnikov interviews; and Loginov, *Soyuz mozhno bylo sokhranit'*, 473 (concerning Shevardnadze). In a memoir, Popov says Yeltsin could have combined the Russian and the Soviet presidencies, and regrets he did not try to convince Yeltsin to do so. Gavriil Popov, *Snova v oppozitsii* (In opposition again) (Moscow: Galaktika, 1994), 260, 269.

113. Second Yeltsin interview; interview with Ruslan Khasbulatov (September 26, 2001). Yeltsin writes in *Zapiski*, 154–55, that he had a mental aversion to replacing Gorbachev: "This path was barred for me. Psychologically, I could not take Gorbachev's place." Gorbachev observed to Shevardnadze on December 10 that if Yeltsin had been willing to take over in August, the decision could have been imposed on him. Loginov, *Soyuz mozhno bylo sokhranit'*, 473.

114. Yevgenii Shaposhnikov, *Vybor* (Choice), 2nd ed. (Moscow: PIK, 1995), 138 (quotation); Shaposhnikov interview.

115. Hough's thesis in *Democratization and Revolution*, 465, is that it was all about power: "Yeltsin's temptation to get rid of Gorbachev by abolishing his job must have been irresistible." This ignores the fact that the disappearance of the Soviet Union downsized Gorbachev's "job." Gorbachev, in his memoirs, portrays Yeltsin at the time as greedy for power and two-faced, but also under the influence of dogmatically anti-USSR advisers such as Gennadii Burbulis.

116. This could not have been the only condition for Yeltsin, since he had accepted treaty drafts that would not have been signed by all the republics. He seemed to assume that Russia's cornucopia of resources, to be sold to nonsignatories at world market prices, would induce them to cooperate. Stewart ("SIC TRANSIT," 322) calls this "the cash and carry solution."

117. These categories were introduced by Roman Szporluk in "Dilemmas of Russian Nationalism," *Problems of Communism* 38 (July–August 1989), 16–23. John Dunlop (*Rise of Russia*, 266–67) says Yeltsin acted like a "velvet imperialist" in the fall of 1991, but I do not find this a helpful label. Yeltsin's vision was centered on the core Russian state, although he hoped it would retain influence in the former Soviet republics.

118. Chernyayev, *1991 god*, 259–60.

119. Boris Yel'tsin, *Prezidentskii marafon* (Presidential marathon) (Moscow: AST, 2000), 31.

120. This phrase comes from Beissinger, *Nationalist Mobilization and the Collapse of the Soviet State*.

Chapter Nine

1. CIA, Director of Central Intelligence, "The Deepening Crisis in the USSR: Prospects for the Next Year," NIE 11-18-90 (November 1990), 15–18; declassified version obtained at http://www.foia.cia.gov.browse_docs.asp?

2. Ibid., 17–18. The 1990 NIE assumed, as almost all forecasts did, that the Soviet state in some form would have to survive for light at the end of the tunnel to be feasible. It did warn that economic difficulties "would make unilateral steps by the republics to assert their economic independence more likely." But, of course, by the end of 1991 events had far outrun this possibility.

3. Vyacheslav Terekhov, interview with the author (June 5, 2001).

4. "Yeltsin Criticizes 'Half-Hearted' Reforms," FBIS-SOV-90-049 (March 13, 1990), 74.

5. Boris Yel'tsin, *Zapiski prezidenta* (Notes of a president) (Moscow: Ogonëk, 1994), 163. In his June 1991 visit to Washington, Yeltsin told President Bush there was no way a military or police coup against Gorbachev would succeed or be attempted. George Bush and Brent Scowcroft, *A World Transformed* (New York: Knopf, 1998), 505.

6. Yel'tsin, *Zapiski*, 33.

7. Pavel Voshchanov, interview with the author (June 15, 2000). Voshchanov was present at the celebration.

8. Yel'tsin, *Zapiski*, 34.

9. Oleg Poptsov, *Khronika vremën "Tsarya Borisa"* (Chronicle of the times of "Tsar Boris") (Moscow: Sovershenno sekretno, 1995), 75.

10. Yu, M. Baturin et al., *Epokha Yel'tsina: ocherki politicheskoi istorii* (The Yeltsin epoch: essays in political history) (Moscow: VAGRIUS, 2001), 148. I will cite this source often in the coming chapters. The coauthors are four former presidential assistants (Yurii Baturin, Mikhail Krasnov, Aleksandr Livshits, and Georgii Satarov), four former speech writers (Aleksandr Il'in, Vladimir Kadatskii, Konstantin Nikiforov, and Lyudmila Pikhoya), and a former press secretary (Vyacheslav Kostikov). I also interviewed six of the coauthors (Baturin, Kostikov, Krasnov, Livshits, Pikhoya, and Satarov).

11. The renaming occurred when the Russian Supreme Soviet was debating ratification of an agreement among CIS members concerning the nuclear arsenal. A deputy noted that Yeltsin had signed as president of "the Russian Federation," and not of the RSFSR. Chairman Ruslan Khasbulatov moved that the name be changed (with "Russia" as an alternative), and the motion passed unanimously.

12. "Minnoye pole vlasti" (The minefield of power), *Izvestiya*, October 28, 1991.

13. Valentina Lantseva, interview with the author (July 9, 2001).

14. Aleksandr Tsipko, "Drama rossiiskogo vybora" (The drama of Russia's choice), *Izvestiya*, October 1, 1991.

15. Details in Marc Zlotnik, "Yeltsin and Gorbachev: The Politics of Confrontation," *Journal of Cold War Studies* 5 (Winter 2003), 159–60. Gorbachev has bitterly reported that the day Yeltsin took over in the Kremlin, December 27, was three days ahead of the agreed-upon date, and that he held uncomely festivities there that morning with Gennadii Burbulis and Ruslan Khasbulatov. Mikhail Gorbachev, *Zhizn' i reformy* (Life and reforms), 2 vols. (Moscow: Novosti, 1995), 2:622.

16. Years later, in January 2000, Vitalii Tret'yakov, as editor of the elite newspaper *Nezavisimaya gazeta,* put out a piece about Yeltsin called "Sverdlovsk Upstart." He had been working on a book on Yeltsin's career which was never published (some draft chapters were serialized in 2006 and have been cited in this book). Gorbachev rang him up with congratulations on the title. Tret'yakov, interview with the author (June 7, 2000).

17. Robert S. Strauss, interview with the author (January 9, 2006).

18. Baturin et al., *Epokha,* 226. Yeltsin described Gorbachev as having made a promise about nonparticipation, in "Boris Yel'tsin: ya ne skryvayu trudnostei i khochu, chtoby narod eto ponimal" (Boris Yeltsin: I do not conceal the difficulties and want the people to understand that), *Komsomol'skaya pravda,* May 27, 1992.

19. It was Yeltsin who had the ban eased to allow Gorbachev to fly to Berlin for the funeral of Willy Brandt, the former German chancellor. He phoned the court chairman, Valerii Zor'kin, to press the case. Jane Henderson, "The Russian Constitutional Court and the Communist Party Case: Watershed or Whitewash?" *Communist and Post-Communist Studies* 40 (March 2007), 7.

20. Yeltsin actually took the initiative to repair relations with Yegor Ligachëv. He had a staffer telephone Ligachëv in 1994 or 1995 and offer to enlarge his pension. Ligachëv hotly refused. Oksana Khimich, "Otchim perestroiki" (Stepfather of perestroika), *Moskovskii komsomolets,* April 22, 2005.

21. Aleksandr Rutskoi, interview with the author (June 5, 2001).

22. Voshchanov interview.

23. Alexei Kazannik, "Boris Yeltsin: From Triumph to Fall," *Moscow News,* June 2, 2004. Cinema director El'dar Ryazanov filmed an interview with Yeltsin and his wife and daughters in the apartment in April 1993. Yeltsin stayed clear of the kitchen stool because it had a nail protruding from the seat; it was one of a set given him by friends in Sverdlovsk on his fortieth birthday in 1971. *Den' v sem'e prezidenta* (A day in the president's family), interviews by Ryazanov on REN-TV, April 20, 1993 (videotape supplied by Irena Lesnevskaya).

24. Tat'yana D'yachenko, "Papa khotel otprazdnovat' yubilei po-domashnemu" (Papa wanted to celebrate his birthday home-style), *Komsomol'skaya pravda,* February 1, 2001.

25. Zavidovo staff reported that Yeltsin's retinue occupied it "in the spirit of conquerors." He first inspected it with Yurii Petrov and Korzhakov in November of 1991. Yurii Tret'yakov, "'Tsarskaya' okhota" (The tsar's hunt), *Trud,* November 20, 2003. Such a perception was inevitable, given the magnitude of the change. The provincial locales all had public park land and commercial facilities as well as a secured compound for the president and other officials. Volzhskii Utës is primarily a healthcare facility. Facilities for the Soviet leadership outside Russia, notably Foros in Ukraine and Pitsunda in Georgia, were, of course, not available to Yeltsin.

26. Boris Yeltsin, third interview with the author (September 12, 2002).

27. Yel'tsin, *Zapiski,* 35.

28. Boris Yel'tsin, *Prezidentskii marafon* (Presidential marathon) (Moscow: AST, 2000), 335. He switched back to a ZIL briefly in 1997, during a campaign against use of expensive foreign vehicles, then went back to the Mercedes. The Ilyushin-62 was replaced in 1996 by a larger Ilyushin-96.

29. Yurii Burtin, "Gorbachev prodolzhayetsya" (Gorbachev is continuing), in Burtin and Eduard Molchanov, eds., *God posle avgusta: gorech' i vybor* (A year after August: bitterness and choice) (Moscow: Literatura i politika, 1992), 61.

30. *Muzhskoi razgovor* (Male conversation), interview of Yeltsin by El'dar Ryazanov on REN-TV, November 7, 1993 (videotape supplied by Irena Lesnevskaya).

31. In some of Yeltsin's comments on the issue, there were intimations of patriotic pride and also of the right to live well, just as his countrymen were all entitled to live now. A campaign pamphlet in 1996 said of his transportation: "The president of Russia, like the president of any other country and like millions of other Russian citizens, does not go to work on a trolley bus." "Special privileges," it said, were an impossibility in post-communist society, in that luxuries were no longer distributed through secret channels and citizens with means could purchase them on the open market: "Ministers travel in Mercedes, yet anyone who is capable of earning enough money can buy a Mercedes. . . . In any department store, you can buy the same suit as [Prime Minister Viktor] Chernomyrdin and the same cap as [Moscow Mayor Yurii] Luzhkov." *Prezident Yel'tsin: 100 voprosov i otvetov* (President Yeltsin: 100 questions and answers) (Moscow: Obshcherossiiskoye dvizheniye obshchestvennoi podderzhki B. N. Yel'tsina, 1996), 18.

32. Vadim Bakatin, the last head of the Soviet KGB, and Yevgenii Shaposhnikov, the last Soviet minister of defense, both appointed with Yeltsin's backing in August, believed Yeltsin wanted more security coordination than obtained but was unable to sell it to the other states. Vadim Bakatin, *Izbavleniye ot KGB* (Deliverance from the KGB) (Moscow: Novosti, 1992), 232–33; author's interviews with Bakatin (May 29, 2002) and Shaposhnikov (May 23, 2000). See also Robert V. Barylski, *The Soldier in Russian Politics: Duty, Dictatorship, and Democracy Under Gorbachev and Yeltsin* (New Brunswick: Transaction, 1998), 173–225.

33. "Yeltsin News Conference with Foreign Journalists," FBIS-SOV-91-174 (September 9, 1991), 66, 69.

34. Author's interviews with Valerii Bortsov (June 11, 2001) and Ivan Rybkin (May 29, 2001); second interview with Sergei Filatov (May 25, 2002); second interview with Aleksandr Yakovlev (March 29, 2004); third Yeltsin interview.

35. Author's first interview with Grigorii Yavlinskii (March 17, 2001). Yeltsin tried but failed to persuade Yavlinskii to tailor the program to Russia and not the USSR, reduce its running time to 400 days (its original length), and omit mention of price hikes. Yavlinskii feels that Yeltsin was fixated on his struggle with Gorbachev and had no intention of doing any serious reform until after his election as president of Russia.

36. Baturin et al., *Epokha,* 190.

37. Bill Keller, "Boris Yeltsin Taking Power," *New York Times,* September 23, 1990.

38. Gwendolyn Elizabeth Stewart, "SIC TRANSIT: Democratization, *Suvereniza-tsiia*, and Boris Yeltsin in the Breakup of the Soviet Union" (Ph.D. diss., Harvard University, 1995), 280. Stewart, working as a photojournalist, taped Yeltsin's remarks on August 24, 1990, in Dolinsk. She calls them "laissez-faire populism." Her illustrated account of Yeltsin on Sakhalin is available at http://www.people.fas.harvard.edu/~gestewar/peopleschoice.html.

39. "B. N. Yel'tsin otvechayet na voprosy 'Izvestii'" (B. N. Yeltsin answers the questions of *Izvestiya*), *Izvestiya*, May 23, 1991.

40. Anatolii Chernyayev, *1991 god: dnevnik pomoshchnika Prezidenta SSSR* (The year 1991: diary of an assistant to the president of the USSR) (Moscow: TERRA, 1997), 260.

41. Yel'tsin, *Zapiski*, 235. As several scholars have pointed out, this sentence is not in the English translation of the memoir.

42. Jonathan Sanders, interview with the author (January 21, 2004).

43. Isaiah Berlin, *Four Essays on Liberty* (Oxford: Oxford University Press, 1969). Berlin thought negative freedom to be superior to positive liberty. Cf. for a different perspective Amartya Sen, *Development as Freedom* (New York: Random House, 1999).

44. Mikhail Fridman, interview with the author (September 21, 2001). His reference is to Milton Friedman, *Capitalism and Freedom* (Chicago: University of Chicago Press, 1962).

45. Yel'tsin, *Zapiski*, 121, 235–36, 238, 392. See Dmitry Mikheyev, *Russia Transformed* (Indianapolis: Hudson Institute, 1996), 70–71, 89; and George W. Breslauer, *Gorbachev and Yeltsin as Leaders* (Cambridge: Cambridge University Press, 2002), 153–54. This therapeutic aspect has sometimes been confused with Social Darwinism, which stresses survival of the fittest and abandonment of the weak. At the societal level, Yeltsin was interested in Russia converging with the West, not competing with it.

46. "Boris Yel'tsin otbyl na otdykh" (Boris Yeltsin has left for a rest), *Izvestiya*, September 25, 1991.

47. Viktor Sheinis, interview with the author (September 20, 2001); V. T. Loginov, ed., *Soyuz mozhno bylo sokhranit'* (The union could have been saved), rev. ed. (Moscow: AST, 2007), 325.

48. Gennadii Burbulis, second interview, conducted by Yevgeniya Al'bats (February 14, 2001). Yeltsin's invitation to Burbulis has never been on the public record.

49. Rutskoi interview; and Mikhail Poltoranin, interview with the author (July 11, 2001).

50. Yurii Petrov, second interview with the author (February 1, 2002). Petrov had looked Yeltsin up while on leave in Moscow at the end of July and told him he was willing to work in his new government. Yeltsin showed him a staff report on organization of the U.S. White House and offered him the job.

51. G. Shipit'ko, "B. Yel'tsin pytayetsya vosstanovit' poryadok v koridorakh vlasti" (Boris Yeltsin tries to restore order in the corridors of power), *Izvestiya*, October 16, 1991. Deputy Premier Igor Gavrilov resigned on October 7 and Economics Minister

Yevgenii Saburov on October 9. The acting chairman of the Supreme Soviet, Ruslan Khasbulatov, accused several ministers and advisers of incompetence and demanded their resignations, whereupon one of them, Sergei Shakhrai, stated that Khasbulatov was mentally unstable. Silayev was taken care of after December: Yeltsin appointed him Russian ambassador to the European Community in Brussels.

52. The "miracle worker" reference comes from Gennadii Burbulis, third interview, conducted by Yevgeniya Al'bats (August 31, 2001). Other information is from Poltoranin interview; interview with Ryzhov (September 21, 2001); and second interview with Yavlinskii (September 28, 2001). Poltoranin came closest to acceptance and wrote up a list of possible ministers, but withdrew because he felt he did not know enough about the economy.

53. Third Burbulis interview.

54. Gaidar's mother was from Sverdlovsk and was the daughter of Pavel Bazhov, a distinguished writer of fairytales set in the Urals. She became friendly with Yeltsin's mother when they were patients at a Moscow hospital. Yegor Gaidar, second interview with the author (January 31, 2002).

55. My reconstruction of the enlistment of Gaidar relies on accounts by him, Yeltsin, and Burbulis. Or see Yel'tsin, *Zapiski*, 163–64: "Why did I choose Yegor Gaidar? . . . Gaidar's theories coincided with my private determination to travel the most painful part of the route [of economic reform] quickly. . . . If our minds were made up, it was time to get going!" For an alternative explanation based on envy and power-seeking, for which no evidence is cited, see Peter Reddaway and Dmitri Glinski, *The Tragedy of Russia's Reforms: Market Bolshevism against Democracy* (Washington, D.C.: U.S. Institute of Peace, 2001), 240–41: "Gaidar's appointment served Burbulis's purpose, because it ensured that Yeltsin would not appoint someone who was either more popular than Burbulis . . . or more influential with Yeltsin . . . thus endangering Burbulis's position at court. One of Yeltsin's reasons for picking Gaidar for the job of 'leading reformer' was that his bland and aloof manner in public made him an unlikely future contender for elective office, even if his reform package were to turn out to be successful and popular."

56. Yegor Gaidar, *Dni porazhenii i pobed* (Days of defeats and victories) (Moscow: VAGRIUS, 1996), 105.

57. Moscow journalist Mikhail Berger, quoted in David E. Hoffman, *The Oligarchs: Wealth and Power in the New Russia* (New York: PublicAffairs, 2002), 180.

58. "Obrashcheniye Prezidenta Rossii k narodam Rossii, k s"ezdu narodnykh deputatov Rossiiskoi Federatsii" (Address of the president of Russia to the peoples of Russia and the Congress of People's Deputies of the Russian Federation), *Rossiiskaya gazeta*, October 29, 1991.

59. On November 3 and 4, Yeltsin remained in contact with Yavlinskii about the possibility of him taking the job. Gaidar says when he heard of it he felt "as if he had just jumped out from under the wheels of an onrushing train." Yavlinskii broke off the negotiations and Gaidar was given the position. Gaidar, *Dni porazhenii i pobed*, 110.

60. Lyudmila Telen', "Izbiratel' Boris Yel'tsin" (Voter Boris Yeltsin), *Moskovskiye novosti*, October 21, 2003. This revealing interview is translated as "Boris Yeltsin: The Wrecking Ball," in Padma Desai, ed., *Conversations on Russia: Reform from Yeltsin to Putin* (Oxford: Oxford University Press, 2006), 79–94. Burbulis, born in 1945, was senior in the new group. Gaidar was born in 1956, Anatolii Chubais (the minister for privatization) in 1955, and Aleksandr Shokhin (labor minister and deputy premier) in 1957. As early as the summer of 1990, Yeltsin had promoted several men in their thirties into high economic posts in the RSFSR—Grigorii Yavlinskii (deputy premier), who was born in 1952, and Boris Fëdorov (finance minister), born in 1958.

61. See Chernyayev, *1991 god*, 265; Carlotta Gall and Thomas de Waal, *Chechnya: Calamity in the Caucasus* (New York: New York University Press, 1998), 99–102; and Sergei Filatov, *Sovershenno nesekretno* (Top nonsecret) (Moscow: VAGRIUS, 2000), 80. Ruslan Khasbulatov writes that Yeltsin was more upset at Gorbachev than at his Supreme Soviet: *Chechnya: mne ne dali ostanovit' voinu* (Chechnya: they did not allow me to halt the war) (Moscow: Paleya, 1995), 20–21.

62. The expression is associated with the views of the economist Jeffrey Sachs. Shock therapy in the narrow sense was first applied in Bolivia in 1985 and, in Eastern Europe, in Poland in 1990. Sachs, then at Harvard University and now at Columbia, modeled his approach on Ludwig Erhard, the architect of West Germany's postwar recovery.

63. Yel'tsin, *Marafon*, 102. The passage on potato planting is mistranslated in the English version of the memoir as "just as potatoes were introduced under Catherine the Great." Peter is thought to have brought potatoes back from Holland around 1700 and to have encouraged their cultivation in the greenhouses at his Strelna Palace, outside St. Petersburg.

64. *Muzhskoi razgovor.* Some leading Russian historians, now free to chastise the past, debunked Peter in the 1990s as a clumsy autocrat, at the same time Yeltsin thought he was imitating him. Ernest A. Zitser, "Post-Soviet Peter: New Histories of the Late Muscovite and Early Imperial Russian Court," *Kritika* 6 (Spring 2003), 375–92.

65. Yel'tsin, *Zapiski*, 235. For roughly the first year after the 1991 coup, Yeltsin often referred to a communist return to power as a real and present danger. In May 1992, for example, he spoke in favor of quick changes to the Russian constitution. "Otherwise those forces that are grouping together right now, the former party apparatus, will develop to the point that it would be very difficult to struggle with them." "Boris Yel'tsin: ya ne skryvayu trudnostei."

66. Burtin, "Gorbachev prodolzhayetsya," 60.

67. Ibid.

68. Yurii Afanas'ev, "Proshël god . . . " (A year has passed), in Burtin and Molchanov, *God posle avgusta*, 9.

69. Telen', "Izbiratel' Boris Yel'tsin."

70. Gaidar, *Dni porazhenii i pobed*, 105.

71. Baturin et al., *Epokha,* 177. Yeltsin said in the speech that the price reform would take place before the end of December. Gaidar and his team had pushed him not to give a definite date.

72. "Yeltsin Discusses Candidacy, Issues, Rivals," FBIS-SOV-91-110 (June 7, 1991), 64–65. During the campaign Yeltsin also made crowd-pleasing promises that were sure to complicate any move to the market, such as indexing minimum wages, pensions, and student stipends at 150 percent of the USSR average. These benefits, he assured voters, would be funded by withholding financial transfers to the Soviet government. In June 1990 he stated that he was working with three alternative schemes for price reform, all of which "foresee a mechanism that will rule out a lowering of living standards." L. N. Dobrokhotov, ed., *Gorbachev–Yel'tsin: 1,500 dnei politicheskogo protivostoyaniya* (Gorbachev–Yeltsin: 1,500 days of political conflict) (Moscow: TERRA, 1992), 205.

73. "Obrashcheniye Prezidenta Rossii."

74. Gaidar, first interview with the author (September 14, 2000). Yeltsin said in his October speech that he had promised improvement by late 1992 in his presidential election campaign; I have not found any such statement. Gaidar writes in his memoir that, beginning with Five Hundred Days, the time limits in various reform plans were useful mostly as hooks for getting Yeltsin and the politicians to sign on to radical reform. "By itself, the realism or unrealism of a program had no significance from an economic point of view. But even a false idea, once taken aboard by the masses, becomes a material force." Gaidar, *Dni porazhenii i pobed,* 65. Yeltsin had to deal with that force before and after Gaidar's exit.

75. Nine percent of Russian workers polled by sociologists in 1993 had not received the previous month's wage in full. This proportion reached 49 percent in 1994 and 66 percent at the beginning of 1996. Eighteen percent of employees in 1994, and 32 percent in 1996, received *no* wages in the previous month. Hartmut Lehmann and Jonathan Wadsworth, "Wage Arrears and the Distribution of Earnings in Russia," William Davidson Institute, University of Michigan, Working Paper 421 (December 2001).

76. Leon Aron, *Yeltsin: A Revolutionary Life* (New York: St. Martin's, 2000), the most adulatory of the Western studies, is no exception. Some of the most positive reviews of Yeltsin's policies have been made by liberal economists. See especially Anders Åslund, *How Russia Became a Market Economy* (Washington, D.C.: Brookings, 1995), and *Building Capitalism: The Transformation of the Former Soviet Bloc* (Cambridge: Cambridge University Press, 2002); and Andrei Shleifer, *A Normal Country: Russia after Communism* (Cambridge, Mass.: Harvard University Press, 2005). Cf. for diametrically opposed analyses Stefan Hedlund, *Russia's "Market" Economy: A Bad Case of Predatory Capitalism* (London: UCL, 1999); Jerry F. Hough, *The Logic of Economic Reform in Russia* (Washington, D.C.: Brookings, 2001); Marshall I. Goldman, *The Piratization of Russia: Russian Reform Goes Awry* (London: Routledge, 2003); and David Satter, *Darkness at Dawn: The Rise of the Russian Criminal State* (New Haven: Yale University Press, 2003).

77. Stephen F. Cohen, *Failed Crusade: America and the Tragedy of Post-Communist Russia* (New York: Norton, 2000), 41, 49, 58. See also Cohen's "Russian Studies Without Russia," *Post-Soviet Affairs* 15 (January–March 1999), 37–55.

78. Reddaway and Glinski, *Tragedy of Russia's Reforms*, 306, 629, 627. Less frequently, and not any more helpfully, Yeltsin has been gibbeted for the opposite vice, of infinite flexibility and unprincipledness. "Like many successful politicians," writes Michael Specter, a Moscow bureau chief of the *New York Times* in the 1990s, "he is a human mood ring, a man whose ideology changes with the seasons, with the country he is visiting, with the phases of the moon. Such tactics work in Russia, which has never really decided whether it belongs in Europe or Asia." Michael Specter, "My Boris," *New York Times Magazine*, July 26, 1998. Another analyst, who met Yeltsin several times in the company of Richard Nixon, writes of him as self-obsessed and "devoid of any meaningful purpose beyond his own political fortunes." Dmitri K. Simes, *After the Collapse: Russia Seeks Its Place as a Great Power* (New York: Simon and Schuster, 1999), 137.

79. Main indicators are conveniently summarized in Åslund, *Building Capitalism*; Shleifer, *Normal Country*; and Peter T. Leeson and William N. Trumbull, "Comparing Apples: Normalcy, Russia, and the Remaining Post-Socialist World," *Post-Soviet Affairs* 22 (July–September 2006), 225–48.

80. The military-industrial complex, currency question, and oil pricing were largely out of Moscow's hands. Not so the London Club (commercial) and Paris Club (sovereign) debts of the Soviet Union. Moscow assumed these $100 billion worth of obligations in exchange for Russia having the agreed-upon status of legal heir to the USSR. It was forced to restructure the sovereign debt twice in the Yeltsin years, in 1996 and 1999, and retired it in 2006.

81. This point is well made in M. Steven Fish, "Russian Studies Without Studying," *Post-Soviet Affairs* 17 (October–December 2001), 332–74, which is a reply to Cohen's "Russian Studies Without Russia." See more generally Steven L. Solnick, *Stealing the State: Control and Collapse in Soviet Institutions* (Cambridge, Mass.: Harvard University Press, 1998).

82. As argued in William Tompson, "Was Gaidar Really Necessary? Russian 'Shock Therapy' Reconsidered," *Problems of Post-Communism* 49 (July–August 2002), 1–10.

83. Andrei Grachëv, *Dal'she bez menya: ukhod prezidenta* (Go ahead without me: the exit of a president) (Moscow: Progress, 1994), 82.

84. Gorbachev arrived in Beijing for a state visit on May 15, 1989, just as the Tienanmen student protest began. The demonstrators were admirers of his and timed their action to coincide with his arrival, so as to deter the police from reprisal. They displayed banners praising Gorbachev, which he would have seen from his motorcade that day. The government declared martial law on May 20, after his departure, and cracked down on the protesters on June 3–4.

85. An excellent treatment of these variables is Kelly M. McMann, *Economic Autonomy and Democracy: Hybrid Regimes in Russia and Kyrgyzstan* (Cambridge: Cambridge University Press, 2006).

86. Yel'tsin, *Zapiski,* 265 (italics added).

87. See on this general point Stephen Hanson, "The Dilemmas of Russia's Anti-Revolutionary Revolution," *Current History* 100 (October 2001), 330–35; and Martin Malia in Desai, *Conversations on Russia,* 344–46.

88. Viktor Sheinis, *Vzlët i padeniye parlamenta: perelomnyye gody v rossiiskoi politike, 1985–1993* (The rise and fall of parliament: years of change in Russian politics, 1985–93) (Moscow: Moskovskii Tsentr Karnegi, Fond INDEM, 2005), 670.

89. "While many complain about 'shock therapy' in Russia, the sad truth is that too little shock was delivered to achieve any therapy, and the actual reforms were far less radical than those in Central Europe." Åslund, *Building Capitalism,* xiii. This is an economist's assessment. A political scientist comes to the same point. Since it scores in about the fortieth percentile among post-communist countries on indices of economic freedom, "gradualism, rather than shock therapy, best characterizes economic policy in post-Soviet Russia." M. Steven Fish, *Democracy Derailed in Russia: The Failure of Open Politics* (Cambridge: Cambridge University Press, 2005), 159–60.

90. Reddaway and Glinski, *Tragedy of Russia's Reforms,* 236.

91. Oleg Poptsov, *Trevozhnyye sny tsarskoi svity* (The uneasy dreams of the tsar's retinue) (Moscow: Sovershenno sekretno, 2000), 311.

Chapter Ten

1. Valerie Bunce and Maria Csanádi, "Uncertainty in the Transition: Post-Communism in Hungary," *East European Politics and Society* 7 (Spring 1993), 269.

2. Irvine Schiffer, *Charisma: A Psychoanalytic Look at Mass Society* (Toronto: University of Toronto Press, 1973), 11. See also Reinhard Bendix, *Max Weber: An Intellectual Portrait* (Garden City: Doubleday, 1962), 300, and the reference to emergencies "associated with a collective excitement through which masses of people respond to some extraordinary experience and by virtue of which they surrender themselves to a heroic leader."

3. Leszek Balcerowicz, "Understanding Postcommunist Transitions," in Larry Diamond and Marc F. Plattner, eds., *Economic Reform and Democracy* (Baltimore: Johns Hopkins University Press, 1995), 96. Balcerowicz, who coined the term "extraordinary politics," was the author of economic shock therapy in post-communist Poland from 1989 to 1991.

4. Yegor Gaidar, *Dni porazhenii i pobed* (Days of defeats and victories) (Moscow: VAGRIUS, 1996), 170.

5. Bunce and Csanádi, "Uncertainty in the Transition," 270 (italics added). It is for this reason that another specialist predicts that, although charismatic leaders may well crop up in post-communist countries, they "will be of real, but limited, consequence—that is, they can affect the distribution of power in a larger or smaller area, but are unable to act as the catalyst for a new way of life." Kenneth Jowitt, *New World Disorder: The Leninist Extinction* (Berkeley: University of California Press, 1992), 266.

6. Yu, A. Levada et al., *Obshchestvennoye mneniye—1999* (Public opinion—1999 edition) (Moscow: Vserossiiskii tsentr izucheniya obshchestvennogo mneniya, 2000), 100–101.

7. Ibid. Another series of polls, using a more simply worded question, traces the decline in Yeltsin's popularity in starker terms. Eighty-seven percent of Russians "fully supported" him in September 1991 and 4 percent said they did not support him. That ratio had dropped to 69 percent to 5 percent in November 1991 and to 43 percent to 19 percent in January 1992; it was 28 percent to 24 percent in March 1992, and 24 percent to 31 percent in July 1992. Leonty Byzov, "Power and Society in Post-Coup Russia: Attempts at Coexistence," *Demokratizatsiya/Democratization* 1 (Spring 1993), 87.

8. Gaidar, *Dni porazhenii i pobed,* 168.

9. Boris Yel'tsin, *Zapiski prezidenta* (Notes of a president) (Moscow: Ogonëk, 1994), 256.

10. Gaidar, *Dni porazhenii i pobed,* 176.

11. Yel'tsin, *Zapiski,* 258.

12. Ibid., 256.

13. Gaidar, *Dni porazhenii i pobed,* 190–91; author's second interview with Yegor Gaidar (January 31, 2002). Yeltsin told Gaidar after the meeting that he had tried unsuccessfully to reach him by phone to tell him of the removal of Lopukhin. Gaidar did not believe it.

14. Yeltsin left Gaidar to sign off on the Gerashchenko appointment on his behalf. Gaidar later called it the worst mistake he made in 1992 and said it would have been much better to go with Gerashchenko's predecessor, Georgii Matyukhin. Yeltsin also told associates he almost immediately regretted the appointment. Gaidar, *Dni porazhenii i pobed,* 195; Yu, M. Baturin et al., *Epokha Yel'tsina: ocherki politicheskoi istorii* (The Yeltsin epoch: essays in political history) (Moscow: VAGRIUS, 2001), 235.

15. Baturin et al., *Epokha,* 251.

16. Vyacheslav Terekhov, interview with the author (June 5, 2001).

17. The greatest controversy was over the exclusion of Khizha, with whom Yeltsin did not want to work closely. One deputy protested that there had been a "gentlemen's agreement" to put him on the final list, but Yeltsin denied it. Interviewed in the lobby after the action, he said,"My opinion had to be taken into account, too." Vladimir Todres, "S"ezd" (The congress), *Nezavisimaya gazeta,* December 15, 1992; Nikolai Andreyev and Sergei Chugayev, "U Gaidara—golosa iskrennikh storonnikov, u Chernomyrdina—doveriye s"ezda" (Gaidar got the votes of sincere supporters and Chernomyrdin got the trust of the congress), *Izvestiya,* December 15, 1992. Khizha left the government in May 1993.

18. Chernomyrdin was deputy minister of the oil and gas industry from 1982 to 1985, answering for the west Siberian fields. His responsibilities included the pipelines being built through Sverdlovsk oblast. He lived at the time, he told me, in the city of Tyumen, the capital of the province bordering Sverdlovsk on the east. He was appointed minister in February 1985 and saw much of Yeltsin when Yeltsin was department head and secretary in the Central Committee apparatus, touring the

Siberian fields with him and Gorbachev in September 1985. Chernomyrdin, as a member of the CPSU Central Committee, attended the October 1987 plenum, where he walked up to Yeltsin and shook his hand at the intermission. Chernomyrdin, interview with the author (September 15, 2000).

19. Yel'tsin, *Zapiski*, 326.

20. "Viktor Stepanovich . . . almost openly sympathized with Gazprom, which he had created practically with his own hands." Boris Yel'tsin, *Prezidentskii marafon* (Presidential marathon) (Moscow: AST, 2000),120.

21. See on this point Daniel S. Treisman, "Fighting Inflation in a Transitional Regime: Russia's Anomalous Stabilization," *World Politics* 50 (January 1998), 250–52.

22. Gaidar, *Dni porazhenii i pobed*, 183.

23. Yel'tsin, *Zapiski*, 256, 258. Not all managers in the petroleum industry favored price controls. As Gaidar describes, quite a few wanted the restrictions to be lifted.

24. Author's interviews with Lev Ponomarëv and Gleb Yakunin (both on January 21, 2001). See also Valerii Vyzhutovich, "My podderzhivayem Yel'tsina uslovno" (We support Yeltsin conditionally), *Izvestiya*, October 7, 1991.

25. Yurii Burtin, "Gorbachev prodolzhayetsya" (Gorbachev is continuing), in Burtin and Eduard Molchanov, eds., *God posle avgusta: gorech' i vybor* (A year after August: bitterness and choice) (Moscow: Literatura i politika, 1992), 60. See for details Viktor Sheinis, *Vzlët i padeniye parlamenta: perelomnyye gody v rossiiskoi politike, 1985–1993* (The rise and fall of parliament: years of change in Russian politics, 1985–93) (Moscow: Moskovskii Tsentr Karnegi, Fond INDEM, 2005), 677–87.

26. Yel'tsin, *Zapiski*, 245.

27. Gennadii Burbulis, second interview, conducted by Yevgeniya Al'bats (February 14, 2001).

28. Baturin et al., *Epokha*, 202.

29. Chernomyrdin interview.

30. Anders Åslund, *How Russia Became a Market Economy* (Washington, D.C.: Brookings, 1995), 198.

31. Boris Fëdorov, interview with the author (September 22, 2001). In September 1993 Yeltsin wanted to have Fëdorov replace Gerashchenko in the central bank, but canned the idea due to Chernomyrdin's strong opposition.

32. Baturin et al., *Epokha*, 256. On fiscal and monetary policy after Fëdorov, see Åslund, *How Russia Became a Market Economy*, 200–203; and Treisman, "Fighting Inflation in a Transitional Regime," 235–65.

33. "Obrashcheniye prezidenta k sograzhdanam" (Address of the president to his fellow citizens), *Rossiiskaya gazeta*, August 20, 1992.

34. In his first book of memoirs, in 1990, he did refer to perestroika as "a revolution from above," but mostly to convey that it did not engage the populace and was resisted by established interests. Boris Yel'tsin, *Ispoved' na zadannuyu temu* (Confession on an assigned theme) (Moscow: PIK, 1990), 103.

35. "B. N. Yel'tsin otvechayet na voprosy 'Izvestii'" (B. N. Yeltsin answers the questions of *Izvestiya*), *Izvestiya*, May 23, 1991.

36. See Yel'tsin, *Marafon*, 236–37.

37. "Obrashcheniye prezidenta k sograzhdanam." The quotation is from Mayakovsky's 1918 poem "Left March," a celebration of the 1917 Revolution.

38. These events are described in Timothy J. Colton, *Moscow: Governing the Socialist Metropolis* (Cambridge, Mass.: Harvard University Press, 1995), 654–57. On August 23 patrolmen and deputies had to escort Yurii Prokof'ev, Yeltsin's successor as Moscow first secretary, from the building of the city party committee adjacent to the Central Committee, after demonstrators refused to let him leave.

39. Yel'tsin, *Zapiski*, 166 (italics added).

40. Lyudmila Pikhoya, interview with the author (September 26, 2001).

41. Patricia Kennedy Grimsted, "Russian Archives in Transition: Caught between Political Crossfire and Economic Crisis," International Research and Exchanges Board, Working Paper, January 1993, 3; conversations with Jonathan Sanders. One mentally deranged American from the Vietnam era was discovered; he stayed in Russia.

42. Mark Kramer, "The Soviet Union and the 1956 Crises in Hungary and Poland: Reassessments and New Findings," *Journal of Contemporary History* 33 (April 1998), 165.

43. Benjamin B. Fischer, "Stalin's Killing Field," https://www.cia.gov/csi/studies/winter99–00/art6.html. For some reason, the Katyn massacre had a special resonance for Yeltsin. He had tears in his eyes at the meeting with the journalists in Moscow. In Warsaw, Fischer maintains, he was likely inspired by Willy Brandt, who as chancellor of West Germany in 1970 fell to his knees after placing a wreath at a memorial to the Warsaw Ghetto destroyed by the Nazis in 1943. Gorbachev acknowledged Soviet responsibility for the Katyn deaths in 1990 but said Lavrentii Beriya, the head of the secret police, made the decision. The documents given to Wałesa in 1992 verify that the decision was taken in March 1940 by Stalin and the Politburo, six of whose members signed the resolution. Soviet propaganda before Gorbachev had claimed that German troops killed the captive Poles.

44. "Beseda zhurnalistov s prezidentom Rossii" (Conversation of journalists with the president of Russia), *Izvestiya*, July 15, 1992.

45. In the former East Germany, all citizens were in 1991 given the right to inspect their files in the archives of the Stasi security service. Millions did so, with devastating results. "There have been countless civil suits initiated when victims uncovered the names of those who had denounced and betrayed them, and many families and friendships were destroyed." John O. Koehler, "East Germany: The Stasi and Destasification," *Demokratizatsiya/Democratization* 12 (Summer 2004), 391. But the policy did shatter the police state, which never happened in Russia.

46. This point is well brought out in Samuel H. Baron and Cathy A. Frierson, eds., *Adventures in Russian Historical Research: Reminiscences of American Scholars from the Cold War to the Present* (Armonk, N.Y.: Sharpe, 2003).

47. Strobe Talbott, *The Russia Hand: A Memoir of Presidential Diplomacy* (New York: Random House, 2002), 162. Yeltsin introduced Volkogonov to Bill Clinton at

a meeting in Moscow several months before the general died of cancer. Volkogonov spoke about his work, and "Yeltsin's face took on a look I'd never seen there before: one of unadulterated compassion, affection, admiration, and sorrow." Ibid.

48. Aleksandr Yakovlev, second interview with the author (March 29, 2004). On the process, see Natal'ya Rostova, "Vozhdi ochen' toropilis'" (The leaders were in a big hurry), *Nezavisimaya gazeta*, October 26, 2001.

49. A variation on the theme that would have been more relevant to Russia was the Truth and Reconciliation Commission in South Africa, chaired by Archbishop Desmond Tutu. But it was appointed only in 1995, after the Russian debate had peaked, and I am unaware of any serious exploration of its applicability. In Latin America after military rule, there have been similar efforts in countries such as Argentina, Chile, El Salvador, and Uruguay.

50. When the communists first presented their suit in the spring, parliamentary deputy Oleg Rumyantsev launched a countersuit signed by more than seventy legislators. The court combined the two cases in May. In November it declined to rule on the legislators' suit. The litigation is ably analyzed in Kathleen E. Smith, *Mythmaking in the New Russia: Politics and Memory in the Yeltsin Era* (Ithaca: Cornell University Press, 2002), 11–29; and Jane Henderson, "The Russian Constitutional Court and the Communist Party Case: Watershed or Whitewash?" *Communist and Post-Communist Studies* 40 (March 2007), 1–16.

51. Victor Yasmann, "Legislation on Screening and State Security in Russia," *RFE/RL Research Report* 2 (August 13, 1993), 11–16; Kieran Williams, Aleks Szczerbiak, and Brigid Fowler, "Explaining Lustration in Eastern Europe: A Post-Communist Politics Approach," European Institute, University of Sussex, Working Paper 62 (March 2003).

52. Yevgenii Krasnikov, "Protivostoyanie" (Opposition), *Nezavisimaya gazeta*, May 7, 1993; Sheinis, *Vzlët i padeniye parlamenta*, 699.

53. Yel'tsin, *Zapiski*, 165.

54. Ibid., 166.

55. Smith, *Mythmaking*, 48.

56. Second Yakovlev interview.

57. The removal of the body was kept secret. The mausoleum was draped in a tarpaulin to fool German bombers, and sentries were still posted. "Ordinary Russians assumed that Lenin was still there, a symbol of resistance and eventual victory." Rodric Braithwaite, *Moscow 1941: A City and Its People at War* (London: Profile, 2006), 95; and more generally I. B. Zbarskii, *Ob"ekt No. 1* (Object No. 1) (Moscow: VAGRIUS, 2000).

58. For comparisons, see Katherine Verdery, *The Political Lives of Dead Bodies: Reburial and Postsocialist Change* (New York: Columbia University Press, 1999). Examples would be Hungary, Rumania, and the post-Yugoslav countries.

59. Most details here are from my second interview with Yeltsin (February 9, 2002); first interview with Georgii Satarov (June 5, 2000); and interview (January 21, 2004)

with Jonathan Sanders, who advised the Reed family. Stalin's office and personal rooms in Building No. 1 were also emptied and the pieces put in storage or sold off.

60. Glinka's song had finished second in a contest for an anthem for the empire in 1833. The contest was won by "God Save the Tsar" by Aleksei L'vov (1798–1870). "The Internationale" was the Soviet anthem until 1944, when the composition by Aleksandr Aleksandrov (1883–1946) and Sergei Mikhal'kov (1913–), its lyrics approved by Stalin, was instated.

61. Yel'tsin, *Marafon*, 172. On the number of awards, see Vladimir Shevchenko, *Povsednevnaya zhizn' Kremlya pri prezidentakh* (The everyday life of the Kremlin under the presidents) (Moscow: Molodaya gvardiya, 2004), 67. The biggest batch of new orders and medals was the several dozen instituted by presidential decree on March 2, 1994. Fifty-two Soviet honorary titles were renewed as Russian awards on December 30, 1995. The Order for Services to the Fatherland, instated on March 2, 1994, was roughly equivalent to the Order of Lenin. The Order of Honor substituted for the Soviet Badge of Honor, the first state award Yeltsin had received in Sverdlovsk in 1966. The most significant reinstatement of a pre-1917 award was of the Order of St. Andrei in 1998.

62. The Prisekin painting can be viewed at http://prisekin.ru. The Ioganson canvas had replaced a pre-1917 portrait of Alexander III, the second-last of the tsars, by Il'ya Repin of the Wanderers school. Alexander Nevsky was known to all Russians of Yeltsin's generation from schoolbooks and from the 1938 film by Alexander Eisenstein, which climaxes in thirty minutes of fighting on the ice, with the music of Sergei Prokofiev in the background.

63. The price tag is unknown. Officials stated that the Grand Kremlin Palace project in Yeltsin's second term cost $335 million. I very much doubt this was all that was spent. Even if it was, other projects would have pushed the total over the $500 million mark.

64. Boris Grishchenko, *Postoronnyi v Kremle: reportazhi iz "osoboi zony"* (A stranger in the Kremlin: reportage from "the special zone") (Moscow: VAGRIUS, 2004), 82–83.

65. "U nas tut vsë nastoyashcheye" (Everything here is genuine), interview with Pavel Borodin in *Kommersant-Daily*, March 24, 1999.

66. Naina Yeltsina, second interview with the author (September 18, 2007); and "U nas tut vsë nastoyashcheye."

67. Aleksandr Gamov, "K dnyu rozhdeniyia Yel'tsina v Kreml' zavezli bulyzhniki iz Sverdlovska" (For Yeltsin's birthday they have brought cobblestones from Sverdlovsk), *Komsomol'skaya pravda*, January 29, 1999.

68. "Vse govoryat—strana v nishchete, a tut takiye khoromy" (Everybody says the country is impoverished, but here we have such mansions), interview with Pavel Borodin in *Kommersant-Daily*, June 19, 1999.

69. The work in the Kremlin had many critics. According to some, preservationists in the Ministry of Culture were not consulted on the contract for Building No. 1

and it was implemented hastily and roughly. Others insisted that many corners were cut both there and in the Grand Kremlin Palace, some ersatz materials were employed, and chandeliers and other objects were sold off below market value. There were also allegations of graft involving the Swiss firm Mabetex. See on this issue Chapter 16.

70. Yel'tsin, *Marafon*, 196–97.

71. Richard J. Samuels, with a debt to the French anthropologist Claude Lévi-Strauss, in *Machiavelli's Children: Leaders and Their Legacies in Italy and Japan* (Ithaca: Cornell University Press, 2003).

72. Five Moscow streets named after Lenin were renamed in the Yeltsin years, and six were unchanged. Of forty-three other Soviet figures after whom streets were named, all references were dropped to nineteen and to twenty-four they were not (for eight of the twenty-four the name was changed in some cases but not in others). Graeme Gill, "Changing Symbols: The Renovations of Moscow Place Names," *Russian Review* 64 (July 2005), 480–503.

73. During his first official visit to France, in February 1992, Yeltsin spoke at Versailles and asked the French to invite persons of Russian origin, many of them members of Parisian high society, to the event. He spoke from the prepared text for a few minutes and then addressed the local Russians directly, pronouncing them welcome in their country of origin and thanking France for having sheltered them. "It was a fantasy moment," recalled one participant, as protocol was abandoned and guests embraced Yeltsin and the Moscow delegation. Hélène Carrère d'Encausse, interview with the author (September 11, 2007).

74. Benjamin Forest and Juliet Johnson, "Unraveling the Threads of History: Soviet-Era Monuments and Post-Soviet National Identity in Moscow," *Annals of the Association of American Geographers* 92 (September 2002), 532.

75. Yel'tsin, *Marafon*, 196. He mentions as one of the practical obstacles differences of opinion over restitution of nationalized property.

76. Vladimir Mezentsev, "Okruzhentsy" (Entourage), part 4, *Rabochaya tribuna*, March 29, 1995. Twenty-nine deputies abstained on the Kryuchkov vote, which was held in July 1989; six voted against.

77. Bakatin, *Izbavleniye ot KGB*, 120. See also J. Michael Waller, "Russia: Death and Resurrection of the KGB," *Demokratizatsiya/Democratization* 12 (Summer 2004), 333–55.

78. Gennadii Burbulis, third interview, conducted by Yevgeniya Al'bats (August 31, 2001).

79. These were not misplaced fears. One of the difficulties in sorting out new responsibilities for the old KGB was that "many of its structures and functions were necessary for the preservation of a democratic society." Waller, "Russia: Death and Resurrection," 347.

80. Aleksandr Korzhakov, *Boris Yel'tsin: ot rassveta do zakata* (Boris Yeltsin: from dawn to dusk) (Moscow: Interbuk, 1997), 175; Aleksandr Korzhakov, interview with the author (January 28, 2002).

81. Decree No. 2233, December 21, 1993, in *Rossiiskaya gazeta,* December 24, 1993.

82. Sergei Kovalëv, interview with the author (January 21, 2001).

83. Second Yakovlev interview.

84. "It is hard labor for me to be filmed, as it is with any regulated, forced behavior. I sweat bullets, and I hate terribly to see myself on the screen." Yel'tsin, *Zapiski,* 37. In Sverdlovsk, Yeltsin shone in televised performances where he did something concrete—answering citizens' letters.

85. Source: interviewers with former staffers. See on this general subject A. L. Il'in et al., *Otzvuk slova: iz opyta raboty spichraiterov pervogo prezidenta Rossii* (Echo of the word: from the work experience of the speech writers of the first president of Russia) (Moscow: Nikkolo M, 1999).

86. Sergei Filatov, *Sovershenno nesekretno* (Top nonsecret) (Moscow: VAGRIUS, 2000), 103.

87. Gorbachev's long-windedness reminded Yeltsin of Leo Tolstoy, whose monumental novels he had not wanted to read as a schoolboy in Berezniki. Yeltsin, second interview with the author (February 9, 2002).

88. Valentina Lantseva, interview with the author (July 9, 2001).

89. Marietta Chudakova, interview with the author (April 14, 2003).

90. Mark Zakharov, interview with the author (June 4, 2002). Yegor Gaidar had a similar conversation with Yeltsin in the spring of 1992, suggesting the Kremlin set up a new unit for selling the reforms. "Yegor Timurovich," he said, "do you want me to re-create the propaganda department of the CPSU Central Committee? Look, as long as I am in charge that won't happen." Oleg Moroz, "Kak Boris Yel'tsin vybiral sebe preyemnika" (How Boris Yeltsin chose his successor), *Izvestiya,* July 7, 2006.

91. Yel'tsin, *Zapiski,* 397; *Marafon,* 63 (italics added). The latter passage is not in the English translation.

92. A large body of research has established the political importance of the speech of U.S. presidents, leaving in dispute whether myth or substance predominates in it. See Jeffrey K. Tulis, *The Rhetorical Presidency* (Princeton: Princeton University Press, 1987); Richard J. Ellis, ed., *Speaking to the People: The Rhetorical Presidency in Historical Perspective* (Amherst: University of Massachusetts Press, 1998); and Shawn J. Parry-Giles, *The Rhetorical Presidency, Propaganda, and the Cold War, 1945–1955* (Westport, Conn.: Praeger, 2002).

Chapter Eleven

1. Boris Yel'tsin, *Zapiski prezidenta* (Notes of a president) (Moscow: Ogonëk, 1994), 166–67.

2. As one scholar says of constitutional politics, it is about the components of a state or would-be state coming together, keeping themselves together, or being held together. The third path applies best to Yeltsin's Russia. Alfred Stepan, "Russian Federalism in Comparative Perspective," *Post-Soviet Affairs* 16 (April–June 2000), 133–76.

3. Ibid., 165.

4. Yevgenia Albats, "Bureaucrats and the Russian Transition: The Politics of Accommodation, 1991–2003" (Ph.D. diss., Harvard University, 2004), 93.

5. For an overview, see Andrew Barnes, *Owning Russia: The Struggle over Factories, Farms, and Power* (Ithaca: Cornell University Press, 2006).

6. Boris Yeltsin, third interview with the author (September 12, 2002).

7. The auction process is analyzed in Chrystia Freeland, *Sale of the Century: Russia's Wild Ride from Communism to Capitalism* (Toronto: Doubleday, 2000), chap. 8; and David E. Hoffman, *The Oligarchs: Wealth and Power in the New Russia* (New York: PublicAffairs, 2002), chaps. 12 and 13.

8. Oleg Poptsov, *Khronika vremën "Tsarya Borisa"* (Chronicle of the times of "Tsar Boris") (Moscow: Sovershenno sekretno, 1995), 71.

9. Yel'tsin, *Zapiski*, 168.

10. See Stephen Holmes, "What Russia Teaches Us Now: How Weak States Threaten Freedom," *The American Prospect* 33 (July–August 1997), 30–39; David Woodruff, *Money Unmade: Barter and the Fate of Russian Capitalism* (Ithaca: Cornell University Press, 1999); William Alex Pridemore, ed., *Ruling Russia: Law, Crime, and Justice in a Changing Society* (Lanham, Md.: Rowman and Littlefield, 2005); and Timothy J. Colton and Stephen Holmes, eds., *The State after Communism: Governance in the New Russia* (Lanham, Md.: Rowman and Littlefield, 2006).

11. Brian D. Taylor, *Politics and the Russian Army: Civil-Military Relations, 1689–2000* (Cambridge: Cambridge University Press, 2003), 307–9.

12. Yel'tsin, *Zapiski*, 259–60.

13. Mark R. Beissinger, *Nationalist Mobilization and the Collapse of the Soviet State* (Cambridge: Cambridge University Press, 2002), 440–41, citing Matthew Wyman, *Public Opinion in Postcommunist Russia* (New York: St. Martin's, 1997), 166–67.

14. Yel'tsin, *Zapiski*, 153, 394. While Yeltsin never described himself as nostalgic for the USSR, his wife did in one interview in 1997: "Like everyone, I have nostalgia for the Soviet Union, when we all lived together like in a big family. And now it is as if everyone has run off. Friends of mine from the institute [UPI] live abroad—in Minsk, in Ukraine, in Kazakhstan." Interview of March 1, 1997, on Ekho Moskvy radio, at http://www.echo.msk.ru/guests/1775.

15. Boris Yel'tsin, *Prezidentskii marafon* (Presidential marathon) (Moscow: AST, 2000), 62.

16. Seventy-one percent of the USSR's 11,000 strategic warheads were based in Russia, 16 percent in Ukraine, 12 percent in Kazakhstan, and 1 percent in Belarus. Russia's control was 100 percent for submarine-launched strategic weapons but only 62 percent for missile-delivered warheads and 24 percent for aircraft-delivered warheads. Yegor Gaidar, *Gibel' imperii: uroki dlya sovremennoi Rossii* (Death of an empire: lessons for contemporary Russia) (Moscow: ROSSPEN, 2006), 421–22.

17. Author's first interview with Andrei Kozyrev (January 19, 2001) and second interview with Yegor Gaidar (January 31, 2002). U.S. President Clinton's main adviser for Russia and Eurasia recalls Kozyrev as "obsessed" with the Yugoslav situation and as worrying that the use of force against the Serbs would stir up nationalist passions and bring "a Russian Milošević" to power. Strobe Talbott, *The Russia Hand: A Memoir of Presidential Diplomacy* (New York: Random House, 2002), 73–74.

18. Stephen Kotkin, *Armageddon Averted: The Soviet Collapse, 1970–2000* (Oxford: Oxford University Press, 2001), 92.

19. First Kozyrev interview.

20. Ambassador Strauss provided informal feedback on a draft of Yeltsin's speech to Congress. Yeltsin asked how members of Congress would question him at the session and was relieved to hear that foreign guests were not interrogated. Author's interviews with Strauss and James F. Collins (both on January 9, 2006). Collins was Strauss's top deputy in the embassy.

21. "Russian President's Address to Joint Session of Congress," *The Washington Post*, June 18, 1992. Richard Nixon, Yeltsin's great admirer, watched the speech on television. "When Yeltsin made statements that Nixon believed were not getting a properly enthusiastic response, he yelled to the Congress through the television, 'Cheer, you jerks!'" Monica Crowley, *Nixon in Winter* (New York: Random House, 1998), 97.

22. Niall Ferguson and Brigitte Granville, "'Weimar on the Volga': Causes and Consequences of Inflation in 1990s Russia Compared with 1920s Germany," *Journal of Economic History* 60 (December 2000), 1061–87.

23. James M. Goldgeier and Michael McFaul, *Power and Purpose: U.S. Policy toward Russia after the Cold War* (Washington, D.C.: Brookings, 2003), 94.

24. Nigel Gould-Davies and Ngaire Woods, "Russia and the IMF," *International Affairs* 75 (January 1999), 7–8. The IMF announced $1 billion in external support to Russia in July 1992, $3 billion in June 1993, and $6.8 billion in April 1995.

25. Talbott, *Russia Hand*, 286. Clinton made this statement to U.S. government officials on a flight to Russia the night of August 31–September 1, 1998.

26. Goldgeier and McFaul, *Power and Purpose*, 54.

27. Talbott, *Russia Hand*, 32, 63.

28. Ibid., 115, 145.

29. Reginald Dale, "Clinton's 'Preposterous' Suggestion," http://www.iht.com/articles/2000/06/09/think.2.t_0.php.

30. Russia requested the Council of Europe seat in May 1992. In May 1998 it ratified the council's Convention for the Protection of Human Rights and Fundamental Freedoms and anti-torture protocol and recognized the right of petition of its citizens to the European Court of Human Rights in Strasbourg. Russians today file more suits with the court than any other nation. To conform to European norms, Yeltsin established a moratorium on executions in 1996 and in June 1999 commuted the sentences of 713 death-row prisoners. Three post-Soviet states (Estonia,

Latvia, and Lithuania) joined the EU in 2004; seven other post-communist countries joined in 2004 and 2007.

31. A. L. Litvin, *Yel'tsiny v Kazani* (The Yeltsins in Kazan) (Kazan: Aibat, 2004), 71.

32. CIA, Directorate of Intelligence, "The Politics of Russian Nationalisms," SOV 91-10044 (October 1991), 13; declassified version obtained at http://www.foia.cia.gov.browse_docs.asp?

33. The republics numbered sixteen until 1991, when four lesser ethnic entities (autonomous oblasts) were reclassified and the Chechen-Ingush republic broke in two, bringing the total to twenty-one. One surviving autonomous oblast and ten "autonomous districts" remained of inferior standing after the reshuffle; three of the eleven voted for sovereignty. The process is well laid out in Jeffrey Kahn, *Federalism, Democratization, and the Rule of Law in Russia* (Oxford: Oxford University Press, 2002), 102–23.

34. Elise Giuliano, "Secessionism from the Bottom Up: Democratization, Nationalism, and Local Accountability in the Russian Transition," *World Politics* 58 (January 2006), 295; Rashit Akhmetov, "Provody" (Sendoff), http://tatpolit.ru/category/zvezda/2007-05-04/285.

35. See Dmitry Gorenburg, *Minority Ethnic Mobilization in the Russian Federation* (Cambridge: Cambridge University Press, 2003), 125. As many as 20,000 protested during the October session of the Tatarstan Supreme Soviet, and more than fifty were injured in clashes with the police. Altogether, 142 nationalist rallies were held in Tatarstan between 1987 and 1993.

36. Aleksandr Tsipko, "Drama rossiiskogo vybora" (The drama of Russia's choice), *Izvestiya*, October 1, 1991. Four of Russia's ethnic republics and twenty-nine of its other territories exceeded the population of Estonia, whose separation from the USSR Yeltsin recognized in August 1991.

37. M. K. Gorshkov, V. V. Zhuravlëv, and L. N. Dobrokhotov, eds., *Yel'tsin–Khasbulatov: yedinstvo, kompromiss, bor'ba* (Yeltsin–Khasbulatov: unity, compromise, struggle) (Moscow: TERRA, 1994), 130.

38. See especially Kahn, *Federalism, Democratization, and the Rule of Law*, 123–32, 153–54 (story about Burbulis at 153); Akhmetov, "Provody" (Shaimiyev's feats); Dmitry Gorenburg, "Regional Separatism in Russia: Ethnic Mobilisation or Power Grab?" *Europe-Asia Studies* 51 (March 1999), 245–74; and Giuliano, "Secessionism from the Bottom Up," 276–310.

39. On August 21, 1991, Yeltsin removed by decree the chief executives of three provinces (Rostov, Samara, and Lipetsk). He first appointed individuals to this office on August 24. But on August 22 Yeltsin asserted the right to name "presidential representatives," who were there independent of the holders of the local office.

40. Outside of war-torn Chechnya, the only republic where Yeltsin ever stepped in to name a president was Karachayevo-Cherkessiya in September 1995, at the request of the local parliament.

41. Secondary accounts mention republic proposals in the provinces of Arkhangel'sk, Irkutsk, Kaliningrad, Krasnoyarsk, Novosibirsk, Orël, Primor'e, St.

Petersburg, Vladivostok, Vologda, and Voronezh. For comparisons, see Philip G. Roeder, *Where Nation-States Come From: Institutional Change in the Age of Nationalism* (Princeton: Princeton University Press, 2007), 192–93; and Yoshiko M. Herrera, *Imagined Economies: The Sources of Russian Regionalism* (Cambridge: Cambridge University Press, 2005), 194–244.

42. Timothy J. Colton and Cindy Skach, "A Fresh Look at Semipresidentialism: The Russian Predicament," *Journal of Democracy* 16 (July 2005), 113–26.

43. Khasbulatov heard about the agreement from news reports while on a visit to South Korea. He wanted to talk about it with Yeltsin by telephone but had to settle for Naina Yeltsina. Rutskoi was informed about the deal by one of Khasbulatov's deputies. Author's interviews with Khasbulatov (September 26, 2001) and Rutskoi (June 5, 2001).

44. Josephine T. Andrews, *When Majorities Fail: The Russian Parliament, 1990–1993* (Cambridge: Cambridge University Press, 2002), 26.

45. Gorshkov, Zhuravlëv, and Dobrokhotov, *Yel'tsin–Khasbulatov*, 201.

46. Khasbulatov interview.

47. Yu, M. Baturin et al., *Epokha Yel'tsina: ocherki politicheskoi istorii* (The Yeltsin epoch: essays in political history) (Moscow: VAGRIUS, 2001), 265. Chernomyrdin had declared in December, when appointed premier, that he intended to work closely with the congress. This prompted Yeltsin's press secretary, Vyacheslav Kostikov, to write a sarcastic pseudonymous article about him in a newspaper. Chernomyrdin complained to Yeltsin, who told Kostikov his criticism was fair but he should keep it to himself, and "I will sort things out with Chernomyrdin myself." Ibid., 322–33.

48. Ibid., 293.

49. Gorshkov, Zhuravlëv, and Dobrokhotov, *Yel'tsin–Khashulatov*, 324–25.

50. Boris Yeltsin, first interview with the author (July 15, 2001).

51. Aleksandr Korzhakov, *Boris Yel'tsin: ot rassveta do zakata* (Boris Yeltsin: from dawn to dusk) (Moscow: Interbuk, 1997), 158–59. He says the agent to be used was chloropicrin, which causes lachrymation and vomiting; in high enough doses, it can lead to serious injury or death.

52. Gorshkov, Zhuravlëv, and Dobrokhotov, *Yel'tsin–Khashulatov*, 369–71.

53. The Constitutional Court had ruled that the results on the third and fourth questions would be binding only if a majority of the entire electorate came out in favor.

54. Dmitri K. Simes, "Remembering Yeltsin," http://www.nationalinterest.org/BlogSE.aspx?id=14110.

55. Leon Aron, *Yeltsin: A Revolutionary Life* (New York: St. Martin's, 2000), 514.

56. Baturin et al., *Epokha*, 345.

57. I owe this point to Valentin Yumashev, who knows Yeltsin's political thinking as well as anyone. Yeltsin describes his conversations with Grachëv about the constitutional crisis, and his confidence in Grachëv's support, in *Zapiski*, 350–51. On September 16 Yeltsin paid a call on the Dzerzhinsky Motorized Rifle Division, which reported to the MVD.

58. Previously undisclosed details from the author's second interview with Vladimir Bokser (May 11, 2001) and interview with Vitalii Nasedkin (June 9, 2001).

59. Baturin et al., *Epokha*, 357.

60. Yel'tsin, *Zapiski*, 347.

61. Ibid., 375; Gorshkov, Zhuravlëv, and Dobrokhotov, *Yel'tsin–Khasbulatov*, 526.

62. Yel'tsin, *Zapiski*, 347.

63. Ibid., 384–86, describes the scene with Grachëv, as does Sergei Filatov, *Sovershenno nesekretno* (Top nonsecret) (Moscow: VAGRIUS, 2000), 317. On the all-important responsibility question, see Robert V. Barylski, *The Soldier in Russian Politics: Duty, Dictatorship, and Democracy Under Gorbachev and Yeltsin* (New Brunswick: Transaction, 1998), 260–62; and especially Taylor, *Politics and the Russian Army*, 295–301.

64. Louis D. Sell, "Embassy Under Siege: An Eyewitness Account of Yeltsin's 1993 Attack on Parliament," *Problems of Post-Communism* 50 (July–August 2003), 61.

65. This act is described in Korzhakov, *Boris Yel'tsin*, 198.

66. Some opposition sources put the death toll much higher, at 500 or even 1,000.

67. Yeltsin's chief of staff, Sergei Filatov, proposed the plebiscite to him on October 5, having fielded a suggestion to this effect from Yurii Ryzhov, the Russian ambassador to Paris (who had heard it from the Sorbonne law professor Michel Lesage). Yeltsin agreed immediately, says Filatov (*Sovershenno nesekretno*, 325–26). But Yeltsin had consistently favored putting a new constitution to the electorate, and so was returning to this idea rather than discovering it.

68. Valerii Zor'kin had favored a "zero option" whereby Yeltsin and parliament would face election at exactly the same time. Yeltsin was never for it, although it would probably have yielded better electoral results for him than those realized in December 1993.

69. "Prezident Rossii otvechayet na voprosy gazety 'Izvestiya'" (The president of Russia answers the questions of the newspaper *Izvestiya*), *Izvestiya*, November 16, 1993.

70. Unnamed speaker on October 23, in *Konstitutsionnoye soveshchaniye: stenogrammy, materialy, dokumenty* (The Constitutional Conference: stenographic records, materials, documents), 20 vols. (Moscow: Yuridicheskaya literatura, 1996), 19:163.

71. Timothy J. Colton, "Public Opinion and the Constitutional Referendum," in Timothy J. Colton and Jerry F. Hough, eds., *Growing Pains: Russian Democracy and the Election of 1993* (Washington, D.C.: Brookings, 1998), 293. Fifty-five percent of the electors voted on the constitution. A Yeltsin decree had set the bar for confirmation at a 50 percent turnout and a 50 percent positive vote. This was much lower than the absolute majority of the entire electorate required by the Russian law on referendums, adopted in October 1990.

72. Even a study deeply critical of Yeltsin stresses the self-isolation of his opponents and that "none of our criticism of Yeltsin implies that a military victory by the White House forces would have set Russia on a better path than it in fact took. That seems most improbable." Peter Reddaway and Dmitri Glinski, *The Tragedy of Russia's Reforms: Market Bolshevism against Democracy* (Washington, D.C.: U.S. Institute of Peace, 2001), 428.

73. "Prezident Rossii otvechayet na voprosy gazety 'Izvestiya.'"

74. In this sense, Yeltsin "sought to construct the presidency as the ruler of those who govern, rather than one who is himself responsible for governing." Alexander Sokolowski, "Bankrupt Government: Intra-Executive Relations and the Politics of Budgetary Irresponsibility in El'tsin's Russia," *Europe-Asia Studies* 53 (June 2001), 543.

75. Some court decisions indicated he should explain his vetoes, but Yeltsin complied selectively and no systematic list of vetoes was published. Yeltsin signed 752 bills from 1994 through 1998 and vetoed 216. Andrea Chandler, "Presidential Veto Power in Post-Communist Russia, 1994–1998," *Canadian Journal of Political Science* 34 (September 2001), 487–516.

76. *Konstitutsionnoye soveshchaniye*, 20:40, which shows Yeltsin's stroke of the pen. This was the most important of the fourteen changes Yeltsin made in the draft transmitted to him on November 7. The final clause of Article 90 did specify that his edicts "should not contradict" the constitution and laws.

77. Because Soviet leaders were primarily party heads, protocol was simple and arrangements were handled by the foreign ministry. Gorbachev created a protocol office in his new presidential establishment in 1990. Yeltsin hired the tactful and decent Shevchenko in January 1992 and upgraded the office. For the arrangements on everything from heraldry to the goblets at Kremlin banquets, see V. N. Shevchenko et al., *Protokol Rossiiskoi Federatsii* (Protocol of the Russian Federation) (Moscow: VAGRIUS, 2000).

78. Gorshkov, Zhuravlëv, and Dobrokhotov, *Yel'tsin–Khasbulatov*, 543.

79. Quoted in Timothy J. Colton, "Introduction," in Colton and Hough, *Growing Pains*, 13. Six cabinet ministers were on the Russia's Choice list but five, including three deputy premiers, ran for other parties and blocs.

80. Details here from Aleksandr Petrov, "Glavnaya tema: 'menya vosprinyali kak yel'tsinskogo palacha'" (Main theme: "they took me for Yeltsin's executioner"), *Moskovskiye novosti*, September 30, 2003.

81. The line of reasoning Kazannik pursued, and it is a debatable one, is that the government might have negotiated peacefully with the rebels on October 3, in the hours after their initial attack on the Ostankino television tower was repulsed. He knew that the trail of responsibility for "criminal orders," if that is what they were, led back to Yeltsin as commander-in-chief, but prosecution of a sitting president was an "extremely complex" problem. Ibid.

82. Ibid.

83. When Khasbulatov sent Yeltsin a letter in 1996 asking to be allowed to use a Kremlin medical clinic, Yeltsin agreed without hesitation. Yevgenii Kiselëv, "Plyaski na grablyakh" (Dancing on horse rakes), *Moskovskiye novosti*, September 30, 2003.

84. Kazannik had him released on bail pending trial due to his heart condition. Yeltsin objected (better to let him die in prison, he said) but let it be. After the amnesty, Barannikov asked Yeltsin to let him live in the apartment building in Krylatskoye in which the president's family was to be registered, and Yeltsin was in favor, until Korzhakov talked him out of it. Petrov, "Glavnaya tema"; Korzhakov, *Boris Yel'tsin*, 143–44. Barannikov died in July 1995.

85. Ligachëv was elected in 1993. In 1995 he was joined in the communist fraction by Anatolii Luk'yanov. Nikolai Ryzhkov was also elected in 1995 and sat in an affiliated group.

86. See Paul Chaisty and Petra Schleiter, "Productive but Not Valued: The Russian State Duma, 1994–2001," *Europe-Asia Studies* 54 (July 2002), 704; and Tiffany A. Troxel, *Parliamentary Power in Russia, 1994–2001: President vs. Parliament* (New York: Palgrave Macmillan, 2003).

87. Thomas F. Remington, "Laws, Decrees, and Russian Constitutions: The First Hundred Years" (unpublished paper, Emory University, 2006). This does not count secret decrees, mostly, one assumes, in the national-security realm. The numbers refer only to "normative" decrees with wide consequences, as opposed to "nonnormative" rulings on particular cases. See also Remington, "Democratization, Separation of Powers, and State Capacity," in Colton and Holmes, *State after Communism*, 261–98; and Scott Parrish, "Presidential Decree Authority in Russia, 1991–1995," in John M. Carey and Matthew S. Shugart, eds., *Executive Decree Authority* (Cambridge: Cambridge University Press, 1998), 62–103.

88. Roeder, *Where Nation-States Come From*, 168–69.

89. Giuliano, "Secessionism from the Bottom Up," 286. The significance of Yeltsin's triumph over his opponents at the center, and the contrast with Gorbachev's weakness in 1990–91, is well drawn in Roeder, *Where Nation-States Come From*, chap. 6.

90. This had been Yeltsin's intent all along, but the plan was upended by his dissolution of provincial legislatures in October 1993, which left half of the proposed representatives to the Federation Council without qualifying office. On the shift to direct election of governors, see Marc Zlotnik, "Russia's Elected Governors: A Force to Be Reckoned With," *Demokratizatsiya/Democratization* 5 (Spring 1997), 184–96.

91. "Mr. Yeltsin proposes that each of these homelands make a treaty with Russia 'on an equal basis,' agreeing on the division of power. His hope is that once they are given full responsibility for their decisions, they will see the folly of economic and political isolation, and the advantages of throwing in with Mr. Yeltsin for greater influence and efficiency. 'I don't know, perhaps you will decide to delegate your foreign relations to Russia,' Mr. Yeltsin suggested. 'Why should you keep 170 embassies in 170 countries?'" Bill Keller, "Kazan Journal: Yeltsin's Response to the Separatists," *New York Times*, September 3, 1990. Shaimiyev has said that the evening of

the Kazan speech Yeltsin asked his advice on what to do next. Shaimiyev suggested a working group to come up with a treaty, and Yeltsin agreed. Anna Rudnitskaya, "Stranno prinyali i stranno otklonili" (Adopted strangely and voted down strangely), http://www.izbrannoe.ru/6077.html.

92. Boris Bronshtein and Vasilii Kononenko, "Lidery demonstratiruyut v Kazani novyye podkhody, a okruzheniyie—ispytannyye priëmy pokazukhi" (The leaders demonstrate new approaches in Kazan, but their entourage engages in tested forms of make-believe), *Izvestiya*, June 1, 1994.

93. Kahn, *Federalism, Democratization, and the Rule of Law*, 165.

94. See especially ibid.; Matthew Crosston, *Shadow Federalism: Implications for Democratic Consolidation* (Aldershot: Ashgate, 2004); and Kathryn Stoner-Weiss, *Resisting the State: Reform and Retrenchment in Post-Soviet Russia* (Cambridge: Cambridge University Press, 2006). Yeltsin did reverse a good many decisions by provincial executives but he did not make it a practice to review provincial legislation. See V. O. Lunich and A. V. Mazurov, *Ukazy Prezidenta RF* (Decrees of the president of the Russian Federation) (Moscow: Zakon i pravo, 2000), 79–86.

95. "Prezident RF otvechayet na voprosy redaktsii 'Truda'" (The president of the Russian Federation answers the questions of the editorial board of *Trud*), *Trud*, August 26, 1994.

96. Daniel S. Treisman, *After the Deluge: Regional Crises and Political Consolidation in Russia* (Ann Arbor: University of Michigan Press, 1999), 75–79.

97. Baturin et al., *Epokha*, 397. A good example of toleration of socialistic policies was Lenin's birthplace, Ul'yanovsk on the south Volga. Under the former CPSU boss Yurii Goryachev, the provincial government controlled food prices and prevented the export of foods to other areas until 1995.

98. Yeltsin, speaking in retirement about his relations with Rossel. Kirill Dybskii, "Ot pervogo litsa: vsë pravil'no" (From the first person: everything is fine), *Itogi*, January 30, 2006. In the Kursk election, the Kremlin supported the incumbent, Vasilii Shuteyev, whom Yeltsin had appointed in 1991. Of the four governors other than Rossel fired by Yeltsin in 1993, three—Yurii Lodkin in Bryansk, Vitalii Mukha in Novosibirsk, and Pëtr Sumin in Chelyabinsk—regained their posts through election in 1995–96. Aleksandr Surat in Amur oblast ran for election in 1997 but lost. Rossel began his comeback by being elected to represent Sverdlovsk in the Federation Council, the national upper house, in December 1993, one month after being fired by Yeltsin; in April 1994 he was chosen chairman of the oblast legislature.

99. Author's interviews with Emil Pain (April 3, 2001), Leonid Smirnyagin (May 24, 2001), and Valentin Yumashev (several, 2006 and 2007). Prusak (born 1960) was the youngest member of this group and Matochkin (born 1931) the oldest. Yeltsin's ties with Guvzhin, Shaimiyev, and Stroyev went back to his apparatchik roots. Mikhail Nikolayev of Sakha fell into the same category, but I omit him from the list because his relations with Yeltsin blew hot and cold. Yeltsin knew Fëdorov, Prusak, and Sobchak from the Soviet congress of deputies and the Interregional Deputies Group, and Nemtsov from the Russian parliament. Fëdorov was Russian minister of

justice from 1990 until his resignation in 1993 but continued to have cordial dealings with Yeltsin after moving to Chuvashiya.

100. He made the remark at the opening of a tennis court, during a tour of Volga cities on the steamboat *Rossiya.* Yeltsin had asked Nemtsov to do something about the nationalist politician Vladimir Zhirinovskii, who was following in his wake in a rented boat, making anti-Yeltsin speeches at every stop. Nemtsov ordered the local water authorities to detain Zhirinovskii's vessel in one of the Volga locks upriver of Nizhnii Novgorod—a peremptory resolution of the problem that Yeltsin loved and in which he surely saw a similarity to his own assertiveness. Yeltsin took Nemtsov with him to the United States and introduced him to President Clinton as a potential heir. "Boris Nemtsov—Yevgenii Al'bats o Yel'tsine" (Boris Nemtsov to Yevgeniya Al'bats about Yeltsin), *Novoye vremya/New Times*, April 30, 2007.

101. "Prezident RF otvechayet na voprosy redaktsii 'Truda.'

102. The 350,000 Chechens affected were part of the 2 million Soviet citizens deported during the war. In the North Caucasus, four other groups—the Balkars, Ingush, Kalmyks, and Karachai—were also deported en masse, and none of them was to reject Russian authority in the 1990s.

103. See Emil Souleimanov, *An Endless War: The Russian-Chechen Conflict in Perspective* (Frankfurt: Peter Lang, 2007), 24–26.

104. Carlotta Gall and Thomas de Waal, *Chechnya: Calamity in the Caucasus* (New York: New York University Press, 1998), 107.

105. Thomas Goltz, *Chechnya Diary: A War Correspondent's Story of Surviving the War in Chechnya* (New York: St. Martin's, 2003), 52.

106. Undated statement shown in *Prezident vseya Rusi* (The president of all Russia), documentary film by Yevgenii Kiselëv, 1999–2000 (copy supplied by Kiselëv), 4 parts, part 4.

107. Gall and de Waal, *Chechnya*, 150–51; John B. Dunlop, *Russia Confronts Chechnya: Roots of a Separatist Conflict* (Cambridge: Cambridge University Press, 1999), 158–60.

108. V. A. Tishkov, Ye. L. Belyayeva, and G. V. Marchenko, *Chechenskii krizis: analiticheskoye obozreniye* (The Chechen crisis: an analytical review) (Moscow: Tsentr kompleksnykh sotsial'nykh issledovanii i marketinga, 1995), 33.

109. Ibid. This conversation with Shaimiyev has been dated variously in March or May of 1994. But Gall and de Waal, *Chechnya*, 146–47, relying on interviews, refer to a conversation on June 10. See also the references to Dudayev's rhetoric in Taimaz Abubakarov, *Rezhim Dzhokhara Dudayeva: zapiski dudayevskogo ministra ekonomiki i finansov* (The regime of Djokhar Dudayev: notes of Dudayev's minister of economics and finance) (Moscow: INSAN, 1998), 167.

110. Anatol Lieven, *Chechnya: Tombstone of Russian Power* (New Haven: Yale University Press, 1998), 69.

111. Korzhakov, *Boris Yel'tsin*, 371.

112. Sergei Yushenkov, chairman of the Duma's defense committee at the time, quoted in Gall and de Waal, *Chechnya*, 161. The statement is reported a little differ-

ently in S. N. Yushenkov, *Voina v Chechne i problemy rossiiskoi gosudarstvennosti i demokratii* (The war in Chechnya and problems of Russian statehood and democracy) (Moscow: Semetei, 1995), 75. Here Lobov is quoted as observing that Clinton's ratings went up after the Haiti operation but not as advocating that Yeltsin intervene in Chechnya for that reason.

113. Oleg Lobov, interview with the author (May 29, 2002).

114. Yel'tsin, *Marafon*, 88. George W. Breslauer, *Gorbachev and Yeltsin as Leaders* (Cambridge: Cambridge University Press, 2002), chap. 9, maintains that Yeltsin began the war as much to recoup lost popularity as to negate the threat to Russia's unity. The argument is well put, but there is no hard evidence to support it.

115. Yel'tsin, *Marafon*, 69.

116. *Muzhskoi razgovor dva* (Male conversation two), interview of Yeltsin by El'dar Ryazanov on ORT-TV, June 16, 1996 (videotape supplied by Irena Lesnevskaya).

117. Yel'tsin, *Marafon*, 69.

Chapter Twelve

1. The phrase is from Arnold M. Ludwig, *King of the Mountain: The Nature of Political Leadership* (Lexington: University Press of Kentucky, 2002), 172–74.

2. Quotations from Sergei Filatov, *Sovershenno nesekretno* (Top nonsecret) (Moscow: VAGRIUS, 2000), 418–19; Vyacheslav Kostikov, *Roman s prezidentom: zapiski press-sekretarya* (Romance with a president: notes of a press secretary) (Moscow: VAGRIUS, 1997), 163; and Tatyana Malkina, interview with the author (June 13, 2001).

3. Boris Yel'tsin, *Zapiski prezidenta* (Notes of a president) (Moscow: Ogonëk, 1994), 308; "Proshchaniye s mamoi" (Farewell to mama), *Argumenty i fakty*, March 24, 1993.

4. Oleg Poptsov, *Khronika vremën "Tsarya Borisa"* (Chronicle of the times of "Tsar Boris") (Moscow: Sovershenno sekretno, 1995), 55.

5. Yeltsin holding his breath is taken from Shamil Tarpishchev, interview with the author (January 25, 2002). For the swims, see Aleksandr Korzhakov, *Boris Yel'tsin: ot rassveta do zakata* (Boris Yeltsin: from dawn to dusk) (Moscow: Interbuk, 1997), 77–78; Lev Sukhanov, *Tri goda s Yel'tsinym: zapiski pervogo pomoshchnika* (Three years with Yeltsin: notes of his first assistant) (Riga: Vaga, 1992), 306–7; and Aleksandr Lebed', *Za derzhavu obidno* (I feel hurt for the state) (Moscow: Moskovskaya pravda, 1995), 380.

6. Shamil' Tarpishchev, *Samyi dolgii match* (The longest match) (Moscow: VAGRIUS, 1999), 300. The transferability of Yeltsin's volleyball skills to tennis makes sense in light of history. William G. Morgan of Holyoke, Massachusetts, invented volleyball in 1895 as a mix of tennis, basketball, and handball.

7. Monica Crowley, *Nixon in Winter* (New York: Random House, 1998), 111. Yeltsin canceled a fourth meeting in 1994 out of unhappiness with Nixon having first met opposition politicians.

8. Tatyana Yumasheva, third interview with the author (January 25, 2007).

9. *Muzhskoi razgovor* (Male conversation), interview of Yeltsin by El'dar Ryazanov on REN-TV, November 7, 1993 (videotape supplied by Irena Lesnevskaya).

10. Boris Yel'tsin, *Prezidentskii marafon* (Presidential marathon) (Moscow: AST, 2000), 337.

11. Natal'ya Konstantinova, *Zhenskii vzglyad na kremlëvskuyu zhizn'* (A woman's view of Kremlin life) (Moscow: Geleos, 1999), 136.

12. *Den' v sem'e prezidenta* (A day in the president's family), interviews of the Yeltsin family by El'dar Ryazanov on REN-TV, April 20, 1993 (videotape supplied by Irena Lesnevskaya).

13. Yel'tsin, *Marafon,* 350. I learned about the philanthropy from my interviews with Irena Lesnevskaya (January 24, 2001) and Galina Volchek (January 30, 2002). Two of the actresses Naina Yeltsina aided were Sof'ya Pilyavskaya (1911–2000) and Marina Ladynina (1908–2003).

14. Konstantinova, *Zhenskii vzglyad,* 225.

15. Kozyrev interviewed in *Prezident vseya Rusi* (The president of all Russia), documentary film by Yevgenii Kiselëv, 1999–2000 (copy supplied by Kiselëv), 4 parts, part 2.

16. Vladimir Shevchenko, third interview with the author (July 15, 2001).

17. Yel'tsin, *Marafon,* 340–41. Yeltsin's declared hard-currency book royalties peaked in 1994 at $280,000. He first made disclosures about his income and property during the 1996 election campaign. See A. A. Mukhin and P. A. Kozlov, *"Semeinyye" tainy, ili neofitsial'nyi lobbizm v Rossii* ("Family" secrets, or unofficial lobbying in Russia) (Moscow: Tsentr politicheskoi informatsii, 2003), 106–9.

18. Boris Yeltsin, *Midnight Diaries,* trans. Catherine A. Fitzpatrick (New York: PublicAffairs, 2000), 314–15. The original is in *Marafon,* 340.

19. Author's interviews with family members. In the late 1990s, for tax purposes, Yeltsin declared the value of the city apartment and the land and dacha at Gorki-10 at about $210,000. In today's prices, the Gorki-10 land alone would be worth many times that. Unverifiable and, to me, implausible claims about the Yeltsins enriching themselves at the public trough can be found at http://compromat.ru/main/eltsyn/a.htm; and http://www.flb.ru/info. Many were originally published in the newspaper *Moskovskii komsomolets.*

20. Yu, M. Baturin et al., *Epokha Yel'tsina: ocherki politicheskoi istorii* (The Yeltsin epoch: essays in political history) (Moscow: VAGRIUS, 2001), 473.

21. Yeltsin's displeasure at Rutskoi that day has been well documented. In one of his press interviews after the death of Yeltsin in 2007, Rutskoi said how impressed he was by the fact that Yeltsin never swore!

22. Aleksandr Korzhakov, interview with the author (January 28, 2002).

23. Vladimir Shevchenko, *Povsednevnaya zhizn' Kremlya pri prezidentakh* (The everyday life of the Kremlin under the presidents) (Moscow: Molodaya gvardiya, 2004), 126–27.

24. Matt Taibbi, "Butka: Boris Yeltsin, Revisited," http://exile.ru/105/yeltsin.

25. Viktor Manyukhin, *Pryzhok nazad: o Yel'tsine i o drugikh* (Backward leap: about Yeltsin and others) (Yekaterinburg: Pakrus, 2002), 178.

26. Yel'tsin, *Zapiski*, 270.

27. Robert S. Strauss, interview with the author (January 9, 2006).

28. Of the German, Yeltsin wrote (*Marafon*, 164), "Kohl and I always found it easy to understand each other psychologically. We resembled one another in terms of our reactions and style of communication and saw the world from the same generational bell tower." Yeltsin used the word "friend" *(drug)* to describe Kohl, Jiang, and Jacques Chirac of France (born in 1932), and mentioned how much he liked speaking Russian with Jiang, who lived in Moscow in the 1950s. He did not discuss Strauss in his memoirs. By contrast, Yeltsin's relations with François Mitterrand, the president of France until January 1996 (born in 1916), were always chilly.

29. Yel'tsin, *Zapiski*, 250.

30. Details from Korzhakov interview. The Sakha visit was in December 1990, when Yeltsin was still parliamentary chairman.

31. Korzhakov, *Boris Yel'tsin*, 391.

32. Yel'tsin, *Zapiski*, 9.

33. The masculine side of comradeship has been revealed in studies of Soviet propaganda, literature, and art. See Eliot Borenstein, *Men without Women: Masculinity and Revolution in Russian Fiction, 1917–1929* (Durham: Duke University Press, 2000).

34. Yel'tsin, *Zapiski*, 198–99.

35. Conversation with Naina Yeltsina during my third interview with Boris Yeltsin (September 12, 2002).

36. Korzhakov, *Boris Yel'tsin*, 458, 19.

37. Viktor Chernomyrdin, interview with the author (September 15, 2000). Chernomyrdin is one of Moscow's most accomplished swearers, and thus had to suppress that habit as well as any chumminess.

38. Yel'tsin, *Marafon*, 176–77; Aleksandr Rutskoi, interview with the author (June 5, 2001).

39. This congruity was stressed in my interviews with Boris Nemtsov.

40. Yegor Gaidar, *Dni porazhenii i pobed* (Days of defeats and victories) (Moscow: VAGRIUS, 1996), 106.

41. Mikhail Gorbachev, *Zhizn' i reformy* (Life and reforms), 2 vols. (Moscow: Novosti, 1995), 1:372. Gorbachev throws in archly that many Soviet builders lied about project completion and made believe that half-finished buildings were ready for occupancy.

42. Other than Yeltsin, the construction engineer who soared highest in Russian politics in the 1990s was the Sverdlovsker Oleg Lobov. Lobov was a level-tempered administrator with none of Yeltsin's quirks.

43. Georgii Shakhnazarov, *S vozhdyami i bez nikh* (With leaders and without them) (Moscow: VAGRIUS, 2001), 376.

44. Yel'tsin, *Zapiski*, 305.

45. Oleg Davydov, "Yel'tsinskaya trekhkhodovka" (The Yeltsin three-step), in A. N. Starkov, ed., *Rossiiskaya elita: psikhologicheskiye portrety* (The Russian elite: psychological portraits) (Moscow: Ladomir, 2000), 65–80.

46. See, for example, "Altered Statesmen: Boris Yeltsin," http://www.discoverychannel.co.uk/alteredstatesmen/features5.shtml. The Wikipedia online encyclopedia now reports as established fact that Yeltsin, along with Winston Churchill, was cyclothymic. Aleksandr Khinshtein, *Yel'tsin, Kreml', istoriya bolezni* (Yeltsin, the Kremlin, the history of an illness) (Moscow: OLMA, 2006), provides what purports to be analysis of other mental conditions, including paranoia, persecution mania, schizophrenia, and "hysterical psychopathy." This text reports a few useful anecdotes, mostly from Korzhakov, but the discussion of Yeltsin's mental state is pure character assassination. Never saying directly that he had most of these conditions, let alone adducing evidence, it prints stylized descriptions of them in boldface in the midst of narration of incidents in his life, leaving it to the reader to draw conclusions. It is also full of basic factual errors. For more responsible discussion of select themes, see Martin Ebon, "Yeltsin's V.I.P. Depression," http://www.mhsource.com/exclusive/yeltsin.html.

47. Anatolii Kulikov, *Tyazhëlyye zvëzdy* (Heavy stars) (Moscow: Voina i mir, 2002), 151; Strobe Talbott, *The Russia Hand: A Memoir of Presidential Diplomacy* (New York: Random House, 2002), 87; Baturin et al., *Epokha*, 367; Sergei Filatov, second interview with the author (January 25, 2002).

48. Tarpishchev interview.

49. Yel'tsin, *Zapiski*, 85–86.

50. *Muzhskoi razgovor.*

51. Baturin et al., *Epokha*, 504.

52. Yel'tsin, *Zapiski*, 304–5.

53. Ibid., 239.

54. Ibid., 293.

55. Ibid.; Korzhakov, *Boris Yel'tsin*, 203.

56. Korzhakov, *Boris Yel'tsin*, 203.

57. This event is reported only in the revised edition of Korzhakov's memoir: *Boris Yel'tsin: ot rassveta do zakata; posleslovive* (Boris Yeltsin: from dawn to dusk; epilogue) (Moscow: Detektiv-press, 2004), 245–46. He told me about it in our interview in 2002. The other men present were reportedly Viktor Ilyushin and Mikhail Barsukov, neither of whom has contradicted Korzhakov's account. Korzhakov knew Yeltsin would not be able to put a bullet in his head but feared, nonetheless, that he might have a heart attack due to the strain.

58. Baturin et al., *Epokha*, 632.

59. Yelena Bonner, interview with the author (March 13, 2001).

60. Yel'tsin, *Marafon*, 23.

61. Yevgenii Primakov, *Vosem' mesyatsev plyus . . .* (Eight months plus) (Moscow: Mysl', 2001), 93.

62. Ludwig, *King of the Mountain*, 233–40. Ludwig (233) includes combinations of the following symptoms: "a melancholy mood, a sleep disturbance, increased or

decreased appetite, lack of energy, excessive tearfulness, a sense of dread or futility, social withdrawal, morbid thoughts, or suicidal preoccupation."

63. Yel'tsin, *Marafon*, 348.

64. Baturin et al., *Epokha*, 505, 507.

65. Third Yeltsin interview.

66. Kostikov, *Roman s prezidentom*, 301, 306–7.

67. Valentin Yumashev, fourth interview with the author (January 22, 2007).

68. Author's first interview with Vladimir Bokser (May 11, 2000) and interviews with Jack Matlock (September 1, 2005), Robert Strauss (January 9, 2006), Valerii Bortsov (June 11, 2001), Aleksandr Rutskoi (June 5, 2001), and Yurii Ryzhov (June 7, 2000); and Aleksandr Korzhakov, "Yel'tsin ne pozvolyal, chtoby v yego kompanii sachkovali s vypivkoi" (Yeltsin did not allow people to goof off because of drink in his company), http://news.rin.ru/news///130889.

69. A reporter in 1991 asked her about Yeltsin's upbringing, and she brushed off reports that he was a drinker: "I know, a lot of rumors are circulating. But I am his mother, I know my son." She then related the story, reported in Chapter 2, of Yeltsin as a teenager in Berezniki pouring another boy's glass of vodka on the ground. Izabella Verbova, "Za tysyachi kilometrov ot Belogo doma" (Thousands of kilometers from the White House), *Vechernyaya Moskva*, October 2, 1991.

70. Talbott, *Russia Hand*, 44–45; Strobe Talbott, interview with the author (January 9, 2006). Given the eight-hour time difference between Washington and Moscow and Clinton's dislike of early-morning appointments, coordination of the two presidents' schedules was no easy task.

71. By evening's end, Yeltsin's skin was stretched across his cheeks and a Clinton adviser knew what people meant when they described someone who had too much to drink as "tight." George Stephanopoulos, *All Too Human: A Political Education* (Boston: Little, Brown, 1999), 140.

72. Hillary Rodham Clinton, *Living History* (New York: Simon and Schuster, 2003), 411–12, 217.

73. Vladimir Bokser, second interview with the author (May 11, 2001); and Bonner interview.

74. Andrei Kozyrev, second interview with the author (September 18, 2001). Kozyrev declined to name the minister.

75. The performance can be viewed at http://www.youtube.com/watch?v=LAr0MgGrwHA.

76. The letter is reproduced in Baturin et al., *Epokha*, 521–23. Korzhakov writes that Pavel Grachëv also signed; the other sources deny it. Yeltsin assistants Yurii Baturin and Georgii Satarov took part in the composition but did not sign, since they had been with him for only a year. The Repin painting in question is the tableau *Reply of the Zaporozh'e Cossacks to Sultan Mehmed IV of Turkey*, completed in 1891.

77. Yel'tsin, *Marafon*, 349.

78. On his visit to Britain in the last week of September, undertaken after his return from Sochi, Yeltsin spent a night at Chequers as a guest of John Major. He and

the prime minister called on an English pub in the village of Great Kimble, knocking on the door to get the owner to open up (Yeltsin said he was the president of Russia and the proprietor replied that he was the kaiser of Germany). That evening at the residence, Yeltsin "came downstairs visibly drunk, and took an immediate dislike to his placement. He picked up his own table card, next door to that of Princess Alexandra, and deposited both the card and himself next to John Major, with whom he chatted amiably, if incoherently, all evening." Max Hastings, *Editor: An Inside Story of Newspapers* (London: Macmillan, 2002), 205.

79. Yel'tsin, *Marafon*, 348–50.

80. "When she caught sight of Korzhakov, she shook" (*Pri vide Korzhakova, yei sotryaslo*). Valentin Yumashev, third interview with the author (September 13, 2006).

81. Baturin et al., *Epokha*, 515.

82. Ibid., 524; Lyudmila Pikhoya, interview with the author (September 26, 2001).

83. Yel'tsin, *Marafon*, 349.

84. Ludwig, *King of the Mountain*, 453.

85. For Churchill in the 1930s, "A typical day's imbibing would begin in midmorning with a whisky and soda and continue through a bottle of champagne at lunch, more whisky and soda in the afternoon, sherry before dinner, another bottle of champagne during dinner, the best part of a bottle of brandy after dinner, and would end with a final whisky and soda before going to bed. On occasions he drank even more than this." Clive Ponting, *Churchill* (London: Sinclair-Stevenson, 1994), 388.

86. Anatolii Chernyayev, *1991 god: dnevnik pomoshchnika Prezidenta SSSR* (The year 1991: diary of an assistant to the president of the USSR) (Moscow: TERRA, 1997), 265.

87. Stephanopoulos, *All Too Human*, 140. Of the correspondence between alcohol consumption and performance in government, Ludwig (in *King of the Mountain*, 230) reports being "astounded by how well certain rulers were able to run their countries and accomplish impressive deeds" despite their periodic abuse of alcohol. He gives Churchill and Atatürk as examples. A counterexample is Harold Wilson, the British prime minister of the 1960s and 1970s who suffered alcoholic dementia by age sixty.

88. I first heard this interpretation of mass attitudes toward Yeltsin's use of alcohol from the pollster Aleksandr Oslon (interview, January 25, 2001).

89. Ruslan Khasbulatov, interview with the author (September 26, 2001).

90. Yel'tsin, *Zapiski*, 156.

91. "Sostoyaniye zdorov'ya Borisa Yel'tsina khorosheye" (The state of Boris Yeltsin's health is good), *Izvestiya*, July 10, 1992.

92. *Muzhskoi razgovor.*

93. Korzhakov's firsthand account stresses Yeltsin's heart pains, but the group had drinks on the ground and in the air. During the 1996 election campaign, Boris Nemtsov, the governor of Nizhnii Novgorod region, who had made cracks about

Shannon, was to accompany him on a snap trip to Chechnya. Nemtsov polished off a quart of vodka on the return flight—Yeltsin had almost none—and was incoherent in front of the press at the Moscow airport. Back in Nizhnii, a telephone call from Yeltsin awakened him the next morning at six A.M., and the president taunted him with the similarity to his mishap in Ireland. "Boris Nemtsov—Yevgenii Al'bats o Yel'tsine" (Boris Nemtsov to Yevgeniya Al'bats about Yeltsin), *Novoye vremya/New Times*, April 30, 2007.

94. The dates of the first two attacks were publicized in 1995. The third was kept secret and is mentioned, without an exact date, in Chazov, *Rok*, 250–51; Korzhakov, *Boris Yel'tsin*, 319; and Yel'tsin, *Marafon*, 22. Chazov speaks of an attack in September 1995, but seems to confuse it with the event of October 26. Yeltsin implies in his memoir that his first full-fledged heart attack (a myocardial infarction, which causes permanent damage to muscle cells) was in December; Chazov, a cardiologist, does not make this distinction.

95. Korzhakov, *Boris Yel'tsin . . . poslesloviye*, 325–26.

96. Chazov, *Rok*, 248–50. In the United States in October, Yeltsin was busy at the bar at the United Nations and the summit with President Clinton in Hyde Park, New York. It was after Hyde Park that Clinton made his oft-quoted one-liner to Strobe Talbott that "Yeltsin drunk is better than most of the alternatives sober." Yeltsin was to claim in *Marafon*, 49, that he was never shown the physicians' report that recommended the angiogram.

97. See the comments on Yeltsin drinking faux vodka toasts with water in Kulikov, *Tyazhëlyye zvëzdy*, 450.

98. Drafts of Article 3 contained a guarantee of "freedom of the means of mass communication." Liberal aides preferred the grander "freedom of mass communication," and won the president over.

99. Quotations from Baturin et al., *Epokha*, 494.

100. Vyacheslav Kostikov, interview with the author (May 28, 2001). Journalists sometimes got phone calls from Yeltsin about particular stories. In September 1992, for example, Yeltsin rang up *Izvestiya*'s diplomatic correspondent and told him his stories about Russian-Japanese relations were "too ironic," but his tone was warm and he did not demand any change. Konstantin Eggert, interview with the author (September 12, 2006).

101. Yakovlev had broadcast a documentary about ethnic relations in the North Caucasus that inflamed local officials; Poptsov was accused of anti-government bias in news coverage. Both moved on to other successes.

102. Ellen Mickiewiecz, *Changing Channels: Television and the Struggle for Power in Russia* (New York: Oxford University Press, 1997); Ivan Zassoursky, *Media and Power in Post-Soviet Russia* (Armonk, N.Y.: Sharpe, 2004).

103. Mayor Anatolii Sobchak of St. Petersburg was involved in the negotiations over its creation, because it initially broadcast on Channel 5, the national station out of the northern capital. NTV moved to Channel 4 in 1994 and was allowed to

broadcast the full day three years later. The first private station in Russia was TV-6, which started in January 1993. Originally partnered with Ted Turner, TV-6 mostly broadcast entertainment.

104. Igor Malashenko, interview with the author (March 18, 2001).

105. Viktor Shenderovich, interview with the author (February 26, 2004); Shenderovich, *Kukliada* (Puppet games) (St. Petersburg: Izdatel'stvo Fonda Russkoi poezii, 1999), 21–44; David E. Hoffman, *The Oligarchs: Wealth and Power in the New Russia* (New York: PublicAffairs, 2002), 291–94. The script for "Lower Depths" is in Shenderovich, *Kukly* (Puppets) (Moscow: VAGRIUS, 1996), 137–44. Hoffman emphasizes Korzhakov as the instigator of the formal charge, but Shenderovich (interview) said it was made at the request of Chernomyrdin.

106. Shenderovich interview. The Hamlet skit is in Shenderovich, *Kukly*, 6–15.

107. Shenderovich, *Kukly*, 121–22.

108. I am grateful to John Dunn of the University of Glasgow for the total number of Yeltsin roles. See his "Humour and Satire on Post-Soviet Russian Television," in Lesley Milne, ed., *Reflective Laughter: Aspects of Humour in Russian Culture* (London: Anthem Press, 2004), 181–222.

109. Shenderovich, *Kukly*, 136.

110. Author's interviews with family members.

Chapter Thirteen

1. The nickname for the route when Stalin was driven up and down it daily was the *amerikanka*, "American way," in reference to its satin-smooth blacktop. Stalin's two main dachas were located off of it, which was one of its attractions to the communist elite. The area it ran through had little industry, was upwind and upriver of Moscow and its pollution, and contained many villas and gentry estates from tsarist times that were adaptable to new needs.

2. As noted in Chapter 10, Yeltsin was in Building No. 14 for about eighteen months in 1994–96. During the reconstruction of Building No. 1, the focal fireplace in the president's ceremonial office was also redone in malachite at his request. Ivan Sautov, director of the Tsarskoye Selo estate near St. Petersburg, supervised the renewal. "Yeltsin was very satisfied and personally thanked many of the builders and subcontractors. He is after all a construction engineer and understands this kind of thing." "U nas tut vsë nastoyashcheye" (Everything here is genuine), interview with Pavel Borodin in *Kommersant-Daily*, March 24, 1999. Lenin, Stalin, and Khrushchev all had their Kremlin offices in Building No. 1, though in different rooms than Gorbachev; Brezhnev's place was in Building No. 14.

3. Boris Yel'tsin, *Prezidentskii marafon* (Presidential marathon) (Moscow: AST, 2000), 166.

4. Quotations from ibid., 167–68.

5. Examples here would be American presidential theory, France's dual executive, and German federalism and electoral legislation.

6. "My mozhem byt' tvërdo uvereny: Rossiya vozroditsya" (We can be certain that Russia will be reborn), *Izvestiya*, July 10, 1991.

7. "Obrashcheniye Prezidenta Rossii k narodam Rossii, k s"ezdu narodnykh deputatov Rossiiskoi Federatsii" (Address of the president of Russia to the peoples of Russia and the Congress of People's Deputies of the Russian Federation), *Rossiiskaya gazeta*, October 29, 1991.

8. Stalin told a relative in the 1930s that the Russians "need a tsar, whom they can worship and for whom they can live and work." He compared himself to Peter the Great, Alexander I, Nicholas I, and the Persian shahs. Georgia, his birthplace, was for centuries part of the Persian empire. Simon Sebag Montefiore, *Stalin: The Court of the Red Tsar* (New York: Random House, 2003), 177.

9. Peter Reddaway and Dmitri Glinski, *The Tragedy of Russia's Reforms: Market Bolshevism against Democracy* (Washington, D.C.: U.S. Institute of Peace, 2001); Lilia Shevtsova, *Yeltsin's Russia: Myths and Reality* (Washington, D.C.: Carnegie Endowment for International Peace, 1999).

10. Boris Nemtsov, *Provintsial* (Provincial) (Moscow: VAGRIUS, 1997), 81–82. The incident in Nizhnii Novgorod is more fully described in Chrystia Freeland, *Sale of the Century: Russia's Wild Ride from Communism to Capitalism* (Toronto: Doubleday, 2000), 38–40.

11. These are the components of the regal bearing given in Arnold M. Ludwig, *King of the Mountain: The Nature of Political Leadership* (Lexington: University Press of Kentucky, 2002), 179–80.

12. The appellation ignored Boris Godunov, whose life was fictionalized in Alexander Pushkin's play and Modest Mussorgsky's opera. Godunov reigned from 1598 to 1605, during the Time of Troubles preceding the Romanov dynasty.

13. His granddaughter Yekaterina related in the late 1980s that when she asked Yeltsin's help with a personal problem (removing the bodyguard attached to her when she enrolled in university), "The tsar resolved the problem in his own manner" and ordered the guard removed. "Sensatsionnoye interv'yu rossiiskoi 'printsessy'" (Sensational interview with a Russian princess), *Moskovskii komsomolets*, January 9, 1998. The piece was first published in *Paris Match* in December 1997.

14. Boris Nemtsov, first interview with the author (October 17, 2000). The exchange in Stockholm occurred on December 2, 1997, in Yeltsin's second term.

15. Pavel Voshchanov, interview with the author (June 15, 2000). That incident occurred in February 1992, just before Voshchanov stepped down, when he questioned a personnel decision by Yeltsin.

16. Boris Yeltsin, third interview with the author (September 12, 2002)

17. Aleksandr Livshits, interview with the author (January 19, 2001).

18. Yu, M. Baturin et al., *Epokha Yel'tsina: ocherki politicheskoi istorii* (The Yeltsin epoch: essays in political history) (Moscow: VAGRIUS, 2001), 424.

19. Yegor Gaidar, second interview with the author (January 31, 2002).

20. Boris Fëdorov, *Desyat' bezumnykh let* (Ten crazy years) (Moscow: Sovershenno sekretno, 1999), 131.

21. Livshits interview.

22. The Kremlin had constitutional authority over 30,000 positions in the executive branch (Donald N. Jensen, "How Russia Is Ruled—1998," *Demokratizatsiya/Democratization* 7 [Summer 1999], 349). But the number Yeltsin attended to was several hundred.

23. Yeltsin concerned himself with golden parachutes only for functionaries who had been close to him. In 1993, for instance, he made Yurii Petrov head of a new State Investment Corporation, in control of several hundred million dollars of capital. When Viktor Ilyushin stepped down as senior assistant in 1996, he was appointed deputy prime minister, and when he left that position he was hired as a vice president of Gazprom. But most of the departed easily found opportunities in the new private sector. As Oleg Soskovets, the ranking member of the Korzhakov group, with whom Yeltsin broke in 1996, put it, "In contemporary Russia, you can use your knowledge outside of the public service. They give you something to occupy yourself with, thank God." Interview with the author (March 31, 2004).

24. Officeholders are given at http://rulers.org/russgov.html. Not counted here are the new defense minister and the new head of internal security appointed in late June 1996.

25. Baturin et al., *Epokha*, 339.

26. Yeltsin allies from the democratic opposition to the Soviet regime criticized the appropriation of the health directorate. See, for example, Ella Pamfilova, "Grustno i stranno" (Sadly and strangely), in Yurii Burtin and Eduard Molchanov, eds., *God posle avgusta: gorech' i vybor* (A year after August: bitterness and choice) (Moscow: Literatura i politika, 1992), 188–89.

27. Quotation from Ivan Goryaev, "The Best of the Empires, Or Crafty Devil of a Manager," http://www.newtimes.ru/eng/detail.asp?art_id=150. Borodin, a former CPSU apparatchik, had been mayor of Yakutsk since 1988 and met Korzhakov while a deputy to the Russian congress in 1990–91. He was named deputy director of the unreformed business department (then called the Main Social-Production Directorate) in the spring of 1993. The USSR Council of Ministers and the Central Committee of the CPSU had separate business offices before 1991. The head of the party unit, Nikolai Kruchina, committed suicide after the August putsch. The presidential equivalent was then kept apart from the government's, and the congress of deputies had its own benefits arm.

28. Boris Fëdorov, interview with the author (September 22, 2001).

29. The involvement in the oil trade came to light in Yevgeniya Al'bats, "Vlast' taino sozdaët svoyu tenevuyu ekonomiku" (The authorities are secretly creating their own shadow economy), *Izvestiya*, February 1, 1995. Borodin is said to have asked for an oil-export quota from the Ministry of Economics after it turned down as unaffordable, and unacceptable to the Duma, his request for funds to pay for the restoration of the Grand Kremlin Palace. An unidentified ministry official recalls: "Pal Palych . . . said, 'Then give me 5 million tons of oil.' I agreed—where else was he going to turn?" Maksim Glikin, "Oni v svoikh koridorakh" (They are in their own

corridors), *Obshchaya gazeta*, February 8, 2001. The quota, the same source said, was later increased to 8 million tons. That much oil would have sold in the late 1990s for the better part of $1 billion, some of which would have gone to Russian producers, to taxes, and no doubt to middlemen.

30. Boris Fëdorov estimated that in his day 1 percent of requests for apartments and the like made their way to Yeltsin. Yeltsin usually routed them to Borodin, sometimes with a handwritten note. On one occasion, Yeltsin offered a toast at a banquet to an official in the executive office, mentioning in passing that this man's housing conditions were poor. Borodin dealt with the problem without further ado. Fëdorov interview and Leonid Smirnyagin, interview with the author (May 24, 2001).

31. In 1994 Borodin controlled twenty premium dachas with a chef and security guards, 150 year-round dachas without these services, and 200 summer-season dachas. Eugene Huskey, *Presidential Power in Russia* (Armonk, N.Y.: M. E. Sharpe, 1999), 52.

32. "Poslaniye Prezidenta Rossiiskoi Federatsii Federal'nomu Sobraniyu, 'Ob ukreplenii rossiiskogo gosudarstva'" (The message of the president of the Russian Federation to the Federal Assembly, "On strengthening the Russian state") (Moscow: Rossiiskaya Federatsiya, 1994), 14.

33. Gennadii Burbulis, second interview, conducted by Yevgeniya Al'bats (February 14, 2001). The idea was not original with Burbulis. The constitutional scholar Avgust Mishin and others had been circulating it for some time.

34. Grigorii Yavlinskii, first interview with the author (March 17, 2001).

35. James MacGregor Burns, *Transforming Leadership: A New Pursuit of Happiness* (New York: Atlantic Monthly Press, 2003), chap. 10.

36. Aleksandr Korzhakov, *Boris Yel'tsin: ot rassveta do zakata* (Boris Yeltsin: from dawn to dusk) (Moscow: Interbuk, 1997), 253–54.

37. Strobe Talbott, *The Russia Hand: A Memoir of Presidential Diplomacy* (New York: Random House, 2002), 177.

38. Baturin et al., *Epokha*, 423.

39. Vyacheslav Kostikov, *Roman s prezidentom: zapiski press-sekretarya* (Romance with a president: notes of a press secretary) (Moscow: VAGRIUS, 1997), 12. The comparisons to a magnetic field or a snake come from my interview with Yevgenii Yasin (May 31, 2001). Gennadii Burbulis (first interview, June 14, 2000) saw a similarity to a wolf lying in ambush.

40. Yel'tsin, *Marafon*, 413.

41. Baturin et al., *Epokha*, 449.

42. Mikhail Zinin,"Yel'tsina zhdët Boldinskaya osen'" (A Boldin-type autumn awaits Yeltsin), *Nezavisimaya gazeta*, September 18, 1991.

43. Yasin interview. Decree No. 226 also relieved lobbying pressure on government bureaucrats. They could now indicate sympathy with the petitioner while saying their hands were tied. See Baturin et al., *Epokha*, 442.

44. Huskey, *Presidential Power in Russia*, 73.

45. Ibid., 40.

46. Anatolii Chubais, first interview with the author (January 18, 2001).

47. Mikhail Bocharov, interview with the author (October 19, 2000).

48. Of the first position, Yeltsin writes (*Zapiski*, 241), "It was thought up 'especially for Burbulis,' to underline his special status." The second was bestowed in part to compensate Burbulis for not being named vice president. Burbulis (second interview) said it was a "role," not a "position."

49. Poltoranin had been minister of the press and information since 1991 and favored a more restrictive attitude toward the media than Fedotov. When Yeltsin, responding to parliamentary sentiment, made Fedotov minister in December 1992 (for the second time), he put Poltoranin in charge of a new Federal Information Center, which duplicated many of the ministry's functions. Ministry and center were both dissolved in December 1993.

50. While all were aware of Yeltsin's dislike of long memos, some found that they could slip in additional information in attachments and illustrative materials. One official took the art to a higher form by throwing in attachments and making references in the body of the note to them. Yeltsin never reprimanded him for this practice. Andrei Kokoshin, interview with the author (June 6, 2000).

51. Baturin et al., *Epokha*, 436.

52. Viktor Chernomyrdin, interview with the author (September 15, 2000).

53. Oleg Poptsov, *Trevozhnyye sny tsarskoi svity* (The uneasy dreams of the tsar's retinue) (Moscow: Sovershenno sekretno, 2000), 100.

54. Boris Yeltsin, first interview with the author (July 15, 2001).

55. Boris Yel'tsin, *Zapiski prezidenta* (Notes of a president) (Moscow: Ogonëk, 1994), 262–63.

56. Oleg Lobov, interview with the author (May 29, 2002).

57. This was made abundantly clear in my interviews with both men. Korzhakov (*Boris Yel'tsin*, 280) describes Soskovets and several others acquiring tape recordings of speeches of the tongue-tied premier and making fun of them.

58. Morshchakov, fifteen years older than Yeltsin, had been his early protector in Sverdlovsk and the organizer of his duck and elk shoots when he was first secretary (see Chapters 3 and 4). Yeltsin first recruited him to work in the Russian Supreme Soviet while he was its chairman. Petrov and Lobov were somewhat younger than Yeltsin. Ilyushin, sixteen years younger, was from Nizhnii Tagil (like Petrov) and had been first secretary of the Sverdlovsk Komsomol and a member of the bureau of the obkom. Lobov was deputy or first deputy premier for four stints (in 1991, 1993, 1996, and 1996–97) and secretary of the Security Council from 1993 to 1996. Another prominent Sverdlovsker was Yevgenii Bychkov, the chairman of the state committee for precious metals and jewels until 1996, but he was appointed to this position by Gorbachev in 1985. One of his deputies after 1991 was Yurii Kornilov, the former chief of the Sverdlovsk KGB.

59. Pikhoya was still in the UPI social sciences department when she joined Yeltsin. Burbulis was affiliated with the institute from 1974 to 1983. Three other UPI faculty members came to Moscow at the same time as Pikhoya.

60. Lyudmila Pikhoya, interview with the author (September 26, 2001).

61. Fëdorov interview.

62. Yeltsin in his memoirs (*Zapiski*, 247) refers to Burbulis as "de facto the head of the Cabinet of Ministers" in the early months. Gaidar soon replaced him as the same. Yeltsin once or twice interceded at cabinet meetings on narrow points. At a session in December 1992, he criticized Andrei Vorob'ëv, the aging health minister, who passed out. Yeltsin fired him days later. Vorob'ëv was to help treat Yeltsin's heart condition in 1996. Sergei Kolesnikov, Chernomyrdin's head speech writer, interview with the author (June 8, 2000).

63. Gennadii Burbulis, third interview, conducted by Yevgeniya Al'bats (August 31, 2001). The State Council replaced a Political Consultative Council Burbulis set up for Yeltsin as head of the Russian parliament in 1990. Besides informing Yeltsin, this earlier body was designed to help him outbid Gorbachev for the affections of the Moscow intelligentsia.

64. The cabinet ministers were Eduard Dneprov (minister of education), Nikolai Fëdorov (justice), Andrei Kozyrev (foreign affairs), Valerii Makharadze (deputy premier), and Aleksandr Shokhin (deputy premier and labor minister). Shakhrai retained the title of state counselor when he became a deputy premier in December 1991.

65. "The creators of the new structure . . . are inspired by the idea of 'the constructive state,' which they juxtapose to 'the corrupting state' based on apparatus 'moves,' 'corridor pragmatism,' and the system of personal connections and mutual favors. To all appearances, the leaders of the State Council see the source of this evil in the old apparatus of the Russian Council of Ministers." Burbulis antagonized others by trying to get a clause in the State Council's charter giving it the right to review all draft presidential decrees. Mikhail Leont'ev, "Rossiya bez pravitel'stva" (Russia without a government), *Nezavisimaya gazeta*, October 5, 1991.

66. Sergei Stankevich, interview with the author (May 29, 2001). The same point was emphasized by Sergei Shakhrai, second interview with the author (January 24, 2001).

67. Yel'tsin, *Zapiski*, 242.

68. Stankevich was to be accused of corruption for an incident in 1993. He fled the country in 1995 and returned in 1999 after the charges were dropped. A group of ten or eleven presidential advisers, most of them unpaid, remained on the roster until the end of 1993. They had very little say collectively or individually. Yeltsin retained a few individuals with that rank in later years.

69. Kostikov, *Roman s prezidentom*, 322. Most speculation about a supercoordinator fastened on the Security Council. Its founding secretary, Skokov, and Aleksandr Lebed, who directed it briefly in 1996, used it as a political bandstand, but its ability to coordinate was slight.

70. See Korzhakov, *Boris Yel'tsin*, 140–50, who says Yeltsin wanted the house to contain a common laundry and an apartment where all the residents would have social events (neither was built). Yeltsin's daughter has said he "spent literally a couple of nights" at the flat between 1994 and 2000. Tat'yana D'yachenko, "Papa khotel

otpraznovat' yubilei po-domashnemu" (Papa wanted to celebrate his birthday home-style), *Komsomol'skaya pravda*, February 1, 2001. Vladimir Shevchenko (*Povsednevnaya zhizn' Kremlya pri prezidentakh* [The everyday life of the Kremlin under the presidents] [Moscow: Molodaya gvardiya, 2004], 36) describes the aversion to the house in the same terms Yeltsin in his memoirs used to describe his overexposure to Gennadii Burbulis: "Psychologically, it was very difficult and untenable to see and converse with the very same people at home and at work."

71. Yel'tsin, *Zapiski*, 341.

72. According to Korzhakov, Yeltsin was "categorically against" admitting Chernomyrdin. Korzhakov convinced him, pointing out that several deputy premiers had been accepted. Aleksandr Korzhakov, *Boris Yel'tsin: ot rassveta do zakata; poslesloviye* (Boris Yeltsin: from dawn to dusk; epilogue) (Moscow: Detektiv-press, 2004), 35.

73. When I spoke to Berezovskii about Yeltsin, one of his opening points was that the president had acknowledged his worth by bringing him into the club. Berezovskii, interview with the author (March 8, 2002). Rybkin also spoke fondly about it, and a half-decade after its dissolution was still carrying a member's card in his wallet (interview, May 29, 2001). The bylaws reserved expulsion for one offense only: betrayal *(predatel'stvo)*, which was to be decided by unanimous vote of the members. When Korzhakov lost his job in June 1996, he was evicted from the club in simpler fashion. Chernomyrdin, a member at Korzhakov's insistence, phoned him and told him not to come around any more. "There was nothing to do. I packed up my things and went to exercise somewhere else." Korzhakov, *Boris Yel'tsin*, 36.

74. Quotation from Valentin Yumashev, fourth interview with the author (January 22, 2007). Membership figure from Shamil' Tarpishchev, *Samyi dolgii match* (The longest match) (Moscow: VAGRIUS, 1999), 294.

75. Yurii Petrov, first and second interviews with the author (May 25, 2000, and February 1, 2002).

76. Yeltsin emphasized his unhappiness at Petrov's tactics in *Zapiski*, 297.

77. Quotation from Yel'tsin, *Marafon*, 257.

78. Huskey, *Presidential Power in Russia*, 58–59.

79. In addition to three or four other policy-specific assistants, the group included service providers such as Yeltsin's protocol chief, head of chancery, and speech writers. The guitar-strumming Lev Sukhanov, who began with Yeltsin in Gosstroi in 1988, remained until 1997. His interest in the occult made him a marginal presence in his last several years in the Kremlin.

80. Baturin et al., *Epokha*, 210. Although Filatov's organization was much bigger, the physical setup privileged Ilyushin. Filatov had his office in Kremlin Building No. 14 and Ilyushin his in Building No. 1, several doors from Yeltsin.

81. For example, on the morning commute with Yeltsin, Korzhakov noted the first secretary's comments about stores they had inspected along the way. He would then telephone the party secretary for trade and services, Alla Nizovtseva, with a report. Nizovtseva, says Korzhakov, did not object to these calls, but Viktor Ilyushin,

then the senior aide to Yeltsin in the gorkom, did object and accused Korzhakov of sticking his nose in other people's business. Ilyushin was further annoyed when Korzhakov and Yeltsin developed their friendship in the summer of 1986. "He became more and more nervous when Boris Nikolayevich assigned me business falling outside the jurisdiction of the guard service." Korzhakov, *Boris Yel'tsin*, 63.

82. Aleksandr Korzhakov, interview with the author (January 28, 2002).

83. Filatov, *Sovershenno nesekretno*, 233. The eavesdropping and its targets, which included Filatov and his family, Viktor Ilyushin, and members of the Chernomyrdin machine, are detailed in Igor' Korotchenko, "Kompromat" (Compromising material), *Nezavisimaya gazeta*, October 12, 1996; and Valerii Streletskii, *Mrakobesiye* (Obscurantism) (Moscow: Detektiv-Press, 1998). The head of research of the Kremlin's executive office was surprised when the surveillance began, associating it with Soviet ways, but thought it deterred the leaking and sale of sensitive information. Mark Urnov, interview with the author (May 26, 2000).

84. Third Yeltsin interview.

85. The outstanding example is Korzhakov's letter to Chernomyrdin of November 30, 1994, about Russian oil exports, in which he advised him to turn over supervision to Soskovets. See Korzhakov, *Boris Yel'tsin*, 406–10; and Irina Savvateyeva, "Kto upravlyayet stranoi—Yel'tsin, Chernomyrdin ili General Korzhakov?" (Who governs Russia—Yeltsin, Chernomyrdin, or General Korzhakov?), *Izvestiya*, December 22, 1994.

86. See, for instance, the description by Yeltsin of Korzhakov's advocacy of Barsukov (*Marafon*, 78); and details on his role in the decision on the procurator general, in Yurii Skuratov, *Variant drakona* (Version of the dragon) (Moscow: Detektiv, 2000), 68–70. The procurator whom Skuratov replaced, Aleksei Il'yushenko (the man who charged NTV with slander for the *Kukly* satire), had also been appointed at Korzhakov's behest in 1994. Korzhakov was godfather of Soskovets's first grandson in 1994, and at the same ceremony Soskovets himself was baptized, with Korzhakov again as godfather.

87. Anatolii Kulikov, *Tyazhëlyye zvëzdy* (Heavy stars) (Moscow: Voina i mir, 2002), 358.

88. Yel'tsin, *Marafon*, 24.

89. Ibid., 78, 256–57.

90. Korzhakov, *Boris Yel'tsin*, 243–46.

91. Yel'tsin, *Zapiski*, 326.

92. Yel'tsin, *Marafon*, 257.

93. Alena V. Ledeneva, *How Russia Really Works: The Informal Practices That Shaped Post-Soviet Politics and Business* (Ithaca: Cornell University Press, 2006), 11.

Chapter Fourteen

1. Aleksandr Korzhakov, *Boris Yel'tsin: ot rassveta do zakata* (Boris Yeltsin: from dawn to dusk) (Moscow: Interbuk, 1997), 308; Nikolai Zen'kovich, *Boris Yel'tsin:*

raznyye zhizni (Boris Yeltsin: various lives), 2 vols. (Moscow: OLMA, 2001), 2:465. In the interview, published in *Komsomol'skaya pravda,* Yeltsin said he favored training a group of twenty leaders from which his successor would be elected. Nothing was done about the suggestion.

2. Dmitri K. Simes, *After the Collapse: Russia Seeks Its Place as a Great Power* (New York: Simon and Schuster, 1999), 139.

3. Strobe Talbott, *The Russia Hand: A Memoir of Presidential Diplomacy* (New York: Random House, 2002), 33.

4. Yu, M. Baturin et al., *Epokha Yel'tsina: ocherki politicheskoi istorii* (The Yeltsin epoch: essays in political history) (Moscow: VAGRIUS, 2001), 525–30; Georgii Satarov, first interview with the author (June 5, 2000).

5. There is scathing commentary in Vyacheslav Kostikov, *Roman s prezidentom: zapiski press-sekretarya* (Romance with a president: notes of a press secretary) (Moscow: VAGRIUS, 1997), 120–21.

6. Sergei Medvedev, interview with the author (May 28, 2001).

7. See http://www.fotuva.org/newsletters/fot13.html.

8. Tatyana Malkina, interview with the author (June 13, 2001).

9. See Korzhakov, *Boris Yel'tsin,* 329–31; and Andrei Shleifer and Daniel Treisman, *Without a Map: Political Tactics and Economic Reform in Russia* (Cambridge, Mass.: MIT Press, 2000), 47.

10. Malkina interview. She added that Yeltsin now and again acted as if he were in a trance or "not of these parts" *(nezdeshnii).*

11. See especially M. Steven Fish, "Russia's Fourth Transition," *Journal of Democracy* 5 (July 1994), 31–42; Marc Morjé Howard, *The Weakness of Civil Society in Post-Communist Europe* (Cambridge: Cambridge University Press, 2003); and Henry E. Hale, *Why Not Parties in Russia? Democracy, Federalism, and the State* (Cambridge: Cambridge University Press, 2006).

12. Source: scattered press reports; second interview with Gennadii Burbulis, conducted by Yevgeniya Al'bats (February 14, 2001); Sergei Stankevich, interview with the author (May 29, 2001).

13. Yevgenii Krasnikov, "Demokraty sozdayut izbiratel'nyi blok" (The democrats create an electoral bloc), *Nezavisimaya gazeta,* June 17, 1993.

14. Details here from Yegor Gaidar, second interview with the author (January 31, 2002). Gaidar was bitter that Yeltsin did not tell him man-to-man that he would not show up for the Russia's Choice congress, but delegated the honor to Viktor Ilyushin. Government minister Aleksandr Shokhin and presidential adviser Sergei Stankevich stood with Shakhrai on the list of his Party of Russian Unity and Accord.

15. Second Gaidar interview. As it was, Russia's Choice received 16 percent of the votes in the party-list half of the vote, 7 points fewer than Vladimir Zhirinovskii's LDPR. Shakhrai's miniparty received 7 percent, which if added to the Russia's Choice vote, even without assistance from Yeltsin, would have put it into a dead heat with the LDPR.

16. Author's first interview with Sergei Filatov (May 25, 2000) and second interview with Aleksandr Yakovlev (March 29, 2004).

17. Ivan Rybkin, interview with the author (May 29, 2001); first Satarov interview.

18. Korzhakov, *Boris Yel'tsin*, 382.

19. Boris Yeltsin, second interview with the author (February 9, 2000).

20. Yevgenii Savast'yanov, interview with the author (June 9, 2000).

21. Viktor Chernomyrdin, interview with the author (September 15, 2000). As prime instigators, he mentioned the Korzhakov-Soskovets group and Viktor Ilyushin. See also Baturin et al., *Epokha*, 541.

22. Oleg Poptsov, *Khronika vremën "Tsarya Borisa"* (Chronicle of the times of "Tsar Boris") (Moscow: Sovershenno sekretno, 1995), 220.

23. Fifteen percent of citizens polled by VTsIOM in September 1994 said they would vote for Yeltsin if an election were held tomorrow. This number slid to 6 percent in March 1995. A poll by the same organization in October 1994 revealed that a mere 3 percent had complete trust in Yeltsin, which were fewer than trusted six other politicians. Oleg Moroz, *1996: kak Zyuganov ne stal prezidentom* (1996: how Zyuganov did not become president) (Moscow: Raduga, 2006), 10–11.

24. Lee Hockstader, "Yeltsin, Communist Zyuganov Launch Presidential Bids," *The Washington Post*, February 16, 1996. The Russian media reported on January 22 that Gaidar was advising Yeltsin not to run at all, saying any Yeltsin candidacy would be "suicidal" and "the best present that could possibly be given to the communists." Yeltsin wrote him a letter on February 2 asking him to be governed "not by emotions but by the interests of Russia." Yegor Gaidar, *Dni porazhenii i pobed* (Days of defeats and victories) (Moscow: VAGRIUS, 1996), 357–58.

25. The most thorough tracking polls on degrees of support were done by the VTsIOM organization, but it did none of this kind between April 1994 and March 1996. Not much seems to have changed through the end of 1995, and so we can take the April 1994 results as indicative. They showed a mere 4 percent of citizens unreservedly supporting Yeltsin and 4 percent supporting him "as long as he is leader of the democratic forces." Thirty-one percent were opposed to him in varying degrees, while a plurality of 42 percent indicated ambivalence. In March 1996 supporters of Yeltsin, by this measure, still came to only 12 percent, with 41 percent opposed and ambivalent citizens coming to 38 percent. Yu, A. Levada et al., *Obshchestvennoye mneniye—1999* (Public opinion—1999 edition) (Moscow: Vserossiiskii tsentr izucheniya obshchestvennogo mneniya, 2000), 100–101.

26. Author's interviews with family members, which directly and persuasively contradict the assertion in Korzhakov, *Boris Yel'tsin*, 316–17, that the family pushed him to run in order to preserve their style of life. Boris Yel'tsin, *Prezidentskii marafon* (Presidential marathon) (Moscow: AST, 2000), 23, notes Naina's opposition.

27. Yel'tsin, *Marafon*, 25.

28. Mark Urnov, interview with the author (May 26, 2000).

29. Yel'tsin, *Marafon*, 24–25.

30. Gaidar, *Dni porazhenii i pobed,* 362.

31. Anatolii Kulikov, *Tyazhëlyye zvëzdy* (Heavy stars) (Moscow: Voina i mir, 2002), 389.

32. L. N. Dobrokhotov, ed., *Ot Yel'tsina k . . . Yel'tsinu: prezidentskaya gonka-96* (From Yeltsin . . . to Yeltsin: the 1996 presidential race) (Moscow: TERRA, 1997), 94.

33. Yel'tsin, *Marafon,* 26. In my interview with him (March 31, 2004), Soskovets would say only that he and Yeltsin had several conversations about the succession question. But Korzhakov (interview with the author, January 28, 2002) and Andranik Migranyan (interview, June 8, 2000) explicitly recalled Yeltsin saying in their hearing that he wanted Soskovets to be president after him.

34. Tat'yana D'yachenko, "Yesli by papa ne stal prezidentom . . . " (If papa had not become president), *Ogonëk,* October 23, 2000.

35. Korzhakov (*Boris Yel'tsin,* 323) notes that she "did not like Soskovets's tone." If she had known more about her father's work as a party functionary, he claims, she would have known that "Soskovets's style was close to that of the early Yeltsin."

36. Irina Savvateyeva, "Boris Yel'tsin predlozhil rossiiskim bankam sotrudnichestvo" (Boris Yeltsin suggests cooperation with Russia's banks), *Izvestiya,* September 1, 1995.

37. Both Soskovets (interview) and Chubais (second interview with the author, March 30, 2004) stressed the role of Soskovets in getting Yeltsin on board for the law. Potanin (interview with the author, September 25, 2001) said Yeltsin took no interest in the auction process. "[He felt that] this was not the king's business, it was very dirty stuff. There are dividing some things up over there—so what? I let them go to work, let them figure it out themselves."

38. The book contract and sponsorship for the club were first revealed in Korzhakov's memoirs and were confirmed in broad outline in my interview with Berezovskii (March 8, 2000).

39. The cars are mentioned in Korzhakov, *Boris Yeltsin,* 284. Some details from an interview with Korzhakov are provided in Paul Klebnikov, *Godfather of the Kremlin: Boris Berezovsky and the Looting of Russia* (New York: Harcourt, 2000), 201. Berezovskii denied having made the gifts in his interview with me. In my second interview with Tatyana (September 11, 2006), she was adamant that she never received them. She purchased a Niva herself in 1992, she said, before ever meeting Berezovskii, and never owned or drove a Blazer.

40. The other partners in Ogonëk were Oleg Boiko and Aleksandr Smolenskii.

41. The timing is important here. Some accounts of the meeting date it in February but others in early to late March. The actual time—the week of Shrovetide—is established by the recollection by Smolenskii that they ate a Shrovetide repast, since this was the time of year. Sergei Agafonov, "Maslenitsa 1996 goda" (Shrovetide in 1996), *Ogonëk,* March 20, 2006. In the Orthodox calendar in 1996, Shrovetide (*Maslenitsa,* in Russian), the feast before the Lenten fast, went from February 19 to February 25.

42. Quotation from Yel'tsin, *Marafon*, 30.

43. Mikhail Khodorkovskii, interview with the author (June 7, 2001); Agafonov, "Maslenitsa 1996 goda." There are also good descriptions of the meeting in David E. Hoffman, *The Oligarchs: Wealth and Power in the New Russia* (New York: PublicAffairs, 2002), 331–33; and Moroz, *1996*, 196–97, which corrects Hoffman on some details but gets the timing wrong.

44. Berezovskii had made Naina Yeltsina's acquaintance in 1993 when a mutual friend asked him to host a benefit reception for a childcare center Yeltsina patronized; Yeltsina, second interview with the author (September 18, 2007). In an interview with David Hoffman in 2000 (*Oligarchs*, 333), Berezovskii said he approached Mrs. Yeltsin with a request for help to speak to Yeltsin privately after the Kremlin meeting. He reminded Yeltsin of the request and they met for several minutes.

45. Some of them, desiring to inflate their influence, were to claim later that it did. Berezovskii, for example, told Hoffman (*Oligarchs*, 333) that Yeltsin reorganized his campaign headquarters "the very next day." This is rubbish. The reorganization occurred on March 19, almost a month later.

46. Baturin et al., *Epokha*, 555–56.

47. Dobrokhotov, *Ot Yel'tsina*, 170.

48. It had been in the making for some time. Soskovets told an American campaign consultant on February 27 that one of his tasks would be to advise "whether we should call it [the election] off if you determine that we're going to lose." Michael Kramer, "Rescuing Boris," *Time*, July 15, 1996. Nikolai Yegorov, the chief of Yeltsin's executive office and an ally of Korzhakov and Soskovets, broached the possibility of postponing the election with governors in a provincial tour in early March, and prevailed on one of them to write to the chairman of the Federation Council in support of the idea. See Dobrokhotov, *Ot Yel'tsina*, 181–82. The fear that Yeltsin would die in a hard-fought campaign played into the calculations of the Kremlin conservatives. If Soskovets were already prime minister, he would have become acting president and presumably would have an excellent chance of winning an election. Chernomyrdin would have that advantage if Yeltsin died while Chernomyrdin was still premier.

49. Baturin et al., *Epokha*, 562.

50. Kulikov, *Tyazhëlyye zvëzdy*, 396–402; Sergei Shakhrai, third interview with the author (June 1, 2001).

51. Talbott, *Russia Hand*, 195; James M. Goldgeier and Michael McFaul, *Power and Purpose: U.S. Policy Toward Russia After the Cold War* (Washington, D.C.: Brookings, 2003), 153.

52. Yel'tsin, *Marafon*, 33; D'yachenko, "Yesli by papa"; Anatolii Chubais, first interview with the author (January 18, 2001). Yeltsin describes the meeting as Tatyana's idea. But Chubais revealed that the idea was his and that he prevailed upon her to get Yeltsin to agree. Yeltsin dates the key meetings on March 23. There is good evidence in other sources that they were held on March 18.

53. Kulikov, *Tyazhëlyye zvëzdy,* 402. Peter Reddaway and Dmitri Glinski, *The Tragedy of Russia's Reforms: Market Bolshevism against Democracy* (Washington, D.C.: U.S. Institute of Peace, 2001), 513, write of the incident: "Contrary to all the wishful thinking in the West about Russian democracy, 'Tsar Boris' had no qualms about throwing the constitution out the window." But he did have such qualms, and he did act on them.

54. Aleksandr Oslon, interview with the author (January 25, 2001). Tatyana's older sister, Yelena Okulova, played a minor advisory role in helping to arrange Naina Yeltsina's campaign schedule.

55. Korzhakov, *Boris Yel'tsin,* 361–69. According to Korzhakov, Chernomyrdin offered to take up the suggestion with Yeltsin; there is no record of him having done so. Korzhakov says that without Chernomyrdin's permission he taped the conversation, which lasted from seven P.M. until almost two A.M., and that the quotations are "almost verbatim" from the transcript.

56. Second Yeltsina interview.

57. David Hoffman, "Yeltsin Vows No Delays in Election," *The Washington Post,* May 7, 1996. Korzhakov gave the interview to the British newspaper *The Observer.* It quickly circulated in Russia.

58. Oslon interview.

59. Dobrokhotov, *Ot Yel'tsina,* 165–69.

60. An eleventh candidate, Aman-Geldy Tuleyev, the governor of Kemerovo province in west Siberia, withdrew on June 5 and threw his support to Zyuganov.

61. Lebed had climbed in the Russian polls shortly after retiring from the army in May 1995. He ran for the Duma in December 1995 on the list of the Congress of Russian Communities, a nationalist organization formed by Yurii Skokov, and was elected in a district in Tula province.

62. Korzhakov, *Boris Yel'tsin,* 363.

63. McFaul, *Russia's 1996 Presidential Election,* 25–26, 109; Baturin et al., *Epokha,* 571.

64. Grigorii Yavlinskii, second interview with the author (September 28, 2001). Yavlinskii's demands were contained in a letter to Yeltsin published in *Izvestiya* and *Nezavisimaya gazeta* on May 18. Korzhakov told Chernomyrdin in mid-April of a conversation Yavlinskii had a few days before with the former vice president of the United States, Dan Quayle—a conversation we must assumed was taped by officers of Korzhakov's guard unit. Yavlinskii is said to have remarked that Zyuganov was his enemy while Yeltsin was a relative, "But you will understand that sometimes a relative is worse than any enemy." Quayle is said to have answered, "I understand." Korzhakov, *Boris Yel'tsin,* 366–67.

65. The Korzhakov-Soskovets group also put an oar in. According to Korzhakov (*Boris Yel'tsin,* 364), Nikolai Yegorov summoned governors to his office in Moscow and "battled in the localities" with holdouts.

66. Igor Malashenko, interview with the author (March 18, 2001).

67. Sara Oates and Laura Roselle, "Russian Elections and TV News: Comparison of Campaign News on State-Controlled and Commercial Television Channels," *Harvard International Journal of Press/Politics* 5 (Spring 2000), 40–41. Korzhakov and his Presidential Security Service complained throughout the campaign that NTV was continuing to criticize the Chechen war, and implicitly Yeltsin's leadership of it, and to refer to Korzhakov and his group as "the party of war." See Aleksandr Korzhakov, *Boris Yel'tsin: ot rassveta do zakata; posleslovіye* (Boris Yeltsin: from dawn to dusk; epilogue) (Moscow: Detektiv-press, 2004), 420–21.

68. Our Home Is Russia got 18 percent of the mentions on the ORT nightly news (Oates and Roselle, "Russian Elections and TV News," 38) but only 10 percent of the popular vote. The KPRF got 13 percent of the mentions and 23 percent of the votes. Russia's Democratic Choice, the liberal party headed by Gaidar, got 12 percent of the mentions and 4 percent of the popular vote.

69. Timothy J. Colton, *Transitional Citizens: Voters and What Influences Them in the New Russia* (Cambridge, Mass.: Harvard University Press, 2000), 61.

70. FOM (Fond "Obshchestvennoye mneniye"), *Rezul'taty sotsiologicheskikh issledovanii* (Results of sociological research), June 13, 1996, 1. The complete run of this in-house bulletin of Aleksandr Oslon's Public Opinion Foundation was supplied to the author by Oslon.

71. See Ellen Mickiewiecz, *Changing Channels: Television and the Struggle for Power in Russia* (New York: Oxford University Press, 1997), 178–84. Even on NTV, though, news anchors opined in the final weeks of the first-round campaign, and reporters subjected Zyuganov's promises and claims to searching questioning while largely sparing Yeltsin.

72. FOM, *Rezul'taty*, June 19, 1996, 1. Surveys by the VTsIOM group show a similar trend. See Stephen White, Richard Rose, and Ian McAllister, *How Russia Votes* (Chatham, N.J.: Chatham House, 1997), 258. VTsIOM data show Yeltsin *fifth* among intended voters in the second half of January, behind Zyuganov, Lebed, Yavlinskii, and Zhirinovskii.

73. Yeltsin led Zyuganov among individuals thirty-five and younger from the beginning; he overtook Zyuganov among persons aged thirty-six to forty-five on April 21, among those forty-six to fifty-five on May 18, and among those older than fifty-five on June 1. He surpassed Zyuganov in March in Moscow and St. Petersburg, in early April in cities of over 1 million in population, in mid-May in other cities and towns, and in the villages of Russia in the first half of June. He won majority support among men and women at about the same time. Poorly educated and low-paid Russians rallied to Yeltsin, and by a narrow margin, only in June; those with a college-level diploma and higher incomes were on his side from the start. FOM, *Rezul'taty*, June 19, 1996, 1–3.

74. Talbott, *Russia Hand*, 161–62; Goldgeier and McFaul, *Power and Purpose*, 196–97. The request had been made by Russian diplomats before Yeltsin discussed it with Clinton in May 1995. Yeltsin first tried to sell Clinton on a delay until after the two of them left office at the end of the decade.

75. Mikhail Rostovskii, "Mutatsiya klana" (Mutation of the clan), *Moskovskii komsomolets*, December 3, 2002 (citing a conversation with Korzhakov).

76. Talbott, *Russia Hand*, 202, 204. Clinton was furious when Yeltsin lectured him in front of the press for the excesses of American foreign policy and Yeltsin left the room before Clinton could reply.

77. Alan Friedman, "James D. Wolfensohn: World Bank and Russian Reform," *International Herald Tribune*, May 27, 1996.

78. Kulikov, *Tyazhëlyye zvëzdy*, 407.

79. Baturin et al., *Epokha*, 658.

80. The revelations about the assassination threat and the white lie to his wife are in "Boris Nemtsov—Yevgenii Al'bats o Yel'tsine" (Boris Nemtsov to Yevgeniya Al'bats about Yeltsin), *Novoye vremya/New Times*, April 30, 2007.

81. FOM, *Rezul'taty*, June 5, 1996, 3. Earlier polls had shown that Chechnya was the single biggest strike against Yeltsin in public opinion and that 70 percent of citizens favored either a pullout or a cessation of hostilities without a pullout.

82. Ibid., April 22, 1996, 2.

83. Ibid., May 10, 1996, 2 (italics added). The bifurcation or polarization gambit is well drawn in McFaul, *Russia's 1996 Presidential Election;* and Leon Aron, *Yeltsin: A Revolutionary Life* (New York: St. Martin's, 2000), chap. 13.

84. Dobrokhotov, *Ot Yel'tsina*, 234–38.

85. Alessandra Stanley, "With Campaign Staff in Disarray, Yeltsin Depends on Perks of Office," *New York Times*, May 13, 1996. Stanley wrote in another story ("A Media Campaign Most Russian and Most Unreal," ibid., June 2, 1996) that the "indirection and goosebumpy emotional tug" of the ads recall General Electric advertising in the United States ("We bring good things to life"). Among the foreign consultants were Sir Tim Bell of the British firm Bell Pottinger (once a counselor to Margaret Thatcher), several media advisers to California governor Pete Wilson, and Richard Dresner, a former business partner of Dick Morris. See Kramer, "Rescuing Boris"; Sarah E. Mendelson, "Democracy Assistance and Political Transition in Russia," *International Security* 25 (Spring 2001), 93–94; and Gerry Sussman, *Global Electioneering: Campaign Consulting, Communications, and Corporate Financing* (Lanham, Md.: Rowman and Littlefield, 2005), 139–40.

86. Source: the survey data used in the writing of Colton, *Transitional Citizens*.

87. Yel'tsin, *Marafon*, 35. See Timothy J. Colton, "The Leadership Factor in the Russian Presidential Election of 1996," in Anthony King, ed., *Leaders' Personalities and the Outcomes of Democratic Elections* (Oxford: Oxford University Press, 2002), 184–209.

88. In the survey (as detailed in Colton, *Transitional Citizens*), 2,456 Russians were interviewed in the weeks after the election runoff and were asked to rate Yeltsin and four of his defeated rivals as possessing or not possessing the five praiseworthy traits. Sixty-four percent reckoned Yeltsin to be intelligent and knowledgeable, 55 percent thought him to have a vision of the future, 45 percent deemed him

strong, and 39 percent saw him as decent and trustworthy. Only 28 percent felt he really cared about people, dwarfed by the 63 percent who rejected this statement. Of respondents who thought the Russian economy was in good shape, 75 percent said Yeltsin cared about people like them; among those who thought the economy to be in bad or very bad shape, only 22 percent agreed. Among persons whose family finances had improved in the past year, 58 percent perceived the president as empathetic; that figure was down to 17 percent in the much larger group whose finances had deteriorated.

89. Daniel Treisman, "Why Yeltsin Won," *Foreign Affairs* 75 (September–October 1996), 67. This article is the best analysis of what Treisman calls the Tammany Hall dimension of the campaign. As Treisman points out, the distribution of benefits preceded the main media campaign, which began only when Yeltsin had already drawn even with Zyuganov in the polls.

90. Baturin et al., *Epokha*, 569.

91. The regiment's "elite soldiers, selected for their Slavic blond looks and six-foot stature, were refitted with pre-revolutionary dress uniforms. Heavy on gold braid and peacock colors, the uniforms were designed by the Bolshoi Theater's costume designers and are meant to evoke the martial splendor of imperial Russia." Alessandra Stanley, "Stripped of Themes, Yeltsin Wraps Himself in Flag," *New York Times*, April 19, 1996.

92. Malashenko interview. The visit was to the Annin Flag Company in Roseland, New Jersey, on September 19, 1988. Malashenko related it to me as having been made by Ronald Reagan, but it hardly matters which U.S. politician he ascribed the scene to in his conversation with Yeltsin.

93. Ibid.

94. Medvedev interview.

95. Lee Hockstader, "Invigorated Yeltsin Hits Hustings," *The Washington Post*, June 1, 1996. The Yeltsin twist can be viewed at http://www.youtube.com/watch?v=d90JtMP2J0Y.

96. Medvedev interview.

97. Alessandra Stanley, "Spendthrift Candidate Yeltsin: Miles to Go, Promises to Keep?" *New York Times*, May 4, 1996.

98. Quoted in Treisman, "Why Yeltsin Won," 70.

99. In *RFE/RL Newsline*, May 27, 1996.

100. The quite unbelievable scene with Denisyuk is captured in *Prezident vseya Rusi* (The president of all Russia), documentary film by Yevgenii Kiselëv, 1999–2000 (copy supplied by Kiselëv), 4 parts, part 2. Yeltsin listens to her request and says, "OK, I will give you a car" *(Ladno, podaryu mashinu)*. He kisses her on both cheeks and assures her that documentation will arrive with the machine. The car came through, and Denisyuk never complained.

101. Baturin et al., *Epokha*, 462.

102. Dobrokhotov, *Ot Yel'tsina*, 296.

103. Ibid., 489.

104. "Yeltsin's earlier television spots were largely upbeat testimonials from average citizens, but those aired today were some of the harshest blasts of the campaign. The ads begin with short statements from Russian men and women saying they do not want to go back to communism; then the announcer, harking back to the Bolshevik Revolution, intones: 'No one in 1917 thought there could be famine.' Grainy black-and-white film shows starving children from Stalin's forced collectivization of agriculture, which killed millions. Also pictured are Russians of the late 1970s lining up at stores whose shelves are empty. The tagline for this and other ads is: 'And the communists didn't even change their name. They won't change their methods.'" David Hoffman, "Yeltsin, Communist Foe Launch TV Attack Ads," *The Washington Post*, June 27, 1996.

105. In the transcript of an intercepted telephone conversation with her husband the morning of June 20, Tatyana is quoted as saying Russians had formed the impression that "these people [Korzhakov and his confrères] are governing the country and not he [Yeltsin]." A bit later, she converses with her mother about the president's options and Naina Yeltsina warns, incorrectly, that Yeltsin would never remove Korzhakov. Aleksandr Khinshtein, *Yel'tsin, Kreml', istoriya bolezni* (Yeltsin, the Kremlin, the history of an illness) (Moscow: OLMA, 2006), 392, 394.

106. Malashenko interview.

107. Yeltsin himself described the scene in *Marafon*, 45.

108. Moroz, *1996*, 459–60.

109. Statistical details here taken from the survey data used in Colton, *Transitional Citizens*. The big change after June 16 was the shift of Lebed voters toward Yeltsin. Oslon's polls as late as the first week of June showed only 27 percent of Lebed supporters intending to support the president in a second round. FOM, *Rezul'taty*, June 13, 1996, 1.

110. Yel'tsin, *Marafon*, 48.

Chapter Fifteen

1. Korzhakov in his memoirs counts the June 26 attack as Yeltsin's fifth, but this includes September 29–30, 1994, when Yeltsin was a no-show for the meeting with Albert Reynolds in Ireland. Most of the medical experts do not classify that event as a full-flown myocardial infarction. Aleksandr Khinshtein, *Yel'tsin, Kreml', istoriya bolezni* (Yeltsin, the Kremlin, the history of an illness) (Moscow: OLMA, 2006), 405–6, gets to five by counting the incident in Kaliningrad on June 23 as a separate heart attack. The physician Vladlen Vtorushin is cited as the source of this information.

2. The text of the letter is in Aleksandr Korzhakov, *Boris Yel'tsin: ot rassveta do zakata* (Boris Yeltsin: from dawn to dusk) (Moscow: Interbuk, 1997), 451 (italics added). Yeltsin reproduced it in *Prezidentskii marafon* (Presidential marathon) (Moscow: AST, 2000), 49, saying that Korzhakov "did not conceal" the content of

the letter but several times told Tatyana Dyachenko "that if something happened to me she would be guilty."

3. Author's interviews with El'dar Ryazanov (May 30, 2001) and Irena Lesnevskaya (January 24, 2001).

4. The chain was instituted in 1994 but Yeltsin's decree specifying its use in the inauguration came out only on August 5, 1996. It consists of a Greek cross, seventeen smaller medals, and links of gold, silver, and white enamel.

5. Yu, M. Baturin et al., *Epokha Yel'tsina: ocherki politicheskoi istorii* (The Yeltsin epoch: essays in political history) (Moscow: VAGRIUS, 2001), 575. Yeltsin wrote later (*Marafon*, 50), "Never in my life had I been so tense" as on August 9.

6. Yeltsin had offered the job to Igor Malashenko of NTV, who pleaded personal circumstances. But it would appear that he made the suggestion first to Chubais and returned to him after Malashenko's refusal.

7. Ye, I. Chazov, *Rok* (Fate) (Moscow: Geotar-Med, 2001), 259.

8. Author's interviews with Sergei Parkhomenko (March 26, 2004) and Viktor Chernomyrdin (September 15, 2000). The article appeared in the *Itogi* of September 10, 1996. It was reported in the press that Chernomyrdin had a bypass operation in 1992, but in fact the procedure he had was an angioplasty.

9. Renat Akchurin, quoted in "Postskriptum" (Postscript), *Izvestiya*, April 28, 2007.

10. "Ekslyuzivnoye interv'yu Prezidenta Rossii zhurnalu 'Itogi'" (Exclusive interview of the president of Russia with the magazine *Itogi*), *Itogi*, September 10, 1996.

11. Yel'tsin, *Marafon*, 53.

12. Lawrence K. Altman, "In Moscow in 1996, a Doctor's Visit Changed History," *New York Times*, May 1, 2007. Citing an interview with DeBakey after Yeltsin's death the previous week, Altman claims that "his Russian doctors said he could not survive such surgery." But the fullest Russian account, by Chazov, says the Russians had already decided that the bypass was necessary and survivable and that they wanted DeBakey for psychological and strategic support. "And that is what happened. Yeltsin confirmed for himself the correctness of his decision, his family calmed down, and the press and television redirected themselves to DeBakey, leaving us finally in peace." Chazov, *Rok*, 262.

13. Yeltsin had communicated his intent to do the temporary transfer in a decree dated September 19. Chernomyrdin took his provisional duties to heart: "He called military specialists in and acquainted himself in detail with the automated system for controlling [Russia's] strategic nuclear forces." Baturin et al., *Epokha*, 725.

14. See on this point Chazov, *Rok*, 271.

15. Akchurin in "Postskriptum."

16. Yel'tsin, *Marafon*, 57.

17. Interviews with family members. Khrushchev put up Vice President Richard Nixon at Novo-Ogarëvo in 1959, since at Gorki-9 "it was not possible to provide the conveniences to which guests were accustomed. For example, there was only one

toilet for everyone, located at the end of the [first-floor] hall. The bath was there, too. By American standards, only people in the slums lived in such conditions." Sergei Khrushchev, *Nikita Khrushchev and the Creation of a Superpower,* trans. Shirley Benson (University Park: Pennsylvania State University Press, 2000), 352.

18. See Sergei Khrushchev, *Pensioner soyuznogo znacheniya* (Pensioner of USSR rank) (Moscow: Novosti, 1991), 69–71.

19. Anatolii Chubais, first interview with the author (January 18, 2001).

20. Yel'tsin, *Marafon,* 58.

21. Madeleine Albright, with Bill Woodward, *Madam Secretary* (New York: Miramax, 2003), 253–54.

22. Strobe Talbott, *The Russia Hand: A Memoir of Presidential Diplomacy* (New York: Random House, 2002), 246.

23. In the VTsIOM tracking poll in April 1997, 3 percent of the electorate gave Yeltsin unqualified support, 7 percent gave him qualified support, 41 percent were opposed to him in one degree or another, and 39 percent were ambivalent. Yu, A. Levada et al., *Obshchestvennoye mneniye—1999* (Public opinion—1999 edition) (Moscow: Vserossiiskii tsentr izucheniya obshchestvennogo mneniya, 2000), 100–101.

24. Korzhakov has said (interview with the author, January 28, 2002) that he was offered $5 million to cancel publication of the book. He thinks the source of the money was a businessman out to protect Yeltsin's interests. I have no corroboration of this claim.

25. Yurii Mukhin, *Kod Yel'tsina* (The Yeltsin code) (Moscow: Yauza, 2005). Like Salii in 1997, Mukhin, a Stalinist and anti-Semite, placed great stock in photographs of hands and other body parts. He has not commented on whether the death and state funeral of the real Yeltsin in 2007 led him to revise his interpretation. One of his other contributions as an analyst is work disclaiming Soviet responsibility for the 1940 massacre of Polish officers at Katyn. A competing version of the trashy tale holds that Yeltsin was an invalid from 1996 until August 6 or 7, 1999, when he died, and that three ringers, controlled by the Yeltsin family and not the CIA, filled in for him before and after his death. "Kozly i molodil'nyye yabloki" (Goats and green apples), http://www.duel.ru/200231/?31_1_3.

26. See Vladimir Shevchenko, *Povsednevnaya zhizn' Kremlya pri prezidentakh* (The everyday life of the Kremlin under the presidents) (Moscow: Molodaya gvardiya, 2004), 106, 138.

27. Yeltsin's office told reporters he played tennis for about ten minutes on July 11, 1997, at Shuiskaya Chupa. That seems to have been the last time.

28. Yelena Tregubova, *Baiki kremlëvskogo diggera* (Tales of a Kremlin digger) (Moscow: Ad Marginem, 2003), 53. Yeltsin in Stockholm was tired after a trip to Beijing. He advised the Swedes to wean themselves from coal and sign a contract with Russia for natural gas deliveries, apparently thinking back to background notes for the China visit. Sweden burns almost no coal; half of its power needs are met by atomic reactors and one-third by hydroelectric stations.

29. For a full early report, see Nikolai Andreyev, "Prezident Rossii postoyanen v svoyei nepredskazuyemosti" (The president of Russia is constant in his unpredictability), *Izvestiya,* May 6, 1992. Compare with Jacob Weisberg, "The Complete Bushisms," www.slate.com/id/76886.

30. See Tregubova, *Baiki kremlëvskogo diggera,* 117.

31. Yelena Dikun, "Yel'tsin v Gorkakh" (Yeltsin in Gorki), *Obshchaya gazeta,* April 2, 1998. *Kukly,* the satire program on the NTV television network, had broadcast a cruel skit comparing Yeltsin to the immobilized Lenin in January 1997.

32. Of recent presidents, Jimmy Carter took the fewest vacation days, seventy-nine over four years. Bill Clinton took 152 over eight years.

33. Anatolii Kulikov, who replaced Viktor Yerin as interior minister in 1995, says that after his operation Yeltsin misaddressed some hand-written notes. "My accurate and delicate attempts to correct the president were not well taken," writes Kulikov. "He would look at me and continue to write." Anatolii Kulikov, *Tyazhëlyye zvëzdy* (Heavy stars) (Moscow: Voina i mir, 2002), 416–17. But most former high officials whom I interviewed, including four second-term prime ministers (Chernomyrdin, Kiriyenko, Primakov, and Stepashin), emphasized his mental acuity and exceptional memory. Primakov and Stepashin, whose tenure was in the second half of term two, also emphasized the limits on his energy. Both felt he was at his full powers for two to three hours per workday. But neither, of course, knew this from direct experience, and family members insist that days this short were the exception rather than the rule.

34. Sergei Stepashin, interview with the author (June 14, 2001).

35. Yel'tsin, *Marafon,* 350.

36. Tatyana Yumasheva, third interview with the author (January 25, 2007). The dilution of the wine was done with Yeltsin's consent. Aleksandr Korzhakov claims that in 1995 he had kitchen staff secretly water down some bottles of vodka to half strength, and that Yeltsin fired several of them for the ruse. Korzhakov, *Boris Yel'tsin,* 303–5.

37. Chazov asserts that Yeltsin violated the restrictions less than a year after his operation, but that in the late 1990s "he finally came to observe the regime and recommendations of the doctors." Chazov, *Rok,* 277. When Yeltsin met with Bill Clinton in Helsinki in March 1997, he was distracted the first evening and consumed a number of glasses of wine; come morning, he "had regained his color and vigor" and seized the initiative in negotiations. At their next meeting, in Birmingham in May 1998, Yeltsin gave, "in both senses of the word, his most sober performance to date." Talbott, *Russia Hand,* 237–38, 269. Talbott records no drinking on Yeltsin's part after Helsinki, and even there the amount was hardly huge and some of it may have come in the form of adulterated wine.

38. Yel'tsin, *Marafon,* 350.

39. Third Yumasheva interview.

40. Yel'tsin, *Marafon,* 82.

41. Vladimir Potanin, interview with the author (September 25, 2001).

42. Those adjustments rarely included strikes or other collective action, mostly because ordinary people could not sort out which culprits to blame for their troubles. See Debra Javeline, *Protest and the Politics of Blame: The Russian Response to Unpaid Wages* (Ann Arbor: University of Michigan Press, 2003). See also Padma Desai and Todd Idson, *Work without Wages: Russia's Nonpayment Crisis* (Cambridge, Mass.: MIT Press, 2000).

43. Kulikov made his allegations about the Russian Legion in a press conference on October 16. There are more details in Kulikov, *Tyazhëlyye zvëzdy*, 469–75. Chubais took the charges seriously and was taken by Lebed's statement to the media that he expected to be president of Russia before 2000, the year the second Yeltsin term was to expire. He communicated his views to Yeltsin by memorandum, since the president did not feel well enough to meet with him. First Chubais interview.

44. Quotations from Yel'tsin, *Marafon*, 74, 77. In addition to stylistic aspects, Lebed shared some physical features with Yeltsin. His nose had been broken repeatedly in boxing matches, and as a party trick he flattened it against his face "like a pancake." Michael Specter, "The Wars of Aleksandr Ivanovich Lebed," *New York Times Magazine*, October 13, 1996.

45. The two had a relationship. Lebed had kept up communication with Korzhakov after his dismissal. When Lebed resigned from his Duma seat, representing Tula province, in order to take up his position with Yeltsin, Korzhakov declared his candidacy. Lebed accompanied Korzhakov to Tula and introduced him as his favored candidate. Korzhakov eventually won the election.

46. Valentin Yumashev, third interview with the author (September 13, 2006).

47. Baturin et al., *Epokha*, 773–74.

48. Yeltsin's chief of staff at the time, Valentin Yumashev, who was new to the job and was rarely involved in security decisions, is quite sure that Yeltsin had lost patience with Rodionov and went in intent on removing him. Third Yumashev interview. For background analysis, see Viktor Baranets, *Yel'tsin i yego generaly* (Yeltsin and his generals) (Moscow: Sovershenno sekretno, 1997); and Dale R. Herspring, *The Kremlin and the High Command: Presidential Impact on the Russian Military from Gorbachev to Putin* (Lawrence: University of Kansas Press, 2006).

49. Rodionov lamented to journalists that the meeting was conducted "in the spirit of a session of the bureau of a [CPSU] obkom." He had told Yeltsin a few days before, he said, that he needed thirty minutes for his report, and the president had not objected. Rodionov claimed that Yeltsin further sliced his time allotment to ten minutes after Rodionov protested the fifteen-minute quota, and then called for a show of hands on dismissing him. Rodionov tried to leave the room at that point but Yeltsin ordered him to stay. Vladimir Kiselëv, "Posle otstavki" (After retirement), *Obshchaya gazeta*, May 29, 1997.

50. Fragments of Yeltsin's remarks can be found in "Yel'tsin o natsional'noi ideye" (Yeltsin on the national idea), *Nezavisimaya gazeta*, July 13, 1996; and Mikhail

Lantsman, "Prezident poruchil doverennym litsam naiti natsional'nuyu ideyu" (The president assigned his campaign aides to find a national idea), *Segodnya*, July 15, 1996.

51. Stepan Kiselëv, "Georgii Satarov: natsional'naya ideya—eto nebol'no" (George Satarov says the national idea will not hurt anyone), *Izvestiya*, July 19, 1996.

52. Details in Bronwyn McLaren, "Big Brains Bog Down in Hunt for Russian Idea," *Moscow Times*, August 9, 1997; Michael E. Urban, "Remythologising the Russian State," *Europe-Asia Studies* 50 (September 1998), 969–92; Kathleen E. Smith, *Mythmaking in the New Russia: Politics and Memory in the Yeltsin Era* (Ithaca: Cornell University Press, 2002), 158–65; and Andrew Meier, *Black Earth: A Journey through Russia after the Fall* (New York: Norton, 2003), 338. The anthology is Georgii Satarov, ed., *Rossiya v poiskakh idei: analiz pressy* (Russia in search of an idea: analysis of the press) (Moscow: Gruppa konsul'tantov pri Administratsii Prezidenta Rossiiskoi Federatsii, 1997). Yeltsin did not mention the national-idea commission in his annual address to parliament, in March 1997, or in the final volume of his memoirs in 2000.

53. Andrei Zagorodnikov, "Svyato mesto pusto ne byvayet" (A holy place is never empty), *Nezavisimaya gazeta*, July 30, 1996.

54. First Chubais interview.

55. Smith, *Mythmaking*, 84.

56. Askar Akayev, interview with the author (September 29, 2004).

57. Yeltsin in *Marafon*, 396, mentioned one invitation, but family members in interviews said there were several.

58. Valentin Yumashev, second interview with the author (September 11, 2006).

59. S. Alekhin, "Boris Yel'tsin: sokhranit' kul'turu—svyataya obyazannost'" (Boris Yeltsin thinks it is a sacred duty to conserve our culture), *Rossiskaya gazeta*, June 10, 1997; Viktoriya Shokhina and Igor' Zotov, "Vizit" (Visit), *Nezavisimaya gazeta*, June 7, 1997.

60. Russians favored reburial by 48 percent to 38 percent when first surveyed in March 1997 and by as much as 55 percent to 34 percent in July 1998. In August 1999 the percentages for and against were tied at 41. A. Petrova, "Lenin's Body Burial," http:/bd.english.fom.ru/report/cat/societas/rus_im/zahoronenie_v_i_lenina/eof993304.

61. An American journalist aptly remarked that some on the Russian left thought communism was only slumbering and that Lenin, "lying in his glass coffin like Sleeping Beauty, is keeping the movement alive." Alessandra Stanley, "Czar and Lenin Share Fate: Neither Can Rest in Peace," *New York Times*, April 9, 1997.

62. Boris Yeltsin, second interview with the author (February 9, 2002).

63. He made this clear in conversations at the time with Boris Nemtsov, who was in charge of the reburial. Nemtsov, second interview with the author (February 6, 2002).

64. This summary does not do justice to the complexity of Russian attitudes toward the last of the Romanovs. They are well analyzed in Wendy Slater, "Relics, Remains, and Revisionism: Narratives of Nicholas II in Contemporary Russia," *Rethinking*

History 9 (March 2005), 53–70. The Orthodox abroad, who had always been strongly anti-communist, had control of a female's finger which they claimed was the only true relic of the family. No tissue attributable to Nicholas and Alexandra's hemophilic son, Aleksei, or their third daughter, Mariya, was found, which fed the suspicion of the clergy abroad. Yekaterinburg archeologists in July 2007 unearthed remains at Koptyaki that seem to be those of Aleksei and Mariya.

65. Wrote one Russian observer, "Yeltsin made a tactical move of genius, making fools out of the rivals who believed his words and refused to participate in the burial." The observer suspected Yeltsin saw the ceremony as the first step toward another election campaign in 2000, and Luzhkov was openly eyeing a presidential run. Melor Sturua, "Puteshestviye iz Moskvy v Peterburg za tsarskiye pokhorony" (A trip from Moscow to St. Petersburg for the tsar's funeral), *Nezavisimaya gazeta*, July 21, 1998. Political calculations aside, it was reported in 1998, and confirmed by Boris Nemtsov in his second interview with me, that Yeltsin resolved his doubts about participating only after a conversation about the merits of the case with Academician Dmitrii Likhachëv, a leading Russian medievalist and Gulag survivor whom he held in high regard.

66. "Vystupleniye Prezidenta RF Borisa Yel'tsina na traurnoi tseremonii v Sankt-Peterburge" (Statement of President Boris Yeltsin at the funeral ceremony in St. Petersburg), *Rossiiskaya gazeta*, July 18, 1998.

67. Iosif Raikhel'gauz, "Kak ya gotovil prezidentskoye poslaniye" (How I prepared the presidential message), *Ogonëk*, November 17, 2000.

68. "Poslaniye Prezidenta Rossiiskoi Federatsii Federal'nomu Sobraniyu, 'Poryadok vo vlasti—poryadok v strane'" (Message of the president of the Russian Federation to the Federal Assembly, "Order in government, order in the country) (Moscow: Rossiiskaya Federatsiya, 1997), 5–6.

69. Ibid., 9, 29.

70. Lebed was more ambitious than Korzhakov and had already had success as an independent politico. But he lacked the resource that was vital to Korzhakov's influence—a friendship with Yeltsin.

71. Eugene Huskey, *Presidential Power in Russia* (Armonk, N.Y.: M. E. Sharpe, 1999), 87–96.

72. Baturin et al., *Epokha*, 719.

73. Yurii Baturin, interview with the author (June 3, 2002). Schooled in rocket science, law, and journalism, Baturin had been rejected by the Soviet program for poor eyesight. He flew to the Mir space station in 1998 and in 2001 to the international space station with Dennis Tito, the world's first space tourist.

74. The membership fluctuated. Valentin Yumashev chaired it after Boiko. Other members of the group in 1996–98 included Tatyana Dyachenko, press secretary Sergei Yastrzhembskii, poll taker Aleksandr Oslon, political consultant Gleb Pavlovskii, Georgii Satarov and Mikhail Lesin of Yeltsin's staff, and Igor Malashenko of NTV.

75. In *Marafon*, 41, Yeltsin says it was Chubais who asked him to clarify her status. Chubais left the Kremlin for the Council of Ministers in mid-March, so the matter took some time to settle and was left to Yumashev to implement.

76. All these points are from the third Yumasheva interview. Yeltsin in his memoirs (*Marafon*, 36) discusses their interaction in the context of the 1996 election campaign. "As a rule, she kept her personal opinion to herself. Tatyana practically never violated this tacit rule of ours. But if she suddenly made an effort—'Papa, I nonetheless think . . . '—I would try to change the subject."

77. The difference between the sisters, and the similarity of Tatyana to their mother, was pointed out by Naina Yeltsina in my second interview with her (September 18, 2007). On disorganization, see the comments of Naina's former press secretary: Natal'ya Konstantinova, *Zhenskii vzglyad na kremlëvskuyu zhizn'* (A woman's view of Kremlin life) (Moscow: Geleos, 1999), 188.

78. Newcomers to the Kremlin team soon learned the utility of the Dyachenko channel if all else failed. But veterans like Pikhoya often refused to use it. She implied in her interview with me (September 26, 2001) that it would have been beneath her dignity.

79. Dikun, "Yel'tsin v Gorkakh."

80. The experience of Anatolii Kulikov, the interior minister from 1995 to 1998, was typical. "The whole time I was minister this weekly report to the president was a ritual that could not be violated under any circumstances." On only one occasion in the three years, when Yeltsin happened to be occupied at the designated hour, did Kulikov miss a planned telephone call. He substituted by calling Chernomyrdin, which infuriated Yeltsin: "The prime minister, that is fine, but you are subordinated to the supreme commander-in-chief and are obligated to report personally to him!" Kulikov, *Tyazhëlyye zvëzdy*, 415.

81. Author's first interview with Mikhail Krasnov (June 5, 2000) and third with Yumashev; and Baturin et al., *Epokha*, 761–66, which relates some details from Krasnov's point of view. Yumashev denies Krasnov's charge that he was indifferent to the reform, saying that the means to implement it were lacking.

82. Yeltsin offered these explanations in my second interview with him. Viktor Ilyushin and Oleg Lobov were the last of the prominent Sverdlovskers to leave high posts, as deputy premier, in March 1997.

83. Kulikov, *Tyazhëlyye zvëzdy*, 417–18. Kulikov seems to have had no awareness that a State Council had existed early in Yeltsin's first term and had been abolished.

84. Sergei Kiriyenko, interview with the author (January 25, 2001).

85. Yel'tsin, *Marafon*, 87.

86. Ibid., 88.

87. Author's interviews with principals; and, on Vyakhirev, "Boris Nemtsov—Yevgenii Al'bats o Yel'tsine" (Boris Nemtsov to Yevgeniya Al'bats about Yeltsin), *Novoye vremya/New Times*, April 30, 2007. Vyakhirev and Chernomyrdin defended the shares deal until December 1997, when Yeltsin, standing behind Nemtsov at a diplomatic reception in Stockholm, Sweden, asked him if a final decision had been made. When Nemtsov said it had not, Yeltsin pulled Vyakhirev aside and said the "bandits' agreement" was to be torn up immediately, which it was.

88. "Boris Nemtsov—Yevgenii Al'bats o Yel'tsine."

89. Thomas F. Remington, "Laws, Decrees, and Russian Constitutions: The First Hundred Years" (unpublished paper, Emory University, 2006). Decrees averaged twenty-one per month in 1992–95 and fifteen per month in 1997–99.

90. "No Improvement in Russian Economy without Land Reform—Yeltsin," http://news/bbc.co.uk/2/hi/world/monitoring/42632.stm.

91. In sequential ballots, the code went from 213 votes in favor to 220 and then to 225, one short of the 226 needed for passage. The Duma determined on July 17 to postpone further consideration.

92. David E. Hoffman, *The Oligarchs: Wealth and Power in the New Russia* (New York: PublicAffairs, 2002), 385. The best accounts of the Svyazinvest auction and the surrounding controversy are to be found in that book and in Chrystia Freeland, *Sale of the Century: Russia's Wild Ride from Communism to Capitalism* (Toronto: Doubleday, 2000), chap. 12.

93. "After the last presidential election, in 1996, the oligarchs captured Yeltsin, his successive governments, and the political process." Lee S. Wolosky, "Putin's Plutocrat Problem," *Foreign Affairs* 79 (March–April 2000), 25. See more broadly Joel S. Hellman, Geraint Jones, and Daniel Kaufmann, *"Seize the State, Seize the Day": State Capture, Corruption, and Influence in Transition*, Policy Research Working Paper 2444 (Washington, D.C.: World Bank, 2000), 1.

94. Author's interviews with Khodorkovskii (June 7, 2001), Fridman (September 21, 2001), and Potanin.

95. Yeltsin's capacity in principle to dictate the terms was mentioned by every businessman I spoke to about 1996, and was especially stressed by Khodorkovskii, who felt Yeltsin was at first affronted by their offer. Yeltsin in his memoirs (*Marafon*, 103) emphasizes that the oligarchs took the initiative. "No one asked them, and there were no obligations incurred to anyone. They came to me not to defend Yeltsin but to defend their own businesses."

96. Second Nemtsov interview.

97. The purpose of Dyachenko's call was to inquire about the status of Yelena Masyuk, an NTV correspondent, and two crew members, who were kidnapped by a splinter group in Chechnya in May; NTV was to pay ransom for their release several weeks later. Berezovskii, speaking as deputy secretary of the Security Council, assured her that everything possible was being done to save them. The record of the conversation, "Zapis' telefonnogo razgovora Borisa Berezovskogo s docher'yu Yel'tsina—Tat'yanoi D'yachenko" (Transcript of a telephone conversation between Boris Berezovskii and Yeltsin's daughter, Tatyana Dyachenko), was leaked in June 1999. It is available at http://www.compromat.ru/main/berezovskiy/dyachenko.htm.

98. Berezovskii called her Tanya and, at one point, Tanyusha, a double diminutive. She called him Boris Abramovich and "you" in the second person plural, and also referred to third parties by name and patronymic.

99. Berezovskii admitted that he personally had not declared all his income and capital on his tax returns. Dyachenko seemed to accept his point that concealment

would continue to be widespread. In that case, though, businessmen "should pay more on the basis of their declared capital," that is, pay at a higher rate and on time.

100. Ul'yan Kerzonov, "Anatolii Chubais stremitsya k polnomy kontrolyu nad Rossiyei" (Anatolii Chubais is striving for complete control over Russia), *Nezavisimaya gazeta,* September 13, 1997. It was widely believed that Kerzonov was a pseudonym for Berezovskii. I heard of the role of the article in my third interview with Yumashev.

101. Potanin interview. I interviewed two other oligarchs who were present, Fridman and Khodorkovskii, and both shared his puzzlement.

102. His comments to Chubais and Nemtsov are related in "Boris Nemtsov—Yevgenii Al'bats o Yel'tsine."

103. One of the authors, Al'fred Kokh, had been dismissed in August in connection with another scandal. Aleksandr Kazakov, Maksim Boiko, and Pëtr Mostovoi were fired in November. Hoffman (*Oligarchs,* 304) presents evidence that the book project was a device for transferring leftover funds from the 1996 campaign.

104. Yel'tsin, *Marafon,* 111.

105. Ibid., 104.

106. Second Nemtsov interview. As Pëtr Aven of Alpha Group put it, "There was a not very explicit but, I would say, implicit understanding that . . . you help us and we'll help you." Aven, interview with the author (May 29, 2001).

107. Hoffman, *Oligarchs,* 386.

Chapter Sixteen

1. Quotations from Boris Yel'tsin, *Prezidentskii marafon* (Presidential marathon) (Moscow: AST, 2000), 113, 119, 118.

2. Ibid., 118.

3. Yu, M. Baturin et al., *Epokha Yel'tsina: ocherki politicheskoi istorii* (The Yeltsin epoch: essays in political history) (Moscow: VAGRIUS, 2001), 778–79; Georgii Satarov, first interview with the author (June 5, 2000).

4. Yel'tsin, *Marafon,* 119–21. The serving ministers on Yeltsin's list were Nikolai Aksënenko (railways), Vladimir Bulgak (communications), and Sergei Kiriyenko (fuel and energy). To legislators and other politicians on April 7, he mentioned as serious candidates Yurii Luzhkov (mayor of Moscow), Yegor Stroyev (governor of Orël province and chairman of the Federation Council), and Dmitrii Ayatskov (Saratov governor), as well as Bulgak, but said nothing about the others whom he later mentioned in the memoir.

5. Ibid., 120–21.

6. In 1984 Nikolayev, as commander of a motorized rifle division in the Urals Military District, spoke at a meeting organized by the Sverdlovsk obkom of the CPSU. First Secretary Yeltsin liked the presentation and said he had "a brilliant future." Igor' Oleinik, "Andrei Nikolayev: genshtabist v politike" (Andrei Nikolayev: a

General Staff officer in politics), http://www.lebed.com/1999/art997.htm. In 1997 Nikolayev submitted his resignation to Yeltsin in an attempt to gain an expression of support. Yeltsin surprised Nikolayev by accepting: "I don't like it when people pressure me in this way." Yel'tsin, *Marafon*, 121.

7. Yel'tsin, *Marafon*, 121.

8. Sergei Kiriyenko, interview with the author (January 15, 2001). In 1994 Kiriyenko spoke as a banker at a dinner for Yeltsin hosted by Nemtsov. Yeltsin asked if he would like to move to Moscow but Nemtsov objected. In August 1997 Kiriyenko, in Nemtsov's company, saw the president at Volzhskii Utës and was invited to dine with the family.

9. Yeltsin's memoir descriptions of them are similar in many ways, but in volume three (*Marafon*, 121–22) he contrasts Kiriyenko's practical experience with Gaidar's lack thereof. He exaggerates the difference and also misleads in speaking of them as being of "a different generation." They were born only six years apart, and when Gaidar was made acting premier in 1992 he was seven months older than Kiriyenko was when Yeltsin nominated him in 1998.

10. This is the sequence as reported in my interview with Kiriyenko, whose memory I trust most on these events. In *Marafon* Yeltsin said he met with Kiriyenko before Chernomyrdin. A recently adopted law on governmental organization specified that only a first deputy premier could be appointed as acting prime minister. Yeltsin was unaware of this detail and, after signing his initial decree, had to retrace his steps, make Kiriyenko a first deputy premier, and then promote him.

11. Quotation from Vladimir Zhirinovskii, interview with the author (January 22, 2002). That the Kremlin paid the LDPR money is widely believed in Moscow. Two persons who served in very high official posts in 1998 said in interviews that cash was provided from pro-government businesses and from a covert item in the federal budget.

12. Ivan Rodin, "Kommunisty predlagayut reshit' uchast' Dumy otkrytym golosovaniyem" (The communists suggest that the Duma make its decision by open vote), *Nezavisimaya gazeta*, April 24, 1998.

13. Baturin et al., *Epokha*, 754.

14. Only twenty-five voted against; almost 200 spoiled ballots, abstained, or stayed out of Moscow; twelve sent in written declarations in favor, which were not counted in the total. Since the ballot was secret, the party breakdown is not known with certainty. But journalists estimated twenty to twenty-five KPRF deputies broke with Gennadii Zyuganov to support Kiriyenko. See Ivan Rodin, "Duma progolosovala za Sergeya Kiriyenko i prodlila svoë sushchestvovaniye" (The Duma voted for Sergei Kiriyenko and prolonged its existence), *Nezavisimaya gazeta*, April 25, 1998; and David Hoffman, "Third Vote Confirms Kiriyenko as New Russian Premier," *The Washington Post*, April 25, 1998.

15. Kiriyenko interview.

16. Mikhail Mikhailovich Zadornov, an economist who worked with Grigorii Yavlinskii on the Five Hundred Days Program in 1990, is not to be confused with Mikhail Nikolayevich Zadornov, the stand-up comedian referred to in Chapter 13.

17. Source: interviews with two of the parties to the affair. Word of it circulated in the press around May 20. Boris Nemtsov had instituted a tender system for most other civilian agencies in 1997.

18. Alexei Goriaev and Alexei Zabotkin, "Risks of Investing in the Russian Stock Market: Lessons of the First Decade," *Emerging Markets Review* 7 (December 2006), 380–97.

19. At one meeting with aides, Yeltsin interrupted to dial Chernomyrdin and ask him what the trend was with Russian treasury notes. "The premier became confused and asked for time to prepare an answer. Yeltsin hung up and remarked, 'Well there you have our premier, and he doesn't know. But I know.' The president beamed: See how I have left him. He wanted to be first in everything." Baturin et al., *Epokha*, 734.

20. Yel'tsin, *Marafon*, 204. Boris Nemtsov, Kiriyenko's mentor and now one of his deputy premiers, believed a stabilizing devaluation could have been done in the first few weeks of the Kiriyenko premiership. Like Yeltsin, he said Kiriyenko would not hear of it. Nemtsov, second interview with the author (February 6, 2002).

21. Yel'tsin, *Marafon*, 203.

22. Aleksandr Livshits, interview with the author (January 19, 2001).

23. Russian GKOs were first issued in February 1993. Coupon-bearing OFZs (Federal Loan Bonds) were introduced in 1995 as a complement, but GKOs defined the market throughout. Western advice paved the way for both types. Although GKOs were denominated in rubles, instruments known as dollar-forward contracts hedged against reduction in the exchange rate. Once the ruble went into collapse, the dollar-forward contracts hastened its demise.

24. See Venla Sipilä, "The Russian Triple Crisis, 1998: Currency, Finance, and Budget," University College London, Centre for the Study of Economic and Social Change in Europe, Working Paper 17 (March 2002); and Padma Desai, "Why Did the Ruble Collapse in August 1998?" *American Economic Review* 90 (May 2000), 48–52. For historical perspective, see Niall Ferguson and Brigitte Granville, "'Weimar on the Volga': Causes and Consequences of Inflation in 1990s Russia Compared with 1920s Germany," *Journal of Economic History* 60 (December 2000), 1061–87.

25. The package, and the expectation that it would be granted, aggravated the crisis by facilitating the conversion of rubles into dollars by Russian and foreign speculators. Brian Pinto, Evsey Gurvich, and Sergei Ulatov, "Lessons from the Russian Crisis of 1998 and Recovery," in Joshua Aizenman and Brian Pinto, eds., *Managing Volatility and Crises: A Practitioner's Guide* (New York: Cambridge University Press, 2005), 406–39.

26. Vera Kuznetsova, "Boris Yel'tsin v ocherednoi raz poobeshchal ne idti na tretii srok" (Boris Yeltsin makes his latest promise not to seek a third term), *Izvestiya*, June 20, 1998. Kuznetsova added that the mill would need to put together a sound business plan to get assistance, but the gist of Yeltsin's remarks was that a subsidy was on the way. For a humorous account of Yeltsin's high spirits and how he mistook a

female journalist for a model from the factory, see Yelena Tregubova, *Baiki kremlëvskogo diggera* (Tales of a Kremlin digger) (Moscow: Ad Marginem, 2003), 81–84.

27. Mikhail Fridman, interview with the author (September 21, 2001).

28. Yel'tsin, *Marafon*, 211–12.

29. Indicative are remarks made by Stephen F. Cohen of New York University on *The NewsHour with Jim Lehrer* on September 14: "The country is in profound crisis. It's coming apart at the seams politically, economically, socially, psychologically. The economy has collapsed. Winter is coming. People have no money. They have no food. There's no medicine. . . . The so-called free market reforms in Russia have collapsed; they're over." Transcript at http://www.pbs.org/newshour/bb/europe/july-dec98/russia_9-14.

30. Sergei Parkhomenko, "Podoplëka" (The real state of affairs), *Itogi*, September 15, 1998.

31. Vitalii Tret'yakov, "Vopros o vlasti" (The question of power), *Nezavisimaya gazeta*, July 10, 1998.

32. Tret'yakov did not explain how to reconcile the council with the constitution or what would happen if its head disagreed with Yeltsin, who would still have the highest standing in the state, or with the prime minister, who would continue to answer to the president.

33. Family members were emphatic on this point in interviews. Some press articles in late August and early September cited Kremlin sources and even provided the date on which Yeltsin would supposedly hand in his resignation.

34. Viktor Chernomyrdin, interview with the author (September 15, 2000); and Valentin Yumashev, fifth interview with the author (September 17, 2007). Yeltsin reiterated in *Marafon*, 219–20, that his former prime minister was not the best leader for the future. But in August 1998 he accepted the Chernomyrdin option. Had the nomination gone through, Yeltsin, Yumashev said, could not have faced up to dismissing him a second time prior to the 2000 election.

35. Strobe Talbott, *The Russia Hand: A Memoir of Presidential Diplomacy* (New York: Random House, 2002), 288.

36. On the way in from the airport on September 1, Chernomyrdin "used the half-hour ride to lobby the president [Clinton] to support his nomination with Yeltsin, who was rumored to be giving up on him." Ibid., 287. Clinton was smart enough not to intrude.

37. Vitalii Tret'yakov, "Vitse-prezident i drugiye" (The vice president and others), *Nezavisimaya gazeta*, September 12, 1998.

38. They were Andrei Kokoshin, secretary of the Security Council; Yevgenii Savast'yanov, deputy head of the Kremlin executive office; and Sergei Yastrzhembskii, press secretary and foreign-policy assistant.

39. Yeltsin felt after his conversations with Yumashev that a Chernomyrdin restored to the prime minister's office would have "the aura of an unjustly offended person." "In that sense, my moral loss would turn out to be a win for Chernomyrdin." *Marafon*, 221

40. Viktor Zorkal'tsev, a Zyuganov deputy, had signed for the KPRF on August 28, and the pact was supported by Nikolai Ryzhkov and other pro-communist factions in the Duma. Chernomyrdin was more favorable to it than Yeltsin.

41. Yevgenii Primakov, *Vosem' mesyatsev plyus* . . . (Eight months plus) (Moscow: Mysl', 2001), 14.

42. In his memoir account (ibid., 7), Primakov says Yeltsin offered the post of prime minister to Maslyukov, in a desperate outburst in the presence of him and Chernomyrdin. Maslyukov, he says, declined the offer but said he would work under Primakov. Valentin Yumashev, who conducted most of the negotiations with other candidates, has strongly denied (interviews) that any such offer was made, as Yeltsin could not accept a member of the KPRF as his head of government. Yeltsin's own memoir only mentions Maslyukov as someone he considered. It is possible that he made a statement that Maslyukov or Primakov misconstrued as an offer, or that he made and retracted one without informing his chief of staff.

43. This success should not be exaggerated. The day before Yeltsin fired him in May 1999, Primakov spoke proudly of having cut the state debt to pensioners in half and of public-sector doctors and teachers waiting two months for their pay instead of five.

44. Yel'tsin, *Marafon*, 239–40.

45. These trends are summarized in Goohoon Kwon, "Budgetary Impact of Oil Prices in Russia," http://www.internationalmonetaryfund.org/external/country/rus/rr/2003/pdf/080103.pdf; and Philip Hanson, "The Russian Economic Recovery: Do Four Years of Growth Tell Us That the Fundamentals Have Changed?" *Europe-Asia Studies* 55 (May 2003), 365–82.

46. Yel'tsin, *Marafon*, 232.

47. Michael R. Gordon, "A Rough Trip for Yeltsin Adds to Worries about Health," *New York Times*, October 13, 1998.

48. Yekaterina Grigor'eva, "Vladimir Shevchenko: za rabotu s Yel'tsinym ya blagodaren sud'be" (Vladimir Shevchenko: I am grateful to fate for the chance to work with Yeltsin), *Izvestiya*, May 21, 2007.

49. Maksim Sokolov, "Zhenikhi v dome Yel'tsina" (The bachelors in Yeltsin's home), ibid., June 17, 1999, 2.

50. Talbott, *Russia Hand*, 350.

51. Quotation from Yelena Dikun, "I prezident imeyet pravo na miloserdiye" (The president, too, has the right to charity), *Obshchaya gazeta*, October 15, 1998. Dikun, reporting on Yeltsin's abbreviated trip to Central Asia, said he had come to resemble Brezhnev and Konstantin Chernenko, and urged family members to take matters into their own hands: "You have nothing to explain, you know perfectly well what is going on. Every person is entitled to grow old, anybody can get unwell—there is nothing in this to be ashamed of. But to turn the process of a person's dying away into a public spectacle or attraction is inhuman and un-Christian."

52. Mikhail Margelov, a then-official in the executive office, interview with the author (May 25, 2000).

53. Yeltsin reclaimed first place in the April poll and held it until September 1999, when Vladimir Putin took the lead.

54. On the phone conversation, revealed to the press by Samuel Berger, Clinton's national-security adviser, see David Stout, "Yeltsin Dismisses Graft Allegations," *New York Times,* September 9, 1999. Pacolli said in 2000 that he had arranged for credit cards for Yeltsin's daughters in 1995; his guarantee expired in two months, and Mabetex paid no bills on their behalf. Carlotta Gall, "Builder in Yeltsin Scandal Discounts Its Gravity," ibid., January 21, 2000. The Swiss case was closed in late 2000.

55. If anyone doubts the downward spiral in Chechnya, read as follows: "There was violation of human rights on a mass scale. . . . A slave market openly operated in the center of Grozny, with hundreds of people (mainly Chechens) held captive as hostages and subjected to violence. Kidnapping people for exchange acquired epidemic proportions, with more than 3,500 Chechens ransomed between 1996 and 1999. Bandits and terrorists killed thousands. . . . Not only did Chechnya become the criminal cesspool of the CIS countries; it also became a base for international terrorism. Terrorists from many different countries became active on its territory, with their activities financed by foreign extremist centers." Dzhabrail Gakaev, "Chechnya in Russia and Russia in Chechnya," in Richard Sakwa, ed., *Chechnya from Past to Future* (London: Anthem, 2005), 32.

56. Yel'tsin, *Marafon,* 253.

57. Yelena Dikun, "Bol'shaya kremlëvskaya rodnya: anatomiya i fiziologiya Sem'i" (The great Kremlin clan: anatomy and physiology of the Family), *Obshchaya gazeta,* July 22, 1999.

58. A hypercritical treatment of Russian politics in the 1990s, for example, writes of Berezovskii both buying the favors of the Yeltsins and blackmailing them. The former assertion rests largely on the testimony of Aleksandr Korzhakov, which is unreliable on the question of Berezovskii's personal favors and presents. The latter assertion is not backed up by hard evidence and does not square with the impression in the book that Yeltsin's daughter Tatyana respected Berezovskii's advice and sought it out. Peter Reddaway and Dmitri Glinski, *The Tragedy of Russia's Reforms: Market Bolshevism against Democracy* (Washington, D.C.: U.S. Institute of Peace, 2001).

59. Leonid Dyachenko first came to public attention when an American investigation into money laundering discovered that he had two sizable bank accounts in the Cayman Islands. No charges were laid. Yurii Skuratov, the procurator general whom Yeltsin forced out of office in the spring of 1999, doubted that the president was informed about Dyachenko's actions. Robert O'Harrow, Jr., and Sharon LaFraniere, "Yeltsin's Son-in-Law Kept Offshore Accounts, Hill Told," *The Washington Post,* September 23, 1999.

60. It was widely reported, for example, that Berezovskii favored the removal of Chernomyrdin in March 1998. But as replacement he advocated Ivan Rybkin, the

former Duma speaker, and not Kiriyenko. Berezovskii, no more consistent in this regard than Yeltsin, was all for the reinstatement of Chernomyrdin in August 1998, and one American journalist wrote at the time that, "More than anyone else, Berezovskii brought back Chernomyrdin to power" (David Hoffman, "Tycoons Take the Reins in Russia," *The Washington Post*, August 28, 1998). As we know, though, Chernomyrdin never came back to power because the Duma refused to confirm him. Primakov, who was confirmed, viewed Berezovskii as a schemer.

61. Yel'tsin, *Marafon*, 109–10. Yeltsin grumbled openly about Berezovskii's pushiness at a ceremony for Russian cosmonauts in April 1998 (Hoffman, *Oligarchs*, 409–10).

62. Yeltsin says in his memoir that he had "several" meetings with Berezovskii. Berezovskii told me (interview, March 8, 2002) there were two conversations during the 1996 campaign and "very few" after that, three or four at most, plus a handful of larger gatherings at which both he and Yeltsin were present.

63. Berezovskii interview.

64. This statement is in Boris Berezovskii, *Iskusstvo nevozmozhnogo* (The art of the impossible), 3 vols. (Moscow: Nezavisimaya gazeta, 2004), 2:250.

65. "Berezovskii said to me that he had a program for psychological influence on Tanya. He could tell her for hours at a time how I, for example, was a scoundrel . . . and, since she was impressionable . . . she in the end had come to hate me fiercely." Second Nemtsov interview. Berezovskii made the claim about meeting Dyachenko every two or three months in a press interview in 1999 (Berezovskii, *Iskusstvo nevozmozhnogo*, 1:142). It is possible that he was exaggerating.

66. Quotations from Berezovskii interview and third interview with Tatyana Yumasheva (January 25, 2007).

67. Valentin Yumashev, fourth interview with the author (January 22, 2007), and third Yumasheva interview; Reddaway and Glinski, *Tragedy of Russia's Reforms*, 606. Dikun, "Bol'shaya kremlëvskaya rodnya," reports yet another example tending in this direction: that Yumashev as Kremlin chief of staff led the opposition to the Sibneft-Yukos merger in 1998. But Yumashev has assured me there is not an ounce of truth to this story.

68. "Pravo pobedilo emotsii" (Law has beaten emotions), *Rossiiskaya gazeta*, November 6, 1998. The Duma brief was not as clear-cut as one might think. In neighboring Ukraine, where the constitutional wording and the status of the incumbent were almost identical, the court ruled in December 2003 in favor of President Leonid Kuchma. He chose not to seek re-election in 2004.

69. Naina Yeltsina, second interview with the author (September 18, 2007).

70. Grigor'eva, "Vladimir Shevchenko." An alternative explanation was that Yeltsin disguised his intentions until the very end, even from close aides.

71. Michael Wines, "Impeachment Also Is Proceeding, in a Convoluted Way, in Russia," *New York Times*, December 19, 1998. The proceedings are described in detail in Kaj Hobér, *The Impeachment of President Yeltsin* (Huntington, N.Y.: Juris,

2004). Some deputies favored a sixth charge blaming Yeltsin for the financial collapse of 1998.

72. Sergei Kovalëv, "Ne zhelayu igrat' v beznravstennyye igry" (I do not wish to play immoral games), *Nezavisimaya gazeta,* May 15, 1999.

73. Strobe Talbott, interview with the author (January 9, 2006).

74. "Confrontation over Pristina Airport," http://news.bbc.co.uk/2/hi/europe/671495.stm.

75. By this time the affair had entered the sphere of theater of the absurd. The government claimed that Skuratov was being blackmailed by the prostitutes and this left him unable to serve.

76. This historical parallel is drawn in Yel'tsin, *Marafon,* 302. Yeltsin was most alarmed by a comment Primakov made in February emphasizing the need to free up cells in Russian prisons for persons who would soon be arrested for economic crimes. He thought it reflected Soviet-era stereotypes.

77. Ibid., 303.

78. The main indicator of favor was seen on the nightly television news on May 5. At a Kremlin meeting that day on preparations for the millennium celebrations, Yeltsin made a show of asking Stepashin to leave his seat at the table and take the chair between him and Patriarch Aleksii II.

79. Natal'ya Konstantinova, "Boris Yel'tsin poshël na politicheskoye obostreniye i otpravil Yevgeniya Primakova v otstavku" (Boris Yeltsin has gone for a sharpening of political tensions and sent Yevgenii Primakov into retirement), *Nezavisimaya gazeta,* May 13, 1999.

80. These maneuvers are analyzed in Aleksandr Sadchikov, "Partiinaya distsiplina ne vyderzhala ispytaniya impichmenta" (Party discipline failed the test of impeachment), *Izvestiya,* May 18, 1999; and Ivan Rodin, "Kak Boris Yel'tsin obygral Zyuganova i Yavlinskogo" (How Boris Yeltsin beat Zyuganov and Yavlinskii), *Nezavisimaya gazeta,* May 18, 1999.

81. Valentin Yumashev, first interview with the author (February 4, 2002). A number of press accounts described Aksënenko as a flunky of Berezovskii's, but I never found any evidence that this was so. He was appointed minister in April 1997 at the initiative of Boris Nemtsov, who was as hostile to Berezovskii as any governmental leader in 1997–98.

82. Yel'tsin, *Marafon,* 315.

83. Yevgenii Yur'ev, "Duma odevayetsya v kamuflyazh" (The Duma is getting dressed in camouflage), *Segodnya,* May 13, 1999.

84. Yel'tsin, *Marafon,* 312, 315. Yeltsin mentioned in that account not revealing his plan to Putin. Tatyana Yumasheva (Dyachenko) told me explicitly in our third interview that her father did not ask her opinion on the selection of Putin.

85. Sergei Stepashin, interview with the author (June 14, 2001).

86. Fifth Yumashev interview.

87. A number of accounts of Yeltsin's last months in power, citing no sources, mention Berezovskii as giving Putin a helping hand. But a journalist who spoke

with Berezovskii in British exile in 2002 reports him as being a detractor of Putin even then: "Berezovsky said he first began to have his doubts about Putin in 1999, when the little-known FSB director was promoted by Yeltsin to prime minister." John Daniszewski, "Former Russian Rainmaker Tries Role of Dissident," *Los Angeles Times*, March 3, 2002.

88. Decree No. 1763, on provisions for retired presidents, was Putin's second as acting president. It provided for retirement pay, security, healthcare, transportation, a state dacha, and other services for all former presidents; one article gave an ex-president lifetime immunity from criminal prosecution and administrative discipline. There was no mention of family members. It was dated December 31 and published on January 5, 2000. Drafts of some parts had been prepared earlier by lawyers in the Kremlin administration, the guards service, and elsewhere. "Naturally, [Yeltsin] and Putin never discussed this question in their meetings before the president's retirement. Boris Nikolayevich would have considered this improper. As far as I know, they never discussed it after his retirement. . . . [Yeltsin considered himself] completely above all this." Valentin Yumashev, personal communication to the author (October 30, 2007). The Putin decree lost effect when it was replaced by a federal statute in February 2001.

89. Yel'tsin, *Marafon*, 254 (italics added). Earlier in the memoir (79), Yeltsin writes of thinking that the generals and security officials with whom he had contact in the first half of the 1990s were inadequate. "I waited for a new general to appear, unlike any other general, or rather one who was like the generals I read about in books when I was young. . . . Time passed, and such a general appeared . . . Vladimir Putin."

90. The plotters were associated with Lev Rokhlin, a retired general and Duma member who was murdered, evidently by his wife, in early July. Rumors of a conspiracy in the Moscow Military District circulated at the time and were confirmed in my fifth interview with Valentin Yumashev.

91. Fifty-two KPRF deputies voted against Putin but thirty-two voted for him. If seven of those thirty-two had voted against, the nomination would have failed.

92. *Ot pervogo litsa: razgovory s Vladimirom Putinym* (From the first person: conversations with Vladimir Putin) (Moscow: VAGRIUS, 2000), 131.

93. "Prezident Rossii Boris Yel'tsin: Rossiya vstupayet v novyi politcheskii etap" (The president of Russia Boris Yeltsin: Russia is entering into a new political phase), *Rossiiskaya gazeta*, August 10, 1999.

94. *Ot pervogo litsa*, 133, 135.

95. Yel'tsin, *Marafon*, 367.

96. See Timothy J. Colton and Michael McFaul, *Popular Choice and Managed Democracy: The Russian Elections of 1999 and 2000* (Washington, D.C.: Brookings, 2003), 173.

97. Yel'tsin, *Marafon*, 387–88.

98. See ibid., 9–21, and *Ot pervogo litsa*, 185–86. Putin's impression that Yeltsin would not be departing until the spring (conveyed to Dyachenko and Yumashev in

a conversation after December 14) is referred to in the communication from Yumashev. Yeltsin met with Putin a second time, on December 29, to discuss a year-end departure.

Chapter Seventeen

1. Boris Yel'tsin, *Prezidentskii marafon* (Presidential marathon) (Moscow: AST, 2000), 397.

2. Michael Wines, "Putin Is Made Russia's President in First Free Transfer of Power," *New York Times*, May 8, 2000.

3. "Boris Yel'tsin: ya khotel, chtoby lyudi byli svobodny" (Boris Yeltsin: I wanted people to be free), *Izvestiya*, February 1, 2006.

4. Comment about the pneumonia in 2001 from Naina Yeltsin, second interview with the author (September 18, 2007).

5. He proudly told a journalist a year after resigning that he was getting up these days at four A.M. "Boris Yel'tsin: ya ni o chëm ne zhaleyu" (Boris Yeltsin: I am not complaining about anything), *Komsomol'skaya Pravda*, December 8, 2000. In later interviews, he gave the time as five or six.

6. The net worth of Deripaska, born in 1968, was estimated at $13.3 billion in 2007, putting him fortieth on *Forbes* magazine's annual world list of wealthy individuals and fifth in Russia. His United Company Rusal is the largest producer of aluminum in the world.

7. A fourth great-grandson was born two months after Yeltsin's death in 2007. Two of the boys were born to Yelena's daughter Yekaterina and two to Yelena's daughter Mariya.

8. Boris Yeltsin, third interview with the author (September 12, 2002). Naina Yeltsina took me through the library during our second interview. It held five or six thousand volumes at the time, and at least that many older books were stored in the Yeltsins' Moscow apartment.

9. "Russian Tennis Remembers Yeltsin," http://leblogfoot.eurosport.fr/tennis/davis-cup/2007/sport_sto1160667.shtml. Yeltsin first displayed his barrier-leaping technique at the Kremlin Cup tournament in Moscow in October 2003. He rushed out onto the court and embraced Anastasia Myskina, who won the women's single title, with parental pride.

10. Yel'tsin, *Marafon*, 405–6.

11. "Boris Yel'tsin: ya ni o chëm ne zhaleyu."

12. Among the foundation's other projects have been help for a Russian-language university in Kyrgyzstan, musical training in orphanages, a pianists' contest in Siberia, a nursing home for army veterans, a clinic for juvenile cancer patients, small war memorials, a film series on "Freedom in Russia," and construction of a tennis and sports complex in Yekaterinburg.

13. Kirill Dybskii, "Ot pervogo litsa: vsë pravil'no" (From the first person: everything is fine), *Itogi*, January 30, 2006.

14. "Boris Yel'tsin: ya ni o chëm ne zhaleyu" (italics added).

15. Ibid.

16. The new lyrics were written by Sergei Mikhal'kov, now eighty-seven, the author of children's books who wrote the original words for the Soviet anthem in 1944. Successive pre-Soviet, Soviet, and post-Soviet Russian anthems can be downloaded from http://www.hymn.ru/index-en.html.

17. Mikhail Kasyanov (born in 1957), Putin's prime minister from 2000 to 2004, had been Yeltsin's last finance minister in 1999. Aleksei Kudrin, the new minister of finance (born 1960), was first deputy minister from 1997 to 1999. The minister of industry and trade, German Gref (born 1964), was first deputy minister of state property from 1998 to 2000.

18. The phrase "restrained support" is from "Boris Yel'tsin: ya ni o chëm ne zhaleyu" and was specifically applied to changes in the federal system. Yeltsin in that interview (December 2000) expressed no reservations about the move against Berezovskii, who he said "did more harm than good." He did not comment on Gusinskii, who had spent several days in jail in May 2000.

19. Yeltsin's rethinking of the first war is apparent in Dybskii, "Ot pervogo litsa." Zelimkhan Yandarbiyev, who negotiated the 1996 cease-fire with Yeltsin and was then acting president of Chechnya, went into exile during the second war and was assassinated by Russian agents in Qatar in 2004. Federal forces killed Aslan Maskhadov, who signed the 1997 peace treaty and was president of the republic until the second Russian invasion, in Chechnya in 2005. Shamil Basayev, the organizer of the 1995 raid on Budënnovsk and the 1999 incursion into Dagestan, was killed in 2006.

20. These actions are well analyzed in Andrew Jack, *Inside Putin's Russia* (Oxford: Oxford University Press, 2004); and Richard Sakwa, *Putin: Russia's Choice*, rev. ed. (London: Routledge, 2008).

21. "Gusinsky's cynical brilliance throughout the campaign against him was to cloak his commercial interests and political ambitious in the language of freedom of speech." Jack, *Inside Putin's Russia*, 155. Berezovskii was less cynical, and had always treated ORT as a source of influence, not a money maker.

22. Boris Nemtsov, third interview with the author (April 12, 2002). Instead of Yeltsin, Yevgenii Primakov headed up the new board. The station was soon converted into a sports channel and went off the air in 2003.

23. Yegor Gaidar, "On ne khotel nasiliya, no tol'ko on ne byl slabakom" (He did not want to use force, but he was no weakling, either), *Novoye vremya/New Times*, April 30, 2007.

24. Details of the interaction from interviews with family members.

25. Author's conversation with Putin on the sidelines of the Valdai Discussion Club, Bocharov Ruchei residence, Sochi, September 14, 2007.

26. Dybskii, "Ot pervogo litsa."

27. Andrei Kolesnikov, "Boris Yel'tsin poproshchalsya so svoyei epokhoi" (Boris Yeltsin said good-bye to his epoch), *Kommersant-Daily*, February 6, 2006.

28. "A Conversation with Billy Graham," http://www/midtod.com/9612/billy graham.phtml.

29. Father Georgii Sudenov in "Ushël Boris Yel'tsin" (Boris Yeltsin has departed), *Izvestiya*, April 24, 2007. Sudenov, the deacon of the church in the Moscow suburb of Troparëvo, was sometimes invited to dine with the Yeltsins. Before eating, he always said grace and Yeltsin joined him in singing the Slavic hymn "Mnogaya leta" (Many years).

30. "Boris Yel'tsin: ya khotel, chtoby lyudi byli svobodny."

31. Second Yeltsina interview.

32. Aleksandr Gamov, "Utraty" (Losses), *Komsomol'skaya pravda*, April 25, 2007.

33. Second Yeltsina interview.

34. Andrei Kolesnikov, "Poslednii put' pervogo prezidenta" (The first president's last road), *Kommersant-Daily*, April 26, 2007. Gorbachev and Yeltsin were both at Putin's first inauguration and a few other ceremonial events but studiously avoided one another. Another notable attendee at the funeral was Aleksandr Rutskoi, the vice president Yeltsin put in jail during the constitutional conflict of 1993. Ruslan Khasbulatov, Rutskoi's ally against Yeltsin, skipped the funeral, as did Aleksandr Korzhakov.

35. The press reported as fact or rumor that Naina's handkerchief contained an icon or a cross. One journalist claimed that the crucifix from Yeltsin's christening in 1931 had been saved all these years and was buried with him. These stories were all untrue.

Coda

1. Mikhail Gorbachev, who attended the funeral, took a moderate but still critical position when he said in a statement that Yeltsin would be remembered for his "tragic fate" and misguided policies. He softened his response in a press interview in which he noted that he and Yeltsin had both set out to improve life for the people.

2. Quoted at http://gazeta.ru/politics/yeltsin/1614107.shtml.

3. Quoted in Yekaterina Grigor'eva and Vladimir Perekrest, "Provodili po-khristianski" (He was given a Christian sendoff), *Izvestiya*, April 26, 2007.

4. Viktor Shenderovich, "Yel'tsin," at http://www.shender.ru/paper/text/?file=154.

5. Commencement address at Washington University, St. Louis, May 19, 2006, at http://www.olin.wustl.edu/discovery/feature.cfm?sid=668&i=30&pg=8.

6. "Boris Yeltsin and His Role in Russian History," at http://bd.english.fom.ru/report/map/dominant/edomt0718_2/ed071820.

7. The latest survey for which data are available was done by the Public Opinion Foundation in February 2006. The question was whether Gorbachev had done more good or more harm to the nation, and a middle category, for good and harm in equal measure, was available. Eleven percent of Russians thought Gorbachev had done more good than harm, 23 percent that he had done them in equal measure,

52 percent that he had done more harm than good, and 14 percent found it hard to answer. "Mikhail Gorbachev, President of the USSR," at http://bd.english.fom.ru/report/cat/societas/rus_im/rus_history/gorbachev_m_s_/etb060812.

8. Sidney Hook, *The Hero in History: A Study in Limitation and Possibility* (New York: Humanities Press, 1943), 156–57. The Russian Lenin was the only one of Hook's examples about whom he wrote an entire chapter. The prevalent image in many recent studies of social and political change is that of "path dependency," whereby positive reinforcement, short time horizons, and inertia keep things on the same track over extended periods of time. See in particular Paul Pierson, *Politics in Time: History, Institutions, and Social Analysis* (Princeton: Princeton University Press, 2004), chap. 1. Before a path can be established, however, it has been pointed out that relatively small factors, such as choices by leaders or bargains struck among different groups, may push things down one of *several* competing paths, so that the pattern is one of "periods of relative (but not total) openness, followed by periods of relative (but not total or permanent) stability." Ibid., 53. Yeltsin made his mark in a period of relative openness in which Hook's metaphor of a fork in the road holds up well.

9. Erik H. Erikson, *Gandhi's Truth: On the Origins of Militant Nonviolence* (New York: Norton, 1969), 113, 402.

10. Gorbachev, of course, addressed these same issues in his own way, and, unlike Yeltsin, he also made conceptual breakthroughs on issues of war and peace. But Gorbachev's reassessments on domestic issues were less thorough than Yeltsin's, which explains why, in the radical climate of the times, Yeltsin consistently outbid him.

11. Isaiah Berlin, "On Political Judgment," *New York Review of Books*, October 3, 1996, 26–30.

12. Robert A. Caro, *The Years of Lyndon Johnson: Master of the Senate* (New York: Knopf, 2002), xx.

13. Sergei Stankevich, interview with the author (May 29, 2001). Stankevich by the time of the interview had no use for Yeltsin and could not be suspected of bias in his favor.

14. Anatolii Kulikov, *Tyazhëlyye zvëzdy* (Heavy stars) (Moscow: Voina i mir, 2002), 410 (italics added).

15. The significance of negative as well as positive choices is clearly drawn in Richard J. Samuels, *Machiavelli's Children: Leaders and Their Legacies in Italy and Japan* (Ithaca: Cornell University Press, 2003), 19.

16. Martin Gilman, "Becoming a Motor of the Global Economy," *Moscow Times*, November 14, 2007.

17. Quotations from Thomas Carothers, "The End of the Transition Paradigm," *Journal of Democracy* 13 (January 2002), 10, 12. Carothers was writing generally of countries that have lost their way in the transition, and not specifically about Russia.

18. Even Putin's treatment of lower-level officials brings to mind Yeltsin's early reputation as boss for the bosses. One observer has called him "the people's czar

who reins in ministers, bureaucrats, tycoons, and even the politicians of the pro-Kremlin United Russia party." Peter Finn, "In a Russian City, Clues to Putin's Abiding Appeal," *The Washington Post*, November 24, 2007.

19. Richard Sakwa, *Putin: Russia's Choice*, rev. ed. (London: Routledge, 2008), xi.

20. Henry Yasas, quoted in Tatyana Gershkovich, "Remembering Yeltsin," *Moscow Times*, September 14, 2007. Some pictures are available at http://www.art4.ru/ru/news/news_detail.php?ID=2994&block_id=28.

21. Gershkovich, "Remembering Yeltsin." Kvaranga's own description of the work in materials distributed at the gallery places more emphasis on the chaos depicted, "without which an absolutely new creation would be impossible." Yeltsin's name, he said, should be read as "fixing in memory either the formation or the crushing of our latest illusion."

22. Gukova's description from the exhibit.

23. Description at the exhibit by Tavasiyev.

24. Description at the exhibit by Leikin and Miturich-Khlebnikova.

Index

PEQUOT LIBRARY
3 4016 09117 4116